Manual:

A Guide to the Development and Use of the Myers-Briggs Type Indicator®

by Isabel Briggs Myers
and Mary H. McCaulley

Consulting Psychologists Press, Inc.
3803 E. Bayshore Road
Palo Alto, CA 94303

Cover color code:

Extravert	orange
Introvert	blue-violet
Sensing	green
Intuition	purple
Thinking	grey
Feeling	red
Judgment	blue
Perception	yellow

Editor: Robert Most
Cover and book designer: MaryEllen Podgorski
Production: Mary Forkner, Publication Alternatives
Manuscript editor: Toni Haskell
Proofreaders: Jennifer N. Nixon, Doreen Finkelstein, Joan Phelan
Compositor: Graphic Typesetting Service

Printed in the United States of America.

02 01 00 99 98 97   22 21 20 19 18 17

Myers-Briggs Type Indicator and MBTI are registered trademarks of Consulting Psychologists Press, Inc.

Introduction to Type is a registered trademark of Consulting Psychologists Press, Inc.

Library of Congress Cataloging-in-Publication Data

Myers, Isabel Briggs.
    Manual, a guide to the development and use
of the Myers-Briggs type indicator.
    Bibliography: p.
    1. Myers-Briggs Type Indicator.   2. Counseling.
I. McCaulley, Mary H.   II. Title.
BF698.8.M94M84 1985   155.2'83   85-17435
ISBN 0-89106-027-8

Acknowledgments
to the First Edition

The writer acknowledges a deep and grateful appreciation to Katharine C. Briggs for her original theory of type which foreshadowed all the preferences except sensation-intuition, for her penetrating analysis of the part played by the judgment-perception preference in her structure of Jungian types, and for her indispensable collaboration in the writing of the Type Indicator and support in its development;

To Clarence G. Myers, for his generous and wholehearted acceptance of the Indicator as a part of the family over the past twenty years;

To David R. Saunders, for his long-standing interest and many contributions toward the improvement of the Indicator, and for his skill in compressing the accumulated wealth of data to proportions usable within the limits of this Manual;

To J.A. Davis, for his very present help in time of stress and for the endless patience and ingenuity he has brought to bear upon each successive difficulty;

To the ETS reviewers, Martin Katz, William E. Coffman, and Frederick R. Kling, for most perceptive and constructive criticism;

To Donald W. MacKinnon and Arthur R. Laney, for generous sharing of their studies of type;

And to all the many others who have helped with information, advice, encouragement, and labor, at ETS and elsewhere.

Isabel Briggs Myers
First Edition, 1962

Acknowledgments
to the Second Edition

The aims of the second edition of the MBTI® Manual are to make available all the research reported by Isabel Briggs Myers in the first edition (Myers, 1962), to clarify points that have been frequently misunderstood, to describe more specifically how to interpret the MBTI, and to add new data from research since the first edition.

Isabel Briggs Myers completed the first draft for the administrative and interpretive sections of this Manual before her death in May 1980. Her work on the first edition has stood up over time and has been extended by many other researchers. To complete this second edition, the second author began by using Isabel Myers' work and adding new data. In the interest of consistency of style, the Myers draft was completely rewritten.

The influence of Isabel Myers permeates this volume. Some sections of this Manual are written by her. In other sections, her ideas are summarized, using written records supplemented by notes of hundreds of hours of discussions over the decade the two authors worked together. Throughout this second edition, there has been an attempt to convey her concern for clarity, accuracy, and interest in "the constructive use of differences." This work reflects Myers' six decades of interest in Jung's theory of psychological types and four decades of research to develop a way of putting Jung's theory to practical use.

The idea of psychological type, and to some extent the theory of Jung, was out of favor in psychology for some decades. Types, temperaments, and traits have been seen by some psychologists as constructs ill-suited to the sophistication of present-day psychology. However, the types described in this Manual have both constitutional and environmental roots; they are developmental and dynamic, not static. Jung's theory provides a powerful way for illuminating everyday observations about individual styles of information gathering and decision making. Because an understanding of Jung's theory is essential for understanding the MBTI, this Manual outlines the theory and then considers the psychometric properties of the MBTI, the interpretation of the MBTI, and practical applications.

Many personality measures are designed to create information for professionals working with clients. The MBTI is designed to provide information that can be given directly to those who have responded to the Indicator. For this reason, this Manual goes into detail to give the interpreter specific steps and cautions when explaining and using the MBTI.

This second edition could not have been completed without the help of many people. Researchers and MBTI users throughout the country have been very generous in sharing their data. Some of these contributions are acknowledged in Appendix A, Description of Samples. Many others have sent data for composite samples, and their contributions are acknowledged here with thanks.

We have tried to give a broad representation of MBTI research; in choosing studies, we tried to select those where researchers understood the theory and the instrument, presenting type tables, and scoring the MBTI as recommended in the Manual. There are many other studies we would like to have included, but space and time are finite. If you are a researcher who has used the MBTI, please believe that whether we used your work or not, we appreciate your contributions to a deeper understanding of type.

Katharine Myers worked with Isabel Myers in preparation of the first draft of this revision, and her valuable suggestions have been incorporated in this work. Richard Cordray reviewed MBTI research early in the process and gave valuable assistance with statistical issues and design. Later, Thomas C. Carskadon, Naomi L. Quenk, and David R. Saunders made suggestions that significantly improved the text. Robert Most was an insightful and supportive editor with a good balance of appreciation and tough-minded skepticism.

This new edition could not have been accomplished without the skill, dedication, and hard work of the staff of the Center for Applications of Psychological Type (CAPT). The Center provided the valuable resources of the Isabel Briggs Myers Memorial Library, and the CAPT MBTI data bank. Special appreciation goes to Gerald P. Macdaid, Richard I. Kainz, and Glenn Granade who made up the research design team. They conducted studies of the MBTI data bank, designed ways to integrate data bank and contributed data, wrote innumerable computer programs to solve problems along the way, and provided valuable ideas for creating and displaying data. Gerald Macdaid supervised the team of CAPT staff and students who worked on Manual projects: secretaries Helen Hunt, M. Catesby Halsey, and Don Prince; psychology students Pilar M.

Cruz, Roy Forest, Jennifer Friedman, Jon C. Mazzoli, Curt M. Schoeneman, James M. Siwy, and Lori Stirrat. The remainder of the staff helped in many big and little ways and put up with the disruptions that this project caused to other CAPT activities. They provided unfailing support.

All of us who have worked on this second edition dedicate it to Isabel Briggs Myers, and to those who use her work to make this world a place of better understanding.

Mary H. McCaulley (INFP)

Gainesville, Florida
February 1985

Contents

Tables and Figures

Chapter 1

Introduction

The purpose of the Myers-Briggs Type Indicator® (MBTI®) is to make the theory of psychological types described by C. G. Jung (1921/1971) understandable and useful in people's lives. The essence of the theory is that much seemingly random variation in behavior is actually quite orderly and consistent, being due to basic differences in the way individuals prefer to use their perception and judgment.

Perception involves all the ways of becoming aware of things, people, happenings, or ideas. Judgment involves all the ways of coming to conclusions about what has been perceived. If people differ systematically in what they perceive and in how they reach conclusions, then it is only reasonable for them to differ correspondingly in their reactions, interests, values, motivations, skills, and interests.

The MBTI is based on Jung's ideas about perception and judgment, and the attitudes in which these are used in different types of people. The aim of the MBTI is to identify, from self-report of easily recognized reactions, the basic preferences of people in regard to perception and judgment, so that the effects of each preference, singly and in combination, can be established by research and put to practical use.

The early chapters in this Manual describe the administration and scoring of the MBTI, Jung's theory of psychological types, and applications of the MBTI in various settings. Later chapters describe the construction and psychometric properties of the MBTI, discuss evidence for reliability and validity, and offer comments about research strategies. Because of the breadth and amount of practical information in this Manual, it is essentially a handbook for using the MBTI.

The MBTI differs from many other personality instruments in these ways:

- It is designed to implement a theory; therefore the theory must be understood to understand the MBTI.

- The theory postulates dichotomies; therefore some of the psychometric properties are unusual.

- Based on the theory, there are specific dynamic relationships between the scales, which lead to the descriptions and characteristics of sixteen "types."

- The type descriptions and the theory include a model of development that continues throughout life.

- The scales are concerned with basic functions of perception and judgment that enter into almost every behavior; therefore, the scope of practical applications is very wide.

Overview of Jung's Theory of Psychological Types

The Four Preferences

The MBTI contains four separate indices (outlined in Table 1.1). Each index reflects one of four basic preferences which, under Jung's theory, direct the use of perception and judgment. The preferences affect not only *what* people attend to in any given situation, but also *how* they draw conclusions about what they perceive.

Extraversion-Introversion (EI). The EI index is designed to reflect whether a person is an extravert or an introvert in the sense intended by Jung (1921/1971, p.160). Jung regarded extraversion and introversion as "mutually complementary" attitudes whose differences "generate the tension that both the individual and society need for the maintenance of life." Extraverts are oriented primarily toward the outer world; thus they tend to focus their perception and judgment on people and objects. Introverts are oriented primarily toward the inner world; thus they tend to focus their perception and judgment upon concepts and ideas.

Sensing-Intuition (SN). The SN index is designed to reflect a person's preference between two opposite ways of perceiving; one may rely primarily upon the process of sensing (S), which reports observable facts or happenings through one or more of the five senses; or one may rely more upon the less obvious process of intuition (N), which reports meanings, relationships and/or possibilities that have been worked out beyond the reach of the conscious mind.

Thinking-Feeling (TF). The TF index is designed to reflect a person's preference between two contrasting ways of judgment. A person may rely primarily on thinking (T) to decide impersonally on the basis of logical consequences, or a person may rely primarily on feeling (F) to decide primarily on the basis of personal or social values.

Judgment-Perception (JP). The JP index is designed to describe the process a person uses primarily in dealing with the outer world, that is, with the extraverted part of life. A person who prefers judgment (J) has reported a preference for using a judgment process (either thinking or feeling) for dealing with the outer world. A person who prefers perception (P) has reported a preference for using a perceptive process (either S or N) for dealing with the outer world.

The Sixteen Types

According to theory, by definition, one pole of each of the four preferences is preferred over the other pole for each of the sixteen MBTI types. The preference on each index is independent of preferences for the other three indices, so that the four indices yield sixteen possible combinations called "types," denoted by the four letters of the preferences (e.g., ESTJ, INFP). The theory postulates specific dynamic relationships between the preferences. For each type, one process is the leading or *dominant* process and a second process serves as an *auxiliary*. Each type has its own pattern of dominant and auxiliary processes and the attitudes (E or I) in which these are habitually used (see Table 1.2 for

Table 1.1 The four preferences of the MBTI

Index	Preferences between	Affects Choices as to
EI	E Extraversion or I Introversion	Whether to direct perception judgment mainly on the outer world (E) or mainly on the world of ideas (I)
SN	S Sensing perception N Intuitive perception	Which kind of perception is preferred when one needs or wishes to perceive
TF	T Thinking judgment F Feeling judgment	Which kind of judgment to trust when one needs or wishes to make a decision
JP	J Judgment P Perception	Whether to deal with the outer world in the judging (J) attitude (using T or F) or in the perceptive (P) attitude (using S or N)

Table 1.2 Processes and attitudes

Attitudes refers to extraversion (E) or introversion (I).

Processes of perception are sensing (or sensation) (S) and intuition (N).

Processes of judgment are thinking (T) and feeling (F).

The style of dealing with the outside world is shown by judgment (J) or perception (P).

---

definitions). The characteristics of each type follow from the dynamic interplay of these processes and attitudes.

In terms of the theory, people may reasonably be expected to develop greater skill with the processes they prefer to use and with the attitudes in which they prefer to use these processes. For example, if they prefer the extraverted attitude (E), they are likely to be more mature and effective in dealing with the world around them than with the introverted world of concepts and ideas. If they prefer the perceptive process of sensing (S), they are likely to be more effective in perceiving facts and realities than theories and possibilities, which are in the sphere of intuition. If they prefer the judgment process of thinking (T), they are likely to have better developed thinking judgments than feeling judgments. And if they prefer to use judgment (J) rather than perception (P) in their attitude to the world around them, they are likely to be better at organizing the events of their lives than they are in experiencing and adapting to them. On the other hand, if a person prefers introversion, intuition, feeling, and the perceptive attitude (INFP), then the converse of the description above is likely to be true.

Further discussion of the preferences, and the specific dynamics of their interactions, are described in Chapter 3 and in *Gifts Differing* (Myers with Myers, 1980).

Identifying the MBTI Preferences

The main objective of the MBTI is to identify four basic preferences. The indices EI, SN, TF, and JP[1] are designed to point in one direction or the other. They are not designed as scales for measurement of traits or behaviors. The intent is to reflect a habitual choice between rival alternatives, analogous to right-handedness or left-handedness. One expects to use both the right and left hands, even though one reaches first with the hand one prefers. Similarly, every person is assumed to use both poles of each of the four preferences, but to respond first or most often with the preferred functions or attitudes.

Items and Scores

The MBTI items scored for each index offer forced choices between the poles of the preference at issue. Choices are between seemingly inconsequential everyday events, chosen by Myers as stimuli to evoke the more comprehensive type preferences. All choices reflect the two poles of the same Jungian preference (e.g., E or I, S or N; never E or N, N or F). Each of the responses for a question may be weighted 0, 1, or 2 points. Responses that best predict to total type with a prediction ratio of 72% or greater carry a weight of 2; items that predict to type with a prediction ratio of 63% to 71% carry a weight of 1; overpopular responses carry a weight of 0. Technical details of item construction, weighting, and prediction ratios are given in Chapter 9.

The totals for weighted scores for each preference are called *points*. Persons with a higher total of points for E than for I are classified as extraverts. The extent of the difference between points for E and points for I is computed by formula[2] to produce an E *preference score*, such as E 13 or E 27. Those with more points for I than for E are classified as introverts and are said to have I preference scores, such as I 13 or I 27. The EI preference score is based on the difference between points for E and points for I.

The letters indicate which of each pair of alternatives the person prefers and presumably has, or can develop, to a greater degree. For example, a preference score letter E suggests that the person prefers extraverting to introverting and probably has spent more time extraverting than introverting. Consequently, the person is likely to be better at activities that call for extraversion than activities that call for introversion and will find more satisfaction from a career that requires extraversion. The characteristics associated with a preference are often less apparent when the numerical portion of the preference score is low. A low score shows almost equal votes for each pole of the preference.

While letters indicate the *direction* of the preference, the number indicates the *strength* of the preference. Preference scores N 9 and N 41 both show a preference for intuition, but the N 41 shows that in the forced-choice format the respondent reported intuition over sensing more often than the respondent with the preference score of N 9. The numerical portion of a score shows how strongly the preference is reported, which is not necessarily the same thing as how strongly it is felt. It is also not necessarily correct to assume that the person with a preference score of N 41 has *developed* the skills of intuition more effectively than the person reporting a score of N 9. Chapter 5 discusses these issues in greater detail.

Letters and Preference Types

The type formula gives letters from all four scores which provide a compact definition of each type (e.g., ESTJ, INFJ, ESFP). The dynamic interrelationships of the preferences are described in Chapter 3 along with the behavioral characteristics associated with each preference pattern. Each pole of the preference is valuable and at times indispensable in its own area of operation. The theory assumes all types are valuable and necessary. Each type has its own special gifts and strengths, its own areas of vulnerability, and its own pathway for development. The *type description* describes these relationships in everyday terms. Each type is described in terms of good development of the functions and attitudes and also in terms of the specific difficulties arising when type is incompletely developed or not used appropriately.

Uses of the Indicator

Almost every human experience involves either perception or judgment and is played out in the world of action or of ideas. Since the MBTI is concerned with individual differences in basic functions and attitudes, the applications of the MBTI potentially cover a broad range of human activities. The differences described by the MBTI are a familiar part of everyday life. Jung's theory offers an explanation for these differences which makes it easier to recognize them and to use them in constructive ways. The theory is indispensable for understanding and using the MBTI, but the MBTI is interesting and valuable to people whose original interest was not in Jung. Some of the ways in which the MBTI is being used are the following:

In Education

- To develop different teaching methods to meet the needs of different types.

- To understand type differences in motivation for learning. In reading, in aptitude, and in achievement, to use the understanding of learning motivation to help students gain control over their own learning and to help teachers reach more students.

- To analyze curricula, methods, media, and materials in light of the needs of different types.

- To provide extracurricular activities that will meet the needs of all types.

- To help teachers, administrators, and parents to work together more constructively.

In Counseling

- To help individuals find direction for their lives by understanding the strengths and gifts of their preferences.

- To help individuals cope with their problems by showing them how to use their problems as a laboratory for developing their powers of perception and judgment and to thereby gain more satisfactory direction in their lives.

- To help couples and families learn the value of both their differences and similarities.

- To help parents accept their children as they are (however different the child's type is from that of the parent).

- To help children follow their different roads to excellence without external disparagement or internal guilt.

In Career Guidance

- To guide individuals in their choice of school majors, professions, occupations, and work settings.

- To consider the opportunities a given career offers for use of the preferred modes of perception and judgment, and the demands that same career makes for use of the least-liked and least-developed modes of perception and judgment.

In Situations Requiring Cooperation and Teamwork

- To select teams, task forces, and work groups with sufficient diversity to solve group problems.

- To help group members recognize, appreciate, and make use of the strengths of each type in the group.

- To help group members grow in their own development, as each learns from the skills of the other.

- To conduct meetings so as to take advantage of the contributions of each type.

- To help those who work or live together to understand how previously irritating and obstructive differences can become a source of amusement, interest, and strength.

In Communications

- To learn the approaches that are most likely to earn agreement and cooperation from each type.

- To increase understanding by "talking the language" of different types in the group.

- To create a climate where differences are seen as interesting and valuable, rather than as problematic.

Chapter 2

Administering and Scoring the MBTI

Populations Suitable for Testing

Reading Level

The original research for the MBTI measured the responses of a variety of populations from fourth grade students to superior adults. When the MBTI is used with high school students and adults who can read at least at the eighth grade level, a counselor can be reasonably confident of the reported type for individual guidance, provided that the reported type never be used as an established fact, but rather as a hypothesis for verification.

The reading level of the phrase questions (Parts I and III of the booklet) is estimated to be seventh to eighth grade with a spread from sixth to eleventh grade, based on the Dale-Chall formula. Almost all word pairs (Part II of the booklet) are above the fourth grade level, but the reading level is not estimated because the Dale-Chall formula is based on the sentence length as well as the word complexity. (Reading level analysis prepared by Janet J. Larsen.)

Age

The MBTI is appropriate for adults and high school students. More caution should be used in interpreting results with middle and junior high school students. These groups can be profitably tested for research, for example, to explore type differences in interest or learning styles.

Translations

Jung's theory is an attempt to describe basic human mental processes; however, until carefully validated translations are available, caution should be used in interpreting the MBTI to non-English-speaking people. Counselors have reported, however, that persons from other cultures tested in English have recognized and found the descriptions of their types quite useful.

Translations of the MBTI are being developed in a number of countries. For information about current published translations, contact Consulting Psychologists Press.

Selection of the MBTI Form

The MBTI is published in three forms—Form F (166 items), Form G (126 items), and Form AV, the Abbreviated Version which is self-scoring (50 items). Both Form F and Form G contain research items as well as the items scored for type; Form AV contains no research items. The Form F and Form G items scored for type are almost identical, but in Form G items are rearranged so that items that best predict to total type are at the beginning, thus increasing the likelihood that respondents who do not finish the MBTI will receive accurate reports of their type.

The Abbreviated Version

The Abbreviated Version (Form AV, earlier referred to as Form H) includes the first 50 items from Form G in a self-scoring format. It is designed for group situations (e.g., workshops) where pretesting and scoring by template are not feasible. Persons will come out the same on Form G and Form AV about 75% of the time. Individuals with greater preference strengths are more likely to have the same type on Form AV as on Form G. Form AV may be used when time pressures preclude administering and scoring Form G and when maximum accuracy is not important. In general, Form AV is not recommended when an accurate assessment of type is required. (See Chapter 9 for details about the Form AV.)

Forms G and F

Form G is now the standard form of the MBTI. Form F is recommended only when researchers or counselors are willing to share their Form F answer sheets with the authors on a confidential basis. Ongoing MBTI research is conducted with Form F. Populations needed for the ongoing MBTI research are persons with high levels of excellence and persons with emotional, social, or physical difficulties.

Administering the MBTI

Preparatory Steps

The MBTI differs from many personality measures in that the results are designed primarily for the respondents. The MBTI is often given to groups with the intent of improving understanding of individual and group dynamics. Before starting the administration of the MBTI, it is important, as with any other assessment measure, to insure that participation is voluntary and to make clear the arrangements for protecting the confidentiality of the results. Some groups are comfortable sharing information, while other groups wish to determine when and whether information will be shared. In organizations, it is important to discuss with the individual whether results will be confidential to them only or whether their results will be placed in personnel files.

Introducing the MBTI

When introducing the MBTI, it is useful to take into account the probable distribution of types in the group.

- Sensing types will need to know that the information will have some practical value.

- Intuitive types will need to see possible future benefits. Intuitive types may also find the choice between alternatives frustrating—all possibilities are in their ken.

- Thinking types can be expected to be skeptical about the MBTI since skepticism is an important aspect of thinking. Acknowledgment of the skepticism and suggestion that they "wait and see" are useful.

- Feeling types can sometimes be more concerned with pleasing the examiner than with reporting their own natural styles.

- Introverts can be expected to be particularly concerned with privacy issues.

The examiner should carefully consider the purposes of using the MBTI and attempt to create an atmosphere in which each individual can respond freely. The examiner should make every effort to create a situation where respondents are interested in the results for their own purposes, not for the benefit of other people. In work situations, particularly, the examiner should be alert to conditions that might cause respondents to report what they believe authority wants to hear. The MBTI items are reasonably transparent and answers can be falsified.

The Mechanics of Administration

The MBTI is virtually self-administering. All necessary instructions are given on the cover of the question booklets and on the response sheets. The same response sheet is used for hand scoring and machine scoring.

When conducting group administration of the MBTI, the examiner should read the instructions aloud, emphasizing the need for carefully filling in the identifying information and matching numbers on the response sheet to the numbers in the response booklet. It is important to have the client fill in the male or female circle on Forms G and F because the TF questions carry different weights as a function of sex. The examiner should make it clear that only one answer is to be given to any question except for the one question where more than one answer is allowed (item 68 on Form F, item 17 on Form G, and the next to the last Part I item on Form AV).

The MBTI has no time limit, but those who are making unusually slow progress may be encouraged to work rapidly and not study the items at length.

In administering the MBTI to poor readers or to younger children, it may be preferable to read the questions aloud; in reading, the examiner should be sure to sound open-minded about both choices, with no bias in either direction.

The examiner should not explain questions or meanings of words to clients who ask about questions. In group testing, group members should not be allowed to discuss the items.

Omissions are permitted if respondents do not understand a question or cannot choose an answer. The reason for permitting omissions is that no item can reliably contribute useful evidence of type unless choices are understood and the question lies within the respondent's experience. (See Table 9.8 for percentages of omissions for Forms F and G.)

Students below eleventh grade should be informed that many of the questions were originally written for adults and that they are not expected to be able to answer every question.

When introducing the MBTI, do not use the word *test*. Use *MBTI* or *the Indicator*. The MBTI is designed to "indicate" equally valuable preferences and does not have right and wrong answers as do achievement tests.

When using the Form G in work situations be alert to employee concerns about the question:

"Are you working?   Yes   No

If you are, what is your occupation?

Do you like it?   A lot   O.K.   Not much"

If respondents are concerned that the information on satisfaction will be relayed to their superiors they can be told to skip that demographic question.

Some people have trouble finding the correct frame of mind for answering the MBTI. When reporting the results to some people, they say they reported their "work self," "school self," "ideal self," or some other self they now consider atypical. The frame of reference desired in respondents is what has been termed the "shoes-off self." The "shoes-off self" fosters an attitude in which one functions naturally, smoothly, and effortlessly, and in which one is not going "against one's grain." The function of the MBTI is to provide the first step toward understanding one's natural preferences.[3]

Using the Stencils

Five stencils are provided for scoring the MBTI Forms G or F: (1) E and I, (2) S and N, (3) T and F male, (4) T and F female, and (5) J and P. Scoring instructions are printed on the stencils. Briefly, the steps are as follows:

Finding the Points

Points are the weighted total of answers for each pole of the four indices. The points are derived as described below:

1. Look over the response sheet for items marked with more than one response. Only one question (#68 on Form F and #17 on Form G) allows scoring for two responses. The stencils also show two questions (#9 and #60 on Form F, #14 and #93 on Form G) with two openings in the stencil. For these questions, if both B and C are marked, B should be counted, but not C. When other questions are marked more than once, cross out the question in red to show that the question should not be counted.

2. Position the scoring stencil over the response sheet so that the appropriate guide mark appears. (The guide mark is a ■ on the Form F response sheet and a * on Form G.) There are two scales on each stencil. For example, the JP stencil has J on the top half and P on the bottom half.

3. Count the respondent's answers that appear as black marks through the stencil holes. Plain circles on the stencil count one point; a circle surrounded by a square and marked "2" on the stencil counts two points. Record the total points in the large circle at the top of the stencil. The maximum number of points for each preference is given on the key. If the total number of circles indicating marks for the scale, plus circles without marks, does not equal the maximum points total on the stencil, recount the stencil.

4. Move the key up so that the guides in the middle of the stencil are positioned over the guidemarks on the answer sheet. Count the points in the same way as described above and record the total in the large circle at the top of this half of the stencil.

5. When scoring the TF stencil, make sure to use the appropriate male or female stencil. The TF stencils have an opening for the male and female circles to provide a check for the scorer. In scoring a group of response sheets, it is best to group male and female response sheets separately. Score the TF stencil first. In this way you will avoid using the wrong stencil. Notice that the male T stencil has a black circle on the stencil which counts as one point in the point total.

6. Continue the steps above until four stencils have been used with two point totals recorded for each stencil.

Converting Points into Preference Scores

The preference score for each index consists of a letter showing the direction of preference and a number showing the reported strength of the preference. Isabel Myers considered the letter to be the more important part of the preference score.

To determine the letter, compare the points for each pole of the preference. The greater number of points indicates the direction of preference and hence the letter part of the preference score. (Example: E 17 and I 9 yield E; E 9 and I 17 yield I.) Record the letter in the scoring box.

To determine the number follow these steps:

• Subtract the smaller number of points from the larger number. (This difference is not recorded on the answer sheet.) Go to the column of the preferred letter side of the stencil (e.g., right side for P or left side for J). Find the difference under the Point Diff. column on the stencil. The preference score is the number under the Score column to the right of the difference score. Record this score in the scoring box, next to the letter. Note that a zero difference appears only under the columns I, N, F, and P.

An example of scoring appears in Table 2.1 and a summary conversion table appears in Table 2.2. In the Table 2.1 example, the points for E are 19 and the points for I are 6. The letter part of the preference score is therefore E and is entered on the top line of the scoring box under Letter. The difference between 19 points and 6 points is 13. The left-hand column of Table 2.2, headed E, S, T, or J, shows that a difference of 13 would yield a preference score of 25. The score for the EI index is therefore written E 25. Table 2.3 shows the preference score ranges for Forms F and G.

Table 2.1 Example of MBTI scoring

Points				Preference Scores Letter plus Number	
E	19	I	6	E	25
S	10	N	17	N	15
T	25	F	7	T	35
J	11	P	11	P	1

Preference scores can also be calculated by formula for those who prefer formulas to tables. The formula is: For E, S, T and J: 2 times (larger points minus smaller points) minus 1. For I, N, F, and P: 2 times (larger points minus smaller points) plus 1. For ties, the preference score will be I 01, N 01, F 01, or P 01. The formula for the EI scale in Table 2.1 would be: 2 times the difference (19 minus 6) equals 26, minus 1 equals E 25.

Continuous Scores

When conducting correlational research with the MBTI, it is useful to treat the dichotomous preference scores as if they were continuous scales. Continuous scores are a linear transformation of preference scores, using the following convention:

• For E, S, T, or J preference scores, the continuous score is 100 minus the numerical portion of the preference score.

• For I, N, F, or P preference scores, the continuous score is 100 plus the numerical portion of the preference score.

For example, a preference score of S 15 is represented by an SN continuous score of 85; a preference score of I 25 is represented by an EI continuous score of 125. The uses of continuous scores in research are discussed in Chapters 9 and 11.

Note that for consistency and ease of interpretation, all notation shows E, S, T, and J on the left and continues toward I, N, F, and P on the right.

Computer Scoring

Computer scoring services are provided for the MBTI and software is available for personal computers. For the latest list of mail-in scoring and software refer to the Consulting Psychologists Press catalog.

Table 2.2 Conversion table for preference scores and continuous scores

E, S, T, or J			I, N, F, or P		
Difference in Points	Preference Score	Continuous Score	Difference in Points	Preference Score	Continuous Score
1	1	99	0	1	101
2	3	97	1	3	103
3	5	95	2	5	105
4	7	93	3	7	107
5	9	91	4	9	109
6	11	89	5	11	111
7	13	87	6	13	113
8	15	85	7	15	115
9	17	83	8	17	117
10	19	81	9	19	119
11	21	79	10	21	121
12	23	77	11	23	123
13	25	75	12	25	125
14	27	73	13	27	127
15	29	71	14	29	129
16	31	69	15	31	131
17	33	67	16	33	113
18	35	65	17	35	135
19	37	63	18	37	137
20	39	61	19	39	139
21	41	59	20	41	141
22	43	57	21	43	143
23	45	55	22	45	145
24	47	53	23	47	147
25	49	51	24	49	149
26	51	49	25	51	151
27	53	47	26	53	153
28	55	45	27	55	155
29	57	43	28	57	157
30	59	41	29	59	159
31	61	39	30	61	161
32	63	37	31	63	163
33	65	35	32	65	165
34	67	33	33	67	167

Table 2.3 Preference score ranges for Form F and Form G

	Form F	Form G
	E53 ... 0 ... I59	E51 ... 0 ... I57
	S67 ... 0 ... N51	S67 ... 0 ... N51
Males	T65 ... 0 ... F39	T65 ... 0 ... F39
Females	T65 ... 0 ... F43	T65 ... 0 ... F43
	J55 ... 0 ... P61	J55 ... 0 ... P61

Chapter 3

The Theory behind the MBTI

It is fashionable to say that an individual is unique. Certainly each individual is a product of heredity and environment and as a result, is different from everyone else. The doctrine of uniqueness, however, gives no practical help in understanding the people whom we must educate, counsel, work with, or deal with in our personal lives.

In practice we tend to assume unconsciously that other people's *minds* work on the same principles as our own. This assumption is not much practical help. All too often the people we interact with do not reason as we reason, do not value the things we value, or are not interested in what interests us.

The merit of the theory underlying the MBTI is that it enables us to expect specific differences in specific people and to cope with the people and their differences more constructively than we otherwise could. Briefly, the theory is that much seemingly chance variation in human behavior is not due to chance; it is in fact the logical result of a few basic, observable preferences.

The Myers-Briggs Type Indicator was designed explicitly to make it possible to test C. J. Jung's theory of psychological types (Jung 1921/1971) and to put it to practical use.[4] Jungian theory was taken into account in every question and in every step of development of the MBTI. Many details of the research leading up to Forms F, G, and AV are described in Chapter 9. The MBTI theory is explained in detail in *Gifts Differing* (Myers with Myers, 1980), a basic reference for all who plan to use the MBTI. In developing the MBTI, Myers and Briggs built on certain statements by Jung that touched on issues relating to the dynamic model. They extended the model in the JP scale by making explicit one aspect of the theory that was implicit but undeveloped in Jung's work. Jungians themselves do not agree about some specifics of Jung's psychological type theory. When the term *type theory* is used in this Manual, it refers to Jung's theory as interpreted by Isabel Myers and Katharine Briggs in the MBTI.

The Four Functions: S, N, T, and F

The essence of Jung's comprehensive theory that relates to psychological types is the belief that everyone uses four basic mental *functions* or *processes* which are called sensing (S), intuition (N), thinking (T), and feeling (F).[5] Everyone uses these four essential functions daily. The sixteen types differ only in the priorities they give to each function and in the attitudes [introversion (I) and extraversion (E)] in which they typically use each function. Chapters in this Manual dealing with type development and dominant and auxiliary functions describe how types differ in these priorities.

The four processes postulated by Jung (S, N, T, and F) represent an individual's orientation to consciousness and are referred to as *orienting functions*. Jung defined a function as "a particular form of psychic activity that remains the same in principle under varying conditions" (Jung 1921/1971, p. 436). Jung's concept of the four functions grew from his empirical observations over many years: Jung concluded "I distinguish these functions from one another because they cannot be related or reduced to one another (Jung, 1921/1971, p. 437). Type theory assumes, therefore, that the many aspects of conscious mental activity can be subsumed under one of these four categories.

To understand Jung's theory it is important to appreciate the critical importance of the uses of the terms *perception* and *judgment*.

Perception includes the many ways of becoming aware of things, people, events, or ideas. It includes information gathering, the seeking of sensation or of inspiration, and the selection of the stimulus to be attended to.

Judgment includes all the ways of coming to conclusions about what has been perceived. It includes decision making, evaluation, choice, and the selection of the response after perceiving the stimulus.

Two Kinds of Perception:
Sensing (S) and Intuition (N)

Jung divided all perceptive activities into two categories—sensing and intuition. He called these *irrational functions* by which he meant that these functions are attuned to the flow of events and operate most broadly when not constrained by rational direction. The modern technique of *brainstorming* uses intuition in Jung's sense as an "irrational" function. During brainstorming, inspirations are encouraged to flow freely, without the constraint of criticism or evaluation.

Sensing Perception (S).
Sensing (S) refers to perceptions observable by way of the senses. Sensing establishes what exists. Because the senses can bring to awareness only

what is occurring in the present moment, persons oriented toward sensing perception tend to focus on the immediate experience and often develop characteristics associated with this awareness such as enjoying the present moment, realism, acute powers of observation, memory for details, and practicality.

Intuitive Perception (N).
Intuition (N) refers to perception of possibilities, meanings, and relationships by way of insight. Jung characterized intuition as perception by way of the unconscious. Intuitions may come to the surface of consciousness suddenly, as a "hunch," the sudden perception of a pattern in seemingly unrelated events, or as a creative discovery. For example, when the sensing function is used to perceive an apple, a person will use terms to describe it like "juicy," "crisp," "red," or "white with black seeds." When the intuitive function is used to perceive the same apple, a person may report "William Tell," "How to keep the doctor away," "Roast pig," or "My grandmother's famous pie."

Intuition permits perception beyond what is visible to the senses, including possible future events. Thus, persons oriented toward intuitive perception may become so intent on pursuing possibilities that they may overlook actualities. They may develop the characteristics that can follow from emphasis on intuition and become imaginative, theoretical, abstract, future oriented, or creative.[6]

Two Kinds of Judgment:
Thinking (T) and Feeling (F)

Jung used the terms *thinking* and *feeling* in specialized ways to refer to the *rational functions* that are directed toward bringing life events into harmony with the laws of reason.

Thinking Judgment (T).
Thinking (T) is the function that links ideas together by making logical connections. Thinking relies on principles of cause and effect and tends to be impersonal. Persons who are primarily oriented toward thinking may develop characteristics associated with thinking: analytical ability, objectivity, concern with principles of justice and fairness, criticality, and an orientation to time that is concerned with connections from the past through the present and toward the future.

Feeling Judgment (F).
Feeling (F) is the function by which one comes to decisions by weighing relative values and merits of the issues. Feeling relies on an understanding of personal values and group values; thus, it is more subjective than thinking. Because values are subjective and personal, persons making judgments with the feeling function are more likely to be attuned to the values of

others as well as their own. Because people oriented toward feeling make decisions by attending to what matters to others, they have an understanding of people, a concern with the human as opposed to the technical aspects of problems, a need for affiliation, a capacity for warmth, a desire for harmony, and a time orientation that includes preservation of the values of the past. The classical distinction in psychology between "tough-minded" and "tender-minded" people is concerned with the TF difference.

The Roles of the Functions

The four functions direct conscious mental activity toward different goals:

- Sensation (S) seeks the fullest possible experience of what is immediate and real.

- Intuition (N) seeks the furthest reaches of the possible and imaginative.

- Thinking (T) seeks rational order and plan according to impersonal logic.

- Feeling (F) seeks rational order according to harmony among subjective values.

The key to the dynamics of the theory lies in the assumption that the four functions pull in different directions. To compare a personality to a ship at sea, we take it for granted that a ship needs a captain with undisputed authority to set the course and bring the ship safely to port. The ship would never reach its destination if each helmsman in turn aimed at a different destination and altered course accordingly. In type theory, one of the four functions is the favorite or dominant function. This dominant function serves as the "captain" of the personality. It determines what is the desired direction and keeps the ship on course. The other functions are important, but are subordinate to and serve the goals of the dominant function. The way in which the dominant and other functions interrelate in each type will be described after the following discussion of extraversion-introversion (EI) and judgment-perception (JP).

The Attitudes: Extraversion (E) and Introversion (I)

The major part of Jung's *Psychological Types* (1921/1971) is devoted to the history and description of extraversion and introversion. These are seen as complementary attitudes or orientations toward life.

The Extraverted Attitude (E)

In the extraverted attitude (E), attention seems to flow ᴄ or to be drawn out, to the objects and people of tʰ environment. There is a desire to act on the environment, tᴄ affirm its importance, to increase its effect. Persons habitually taking the extraverted attitude may develop some or all of the characteristics associated with extraversion: awareness and reliance on the environment for stimulation and guidance; an action-oriented, sometimes impulsive way of meeting life; frankness; ease of communication; or sociability.

The Introverted Attitude (I)

In the introverted attitude (I), energy is drawn from the environment, and consolidated within one's position. The main interests of the introvert are in the inner world of concepts and ideas. Persons habitually taking the introverted attitude may develop some or all of the characteristics associated with introversion: interest in the clarity of concepts and ideas; reliance on enduring concepts more than on transitory external events; a thoughtful, contemplative detachment; and enjoyment of solitude and privacy.

In everyday usage, the term *extravert* often means *sociable*, and *introvert* means *shy*. Jung's concept, and Myers' descriptions are much broader than the layperson's view. Extraverts and introverts are assumed to be variants of normal human personality, recognized through history and literature, and each with major contributions to society.

Judgment (J) and Perception (P): Orientation to the Outer World

Jung described extraversion-introversion (EI), sensing-intuition (SN), and thinking-feeling (TF) explicitly in his work; the importance of judgment and perception was implicit in Jung's work, and was made explicit by Isabel Myers and Katharine Briggs in the development of the MBTI. The JP preference has two uses. First, it describes identifiable attitudes[7] and behaviors to the outside world. Second, it is used, in conjunction with EI, to identify which of the two preferred functions is the leading or dominant function and which is the auxiliary. The recognition and development of facts about the JP function are a major contribution of Briggs and Myers to the theory of psychological types.

The JP attitude was derived before the MBTI was begun from close observations of behavior over a period of several decades. Behaviors characteristic of persons who used either thinking or feeling in their outer life (i.e., who extraverted one of the judgment functions) formed the basis for the J pole of the JP preference. Behaviors characteristic of persons who used either sensing or intuition in their outer life (i.e., who extraverted a perceptive function) formed the basis of the P pole of the JP preference. One of the most overlooked characteristics of the JP scale is that *for every type* it describes the orientation to the outer or extraverted world. Since extraverted activities are by definition more apparent in behavior than introverted activities, the JP attitude is often one of the earliest recognized.

In any new activity, it is appropriate first to use a perceptive function (S or N) to observe or take in the situation; then it is appropriate to use a judgment function (T or F) to decide on the appropriate action. Perceptive types typically remain longer in the observing attitude; judging types move more quickly through perception in order to reach conclusions.

The Perceptive Attitude (P)

In the *perceptive attitude* (P), a person is attuned to incoming information. For sensing-perceptive (SP) types the information is more likely to be the immediate realities. For intuitive-perceptive (NP) types the information is more likely to be new possibilities. But for both SP and NP types the perceptive attitude is open, curious, and interested. Persons who characteristically live in the perceptive attitude seem in their outer behavior to be spontaneous, curious, and adaptable, open to new events and changes, and aiming to miss nothing.

The Judging Attitude (J)

In the *judging attitude* (J), a person is concerned with making decisions, seeking closure, planning operations, or organizing activities. For thinking-judging (TJ) types the decisions and plans are more likely to be based on logical analysis; for feeling-judging (FJ) types the decisions and plans are more likely to be based on human factors. But for all persons who characteristically live in the judging (J) attitude, perception tends to be shut off as soon as they have observed enough to make a decision. (In contrast, persons who prefer the perceptive attitude will often suspend judgment to take another look, reporting "We don't know enough yet to make a decision.") Persons who prefer J often seem in their outer behavior to be organized, purposeful, and decisive.

Procrastination comes from perception with a deficit of judgment. Prejudice comes from judgment with a deficit of perception. Persons new to the MBTI sometimes assume that judging types are necessarily judgmental. It is important to make sure it is understood that judgment refers to decision making, the exercise of judgment, and is a valuable and indispensable tool.

The Theory of Type Development

Type theory assumes that children are born with a predisposition to prefer some functions over others. Children are most interested in the domain of their preferred function. They are motivated to exercise their dominant function, becoming more skillful, adept, and differentiated in its use. With the reinforcement of constant practice, the preferred function becomes more controlled and trustworthy. A sense of competence comes from exercising a function well. The pleasure of using the function generalizes to other activities requiring use of the function, and leads to the surface traits, behaviors, and skills associated with the function.

While this development of a preferred function is occurring, there is *relative* neglect of the opposite pole of the same preference. In this sequence of events, for example, a child who prefers sensing perception and a child who prefers intuitive perception will develop along divergent lines. Each will become *relatively* differentiated in an area where the other remains undifferentiated. Both channel their interests and energies into activities that give them a chance to use their minds in the ways they prefer, and each acquires the set of surface traits that grow out of the basic preferences beneath.

For example, a person who develops sensing in a highly differentiated way is likely to become an astute observer of the immediate environment. As development occurs, the person develops some of the characteristics assumed to follow from this acute awareness: realism, practicality, and common sense. While attention is being given to the specifics of the environment, the person spends less time and energy using intuition, which is the perceptive function opposite to sensing. Focusing on the present (S) gives people who prefer the sensing function less time for focusing on the future (N); focusing on the concrete (S) gives them less energy for focusing on the abstract (N); focusing on practical applications (S) gives them less interest in theoretical issues (N); and focusing on reality (S) gives them less time for focusing on imagination (N).

In this model, *environment* becomes extremely important because environmental factors can foster development of each person's natural preferences, or it can discourage their natural bent by reinforcing activities that are less satisfying and less motivating, making skill development more difficult. Environmental interference with type development can result in a "falsification" of type. Falsified individuals may become skillful in using an initially less-preferred function, but may also be less content, may feel less competent, or may be out of touch with their own best gifts. When an individual answers the MBTI, one cannot know the extent to which natural development has been fostered or thwarted. Chapter 5 will discuss some of the strategies for helping individuals identify their true preferences.

Type development is seen as a lifelong process of gaining greater command over the functions or powers of perception and judgment. For each type, two of the four functions are assumed to be more interesting and more likely to be consciously developed and used. The other two less-preferred functions are assumed to be less interesting and are likely to be relatively neglected. Development comes from striving for excellence in those functions that hold the greatest interest and from becoming at least passable in the other less interesting, but essential functions. In youth, the task is to develop the first (*leading or dominant*) and the second (*auxiliary*) functions; in midlife one can gain greater command over the less preferred third and fourth (or inferior) functions. A very few exceptional persons may reach a stage of individuation where they can use each function easily as the situation requires. The theory assumes that youth is the time for specialization and that midlife is the time to become a generalist.

Some people dislike the idea of a dominant function and prefer to think of themselves as using all the functions equally. Jung said that such impartiality, where it actually exists, keeps all the functions undeveloped and produces a "primitive mentality." Optimum use of the four functions, therefore, is not to be obtained through a strict level of equality, but through selective development of each function in proportion both to its relative importance to the individual and to its useful relationship to the other processes. This development will require:

- Development of excellence in the favorite, dominant process.

- Adequate but not equal development of the auxiliary for balance.

- Eventual admission of the least developed processes to conscious, purposeful use in the service of the dominant process, even though this use may require the dominant and auxiliary to temporarily relinquish control in consciousness so that the third or fourth function can become more conscious.[8]

- Use of each of the functions for the tasks for which they are best fitted.

The Dynamic Interaction of Preferences

When a person answers the MBTI, votes are cast for extraversion (E) or introversion (I), sensing (S) or intuition (N), thinking (T) or feeling (F), and judgment (J) or perception (P).[9]

The letters for the chosen preferences appear in the type formula in this order: E or I, S or N, T or F, J or P. All sixteen possible combinations of letters occur—ESTJ, ISFP, INFJ, ENTP, and so on. The four-letter type formulas stand for a complex set of dynamic relationships between the functions (S, N, T, and F), the attitudes (E and I), and the orientation to the outer world (J and P).

Jung (1921/1971) first described eight preference types:

Extraverts with dominant sensing
Introverts with dominant sensing

Extraverts with dominant intuition
Introverts with dominant intuition

Extraverts with dominant thinking
Introverts with dominant thinking

Extraverts with dominant feeling
Introverts with dominant feeling

Jung described, but did not go into great detail concerning, the need for an auxiliary function that was "in every respect different from the nature of the primary function" (Jung, 1921/1971, p. 406). In writing about introverted thinking types (p. 307), Jung commented that in introverts with thinking dominant the counterbalancing functions have an extraverted character. Myers and Briggs used these ideas in their dynamic representation of the MBTI types. They assumed:

1. For each type, one function will lead or be dominant. This is the first function.

2. Members of each type will mainly use their first function in the favorite attitude. That is, extraverts use the first function mainly in the outer world of extraversion; introverts use the first function mainly in the introverted world of concepts and ideas.

3. In addition to the first or dominant function, a second or auxiliary function will be developed to provide balance.

4. The second function provides balance between extraversion and introversion. For extraverts, the first or

dominant function will be extraverted, and the second or auxiliary will typically be used in the inner world. For introverts, the first or dominant function will be introverted and the second or auxiliary will typically be used in the outer world. In the development of the auxiliary or second function, therefore, a person develops skills in living in both the outer world and the inner world.

Notice that in this model, extraverts show their first or best function to the world; introverts show their second-best function to the outside world, saving their best function for the inner world of ideas. It follows, therefore, that introverts are more likely to be underestimated in casual contacts, since they show their second-best, not their best function.

The fact that the second function provides balance between extraversion and introversion also provides an answer to a common misconception of persons first learning type theory. Extraverts may assume that type theory says they never like to be alone, and introverts may assume that type theory says they never like to be sociable. Type theory, however, assumes that everyone lives in both the extraverted and introverted worlds to some extent (with many attaining competence in both worlds) but that for each person one attitude is preferred. A well-developed introvert can deal ably with the extraverted world, when necessary, but works best, most easily, and most enjoyably with ideas. A similarly well-developed extravert can deal effectively with ideas, but works best, with most interest and satisfaction, externally in action. Good type development fosters the ability to extravert comfortably and to introvert comfortably, but assumes also a natural preference for one attitude or the other.

5. The second function also provides balance between perception and judgment. If the first function is a perceptive function (S or N), the second function will be a judgment function (T or F). Or, if the first function is a judgment function (T or F), the second function will be a perceptive function (S or N). In the development of the auxiliary, therefore, the person gains command of both perception and judgment, that is, of taking in information and making decisions or of seeing the stimulus and making the response.

6. The JP preference, as noted earlier, points to the function used in the extraverted attitude, for *both extraverts and introverts.*

7. If the dominant function is typically extraverted, the other three functions will be typically introverted. If the dominant function is typically introverted, the other three functions are typically extraverted.[10]

8. The function opposed to the dominant is typically the least developed or inferior function.[11] It can also be referred to as the fourth function.

9. The function opposite to the auxiliary is the third or tertiary function.

These assumptions make it possible to use the type formula to identify the use of the first (dominant), second (auxiliary), third, and fourth (inferior) functions for each of the sixteen types.

Identifying the Dynamics from the Type Formula

The type formula shows the preferences in a fixed order (see also Table 3.1):

First letter: preference for E or I.

Second letter: preference for the perceptive function S or N.

Third letter: preference for the judgment function T or F.

Fourth letter: JP index used to point to the visible, extraverted function. This is the first step in identifying the first or dominant function.

Identifying Dynamic Relationships for *Extraverted* Types

Step One: Look at the fourth letter. If it is J, it points to the third letter, since the third letter gives the chosen judgment function. If it is P, it points to the second letter, where the chosen perceptive function appears.

**Example: E S T J—J points to T.
            E N F P—P points to N.**

Step Two: By definition, JP points to that one of the preferred functions which is typically extraverted. The other preferred function will typically be introverted.

Example: E S T J—T is extraverted, S is introverted.

Table 3.1 Positions of preferences in type formula

EI	SN	TF	JP
Extraversion or introversion	Sensing or intuition	Thinking or feeling	Judgment or perception
Attitudes	Perception functions	Judgment functions	Attitudes or orientation to outer world

E N F P—N is extraverted, F is introverted.

Step Three: For extraverted types, the extraverted function is dominant and the introverted function is auxiliary.

Example: **E S T J—T is extraverted so must be the first or dominant. S is introverted so must be the second or auxiliary.**

E N F P—N is extraverted so must be the first or dominant. F is introverted so must be the second or auxiliary.

Step Four: For all types, the third function is the opposite of the second, and the fourth or inferior function is the opposite of the first.

Example: **E S T J—T is #1, S is #2, N is #3, and F is #4. E N F P—N is #1, F is #2, T is #3, and S is #4.**

Identifying Dynamic Relationships for *Introverted* Types

Step One: (same as for extraverts)—Look at the fourth letter. If it is J, it points to the third letter, since the third letter gives the chosen judgment function. If it is P, it points to the second letter, where the chosen perceptive function appears.

Example: **I S T J—J points to T. I N F P—P points to N.**

Step Two: (same as for extraverts)—JP points to the extraverted function, therefore:

Example: **I S T J—T is extraverted, S is introverted. I N F P—N is extraverted, F is introverted.**

Step Three: For introverted types, the extraverted function is auxiliary and the introverted function is dominant.

Example: **I S T J—T is extraverted so must be the second or auxiliary. S is introverted so must be the first or dominant.**

I N F P—N is extraverted so must be the second or auxiliary. F is introverted so must be the first or dominant.

Step Four: For all types, the third function is the opposite of the second, and the fourth or inferior function is opposite the first.

Example: **I S T J—S is #1, T is #2, F is #3, and N is #4. I N F P—F is #1, N is #2, S is #3, and T is #4.**

Once the principles are grasped, one can use the brief rule: JP points to the dominant for extraverts and to the auxiliary for introverts. Table 3.2 shows the theoretical uses of the four functions for each of the sixteen types.

Example of Dynamics in Type ENTP

ENTP is an extravert with intuition (N) the dominant, extraverted function and thinking (T) the auxiliary, introverted function.

In theory, therefore, ENTPs trust intuition (#1) most, use it most, develop it most, and shape their lives to give the maximum freedom for pursuing their intuitive goals. They use their thinking (#2) in pursuit of something challenging to their intuition, but may not let their thinking (#2) veto anything their intuition (#1) seriously desires. Being oriented to the challenge of new possibilities (N #1) in the outer world (E), they may often find themselves over-committed to too many projects. (This is especially likely

Table 3.2 Priorities and direction of functions in each type

ISTJ				ISFJ				INFJ				INTJ			
#1	DOMINANT	S	(I)	#1	DOMINANT	S	(I)	#1	DOMINANT	N	(I)	#1	DOMINANT	N	(I)
#2	AUXILIARY	T	(E)	#2	AUXILIARY	F	(E)	#2	AUXILIARY	F	(E)	#2	AUXILIARY	T	(E)
#3	TERTIARY	F	(E)	#3	TERTIARY	T	(E)	#3	TERTIARY	T	(E)	#3	TERTIARY	F	(E)
#4	inferior	N	(E)	#4	inferior	N	(E)	#4	inferior	S	(E)	#4	inferior	S	(E)
ISTP				**ISFP**				**INFP**				**INTP**			
#1	DOMINANT	T	(I)	#1	DOMINANT	F	(I)	#1	DOMINANT	F	(I)	#1	DOMINANT	T	(I)
#2	AUXILIARY	S	(E)	#2	AUXILIARY	S	(E)	#2	AUXILIARY	N	(E)	#2	AUXILIARY	N	(E)
#3	TERTIARY	N	(E)	#3	TERTIARY	N	(E)	#3	TERTIARY	S	(E)	#3	TERTIARY	S	(E)
#4	inferior	F	(E)	#4	inferior	T	(E)	#4	inferior	T	(E)	#4	inferior	F	(E)
ESTP				**ESFP**				**ENFP**				**ENTP**			
#1	DOMINANT	S	(E)	#1	DOMINANT	S	(E)	#1	DOMINANT	N	(E)	#1	DOMINANT	N	(E)
#2	AUXILIARY	T	(I)	#2	AUXILIARY	F	(I)	#2	AUXILIARY	F	(I)	#2	AUXILIARY	T	(I)
#3	TERTIARY	F	(I)	#3	TERTIARY	T	(I)	#3	TERTIARY	T	(I)	#3	TERTIARY	F	(I)
#4	inferior	N	(I)	#4	inferior	N	(I)	#4	inferior	S	(I)	#4	inferior	S	(I)
ESTJ				**ESFJ**				**ENFJ**				**ENTJ**			
#1	DOMINANT	T	(E)	#1	DOMINANT	F	(E)	#1	DOMINANT	F	(E)	#1	DOMINANT	T	(E)
#2	AUXILIARY	S	(I)	#2	AUXILIARY	S	(I)	#2	AUXILIARY	N	(I)	#2	AUXILIARY	N	(I)
#3	TERTIARY	N	(I)	#3	TERTIARY	N	(I)	#3	TERTIARY	S	(I)	#3	TERTIARY	S	(I)
#4	inferior	F	(I)	#4	inferior	T	(I)	#4	inferior	T	(I)	#4	inferior	F	(I)

to happen to an ENTP because intuitive types typically underestimate the time it takes to bring activities to completion.) When the ENTP decides there are too many activities for the available time, the thinking (#2) function is needed. The ENTP withdraws into the inner world (I), analyzes the costs and consequences of continuing or dropping each activity, and makes a logical judgment (#2) about which projects to drop. With more mature type development, the ENTP may learn to take time to pull back from the exciting challenges (N #1) for action (E) and consider (I) whether the costs permit adding new activities (T #2), *before* taking on new commitments.

The fourth or inferior function of ENTP is sensing (#4); ENTPs need to train themselves not to neglect realities (#4) in the enthusiasm for possibilities (#1). Type theory says that sensing (#4) and feeling (#3) develop more slowly for an ENTP. One way to develop sensing and feeling is on a project chosen by intuition (#1). To accomplish the project the ENTP will need to know many facts and be able to solve many practical details; thus sensing (#4) comes into

play to help intuition (#1). Further, the project may require working in a team or persuading other people; thus feeling (#3) also comes in to help intuition (#1).

Dynamics of the Type Descriptions

The descriptions of each of the types are built on dynamic principles as shown in the description of ENTP. A valuable guide for describing the MBTI types is the *Introduction to Type®* guide (Myers, Fifth Edition, 1993).

Notice that in this Manual, descriptions for the extraverted and introverted version of each function are on facing pages for comparison and study. In *Introduction to Type*, descriptions for types with the same dominant function appear on facing pages. The descriptions typically begin with the characteristics of the dominant and auxiliary functions. A discussion of type development follows, showing the difficulties if the dominant and auxiliary functions are not developed to provide balance. The descriptions also discuss development issues around the tertiary and inferior functions. It is important to understand that the type descriptions, which may seem like horoscopes to the uninitiated, are firmly based on the dynamics of type theory, supplemented by years of observation of the types and empirical results from research. (See Chapter 5 for ways of explaining type description to respondents.)

Table 3.3 shows brief descriptions of preferences as they appear on page 7 of *Introduction to Type*. Tables 3.4–3.11 show the guide's dynamic descriptions as they appear on pages 8–23.

Types are Created by Exercise of Preferences

In summary, the MBTI contains four separate indices: EI, SN, TF, and JP. Two of these, SN and TF, reflect basic preferences for use of perception and judgment. The other two, EI and JP, reflect attitudes or styles of orientation to the inner and outer world. Together, these functions and orientations influence how a person perceives a situation and decides on a course of action. Each of these choices is like a fork in the road of human development, offering different paths that lead toward different kinds of excellence. How far different individuals will go, how much excellence they will actually achieve, depends, in part, upon their energy and aspirations. *The kind of excellence toward which they are headed* is determined, according to type theory, by the inborn preferences that direct them at each fork of the road.

Under this theory people create their "type" by the exercise of their preferences with regard to their use of perception and judgment. People who have the same preferences tend to have in common whatever qualities *result* from the exercise of those preferences. The interests, values, needs, and habits of mind that naturally result tend to produce a recognizable kind of person. We can therefore *partly* describe individuals by stating their preferences as ENTP, ESFJ, INFP, or whatever the case may be.

We can also begin intelligently to expect ENTPs to be different from others in ways characteristic of previously known ENTPs. To describe them as belonging to that type (if they agree that it *is* their type) in no way infringes on their right to be what they like. They were exercising that right when they found, consciously or unconsciously, that they liked extraverting, intuition, thinking, and the perceptive attitude.

When we aim, in dealing with people, to keep their type in mind, we are respecting not only their abstract right to develop along lines of their own choosing, but also *the importance of qualities they have developed by that choice.*

Learning Type through Study of Individual Descriptions

Once the principles of dynamics of type are understood, the next step is to study the descriptions to master the characteristics of each type. Isabel Myers recommended several strategies for this learning. One is to enter the names of persons with known types on the type description pages. Study the description of their type in this Manual and in *Gifts Differing* (Myers, 1980). Consider how many of their characteristics could have developed out of preferences they expressed on the MBTI. Your knowledge of each person enriches your knowledge of type.

Where you find your observations confirming theory, and where you find the theory sharpening your observations, you will be able to draw more useful conclusions about the types of other people. Type theory seems simple, but it is in fact rich and complex. People of the same type differ in many ways. The ways in which type preferences appear are affected by cultural pressures and by the stage of type development a person has reached. To truly understand type, there is no substitute for a prolonged period of interested skepticism in which you match your observations and knowledge of people with predictions from Jung's theory.

Other strategies for understanding the types are described in the next chapter.

Table 3.3 Characteristics frequently associated with
each type

Sensing Types

ISTJ	ISFJ
Serious, quiet, earn success by concentration and thoroughness. Practical, orderly, matter-of-fact, logical, realistic, and dependable. See to it that everything is well organized. Take responsibility. Make up their own minds as to what should be accomplished and work toward it steadily, regardless of protests or distractions.	Quiet, friendly, responsible, and conscientious. Work devotedly to meet their obligations. Lend stability to any project or group. Thorough, painstaking, accurate. Their interests are usually not technical. Can be patient with necessary details. Loyal, considerate, perceptive, concerned with how other people feel.
ISTP	**ISFP**
Cool onlookers—quiet, reserved, observing and analyzing life with detached curiosity and unexpected flashes of original humor. Usually interested in cause and effect, how and why mechanical things work, and in organizing facts using logical principles. Excel at getting to the core of a practical problem and finding the solution.	Retiring, quietly friendly, sensitive, kind, modest about their abilities. Shun disagreements, do not force their opinions or values on others. Usually do not care to lead but are often loyal followers. Often relaxed about getting things done because they enjoy the present moment and do not want to spoil it by undue haste or exertion.
ESTP	**ESFP**
Good at on-the-spot problem solving. Like action, enjoy whatever comes along. Tend to like mechanical things and sports, with friends on the side. Adaptable, tolerant, pragmatic; focused on getting results. Dislike long explanations. Are best with real things that can be worked, handled, taken apart, or put together.	Outgoing, accepting, friendly, enjoy everything and make things more fun for others by their enjoyment. Like action and making things happen. Know what's going on and join in eagerly. Find remembering facts easier than mastering theories. Are best in situa-tions that need sound common sense and practical ability with people.
ESTJ	**ESFJ**
Practical, realistic, matter-of-fact, with a natural head for business or mechanics. Not interested in abstract theories; want learning to have direct and immediate application. Like to organize and run activities. Often make good administrators; are decisive, quickly move to implement decisions; take care of routine details.	Warm-hearted, talkative, popular, conscientious, born cooperators, active committee members. Need harmony and may be good at creating it. Always doing something nice for someone. Work best with encouragement and praise. Main interest is in things that directly and visibly affect people's lives.

Introverts

Extraverts

Intuitive Types

INFJ

Succeed by perseverance, originality, and desire to do whatever is needed or wanted. Put their best efforts into their work. Quietly forceful, conscientious, concerned for others. Respected for their firm principles. Likely to be honored and followed for their clear visions as to how best to serve the common good.

INTJ

Have original minds and great drive for their own ideas and purposes. Have long-range vision and quickly find meaningful patterns in external events. In fields that appeal to them, they have a fine power to organize a job and carry it through. Skeptical, critical, independent, determined, have high standards of competence and performance.

INFP

Quiet observers, idealistic, loyal. Important that outer life be congruent with inner values. Curious, quick to see possibilities, often serve as catalysts to implement ideas. Adaptable, flexible, and accepting unless a value is threatened. Want to understand people and ways of fulfilling human potential. Little concern with possessions or surroundings.

INTP

Quiet and reserved. Especially enjoy theoretical or scientific pursuits. Like solving problems with logic and analysis. Interested mainly in ideas, with little liking for parties or small talk. Tend to have sharply defined interests. Need careers where some strong interest can be used and useful.

ENFP

Warmly enthusiastic, high-spirited, ingenious, imaginative. Able to do almost anything that interests them. Quick with a solution for any difficulty and ready to help anyone with a problem. Often rely on their ability to improvise instead of preparing in advance. Can usually find compelling reasons for whatever they want.

ENTP

Quick, ingenious, good at many things. Stimulating company, alert and outspoken. May argue for fun on either side of a question. Resourceful in solving new and challenging problems, but may neglect routine assignments. Apt to turn to one new interest after another. Skillful in finding logical reasons for what they want.

ENFJ

Responsive and responsible. Feel real concern for what others think or want, and try to handle things with due regard for the other's feelings. Can present a proposal or lead a group discussion with ease and tact. Sociable, popular, sympathetic. Responsive to praise and criticism. Like to facilitate others and enable people to achieve their potential.

ENTJ

Frank, decisive, leaders in activities. Develop and implement comprehensive systems to solve organizational problems. Good in anything that requires reasoning and intelligent talk, such as public speaking. Are usually well informed and enjoy adding to their fund of knowledge.

Introverts

Extraverts

Table 3.4 Extraverted Thinking Types descriptions

ESTJ   Extraverted Thinking with Introverted Sensing

At Their Best

People with ESTJ preferences like to organize projects, operations, procedures, and people, and then act to get things done. They live by a set of clear standards and beliefs, make a systematic effort to follow these, and expect the same of others. They value competence, efficiency, and results.

ESTJs can be quite gregarious and generally enjoy interacting with people, especially around tasks, games, traditions, and family activities. They take relationship roles seriously and fulfill them responsibly. Others usually see ESTJs as

- conscientious and dependable
- decisive, outspoken, and self-confident

Characteristics of ESTJs

ESTJs take an objective approach to problem solving and are tough when the situation requires toughness. They use their Thinking primarily externally to organize their lives and work, and have little patience with confusion, inefficiency, or halfway measures. ESTJs are likely to be

- logical, analytical, objectively critical
- decisive, clear, and assertive

ESTJs focus on the present—what is real and actual. They apply and adapt relevant past experience to deal with problems, and they prefer jobs where results are immediate, visible, and tangible. ESTJs are likely to be

- practical, realistic, and matter-of-fact
- systematic and pragmatic

ESTJs are excellent administrators because they understand systems and logistics. They can project the steps needed to accomplish a task, foresee potential problems, assign responsibilities, and marshal resources. They cover all the bases, leave no loose ends, and get things done on time. When they see things are not working, they will plan and act to correct the situation. Otherwise, they prefer proven procedures and systems. Their orientation is to tasks, action, and the bottom line.

How Others May See Them

Because they naturally devise systems, procedures, and schedules, others rely on ESTJs to take charge and get things done. Others may also find them overpowering—ESTJs are so certain about how things should be! Because they are clear and straightforward in their communication, people seldom have to wonder where they stand.

Potential Areas for Growth

Sometimes life circumstances have not supported ESTJs in the development and expression of their Sensing and Thinking preferences.

- If they've not developed their Sensing, ESTJs may decide too quickly before taking in enough information. Then their decisions will reflect their previously-formed judgments or biases.
- If they've not developed their Thinking, they may not have a reliable way of evaluating information and thus end up making inconsistent or overly harsh decisions.

If ESTJs do not find a place where they can use their gifts and be appreciated for their contributions, they usually feel frustrated and may

- become rigid and dogmatic,
- become intrusive, "know-it-all" experts, overpowering others and refusing to listen, and
- get picky about details and be impatient with those who do not follow procedures exactly.

It is natural for ESTJs to give less attention to their non-preferred Feeling and Intuitive parts. If they neglect these too much, however, they may

- apply logic even when feelings and impacts on people need primary consideration,
- fail to respond to others' needs for intimate connection and processing of feelings, and
- not always see the wider ramifications of a seemingly simple, direct action.

Under great stress, ESTJs may feel alone and unappreciated, and be unable to communicate their inner feeling of distress and despair.

ENTJ   Extraverted Thinking with Introverted Intuition

At Their Best

People with ENTJ preferences are natural leaders and organization builders. They conceptualize and theorize readily and translate possibilities into plans to achieve short-term and long-term objectives. They readily see illogical and inefficient procedures and feel a strong urge to correct them—to organize people and situations to get them moving in the right direction.

ENTJs prefer that things be settled and clear, but their love of ideas can pull them into wide-ranging Intuitive exploration and discussions. Their verbal fluency, decisiveness, self-confidence, and urge to organize others can overpower people at times. Others usually see ENTJs as

- direct, challenging, and decisive
- objective, fair, and stimulating

Characteristics of ENTJs

ENTJs use their Thinking primarily externally and are, thus, natural critics. They set their own standards and are forceful in applying these to others, to organizations, and to themselves. They value intelligence and competence and abhor inefficiency. They can be tough when the situation calls for toughness. ENTJs are likely to be

- analytical, logical, and objectively critical
- decisive, clear, and assertive

ENTJs are intellectually curious, seek new ideas, and like complex problems. They use their Intuition primarily internally to conceive possibilities and create the insights they use in making decisions and plans. ENTJs are likely to be

- conceptual
- innovative theorizers and planners

ENTJs are excellent solvers of organizational problems. They are keenly aware of the intricate connections within organizations and are action-oriented and strategic—they think ahead, anticipate problems, devise broad plans and systems, and marshall the human and material resources to achieve goals. They are generally disinterested in routine maintenance activities, preferring the stimulation of new challenges.

How Others May See Them

ENTJs love, and are energized by, stimulating interactions with people. They often challenge statements and behaviors, expecting that others will defend them and that, as a result, mutual learning will take place. ENTJs admire and seek out people who stand up to them, say what they think, and argue persuasively.

Potential Areas for Growth

Sometimes life circumstances have not supported ENTJs in the development and expression of their Intuitive and Thinking preferences.

- If they've not developed their Intuition, ENTJs may make decisions too quickly without considering alternatives or exploring possibilities. In this case, their decisiveness can become dictatorial.
- If they've not developed their Thinking, they may not have a reliable way to evaluate their insights and make plans. Then their decision making will be inconsistent and changeable.

If ENTJs do not find a place where they can use their gifts and be appreciated for their contributions, they usually feel frustrated and may

- become overly impersonal and critical,
- be intrusive and directive—giving orders without listening, and
- become abrasive and verbally aggressive.

It is natural for ENTJs to give less attention to their non-preferred Feeling and Sensing parts. If they neglect these too much, however, they may

- fail to notice or value another's need for personal connection, appreciation, and praise,
- fail to factor into their plans the needs of others for support and processing time, and
- overlook specifics and realistic factors that are necessary to carry their plans to completion.

Under great stress, ENTJs can be overwhelmed by self-doubt, feel alone and unappreciated, and feel unable to express their distress to others.

Table 3.5 Introverted Thinking Types descriptions

ISTP Introverted Thinking with Extraverted Sensing

At Their Best

People with ISTP preferences carefully observe what is going on around them. Then, when the need arises, they move quickly to get to the core of a problem and solve it with the greatest efficiency and the least effort. They are interested in how and why things work, but find abstract theories uninteresting unless they can quickly apply them. They often function as troubleshooters.

ISTPs resist regimentation and rules, thrive on variety and novelty, and enjoy the challenge of solving a new, concrete, extensive problem.

Characteristics of ISTPs

ISTPs use their Thinking primarily internally to see the essential structure underlying the facts. Their minds work almost like computers, reasoning impersonally and objectively. They make rational decisions based on a great deal of concrete data. ISTPs are likely to be

- detached and objectively critical
- analytical and logical problem-solvers

ISTPs are realists, focusing on what is and what can be done with it, rather than on theoretical possibilities. They are often good at hands-on activities and enjoy sports and the outdoors. ISTPs are likely to be

- practical and realistic,
- factual and pragmatic

ISTPs are expedient and believe in economy of effort—doing only what's needed with the least possible discussion and fuss. If they neglect the desired results.

How Others May See Them

ISTPs are egalitarian and generally tolerant of a wide range of behavior—until their ruling, logical principles are attacked. At that point, they can surprise others by expressing their firm and clear judgments. ISTPs listen and seem to agree because they are not disagreeing; later, others may find the ISTP was analyzing and making judgments within.

With their constant scanning for information and focus on results, ISTPs will change course readily if they see another, more efficient way. Because of this, others

sometimes have trouble "reading" them. They tend to be quiet and reserved, though they can be quite talkative in areas where they have a lot of knowledge. Others usually see ISTPs as

- adaptable, action-oriented risk-takers
- confident, independent, and self-determined

Potential Areas for Growth

Sometimes life circumstances have not supported ISTPs in the development and expression of their Sensing and Thinking preferences.

- If they've not developed their Sensing, ISTPs may have no reliable way of getting accurate data about the external world or of translating their thoughts into action.
- If they've not developed their Thinking, they may get caught up in the realities around them and not take time to do the internal logical processing they need to make good decisions. Then their actions may be haphazard responses to immediate needs.

If ISTPs do not find a place where they can use their gifts and be appreciated for their contributions, they usually feel frustrated and may

- become cynical and negative,
- withdraw their attention and energy, and
- put off decisions.

It is natural for ISTPs to give less attention to their non-preferred Feeling and Intuitive parts. If they neglect these too much, however, they may

- overlook others' emotional needs and values,
- not give sufficient weight to the impacts of their decisions on people, and
- focus so much on immediate results that they lose track of the long-term ramifications of their decisions and actions.

Under great stress, ISTPs may erupt outwardly in inappropriate displays of emotion. The resulting explosive anger or hurt tearfulness is quite unnerving to others and embarrassing to the usually calm and controlled ISTP.

INTP Introverted Thinking with Extraverted Intuition

At Their Best

People with INTP preferences are independent problem-solvers who excel at providing a detached, concise analysis of an idea or situation. They ask the hard questions, challenging others and themselves to find new logical approaches.

Characteristics of INTPs

INTPs use their Thinking primarily internally to find or develop underlying principles and logical structures for understanding and explaining the world. They approach almost everything with skepticism, form their own opinions and standards, and apply these standards rigorously to themselves. They highly value intelligence and competence. INTPs are likely to be

- logical, analytical, and objectively critical
- detached and contemplative

INTPs see possibilities beyond the present and obvious. They love to theorize and discuss abstractions. INTPs are usually

- mentally quick, insightful, and ingenious
- intensely curious about ideas and theories

INTPs quickly see inconsistencies and illogicality and enjoy taking apart and reworking ideas. They naturally build complex theoretical systems to explain the realities they see. They find it difficult to work on routine things, but bring great energy, intensity, and focus to research-ing or analyzing a problem that arouses their curiosity.

How Others May See Them

INTPs are usually quiet and reserved though they can be talkative in areas where they are especially knowledge-able. Unless their work requires action, they are more interested in the challenge of finding solutions than in putting solutions to practical use. They prefer not to organize people or situations.

INTPs are tolerant of a wide range of behavior, arguing and raising issues only when they believe it is reasonable to do so. This flexibility disappears, however, when their ruling principles are challenged; then they stop adapting.

INTPs prize precision in communication and dislike redundancy or stating the obvious. They want to state

the exact truth, but may make it so complex that others have difficulty understanding. Others usually see INTPs as

- quiet, contained, calm, and detached observers
- independent, valuing autonomy

Potential Areas for Growth

Sometimes life circumstances have not supported INTPs in the development and expression of their Intuitive and Thinking preferences.

- If they've not developed their Intuition, INTPs may have no reliable way for taking in information and be immersed in their internal logical systems. Then they find it difficult to communicate or actualize their ideas.
- If they've not developed their Thinking, they may go from insight to insight, never analyzing them with a critical eye or integrating them into a whole.

If INTPs do not find a place where they can use their gifts and be appreciated for their contributions, they usually feel frustrated and may

- become cynical and negative,
- be sarcastic and destructively critical,
- isolate themselves and put off action, and
- engage in verbal sparring and arguments.

It is natural for INTPs to give less attention to their non-preferred Feeling and Sensing parts. If they neglect these too much, however, they may

- be insensitive to the needs of others for information and emotional connection,
- decide something they or others value is not important because it's "not logical,"
- fail to consider the impact of their ideas on people, and
- be impractical—forgetting details such as appropriate dress, paying bills, physical needs.

Under great stress, INTPs may erupt outwardly in inappropriate displays of emotion. The resulting explosive anger or hurt tearfulness is quite unnerving to others and embarrassing to the usually calm and controlled INTP.

Table 3.6 Extraverted Feeling Types descriptions

ESFJ Extraverted Feeling with Introverted Sensing

At Their Best

People with ESFJ preferences like to organize people and situations and then work with others to complete tasks accurately and on time. They are conscientious and loyal, following through even in small matters, and they want others to be the same. They value security and stability.

Sociable and outgoing, ESFJs are great at celebrations and traditions. They bring a very personal caring to the workplace and home. ESFJs want to be appreciated for themselves and for what they give to others.

Characteristics of ESFJs

ESFJs use their Feeling primarily externally, and radiate warmth and energy. They are encouraged by approval and hurt by indifference or unkindness. Conflict-filled or tense situations make them uncomfortable, and they work to insure these don't occur. ESFJs are likely to be

- warm, sympathetic, and helpful
- personable, cooperative, and tactful
- decisive, thorough, and consistent

ESFJs focus on the present and base decisions on experience and facts. Though they enjoy variety, they adapt well to routine and don't like work which demands mastery of abstract ideas or impersonal analysis. They enjoy their possessions and take good care of them. ESFJs are likely to be

- practical, realistic, and down-to-earth
- decisive, thorough, and consistent

ESFJs are sensitive to the needs of others and good at providing practical caring. Much of their pleasure and satisfaction comes from the comfort and pleasure of people around them.

How Others May See Them

ESFJs are energized by interaction with others and genuinely interested in others' lives and concerns. They feel most comfortable in structured situations and enjoy creating order, structure, and schedules. They prefer to do things the traditional and accepted way.

For the sake of harmony, ESFJs will agree with others when they can. However, they also have strong values which they express clearly and confidently when they think it is appropriate.

ESFJs value family and social ties. They enjoy belonging and are good at celebrations and traditions. Others usually see ESFJs as

- sociable, out-going, enthusiastic, and energetic
- organized and orderly
- committed to preserving traditions

Potential Areas for Growth

Sometimes life circumstances have not supported ESFJs in the development and expression of their Sensing and Feeling preferences.

- If they've not developed their Sensing, ESFJs may not take in much information before making decisions and will then jump to conclusions before fully understanding a situation.
- If they've not developed their Feeling, they may be tentative and uncertain, accepting the judgments of others too quickly.

If ESFJs do not find a place where they can use their gifts and be appreciated for their contributions, they usually feel frustrated and may

- doubt themselves and focus their attention entirely on satisfying the needs of others,
- become overly sensitive, imagining slights where none were intended.

It is natural for ESFJs to give less attention to their non-preferred Thinking and Intuitive parts. If they neglect these too much, however, they may

- find it difficult to acknowledge and deal with the truth of problems with people or things they care about,
- support those in charge or the standard procedures too uncritically, and
- fail to see wider possibilities or alternative ways of doing things.

Under great stress, ESFJs may find themselves uncharacteristically critical of others and of themselves. Their negative thoughts and opinions often trouble them greatly.

ENFJ Extraverted Feeling with Introverted Intuition

At Their Best

People with ENFJ preferences are highly attuned to others, using empathy to quickly understand emotional needs, motivations, and concerns. Their focus is on supporting others and encouraging their growth. ENFJs are catalysts, drawing out the best in others, and they can be inspiring leaders as well as loyal followers.

Characteristics of ENFJs

ENFJs base decisions on personal values. They use their Feeling primarily externally, radiating warmth and energy. They look for and find the best in others and prize harmony and cooperation. They are warmed by approval—responding with energy and devotion—and especially sensitive to criticism or tensions. ENFJs are likely to be

- warm, compassionate, and supportive
- loyal and trustworthy

ENFJs see meanings and connections where others do not. They are curious about new ideas and stimulated by possibilities for contributing to the good of humanity. ENFJs are likely to

- be imaginative
- like variety and new challenges

ENFJs naturally see the potential for growth in others and devote energy to help others achieve it. They are sensitive facilitators. ENFJs take responsibility to organize interactions of colleagues, friends, or family so that all are involved, harmony prevails, and people have fun.

How Others May See Them

ENFJs are energetic, enthusiastic, and very aware of others. Their genuine interest can usually draw out and involve even the most reserved person. They listen to and support others, but also have very definite values and opinions of their own which they will express clearly. ENFJs are energized by people and are socially adept; however, they also have a strong need for authentic intimate relationships. They bring great enthusiasm and intensity to creating and maintaining these.

ENFJs like their lives to be organized and will work to bring closure to ambiguous relationships or situations. However, if people's needs conflict with schedules and rules, they will put people first. Others usually see ENFJs as

- sociable, personable, congenial, and gracious
- expressive, responsive, and persuasive

Potential Areas for Growth

Sometimes life circumstances have not supported ENFJs in the development and expression of their Intuitive and Feeling preferences.

- If they've not developed their Intuition, ENFJs may not see possibilities, making decisions too quickly without taking in enough information or considering factors beyond their own personal values.
- If they've not developed their Feeling, their decisions may be inconsistent and poorly formulated. They may then accept the judgments of others too readily.

If ENFJs do not find a place where they can use their gifts and be appreciated for their contributions, they usually feel frustrated and may

- worry, feel guilty, and doubt themselves,
- become insistent and controlling in their desire for harmony, and
- become overly sensitive to criticism—real or imagined.

It is natural for ENFJs to give less attention to their non-preferred Thinking and Sensing parts. If they neglect these too much, however, they may

- make decisions based solely on personal values when logic is needed also,
- find it difficult to admit to problems or disagreements with people they care about, and
- overlook details required to realize their ideals.

Under great stress, ENFJs may find themselves suddenly and uncharacteristically critical and fault-finding with others. They generally keep these negative opinions to themselves, but they find such thoughts troubling and upsetting.

Table 3.7 Introverted Feeling Types descriptions

ISFP Introverted Feeling with Extraverted Sensing

At Their Best

ISFPs live in the present with a quiet sense of joyfulness and want to have time to experience each moment. They prize the freedom to follow their own course, have their own space, and set their own time frame. They are faithful in fulfilling obligations to people and things that are important to them.

ISFPs may be underestimated by others and may also underrate themselves. They often take for granted what they do well and make too much of the contrast between their inner standards and their actual behavior and accomplishments. Others usually see ISFPs as

- quiet, reserved, and private—hard to know well
- spontaneous and tolerant

Characteristics of ISFPs

ISFPs are guided by a strong core of inner values and want their outer life to be congruent with those. They want their work to be more than just a job; they want to contribute to people's well-being or happiness. They don't enjoy routine, but will work with energy and dedication when doing something they believe in. ISFPs are likely to be

- trusting, kind, and considerate
- sensitive and gentle

ISFPs are acutely aware of the specifics and realities of the present—people and the world around them. They learn by doing more than by reading or hearing. ISFPs are likely to be

- observant
- realistic, practical, concrete, and factual

ISFPs are attuned to the feelings and needs of others and are flexible in responding to them. They often have an affinity for nature and for beauty in all living things—people, plants, and animals. They prize most those who take time to understand the ISFPs' values and goals and support ISFPs in achieving their goals in their own way.

How Others May See Them

ISFPs are adaptable and flexible unless something which matters deeply to them is endangered; then they stop adapting. They care deeply about people, but may show it through doing things for others more than through words.

ISFPs tend to be quiet and unassuming, and their warmth, enthusiasm, and playful humor may not be apparent to people who don't know them well. They prefer not to organize situations, but instead to observe and support; they have little wish to dominate.

Potential Areas for Growth

Sometimes life circumstances have not supported ISFPs in the development and expression of their Sensing and Feeling preferences.

- If they've not developed their Sensing, ISFPs may have no reliable way of getting accurate data about the external world or of actualizing their values. Their decisions will be based on little information and be overly personal.
- If they've not developed their Feeling, they may get caught up in Sensing realities and not take time to do the internal valuing process by which they make their best decisions. They may avoid decision making, allowing others or circumstances to decide for them.

If ISFPs do not find a place where they can use their gifts and be appreciated for their contributions, they usually feel frustrated and may

- withdraw from people and situations,
- passively resist structures and rules,
- be excessively self-critical, and
- feel unappreciated and undervalued.

It is natural for ISFPs to give less attention to their non-preferred Thinking and Intuitive parts. If they neglect these too much, however, they may

- reject or not take seriously logical systems,
- feel ill-equipped to deal with complexity,
- be excessively self-critical, and
- not always see the wider ramifications of their specific, immediate decisions.

ISFPs can, under extreme pressure, become uncharacteristically critical of themselves and others, verbalizing harsh and negative judgments.

INFP Introverted Feeling with Extraverted Intuition

At Their Best

People with INFP preferences have an inner core of values that guides their interactions and decisions. They want to be involved in work that contributes to their own growth and inner development and to that of others—to have a purpose beyond their paycheck. INFPs make a priority of living in congruence with their values.

Characteristics of INFPs

INFPs primarily use their Feeling preference internally where they make decisions based on valuing self-understanding, individuality, and growth. Moral commitment to what they believe in is crucial to INFPs. They are likely to be

- sensitive, concerned, and caring
- loyal to people or a cause

INFPs enjoy reading, discussing, and reflecting on possibilities for positive change in the future. They are quick to see connections and meanings. INFPs are likely to

- be curious and creative
- have long-range vision

INFPs are fascinated by opportunities to explore the complexities of human personality—their own and others'. They tend to work in bursts of energy and are capable of great concentration and output when fully engaged in a project. They are generally faithful in fulfilling obligations related to people, work, or ideas to which they are committed, but can have difficulty performing routine work with little meaning for them.

How Others May See Them

INFPs find structures and rules confining and prefer to work autonomously. They are adaptable and flexible until something violates their inner values. Then they stop adapting. The resulting expression of value judgments can come out with an intensity that is surprising to others.

INFPs tend to be reserved, being selective about sharing their most deeply held values and feelings. They value relationships based on depth, authenticity, true connection, and mutual growth. INFPs prize most those who take time to understand their values and goals. Others usually see INFPs as

- sensitive, introspective, and complex
- original and individual

Potential Areas for Growth

Sometimes life circumstances have not supported INFPs in the development and expression of their Intuitive and Feeling preferences.

- If they've not developed their Intuition, INFPs may not have reliable ways of taking in information and will then fail to notice the realities. Then they make decisions based solely on personal values and find it difficult to translate their values into action.
- If they've not developed their Feeling, they may not take time to do the inner valuing process by which they make their best decisions, instead going from one exciting possibility to another, achieving little.

If INFPs do not find a place where they can use their gifts and be appreciated for their contributions, they usually feel frustrated and may

- have uncharacteristic difficulty expressing themselves verbally,
- withdraw from people and situations, and
- not give enough information to others, especially about important values.

It is natural for INFPs to give less attention to their non-preferred Thinking and Sensing parts. If they neglect these too much, however, they may

- become easily discouraged about the contrast between their ideals and accomplishments,
- reject logical reasoning even in situations that require it, asserting the supremacy of their internal viewpoint, and
- be impractical, have difficulty estimating the resources required to reach a desired goal.

Under great stress, INFPs may begin seriously doubting their own competence and that of others, becoming overly critical and judgmental.

Table 3.8 Extraverted Sensing Types descriptions

ESTP Extraverted Sensing with Introverted Thinking

At Their Best

People with ESTP preferences are energetic, active problem-solvers, responding creatively to challenging situations in their environment. They seldom let rules or standard procedures interfere, finding new ways to use existing systems. They develop easy ways to do hard things and make their work fun. They are flexible, adaptable, inventive, and resourceful, can pull conflicting factions together, and are good team members.

They are popular companions for activities (parties, sports, or work) because of their zest for life and their enjoyment of the moment.

Characteristics of ESTPs

ESTPs are interested in everything going on around them—activities, food, clothes, people, and the outdoors—everything that offers new experiences. Because they learn more from doing than from studying or reading, they tend to plunge into things, learning as they go along, trusting their ability to respond. ESTPs are likely to be

- practical and realistic
- observant
- focused on immediate experience

ESTPs make decisions by logical analysis and reasoning and can be tough when the situation calls for toughness. For the most part, however, they prefer to deal flexibly with what is, rather than make judgments. ESTPs usually are

- analytical, rational problem-solvers
- straight-forward and assertive

ESTPs are expert at seeing the need of the moment and reacting quickly to meet it. They good-naturedly take things as they are and seek satisfying solutions, rather than imposing a "should" or "must" of their own.

How Others May See Them

ESTPs are strong in the art of living. Others respond to their enthusiasm and good humor; they love life and immerse themselves in it. ESTPs are people of action. They dislike and avoid theory and written directions. Traditional schools can be difficult for people with these preferences, though ESTPs do well when they see the

relevance and are allowed to experiment. Others usually see ESTPs as

- gregarious, fun-loving, and spontaneous
- adventurous risk-takers
- pragmatic trouble-shooters

Potential Areas for Growth

Sometimes life circumstances have not supported ESTPs in the development and expression of their Thinking and Sensing preferences.

- If they've not developed their Thinking, ESTPs will not have a useful way of selecting amongst the barrage of incoming sensory data. They may then make ill-founded decisions and have difficulty setting priorities.
- If they've not developed their Sensing, they may focus on the Sensing data that are immediately available. Their decisions then may be limited to gratification of their sensual desires, particularly those involving physical challenge and risk.

If ESTPs do not find a place where they can use their gifts and be appreciated for their contributions, they usually feel frustrated and may

- have trouble accepting structure and meeting deadlines,
- focus entirely on excitement and activity, get completely caught up in external activities, and put enjoying life ahead of important obligations.

It is natural for ESTPs to give less attention to their non-preferred Intuitive and Feeling parts. If they neglect these too much, however, they

- may not see the wider ramifications of their actions and decisions,
- may forget dates and events which have special meaning to others,
- may be unaware of the impact of their actions on others, and
- may be impatient with discussion or exploration of relationships.

Under great stress, ESTPs may experience negative fantasies inside. They may imagine that others do not really care about them, then marshall and distort their Sensing data to provide themselves with "evidence" of this neglect.

ESFP Extraverted Sensing with Introverted Feeling

At Their Best

People with ESFP preferences are exuberant lovers of life. They live in the moment and find enjoyment in people, food, clothes, animals, the natural world, and activities. They seldom let rules interfere with their lives, focusing on meeting human needs in creative ways.

ESFPs are excellent team players, oriented to getting the task done with a maximum amount of fun and a minimum amount of fuss.

Characteristics of ESFPs

ESFPs are interested in people and new experiences. Because they learn more from doing than from studying or reading, they tend to plunge into things, learning as they go. They appreciate their possessions and take pleasure in them. ESFPs are likely to be

- practical, realistic, and specific
- observant
- focused on current realities

ESFPs make decisions by using their personal values. They are good at interpersonal interactions and often play the role of peacemaker. Many feel a special affinity for children and animals. They primarily use their feeling internally to make decisions by identifying and empathizing with others. Thus, ESFPs are likely to be

- generous, optimistic, and persuasive
- warm, sympathetic, and tactful

ESFPs are keen observers of human behavior. They seem to sense what is happening with other people and respond quickly to their practical needs. They are especially good at mobilizing people to deal with crises.

How Others May See Them

ESFPs get a lot of fun out of life and are fun to be with; their exuberance and enthusiasm draw others to them. They are flexible, adaptable, congenial, and easy-going. They seldom plan ahead, trusting their ability to respond in the moment and deal effectively with whatever presents itself. They hate structure and routine and will generally find ways to get around it.

ESFPs tend to learn by doing, by interacting with their environment. They dislike theory and written explanations. Traditional schools can be difficult for ESFPs, though they do well when they see the relevance and are allowed to interact with people or the topics being studied. Others usually see ESFPs as

- resourceful and supportive
- gregarious, fun-loving, playful, spontaneous

Potential Areas for Growth

Sometimes life circumstances have not supported ESFPs in the development and expression of their Feeling and Sensing preferences.

- If they've not developed their Feeling, ESFPs may get caught up in the interactions of the moment, with no mechanism for weighing, evaluating, or anchoring themselves.
- If they've not developed their Sensing, they may focus on the sensory data available in the moment. Their decisions then may be limited to gratification of their sensual desires, particularly those involving interactions with other people.

If ESFPs do not find a place where they can use their gifts and be appreciated for their contributions, they usually feel frustrated and may

- become distracted and overly impulsive,
- have trouble accepting and meeting deadlines, and
- overpersonalize others' actions and decisions.

It is natural for ESFPs to give less attention to their non-preferred Intuitive and Thinking parts. If they neglect these too much, however, they may

- fail to look at long-term consequences, acting on immediate needs of themselves and others,
- avoid situations and people filled with complexity or ambiguity, and
- put enjoyment ahead of obligations.

Under great stress, ESFPs may feel overwhelmed internally by negative possibilities. They then put energy into developing simplistic global explanations for their negative pictures.

Table 3.9 Introverted Sensing Types descriptions

ISTJ Introverted Sensing with Extraverted Thinking

At Their Best

ISTJs have a strong sense of responsibility and great loyalty to the organizations, families, and relationships in their lives. They work with steady energy to fulfill commitments as stated and on time. They go to almost any trouble to complete something they see as necessary, but balk at doing anything that doesn't make sense to them.

ISTJs generally prefer to work alone and be accountable for the results; however, they are comfortable working in teams when it is necessary to do the job right, when roles are clearly defined, and when people fulfill assigned responsibilities.

Characteristics of ISTJs

ISTJs have a profound respect for facts. They use their Sensing primarily internally where they have a storehouse of information which they draw on to understand the present. Thus, they are likely to be

- practical, sensible, and realistic
- systematic

ISTJs use Thinking in decision making, taking an objective, logical, and tough-minded approach. Their focus is on the task or system as a whole, rather than individuals. ISTJs tend to be

- logical and analytical
- detached and reasonable

ISTJs are clear and steadfast in their opinions because they have arrived at them by applying logical criteria based on their experience and knowledge. They believe standard procedures exist because they work. ISTJs will support change only when facts demonstrate it will bring better results.

How Others May See Them

ISTJs are sociable when comfortable in the roles they are playing; however, they generally do not share their wealth of rich Sensing observations and memories except with close friends. Others see their standards and judgments, their desire for structure and schedules, but may not see their individual, sometimes humorous, private reactions.

It can be hard for ISTJs to see the sense in needs that differ widely from their own; but, once they are convinced that something matters to a person they care about, that need becomes a fact. They then go to generous lengths to meet the need, even while continuing to think it doesn't make sense. Others usually see ISTJs as

- calm, reserved, and serious
- consistent and orderly
- valuing traditions

Potential Areas for Growth

Sometimes life circumstances have not supported ISTJs in the development and expression of their Thinking and Sensing preferences.

- If they've not developed their Thinking, ISTJs may not have reliable ways for dealing with the world and instead may be preoccupied with their internal memories.
- If they've not developed their Sensing, they may rush into premature judgments and actions without considering new information.

If ISTJs do not find a place where they can use their gifts and be appreciated for their contributions, they usually feel frustrated and may

- become rigid about time, schedules, and procedures —go "by the book,"
- be critical and judgmental of others, and
- find it hard to delegate—to trust anyone else to do the job right.

It is natural for ISTJs to give less attention to their non-preferred Intuitive and Feeling parts. If they neglect these too much, however, they may

- not see the wider ramifications of current, expedient decisions,
- concentrate on logic so much they don't consider impacts on people, and
- not respond appropriately to others' need for connection and intimacy.

Under great stress, ISTJs may be unable to use their customary calm, reasonable judgment and get caught up in "catastrophizing"—imagining a host of negative possibilities for themselves and others.

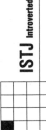

ISFJ Introverted Sensing with Extraverted Feeling

At Their Best

People with ISFJ preferences are dependable and considerate, committed to the people and groups with which they are associated, and faithful in carrying out responsibilities. They work with steady energy to complete jobs fully and on time. They will go to great trouble to do something they see as necessary, but dislike being required to do anything that doesn't make sense to them.

ISFJs focus on what people need and want, and they establish orderly procedures to bring these about. They take roles and responsibilities seriously and want others to do the same.

Characteristics of ISFJs

ISFJs have a realistic and practical respect for facts. They use their Sensing primarily internally where they have a wealth of stored information. They remember clearly the details of things that have personal meaning for them such as tones of voice or facial expression. ISFJs are likely to be

- practical and realistic
- concrete and specific

ISFJs use Feeling to make decisions based on personal values and concern for others. They value harmony and cooperation and work to create them. Thus, they are likely to be

- cooperative and thoughtful of others
- kind and sensitive

Their opinions are firm because their decisions are based on their clear values and their wealth of stored data. ISFJs respect established procedures and authority, believing that these have persisted because they function well. Therefore, they will support change only when new data show it will be of practical benefit to people.

How Others May See Them

ISFJs are unassuming and quiet in their interactions, often putting the needs of others—especially family members—ahead of their own. They are uncomfortable with confrontation and will go a long way to accommodate others, though their respect for traditions and

people's feelings can lead them to challenge others. People see their values, their desire for structure and closure, their kindness. What others may not see is the wealth of rich, accurate internal Sensing impressions and memories. Others usually see ISFJs as

- quiet, serious, and conscientious
- considerate, good caretakers
- honoring commitments, preserving traditions

Potential Areas for Growth

Sometimes life circumstances have not supported ISFJs in the development and expression of their Feeling and Sensing preferences.

- If they've not developed their Feeling, ISFJs may not have reliable ways for dealing with the world and instead be preoccupied with their Sensing memories and impressions.
- If they've not developed their Sensing, they may rush into judgments and actions without considering new information.

If ISFJs do not find a place where they can use their gifts and be appreciated for their contributions, they usually feel frustrated and may

- become rigid in supporting hierarchy, authority, and procedures,
- feel unappreciated, resentful—complain a lot, and
- be overly focused on immediate impacts of decisions on people.

It is natural for ISFJs to give less attention to their non-preferred Intuitive and Thinking parts. If they neglect these too much, however, they may

- not see the wider ramifications of current decisions or procedures,
- find it difficult to assert their needs, and
- be uncomfortable applying impersonal logic to decisions, even when it's needed.

Under great stress, ISFJs can get caught up in "catastrophizing"—imagining a host of negative possibilities. They may then express these without their usual consideration for their impact on people around them.

Table 3.10 Extraverted Intuitive Types descriptions

ENTP   Extraverted Intuition with Introverted Thinking

At Their Best

People with ENTP preferences constantly look to the environment for opportunities and possibilities. They see patterns and connections not obvious to others and, at times, seem able to see into the future. They are adept at generating conceptual possibilities and then analyzing them strategically.

ENTPs are good at understanding how systems work and are enterprising and resourceful in maneuvering within them to achieve their ends.

Characteristics of ENTPs

ENTPs are enthusiastic innovators. Their world is full of possibilities, interesting concepts, and exciting challenges. They are stimulated by difficulties, quickly devising creative responses and plunging into activity, trusting their ability to improvise. They use their Intuition primarily externally and enjoy exercising ingenuity in the world. ENTPs are likely to be

- creative, imaginative, and clever
- theoretical, conceptual, and curious

ENTPs use their Thinking primarily internally to analyze situations and their own ideas and to plan. They admire competence, intelligence, precision, and efficiency. ENTPs are usually

- analytical, logical, rational, and objective
- assertive and questioning

ENTPs are enterprising and resourceful. The more challenging the problem, the better—and the more complex the solution they will create. They can do almost anything that captures their interest.

How Others May See Them

ENTPs are spontaneous and adaptable. They find schedules and standard operating procedures confining and work around them whenever possible. They are remarkably insightful about the attitudes of others, and their enthusiasm and energy can mobilize people to support their vision.

Their conversational style is customarily challenging and stimulating because they love to debate ideas. They are fluent conversationalists, mentally quick, and enjoy verbal sparring. When they express their underlying Thinking principles, however, they may feel awkward and speak with uncharacteristic intensity and abruptness. Others usually see ENTPs as

- independent, autonomous
- lively, enthusiastic, and energetic
- assertive and outspoken

Potential Areas for Growth

Sometimes life circumstances have not supported ENTPs in the development and expression of their Thinking and Intuitive preferences.

- If they've not developed their Thinking, they may not have reliable ways to evaluate their insights and make plans to carry them through. Then they go from enthusiasm to enthusiasm with little to show for it.
- If they've not developed their Intuition, they may not take in relevant information and have "insights" unrelated to current reality.

If ENTPs do not find a place where they can use their gifts and be appreciated for their contributions, they usually feel frustrated and may

- become brash, rude, and abrasive,
- criticize others, especially those who seem to the ENTP to be inefficient or incompetent,
- become rebellious and combative, and
- be scattered—unable to focus.

It is natural for ENTPs to give less attention to their non-preferred Sensing and Feeling parts. If they neglect these too much, however, they may

- not take care of the details and routine required to implement their insights,
- not give enough weight to the impact of their ideas and plans on people, and
- be excessively and inappropriately "challenging and stimulating."

Under great stress, ENTPs can be overwhelmed by detail, losing their ability to generate possibilities. Then they focus on a minor or distorted detail, thinking that it is supremely important.

ENFP   Extraverted Intuition with Introverted Feeling

At Their Best

For people with ENFP preferences, life is a creative adventure full of exciting possibilities. They are keenly perceptive of people and the world around them and insightful about the present and future. ENFPs experience a wide range of feelings and intense emotions. They need affirmation from others and readily give appreciation and support to others.

Characteristics of ENFPs

ENFPs are innovators, initiating projects and directing great energy into getting them underway. Using Intuition primarily externally, they are stimulated by new people, ideas, and experiences. They find meaning and significance readily and see connections that others don't. They are likely to be

- curious, creative, and imaginative
- energetic, enthusiastic, and spontaneous

ENFPs value harmony and good will. They like to please others and will adapt to others' needs and wishes when possible. ENFPs primarily use Feeling internally, making decisions by applying personal values through identification and empathy with others. ENFPs are likely to be

- warm, friendly, and caring
- cooperative and supportive

ENFPs have exceptional insight into possibilities in others and the energy to help actualize them.

How Others May See Them

ENFPs are usually lively, gregarious, and sociable, with a large circle of friends. They are interested in almost everything and bring a zest to life that draws others to them. At the same time, they value depth and authenticity in their close relationships and direct great energy to creating and supporting open and honest communication.

ENFPs hate routine, schedules, and structure, and usually manage to avoid them. They are normally verbally fluent, even in extemporaneous situations; however, when their deepest values need expression, they may suddenly be awkward. Their articulation of their judgments will often come out with great intensity. Others usually see ENFPs as

- personable, perceptive, and persuasive
- enthusiastic, spontaneous, and versatile
- giving affirmation and wanting to receive it

Potential Areas for Growth

Sometimes life circumstances have not supported ENFPs in the development and expression of their Feeling and Intuitive preferences.

- If they've not developed their Feeling, they may go from enthusiasm to enthusiasm, never committing the energy necessary to actualize their insights.
- If they've not developed their Intuition, they may overly on personal value judgments and fail to take in enough information. They then will not trust their own insights, be uncertain, and accept others' perceptions too quickly.

If ENFPs do not find a place where they can use their gifts and be appreciated for their contributions, they usually feel frustrated and may

- become scattered, have trouble focusing, be easily distracted,
- become rebellious, excessively nonconforming, and
- ignore deadlines and procedures.

It is natural for ENFPs to give less attention to their non-preferred Sensing and Thinking parts. If they neglect these too much, however, they may

- not take care of the details and routine required for implementing their inspirations,
- overextend themselves—have trouble saying no to interesting possibilities and people, and
- fail to apply reason and logic to their judgments about people and their inspirations.

Under great stress, ENFPs may become overwhelmed by detail and lose their normal perspective and sense of options. They then tend to focus on an unimportant or distorted detail, letting it become the central fact of their universe.

Table 3.11 Introverted Intuitive Types descriptions

INTJ Introverted Intuition with Extraverted Thinking

At Their Best

People with INTJ preferences have a clear vision of future possibilities and the organization and drive to implement their ideas. They love complex challenges and readily synthesize complicated theoretical and abstract matters. They create a general structure and devise strategies to achieve their goals.

INTJs value knowledge highly and expect competence of themselves and others. They especially abhor confusion, mess, and inefficiency.

Characteristics of INTJs

INTJs see things from a global perspective and quickly relate new information to overall patterns. They trust their insightful connections regardless of established authority or popular opinions. Dull routine smothers their creativity. INTJs use their Intuition primarily internally, where they develop complex structures and pictures of the future. They are likely to be

- insightful, creative synthesizers
- conceptual, long-range thinkers

INTJs use their Thinking to make logical decisions. They assess everything with a critical eye and are tough and decisive when the situation calls for toughness. INTJs tend to be

- clear and concise
- rational, detached, and objectively critical

INTJs are excellent long-range planners and often rise to positions of leadership in groups or organizations. They are independent, trust their own perceptions and judgments more than those of others, and apply their high standards most strongly to themselves.

How Others May See Them

INTJs usually don't directly express their most valued and valuable part—their creative insights. Instead, they translate them into logical plans and decisions. Because of this, others sometimes experience INTJs as intractable, much to the surprise of the INTJ who is very willing to change an opinion when new evidence emerges. They present a calm, decisive, and assured face to the world,

though they often find it difficult to engage in social conversation. Others usually see INTJs as

- private, reserved, hard to know, even aloof
- conceptual, original, and independent

Potential Areas for Growth

Sometimes life circumstances have not supported INTJs in the development and expression of their Thinking and Intuitive preferences.

- If they've not developed their Thinking, INTJs may not have reliable ways for translating their valuable insights into applications that can be realized.
- If they've not developed their Intuition, they may not take in enough information or take in only that information that fits their insights. Then they may make ill-founded decisions based on limited or idiosyncratic information.

If INTJs do not find a place where they can use their gifts and be appreciated for their contributions, they usually feel frustrated and may

- become aloof and abrupt, not giving enough information about their internal processing, and be critical of those who do not see their vision quickly; then they become single-minded and unyielding in pursuing it.

It is natural for INTJs to give less attention to their non-preferred Sensing and Feeling parts. If they neglect these too much, however, they may

- overlook details or facts that do not fit into their Intuitive patterns,
- engage in "intellectual games," "quibbling over abstract issues and terms that have little meaning or relevance to others.
- not give enough weight to the impacts of their decisions on individuals, and
- not give as much praise or intimate connection as others desire.

Under extreme stress, INTJs can overindulge in Sensing activities—watching TV reruns, playing cards, overeating,—or become overly focused on specific details that they normally do not notice or usually see as unimportant.

INFJ Introverted Intuition with Extraverted Feeling

At Their Best

People with INFJ preferences have a gift for intuitively understanding complex meanings and human relationships. They have faith in their insights, which often take on a sense of sureness, of "knowing." They find they often empathically understand the feelings and motivations of people before the others are themselves aware of them.

Characteristics of INFJs

INFJs seek meaning and connection in their lives and have little use for details unless the details verify their inner vision. They use their Intuition primarily internally, where they develop complex pictures and understandings. INFJs are likely to be

- insightful, creative, and visionary
- conceptual, symbolic, and metaphorical
- idealistic, complex, and deep

INFJs apply personal values and empathize to understand others and make decisions. They are loyal to people and institutions that exemplify their values. INFJs prefer to lead persuasively by sharing their vision. They are likely to be

- sensitive, compassionate, and empathic
- deeply committed to their values

INFJs want meaning and purpose in their work, their relationships, even their material possessions. They are invested in growth and development for themselves and significant others and are willing to consider unconventional paths to achieve these. They value the depth and complexity of their insights and creative gifts as well as those of others. They want to see these insights realized in the world.

How Others May See Them

INFJs readily show compassion and caring for others, but they share their internal intuitions only with those they trust. Others, then, may find them difficult to know. When they try to communicate their internal sense of "knowing," they often express it metaphorically and with complexity. They especially value authenticity and commitment in relationships.

Though INFJs are usually reserved, they don't hesitate to assert themselves when their values are violated. Then they can be persistent and insistent. Others usually experience INFJs as

- private and mysterious
- intense and individualistic

Potential Areas for Growth

Sometimes life circumstances have not supported INFJs in the development and expression of their Feeling and Intuitive preferences.

- If they've not developed their Feeling, INFJs may not have reliable ways of accomplishing their goals. Then, their valuable insights and creativity stay locked inside.
- If they've not developed their Intuition, they may not take in enough information or take in only what fits with their internal pictures. Then, they will make ill-founded decisions based on distorted or limited information.

If INFJs do not find a place where they can use their gifts and be appreciated for their contributions, they usually feel frustrated and may

- not give others the information they used to arrive at a decision, and thus seem arbitrary,
- base their judgments on little data, on a sense of "knowing" that has little basis in reality,
- withdraw their energy and insight, and
- become resentful and critical.

It is natural for INFJs to give less attention to their non-preferred Sensing and Thinking parts. If they neglect these too much, however, they may

- be unable to verbalize their inner insights in a way that others can understand,
- fail to expose their insights to reason and practicality and end up following a vision that has little possibility to be realized, and
- become single-minded in pursuit of a vision.

Under great stress, INFJs may become obsessed with data they usually consider irrelevant or overindulge in Sensing activities such as watching TV reruns, overeating, or buying things with little meaning for them.

Chapter 4

Understanding the Sixteen Types

When making practical use of type theory and data, it is important to consider not only what can in theory be expected of a person with a given set of preferences, but also what has been observed in people of that type. The usefulness of counseling feedback to any respondent may depend to a large extent upon the interpreter's knowledge of type characteristics.

It is *not* helpful to try to memorize the characteristics of the sixteen types. The best way to keep the types and their characteristics in mind is through understanding the dynamics outlined in Chapter 3 and by using the *type table* which presents the sixteen types in a logical relationship.

There is much to be learned from type tables, which show the frequencies of types in groups with characteristics in common, for example, common occupation, college major, or avocation. Such tables show the results of choices. If an occupation requires attention to detail, system, and order and if that occupation attracts the types who in theory should prefer attention to detail, system, and order,—the SJ types—then the table provides construct validity for type theory *and* information about the occupation and the people attracted to it, for career counseling.

The following sections describe theoretical predictions for grouping the types and give examples of particular populations. In these examples, notice where concentrations of types occur and where types are infrequent.

Placement of Types on the Type Table

The type table is designed to highlight similarities and differences of the types by their placement (see Figure 4.1 for the format of the type tables). Each type has three letters in common with any adjacent type.

Extraverts (E) and Introverts (I)

Introverted (I) types appear in the first and second rows of the type table. Extraverted (E) types appear in rows three and four. Isabel Myers' mnemonic aid for EI placement is that introverts are more likely to have their heads *up* in the clouds; and extraverts are more likely to have their feet *down* on the ground.

Sensing (S) and Intuition (N)

Sensing types (S) and intuitive types (N) are positioned on the type table in the same order as in the name of the SN index, namely with sensing on the left and intuition on the right.

Thinking (T) and Feeling (F)

The thinking types compose the two outer columns of the table. Feeling types are contained on the two inner columns. Myers chose this placement so that it would be easy to remember by considering that the feeling (F) types, with their higher need for affiliation, are in the middle columns, surrounded by other types. The more objective thinking (T) types are in the outer columns with unpeopled space beside them.

Judgment (J) and Perception (P)

Note that the decisive judging types are on the top and bottom rows, while the more adaptable perceptive types are in the middle rows.

The aim of one using the MBTI should be to understand the type table so well that a glance at a population distribution will give maximum information about the characteristics of the sample. Table 4.1 shows the sixteen types in the conventional order, with the contribution that each preference makes to each type.

Terminology for Identifying Combinations of Types

Since Jung's descriptions of the types take no account of the auxiliary function, the Jungian terms always refer to the dominant or first function. For example, when Jungians refer to *extraverted thinking* types, or *extraverted thinkers*, they mean the extraverts with thinking dominant. In MBTI letters these are ESTJ and ENTJ.

The term *extraverts with thinking* stands for all four types that contain E and T, regardless of whether thinking is the dominant or the auxiliary function. The letter designation for extraverts with thinking is the E–T– types (or ET types in standard usage).[12]

In the interests of clarity, MBTI terminology refers to combinations of types by letter designations. Table 4.2

Figure 4.1 Format of type tables

ISTJ	ISFJ	INFJ	INTJ
ISTP	ISFP	INFP	INTP
ESTP	ESFP	ENFP	ENTP
ESTJ	ESFJ	ENFJ	ENTJ

Extraversion-Introversion

I
E

Sensing-Intuition

S	N

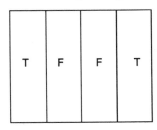

Thinking-Feeling

T	F	F	T

Judgment-Perception

J
P
P
J

gives the letters and names for common combinations. Characteristics of these and other combinations are given in the section to follow.

Characteristics of Groups of the Types

It is often useful to describe a set of types with identical common characteristics. The main problem in grouping types is to restrict the description to the common characteristics found in every type in the group. Characteristics found in only one or two types in a group of four should not be reported as typical of the whole group. A number of observers have begun to focus on specific type groupings, naming them and describing their characteristics. The research to bring together these observations and test them empirically is still in the early stages. The following

Table 4.1 Contributions made by each preference to each type

	Sensing Types		Intuitive Types	
	With Thinking	With Feeling	With Feeling	With Thinking
Introverts — Judging Types	**ISTJ** I Depth of concentration S Reliance on facts T Logic and analysis J Organization	**ISFJ** I Depth of concentration S Reliance on facts F Warmth and sympathy J Organization	**INFJ** I Depth of concentration N Grasp of possibilities F Warmth and sympathy J Organization	**INTJ** I Depth of concentration N Grasp of possibilities T Logic and analysis J Organization
Introverts — Perceptive Types	**ISTP** I Depth of concentration S Reliance on facts T Logic and analysis P Adaptability	**ISFP** I Depth of concentration S Reliance on facts F Warmth and sympathy P Adaptability	**INFP** I Depth of concentration N Grasp of possibilities F Warmth and sympathy P Adaptability	**INTP** I Depth of concentration N Grasp of possibilities T Logic and analysis P Adaptability
Extraverts — Perceptive Types	**ESTP** E Breadth of interests S Reliance on facts T Logic and analysis P Adaptability	**ESFP** E Breadth of interests S Reliance on facts F Warmth and sympathy P Adaptability	**ENFP** E Breadth of interests N Grasp of possibilities F Warmth and sympathy P Adaptability	**ENTP** E Breadth of interests N Grasp of possibilities T Logic and analysis P Adaptability
Extraverts — Judging Types	**ESTJ** E Breadth of interests S Reliance on facts T Logic and analysis J Organization	**ESFJ** E Breadth of interests S Reliance on facts F Warmth and sympathy J Organization	**ENFJ** E Breadth of interests N Grasp of possibilities F Warmth and sympathy J Organization	**ENTJ** E Breadth of interests N Grasp of possibilities T Logic and analysis J Organization

characterizations are a first step toward listing the expected characteristics of type groupings.

The Rows of the Type Table (IJ, IP, EP, EJ)

The rows of the type table group the introverted and extraverted irrational types (IJs and EPs) and the introverted and extraverted rational types (IPs and EJs).

I—J: The decisive introverts

A judgment function (T or F) is extraverted and auxiliary; a perceptive function (S or N) is introverted and dominant.

IJs are introspective, persevering, and hard to convince or change.

I—P: The adaptable introverts

A perceptive function (S or N) is extraverted, but a judgment function (T or F) is introverted and dominant.

IPs are introspective, adaptable in little things, and firm on important issues.

E—P: The adaptable extraverts

A perceptive function (S or N) is extraverted and dominant; a judgment function (T or F) is introverted and auxiliary.

EPs are active, energetic, sociable, and always seeking new experiences.

E—J: The decisive extraverts

A judgment function (T or F) is extraverted and dominant; a perceptive function (S or N) is introverted and auxiliary.

EJs are fast moving, decisive, confident looking, and they enjoy making things happen.

Less attention has been paid to the above combinations than to others. Two examples of representative data illustrate the differences between the row type groupings. Data from the 16PF Leadership Scale (Camiscioni, 1974) of two samples of Ohio State University medical students showed significant differences between the row type groupings. EJ types scored the highest in leadership, followed by EP

types, IJ types, and IP types. It appears that the kind of leadership described by the 16PF is active decision making.

Other data from the Ohio medical students were based on an entry questionnaire that asked about the students' decision to enter medical school. The decisive extraverts (EJ types) said significantly more often that they decided on medicine early and were confident they were in the right field. The thoughtful introverts (IP types) said that they decided late and, even though they were then in medical school, they were not confident about their decision.

Combinations of Perception and Judgment: ST, SF, NF, NT

Isabel Myers considered the columns[13] of the type table to be the most important of the groupings of the types, particularly when career choices are concerned. These groups focus on the combinations of perception (S and N) with judgment (T and F). The type characteristics are assumed to stem from the preferred use of these mental functions.

–ST–: The practical and matter-of-fact types

ST people rely primarily on sensing for purposes of perception and on thinking for purposes of judgment. Their main interests focus on facts, because facts can be collected and verified directly by the senses—by seeing, hearing, touching, counting, weighing, and measuring. The ST types typically approach their decisions regarding facts by impersonal analysis, because what they trust is thinking, with its step-by-step logical process of reasoning from cause to effect, from premise to conclusion.

In consequence, STs tend to be practical and matter-of-fact. Type theory predicts that their best chances for success and satisfaction lie in fields that demand impersonal analysis of concrete facts, such as economics, law, surgery, business, accounting, production, and the handling of machines and materials.

–SF–: The sympathetic and friendly types

Table 4.2 Terminology for describing combinations of the types

MBTI Letters	Terminology	MBTI Letters	Terminology
	The Eight Jungian Types		The Functions Combined with Extraversion and Introversion
ES–P	Extraverted sensing types (extraverts with S dominant)	ES— types	Extraverts with sensing (the four types with E and S)
IS–J	Introverted sensing types (introverts with S dominant)	ES–P types	Extraverted sensing types (the two E types with S dominant)
EN–P	Extraverted intuitive types (extraverts with N dominant)	IS— types	Introverts with sensing (the four types with I and S)
IN–J	Introverted intuitive types (introverts with N dominant)	IS–J types	Introverted sensing types (the two I types with S dominant)
E–TJ	Extraverted thinking types (extraverts with T dominant)	EN— types	Extraverts with intuition (the four types with E and N)
I–TP	Introverted thinking types (introverts with T dominant)	EN–P types	Extraverted intuitive types (the two E types with N dominant)
E–FJ	Extraverted feeling types (extraverts with F dominant)	IN— types	Introverts with intuition (the four types with I and N)
I–FP	Introverted feeling types (introverts with F dominant)	IN–J types	Introverted intuitive types (the two I types with N dominant)
	Single Preferences	E–T– types	Extraverts with thinking (the four types with E and T)
E types	All eight types preferring extraversion to introversion	E–TJ types	Extraverted thinking types (the two E types with T dominant)
I types	All eight types preferring introversion to extraversion	I–T– types	Introverts with thinking (the four types with I and T)
S types	All eight types preferring sensing to intuition (whether S is dominant or not)	I–TP types	Introverted thinking types (the two I types with T dominant)
N types	All eight types preferring intuition to sensing (whether N is dominant or not)	E–F– types	Extraverts with feeling (the four types with E and F)
T types	All eight types preferring thinking to feeling (whether T is dominant or not)	E–FJ types	Extraverted feeling types (the two E types with F dominant)
F types	All eight types preferring feeling to thinking (whether F is dominant or not)	I–F– types	Introverts with feeling (the four types with I and F)
J types	All eight types preferring the judging attitude to the perceiving attitude	I–FP types	Introverted feeling types (the two I types with F dominant)
P types	All eight types preferring the perceptive to the judging attitude		

SF people, like ST people, rely primarily on sensing for purposes of perception, but they prefer feeling for purposes of judgment. They too are mainly interested in facts that they can gather directly through the senses, but they approach their decisions with more subjectivity and personal warmth. The subjectivity and warmth comes from their trust of feeling, with its power to weigh how much things matter to themselves and others. They are more interested in facts about people than in facts about things.

In consequence of their preferences for sensing and feeling, SFs tend to be sympathetic and friendly. In theory, their best chances for success and satisfaction lie in fields where their personal warmth can be effectively applied to concrete situations. The combination of sensing and feeling can be valuable in selling tangibles, service-with-a-smile jobs, teaching (especially in the early grades and applied fields), nursing, pediatrics, and other health fields involving direct patient care.

–NF–: The enthusiastic and insightful types

NF people typically possess the same personal warmth as SF people, since they use feeling for purposes of judgment. However, since they prefer intuition to sensing for purposes of perception, they do not center their attention upon concrete situations. Instead, they focus their interest upon possibilities, such as new projects, things that have never happened but might be made to happen, or truths that are not yet known but might be. NF types are typically interested in the complexities of communication. Intuition provides an interest in patterns underlying immediate facts, symbolic meanings, and theoretical relationships. Feeling provides the interest in using these intuitive insights in human relationships.

The personal warmth and commitment with which NF people seek and follow up possibilities tend to make them enthusiastic as well as insightful. Often they have a marked gift for the spoken or written word and can communicate both the possibilities they see and the values they attach to those possibilities. Their best chance for success and satisfaction lies in work that involves the unfolding of possibilities, especially possibilities for people, such as in teaching (particularly in the upper grades and college), selling intangibles, counseling, writing, and research.

–NT–: The logical and ingenious types

Like NF people, NT people prefer intuition for purposes of perception, but they prefer the objectivity of thinking for purposes of judgment. They too focus on possibilities, theoretical relationships, and abstract patterns, but they judge these with impersonal analysis. Often the possibility they pursue is a technical, scientific, theoretical, or executive one, with the human element subordinated.

NTs tend to be logical and ingenious. They are best in solving problems within their field of special interest, whether scientific research, mathematics, the more intricate aspects of finance, or any sort of development or pioneering in technical or administrative areas.

Some of the comparisons between the column types appear in Table 4.3.

Table 4.3 The combinations of perception and judgment

	ST	SF	NF	NT
People who prefer	Sensing and thinking	Sensing and feeling	Intuition and feeling	Intuition and thinking
Focus attention on	Facts	Facts	Possibilities	Possibilities
And handle these with	Impersonal analysis	Personal warmth	Personal warmth	Impersonal analysis
Thus they tend to become	Practical and matter-of-fact	Sympathetic and friendly	Enthusiastic and insightful	Logical and ingenious
And find scope for their abilities in	Technical skills with facts and objects	Practical help and services for people	Understanding and communication with people	Theoretical and technical developments

SJ, SP, NP, and NJ

The SJ, SP, NP, and NJ grouping of types combines differences in perception (S and N) and the use of perception or judgment in outer behavior (J or P).

–S–J: The realistic decision-makers

SJs use a judgment function (T or F) in their outer behavior, but their inner world focuses on facts of immediate experience (S).

SJs seek order in their environment. They are organized, dependable, and conservative. They tend to solve problems by reliance on past experiences, and they dislike ambiguity.

–S–P: The adaptable realists

SPs focus on facts of immediate experience in their outer behavior (S), and their inner world uses a judgment function (T or F).

SPs seek new experiences in the present moment. They are curious about the world around them. They adapt to situations as they arise and are good observers of the immediate situation.

–N–P: The adaptable innovators

The outer behavior of NPs focuses on possibilities for the future (N), and their inner world uses a judgment function (T or F).

NPs constantly seek the challenge of the new. They adapt to new possibilities as they arise. They are unconventional, independent spirits who hate to be fenced in.

–N–J: The visionary decision makers

NJs use a judgment function (T or F) in their outer behavior, but their inner world focuses on future possibilities.

NJs strive to accomplish goals of inner vision. They are driving, persistent, and determined.

TJ, TP, FP, and FJ

The grouping of types TJ, TP, FP, and FJ combines the functions of judgment (T and F) and use of perception or judgment in outer behavior (J or P).

—TJ: The logical decision makers

The outer behavior of TJs shows their use of the thinking judgment function.

TJs are tough-minded, executive, analytical, and instrumental leaders.

—TP: The adaptable thinkers

TPs use a perceptive function (S or N) in their outer behavior, but their inner world focuses on the impersonal logic of events.

TPs are objective, skeptical, observant, and curious, especially about materials, events, or possibilities that have or can be made to fit into consistent and orderly frameworks.

—FP: The gentle types

FPs use a perceptive function (S or N) in outer behavior, but in their inner world they focus on subjective values (F).

FPs are adaptable, affiliative harmony seekers who are concerned with the human aspects of problems.

—FJ: The benevolent administrators

FJs use feeling, whether dominant or auxiliary, in their outer behavior.

FJs are observant about people and their needs. They spend energy in making people happy and in bringing harmony into relationships. They are expressive leaders.

IN, EN, IS, and ES

The grouping of IN, EN, IS, and ES is referred to as "the quadrants" because these types make up the four quadrants of the table. They combine the functions of perception (S and N) with the extraverted or introverted attitude. The quadrants are listed in this order because they are useful for looking at differences in academic aptitude and achievement. The expectation for academic measures is that the quadrants will rank in the order shown.

IN—: The thoughtful innovators

INs have introversion combined with intuition which may be dominant or auxiliary.

INs are introspective and scholarly. They are interested in knowledge for its own sake, as well as ideas, theory, and depth of understanding. They are the least practical of the types.

EN—: The action-oriented innovators

ENs combine extraversion with intuition, which may be dominant or auxiliary.

ENs are change agents; they see possibilities as challenges to make something happen. They have wide-ranging interests and like to see new patterns and relationships.

IS—: The thoughtful realists

ISs combine introversion with sensing, which may be dominant or auxiliary.

ISs like to test ideas to see whether they are supported by facts. They like to deal with what is real and factual in a careful, unhurried way.

ES—: The action-oriented realists

ESs combine extraversion with sensing, which may be dominant or auxiliary.

ESs are active, realistic doers. ESs are the most practical of the types. They learn best when useful applications are obvious.

ET, EF, IF, and IT

The grouping of ET, EF, IF, and IT does not appear on the standard type table (for reasons of space, not of theory), but it is shown on the type table worksheets.

E–T–: The action-oriented thinkers

ETs join extraversion with thinking, whether dominant or auxiliary.

ETs are active and energetic. They are objective, and they like to make things happen in reasoned, analytical, and logical ways.

E–F–: The action-oriented cooperators

EFs join extraversion with feeling, whether dominant or auxiliary.

EFs are sociable, friendly, and sympathetic. They like to make things happen for the pleasure or welfare of others.

I–F–: The reflective harmonizers

IFs join introversion with feeling, whether dominant or auxiliary.

IFs are quiet and caring. They have concern for deep and enduring values, as well as for people.

I–T–: The reflective reasoners

ITs combine introversion with thinking, whether dominant or auxiliary.

ITs are quiet and contemplative. They have concern for basic principles that explain the causes and consequences of events or the workings of things. ITs are the most removed from daily social intercourse with people and are the slowest to develop social skills.

The brief descriptions above are not meant to be exhaustive or final, but are designed to show how to interpret patterns that appear in the type table. A great deal is known about some of the groups; very little is known about other of the groupings. For example, the tough-minded TJs turn up in large numbers among business executives, and the benevolent FJs are found in the clergy. The organized and detail-minded SJs are frequent among pharmacists, medical technologists, and teachers (especially in the lower grades); the free-spirited NP types appear in academic independent study programs. The practical and matter-of-fact STs are found in production, accounting, civil engineering; the sympathetic and friendly SFs are frequent at all levels of direct patient care. The enthusiastic and insightful NFs appear in all fields directly or indirectly related to communications; and the logical and ingenious NTs appear in science and technologies where logical models are needed to deal with complexities.

Type tables and type groupings present data on the construct validity of the MBTI and illuminate the characteristics of the types.

Representative Type Tables

The following section gives examples of type tables from different populations (see also Myers with Myers, 1980). The illustrative tables serve two purposes. First, they offer practice in recognizing the meanings of the letter combinations. Second and more important, they illustrate the use of greater-than-expected (or fewer-than-expected) frequencies for making or testing hypotheses about types. If certain types occur in a given population more or less frequently than expected by chance, the theory can be used to suggest why the phenomenon occurs.

Expected Frequencies

In exploring hypotheses about type and sample populations, it is necessary to adopt some reasonable estimate of the frequencies to be expected in some comparison population. The obvious statistical approach would be to expect one-sixteenth (6.25%) of the population to fall in each of the sixteen types. The fact is that even distributions of types are very rare.[14]

The following type tables show the numbers and percentages in each type and type group. In addition, the convention for making trends visible is followed; that is, each 1% of the sample is designated by the symbol ¤.

Example of Data on School Administrators

A typical sample of executives is shown by the distribution of Canadian school administrators (von Fange, 1961) in Table 4.4. The decision-making J types greatly outnumber the P types.

Graduate Students in Business

The data in Table 4.5 were shared by R. L. Cacioppe in 1980. The sample, from the Management Studies Centre of Macquarie University in New South Wales, is heavily T and J, with the tough-minded TJs accounting for 62% of the

Table 4.4 Canadian school administrators (*N* = 124)

Sensing Types		Intuitive Types				
With Thinking	With Feeling	With Feeling	With Thinking		Number	Percent
ISTJ *N* = 14 % = 11.29 □□□□□□□□□□ □	**ISFJ** *N* = 12 % = 9.68 □□□□□□□□□	**INFJ** *N* = 9 % = 7.26 □□□□□□□	**INTJ** *N* = 10 % = 8.06 □□□□□□□□	Judging / Introverts	E 74 I 50	59.68 40.32
					S 73 N 51	58.87 41.13
					T 68 F 56	54.84 45.16
ISTP *N* = 0 % = 0.0	**ISFP** *N* = 1 % = 0.81 □	**INFP** *N* = 3 % = 2.42 □□	**INTP** *N* = 1 % = 0.81 □	Perceptive	J 107 P 17	86.29 13.71
					IJ 45 IP 5 EP 12 EJ 62	36.29 4.03 9.67 50.00
ESTP *N* = 1 % = 0.81 □	**ESFP** *N* = 3 % = 2.42 □□	**ENFP** *N* = 6 % = 4.84 □□□□□	**ENTP** *N* = 2 % = 1.61 □□	Perceptive / Extraverts	ST 42 SF 31 NF 25 NT 26	33.87 25.00 20.16 20.97
					SJ 68 SP 5 NP 12 NJ 39	54.84 4.03 9.68 31.45
ESTJ *N* = 27 % = 21.77 □□□□□□□□□□ □□□□□□□□□□ □□	**ESFJ** *N* = 15 % = 12.10 □□□□□□□□□□ □□	**ENFJ** *N* = 7 % = 5.65 □□□□□□	**ENTJ** *N* = 13 % = 10.48 □□□□□□□□□□	Judging	TJ 64 TP 4 FP 13 FJ 43	51.61 3.23 10.48 34.70
					IN 23 EN 28 IS 27 ES 46	18.55 22.58 21.77 37.10

Note: □ = 1% of sample.
Source of data: von Fange, E. A. Implications for School Administration of the Personality Structure of Educational Personnel. Unpublished doctoral dissertation, University of Alberta, 1961.

Table 4.5 Australian postgraduate students in business administration (*N* = 228)

	Sensing Types		Intuitive Types					Number	Percent
	With Thinking	With Feeling	With Feeling	With Thinking					

Sensing Types — With Thinking	Sensing Types — With Feeling	Intuitive Types — With Feeling	Intuitive Types — With Thinking
ISTJ *N* = 47 % = 20.6 ❑❑❑❑❑❑❑❑❑❑ ❑❑❑❑❑❑❑❑❑❑ ❑	**ISFJ** *N* = 7 % = 3.1 ❑❑❑	**INFJ** *N* = 3 % = 1.3 ❑	**INTJ** *N* = 31 % = 13.6 ❑❑❑❑❑❑❑❑❑❑ ❑❑❑❑
ISTP *N* = 14 % = 6.1 ❑❑❑❑❑❑	**ISFP** *N* = 0 % = 0.0	**INFP** *N* = 2 % = 0.9 ❑	**INTP** *N* = 23 % = 10.1 ❑❑❑❑❑❑❑❑❑❑
ESTP *N* = 5 % = 2.2 ❑❑	**ESFP** *N* = 1 % = 0.4 ❑	**ENFP** *N* = 6 % = 2.6 ❑❑❑	**ENTP** *N* = 19 % = 8.3 ❑❑❑❑❑❑❑❑
ESTJ *N* = 31 % = 13.6 ❑❑❑❑❑❑❑❑❑❑ ❑❑❑❑	**ESFJ** *N* = 3 % = 1.3 ❑❑❑❑❑❑❑	**ENFJ** *N* = 3 % = 1.3 ❑	**ENTJ** *N* = 33 % = 14.5 ❑❑❑❑❑❑❑❑❑❑ ❑❑❑❑

Right margin labels: Judging / Introverts / Perceptive / Perceptive / Extraverts / Judging

	Number	Percent
E	101	44.3
I	127	55.7
S	108	47.4
N	120	52.6
T	203	89.0
F	25	11.0
J	158	69.3
P	70	30.7
IJ	88	38.6
IP	39	17.1
EP	31	13.6
EJ	70	30.7
ST	97	42.5
SF	11	4.8
NF	14	6.1
NT	106	46.5
SJ	88	38.6
SP	20	8.8
NP	50	21.9
NJ	70	30.7
TJ	142	62.3
TP	61	26.8
FP	9	3.9
FJ	16	7.0
IN	59	25.9
EN	61	26.8
IS	68	29.8
ES	40	17.5

Note: ❑ = 1% of sample.
Source of data: R. L. Cacioppe, Management Studies Centre, Macquarie University, North Ryde, New South Wales, 12–80. Used with permission.

students. Other data on business schools show relatively more S types in undergraduate programs and relatively more N types in graduate programs.

Professional Fine Artists in San Diego

A group of professional fine artists in San Diego were studied by R. S. Simon (1979). Since intuition is the function concerned with imagination, new possibilities, and creativity, one would expect creative samples to have many intuitive types, as shown in Table 4.6. Note that 91% of the fine artists preferred intuition. Simon also reported on peer ratings of the artists; of those rated as the most highly creative, 95% preferred intuition. Because true creativity in the arts requires highly differentiated use of tools and materials, one might expect artists to prefer sensing perception

Table 4.6 Professional fine artists (*N* = 114)

	Sensing Types		Intuitive Types				
	With Thinking	With Feeling	With Feeling	With Thinking		Number	Percent
	ISTJ *N* = 2 % = 1.75 □□	**ISFJ** *N* = 3 % = 2.63 □□□	**INFJ** *N* = 19 % = 16.67 □□□□□□□□□ □□□□□□□	**INTJ** *N* = 8 % = 7.02 □□□□□□□	Judging		
	ISTP *N* = 0 % = 0.0	**ISFP** *N* = 1 % = 0.88	**INFP** *N* = 25 % = 21.93 □□□□□□□□□□ □□□□□□□□□□ □□	**INTP** *N* = 12 % = 10.53 □□□□□□□□□□ □	Perceptive		
	ESTP *N* = 1 % = 0.88 □	**ESFP** *N* = 0 % = 0.0	**ENFP** *N* = 16 % = 14.04 □□□□□□□□□□ □□□□	**ENTP** *N* = 0 % = 0.0	Perceptive		
	ESTJ *N* = 1 % = 0.88 □	**ESFJ** *N* = 2 % = 1.75 □□	**ENFJ** *N* = 14 % = 12.28 □□□□□□□□□□ □□	**ENTJ** *N* = 10 % = 8.77 □□□□□□□□□	Judging		

Introverts / *Extraverts* labeled on right side of grid.

	Number	Percent
E	44	38.60
I	70	61.40
S	10	8.77
N	104	91.23
T	34	29.82
F	80	70.18
J	59	51.75
P	55	48.25
IJ	32	28.07
IP	38	33.33
EP	17	14.91
EJ	27	23.68
ST	4	3.51
SF	6	5.26
NF	74	64.91
NT	30	26.32
SJ	8	7.02
SP	2	1.75
NP	53	46.49
NJ	51	44.74
TJ	21	18.42
TP	13	11.40
FP	42	36.84
FJ	38	33.33
IN	64	56.14
EN	40	35.09
IS	6	5.26
ES	4	3.51

Note: □ = 1% of sample.
Source of data: Simon, R. S. *Jungian Types and Creativity of Professional Fine Artists.* Unpublished doctoral dissertation, United States International University, 1979. Used with permission. Data collected by Robert S. Simon from professional fine artists in San Diego, California. (Males: *N* = 36, Females: *N* = 78.)

rather than intuition. Empirically, N types outnumber S types in art students and among artists. The theoretical explanation is that the insights and inspirations provided by intuition are more important, but true artistic skill requires the development of S skills for use in the service of N inspirations.

Independent Study in High School

E. Barberousse (1975) reported on an experimental humanities program in a traditional, highly competitive suburban high school. One hundred students were randomly selected for the program from 177 volunteers out of a class of 750 seniors. The program, in offering an interdisciplinary approach to such themes as Man and Self and Man and Earth, was very different from the standard program. A small group of students who still felt constrained by the experimental program received permission to learn the work by independent study. The preferences most associated with students involved in independent study were N (future possibilities are more interesting than conventional realities), P (openness is more valuable than structure), and to a certain extent I (ideas and concepts are more trustworthy than transitory external conditions). The humanities students were 50% I, 79% N, 75% F, and 77% P. Their fellows doing the independent study are shown in Table 4.7. They were 55% I, 93% N, 81% F, and 90% P, with 86% in the four NP types.

In a similar study, Rezler and Johns (1973) collected data on four classes of medical students electing independent study. In their study, the 72 independent scholars were

Table 4.7 High school seniors who selected an independent study program (*N* = 42)

	Sensing Types		Intuitive Types			Number	Percent
	With Thinking	With Feeling	With Feeling	With Thinking			
	ISTJ N= 0 %= 0.0	ISFJ N= 1 %= 2.38 •	INFJ N= 1 %= 2.38 •	INTJ N= 0 %= 0.0	Judging (Introverts)	E 19 / I 23	45.24 / 54.76
						S 3 / N 39	7.14 / 92.86
						T 8 / F 34	19.05 / 80.95
	ISTP N= 0 %= 0.0	ISFP N= 0 %= 0.0	INFP N= 17 %= 40.48 •••••••••• •••••••	INTP N= 4 %= 9.52 ••••	Perceptive (Introverts)	J 4 / P 38	9.52 / 90.48
						IJ 2 / IP 21 / EP 17 / EJ 2	4.76 / 50.00 / 40.48 / 4.76
						ST 0 / SF 3 / NF 31 / NT 8	0.00 / 7.14 / 73.81 / 19.05
	ESTP N= 0 %= 0.0	ESFP N= 2 %= 4.76 ••	ENFP N= 12 %= 28.57 •••••••••• ••	ENTP N= 3 %= 7.14 •••	Perceptive (Extraverts)	SJ 1 / SP 2 / NP 36 / NJ 3	2.38 / 4.76 / 85.71 / 7.14
						TJ 1 / TP 7 / FP 31 / FJ 3	2.38 / 16.67 / 73.81 / 7.14
	ESTJ N= 0 %= 0.0	ESFJ N= 0 %= 0.0	ENFJ N= 1 %= 2.38 •	ENTJ N= 1 %= 2.38 •	Judging (Extraverts)	IN 22 / EN 17 / IS 1 / ES 2	52.38 / 40.48 / 2.38 / 4.76

Note: • = one student.
Source of data: Humanities Pilot Program at Walt Whitman High School during school session of 1969–70. Data collected by E.H. Barberousse. Used with permission.

57% I, 86% N, 60% F and 60% P, with 57% in the four NP types.

Clergymen from Various Denominations

Since the F function is concerned with values, the prediction from theory is that there should be more F types than T types in religious samples. The clergy in Table 4.8 are a composite of different denominations brought together from the MBTI data bank. 78% of this sample prefer the feeling judgment. What had not been expected from theory was the large number of J types in this and other samples of religious workers. One interpretation of the table is that the clergy rely primarily on their values, *and* they have a vocation that requires they be the "value executives" for their parishioners.

Table 4.8 Male clergy from Protestant denominations ($N = 1,458$)

Sensing Types		Intuitive Types			Number	Percent
With Thinking	With Feeling	With Feeling	With Thinking			
ISTJ $N = 60$ $\% = 4.12$ ¤¤¤¤	**ISFJ** $N = 150$ $\% = 10.29$ ¤¤¤¤¤¤¤¤¤¤	**INFJ** $N = 149$ $\% = 10.22$ ¤¤¤¤¤¤¤¤¤¤	**INTJ** $N = 62$ $\% = 4.25$ ¤¤¤¤	Judging / Introverts	E 855 I 603 S 561 N 897	59.64 41.36 38.48 61.52
ISTP $N = 8$ $\% = 0.55$ ¤	**ISFP** $N = 33$ $\% = 2.26$ ¤¤	**INFP** $N = 121$ $\% = 8.30$ ¤¤¤¤¤¤¤¤	**INTP** $N = 20$ $\% = 1.37$ ¤	Perceptive	T 337 F 1121 J 996 P 462 IJ 421 IP 182 EP 280 EJ 575	23.11 76.89 68.31 31.69 28.88 12.48 19.20 39.44
ESTP $N = 7$ $\% = 0.48$	**ESFP** $N = 42$ $\% = 2.88$ ¤¤¤	**ENFP** $N = 200$ $\% = 13.72$ ¤¤¤¤¤¤¤¤¤¤ ¤¤¤¤	**ENTP** $N = 31$ $\% = 2.13$ ¤¤	Perceptive / Extraverts	ST 143 SF 418 NF 703 NT 194 SJ 471 SP 90 NP 372 NJ 525	9.81 28.67 48.22 13.31 32.30 6.17 25.51 36.01
ESTJ $N = 68$ $\% = 4.66$ ¤¤¤¤¤	**ESFJ** $N = 193$ $\% = 13.24$ ¤¤¤¤¤¤¤¤¤¤ ¤¤¤	**ENFJ** $N = 233$ $\% = 15.98$ ¤¤¤¤¤¤¤¤¤¤ ¤¤¤¤¤¤	**ENTJ** $N = 81$ $\% = 5.56$ ¤¤¤¤¤¤	Judging	TJ 271 TP 66 FP 396 FJ 725 IN 352 EN 545 IS 251 ES 310	18.59 4.53 27.16 49.73 24.14 37.38 17.22 21.26

Note: ¤ = 1% of sample.
Source of data: Ruppart, R.E. (1985). *Psychological types and occupational preferences among religious professionals: A psychosocial, historical perspective.* Doctoral dissertation, New York University. Used with permission.

Counselors from the MBTI Data Bank

Counselors have diverse interests, but share a concern for unraveling the intricacies of behavior and for finding patterns in a complex and nebulous world. One might predict, therefore, that counselors would be more interested in perceiving the intangible (N) than the tangible (S). Composite samples of people referring to themselves as counselors on MBTI response sheets and scored by CAPT (McCaulley, 1978) show a greater percentage of N types (see Table 4.9).

Table 4.9 Practicing counselors (*N* = 359)

Sensing Types With Thinking	Sensing Types With Feeling	Intuitive Types With Feeling	Intuitive Types With Thinking		Number	Percent
ISTJ *N* = 21 % = 5.8 □□□□□□	**ISFJ** *N* = 20 % = 5.6 □□□□□□	**INFJ** *N* = 28 % = 7.8 □□□□□□□□	**INTJ** *N* = 11 % = 3.1 □□□	Judging / Introverts	E 200 I 159 S 118 N 241 T 85 F 274	55.71 44.29 32.87 67.13 23.68 76.32
ISTP *N* = 4 % = 1.1 □	**ISFP** *N* = 16 % = 4.5 □□□□□	**INFP** *N* = 50 % = 13.9 □□□□□□□□□□□□□□	**INTP** *N* = 9 % = 2.5 □□□	Perceptive / Introverts	J 170 P 189 IJ 80 IP 79 EP 110 EJ 90	47.35 52.65 22.28 22.01 30.64 25.07
ESTP *N* = 4 % = 1.1 □	**ESFP** *N* = 11 % = 6.1 □□□□□□	**ENFP** *N* = 84 % = 23.4 □□□□□□□□□□□□□□□□□□□□□□□	**ENTP** *N* = 11 % = 3.1 □□□	Perceptive / Extraverts	ST 47 SF 71 NF 203 NT 38 SJ 83 SP 35 NP 154 NJ 87	13.09 19.78 56.55 10.58 23.12 9.75 42.90 24.23
ESTJ *N* = 18 % = 5.0 □□□□□	**ESFJ** *N* = 24 % = 6.7 □□□□□□□	**ENFJ** *N* = 41 % = 11.4 □□□□□□□□□□□	**ENTJ** *N* = 7 % = 1.9 □□	Judging / Extraverts	TJ 57 TP 28 FP 161 FJ 113 IN 98 EN 143 IS 61 ES 57	15.88 7.80 44.85 31.48 27.30 39.83 16.99 15.88

Note: □ = 1% of sample.
Source of data: Sample reported by M. H. McCaulley in *Application of the Myers-Briggs Type Indicator to Medicine and Other Health Professions: Monograph I,* 1978. Used with permission.

Estimates of Frequencies of Types in the General Population

One of the first questions people ask when learning about type is, "How frequent is my type?" No definitive answer can yet be given to this question, but estimates are possible. The following sections show various estimations of MBTI types in the general population.

Myers' Estimates of Type Distributions

Isabel Myers (1962) made the following estimates of type in the general population:

> **About 75% of the population in the United States prefer E.**
>
> **About 75% of the population in the United States prefer S.**
>
> **About 60% of males in the United States prefer T.**
>
> **About 65% of females in the United States prefer F.**
>
> **About 55% to 60% of the population in the United States prefer J.**

An estimate of type in the general population can be based on Myer's sample of eleventh and twelfth grade high school students from Pennsylvania, tested with Form D2 of the MBTI in the spring of 1957 (see Tables 4.10 and 4.11). These students came from 27 high schools with both college preparatory and noncollege preparatory programs. This sample can be expected to have more introverts and intuitive types than the general population, since Myers' studies of high school dropouts found a greater proportion of extraverts and sensing types.

Estimates from the MBTI Data Bank

Population frequencies can be estimated from the Center for Applications of Psychological Type (CAPT) MBTI data bank of response sheets sent in for computer scoring. The data shown in Tables 4.10 and 4.11 include response sheets for Form F submitted for scoring from March 1978 through December 1982. The CAPT MBTI data bank has a bias, of undetermined amount, toward intuition and introversion, since many of the professionals submitting cases for scoring are working in educational institutions. The percentage from the data bank of persons who have completed at least one year of college is 63% for males and 50% for females on Form F, and 50% for males and 54% for females on Form G (the Form G data bank is in Tables 4.12 and 4.13). The adults with lower educational levels

were included in the data bank sample because their response sheets were submitted in conjunction with some professional activity. The Form G data bank includes over 3,500 engineering students in the Engineering Consortium Study, increasing the percentage of T types for males and females.

MBTI response sheets ask respondents to indicate the number of years of education *completed*. Tables 4.10 and 4.11 show the percentage at each level completed for males and females, tested after the ages when they might reasonably be in school.

Despite the limitations of the MBTI data bank and sampling variations from year to year, certain trends in type distributions of populations are indicated. Females have relatively more F types and males have relatively more T types. The STJ types are frequent among males, and the SFJ types are more frequent among females. The IN types are relatively rare, but their numbers are more frequent at higher educational levels.

Estimates from SRI International Longitudinal Study of Values

A third estimate of the population comes from smaller samples collected by Brooke H. Warrick as part of an ongoing study at SRI International on American Values and Life Styles (VALS) (see Tables 4.12 and 4.13). The MBTI was administered to a random national sample to determine whether a relationship existed between values and the MBTI dimensions. The study was based on a national random sample of households with telephones (excluding military and other institutions) in 300 counties across the continental United States. Half of the sample was allocated to the ten metropolitan areas. The MBTI was distributed during the summer of 1983 to 2,000 respondents and had a return rate of 55% (446 males and 659 females). The sample is the closest currently available on a nationwide random basis, but is somewhat biased toward more affluent groups. A noteworthy fact is that the sample for both males and females includes more introverts than extraverts. Warrick (personal communication) reported that the SRI VALS data indicated a clear trend toward people reporting more introverted values than in the past decade. The same trend toward introverted values is mentioned in Yankelovich (1981, p. 5).

The VALS sample also has a surprisingly large proportion of the dependable ISJ types. One confounding factor may be that ISJ types tend to be more conscientious in meeting research commitments.

The SRI sample shows a trend found in other samples which suggests that there are more extraverts in female samples than in comparable male samples.

Table 4.10 Male distribution of types by educational level (*N* = 12,860 males)

Students	ISTJ Number	ISTJ Percent	ISFJ Number	ISFJ Percent	INFJ Number	INFJ Percent	INTJ Number	INTJ Percent
Jr.H.S.	88	9.59	39	4.25	25	2.72	48	5.23
Sr.H.S.	14	9.21	3	1.97	2	1.32	2	1.32
T.Coll.	597	10.60	353	6.27	165	2.93	243	4.31
N.Coll.	155	17.20	51	5.66	19	2.11	54	5.99
Nonstudents								
Sch.D.	30	14.63	20	9.76	6	2.93	8	3.90
H.S.Gr.	137	22.61	46	7.59	7	1.16	14	2.31
Coll.G.	761	17.12	200	4.50	145	3.26	425	9.56

Students	ISTP Number	ISTP Percent	ISFP Number	ISFP Percent	INFP Number	INFP Percent	INTP Number	INTP Percent
Jr.H.S.	61	6.64	47	5.12	69	7.52	62	6.75
Sr.H.S.	23	15.13	4	2.63	8	5.26	11	7.24
T.Coll.	380	6.75	287	5.10	329	5.84	327	5.81
N.Coll.	61	6.77	25	2.77	47	5.22	62	6.88
Nonstudents								
Sch.D.	12	5.85	8	3.90	7	3.41	6	2.93
H.S.Gr.	38	6.27	13	2.15	5	0.83	17	2.81
Coll.G.	144	3.24	85	1.91	203	4.57	248	5.58

Students	ESTP Number	ESTP Percent	ESFP Number	ESFP Percent	ENFP Number	ENFP Percent	ENTP Number	ENTP Percent
Jr.H.S.	79	8.61	66	7.19	93	10.13	78	8.50
Sr.H.S.	24	15.79	9	5.92	16	10.53	10	6.58
T.Coll.	364	6.46	304	5.40	421	7.48	347	6.16
N.Coll.	22	2.44	23	2.55	47	5.22	42	4.66
Nonstudents								
Sch.D.	10	4.88	6	2.93	7	3.41	8	3.90
H.S.Gr.	33	5.45	12	1.98	9	1.49	17	2.81
Coll.G.	117	2.63	69	1.55	264	5.94	251	5.65

Students	ESTJ Number	ESTJ Percent	ESFJ Number	ESFJ Percent	ENFJ Number	ENFJ Percent	ENTJ Number	ENTJ Percent
Jr.H.S.	73	7.95	43	4.68	14	1.53	33	3.59
Sr.H.S.	11	7.24	4	2.63	6	3.95	5	3.29
T.Coll.	633	11.24	371	6.59	208	3.69	303	5.38
N.Coll.	138	15.32	63	6.99	35	3.88	57	6.33
Nonstudents								
Sch.D.	38	18.54	11	5.37	5	2.44	23	11.22
H.S.Gr.	186	30.69	38	6.27	8	1.32	26	4.29
Coll.G.	683	15.36	158	3.55	185	4.16	508	11.43

Table 4.12 shows for males the percentages in each type for the Myers samples, the data bank samples, and the VALS study samples. Table 4.13 shows comparable data for females. As expected, more males report a preference for T and more females report a preference for F.

The samples did not have the 75% extraverts expected by Myers. The Myers sample showed 61% E for males and 68% E for females. The data bank samples for males show 51% E for Form F and 49% E for Form G. The female data were 56% E for Form F and 55% E for Form G. The VALS data showed 36% E for males and 43% E for females. Female samples all had more extraverts than male samples. It is not clear whether Isabel Myers' estimated percentage of 75% E is too high, whether current sampling includes fewer extraverts because they are more likely to drop out of high school, or whether a demonstrable trend is occurring. Whatever the reason, it is important for MBTI users to watch the EI scale in sample distributions.

Given the problems of reaching and testing representative samples with any written questionnaire, the true distribution (which must include school dropouts) may never be known. It is clear that in the samples collected by professionals using the MBTI, Is and Ns occur more frequently than in Myers' estimates. To the extent that T and F concern decision making, the rapid changes in society can be expected to make people uncertain of the basis for their decisions; if so, clear and consistent preferences for T or for F may be difficult to develop. The JP preference can be affected developmentally by cultural uncertainties, as some people may cling to the certainty promised by J, while others give up trying to control their lives and opt for the adaptability of P.

Population norm tables are useful for counseling because they show that all types exist, although not in equal numbers, and that if one seeks judiciously, kindred spirits can be found. The utility of population norms for researchers is that populations can differ markedly in the distributions of types, and these differences can affect weights in research data.

Understanding of Type through the Personal Type Table

The personal type table is a useful tool for understanding MBTI types. Create a personal table by entering onto a blank type table the names of family, friends, colleagues, students, or clients as their types become known. Study the table for similarities among people of neighboring types, and differences among people in types far apart on the table. (Note that the type table can be rolled like a cylinder so that J types are next to each other. It can be rolled in the other direction to bring T types together.)

As the personal type table grows, study it periodically and ask questions such as:

1. Are the sensing types (S types) on the left half more interested in facts than the intuitive types (N types) on the right half? Are the N types more interested in possibilities than the S types?

2. Are the thinking types (T types) on the outer columns

Notes: Student samples include answer sheets where "Are you a student?" was answered "yes."
Jr.H.S. includes students in seventh, eighth, or ninth grade (highest grade completed 6–8).
Sr.H.S. includes students in tenth, eleventh, or twelfth grade (highest grade completed 9–11).
T.Coll. refers to college students of traditional age (highest grade completed 12–15 and age from 18–24 inclusive).
N.Coll. refers to college students of nontraditional age (highest grade completed 12–15 and age 25 or older).

Nonstudent samples include answer sheets where "Are you a student?" was answered "no" and ages were given as over 24.
Sch.D. refers to high school dropouts and includes nonstudent males over age 24 whose highest grade completed was 11 or lower.
H.S.Gr. refers to nonstudent males over age 24 whose highest grade completed was 12.
Coll.G. refers to nonstudent males over age 24 whose highest grade completed was 16.

Source of data: All data are from the MBTI Form F Data Bank of cases scored between March 1978 and December 1982.

Table 4.11 Female distribution of types by education level ($N = 20,006$ females)

	ISTJ		ISFJ		INFJ		INTJ	
Students	*Number*	*Percent*	*Number*	*Percent*	*Number*	*Percent*	*Number*	*Percent*
Jr.H.S.	58	4.51	117	9.11	43	3.35	16	1.25
Sr.H.S.	6	3.11	12	6.22	4	2.07	3	1.55
T.Coll.	578	6.01	1179	12.26	366	3.81	183	1.90
N.Coll.	254	10.40	315	12.89	114	4.67	75	3.07
Nonstudents								
Sch.D.	49	12.37	78	19.70	10	2.53	12	3.03
H.S.Gr.	129	9.65	256	19.15	48	3.59	32	2.39
Coll.G.	485	10.24	575	12.14	325	6.86	274	5.79

	ISTP		ISFP		INFP		INTP	
Students	*Number*	*Percent*	*Number*	*Percent*	*Number*	*Percent*	*Number*	*Percent*
Jr.H.S.	29	2.26	100	7.78	120	9.34	29	2.26
Sr.H.S.	6	3.11	13	6.74	15	7.77	6	3.11
T.Coll.	213	2.22	590	6.14	556	5.78	187	1.94
N.Coll.	73	2.99	159	6.51	133	5.44	70	2.87
Nonstudents								
Sch.D.	17	4.29	32	8.08	18	4.55	7	1.77
H.S.Gr.	41	3.07	106	7.93	71	5.31	18	1.35
Coll.G.	66	1.39	144	3.04	351	7.41	168	3.55

	ESTP		ESFP		ENFP		ENTP	
Students	*Number*	*Percent*	*Number*	*Percent*	*Number*	*Percent*	*Number*	*Percent*
Jr.H.S.	35	2.72	162	12.61	247	19.22	48	3.74
Sr.H.S.	12	6.22	27	13.99	25	12.95	9	4.66
T.Coll.	246	2.56	821	8.54	1185	12.32	294	3.06
N.Coll.	54	2.21	114	4.67	211	8.64	79	3.23
Nonstudents								
Sch.D.	10	2.53	23	5.81	20	5.05	4	1.01
H.S.Gr.	35	2.62	108	8.08	81	6.06	19	1.42
Coll.G.	40	0.84	142	3.00	453	9.57	193	4.08

	ESTJ		ESFJ		ENFJ		ENTJ	
Students	*Number*	*Percent*	*Number*	*Percent*	*Number*	*Percent*	*Number*	*Percent*
Jr.H.S.	70	5.45	124	9.65	66	5.14	21	1.63
Sr.H.S.	9	4.66	28	14.51	9	4.66	9	4.66
T.Coll.	724	7.53	1558	16.20	662	6.88	274	2.85
N.Coll.	237	9.70	309	12.65	145	5.94	101	4.13
Nonstudents								
Sch.D.	47	1.87	41	10.35	15	3.79	13	3.28
H.S.Gr.	126	9.42	189	14.14	39	2.92	39	2.92
Coll.G.	400	8.45	423	8.93	376	7.94	321	6.78

more given to logic and analysis than the feeling types (F types) in the center columns? Do the F types appear warmer or more sympathetic than the T types?

3. Do the extraverts (E types) in the lower half of the table appear more at home in the outer world than the introverts (I types)? Are I types more interested in the world of ideas than the E types?

4. Are the judging types (J types) in the top and bottom rows more decisive and organized than the perceptive types (P types) in the middle rows? Are the P types more spontaneous or adaptable than the J types?

5. How are people of the same type alike? and different?

Many people are surprised to find that most of their friends are in the same area of the type table and they may have no acquaintances at all in some of the types. This exercise is useful for alerting MBTI users to seek out and learn more about persons of types relatively unknown to them.

Notes: Student samples include answer sheets where "Are you a student?" was answered "yes."
Jr.H.S. includes students in seventh, eighth, or ninth grade (highest grade completed 6–8).
Sr.H.S. includes students in tenth, eleventh, or twelfth grade (highest grade completed 9–11).
T.Coll. refers to college students of traditional age (highest grade completed 12–15 and age from 18–24 inclusive).
N.Coll. refers to college students of nontraditional age (highest grade completed 12–15 and age 25 or older).

Nonstudent samples include answer sheets where "Are you a student?" was answered "no" and ages were given as over 24.
Sch.D. refers to high school dropouts and includes nonstudent females over age 24 whose highest grade completed was 11 or lower.
H.S.Gr. refers to nonstudent females over age 24 whose highest grade completed was 12.
Coll.G. refers to nonstudent females over age 24 whose highest grade completed was 16.

Source of data: All data are from the MBTI Form F Data Bank of cases scored between March 1978 and December 1982.

Table 4.12 Four male normative samples

ISTJ	ISFJ	INFJ	INTJ
Myers H.S 8.76%	4.48%	1.60%	3.69%
MBTI data bank			
Form F 13.93%	5.34%	3.15%	6.54%
Form G 15.45%	4.42%	2.63%	7.28%
SRI VALS 30.72%	7.62%	1.79%	4.93%

ISTP	ISFP	INFP	INTP
Myers H.S 6.12%	5.17%	3.49%	4.78%
MBTI data bank			
Form F 5.04%	3.32%	5.51%	5.77%
Form G 6.07%	3.00%	4.76%	7.05%
SRI VALS 8.30%	2.91%	3.59%	3.81%

ESTP	ESFP	ENFP	ENTP
Myers H.S 8.90%	7.18%	5.98%	6.41%
MBTI data bank			
Form F 4.77%	3.51%	6.76%	6.00%
Form G 5.90%	3.12%	5.38%	6.86%
SRI VALS 4.93%	1.79%	1.79%	3.14%

ESTJ	ESFJ	ENFJ	ENTJ
Myers H.S 17.07%	8.21%	2.84%	5.33%
MBTI data bank			
Form F 13.77%	5.09%	3.76%	7.74%
Form G 14.01%	4.39%	2.74%	6.93%
SRI VALS 12.33%	4.26%	1.57%	6.50%

Notes: *Myers H.S.* refers to Myers' sample of eleventh and twelfth grade high school males (N = 4,933).
MBTI data bank refers to males in the MBTI data banks whose records were scored between March 1978 and December 1982. For Form F, N = 23,240; for Form G, N = 15,791.
SRI VALS refers to data from the Values and Lifestyles Program (VALS) (N = 446) made available by Brooke H. Warrick, Senior Consultant, SRI International, Menlo Park, California. Used with permission.

Table 4.13 Four female normative samples

ISTJ	ISFJ	INFJ	INTJ
Myers H.S 4.86%	9.46%	2.01%	1.41%
MBTI data bank			
Form F 7.80%	11.70%	4.66%	3.44%
Form G 9.77%	10.30%	4.77%	4.00%
SRI VALS 11.23%	20.94%	3.79%	2.12%

ISTP	ISFP	INFP	INTP
Myers H.S 1.96%	5.65%	4.35%	2.14%
MBTI data bank			
Form F 2.06%	5.32%	6.59%	2.72%
Form G 2.67%	4.27%	6.32%	3.20%
SRI VALS 4.55%	9.26%	3.95%	.91%

ESTP	ESFP	ENFP	ENTP
Myers H.S 3.85%	11.83%	9.41%	3.19%
MBTI data bank			
Form F 2.25%	6.64%	11.28%	3.68%
Form G 2.78%	5.73%	9.80%	4.11%
SRI VALS 3.34%	7.89%	5.01%	1.37%

ESTJ	ESFJ	ENFJ	ENTJ
Myers H.S 12.61%	20.45%	4.47%	2.35%
MBTI data bank			
Form F 8.13%	12.49%	6.72%	4.53%
Form G 10.07%	10.66%	6.38%	5.17%
SRI VALS 8.35%	12.44%	2.73%	2.12%

Notes: *Myers H.S.* refers to Myers' sample of eleventh and twelfth grade high school females ($N = 4,387$).
MBTI data bank refers to females in the MBTI data banks whose records were scored between March 1978 and December 1982. For Form F, $N = 32,731$. For Form G, $N = 16,880$.
SRI VALS refers to data from the Values and Lifestyles Program (VALS) ($N = 659$) made available by Brooke H. Warrick, Senior Consultant, SRI International, Menlo Park, California. Used with permission.

Chapter 5

Initial Interpretation and Verification

This chapter reviews issues in explaining MBTI results to clients. Because MBTI reports are designed to be given directly to respondents, interpretation necessarily includes steps to help respondents verify the accuracy of these reports based on their knowledge of themselves. The interpreter is a teacher of the theory, since the MBTI type description is essentially a report of predictions from theory. The first section of this chapter gives Isabel Myers' guidelines for using the MBTI report form and *Introduction to Type*. The last section of this chapter discusses interpreting scores to identify the preferred type.

In counseling situations, about 75% of clients agree with their reports and the main part of the session is concerned with how type preferences appear in their behaviors. This chapter gives reasons why people may *not* agree with their reports, and stresses the responsibilities of the interpreter. Professionals are rightly skeptical about the capability of any personality measure to reflect the complexity of either human behavior or personality. On the other hand, laypeople may put too much reliance on psychological data. Since type descriptions are designed to be given directly to respondents, it is particularly important for interpreters to use strategies that encourage respondents to verify the report against their own experience.

Introducing the Interpretation

Interpretation of MBTI results should be a joint process between the professional giving the interpretation and the respondent reacting. One should never say flatly "You *are* such and such a type." The statement not only sounds arbitrary and limiting, but it may not be true. MBTI results are, of course, not always right. The reported type should be submitted to the respondent's judgment, with statements like, "This shows how you *came out*. Would you say that is right?"

As with any self-report instrument, the correctness of the results depends in part on how well the questions have been answered. If people answering the MBTI feel that they have nothing to gain, they may answer carelessly or even at random. If they fear they have something to lose, they may answer as they assume they *should*. But if they understand before answering that they will be told how they come out and will be invited to confirm or correct the report of their type, their answers are more likely to be genuine.

First Steps

1. No questions, however accurate, can explain all human complexity. The MBTI results are a first step toward understanding the respondent's true preferences.

2. In answering the MBTI, the respondent chose between a series of preferences. These choices may have seemed difficult, because all the choices described activities that are necessary and valuable. Such choices are more difficult than choices between things considered good or bad. (It is often useful to describe the process of responding to the MBTI as one of casting votes in four "elections," each with two good candidates.)

3. The terms and letters may seem a little strange at first, but the behaviors described by those terms should be familiar to the respondent.

4. The MBTI is an Indicator, not a test. There are no right or wrong answers. There are also no good or bad, or sick or well types. All types are valuable.

5. Whatever the type, one *does use* both sides of each preference, though not with equal liking. A useful analogy is that preferences are like handedness; one uses both hands, but reaches first with the preferred hand which is probably more adept.

6. Typically people use and develop more skills with the processes they like.

7. The preferences described are important for understanding how people assimilate information and make decisions. They describe processes that will seem familiar. One value of type is that it helps people use the information they already know in more organized and practical ways.

8. If the reported process or type does not seem right, respondents can discover and decide for themselves, with help from the interpreter, which processes or which type more accurately describes them.

These cautions are more important for the MBTI than for instruments where scores are reported on a continuum, because types are reported in letters and descriptions which can give a sense of certainty that goes beyond the data.

Explaining the Preferences

The next step is to explain the nature of the preferences. Describe for each preference the ways in which people who prefer one pole of a preference differ from those who prefer the opposite pole (see Table 5.1).

Vary the descriptions of the preferences depending on the respondent's type and the time available. Concrete behavioral examples of the preferences are helpful for bringing the theoretical abstractions into everyday experiences; such examples are particularly important when explaining type concepts to sensing types. Visual aids can be helpful; for example, *Looking at Type* (Page, 1983) describes the preferences with cartoon characters.

By explaining type characteristics, the interpreter provides both an illustration of type differences, and also a first check on whether the reported type is correct. If respondents confirm that all four preferences are indicative of their behavior and personality, the correctness of the reported type is tentatively confirmed. When a characteristic is not confirmed, the preference in question should be considered to be in doubt and evaluated further.

Brief Descriptions of Each Type

Another means for checking the reported type is through the use of "Characteristics Frequently Associated with Each Type" on the back of the handscoring profile sheet. This table contains short type sketches. People not given to introspection (particularly ES types) often find it easier to recognize themselves among these miniature portraits than to recognize their preferences one at a time.

When using the brief type tables for verification, the individual's type description should be read to him or her first, then compared with neighboring type descriptions. Should another type description seem to fit the client as well or better, that type should be respectfully included for consideration as the individual's "true" type.

Introduction to Type as a Verification Tool

If people who take the MBTI are to make real use of the results, they need more information than is in the report form and more than they can remember from a verbal explanation.

Table 5.1 Choices of the four preferences

E: With an E for extraversion, you probably are more at home in the outer world of people and things than in the inner world of ideas.

I: With an I for introversion, you probably are more at home in the inner world of ideas than in the outer world of people and things.

S: With an S for sensing, you probably would rather work with known facts than look for possibilities and relationships.

N: With an N for intuition, you probably would rather look for possibilities and relationships than work with known facts.

T: With a T for thinking, you probably base your judgments more on impersonal analysis than on personal values.

F: With an F for feeling, you probably base your judgments more on personal values than on impersonal logic.

J: With a J for judging, you probably like a planned, decided, orderly way of life better than a flexible, spontaneous way.

P: With a P for perception, you probably like a flexible, spontaneous way of life better than a planned, orderly way.

To meet this need, *Introduction to Type* was written to be used as an interpretive tool. To appeal to different types, it describes type in words for each type that will best communicate with that type. When MBTI results are explained to individuals or groups, the task is made simpler when people have the booklet in front of them, which allows them to see the type contrasts while they are being explained. Respondents are more likely to "put it all together" with *Introduction to Type* for reference.

Introduction to Type is arranged to make the differences between types as self-evident as possible, and to show that these differences are not only logical (which is important to thinking types) but also valuable (which is important to feeling types). The opening pages are devoted to definitions of the preferences and a brief introduction to type theory.

Combinations of Perception and Judgment

Following the basic principles of type, *Introduction to Type* provides a section on applications, including descriptions of the combinations of perception and judgment, ST, SF, NF, and NT. Each of these four combinations produces a different set of characteristics, that is, different interests, values, needs, abilities, habits of mind, and surface traits.

If you ask clients to ascertain which column comes closest to describing them, they will have evidence about which two processes they typically depend on. One of these two will be their "favorite" or dominant process and the other will be the auxiliary, which provides balance.

Making Full Use of Perception and Judgment

People's main strengths come from the processes of perception and judgment that they like best, have trusted, and developed at the expense of those they like less. For some purposes, however, their less-liked modes of perception and judgment can serve them better and therefore should not be ignored. Each process can be seen as a tool, indispensable in its own area.

Page 29 of *Introduction to Type* offers a technique for making full use of the processes of perception and judgment. It is valuable for introducing the MBTI, but it is even more useful for guiding individuals toward full type development. The technique requires use of *both* kinds of perception and *both* kinds of judgment, preferred and less preferred, *each for the right purpose and in the right order.*

Since perception should always precede judgment, the order is described as follows:

When there is a problem or situation to deal with:

1. Use sensing to *gather* the relevant facts and to face them realistically.

2. Use intuition to discover *new possibilities* and all the actions that might be taken to improve the matters.

3. Use thinking-judgment to analyze all the *consequences,* good or bad, of each action that might be taken.

4. Use feeling-judgment to weigh the *value,* to self and to others, of what will be gained or lost by these solutions.

Faithfully taken, these steps lead to a better solution than would otherwise be reached. They strengthen both perception and judgment for use in the next problem.

If there is doubt about which are one's true preferences, these steps offer another way for discovering an individual's preferences. The step that sounds hardest to take to the client tends to be the step that demands the use of the least-liked, least-developed kind of perception or judgment (the inferior function). For example, if the idea of looking logically and analytically (T) at every good and bad outcome of possible actions sounds difficult and depressing, then thinking may be one's inferior function and feeling one's dominant function.

Mutual Usefulness of Opposites

Page 24 of *Introduction to Type* illustrates the mutual usefulness of opposite types by listing ways in which opposites on SN or TF can supplement each other. For instance, an intuitive type needs a sensing type to bring up pertinent facts and a sensing type needs an intuitive type to bring up new possibilities. A feeling type needs a thinking type to analyze; a thinking type needs a feeling type to persuade.

When an individual's preferences are in doubt, a study of the lists in *Introduction to Type* can be useful for identifying actions that seem relatively easy or hard. Easier actions are more likely to be associated with preferred processes. A second use of the lists is to continue to build an appreciation of differences. By building appreciation, members of each type will be more ready to recognize and gratefully accept the expertise of people with preferences different from their own, without feeling inferior or diminished.

Dominant and Auxiliary

Page 6 of *Introduction to Type* introduces the concepts of (but not the terms) dominant and auxiliary functions and briefly explains how they work differently with extraverts and introverts. It is not necessary for people to grasp or remember an explanation of dominant and auxiliary until later when they are much more familiar with the structure of type. Until this time, however, it may be useful to be able to determine quickly the individual's dominant and auxiliary functions. The type descriptions in *Introduction to Type* are titled so they can be used for this purpose. Also, a summary of type dynamics appears as Table 3.2 in this Manual.

Full-Page Descriptions of the Types

When initially interpreting the MBTI, the most important activity is to discuss the full-page description of the individual's type sentence by sentence. As in the preliminary steps, this reading should be with an attitude of inquiry. The purpose is to discover where the description fits and where it does not fit. Respondents often bring up examples substantiating statements in the description. Uncertainties about preferences may be dispelled at this stage.

In reading the type descriptions, it is important to remember that not *everything* in the type description can be expected to fit. There is a great deal of variation within every type, since different people with the same preference may exercise that preference in a wide variety of ways. For example, one member of a type with dominant sensing may use sensing in the details of accounting, another in building construction, and a third in taking care of patients. All three share an interest in paying attention to realistic, here-and-now events. The characteristics cited in the type descriptions are related to the effects of the dominant, auxiliary, and inferior functions, and the attitudes in which they occur. These characteristics are likely to be seen as accurate, but more specific comments in the descriptions, especially descriptions about careers, may not necessarily fit a particular member of the type.

The type descriptions from *Introduction to Type* are reproduced two per table.

The descriptions apply to each type at its best, as exemplified by normal, well-balanced, effective people. In theoretical terms, the descriptions assume adequate development of two processes, the dominant and auxiliary.

Each table provides a description of a pair of types with the same dominant process. The pair differs only in their auxiliary process. For example, for the two extraverted thinking types, the descriptions are headed ESTJ and ENTJ and discuss the characteristics these two types share, particularly the characteristics due to their dominant process, extraverted thinking. Also included in each description are the characteristics associated with each type's auxiliary functions. These sections show, for example, how extraverted thinkers who use sensing as auxiliary (ESTJ) tend to differ from extraverted thinkers who use intuition as auxiliary (ENTJ).

Effect of an Undeveloped Auxiliary

Each type description contains statements describing the effect of an inadequately developed auxiliary process. These statements do *not* apply to members of the type in general, but only to those who have not developed their auxiliary enough to give them balance. The reason for including the warning statements (introduced by *if*) is to emphasize the importance of the auxiliary to effective type functioning. Without a good auxiliary, the main body of the description will not be true.

Effects of the Types in Work Situations

The effects of each preference in work situations, as presented on page 25 of *Introduction to Type,* describe differences typically found in persons with opposite preferences. Discussion of these differences can sometimes help an individual resolve a doubtful preference. None of these effects are certain to be found in *every* member of that type. They will, however, be found more often in members of that type than in members of the opposite type. This section is especially useful in career counseling for judging how satisfying tasks for any specific job are likely to be to an individual with a particular set of preferences.

Final Steps in Verification of Type

The following checklist contains key points to remember when explaining type from the perspective of being a teacher of type to an individual learning type theory. These points were developed by Gordon Lawrence (1982) and are used with his permission.

Guidelines for Teaching and Explaining the MBTI

Explain the Nature of the MBTI as an Instrument

- The MBTI is concerned with differences in incorporating information and making decisions.

- The MBTI shows interesting and important behavioral patterns. Knowledge of these patterns is useful for understanding people and their interaction.

- The MBTI is not a "test" but an "indicator." There are no right or wrong answers.

- There are no good or bad, or sick or well profiles.

- Each type has its own gifts and its own blind spots.

- Scores do not show maturity or excellence. They show only the strength of the preference of one element over the other.

Explain the Nature of Typology

- Use language that is appropriate for the student.

- Type is a shorthand way for describing four sets of mental processes.

- Types are not pigeonholes, but describe preferred ways of functioning.

- All types are valuable.

- Describe the four processes or functions (SN and TF) and four attitudes (EI and JP). Describe them correctly showing how each preference has polar opposites (EI, SN, TF, and JP).

- Everyone uses all the processes and attitudes but in theory each person likes some more than others.

- Give examples of each set of elements (SN, TF, EI, JP). Include personal examples.

- Use graphics such as those in *Looking at Type* (Page, 1983).

Help Students to Interpret Their Results

- Reassure the student. Being confused at first is normal.

- Show how the elements combine to make up a type. Show how the student's type is composed from the poles of elements.

- Guide the student through *Introduction to Type*.

- Help the student to see applications in his or her own experience.

- Tell the student that one's frame of mind (i.e., "work self" or "home self") can influence one's MBTI score.

- Stress that it is the learner's responsibility for recognizing his or her own type, beyond the MBTI scores.

- Help the student to see that trusting one's favorite processes is a key to personal development.

- Encourage questions and comments.

- Make your nonverbal behavior consistent with your verbal explanation. For example, do not state that all types are equally valuable and contradict this by your nonverbal signs showing a belief that some types are better than others.

- Avoid statements such as, "This is how you are." Use a questioning approach such as, "Is this true for you?"

Each stage of the interpretive process gives information which the respondent can consider and use in evaluating the accuracy of his or her type. In some cases, there is instant recognition of the correctness of the results. For these people, most of the time spent on the interpretive should be type examples and practical applications. Other individuals have doubts about their type, and the steps described above are designed to bring out new information that may help to resolve questions about which is their correct type.

Throughout the explanation process, the interpreter should keep in mind possible reasons why the MBTI results may not be a true measure of that person's type. The working assumption of type theory is that each person has "true" preferences. The goal of development is to become differentiated with the preferred processes, and at least passable with the less-preferred processes. It is important to be aware of reasons why type preferences may be incorrectly reported. These include:

- There may be a lack of differentiation of type. Such a lack occurs more often in young people.

- There may be difficulty choosing between the expectations of one's parents and one's own preferences.

- The respondent may feel torn between demands of work and his or her own preferences.

- The respondent is in a life crisis and is not using his or her typical mode of coping.

- The MBTI was administered in a situation involving authority (e.g., for employment) and questions were answered in terms of one's perception of that authority's preferences instead of one's own.

- The terms used in the MBTI were misunderstood and the respondent rejected the term because of an assumed negative connotation, such as when introversion is interpreted to mean "neurotic" or "shy," when judgment is interpreted to mean "judgmental," or when feeling is interpreted to mean "overemotional." When explaining the MBTI, you may need to repeat a discussion of the meanings of these terms in the context of the MBTI.

- The individual was confused because of perceived social pressures. This confusion is most likely to occur with the TF scale if the respondent equates thinking with masculinity and feeling with femininity.

- The respondent believed that the type description must fit his or her own characteristics perfectly to be accepted. The interpreter should repeat the discussion about how there are *individual differences* within any particular type.

- The respondent may be in a growth period in which previously unused or unappreciated processes are being developed. During such a period there may be uncertainty about previously trusted processes as the less-developed processes become differentiated.

All self-report instruments are subject to the effects described above, and to many other effects not intended by those who administer them. Since the MBTI dichotomizes responses, and since the theory postulates "true preferences," the MBTI interpreter should be particularly careful during each stage of the interpretation to help individuals discover for themselves which preferences best fit them.

It is not necessary for the respondent to discover "true preferences" during the introductory session, but it *is* necessary to set the stage for the search. A key tool during interpretation is the full-page type description. Any qualms or demurs should be taken seriously. With experience, an interpreter can judge which of the above steps are necessary for a particular client and which may be omitted. The issues and strategies discussed above should be kept in mind during any interpretation.

Interpretation of MBTI Scores

Quantitative interpretation of the MBTI scores is not recommended. Scores were designed to show the direction of a preference, not its intensity. Any questions concerning scores should be used for joint exploration of the preference at issue. Scores can sometimes provide information on (a) the likelihood that the preference has been correctly reported and (b) the importance of the preference to the respondent.

Strength Does Not Imply Excellence

The most frequent error that occurs when interpreting the numerical portion of MBTI scores is assuming that strength of preference implies excellence; it is incorrect to assume that a person with a score of N 47 has a better command of intuition than a person with an N 19 score. A larger score simply means that the respondent, *when forced to choose*, is more clear about what he or she prefers. While it frequently happens (and is reasonable to expect) that those who report clear preferences, (a) exercise them more, and thus (b) are more likely to have developed the skills associated with those preferences, and further (c) are more likely to develop the traits and habits associated with exercise of those skills, this sequence may have been interrupted in any given individual.

Interpreting Levels of Preference

The following guidelines may be useful for looking at preference scores. The cutoff points were established by Isabel Myers; they should be treated as approximations, not as precise division points. Table 5.2 shows the percentage frequencies of male and female cases from the CAPT MBTI data bank.

Very Clear Preferences (41 or higher, or 31 for F). Respondents who report very clear preference scores (roughly 41 or more, or for the feeling pole 31 or more) usually agree that they hold the preferences reported by the MBTI, and often the attitudes and skills that accompany those preferences. Because their vote for the preference is so one-sided, it can be useful to inquire whether they can comfortably use the less-preferred choice if the situation demands it. The interpreter should make sure this is an

inquiry, not an accusation. For example, one might inquire about meeting deadlines for respondents with preference scores of P 59. However, do not be surprised to find some respondents who are always on time despite their clear preference for P.

Clear Preferences (21–39, or 29 for F). When an individual's preference scores are 21 through 39 (29 for F) there is a reasonable probability that the respondent holds and acts on the reported preference.

Moderate Preferences (11–19). When preference scores are 11 through 19, the respondent may still most often agree with the description of the reported preference, but the interpreter should inquire whether the interpretation fits and should be alert for questions about preference during the explanation.

Slight Preferences (1–9). When preference scores are 1 through 9, a change of one or two questions could change the letter designation. The respondent has essentially "split the vote." The interpreter should encourage the respondent to consider whether he or she prefers and adequately uses the reported preference. Low scores are often associated with a sense of tension between the poles of the low preference. (For example, low TF scores are often associated with reports of trouble in knowing whether "to follow my head or my heart.")

Social pressures can also provide different pressures for men and women on the TF scale. Men are encouraged more toward T activities and women toward F activities. Note that in Table 5.2 one-fifth or one-fourth of males and females have slight preferences for all scales but TF. On the TF scale, two-fifths of males preferring F and females preferring T reported only slight preferences on TF. It is useful to inquire whether the low scores indicate clear preferences that seem less clear to the respondent because he or she answered in a socially expected manner, or whether the low scores indicate a conflict between sex-role expectations and type preferences.

Respondents will sometimes interpret low scores as advantageous, interpreting the score to indicate that they have good command of both preferences. In reality, low scores are more often a reflection of tension between the opposite poles of the preference than an indication of equal excellence in both.

Comparison of Dominant and Auxiliary

When there is doubt about the respondent's type, it is sometimes useful to compare scores for the dominant and auxiliary. According to theory, the dominant function will show a clearer preference than will the auxiliary. (The SN

Table 5.2 Percentage of males and females at each level of preference

Form F
Males (N = 23,240)
Scale Percent for Each Degree of Preference

Degree of preference	E	I	S	N	T	F	J	P
Slight	25.4	24.5	22.5	25.4	24.5	39.8	20.2	26.6
Moderate	24.7	25.3	22.3	21.8	23.5	31.9	19.8	23.4
Clear	39.7	37.2	36.8	38.1	35.6	20.2	39.8	34.3
Very clear	10.2	13.0	18.4	14.7	16.4	8.1	20.2	15.7

Form F
Females (N = 32,731)
Scale Percent for Each Degree of Preference

Degree of preference	E	I	S	N	T	F	J	P
Slight	22.6	26.3	22.7	25.7	38.1	25.4	21.7	27.7
Moderate	23.2	24.6	22.9	21.2	27.4	28.7	22.2	24.0
Clear	41.4	37.3	37.6	37.9	27.7	26.6	39.2	33.5
Very clear	12.8	11.2	16.5	12.6	6.8	2.5	16.9	14.8

Form G
Males (N = 15,791)
Scale Percent for Each Degree of Preference

Degree of preference	E	I	S	N	T	F	J	P
Slight	27.7	25.5	22.1	27.5	22.7	44.2	21.9	26.5
Moderate	26.8	24.0	23.8	23.3	23.2	30.6	21.9	23.3
Clear	37.7	38.6	38.2	36.6	36.1	19.0	39.9	33.4
Very clear	7.8	11.9	15.9	12.6	18.0	6.2	16.3	16.8

Form G
Females (N = 16,880)
Scale Percent for Each Degree of Preference

Degree of preference	E	I	S	N	T	F	J	P
Slight	24.8	28.1	22.8	27.6	37.0	30.3	20.6	29.4
Moderate	25.7	25.2	23.2	22.9	27.0	29.9	23.3	24.3
Clear	40.0	35.9	38.5	37.1	29.2	24.6	40.0	32.3
Very clear	9.5	10.8	15.5	12.4	6.8	15.2	16.1	14.0

Notes: Data are from the MBTI data bank. The preference score limits are: slight 1 to 9, moderate 11 to 19, clear 21 to 39, and very clear 41 or over. For preference F, clear is 21 to 29, and very clear is 31 or over.

scale sometimes has an auxiliary score greater than the dominant score. This can occur because the range for the SN score is greater than the TF range. The larger range increases the number of cases with high SN scores and thus the number of cases in which SN is greater than TF.)

Table 5.3 shows the percentage of cases where the dominant is greater than the auxiliary for each of the sixteen types. Scores for the dominant are greater than those for the auxiliary in only about half the types with a range from 69% to 31%. These percentages are similar to the percentages of dominant higher than auxiliary reported by Carlyn (1975) for 101 preservice and inservice teachers (55%), by McCarley and Carskadon (1983) for 62 female undergraduate psychology students (53%), and by Williams and Carskadon (1983) for 80 normal adults and 80 adults under stress (44%).

The dominant-auxiliary comparison should, therefore, be considered as an "alert" to the interpreter, but not as a "clinical sign." The dominant-auxiliary comparison is most useful in alerting the interpreter to a possible error in the type reported by the MBTI. Such an error is quite possible when the dominant preference is weak (indicated by a low score) and when the auxiliary preference is clear (indicated by a high score).

The interpreter should inquire more thoroughly about low scores for the dominant function than when another preference has a low score. When the dominant has a low score, the respondent has not reported a clear preference for the function which, in theory, should be most trustworthy and differentiated for his or her type. Sometimes it is useful to look at scores on EI or JP when the preference for the dominant is low. For example:

Case A	Case B	Case C
E 09	E 31	E 27
S 35	S 35	S 35
F 07	F 07	F 31
J 39	J 07	J 39

Table 5.3 Percentage of each type with higher scores for dominant function

ISTJ Form	Number	Percent	ISFJ Form	Number	Percent	INFJ Form	Number	Percent	INTJ Form	Number	Percent
F	3,399	58.69	F	3,420	67.44	F	1,157	51.29	F	1,131	42.73
G	2,267	55.44	G	1,681	69.01	G	633	51.84	G	748	40.99

ISTP Form	Number	Percent	ISFP Form	Number	Percent	INFP Form	Number	Percent	INTP Form	Number	Percent
F	763	41.35	F	1,084	43.14	F	1,260	36.65	F	863	38.70
G	666	47.23	G	470	39.33	G	594	32.66	G	675	40.79

ESTP Form	Number	Percent	ESFP Form	Number	Percent	ENFP Form	Number	Percent	ENTP Form	Number	Percent
F	982	53.28	F	1,358	45.43	F	3,031	57.60	F	1,593	61.27
G	655	46.79	G	771	52.84	G	1,499	59.84	G	954	53.72

ESTJ Form	Number	Percent	ESFJ Form	Number	Percent	ENFJ Form	Number	Percent	ENTJ Form	Number	Percent
F	2,338	39.90	F	1,797	34.09	F	1,422	46.21	F	1,679	51.17
G	1,688	43.15	G	777	31.17	G	655	43.41	G	1,051	53.43

Note: *Number* refers to the total number in each type. *Percent* refers to the percentage of total number of cases where preference for the dominant function is greater than preference for the auxiliary function. Data are from the MBTI Form F and Form G data banks.

All three cases came out ESFJ, a type where F is dominant and S is auxiliary; in all three cases there is a reported preference for the auxiliary S over the dominant F.

In Case A, E is low and S is high. The EI and TF preferences have low scores. If the respondent decided ISFJ fitted better than ESFJ than S would be dominant and the dominant score would be greater than the auxiliary.

In Case B, the TF and JP preferences have low scores. In this case, there is little question about the EI preference, but there is a possibility that P could fit better than J. Note that if the respondent decided that ESFP was his or her type, then S would be the dominant function and the score for the dominant would be greater than the score for the auxiliary.

In Case C, there is a clear preference for both S and for F, and the fact that S is slightly preferred over F can be treated as inconsequential since both are about equally high.

In general, a comparison of dominant and auxiliary scores can be useful if, (*a*) there is a wide gap between them, (*b*) if the score for the dominant is low, and (*c*) if either EI or JP is also questionable. It is important to remember that the interpreter should not try to persuade a respondent to change a preference simply to make the scores fit the theory.

Dynamics of the Phrase Questions and Word Pairs

The preference scores for EI, SN, TF, and JP can be divided into that portion of the score which is scored from the Phrase Questions (Parts I and III in Forms F and G) and the portion scored from Word Pairs (Part II in Forms F and G).

Isabel Myers made the following hypotheses about the dynamics of the Phrase Questions and the Word Pairs:

Hypothesis One. People who wish they were a different type may tend to answer the Phrase Questions according to what they are and the Word Pairs according to what they would like to be, that is, what "appeals" to them.

Hypothesis Two. People who feel insecure about the worth of their type may tend to reverse the process and answer the Phrase Questions with what seem "right answers" and the Word Pairs with answers reflecting what they really feel they are.

Hypothesis Three. People who are secure and confident in their type but are working to develop their less-liked processes may tend to present a mixed picture on the Word Pairs versus Phrase Questions.

There is little research dealing with differential responses to Word Pairs and Phrase Questions. However, Nechworth & Carskadon (1979) asked 192 students who had recently taken the MBTI under normal instructions to retake it answering it as they would like to be. In this condition, each of the four scale scores on the Phrase Questions changed significantly while scores on Word Pairs did not. Students' ideal types moved toward E, N, T, and J with the largest change toward extraversion. This study supports Myers' first hypothesis.

Table 5.4 shows that three-fourths of cases will have a discrepancy between Word Pairs and Phrase Questions on at least one preference.

Table 5.4 Similarity in scores for Phrase Questions and Word Pairs

		Percent Agreeing in Phrase Questions and Word Pairs				
Sample	N	EI	SN	TF	JP	All
McCarley and Carskadon (1983)	62	79%	77%	63%	71%	26%
Williams and Carskadon (1983)						
Normal subjects	80	—	—	—	—	26%
Stressed subjects	80	—	—	—	—	15%
MBTI data bank						
Form F males	23,240	68%	76%	70%	72%	36%
Form F females	32,731	68%	77%	70%	63%	37%
Form G males	15,791	70%	75%	73%	72%	36%
Form G females	16,880	69%	76%	66%	66%	35%

Table 5.4 shows that for particular scales there is good consistency, but that three-fourths of subjects can be expected to show a discrepancy on at least one scale. When subjects are queried, discrepancies such as I 35 on Phrase Questions and E 03 on Word Pairs are usually not considered meaningful. Discrepancies such as S 15 and N 17 are usually reflected in descriptions of tension by respondents. In this SN example, the tensions would be between being practical (S) or following one's dream (N).

The suggestions in this chapter are designed to cover issues to take into account when interpreting the MBTI and describing type. These sections are designed to alert an interpreter to reasons why a type reported from the MBTI may not be considered accurate by the respondent. The strategies above are designed to help the respondent determine which preferences seem accurate.

The interpreter's role is not to determine the accuracy of the MBTI. The interpreter's task is to provide ways in which respondents can understand their best and most trustworthy way of functioning. While experience generally shows that clear preference scores are likely to be seen as accurate, the interpreter should be prepared for the occasional case in which very strongly reported preferences are the result of defensive overreaction to the individual's doubts about the opposite pole, which is actually the one the individual prefers. There are also cases where low preference scores are subjectively experienced by respondents as clear and consistent. As with all psychological instruments, the interpreter should keep in mind that self-report from a limited number of questions, no matter how carefully validated, cannot completely describe any human being.

Chapter 6

Use of Type in Counseling

The MBTI is useful for short-term counseling (such as academic advising; study skills counseling; career counseling; marriage, family, and other relationship counseling) and more extensive life counseling. The issues outlined in this chapter are designed to demonstrate how the theory of Jungian typology as developed in the MBTI can be useful for counseling.

Initial Interpretation

When type theory is used in counseling, the first step is to discover the client's true preferences. The theory behind the MBTI assumes that preferences are inborn and can be falsified by family and other environmental pressures. Therefore, each stage of interpreting the MBTI results is essentially testing the hypothesized type based on the indicator and theory against the respondent's experiences of his or her behavior. Refer to Chapter 5 for ways respondents can use the MBTI to indicate their inherent preferences.

Understanding and Accepting Preferences

Counselors have said that what they like most about type is that it gives clients a sense of worth and dignity concerning their own qualities. Counselees can be assured by the counselor at the beginning that finding out about type, one's own and other people's, is a releasing experience, not a restricting one as may have been feared. Finding out about type frees one to recognize one's own natural bent and to trust one's own potential for growth and excellence. There is no obligation or need to be like others, however admirable others may be in their respective ways.

People often come to counseling because of a long period of disconfirmation by others. When they see a road toward excellence and happiness which they can travel by discovering and following their own intrinsically valuable preferences, they often become more hopeful. As the model is explained to the client, problems and liabilities can be seen as a neglect of less-preferred functions while more-preferred were being developed. The stage can be set for looking at the client's problems from the perspective of gaining more command over all his or her powers, not only the preferred, but also the less-preferred functions when these are needed. For example, the intuitive sees that the dream of the future is valued, but that present realities may have been overlooked and need more attention. The sensing type sees that the skills of dealing with present realities are valuable, but that learning to use intuition also will open up more practical options.

Positive insights can come from seeing type distributions. The intuitive who discovers that everyone else in the family prefers sensing gains a new perspective on his or her long-time experience of feeling like an outsider. The spontaneous extravert in a career attractive to organized introverts discovers why work feels unsatisfying.

A counselor will notice that clients who have correctly reported their preferences will evidence a sense of release when reading their type descriptions. Such clients will adduce the consequent aspects of their type and will readily discuss the negative aspects of their type in a nondefensive way. The negative aspects are seen as simply the opposite side of the strengths.

Isabel Myers believed that type preferences were inborn, but that environmental pressures were important in determining the likelihood of optimum type development. Causes of falsification of type are described in Chapter 5 and in *Gifts Differing* (Myers with Myers, 1980, pp. 189–92). Jung (1921/1971, p. 548) and Myers with Myers (1980, p. 189) wrote that when external influences cause falsification of type, emotional difficulties will follow. It is for this reason that this Manual cautions counselors to carefully check with their clients and with their own observations of their clients for evidence of type falsification. This is particularly important in counseling because a goal of treatment is to identify and strengthen the inherent preferences, not to continue the falsification process.

Identifying True Preferences

If the client has doubts about the accuracy of the reported preference, you should be alert to the client's tone when discussing activities. Activities associated with true preferences are usually described with pleasure, or with an off-handed manner taking them for granted. When the client follows these activities they are motivated and energetic. Activities associated with less-preferred processes are often described in terms of effort, struggle, or discomfort. Following such activities is tiring and can be depressing.

Usually, the client's true preferences are recognized early in the counseling process or even in the first interpretive session. In some cases, one or more preferences remain in

question at the end of the session. The counselor and client can agree to proceed with what is known about the clear preferences while investigating further those that are not clear. For example, if intuition is clear, but there is doubt whether thinking or feeling is preferred, the counselor and client can discuss the implications of preferring intuition. Between sessions the client can observe his or her experience during decision making, noting: Which options occur first? Which carry the most weight? When a decision turns out to be good, how was it made? When a decision turns out to be bad, how was it made? This exercise is most useful when the decisions seem relatively minor, such as where to go for dinner or how to schedule a day.

Counseling for Type Development

The MBTI model of Jung's theory assumes that type development is a lifelong process of increasing consciousness, differentiation, and direction of one's processes. In *Psychological Types,* Jung (1921/1971) gave the following criteria for differentiation:

> **Whether a function is differentiated or not can easily be recognized by its strength, stability, consistency, reliability, and adaptedness. (p. 540)**

Isabel Myers described the steps of type development:

> **The kind of perception one prefers and the kind of judgment one prefers determine, between them, the directions in which one can develop most fully and effectively with the most satisfaction to oneself.**

> **It is sometimes said that both kinds of perception and both kinds of judgment should be developed equally. The answer is that such a dead level of uniformity leaves one with no stable direction for one's life. Each of the four processes has its own objectives, its own fulfillments. The goals of the opposite processes are not compatible. Intuition does not want the same things as sensing. Feeling is not satisfied by what satisfies thinking. One cannot direct one's life effectively toward a desired result until one's best-trusted kind of perception and best-trusted kind of judgment are agreed as to *what* is to be desired.**

This is not to say, however, that the least-trusted processes can safely be ignored. The two kinds of perception and the two kinds of judgment are as necessary to us as tools are to a carpenter. Each has its uses, and serves increasingly as we grow more familiar with what it can and cannot do. We need to know how to handle each tool and know when to lay one down and pick up another.

Full development of one's type is a lifelong adventure. It involves getting to be very good with the favorite, best-trusted process, the *dominant process*. The dominant process outranks the other three and sets the major goals of one's life. Full development of one's type also involves getting to be good, though not *as* good, with the second-best process, the *auxiliary process*. It is the job of the auxiliary process to do the things that the dominant process cannot and/or does not want to do. The auxiliary process supplies judgment if the dominant process is perceptive, or perception if the dominant process is judging. Finally, full type development involves learning to use one's two less-favored, less-developed processes when these processes are needed.

Each step toward full command of one's natural gifts is rewarding. Good type development is a journey which opens up new abilities and understanding.

Type development is a process of getting greater command of preferred functions, adequate command of less-preferred functions, and comfort in both the extraverted and introverted attitudes. Type development provides confidence and self-direction. A greater appreciation for the aspects of one's life that come easily, and those that are difficult, also brings an appreciation and respect for individuals of different types whose strengths and struggles are different from one's own. A first step in the path to type development is to know which functions and attitudes are being used at any given time.

Fostering Type Development

The strategies for fostering type development include: (*a*) learning to identify the functions and attitudes,

(*b*) understanding the dynamics of type, (*c*) using the processes appropriately, and (*d*) overcoming type falsification.

Learning to Identify the Functions and Attitudes. The four processes, S, N, T, and F, are indispensable tools. In counseling, the counselor can ask questions to teach the processes and bring them into the client's awareness. Examples of such questions are:

Were you using sensing or intuition at that point?

What kind of decision would your feelings make here? What kind would your thinking make?

At this point did the situation call more for sensing or for intuition? Which one were you using?

Isabel Myers' prescription for development of perception and judgment appears below. It can be used as a model for group or individual problem solving.

Making Full Use of Perception and Judgment

Whenever you have a problem, a decision to make, or a situation to deal with, try exercising:

- One process at a time
- Consciously and purposefully
- Each process in its own field
- Without interference by any other process
- And in this order

Use your sensing for facing the facts; being realistic; finding exactly what the situation is, what you are doing, and what other people are doing. Try to put aside all wishful thinking or sentiment that may blind you to realities. Ask yourself how the situation would look to a wise, impartial bystander.

Use your intuition to discover all the possibilities, that is, all the ways in which you might change a situation, your handling of it, or other people's attitudes toward it. Try to put aside your natural assumption that you have been doing the one and only obviously right thing.

Use your thinking-judgment in an impersonal analysis of cause and effect. Include all the consequences of the alternative solutions, pleasant and unpleasant. Include consequences that weigh against the solution you prefer as well as those that are in its favor. Try to count the full cost of everything that would be a consequence of the decision. Examine every misgiving you may have been suppressing out of loyalty to someone, a liking for something, or reluctance to change your stand on the decision.

Use your feeling-judgment to weigh how deeply you care about the things that will be gained or lost by alternative solutions. Make a fresh appraisal; try not to let the temporary outweigh the permanent, however agreeable or disagreeable the immediate prospect may be. Consider how the other people concerned will feel about the outcomes, even if you think it may be unreasonable of them to feel that way. Include their feelings and your own feelings along with the facts when deciding which solution will work out best.

By following this exercise you will probably make your usual choice, a solution that appeals to your favorite process, but the decision will be made on a sounder basis because you will have considered facts, possibilities, consequences, and human values. Ignoring any one of these may lead to trouble. Intuitives may base a decision on some possibility without discovering facts that will make it impossible. Sensing types may settle for a faulty solution to a problem because they assume no better one is possible. Thinking types may ignore human values, and feeling types may ignore consequences.

You will find some steps in this exercise easier than others. The ones that use your best processes are rather fun. The others are harder but worthwhile. If feeling is your favorite process, the attempt to see *all* the consequences of an act may show you that even the best intentions can go wrong unless thought through. If thinking is your favorite process, the attempt to learn how others *feel* about your plans may show why you meet so much opposition.

What makes the hard steps hard is that they call for the strengths of opposite types.

When your problem is important, you may be wise to consult someone to whom these strengths come naturally. It is startling to see how differently a given situation can look to a person of the opposite type. Consulting with others of opposite type will help you to understand and use the neglected opposite side of yourself.

Development of EI and JP. For extreme extraverts, a major value of counseling is the teaching of introversion. Teach extraverts to slow down and consider their behavior before they act, then to consider it again after they act. Teach introverts to practice more actions and outward expression of opinions.

Clients can be taught to identify when they are using judgment and when they are using perception. For example, a parent describing a child's behavior in a judging manner can be shown that their every description is full of judgments ("This is wrong." "He shouldn't have done that." "I made a mistake"). Practice in the perceptive attitude can lead to statements such as: "Why did it look like that to him?" "I wonder if he did it because? . . ." The essence of the perceptive attitude is that a topic opens up new questions and creates curiosity for learning more about a situation. Judgment closes the issues; perception opens it up for new discoveries. Many J types benefit from learning to stay longer in the perceptive attitude; many P types benefit from learning to come to closure.

Identifying the Dynamics of Type Development. The MBTI provides a general model that builds on strength first before dealing with weaknesses. The steps are:

Assessment of the dominant. Since the dominant function in theory gives direction and is the most trustworthy, the counselor should listen for evidence that the dominant process is trusted and giving directions. If the dominant is sensing, does the person have a good sense of reality, do practical things well, and enjoy the little pleasures of everyday life? If the dominant is intuition, do insights stand up under verification? If the dominant is feeling, are values securely in place and can the client live by his or her values comfortably? If the dominant is thinking, does the client see consequences clearly and take them into account when governing his or her behavior? The assumption in using the dominant process is that relying on well-differentiated, trustworthy processes will lead to more positive outcomes and a greater sense of autonomy for the individual.

A counselor should seriously consider any difficulties an individual is having in the aspects of life related to the dominant function. For example, impracticality in a sensing type is more serious than impracticality in an intuitive type, since realism should be an essential characteristic of those who prefer the sensing perception.

Assessment of the auxiliary. Many problems encountered in counseling situations are related to failure to develop the auxiliary. Isabel Myers' type descriptions all discuss the consequences of failure to develop the auxiliary, and a discussion of these consequences should enter into the interpretive interview. The auxiliary provides the balance between perception and judgment. Myers with Myers (1980, p. 182) wrote about this balance: "In type theory balance does not mean equality of two processes or of two attitudes; instead, it means superior skill in one, supplemented by a helpful but not competitive skill in the other." Some of the effects of failure to develop the auxiliary are:

- Extraverts will place so much reliance on the outer world that they will not be in touch with their own inner ideas.

- Introverts will be so caught up in their inner world that they will be ineffective in the outer world.

- Types with sensing or intuition dominant (IJ and EP types) can be so caught up in experiencing life that they fail to direct their activities.

- Types with thinking or feeling dominant (IP and EJ types) can be so caught up with controlling their worlds that they fail to understand their experiences.

Lack of developing the auxiliary is most visible in extraverts, but counselors should recognize that such a lack can be very important in introverts, since it is through the auxiliary process that introverts deal with the outer world.

The third and fourth processes. In theory, individuals are least effective and most vulnerable in the areas of their third and fourth processes, especially the fourth or inferior process. Counselors new to type theory may take the position that if clients have dominant feeling, the most helpful counseling strategy is to help them develop their inferior thinking. This is not the approach taken in developmental counseling, which builds on strengths to get to weakness by encouraging the client to use the dominant and auxiliary to strengthen the inferior functions.

Counselors and clients can become aware of the manifestation of less-preferred and inferior processes. They are likely to be experienced in eruptions, or as behaviors that are unexplainable or alien. The strategy for developing the less-preferred functions is to use them to help achieve goals set by the dominant and auxiliary. For example, an ENFP in theory would be caught up with new possibilities (dominant N) for people (auxiliary F). It is difficult for an ENFP

to deal with matters in a tough-minded fashion (third function T) or with a large amount of practical details (inferior process S). If the ENFP is enthusiastic about a project that captures N and F, S and T will be used in the service of N and F to accomplish the practical aspects of the project. This exercise is valuable for teaching full use of perception and judgment and helps clients to identify which functions are easier or more difficult for them.

Processes are developed through practice, not through understanding alone. First teach clients to identify their processes; then teach them to practice using the processes. Small tasks which may seem inconsequential to outsiders are better for learning to develop processes than are major life decisions. The process of choosing a meal in a restaurant is a better place to practice a new skill than the process of choosing a career. Small tasks are especially important for practicing less-preferred processes, since initial failures can be interesting experiments, not blows to self-esteem.

Using Preferences Appropriately

The preferences are tools. Part of the counselor's task is helping the client recognize which tool is needed for a given situation.

Use of Judgment. The place to use judgment is in monitoring one's behavior and in choosing a course of action given everything that has been perceived. Judgment begins with one's personal standards that must be met for self-approval, and with one's long-range goals. Judgment is *not* best used to impose standards on others. The terms *judgmental* and *authoritarian* describe the misplacement of judgment from one's own goals to those of others.

One's natural tendency is to leave decisions, wherever possible, to the kind of judgment one likes and trusts. Both thinking and feeling have their utilities. In practical matters, thinking links cause and effect and provides respect for the consequences of a decision. Thinking uses logic to determine the probable cause of an unfortunate effect, or the probable result of a proposed action. Feeling is useful in attaching value to people, things, ideas, and ideals, and respecting the values of others. People who strongly prefer thinking are often long on logic and short on appreciation, while people who strongly prefer feeling are often long on appreciation and short on logic, but not necessarily. If the merits of each kind of judgment are understood, a thinking type can use feeling to admire what truly is admirable, and a feeling type can use thinking to take a careful look at consequences. Such understanding of the opposite type can provide a substantial increase in effectiveness and satisfaction.

Unfortunately, the reverse is also possible. People who are unaware of the proper use of the two kinds of judgment, or perhaps even of their existence, may use both the wrong way. Their thinking may overlook the consequences of their own actions and concentrate on instances of other people's actions, believing that if the other person had acted differently, the result would have been more desirable. If such people comment on all such instances, they subject the people around them to a constant barrage of criticism, much of it trivial and none of it useful. Consequently, the people who are always being criticized will stop their ears against all criticism, however appropriate. Feeling judgment can be as badly misused as thinking. People misusing feeling judgment concentrate on negative instead of positive valuations, disliking what people do, say, or are imagined to think, and thus "getting their feelings hurt" on every possible occasion. Touchy oversensitivity is *not* an admirable or useful form of feeling, just as constant criticism of others is *not* an admirable or useful form of thinking.

The role of the counselor is to help the client identify and use thinking and feeling appropriately, and to differentiate the two.

Use of Perception. Since the accuracy of judgment rests on the accuracy of the information on which the judgment is based, good type development involves accurate perception before judgment. Sensing provides awareness of the actual, existing situation and relevant facts. Intuition involves perception of new ways of looking at events and new ways of solving problems. The counselor should guide clients to the proper use of perception.

Examples of Counseling Issues for Each Preference

The following descriptions are designed to alert counselors to issues frequently associated with each MBTI preference. For other discussions of the topic see Jones and Sherman (1979), Newman (1979), and von Franz (1971).

Extraversion and Introversion (EI)

Issues related to the EI attitude focus on the orientation of the conscious attitude toward the outer world (E) or the world of concepts and ideas (I).

Extraversion. Extraverts can be expected to look outward before they look inward for explanation of events that occur in their lives. They are more likely, therefore, to be extrapunitive than intrapunitive.

Extraverts gain insight more easily after experience. Therefore, counseling sessions are likely to be devoted to developments of the past week, seeking explanations of past events.

Extraverts can become uncomfortable if the counselor is very quiet. They seek active interaction as a verification that they have been heard.

Extraverts can present such an active, competent face (especially EJ types) that it is easy to miss signs of distress and lack of confidence.

For extreme extraverts, the developmental task is balancing their E with their I. They need to learn in small doses to consider (use I) before acting, and learn to find pleasure in solitude and their own company (I).

Introversion. Introverts are more likely to look to themselves first for causes of difficulties. They are more intrapunitive than extrapunitive. The counselor may need to focus their attention on the fact that some problems have their source in the environment.

Introverts gain experience more easily after they have a conceptual framework. Therefore, introverts benefit from comments that help them clarify the concepts behind their own behavior and that of others. Principles that explain why people behave in certain ways make the environment more understandable and therefore safer, so that action can be attempted.

Sessions with introverted clients often have long pauses (which may cause discomfort to extraverted counselors) while the introvert clarifies what has been said internally, or gains the courage to test another idea on the counselor.

A counselor can discuss how the introvert can attempt more extraverted activities, and the counselor can prepare the introvert for experimenting with extraversion between counseling sessions.

Sensing and Intuition

The counseling issues related to sensing and intuition are the different ways clients see or experience themselves or the world.

Sensing. When counseling a sensing type, dynamic issues should be discussed in concrete terms, and comments are best understood by the client when they are tied to concrete examples.

Sensing clients are more likely to see their view of the situation as permanent or a given. The counselor can provide intuition by describing alternatives. The client can assess the practicality of the alternatives. The goal of modeling intuition is to teach the client that intuition can open new possibilities. Counseling should teach skills for seeing others' intuition and for using one's own intuition when sensing does not provide answers. When intuition is the inferior process (ISJ and ESP types), the client may suggest more negative than positive possibilities. In this case the client should be helped to develop strategies to counteract the "black cloud effect."

Therapeutic strategies that involve activity can be helpful for grounding sensing types whose comfort in reality is shaken. Such activities include involvement in nature, hobbies requiring motion and touch, and the carrying out of daily activities.

Intuition. Intuitive clients are likely to use more abstract or symbolic terminology and respond to symbolism from the counselor.

Intuitive types can be so caught up in possibilities that they (*a*) overlook the facts and the limitations facts impose (*b*) assume they already know all the facts or (*c*) assume that facts are unimportant. A counselor may need to push intuitive clients to turn on their sensing to assess the practical steps needed to make their possibilities realities.

Intuitives tend to be independent, and counselors will do well to let them find their own solutions with a minimum of direction.

Intuition sees new possibilities; intuitive clients often take the position that there must be an answer if they look long enough. This stance can provide hope and optimism in treatment but a counselor may need to ask whether the client's energy might be better spent on goals that provide more immediate possibilities.

Intuitive types often underestimate the time needed to accomplish tasks. Counselors can inject a note of realism that can help intuitives better manage their time.

Thinking and Feeling

Issues related to decision making involve the difference between thinking and feeling.

Thinking. A thinking type is naturally skeptical and critical, and can be expected to be so in the counseling session. A counselor therefore should be prepared to back up his or her statements with evidence.

Thinking types often disregard what matters to them (F issues) because "It isn't logical to care so much." At some stage it is important for them to accept and integrate their values.

In early sessions it is not useful to ask a thinking type to describe feelings. It is also not useful for counselors to label thinking types "defensive" or "intellectualizing" when they have trouble putting feeling into words, or when their words for feelings sound analytical.

Thinking types (especially introverts) are often later than other types in discovering social skills. Social skills training with easy exercises can be useful when the client sees the logic of learning these skills.

Examination of the cause-effect formulas used by thinking clients for directing their lives can lead to more effective or more relevant formulas, especially with regard to interpersonal relationships.

A useful exercise for thinking types is learning to appreciate other people.

Feeling. When counseling feeling types it is important for a counselor to help clarify values and discuss choices between short-range and long-range goals.

Cynicism undermines valuing and counselors should take cynicism seriously, especially in types where feeling is dominant (EFJ and IFP). A client will benefit from finding a person, animal, idea, or goal that is safe to care about.

Feeling types are likely to ignore unpleasant facts that conflict with their values; they can benefit from *gentle* confrontations with these discrepant facts.

Feeling types are more likely to try to discover what the counselor considers to be a "good patient" and live up to this role to the detriment of finding their own way.

Feeling types, especially EFJ types, are most likely of all types to experience overvaluation of the counselor and rely on the counselor instead of finding their own values.

For feeling types, the counselor's interpretations, even mild comments, may be taken as harsh criticism.

Feeling types may devote so much energy to other people's needs that they have insufficient time for themselves. It can be a slow process to help a feeling type balance the nurturance that is intrinsic and satisfying for them against the legitimate attention to their own desires. A counselor trying to help feeling types care for themselves is likely to be accused of preaching selfishness.

Extravert feeling types (EFJ) may express their values in all-or-none, rigid terms and need help in taking the circumstances of individual cases into account (i.e., to differentiate their F).

Feeling types may hesitate to state their wishes clearly, because they assume that other people ought to know without being told. It is useful to point out that thinking types may not know what matters to another person and that it is unkind to make them guess when such information could be provided.

Judgment and Perception

Judgment and perception are relevant to counseling when clients have concerns about controlling their lives or adapting to life's demands.

Judgment. Judging types bring issues relating to control and authority into counseling sessions. They may fear losing control of their own or others' behaviors.

Adapting to changes, especially when their previous strategies have proven ineffective, can be particularly stressful to judging types.

One experiment for learning perception is to have judging types let go of control for a limited time or in a limited area. The client can "plan to be flexible."

It is useful to teach strategies for using perception to understand one's own or other people's behavior. Judging clients should be taught to ask questions where they thought they had answers. An example is: instead of "My son is bad because he . . ." becomes "Why do you suppose he does? . . ."

Perception. Extremes in the perceptive type may show problems related to diffusion, drifting, procrastination, and confusion over direction.

A client with a very strong preference for perception may see even modest structure as unduly restricting. Behavior that seems irresponsible to others is seen by the client as a valuable exercise in freedom.

TP clients can learn the use of J skills by considering the negative consequences of not coming to closure or being late. FP clients can consider the harm they may be doing to others by not coming to closure.

Perceptive types benefit from examining what happens when they have difficulties with decision making, asking themselves what facilitates decisions for them? What blocks decisions? If the person has never learned time management or similar J skills, these can be taught. But it is usually more useful to mobilize the energy of the decision making functions, T or F, to understand and overcome blocks to decision making.

The teaming of perceptive clients with people skilled in judging, especially SJ types, can be useful for teaching judging skills.

For NP types overwhelmed with too many options, practice in collecting facts will often eliminate most options as impractical and make their choices manageable. Counselors should help J types avoid premature closure and P types to come to closure.

Communication Styles for Counselors

The counseling session offers a laboratory for Isabel Myers' prescription for successful communication (Myers with Myers, 1980): "In order to be successful, a communication needs to be listened to without impatience and understood without hostility."

Clients best understand counseling interventions couched in the clients' own type of language. Sensing language is more concrete; intuitive language is more abstract and symbolic. Thinking language is more objective and analytical; feeling language is more personal. With practice and an attentive ear, counselors can use words that help the client feel understood. When introducing a topic to a group, a reference to practical issues (S), new possibilities

(N), long-range consequences (T), and help for people (F) will provide motivation for each of the processes.

Sensing types, particularly ISJ types, often describe events with many circumstantial details. Intuitive counselors who immediately see what the client is leading up to can be tempted to interrupt. Interruptions can be seen by the client as a disconfirmation of the client's own style, a lack of understanding or respect.

Intuitive types who often use abstract or symbolic terms can mislead counselors into believing they understand the client. The counselor should investigate whether the meaning he or she attributes to these terms matches the meaning the client wishes to convey.

Communication with thinking types should begin with the facts and reasons given by the thinking type. New information from the counselor should be given in a brief, orderly style with a clear beginning, middle, and end.

Communication with feeling types should clearly acknowledge the areas of agreement before raising questions. Feeling types, especially those in distress, are hypersensitive to indications that the counselor may not be on their side.

Yeakley (1982, 1983) developed Communication Style Preferences for each of the types, based on the similarity of functions that are extraverted. Preliminary studies by Yeakley indicate that high similarity in communications style is significantly associated with effective communication in marriage, in manager-subordinate relationships in business, in the grades teachers give students, in sales to life insurance prospects, and in the types of parishioners ministers attract. In summarizing his findings, Yeakley (1983, p. 22) stressed the need for two people to use the same communication style at the same time. Yeakley's (1983, p. 22) descriptions of "styles of listening" provide useful suggestions for counselors:

> **Listening in the sensing style means** *interpreting* **at a very practical level and asking questions such as:**
>
> > What is the speaker saying?
> > How should the words be decoded?
> > How should the message be perceived?
>
> **Listening in the intuitive style means** *understanding* **at a much deeper level and asking questions such as:**
>
> > What does the speaker really mean?
> > What are the assumptions underlying the message?
> > What are the implications of the message?
> > What are the possibilities suggested by the
> > message?

Listening in the thinking style means *analyzing* and *organizing* while asking questions such as:

What is the structure of the message?
What is the central idea?
What are the main points?
What are the subpoints?
How are the various points related?
Is there adequate evidence to justify each claim?
Is the reasoning logical?
Are the claims true or false?

Listening in the feeling style means *evaluating* and *appreciating* while asking questions such as:

What are the values suggested by the message?
Should these values be accepted or rejected?
How do I feel about the message?
How do I feel about the speaker?

Counseling with Couples and Families

When using the MBTI in counseling couples and families the goal is to help them use differences in type constructively rather than destructively. Couples often ask how common it is to marry their own type or an opposite type. Table 6.1 shows data from two samples of couples. One set is from Myers with Myers (1980, p. 128), and the other set was accumulated by the Center for Applications of Psychological Type (CAPT) from the literature and various researchers. It is clear from Table 6.1 that people marry their own type or opposite types less frequently than they

marry persons similar on two or three preferences. The comparison to random assortment of types in Table 6.1 indicates that people are a little more likely to marry a similar type than a more opposite type.

Counseling Issues for Each Preference

Happy and unhappy marriages are found in all type combinations. Counseling issues vary with the location of differences. Table 6.2 is valuable for discussing the mutual usefulness of opposite types.

EI Differences. When counseling differences in EI, issues of sociability (E) and privacy (I) will need to be resolved. The extravert needs to have sufficient external stimulation and the introvert needs sufficient time alone. A first step is getting each partner to recognize the legitimate but different needs of the other partner. Such recognition is difficult when the husband is introverted, and expends extraversion at work all day; typically, he has little left for sociability in the evening. Sherman (1981) studied aspects of marital satisfaction and found more problems reported between couples where the wife was extraverted and the husband introverted.

Couples who differ on EI may also have a problem communicating, since the E partner is more likely to reach decisions by talking them out and getting feedback, while the I partner is more likely to process issues internally, sharing only the final conclusion. This difference leaves the E partner feeling excluded from an important satisfaction—mutual sharing.

SN Differences. When a couple differs in SN, misunderstandings can occur because the couple often look very differently at the same event. It is important that they define terms carefully. Intuitive partners with rapid insights can

Table 6.1 Similarities and differences in married couples

Number of Similar Preferences	Myers Sample (375 Couples)	CAPT Composite (571 Couples)	Random Assortment
All four	9%	10%	6.25%
Three	35%	28%	37.5%
Two	33%	38%	37.5%
One	19%	18%	25%
None	4%	6%	6.25%

Note: Samples are from Myers with Myers (1980) and an accumulation of studies assembled by CAPT.

Table 6.2 Mutual usefulness of opposite types

Intuitives Need Sensing Types:	Sensing Types Need Intuitives:
To bring up pertinent facts	To bring up new possibilities
To apply experience to problems	To supply ingenuity on problems
To read the fine print in a contract	To read the signs of coming change
To notice what needs attention now	To see how to prepare for the future
To have patience	To have enthusiasm
To keep track of essential details	To watch for new essentials
To face difficulties with realism	To tackle difficulties with zest
To show that the joys of the present are important	To show that the joys of the future are worth working for

Feeling Types Need Thinking Types:	Thinking Types Need Feeling Types:
To analyze	To persuade
To organize	To conciliate
To find the flaws in advance	To forecast how others will feel
To reform what needs reforming	To arouse enthusiasm
To hold consistently to a policy	To teach
To weigh "the law and the evidence"	To sell
To fire people when necessary	To advertise
To stand firm against opposition	To appreciate the thinker

make sensing partners feel slow and mundane. Sensing partners with a solid sense of reality cause intuitive partners to feel impractical and unobservant.

TF Differences. When a couple differs in TF, decision-making issues can be a source of difficulty, since one partner will prefer objectivity and the other subjectivity. Thinking types can become irritated with what seems the incomprehensible lack of logic of feeling types, and feeling types often accuse thinking partners of being cold.

Thinking types can improve relationships by refraining from all but necessary criticism, and by voicing appreciation. Feeling types can improve relationships by stating their wishes clearly, so that the thinking type does not have to guess their wishes.

Feeling types can avoid hurt feelings by learning to identify those comments which sound like personal criticism but which were merely impersonal comments from the viewpoint of their thinking partner.

JP differences. Issues of order, territory, and life-style are typically associated with the JP preference. If the male is J and the female P, their styles fit cultural expectations; J wives and P husbands may have more issues around "who wears the pants in the family." Order in the surroundings is often more important to the J partner; spontaneity and freedom are more important to the P partner. As a counseling

technique, have the couple discuss how they have planned for vacations. This exercise can be enlightening to couples with clear JP differences.

Couple Type Indicators

When interpreting results of the MBTI to a couple, it is useful to let partners guess their preferences as they are discussed and to compare these with the answers given on the indicator. Both partners can be asked to comment on the accuracy of type descriptions in describing both themselves and their partner, and to discuss type characteristics as they affect their relationship.

One strategy in working with couples is to ask each partner to answer the MBTI twice: once for oneself and once estimating one's partner's responses. The counselor can compare each spouse's two sets of responses and discuss the perception of the other's type as opposed to what each reports as his or her type by their indicator responses. The task of counseling is quite another matter for a couple of different types who understand their type differences as opposed to a couple who are also quite different in type but who see themselves as similar to one another. Another situation is that a couple may identify differences and expand them; that is, a husband may report himself as an I 19 but be seen by an extraverted wife as an I 39.

Type with Family Counseling

Type concepts can be useful in family counseling. The type distribution of the family provides a language for talking about alliances, difficulties in communication, allocation of household tasks, differences over child rearing, and discussions of children's career plans.

When working with families it is particularly relevant to discuss the value of type differences. Any relationship suffers if the oppositeness of preference is treated as an inferiority. The parent-child relationship suffers severely if a parent tries to make a child into a carbon copy of him- or herself. It is hard on children to find that a parent wishes they were something they definitely are not. Children who are feeling types may try to falsify their type in the desired direction; thinking types may resist their parent's expectations with hostility. Neither reaction repairs the damage done to the child's self-confidence.

It can be helpful for the counselor to give parents a perspective on how parenting differs based on the type of the child. It is easier for an orderly, practical SJ parent to raise an SJ child who has a desire to conform to structure, than it is for him or her to rear an independent NP child who finds structure an anathema. Understanding type differences can reduce guilt in the relationship and promote problem solving on the part of both parent and child.

Type Differences and Issues in Providers of Psychological Services

Type theory can illuminate many of the personality and behavior differences among providers of psychological services, and it raises new issues about the delivery of health care. For a review of type in relation to type and counseling, see Carskadon (1979a).

Providers of Psychological Services

All sixteen types are represented by providers of psychological services, and all sixteen types become clients, but the distributions of both differ from the general population. In theory, helping people through psychological methods requires more intuitive than sensing skills, since intuition is concerned with perception of patterns, recognition of inferred meanings, and intangible relationships. In a study by Newman (1979), N types scored significantly higher than S types on ability to identify inferred meanings. A study by DiTiberio (1977) found Ns higher for covert feeling messages.

Any career that deals mainly with people tends to attract more feeling than thinking types. Table 6.3 shows the types reported over a number of samples of psychological service providers.

Across all the studies in Table 6.3, intuition and feeling tend to predominate. Occupations that require practitioners to deal with large numbers of people tend to have more extraverts. There are relatively more sensing types in the occupations where counseling is accompanied with more paperwork. Given that the majority of the population prefers sensing, the fact that most counselors prefer intuition creates a responsibility for counselors to learn methods for communicating and treating sensing clients.

Type Differences in Professional Orientation

In theory, extraverts should prefer to focus on environmental issues and to work with larger numbers of individuals and groups. Introverts should prefer to focus on intrapsychic therapy, to work with individuals, and to provide longer-term treatment. Sensing types should prefer to use more applied methods; intuitives should prefer more dynamic approaches. Thinking types should prefer more analytical, "tough-minded" approaches, and feeling types should be drawn to approaches that involve understanding the client's goals and values. Judging types should prefer more directive and controlled kinds of treatment, while perceptive types should favor methods that emphasize understanding the client. Examples of significant differences ($p<.05$) among counselors of different types appear in Table 6.4.

Treatment Strategies

Very little work has been conducted on the appropriate treatment method for any given type. However, there is some evidence about the counseling expectations of different types.

Carskadon (1979) asked college students about what qualities they value in a counselor. Thinking types rated behavioral characteristics higher, and feeling types rated humanistic characteristics higher. In a study of college students Weir (1976) found that feeling types who listened to an audiotape of a counselor demonstrating high unconditional positive regard were significantly more likely to prefer this approach than were other types. A study by Arain (1968) found that among high school students seeking counseling, thinking types preferred cognitive characteristics in prospective counselors and feeling types preferred affective characteristics.

College undergraduates who volunteered for a small group "self-understanding" research project were 84% N (and 51% NF) types (McCary, 1970). In a group of medical students asked "How important is it for the faculty to help you with your own personal development and self-under-

Table 6.3 MBTI types of professionals providing psychological services

Source	Sample	N	EI	SN	TF	JP	Comments
			Percentages				
Levell (1965)	Counselor trainees	117	E75	N67	F71	P57	NF 45%
Terrill (1970)	Secondary school counselors	58	—	—	—	—	FP "tendency"
Braun (1971)	VA therapists	48	—	—	—	—	NF "consistent"
Beck (1973)	Counseling supervisees	115	—	—	—	—	NF "majority"
Schilling (1972)	Residence hall assistants	57	E75	N67	F70	P52	NF 49%
Frederick (1974)	Doctoral students Helping professionals	46	—	—	—	—	I,N,F,P modal
Elliott (1975)	Counselors of runaway youth	119	E51	N70	F74	P63	NF 70%
Galvin (1976)	Crisis center staff	42	E67	N93	F79	P64	NF 76%
Newman (1979)	Counseling students	251	I53	N66	F84	P63	NF 59%
Perry (1975)	APA psychologists (Clin., Couns.)	25	E66	N96	F76	J66	NF 72%
McCaulley (1977)	Myers' followup: Psychiatrists	415	I55	N78	T55	P60	NF 35% NT 43%
	Child psychiatrists	91	I58	N81	T51	P59	NF 42% NT 40%

standing?", ST types reported low interest in self-understanding and NF types reported high interest in self-understanding. The ST types also reported that the faculty placed more emphasis on self-understanding than they wanted. NF students in the same classes felt that the faculty was neglecting this part of their education (Otis as reported in McCaulley, 1978, p. 188).

In the 1960s Mendelsohn and his associates (Mendelsohn, 1966; Mendelsohn and Kirk, 1962; Mendelsohn and Geller, 1963, 1965, 1967) reported on a series of students coming to the Counseling Center of the University of California, Berkeley. Their analyses were concerned more with scores than with hypotheses about individual types, but they found the following significant differences: (a) compared to their peers, Ns, Ts, and Ps were more likely to be clients of the center; (b) when the students had similar types as their counselors, they came for more sessions overall, but they also missed more sessions during treatment; (c) students with different types from their counselors almost always came for only a few sessions; (d) students who were more like or more unlike counselors later rated the counseling experience less favorably than students of middle similarity.

In an unpublished study in 1966, Grant (1966) compared the type distribution of 114 students coming to the counseling center at Auburn with personal problems to the distribution of the student body. Types overrepresented in the "problem group" were INFJ, INFP, INTJ, ISFP, ENFP, and ENTP. Students underrepresented were ESTP, ISFJ, ENFJ, ESFJ, ESFP, and ESTJ. ENFPs had the

Table 6.3 MBTI types of professionals providing psychological services

Source	Sample	N	Percentages				Comments
			EI	SN	TF	JP	
Levin (1978)	Psychotherapists	91	E52	N91	F61	J56	INFP modal
	Psychoanalytic	15	I67	N93	F67	J80	INFJ modal
	Rational emotive	24	E62	N83	T58	J71	ENTJ modal
	Gestalt	12	E/I50	N92	F75	P75	E/I NFP modal
	Behavioral	15	I53	N87	T60	J53	ENTJ modal
	Experiential	25	E56	N96	F84	P56	ENFP modal
McCaulley (1978)	Psychol. Services	2,453	E54	N67	F69	P54	NF 50%
	Students	1,247	E52	N69	F70	P59	NF 51%
	Practicing	1,206	E57	N65	F67	J50	NF 48%
	Psychologists	289	I51	N81	F58	P56	NF 50%
	Vocational Counselors	53	E60	N53	F68	J55	NF 42%
	Rehabilitation Counselors	142	E60	S51	F61	P51	NF 37%
	Counselors	359	E56	N67	F76	P53	NF 57%
	School counselors	287	E64	N61	F70	J52	NF 48%
	College counselors	67	E64	N58	F58	J57	NF 40%
	Paraprofessionals/ Volunteers	126	E56	S60	F65	J58	NF 28% SJ 44%
	Social Work	169	E 62	N69	F72	P53	NF 55%
Coan (1979)	Psychologists	61	E66	N80	F52	J56	
		43F	I58	N88	F65	P53	
Casas & Hamlet (1984)	Canadian student counselors	50	I62	N72	T56	J62	NF 36%
Macdaid (1984b)	Crisis center volunteers	145	E50	N80	F61	P54	NF 50%

largest number of people with problems, but INFPs came for more counseling sessions.

In these few studies, it appears that intuitives, who are more interested in psychological approaches to life, are also more likely to seek psychological solutions to their problems. The studies also suggest that there may be a match between the kinds of treatments preferred by clients of a particular type and the kind of treatment offered by practitioners of the same type. In the future, any research on therapist-client relationships will have to take into account the relative similarity of types among therapists as compared to the diversity of types in the general population.

Table 6.4 Type differences in counselor orientation

		MBTI Preference	
Source of Data	Theoretical Orientation	Males	Females
Coan (1979)	Environmental determinism	E- - -	E- F-
(N = 104)	Biological determinism	I- - -	I- T-
	Nature (endogenism)	I- - -	I- T-
	Nurture (exogenism)	E- - -	E- F-
	Behavioral content emphasis	- STJ	- ST-
	Experiential content emphasis	- NFP	- NF-
	Factual orientation	- S- -	- - - -
	Theoretical orientation	- N- -	- - - -
	Objectivism	- - T-	- - TJ
	Subjectivism	- - F-	- - FP
	Physicalism	- - T-	- - T-
	Quantitative orientation	- - - -	- - TJ
	Qualitative orientation	- - - -	- - FP
	Impersonal causality	- - T-	- - - -
	Personal will	- - F-	- - - -
	Elementarism	- - - -	- - - J
	Holism	- - - -	- - - P

		Males and Females
Levin (1978)		
(N = 25)	Experiential orientation	- - F-
(N = 15)	Psychoanalytic orientation	- - - J
(N = 24)	Rational-emotive orientation	- - T-
Perelman (1978)	Client-Counselor relationship	
(N = 8)	among counseling students	
	Focus on quality relationship	- - F-
	Focus on distinctive behaviors	- - T-
Witzig (1978)	Client assignment to mode of treatment	
(N = 2 cases each	Assigned informational/cognitive	- -T-
by 102 therapists)	Assigned symbolic/intuitive	-N- -

Chapter 7

Using Type
in Career Counseling

Introduction

The MBTI is especially useful in career counseling for providing clients with an understanding of their interests and how they may wish to live their lives. In theory, occupations should attract particular types, and similar occupations should have similar type distributions.

The Center for Applications of Psychological Type (CAPT) has collected data on occupations listed on response sheets and the MBTI type. All occupations collected have individuals from all sixteen types, but each occupation attracts some types more than others. The SN preference appears to be the most important in choice of occupation; that is, there are more statistically significant relationships relevant to occupations on the SN preference. The EI preference seems to be most important for finding an appropriate work setting within a particular occupation. Information on type and occupations came from tables of students and practitioners in particular careers, supplemented by data on dropouts and career satisfaction.

Type Development
and Career Counseling

People choose occupations for many reasons including challenge, money, location, family encouragement, influence of charismatic teachers, desire to serve others, opportunity for leisure time, and liking for co-workers. The basic assumption when using the MBTI in career counseling is that one of the most important motivations for career choice is a desire for work that is intrinsically interesting and satisfying and that will permit use of preferred functions and attitudes, with relatively little need for using less-preferred processes. No occupation provides a perfect match between type preferences and work tasks, but good occupational choices can prevent major mismatches.

When there is a mismatch between type and occupation, the client usually reports feeling tired and inadequate. According to type theory, the mismatch causes fatigue because it is more tiring to use less-preferred processes. A mismatch also causes discouragement, because despite the greater expenditure of effort, the work product is less likely to show the quality of products that would be developed if the preferred process were utilized. Tasks that call on preferred and developed processes require less effort for better performance, and give more satisfaction.

Work can become a good arena for type development. Every job has tasks that require the use of less-preferred processes. Counselors can help clients see that disliked tasks can be good tools for developing less preferred functions. For example, a thinking type can use a public relations assignment to develop feeling, and an intuitive type can use a production assignment to develop sensing. Most people can benefit from assignments that force them to develop less-used processes. However, few people want the major part of their time and effort to be used on less preferred processes at the sacrifice of their major interests. When mismatched work assignments are necessary, they can be made more palatable if they are construed as challenges for personal growth.

Clients should never be discouraged from entering an occupation on the basis that they are "not the type." If that occupation is seldom chosen by people of their type, or in their type's column (ST, SF, NF, or NT), it is prudent for them to investigate the proposed occupation carefully. There may be reasons, not apparent to them at first, that would make the work less appealing. If after researching the occupation, there is still a desire to enter the occupation, the clients do so knowing that they will be different from many of their co-workers. Being in a situation of *consciously chosen* difference is very different from being in a situation where one expects to fit in and does not understand why one feels like an outsider. The result of the atypical choice can be positive. A rare type in a field can bring new viewpoints to the occupation that can lead to progress in the field. Very often, a niche can be found to use atypical talents. For example, an ENTP medical technologist on a hospital team became the troubleshooter, while the more typical SJ medical technologists made sure normal operations ran smoothly.

Expectations of Work Choices for Each MBTI Preference

Isabel Myers developed the following work expectations for each preference.

Extraverts: Work interactively with a succession of

people, or with activity outside the office or away from the desk.

Introverts: Work that permits some solitude and time for concentration.

Sensing types: Work that requires attention to details and careful observation.

Intuitive types: Work that provides a succession of new problems to be solved.

Thinking types: Work that requires logical order, especially with ideas, numbers, or physical objects.

Feeling types: Work that provides service to people and a harmonious and appreciative work environment.

Judging types: Work that imposes a need for system and order.

Perceptive types: Work that requires adapting to changing situations, or where understanding situations is more important than managing them.

Once people understand their MBTI preferences, they can begin to build a picture of an "ideal job" that would let them fully use their preferences, with relatively little demand on their less-developed processes and attitudes. Counselors can suggest occupations, and work settings within an occupation, that contain features of the "ideal job."

Tables 7.1, 7.2, 7.3, and 7.4 contain contrasting examples of the "Effects of Each Preference in Work Situations" (also see page 25 of *Introduction to Type*). These can be used as a checklist for identifying work preferences. The tables include comments for the counselor showing where specific preferences can affect these generalized statements. For example, all extraverts are not alike in the other preferences (SN, FT, or JP), so extravert work preferences may fit some extraverted types better than other extraverted types. Most people will check some statements in both preference columns. The aim in using the table is not to find a perfect fit between type preferences and career preferences, but to use the contrasts for looking at career goals in a new way.

Occupation and MBTI Preference

Appendix D shows tables of occupations empirically attractive to EI, SN, TF, JP, and to the sixteen types. The data for these tables come from the CAPT MBTI data bank

Table 7.1 Effects of extraversion-introversion in work situations

Extraverts	Introverts
Like variety and action.	Like quiet for concentration.
Tend to be faster, dislike complicated procedures (especially ES types).	Tend to be careful with details, dislike sweeping statements (especially IS types).
Are often good at greeting people (especially EF types).	Have trouble remembering names and faces (especially IT types).
Are often impatient with long, slow jobs.	Tend not to mind working on one project for a long time uninterruptedly.
Are interested in the results of their job, in getting it done, and in how other people do it.	Are interested in the idea behind their job.
Often do not mind the interruption of answering the telephone (especially EF types).	Dislike telephone intrusions and interruptions (especially IT types).
Often act quickly, sometimes without thinking.	Like to think a lot before they act, sometimes without acting.
Like to have people around (especially EF types).	Work contentedly alone (especially IT types).
Usually communicate freely (especially EF types).	Have some problems communicating (especially IT types).

(described in Appendix B). MBTI response sheets contain a line for individuals to write their occupation. When these response sheets are sent to CAPT for scoring, the occupations are coded by a system modified from the *Dictionary of Occupational Titles* (U.S. Department of Labor, 1977). Data are included in the Appendix D tables when an occupation is represented by at least fifty people. No attempt has been made to group occupations by families because it is often instructive to see which occupations attract people of the same preference. Note that these are samples of convenience, not randomly selected samples. In addition, respondents differ in the precision with which they name their occupation. Despite these limitations, the listings are consistent with the theory and commonsense understanding of the occupation and the MBTI. Readers with a special interest in medicine and other health occupations will find similar summary information in McCaulley and Morgan (1982) and McCaulley (1977, 1978).

Guidelines for Using the Career Listings in Appendix D

1. Look at the occupations at the top and the bottom of the table. Notice how they are different.

2. Consider whether any of the occupations at the high preference end of the table are attractive to the person seeking career information. Consider also the attractiveness of occupations at the bottom of the table.

3. Discuss how the high and low attraction occupations are or are not related to type preferences. This discussion and the search for patterns can be the most enlightening use of the data for career planning.

4. Notice the number of cases in the data bank for occupations of particular interest. Percentages for occupations with several hundred cases are more likely to be stable.

Table 7.2 Effects of sensing-intuition in work situations

Sensing Types	Intuitive Types
Dislike new problems unless there are standard ways to solve them.	Like solving new problems.
Like an established order of doing things (especially SJ types).	Dislike doing the same thing repeatedly (especially NP types).
Enjoy using skills already learned more than learning new ones.	Enjoy learning a new skill more than using it.
Work more steadily, with realistic idea of how long it will take (especially IS types).	Work in bursts of energy, powered by enthusiasm, with slack periods in between (especially EN types)
Usually reach a conclusion step by step (especially IS types).	Reach a conclusion quickly (especially EN types).
Are patient with routine details (especially ISJ types).	Are impatient with routine details (especially ENP types).
Are impatient when the details get complicated (especially ES types).	Are patient with complicated situations (especially IN types).
Are not often inspired, and rarely trust the inspiration when they are inspired.	Follow their inspirations, good or bad (especially with inadequate type development).
Seldom make errors of fact.	Frequently make errors of fact.
Tend to be good at precise work (especially IS types).	Dislike taking time for precision (especially EN types).

Percentages can change when new cases are added to small samples. All of the occupations listed contain at least fifty cases.

Extraversion and Introversion and Occupational Choices

Table 7.1 shows Isabel Myers' description of work aspects of extraversion and introversion. Appendix D contains occupations from the MBTI data bank in order of interest to extraverts and introverts. In Appendix D occupations attracting the most extraverts and fewest introverts appear at the top of the column; occupations attracting the fewest extraverts and most introverts appear at the bottom.

Sensing and Intuition and Occupational Choices

Table 7.2 contains a description of the effects of sensing and intuition in work situations with comments for the

counselor. Appendix D shows occupations empirically attractive to sensing versus intuition.

The SN preference is important because it points to those aspects of work most likely to be motivating and to require the most attention. A person whose interest lies in direct experience is therefore predicted to find applied occupations more motivating (e.g., civil engineering) than occupations where theory is of paramount importance (e.g., nuclear physics).

Thinking and Feeling and Occupational Choices

Most occupations have a technical/scientific component and a communications/interpersonal component. Type theory suggests that the technical/scientific aspects will be more important to thinking types, and the communications/interpersonal aspects to feeling types. Counselors should be alert to the fact that many helping professions, particularly

Table 7.3 Effects of thinking-feeling in work situations

Thinking Types	Feeling Types
Do not show emotion readily and are often uncomfortable dealing with people's feelings (especially IT types).	Tend to be very aware of other people and their feelings (especially EF types).
May hurt people's feelings without knowing it.	Enjoy pleasing people, even in unimportant things.
Like analysis and putting things into logical order. Can get along without harmony.	Like harmony. Efficiency may be badly disrupted by office feuds.
Tend to decide impersonally, sometimes paying insufficient attention to people's wishes.	Often let decisions be influenced by their own or other people's personal likes and dislikes.
Need to be treated fairly.	Need occasional praise.
Are able to reprimand people or fire them when necessary.	Dislike telling people unpleasant things.
Are more analytically oriented— respond more easily to people's thoughts (especially IT types).	Are more people oriented—respond more easily to people's values.
Tend to be firm-minded.	Tend to be sympathetic.

those in health, require technical knowledge, and many technical fields require good communications skills. Thinking types can develop communications skills (F) when they perceive a logical reason to do so; feeling types can develop technical skills (T) when these are needed to care for others.

Table 7.3 presents descriptions of thinking and feeling in work situations with comments for counselors (also on page 25 of *Introduction to Type*). Appendix D presents a ranking of occupations according to preferences for thinking and feeling.

Judgment and Perception and Occupational Choices

Judgment and perception are related to the style of working more than to the tasks themselves. Certain fields have more judging types because an orderly approach is essential (such as in the health professions), or because decision making is important (as in management). Perception is found most often in occupations that require openness and understanding (as in nondirective counseling), or where adaptability to change is essential (as in troubleshooting).

Table 7.4 presents descriptions of judgment and perception in work situations with comments for counselors (also on page 25 of *Introduction to Type*).

Using Type Data in Counseling

Counselors using MBTI career data should take into account two main factors: (*a*) at what point the data were collected in relation to the career stage of the individuals in the sample (i.e., student, entry, or established) and (*b*) whether the data are based on absolute numbers, percentages, or on ratios that may be called "selection ratios," "dropout ratios," or "satisfaction ratios."

Research Steps for Type and Career. When researching type and career, the following steps are relevant:

1. *Interest:* Determine the distribution of types interested in the occupation under study. Which types are over-

Table 7.4 Effects of judgment-perception in work situations

Judging Types	Perceptive Types
Work best when they can plan their work and follow the plan.	Adapt well to changing situations.
Like to get things settled and finished.	Do not mind leaving things open for alterations.
May decide things too quickly (especially EJ types).	May have trouble making decisions (especially IP types).
May dislike to interrupt the project they are on for a more urgent one (especially ISJ types).	May start too many projects and have difficulty in finishing them (especially ENP types).
May not notice new things that need to be done.	May postpone unpleasant jobs.
Want only the essentials needed to begin their work (especially ESJ types).	Want to know all about a new job (especially INP types).
Tend to be satisfied once they reach a judgment on a thing, situation, or person.	Tend to be curious and welcome a new light on a thing, situation, or person.

selecting or underselecting the field, compared to a base population?

2. *Selection:* Determine the types selected for training. Which types are overselected and which are underselected from the applicant pool?

3. *Dropouts:* Study the rates of graduation or dropout for each type compared to the population distribution of entering students. Identify the types most likely to leave because of academic failure, lack of interest, or other causes.

4. *Practice:* Study practitioners to determine whether some types are more likely to practice and others to leave the occupation.

5. *Specialty choice:* Study the types attracted to occupational specialties and particular settings. Determine whether some specialties and settings are more attractive to some types than to others, given the particular occupation.

6. *Satisfaction and competence:* Determine which types within the occupation show the most satisfaction and competence at the job. Study how the theoretical characteristics of the successful types relate to interest, motivation, methods of work, job satisfaction, and competence for the particular occupation.

Data from Absolute Frequencies or from Selection Ratios. Relevant to occupational research is the selection of occupations as a function of type. For example, one might wish to know the types attracted to accounting, nuclear engineering, or fine arts in a given university (where all freshmen have answered the MBTI and the type distribution is known). The null hypothesis is that the percentages of the sixteen types will be the same for any given occupation as for the total freshman class. That is, if 6.5% of the freshmen are ISTJ, then 6.5% of students in accounting, nuclear engineering, and history are expected to be ISTJs.[15]

Assume that in actuality 9.8% of accounting students are ISTJ, 3.1% of nuclear engineering students are ISTJ, and 0.3% of fine arts students are ISTJ. One can now compute the ratio of the actual frequencies to the expected frequency (based on 6.5% expected for ISTJ in each major) to determine the *relative* attraction of the three fields of study to the ISTJ students. In this case, the ratios of attraction, or "selection ratios," are 1.51 for accounting, .48 for nuclear engineering, and .05 for fine arts. Ratios greater than 1.00 indicate that more ISTJs have selected the major than would be expected from their numbers among the freshmen; ratios less than 1.00 indicate that fewer ISTJs than expected have chosen the major in question. Type theory predicts that ISTJ, a thorough, thoughtful type with sensing as a dominant function, would be more attracted to accounting, since it requires careful attention to detail, than to nuclear engineering, one of the more theoretical of the engineering specialties, or to fine arts where the creative use of intuition is more important.

When type distributions are used to test hypotheses about types, it is important to choose populations that provide a reasonable basis for expected frequencies. For example, it is reasonable to use college freshmen or high school seniors to provide base rate frequencies for college majors. It is reasonable to use college graduates to provide base rate frequencies for fields of graduate study. It is reasonable to use entering students to provide base rate frequencies for a study of dropouts. It is less reasonable to use ninth grade students to provide base rate frequencies for practicing architects.

Interpretation of Absolute Numbers and Ratios. For some purposes, a career counselor will be most interested in the absolute numbers of a type within a given occupation. For other purposes, it is more important to know whether the field is *relatively* more or less attractive to a given type, in comparison to some normative (or base) population. Relative attraction is shown by ratios; absolute frequencies are shown by percentages.

The following example shows how absolute numbers and ratios can be used. The example comes from a comparison of experimental and clinical psychologists (Perry, 1975).

Data collected by Perry (1975) from members of the American Psychological Association show significant differences in type for twenty-five clinical psychologists (members of the Divisions of Clinical, Counseling, Humanistic Psychology, and Psychotherapy) and thirty experimental psychologists (members of Divisions of Physiological and Comparative, Experimental Psychology, and the Experimental Analysis of Behavior). The total sample included a third group which the author called "buffer group" (seventeen members of Divisions for Developmental, Educational, and Personality and Social Psychology).

Table 7.5 shows the distribution of seventy-two psychologists consisting of Perry's total sample of experimental, clinical, and "buffer group" psychologists. Table 7.6 shows the distribution and selection ratios for the twenty-five clinical psychologists. Table 7.7 shows the distribution and selection ratios for the thirty experimental psychologists.

The selection ratios for clinical and experimental psychologists are calculated based on the total sample of seventy-two psychologists in the Perry data. The null hypothesis is that both experimental and clinical psychologists will have the same percentage in each type as Perry found in his total sample. These small distributions are worth careful study because they demonstrate important principles in using the MBTI for career counseling. The following questions might arise during a counseling interview with a prospective psychologist. The counselor should be very cautious about generalizing from such small samples, but for purposes of demonstration please assume that the data have been verified on larger populations.

Q. What types go into psychology?

A. All sixteen types enter psychology, but intuitive types are much more likely to choose psychology than sensing types (N 81.9%).

Q. I am a sensing type and I want to be a psychologist. Where will I fit?

A. You are more likely to find other sensing types if you consider one of the experimental fields (S ratio 1.8, *p*<.01). About one-third of experimental psychologists prefer sensing and two-thirds prefer intuition. You would still be in the minority in experimental psychology, but not so much as you would be if you entered clinical psychology, where only about five percent are sensing types. There are many practical applications of psychological principles, and you might want one of the fields where you can see tangible results of your efforts.

Q. I am an ISTJ and want to enter psychology. Where would I fit?

A. You are more likely to like the work of an experimental psychologist. In one study, more than twice the expected number of ISTJs chose experimental (I ratio 2.4,

Table 7.5 Practicing psychologists from a range of disciplines (*N* = 72)

Sensing Types		Intuitive Types				
With Thinking	With Feeling	With Feeling	With Thinking		*N*	Percent
ISTJ *N* = 5 % = 6.9 ооооооо	ISFJ *N* = 2 % = 2.8 ооо	INFJ *N* = 7 % = 9.7 оооооооооо	INTJ *N* = 2 % = 2.8 ооо	Judging / Introverts	E 34 I 38 S 13 N 59 T 35 F 37	47.22 52.78 18.06 81.94 48.61 51.39
ISTP *N* = 0 % = 0.0	ISFP *N* = 1 % = 1.4 о	INFP *N* = 10 % = 13.9 оооооооооо оооо	INTP *N* = 11 % = 15.3 оооооооооо ооооо	Perceptive / Introverts	J 34 P 38 IJ 16 IP 22 EP 16 EJ 18	46.61 52.78 22.22 30.56 22.22 25.00
ESTP *N* = 2 % = 2.8 ооо	ESFP *N* = 1 % = 1.4 о	ENFP *N* = 7 % = 9.7 оооооооооо	ENTP *N* = 6 % = 8.3 оооооооо	Perceptive / Extraverts	ST 9 SF 4 NF 33 NT 26 SJ 9 SP 4 NP 34 NJ 25	12.50 5.56 45.83 36.11 12.50 5.56 47.22 34.72
ESTJ *N* = 2 % = 2.8 ооо	ESFJ *N* = 0 % = 0.0	ENFJ *N* = 9 % = 12.5 оооооооооо оо	ENTJ *N* = 7 % = 9.7 оооооооооо	Judging / Extraverts	TJ 16 TP 19 FP 19 FJ 18 IN 30 EN 29 IS 8 ES 4	22.22 26.39 26.39 25.00 41.67 40.28 11.11 6.94

Note: о = 1% of sample.

Source: *Interrelationships among Selected Personality Variables of Psychologists and Their Professional Orientation* by H. W. Perry. Doctoral dissertation. Notre Dame University, 1974. Adapted by permission.

p<.01). In fact, all the ISTJs in that study chose one of the experimental fields. Remember that most of your colleagues are likely to prefer intuition, but you will probably find more people who share your interests in the experimental fields.

Q. I know I want psychology, but I'm not sure which field to choose. What is the difference between clinical and experimental psychology?

A. Clinical psychology attracts more

Table 7.6 Selection ratios for clinical psychologists (*N* = 25)

Sensing Types		Intuitive Types				
With Thinking	With Feeling	With Feeling	With Thinking			

					N	Percent	Index

ISTJ
N = 0
% = 0.0

I   0.0

ISFJ
N = 0
% = 0.0

I   0.0

INFJ
N = 6
% = 24
¤¤¤¤¤¤¤¤¤
¤¤¤¤¤¤¤¤¤
¤¤¤¤

I   2.5**

INTJ
N = 0
% = 0.0

I   0.0

(Judging / Introverts)

ISTP
N = 0
% = 0.0

I   0.0

ISFP
N = 1
% = 4.0
¤¤¤¤

I   2.9

INFP
N = 4
% = 16.0
¤¤¤¤¤¤¤¤¤
¤¤¤¤¤¤

I   1.2

INTP
N = 0
% = 0.0

I   0.0**

(Perceptive / Introverts)

ESTP
N = 0
% = 0.0

I   0.0

ESFP
N = 0
% = 0.0

I   0.0

ENFP
N = 3
% = 12.0
¤¤¤¤¤¤¤¤¤
¤¤

I   1.2

ENTP
N = 3
% = 12.0
¤¤¤¤¤¤¤¤¤
¤¤

I   1.4

(Perceptive / Extraverts)

ESTJ
N = 0
% = 0.0

I   0.0

ESFJ
N = 0
% = 0.0

I   0.0

ENFJ
N = 5
% = 20.0
¤¤¤¤¤¤¤¤¤
¤¤¤¤¤¤¤¤¤

I   1.6

ENTJ
N = 3
% = 12.0
¤¤¤¤¤¤¤¤¤
¤¤

I   1.2

(Judging / Extraverts)

	N	Percent	Index
E	14	56.0	1.2
I	11	44.0	0.8
S	1	4.0	0.2*
N	24	96.0	1.2*
T	6	24.0	0.5**
F	19	76.0	1.5**
J	14	56.0	1.2
P	11	44.0	0.8
IJ	6	24.0	1.1
IP	5	20.0	0.7
EP	6	24.0	1.1
EJ	8	32.0	1.3
ST	0	0.0	0.0*
SF	1	4.0	0.7
NF	18	72.0	1.6**
NT	6	24.0	0.7
SJ	0	0.0	0.0*
SP	1	4.0	0.7
NP	10	40.0	0.8
NJ	14	56.0	1.6**
TJ	3	12.0	0.5
TP	3	12.0	0.5*
FP	8	32.0	1.2
FJ	11	44.0	1.8**
IN	10	40.0	1.0
EN	14	56.0	1.4*
IS	1	4.0	0.4
ES	0	0.0	0.0

Note: ¤ = 1% of sample.
I = Index of attraction (ratio of observed to expected frequency, based on the proportion of the type in the total sample of seventy-two psychologists).
* *p* < .05. ** *p* < .01.
"Clinical" psychologists responded to author's inquiry to American Psychological Association Divisions of Clinical, Counseling, Humanistic Psychology and Psychotherapy.

Source: *Interrelationships among Selected Personality Variables of Psychologists and Their Professional Orientation* by H. W. Perry. Doctoral dissertation. Notre Dame University, 1974. Adapted by permission.

Table 7.7 Selection ratios for experimental psychologists (*N* = 30)

Sensing Types		Intuitive Types			*N*	Percent	Index
With Thinking	With Feeling	With Feeling	With Thinking				

ISTJ (Judging, Introverts)
N = 5
% = 16.7
I = 2.4**

ISFJ
N = 2
% = 6.7
I = 2.4

INFJ
N = 1
% = 3.3
I = 0.3

INTJ
N = 1
% = 3.3
I = 1.2

ISTP (Perceptive)
N = 0
% = 0.0
I = 0.0

ISFP
N = 0
% = 0.0
I = 0.0

INFP
N = 2
% = 6.7
I = 0.5

INTP
N = 6
% = 20.0
I = 1.3

ESTP (Perceptive, Extraverts)
N = 1
% = 3.3
I = 1.2

ESFP
N = 0
% = 0.0
I = 0.0

ENFP
N = 1
% = 3.3
I = 0.3

ENTP
N = 3
% = 10.0
I = 1.2

ESTJ (Judging)
N = 2
% = 6.7
I = 2.4

ESFJ
N = 0
% = 0.0
I = 0.0

ENFJ
N = 4
% = 13.3
I = 1.1

ENTJ
N = 2
% = 6.7
I = 0.7

	N	Percent	Index
E	13	43.3	0.9
I	17	56.7	1.1
S	10	33.3	1.8**
N	20	66.7	0.8**
T	20	66.7	1.4**
F	10	33.3	0.6**
J	17	56.7	1.2
P	13	43.3	0.8
IJ	9	30.0	1.4
IP	9	26.7	0.9
EP	5	16.7	0.8
EJ	8	26.7	1.1
ST	8	26.7	2.1**
SF	2	6.7	1.2
NF	8	26.7	0.6**
NT	12	40.0	1.1
SJ	9	30.0	2.4**
SP	1	3.3	0.6
NP	12	40.0	0.8
NJ	8	26.7	0.8
TJ	10	33.3	1.5
TP	10	33.3	1.3
FP	3	10.0	0.4**
FJ	7	23.3	0.9
IN	10	33.3	0.8
EN	10	33.3	0.8
IS	7	23.3	2.1**
ES	3	10.0	1.4

Note: ¤ = 1% of sample.
I = Index of attraction (ratio of observed to expected frequency, based on the proportion of the type in the total sample of seventy-two psychologists).
* *p* < .05, ** *p* < .01, *** *p*.<.001.
Experimental psychologists responded to author's inquiry to American Psychological Association Divisions of Experimental, Comparative, and Physiological Psychology and Experimental Analysis of Behavior.

Source: *Interrelationships among Selected Personality Variables of Psychologists and Their Professional Orientation* by H. W. Perry. Doctoral dissertation. Notre Dame University, 1974. Adapted by permission.

psychologists who are concerned with possibilities (N) for people (F) (NF 72%, ratio 1.6, *p*<.01). Experimental psychology attracts more people interested in theory (N) and logical analysis (T), but there is also a sizable number of more practical people in experimental psychology (S ratio 1.8, *p*<.001). You will find all types in each area, but these facts may help you think about how your interests relate to the psychological specialties.

Q. I am going to hire several experimental psychologists. What types are they likely to be?

A. Any of the MBTI types may enter experimental psychology. However, your candidates probably will be logical, analytic, and intuitive types (T 66.7%, N 66.7%, NT 40%). You might also find some more practical, detail-minded psychologists in your applicant pool (S 33.3%, ratio 1.8, *p*<.05). Have you thought through what skills you want in your hire? If your research is primarily theoretical, you may want to interview applicants about their interest in theory and abstract, logical models (i.e., interview for an NT). If your projects are more applied, you might want to question applicants about the practical details relevant to psychological work (i.e., interview for an ST). Keep in mind that if your research will be in an interpersonally sensitive area, you might want to look for an experimental psychologist with good people skills; insightful types who usually enter counseling fields also choose experimental psychology, but not as frequently (NF 26.7%; ratio 0.6, *p*<.01).

These oversimplified answers demonstrate that percentages are important when asking about manpower trends, or applicant pools. Ratios are more important when working with individuals to determine relative attraction to particular occupations or specialties.

SCII General Occupational Themes and the MBTI

Many counselors use the MBTI along with the Strong-Campbell Interest Inventory (SCII) or other career interest

inventories. When the SCII and the MBTI are used together, the SCII points to specific careers of interest, and the MBTI shows the reasons why the careers are attractive. Correlations between the scales of several interest inventories and the MBTI are listed in Table 11.1. An example of the relationship between the SCII General Occupational Themes (GOT) and the MBTI is provided in Table 7.8, which shows data from five student samples. For the Lacy (1984), and Kauppi (1982) samples, students who scored more than one-half a standard deviation above the sample mean for each GOT were designated as high scorers, and students who scored more than one-half a standard deviation below the sample mean for each GOT were designated as low scorers. High-scoring and low-scoring students on each GOT were compared to the type table for the total group using the Selection Ratio Type Table Program (SRTT). Table 7.8 shows the GOTs that were significantly represented in the type table cell as indicated by the SRTT.

As predicted, N types scored higher on artistic, SJ types on conventional, F types on social, and IN and NT on investigative scales. Sensing types, especially extraverts with sensing, scored higher on enterprising. The pattern for realistic is less clear. Campbell (1977) describes the realistic scale as follows (predicted MBTI preferences shown in parentheses): robust, rugged, practical (S), concrete (S), good motor skills (ES) but lacking verbal and interpersonal skills (not ENF), stable (EST), natural (ES), persistent (J), conventional (SJ), liking to build with tools (ST). Table 11.1 shows that the realistic scale does not correlate consistently with any MBTI preference, perhaps because its characteristics include aspects of more than one MBTI preference. One interesting artifact of the GOT data is that females show a stronger relationship between thinking and realistic than do men.

Career Choices of ST, SF, NF, and NT Types

Table 4.3 described the theoretical expectations for career interests of the ST, SF, NF, and NT groups. Appendix D presents percentage distributions of a number of samples from different occupations. These tables can be used to understand the relationships between types and occupational groups.

Occupations Attractive to the Sixteen Types

Tables in Appendix D list occupations from the CAPT MBTI data bank for persons who described their occupations on their response sheets. The CAPT data bank is described in Appendix B. To create these occupational tables, a type table was created for each occupation showing the percentage in each type making up the total number in the

Table 7.8 SCII General Occupational Themes (GOT) and the MBTI

ISTJ	ISFJ	INFJ	INTJ
High scores	*High scores*	*High scores*	*High scores*
Conventional B Investigative D Realistic E	Conventional ABDE Enterprising AD	Artistic A	Investigative ABE Realistic B
Low scores	*Low scores*	*Low scores*	*Low scores*
Artistic AB Social AB	Artistic BD Investigative B	Enterprising B	Social AB

ISTP	ISFP	INFP	INTP
High scores	*High scores*	*High scores*	*High scores*
Realistic E	Conventional E	Artistic ABE	Investigative AE Realistic B
Low scores	*Low scores*	*Low scores*	*Low scores*
Enterprising B Social BD	Investigative A	Conventional AB Enterprising A	Conventional A Social A

ESTP	ESFP	ENFP	ENTP
High scores	*High scores*	*High scores*	*High scores*
Conventional A Enterprising E	Realistic E	Artistic AB Realistic B Social ADE	
Low scores	*Low scores*	*Low scores*	*Low scores*
Artistic AD Investigative A Realistic B Social B	Artistic D		Conventional B

ESTJ	ESFJ	ENFJ	ENTJ
High scores	*High scores*	*High scores*	*High scores*
Conventional AB Enterprising E	Conventional B Enterprising B Social AE	Artistic B Social BDE	Investigative A
Low scores	*Low scores*	*Low scores*	*Low scores*
Artistic B	Artistic B Realistic B		

Notes: Groups A and B are students from Franklin and Marshall College from Lacy (1984) (Group A, 912 males; Group B, 848 females). Group D are 134 male and female high-achieving students studied by Kauppi (1982). Group E includes 314 male and female students at the University of Guelph and Waterloo University studied by Walsh (1984).

occupation. These type percentages were then ranked from high to low. Data were collected from response sheets scored in the 1970's until 1984.

Example of Consistency in a Business Occupation. Table 7.9 was designed to demonstrate consistency of main trends in types attracted to an occupation, and the importance of taking into account differences as well as similarities within a sample. Table 7.9 shows the percentages of each type in samples of business executives. Note that in samples with line responsibilities S types outnumber N types. Samples with long-range planning responsibilities tend to have more N types. The samples also show a strong selection for tough-minded, logical, analytical, and decisive TJ types, and a relative scarcity of FP types. This table could be useful for counseling an INFP promoted to an executive post. The counselor might discuss the reasons why the INFP often feels in alien territory or isolated in the executive suite. A discussion of the humanistic values and interpersonal sensitivity that the INFP might bring to a TJ environment might give the INFP a new perspective and sense of confidence.

Table 7.9 might also be useful in working with TJ executives, by discussing how a lack of F and P in the executive suite might be causing problems. The discussion could lead the TJ to recognize the need for more gestures of appreciation (F), more attention to interpersonal issues (F), and the need to collect more input (P) before rushing into decisions (J).

Other Issues in Careers and MBTI Types

The Effect of Occupation on Type Preferences

Counselors are often asked whether occupations might not cause MBTI preferences. For example, "I have been an accountant for 25 years. Perhaps my needing to be concerned about details over the years made me report myself ISTJ."

Type theory predicts that a priori type preferences are more important for determining occupational choice than are occupational environments for determining type preferences. Myers (McCaulley, 1979) conducted a large longitudinal study that is relevant to this issue. In the early 1950s she tested 5,355 medical students from forty-five schools. Most were in their freshman year of medical school. Twelve years later she identified their specialty choices from the *Directory of the American Medical Association*. Students had significantly chosen specialties which in theory would attract their types. Ten years later McCaulley (1979, p. 98) followed up the sample to investi-

gate specialties, work settings, professional memberships, and faculty appointments. Of the original sample, 4,953 or 92% were practicing medicine; of these, 963 or 19% had changed their major specialty in the decade between followups. Changes were significantly more likely to be toward specialties more compatible with the type preferences measured in their freshman year (chi-square 46.87, $p<.001$). Introverts (ratio 1.22, $p<.05$), intuitive types (ratio 1.41, $p<.001$), and perceptive types (ratio 1.18, $p<.05$) were significantly more likely to change to specialties typical of their type. Among the introverts, INFP made the most shifts toward a typical specialty (ratio 2.86, $p<.001$). Two types, ESTJ (ratio 0.28, $p<.001$) and ESFJ (ratio 0.41, $p<.001$) moved significantly toward *less* typical specialties. Part of this finding may be an artifact. Both ESTJ and ESFJ had large numbers in general practice at the first follow-up, and almost any move away from general practice decreased their ratio.

The fact that types in specialties not typical of their type change to specialties more typical of their type indicates that people are more likely to change their work environment to match their type than to change their type to match their work environment. More longitudinal studies are needed, but for the present, counselors can reasonably assume that type is more likely to affect the choice of career than vice versa.

Unfortunately, some counselors ask clients to answer the MBTI in their "work self" frame of mind. Clients then describe themselves according to a stereotype of the ideal person in that occupation. Counselors who adopt this strategy (which is not recommended) lose a major advantage of the MBTI in career planning, the ability to focus on similarities or conflicts between the individual's interests and the occupation's demands.

Work Setting and Type

Since all careers studied contain members from all sixteen types, it is important to know more about how the rare types in an occupation function. Do they find a niche where they are happy and effective, or do they find themselves unhappy and drained? Quenk (1975), Quenk and Albert (1975), and McCaulley (1977, pp. 204–9) studied type differences in a work setting. They sampled a nationwide group of 476 physicians who responded to the MBTI and a *Physician Work Setting Instrument* (PWSI) developed by the authors. Data on the PWSI were reduced by cluster analysis to seven dimensions. Further analyses of the dimension scores for each physician identified seven "niches." Reports on the common demographic characteristics and attitudes of physicians in each niche cover specialties, education, work history, work setting, demographic characteristics, and satisfaction. Table 7.10 shows significant rela-

Table 7.9 Percentages of MBTI types in samples of managers

	ISTJ Number	ISTJ Percent	ISFJ Number	ISFJ Percent	INFJ Number	INFJ Percent	INTJ Number	INTJ Percent
A	83	26.27	7	2.22	1	0.32	10	3.16
B	43	28.67	8	5.33	2	1.33	4	2.67
C	128	16.93	29	3.84	8	1.06	37	4.89
D	7	5.93	5	4.24	2	1.69	19	16.10
E	202	23.79	55	6.48	20	2.36	55	6.48
F	23	22.72	2	1.98	0	0.00	9	8.91
G	584	15.88	225	6.12	99	2.69	198	5.38
H	202	23.41	16	1.85	13	1.51	99	11.47
I	8	5.76	5	3.60	3	2.16	11	7.91

	ISTP Number	ISTP Percent	ISFP Number	ISFP Percent	INFP Number	INFP Percent	INTP Number	INTP Percent
A	4	1.27	1	0.32	0	0.00	5	1.58
B	10	6.67	3	2.00	0	0.00	1	0.67
C	29	3.84	16	2.12	21	2.78	25	3.31
D	1	0.85	2	1.69	0	0.00	3	2.54
E	37	4.36	10	1.18	26	3.06	25	2.94
F	3	2.97	2	1.98	1	0.10	3	2.97
G	112	3.05	103	2.80	158	4.30	149	4.05
H	36	4.17	3	0.35	21	2.43	56	6.49
I	3	2.16	1	0.72	6	4.32	12	8.63

	ESTP Number	ESTP Percent	ESFP Number	ESFP Percent	ENFP Number	ENFP Percent	ENTP Number	ENTP Percent
A	8	2.53	3	0.95	1	0.32	5	1.58
B	11	7.33	6	4.00	3	2.00	3	2.00
C	32	4.23	15	1.98	28	3.70	50	6.61
D	10	8.47	7	5.93	5	4.24	3	2.54
E	33	3.89	10	1.18	25	2.94	36	4.24
F	4	3.96	0	0.00	5	4.95	7	6.93
G	108	2.94	113	3.07	237	6.44	181	4.92
H	29	3.36	11	1.27	22	2.55	45	5.21
I	5	3.60	0	0.00	22	15.83	12	8.63

	ESTJ Number	ESTJ Percent	ESFJ Number	ESFJ Percent	ENFJ Number	ENFJ Percent	ENTJ Number	ENTJ Percent
A	147	46.52	8	2.53	1	0.32	32	10.13
B	42	28.00	6	4.00	0	0.00	8	5.33
C	193	25.53	50	6.61	22	2.91	73	9.66
D	25	21.19	6	5.08	4	3.39	19	16.10
E	176	20.73	50	5.89	14	1.65	75	8.83
F	27	26.73	0	0.00	2	1.98	13	12.87
G	645	17.54	242	6.58	151	4.11	373	10.14
H	172	19.93	23	2.67	10	1.16	105	12.17
I	13	9.35	6	4.32	8	5.76	24	17.27

Notes: Samples are described in Appendix B. Managers in the samples are described as: A, Retail store managers (Gaster, 1982); B, Managers of small businesses (Hoy and Hellriegel, 1982); C, Bank and financial managers (MBTI data bank); D, Chief executives of large Japanese companies (Ohsawa, 1981); E, English managers of small businesses (Margerison & Lewis, 1981); F, Executives in a regional telephone company (Dietl, 1981); G, Managers and Administrators (MBTI data bank); H, Male participants in Center for Creative Leadership Program (Van Velsor, 1983); I, Female participants in Center for Creative Leadership program (Van Velsor, 1983).

Table 7.10 Physician work settings and MBTI preferences

Physician Work Setting Items	EI	SN	TF	JP
Personal patient involvement				
Counseling patients and families	E**	N*	F***	—
Direct patient contact	—	—	F*	
Dealing with patients' emotional problems	E***	N**	F***	P**
Referring patients	E***	—	—	—
Chance for appreciation from public	E***	—	—	—
Reviewing charts and test results	—	—	T***	—
Performing diagnostic procedures	—	—	T**	J**
Giving care outside of major setting	E**	—	F***	—
Habitual and nonvarying activities	—	S**	—	J**
Seeing more patients per week	—	S**	—	—
Physician-teacher				
Supervising students or staff	—	N**	T*	—
Affiliation with medical school	—	N***	T***	—
Presenting cases to an audience	—	N**	T*	—
Committee work, policy development	—	—	T*	—
Supervision of subordinates	—	—	F***	—
Personal control of professional life				
Maintaining preferred pace of life	—	S***	—	J*
Time for family and outside activity	E**	S*	—	J***
Determining free time/vacation	—	S**	—	J***
Taking less than entitled vacation	I**	—	—	—
Working in more than one setting	—	N**	—	—
Time wasted in travel between settings	—	N***	—	—
Ideal care prevented by financial constraints	—	N**	F**	—
Chance for spouse to follow own career	—	N***	F***	—
Responsibility to define own activities	E***	—	T***	—
Medical innovation				
Trying out new ideas	—	N**	T**	—
Expanding knowledge in area of medicine	—	N**	T***	—
Delegating tasks to subordinates	—	—	T***	J*
Personal control of income				
Handling practice finances personally	E***	S*	—	J**
Personal control of time in care	E***	—	—	—
Higher income from practice	—	S*	—	J**
Interaction with medical community				
Accessibility of consultation services	E**	N*	—	—
Isolation from other physicians	I*	—	—	P***
Professional ambition				
Chance for professional advancement	—	—	T***	—
Chance for prestige among colleagues	E***	—	T*	—
Active in nonmedical community affairs	E***	—	F**	—
With community boards	E**	—	—	P*
Stayed longer in present community	—	S***	T*	J***
Living in smaller community	—	S***	—	—

Note: MBTI letters show the preference with the higher score when items were compared for differences in mean scores of E physicians versus I physicians, S versus N, T versus F, and J versus P.

*$p < .05$ **$p < .01$ ***$p < .001$

tionships between MBTI preference scores and the PWSI. In 284 comparisons, 97 were significantly related to type preferences. Many of these work characteristics are also found in fields outside medicine.

Retention and Turnover

Laney (1949) used the MBTI to understand turnover in utility jobs. The study sampled all men hired by Washington Gas Light Company from 1945 through 1947. Form C of the MBTI was administered at the time of hiring, but the results were not used in selection, or job assignment, nor were they communicated to supervisors. Turnover data were based on the employees remaining with the company until December 15, 1948. Table 7.11 shows the turnover rates for SN, JP, and their combinations. Turnover was measured by the percentage of each type who had left the company.

The less frequent intuitive types (N) and perceptive types (P) had turnover rates significantly higher than the more frequent sensing types (S) and judging types (J). The NPs in theory are the most independent spirits with the greatest need for change and challenge. The SJs are most attuned to repetitive work with order and schedules.

Turnover in Mechanical and Clerical Assignments. Laney (1949) also studied turnover by types of jobs, as shown in Table 7.12. When jobs are divided into Clerical, Mechanical, and Other, turnover rates for Ns are at least one third higher than rates for Ss; rates for Ps are at least one-fifth higher than rates for Js. The highest excess turnover for Ns and Ps is in Mechanical jobs.

Turnover Related to Work Setting. The relationship of EI to turnover in the Washington Gas Light study appears to relate to work setting. To investigate the relationship of settings and type, Laney selected a sample of men with IQ scores of 100 or higher. The hypothesis was that clerical jobs, being quiet and demanding more sustained concentration, would be more congenial for introverts and that active jobs, such as mechanical tasks and meter reading,

would be more congenial for extraverts. Table 7.13 showed turnover was significantly higher for employees placed in unsuitable jobs (introverts in active jobs, extraverts in clerical jobs). After turnover, introverts held 48% of clerical jobs but only 18% of active jobs (chi-square 9.18, $p<.01$).

Turnover Related to Sales and Customer Relations Assignments. Laney also investigated the hypothesis that Es and Fs would predominate in sales and customer relations jobs. Since the number of men hired for these positions during the study was only 14, this analysis includes all employees engaged in sales or customer relations as of December 15, 1948. Table 7.14 shows that extraverts and feeling types were significantly overrepresented in sales/customer relations, compared to a base population of new employees over the three years of Laney's study.

In a follow-up of his sample nine years later, Laney (personal communication) reported that four of the original eighteen thinking types and thirty-three of the original forty-two feeling types remained in customer relations positions. This contrast shows that feeling types significantly more often remained in customer relations (chi-square 16.92, $p<.001$).

Intelligence and Turnover. In Laney's study, the N and P types, like those in other studies, had significantly higher mean intelligence than their opposites. Since the N and P types also had higher turnover rates, the mean intelligence of those leaving the company was naturally higher than the intelligence of employees who stayed. There is an obvious temptation to explain the group differences in turnover to the group differences in intelligence. Is turnover a function of type or intelligence? If higher intelligence is a source of turnover, it should be evident in all types. Laney (personal communication) reported a correlation r −.01 between the Wonderlic Personnel Test intelligence scores and the number of months of employment for the 228 SJ types (the least turnover-prone of the types), evidencing no relationship to intelligence.

Table 7.11 Turnover rate of utility workers

SN		JP		SN/JP	
N Turnover Rate		*N* Turnover Rate		*N* Turnover Rate	
S 425	41.4%	J 307	39.1%	NP 35	68.6%
N 78	62.8%	P 129	52.7%	NJ 25	60.0%
Chi-square 12.03 $p<.001$		Chi-square 6.88 $p<.01$		SP 73	47.9%
				SJ 244	35.2%

Management Performance. In an early study, Hay (1964) asked sixty-two engineering managers in three oil refineries to describe themselves on fifty statements of management behaviors. In the first description they described their behavior as they saw it; then a week later they described how they would *like* to function. The self-ideal congruence of the measures was related to other instruments and to supervisors' ratings. Introverts who in theory should be relatively less influenced by outside opinions, reported higher self-ideal congruence (r .25, p<.05). Supervisors rated engineering managers more highly who had higher self-ideal congruence (r .40, p<.01). Supervisors also slightly favored intuitive preferences (r .27, p<.05) and perceptive preferences (r .32, p<.05) in their ratings.

Other relationships between type and careers, including correlations between the MBTI and career interest inventories, appear in Chapter 11.

Table 7.12 Type differences in turnover in relation to work classified by clerical or mechanical tasks

Employee Group	*N*	Clerical	Mechanical	Other
N employees	78	63.2%	63.0%	62.5%
S employees	425	47.1%	36.0%	46.8%
Excess turnover	N>S	16.1%	27.0%	15.7%
P employees	129	61.5%	50.8%	50.0%
J employees	307	50.7%	33.3%	41.1%
Excess turnover	P>J	10.8%	17.5%	8.9%

Table 7.13 Turnover in jobs classified by activity level

Employees				

		Turnover Rates		
Employees	*N*	Introverts	*N*	Extraverts
Active jobs	34	64.7%	79	31.6%
Clerical jobs	21	33.3%	39	61.5%
Excess turnover		31.4%		29.9%
Chi-square		5.13, p<.03		9.61, p<.01

Table 7.14 Assignments to sales and customer relations

	E	I	T	F
Customer relations jobs	54	4	18	42
New employees (three-year sample)	321	110	232	174
Chi-square	9.92, p<.002		15.49, p<.001	

Chapter 8

Uses of Type in Education

The MBTI is used in education to understand students, teachers, and the education system. This chapter will provide a conceptual framework and practical suggestions for using type theory in educational settings. Anyone using type theory in education should be familiar with the discussion of early influences of type in learning in Myers with Myers (1980, pp. 137–58). This chapter reports Isabel Myers' data related to type in education and extends her results to new populations.

Type and Learning

Consistent with the expectation of type theory, the type classifications relate to three aspects of educational achievement: *aptitude, application,* and *interest.* When predicting performance, aptitude is the most measurable. When aptitude appears insufficient to account for high academic achievement, then the presence of some other favorable characteristic may be inferred; for example, greater than average application or greater than average interest. Application produces one kind of achiever, interest another.

This section is designed to show how type differences appear in aptitude, application, interest, and achievement, and how type theory accounts for the different effects of these characteristics. Aptitude will be discussed mainly in relation to how an interest in concepts and ideas (I) and symbols, imagination, and theory (N) contributes to an individual's academic aptitude. Application will be discussed mainly in relationship to the JP preference. Other things being equal, judging types seem more willing to apply themselves to required tasks, even if those tasks are not interesting in themselves. The role that interest plays in career choice has been discussed in Chapter 7. This chapter will discuss the relationship of type differences to the patterns of achievement of students in various fields of study.

Theoretical Expectations
of Type Differences in Learning

Academic achievement requires the capacity to deal intensively with concepts and ideas, which are mainly the province of *introversion*. It also requires the capacity to work with abstraction, symbols, and theory, which are the province of *intuition*. The prediction from type theory is that persons who prefer introversion and intuition will show greater academic aptitude than persons who prefer extraversion and sensing perception and whose best gifts lie in the practical world of action. Obviously, all types may perform well in college and graduate school. Type theory predicts, however, that types with introversion and intuition (IN types) will have a *relative* advantage, since their interests match academic tasks.

In examining the data that follow, it is important to keep in mind that academic aptitude tests are designed primarily to measure knowledge and aptitude in the IN domain; there are many other interests and capabilities that aptitude tests are not designed to measure. It is unfortunate that aptitude tests are often interpreted as being equivalent to measures of intelligence. Their scope is more limited.

Thinking and *feeling* are predicted to have a lesser relationship to academic aptitude than introversion and intuition. However, academic tasks requiring logical analysis favor thinking types, and academic tasks requiring understanding of human motivations favor feeling types.

The JP preference is predicted to differentiate to some small extent between aptitude and achievement. The *perceptive attitude* (open, spontaneous, and curious) favors a wide acquaintance with many subjects, which may lead to increased scores on aptitude measures. The *judging attitude* (planful, focused, and organized) is related to application and is often associated with higher grades.

Grades are a relevant measure because they are the end product of the interaction between aptitude, application, and interest. The theory and data on type differences in education help explain underachievement and overachievement. Type theory permits an educated guess about the application and interest students will bring to their studies, and permits more accurate interpretation of their aptitude scores. Since the aim of education is for all types to achieve and complete their studies creditably, the importance of the data on type differences lies in understanding why the differences occur, so that students can plan their learning and teachers their instruction to maximize the aptitude, interest, and application of all types.

Type Differences in Aptitude

Scholastic aptitude measures are concerned with a student's abilities to deal with concepts and ideas (I) and with symbols, abstraction, and theory (N). These relationships can be seen in (*a*) mean scores of preferences for IN, EN, IS, and ES, (*b*) shifts in aptitude scores as a function of the strength of EI and SN preferences, or (*c*) correlations between EI, SN, TF, and JP continuous scores and aptitude scores.

Differences in Aptitude Scores for the Four MBTI Preferences. Table 8.1 compares mean Scholastic Aptitude Test-Verbal (SAT-V) scores for male students in eight colleges. The table shows the difference between the mean score for each preference and the mean score for all students in the school. Introverts consistently scored higher than extraverts on the SAT-V, intuitives scored higher than sensing types, and the SN differences are greater than the EI differences. Although the differences are small, they are consistent in direction for all eight schools, except for TF where no differences in aptitude were predicted. It is often assumed that thinking types will have an advantage over feeling types in aptitude, and they may score higher in quantitative and scientific aptitude. In general, however, TF is much less important in understanding aptitude than EI, SN, and to some extent JP.

Note that in Table 8.1 the JP preference is also associated with aptitude. As noted above, P types, who in theory are more open to new information, average somewhat higher on aptitude tests than do J types, whereas J types average somewhat higher in grades.

The following tables show data from a series of studies of aptitude, achievement, and attitudes toward school. The populations are students from seventh to twelfth grades at The Florida State University Developmental Research School (McCaulley and Natter, 1974), a longitudinal study of University of Florida freshmen (McCaulley, 1973), and data from medical samples (McCaulley, 1977, 1978).

Table 8.2 shows the data for differences between extraverts and introverts. Though introverts more often score higher than extraverts in aptitude, the differences were seldom statistically (or practically) significant.

Table 8.3 shows the differences on the same measures as Table 8.2 for sensing and intuitive types. Most of these differences are statistically significant. There were larger differences for scales requiring high levels of abstraction or verbal ability, and smaller differences for tests of more practical skills.

Table 8.4 shows the differences on the same measures for thinking and feeling types. As predicted, there are relatively few significant differences. Most differences are in the mathematical or scientific subjects, which are of special interest to thinking types.

Table 8.5 shows the differences in mean scores of the same aptitude measures for judging and perceptive types. In most of the comparisons, perceptive types averaged slightly

Table 8.1 Deviations from SAT–V sample means for EI, SN, TF, and JP

		Deviation from School Mean Score on Scholastic Aptitude Test–Verbal							
Sample	*N*	E	I	S	N	T	F	J	P
Liberal arts students									
Amherst, 1962	245	−15	+12	−31	+20	+ 5	− 4	−11	+15
Amherst, 1963	246	−14	+11	−37	+14	+ 2	− 2	− 6	+ 6
Brown, 1962	591	−15	+19	−26	+19	+10	−10	− 6	+ 6
Dartmouth, 1961	663	− 6	+ 9	−22	+24	+ 1	0	−10	+10
Dartmouth, 1963	815	−10	+15	−22	+17	+ 9	−11	−11	+13
Stanford, 1963	713	− 8	+ 8	−29	+20	− 5	+ 5	−13	+17
Wesleyan, 1963	236	−20	+23	−28	+12	+ 7	− 7	− 9	+ 8
Weighted mean		−11	+13	−26	+19	+ 4	− 4	−10	+11
Standard error of mean		1.71	1.93	1.98	1.68	1.77	1.87	1.75	1.87
Weighted difference		24***		45***		8**		21***	
Engineering students									
Caltech, 1958–61	504	− 5	+ 3	−18	+ 5	− 2	+ 4	− 7	+ 6
Caltech, 1962	201	− 6	+ 3	−23	+ 2	+ 4	−12	− 7	+10
Cornell, 1964	498	− 7	+ 8	−23	+18	0	− 1	− 8	+14
Rensselaer Polytechnic, 1962	771	−11	+13	−25	+18	+ 3	− 6	− 6	+13
Weighted mean		− 8	+ 8	−23	+12	+ 1	− 3	− 7	+10
Standard error of mean		2.45	2.38	2.94	2.09	2.11	2.99	2.18	2.72
Weighted difference		16***		35***		4		17***	

Note: Significance is computed for total group t tests, not separate institutions.

* *p*<.05, ** *p*<.01, ****p*<.001.

higher in achievement, as predicted, but few of the differences were statistically significant.

Effect of Consistency of Preference on Aptitude.
There is some evidence that clarity or consistency of preferences is associated with higher scores on aptitude measures. Examples in Chapter 9 show a tendency for students with clearer preferences on E and I, T and F, and J and P to average higher on aptitude measures than students whose preference scores are low. An exception is the SN scale where clear preferences on N are associated with higher aptitude scores, but clear preferences on S do not lead to higher aptitude scores. At all levels of preference, sensing types score about the same in aptitude.

Myers (1962) analyzed Terman's Concept Mastery Test (CMT) scores and MBTI preferences for college freshmen from Brown (525 students) and Wesleyan (236 students). The CMT is designed to measure high ranges of vocabulary and verbal reasoning. The advantage of introversion over extraversion was greater than the advantage of intuition over sensing in both schools (Brown: I>E 12.2 points, N>S 11.3 points; Wesleyan: I>E 14.9 points, N>S 11.4 points). Myers' interpretation of the greater impact of introversion than intuition on the CMT scores was that the CMT is untimed; thus, the intuitives' speed was of no particular asset, and the introverts' depth was fully utilized.

The Brown University sample was then divided into six groups: mild, moderate, or clear preferences for S; and mild, moderate, or clear preferences for N. Mean Concept Mastery

Table 8.2 Mean aptitude scores for extraversion and introversion

Aptitude Measures	Extraversion			Introversion			
	N	Mean	SD	N	Mean	SD	t
High School Students							
Florida Eighth Grade Test[a]							
Computation	90	62.8	25.0	65	61.5	27.0	.31
Problem solving	90	66.7	26.6	65	69.0	25.6	.52
Everyday living math	90	20.2	4.3	64	20.7	4.7	.62
Everyday living reading	92	39.5	4.9	65	39.4	6.2	.22
Study skills	92	63.3	26.4	65	62.6	29.2	.15
Florida Ninth Grade Test[a]							
Verbal	81	62.4	23.5	82	65.4	26.4	.77
Quantitative	81	61.6	27.0	82	68.0	28.4	1.48
Social studies	81	57.2	25.5	82	62.2	27.5	1.20
English	81	57.2	25.6	82	63.3	25.0	1.54
Mathematics #1	80	62.6	26.8	83	66.3	28.7	.85
Mathematics #2	80	67.8	26.1	83	69.7	29.1	.42
Science	80	54.5	24.6	83	60.3	30.0	1.33
Florida Twelfth Grade Placement Test[a]							
Aptitude	40	59.9	26.5	46	72.3	26.6	2.15*
English	40	56.0	27.9	46	66.2	28.0	1.69
Social studies	40	52.1	25.9	46	62.2	26.6	1.77
Reading index	40	54.5	26.8	46	66.2	26.6	2.03*
Natural science	40	44.4	26.7	46	55.9	29.9	1.86
Mathematics	40	60.6	25.3	46	72.7	26.1	2.17*
PSAT[a]							
Verbal	38	43.3	10.0	38	47.3	13.1	1.45
Mathematics	39	47.9	13.7	38	57.1	11.8	3.16**
Gates Reading Test[a]							
Vocabulary	164	55.7	27.1	134	60.7	30.5	1.49
Comprehension	164	57.1	28.8	134	62.2	31.3	1.47

(continued)

scores were computed for extraverts and introverts separately. The results are shown in Figure 8.1. Among students with clear preferences for S, extraverts and introverts scored the same on the CMT. Introverted students had higher mean CMT scores at each stage of greater intuition. At all stages, introverts scored higher than extraverts. Myers (1962) interpreted the data as confirming an interest in concepts and ideas among introverts. "The almost 20-point difference in Concept Mastery scores of mildly intuitive students (N 1 – N 17) depending on whether they are introverts or extraverts, suggests that introverts use their minds, including their intuition, in a way that is different and advantageous for dealing with the intricacies of language and thought" (1962, p. 37).

Product Moment Correlations of Aptitude Scores and MBTI Preferences. Table 8.6 shows the product-moment correlations of aptitude scores and MBTI continuous scores for EI, SN, TF, and JP. Correlations are in the direction of I, N, P, and sometimes T. The correlations tend to be higher for verbal than for mathematical measures. For heterogeneous groups, such as the applicants to the California Institute of Technology, the correlations are larger than correlations for more homogeneous classes

Table 8.2 Mean aptitude scores for extraversion and introversion

Aptitude Measures	Extraversion			Introversion			
	N	Mean	SD	*N*	Mean	SD	*t*
High School Students							
Armed Services Vocational Aptitude Battery[a]							
Electrical	38	38.7	23.4	37	45.1	25.4	1.12
Motor mechanical	35	34.8	16.4	36	39.2	20.2	1.12
General mechanical	35	36.6	18.7	36	40.6	19.1	.90
Clerical/administrative	35	67.2	12.6	36	61.9	20.5	1.30
General technical	35	60.7	17.6	36	65.0	20.9	.92
California Test of Mental Maturity[a]							
IQ	253	106	14.7	205	107	16.9	.38
College and University Students							
University of Florida freshmen and transfers[b]							
Florida Twelfth Grade Placement Test							
	1457	394.3	67.74	1337	412.5	66.25	7.18***
Scholastic Aptitude Test							
Math	700	545.7	85.94	621	568.7	89.53	4.77***
Verbal	692	504.7	84.49	613	539.8	86.92	7.39***
Medical School Students							
Myers' Longitudinal Study[c]							
Medical School Aptitude Test							
Verbal	2203	506.4	90.6	2121	538.3	96.4	11.21***
Quantitative	2203	511.8	92.6	2121	536.1	92.7	8.63***
General information	2203	500.5	93.6	2121	527.7	96.6	7.16***
Science	2203	514.8	88.5	2121	545.4	91.1	11.21***

* $p<.05$, ** $p<.01$, *** $p<.001$.

Sources and sample descriptions are listed in Appendix B.
[a] McCaulley and Natter (1974)
[b] McCaulley and Kainz (1974)
[c] McCaulley (1977)

of students who have been admitted. The correlations in Table 8.6 support the theoretical expectations that IN and P types have an advantage on aptitude measures. Like most comparisons of aptitude and personality, the correlations in Table 8.6 are low.

Type Differences in Application

Isabel Myers described application from Webster's definition as "persistence in fixing one's attention and assiduity in the performance of what is required." She considered ap-

plication to be one of the three main components of scholastic success (with aptitude and interest).

Table 11.1 shows correlations of MBTI preferences with faculty ratings of students on a bipolar rating scale. These data were part of the College Students Characteristics Study (Ross, 1961). The sample is based on 249 male students selected with no known biases. The faculty attributed the following description to J students more than to P students: thorough, responsible, dependable, good on details, performs up to capacity, meets deadlines, works steadily, fond of work, industrious, and completes undertakings. If all of

Figure 8.1 Mean Concept Mastery scores of extraverts and introverts at different levels of preference for S and N

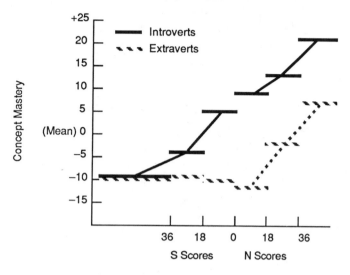

these traits, or any major portion of them, are more highly developed in J students, then, other things being equal, the grades of J students should be higher in proportion to their aptitude than the grades of P students.

Type Differences in Interest

Previous sections have considered the relationship of aptitude and application to academic success, and have shown that types differ on these variables in predictable ways. Isabel Myers also considered *interest* as important to academic success. This section describes type differences in interests and the next section gives representative data from Myers' early work showing the patterns of achievement and type in liberal arts, business, and engineering.

The response sheet for Form G of the MBTI asks the question, "Which do you like best—math, English, science, history, practical skills, music, art?" Table 8.7 shows the responses by the sixteen types to this question for 27,787 response sheets scored by the CAPT MBTI data bank. The table shows subjects significantly chosen by each type, using the Selection Ratio Type Table program (SRTT) described in Chapter 7.

Practical skills was chosen by six of the eight sensing types and none of the intuitive types. Mathematics was chosen by ST types and science by NT types. At the educational levels most respondents would have in mind when responding to the question, mathematics would connote clarity, certainty, and accuracy, which would appeal to sensing and thinking; science would connote discovery, analysis, and theory, which would appeal to intuition and thinking. The humanities were chosen by the intuitive types, especially the NF types who in theory have a special

interest in communication. An interesting part of the data was the choice of history by the extraverted sensing types, ESTP and ESFP. These two types who in theory have the least natural interest in the academic may have their interest captured by reading about what real people did in other times. The data in Table 8.7 can suggest the topic areas that may interest students of each type.

Myers (1962) displayed data on the numbers and percentages of E, I, S, N, T, F, J, and P in samples at different levels of education and with different kinds of interests. The Myers (1962) table is reproduced in Table 8.8. These data are useful for comparing interests associated with different preferences. The size of preference scores is evidence for the relationship between the preference and the interest.

Myers (1962) discussed the Table 8.8 data in terms of scholastic potential. The two samples at the junior high level offer a contrast between very good and extraordinarily good academic aptitude. The pre-academic sample consists of seventh and eighth grade students in a college town where the average IQ for eighth grade was 114 and where most students were destined for academic courses. The gifted sample consists of seventh, eighth, and ninth grade students in special classes for the gifted in a suburban public school system; all students had very high intelligence and ranked at the 95th percentile or higher on achievement tests.

Table 8.8 indicates that certain preferences are conspicuously more frequent in the gifted sample as compared to the very good pre-academic sample. Seventy-nine percent of male gifted students were intuitive types, compared to 28% of pre-academic males ($p < .001$). The frequency of introverts in the male gifted sample is 50% compared to 32%, and the relationship of perceptives is 62% compared to 51%. The proportions for female gifted compared to pre-academic students are similar: 88% intuitives compared to 30%, 42% introverts compared to 25%, and 65% perceptives compared to 53%. The differences between EI and SN for the two groups are statistically significant (EI, $p < .01$; SN, $p < .001$).

The preferences for N and for I, and perhaps P, are consistent with early data on academic potential. It follows that introverts and intuitives should be more frequent in academic twelfth grade than in junior high school before attrition, and even more frequent in highly selective liberal arts and engineering colleges.

Table 8.8 is useful for comparing the direction of preferences and strength of preferences in samples at different educational levels. For further discussion of Table 8.8 see Myers (1962).

Type Differences in Achievement

Type differences enter into academic achievement in many ways. Scholarly learning requires understanding of concepts

Table 8.3 Mean aptitude scores for sensing and intuition

Aptitude Measures	Sensing			Intuition			
	N	Mean	SD	N	Mean	SD	t
Junior High School Students							
California Test of Mental Maturity[a]							
Overall IQ	118	101.3	14.2	56	112.2	13.6	4.82***
Florida Eighth Grade Test[b]							
Vocabulary	88	62.0	25.4	65	73.9	25.5	2.84**
Comprehension	87	62.7	25.2	66	72.1	24.8	2.32*
Computation	89	60.6	25.8	66	64.5	25.8	.94
Problem solving	89	64.0	26.5	66	72.6	24.9	2.05*
Everyday living math	88	20.0	4.3	66	21.0	4.6	1.36
Everyday living reading	89	38.9	5.8	68	40.2	4.9	1.47
Study skills	89	58.9	25.9	68	68.3	28.8	2.14*
Florida Ninth Grade Test[b]							
Verbal	92	55.0	24.1	71	75.4	21.1	5.63***
Quantitative	92	57.4	27.1	71	74.4	25.9	4.04***
Social studies	92	50.5	24.0	71	71.8	25.0	5.50***
English	92	52.9	24.2	71	69.9	23.8	4.50***
Mathematics #1	92	56.5	27.2	71	74.7	25.2	4.38***
Mathematics #2	92	61.6	27.8	71	78.1	24.6	3.95***
Science	92	47.8	25.1	71	70.0	25.7	5.54***
Florida Twelfth Grade Placement Test[b]							
Aptitude	48	59.6	26.4	38	75.2	25.7	2.76**
English	48	53.2	27.8	38	71.8	25.5	3.19**
Social studies	48	49.9	22.8	38	67.1	28.2	3.11**
Reading index	48	52.3	25.4	38	71.4	25.9	3.43***
Natural science	48	39.9	23.3	38	64.0	29.9	4.20***
Mathematics	48	61.9	24.5	38	73.6	27.3	2.08*
PSAT[b]							
Verbal	38	39.3	8.3	38	51.4	11.6	5.17***
Mathematics	38	48.6	11.6	39	56.1	14.5	2.49**
Gates Reading Test[b]							
Vocabulary	174	51.1	27.7	124	67.7	27.4	5.11***
Comprehension	174	53.6	27.8	124	67.5	31.2	4.03***
Armed Services Vocational Aptitude Battery[b]							
Electrical	44	37.2	22.7	31	48.4	25.7	1.99
Motor mechanical	40	35.3	18.4	31	39.7	18.5	1.00
General mechanical	40	35.4	20.5	31	42.8	16.0	1.64
Clerical/administrative	40	59.2	16.3	31	71.4	15.9	3.16**
General Technical	40	57.4	16.3	31	70.0	20.9	2.85**
California Test of Mental Maturity[b]							
IQ	271	104.0	15.4	187	112.0	14.8	6.11***

(continued)

Table 8.3 Mean aptitude scores for sensing and intuition

Aptitude Measures	Sensing			Intuition			
	N	Mean	SD	N	Mean	SD	t

College and University Students

University of Florida freshmen and transfers[c]
Florida Twelfth Grade Placement Test

	1307	387.2	71.97	1487	416.9	66.28	11.86***
Scholastic Aptitude Test							
Math	561	544.1	86.84	760	565.7	88.42	4.42***
Verbal	558	495.4	84.03	747	540.4	84.89	9.52***

Medical School Students
Myers' Longitudinal Study[d]
Medical School Aptitude Test

Verbal	1994	486.6	83.8	2330	552.3	93.2	24.21***
Quantitative	1994	506.4	92.2	2330	538.6	92.0	11.43***
General Information	1183	483.5	88.3	1330	539.7	94.7	15.34***
Science	1992	505.5	86.1	2329	550.6	90.1	16.75***

* $p<.05$, ** $p<.01$, *** $p<.001$.

Sources and sample descriptions are listed in Appendix B.
[a] May (1971)
[b] McCaulley and Natter (1974)
[c] McCaulley and Kainz (1974)
[d] McCaulley (1977)

and the ability to deal with theory and abstraction, which are primarily the domain of I and N.

Learning typically does not occur without concentration and effort. The greater tendency for judging types to focus their energies is an important aspect of application.

Type preferences are also related to interest. The interest students bring to learning is expected to relate to the match or mismatch between their type preferences and the content to be learned or the way the content is taught.

The extent to which a student has aptitude, interest, and application for learning depends on many other factors such as age, previous achievements, life events, and level of type development. When a student learns something new, type theory predicts that he or she will find some tasks that use their preferred functions; these are tasks that seem interesting, with challenges that are fun and exciting. Other tasks require use of less-preferred functions and attitudes. These are tasks that seem difficult and are accomplished with a sense of drudgery and use of willpower. Data on academic achievement report only the end product of these positive or negative learning experiences. Because of the many

and conflicting influences on learning, correlations of personality variables with academic achievement are typically low; this is also the case with the MBTI. The data presented later in this chapter can be used to evaluate the construct validity of the MBTI, and to understand how influences on learning relate to different types.

Achievement as Reflected in Correlations. Earlier tables have shown correlations of MBTI preferences with aptitude measures. Table 8.9 shows correlations of MBTI preferences with measures of achievement. The data include samples of high school and college students.

While Table 8.6 shows higher aptitude for Ns and Ps, Table 8.9 shows higher achievement for Ns and Js. In Table 8.9 the coefficients are in no case large; however, with the exception of TF, they are completely consistent in direction of preference. Except for one zero the EI and SN correlations are all positive, indicating that introverts and intuitives tend to have higher grades. This would be expected from their higher aptitude. Every correlation with JP is negative, which indicates that J students also tend to have

Table 8.4 Mean aptitude scores for thinking and feeling

Aptitude Measures	Thinking			Feeling			
	N	Mean	SD	N	Mean	SD	t
High School Students							
Florida Eighth Grade Test[a]							
Vocabulary	43	65.0	27.0	110	67.9	25.7	.62
Comprehension	44	68.3	25.5	111	66.0	25.4	.50
Computation	44	62.5	25.3	111	62.1	26.1	.09
Problem solving	44	69.4	25.4	111	67.0	26.5	.52
Everyday living math	44	20.8	4.4	110	20.3	4.5	.62
Everyday living reading	44	38.7	5.7	113	39.8	5.3	1.16
Study skills	44	62.0	28.3	113	63.4	27.3	.28
Florida Ninth Grade Test[a]							
Verbal	46	64.6	23.8	117	63.6	25.5	.22
Quantitative	46	69.4	26.1	117	63.0	28.3	1.33
Social studies	46	65.7	25.6	117	57.4	26.7	1.79
English	46	59.8	26.6	117	60.5	25.0	.14
Mathematics #1	46	67.7	26.7	117	63.2	28.2	.93
Mathematics #2	46	71.0	27.2	117	67.9	27.8	.65
Science	46	63.3	25.8	117	55.1	28.0	1.73
Florida Twelfth Grade Placement Test[a]							
Aptitude	24	66.5	30.6	62	66.5	25.9	.02
English	24	60.7	31.1	62	61.7	27.3	.15
Social studies	24	64.2	24.0	62	54.9	27.3	1.46
Reading index	24	62.7	29.9	62	60.0	26.3	.41
Natural science	24	56.5	30.4	62	48.3	28.2	1.19
Mathematics	24	66.6	29.5	62	67.2	25.2	.10
PSAT[a]							
Verbal	26	46.1	12.3	50	44.9	11.5	.42
Mathematics	26	53.3	13.0	51	52.0	13.9	.40
Gates Reading Test[a]							
Vocabulary	89	59.6	28.3	209	57.3	28.9	.62
Comprehension	89	62.4	29.2	209	58.2	30.3	1.11
Armed Services Vocational Aptitude Battery[a]							
Electrical	18	52.6	27.2	57	38.4	22.7	2.20*
Motor mechanical	17	47.3	20.2	54	34.1	16.8	2.68**
General mechanical	17	46.7	22.5	54	36.1	17.1	2.06*
Clerical/administrative	17	67.5	21.4	54	63.6	15.7	.82
General technical	17	71.2	20.0	54	60.3	18.6	2.07*
California Test of Mental Maturity[a]							
Overall IQ	137	109.0	16.3	321	107.0	15.5	1.13

(continued)

Table 8.4 Mean aptitude scores for thinking and feeling

Aptitude Measures	Thinking			Feeling			
	N	Mean	SD	*N*	Mean	SD	*t*
College and University Students							
University of Florida freshmen and transfers[b]							
Florida Twelfth Grade Placement Test							
	1018	403.6	71.00	1776	402.7	65.58	.28
Scholastic Aptitude Test							
Math	483	564.3	88.60	838	552.0	87.97	2.45**
Verbal	479	526.9	94.13	826	517.8	83.09	1.83*
Medical School Students							
Myers' Longitudinal Study[c]							
Medical School Aptitude Test							
Verbal	2344	519.9	96.4	1980	524.5	92.9	1.59
Quantitative	2344	524.0	95.3	1980	523.4	91.2	.15
General information	1391	513.1	97.8	1122	513.5	93.6	0.00
Science	2342	533.3	92.9	1979	525.7	88.7	2.72**

* $p<.05$, ** $p<.01$, *** $p<.001$.

Sources and sample descriptions are listed in Appendix B.
[a] McCaulley and Natter (1974)
[b] McCaulley and Kainz (1974)
[c] McCaulley (1977)

higher grades in spite of lower aptitude (in Table 8.6). The correlations with TF are smaller and, like the correlations of TF with aptitude, are somewhat less consistent. Thus, the three preferences that make the main contributions to scholastic success are I, N, and J.

If it could be assumed that all these correlations are linear and that they do not interact, their net effect could be expressed in a multiple regression coefficient. Unfortunately, the preferences are not linear. Data reported in Chapter 9 show that plots of preference scores and academic variables tend to be far from linear. Students with clearer MBTI preferences tend to score higher on aptitude measures, with the exception of the preference for sensing. Isabel Myers (1962) reported a supplementary analysis to the data in Table 8.9. She computed correlations for sensing types and intuitive types separately. These data are reported in Table 8.10.

Myers (1962) commented on the data in Table 8.10:

For instance, when the correlations of SN with grade point average . . . are computed separately for S people and N people, the relationship is found to reside solely on the

N side and in the difference between intuitives and sensing people as a group. Among N students, stronger N appears to conduce to higher grades. Among S students in the present college samples, however, the correlation of grade-point average with the *preference* score (that shows simply the reported strength of the preference for S) is as often positive as negative. It would thus be a mistake to assume that grades become lower and lower as S gets stronger. (pp. 39–40)

Achievement as Reflected in Mean Scores of Achievement Measures. Table 8.11 shows grades or other academic measures for student populations, some of whose aptitude data were given in Tables 8.2 through 8.5.

The patterns shown in the correlations appear also in the mean gradepoint averages. The trends shown in previous tables continue with Is scoring somewhat higher than Es, Ns higher than Ss, Ts and Fs with no clear pattern, and Js receiving higher grades than Ps.

Table 8.5 Mean aptitude scores for judgment and perception

Aptitude Measures	Judgment			Perception			
	N	Mean	SD	*N*	Mean	SD	*t*

High School Students

Florida Eighth Grade Test[a]

Vocabulary	62	62.3	27.8	91	70.3	24.4	1.89
Comprehension	62	62.2	27.8	93	69.6	23.3	1.79
Computation	62	58.2	26.2	93	65.0	25.2	1.63
Problem solving	62	62.5	28.4	93	71.1	24.0	2.02*
Everyday living math	61	19.5	4.6	93	21.0	4.3	2.00*
Everyday living reading	63	37.9	6.3	94	40.5	4.5	2.96**
Study skills	63	55.8	27.3	94	67.8	26.7	2.74**

Florida Ninth Grade Test[a]

Verbal	43	57.6	25.6	120	66.1	24.4	1.94
Quantitative	43	58.7	29.0	120	67.0	27.1	1.69
Social studies	43	58.1	24.2	120	60.4	27.4	.49
English	43	54.0	25.6	120	62.6	25.0	1.93
Mathematics #1	43	58.2	29.1	120	66.7	27.0	1.74
Mathematics #2	43	62.6	29.1	120	71.0	26.8	1.72
Science	43	52.0	26.8	120	59.4	27.7	1.52

Florida Twelfth Grade Placement Test[a]

Aptitude	26	62.2	29.9	60	68.4	25.8	.96
English	26	54.9	32.1	60	64.3	26.2	1.43
Social studies	26	58.1	24.9	60	57.3	27.5	.13
Reading index	26	56.7	29.1	60	62.5	26.4	.90
Natural science	26	49.2	28.1	60	51.2	29.4	.28
Mathematics	26	63.0	29.1	60	68.8	25.0	.95

PSAT[a]

Verbal	19	42.3	11.8	57	46.3	11.6	1.28
Mathematics	20	48.5	18.0	57	53.8	11.5	1.53

Gates Reading Test[a]

Vocabulary	103	56.0	26.7	195	59.0	29.7	.88
Comprehension	103	56.4	30.1	195	61.0	29.9	1.25

Armed Services Vocational Aptitude Battery[a]

Electrical	24	45.7	24.9	51	40.0	24.3	.93
Motor mechanical	23	36.0	16.6	48	37.8	19.4	.38
General mechanical	23	38.2	21.1	48	38.8	18.0	.13
Clerical/administrative	23	61.0	19.6	48	66.3	15.8	1.22
General technical	23	58.4	23.0	48	65.0	17.2	1.35

California Test of Mental Maturity[a]

IQ	171	104	16.0	287	109	15.3	3.20**

(continued)

Table 8.5 Mean aptitude scores for judgment and perception

Aptitude Measures	Judgment			Perception			
	N	Mean	SD	*N*	Mean	SD	*t*
College and University Students							
University of Florida freshmen and transfers[b]							
Florida Twelfth Grade Placement Test							
	1406	397.6	68.45	1388	408.5	66.38	4.25***
Scholastic Aptitude Test							
Math	635	554.6	88.84	686	558.2	87.96	.75
Verbal	629	514.2	90.00	686	527.7	84.42	2.79**
Medical School Students							
Myers' Longitudinal Study[c]							
Medical School Aptitude Test							
Verbal	2000	504.7	93.3	2324	537.0	93.6	11.34***
Quantitative	2000	507.6	91.9	2324	537.7	92.6	10.70***
General information	1202	494.6	93.7	1311	530.3	94.8	9.47***
Science	1999	514.1	90.9	2322	543.4	89.1	10.65***

* $p<.05$, ** $p<.01$, *** $p<.001$.

Sources and sample descriptions are listed in Appendix B.
[a] McCaulley and Natter (1974)
[b] McCaulley and Kainz (1974)
[c] McCaulley (1977)

Achievement of the Sixteen Types Considered Individually. The MBTI is used with individuals, and individuals' types are the result of the interaction of preferences. Useful information beyond the correlations of the previous sections can be gained by plotting the mean performance of people of each type in terms of various measures. This approach makes it possible to see the outcome of whatever interactions occur among the four preferences in each of the sixteen types. In this section are a series of such plots from data reported by Myers (1962) with her comments about how these data can help a teacher or counselor understand what to expect from each type in learning situations. The data are also relevant to the construct validity of the Indicator.

The plots compare aptitude (as measured by intelligence or scholastic aptitude tests) and achievement (as estimated by grade point averages). Myers explains why the positions of the types shift from sample to sample. She cautions that if one wants an *accurate* portrayal of the natural scholastic behavior of each type, the plots would have to be done at the high school level before dropouts, and before self-selection to careers and the sorting of students into different institutions and different fields of study by selection committees.

Aptitude and Achievement for the Sixteen Types in High School. Figure 8.2 shows the positions of the types when grade point average is plotted against intelligence scores in a sample of 3,503 male college preparatory high school students from twenty-seven Pennsylvania high schools.

The regression line is drawn to represent the correlation of .47 between grades and IQ in the total sample. A number of facts can be seen from Figure 8.2:

1. All the J types but ESFJ are above the line and all P types but INTP are below the line. The J types consistently achieve higher grades for a given amount of aptitude; that is, they overachieve. The P types get grades lower than expected for their level of aptitude; that is, they underachieve.

2. Both INT types are high, but INTJ is three times as far above the line as INTP. Both ESF types are low, but

ESFP is two and one-half times as far below as ESFJ. These differences show the clear advantage of J.

3. The range of grade point average mean scores extends more than one standard deviation, from INTJ at the top to ESFP at the bottom.

4. The S types fall near or below the mean in IQ for their classes, and the N types fall near or above the mean.

5. The three preferences that appear to contribute most to scholastic success are I, N, and J. The types that possess all three of these "scholastic preferences," INTJ and INFJ, are quite high. The six types that have two scholastic preferences are well above the sample mean GPA. On the right with higher intelligence scores are the two IN–P types, highly endowed but apt to let their need for autonomy get in the way of "assiduity in the performance of what is required." Nearer the sample mean in intelligence are the EN types, whose assiduity has to compete with the extracurricular activities which relates to the E–T's need for dominance and the E–F's need for affiliation.

6. At the left are the IS–J types whose introverted interest in concepts and ideas combines with the application of J to produce a solid, even, scholastic performance which surpasses their apparent aptitude. The remaining intuitive types, ENTP and ENFP, have achievement near the sample mean, though below their own capabilities as measured by intelligence scores. The rest of the sensing types all average lower on achievement, with three of the bottom four places being held by types with both S and P.

7. The slope of .47 between achievement and aptitude reflects a difference in grades for the types which is greater than can be accounted for by intelligence. The fact that introverts with intuition have the highest mean intelligence scores makes it easy to accept that they also have the highest grades; that is that INFJ and INTJ have the highest grade point average of the J types, and INTP and INFP have the highest grade point average of the P types. It is worthwhile, however, to learn how much of the high achievement of the IN types is accounted for by their type, irrespective of their level of intelligence.

To look at the IN type controlling for intelligence, Table 8.12 compares the IN types that have both intuition and introversion with the corresponding ES types that have neither; this comparison allows a "partialing out" of the effect of preferences except for I and N. The following discus-

Figure 8.2 Comparison of intelligence and grades of the sixteen types in high school

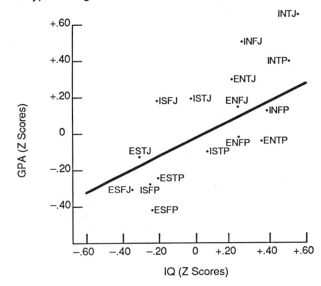

sion gives Isabel Myers' guidelines for interpreting Figure 8.2 and similar figures in the next section.

In the type-to-type comparisons of Table 8.12 the difference between mean IQ of INTJ and ESTJ students, for example, is used to find the expected difference in GPA for those types. The expected difference is estimated, using the correlation of .468 between grades and intelligence in this sample. Of the difference of .794 standard scores between INTJ and ESTJ, intelligence accounts for .399 of the difference, which leaves an equal share of the difference, .395, *not* attributable to intelligence and presumably attributed to other characteristics of IN types.

Table 8.12 demonstrates that a very substantial part of the superior scholastic achievement of the IN types as compared with the ES types cannot be attributed to their intelligence as measured by high school intelligence tests, or to application as measured by preference for J, since the types compared on this table are matched on J and P. Some other influence must be operating, which is strongly associated with the preference for I and N. IN makes approximately as great a difference in scholastic achievement as does the .60 to .85 standard deviations of intelligence that separates the ES types from the IN types of Table 8.12.

Theory and observation favor the hypothesis that the essential difference between IN and ES is a habit of mind that produces, among other results, a characteristic level of interest in activities that suit each type, and a lack of interest in activities that do not. Under this hypothesis, the IN

Table 8.6 Product-moment correlations of intelligence and aptitude tests with MBTI continuous scores

Source and Sample	Measure	N	EI	SN	TF	JP	Relationship
			High School Samples				
(1) High School males	IQ	3,503	.11**	.28**	−.10**	.08	INT-
(1) High School females	IQ	2,511	.10**	.34**	−.01	.14**	IN-P
			College and University				
Liberal arts colleges							
(1) Amherst, males, 1962	SAT-V	245	.19**	.39***	−.05	.20**	IN-P
(1)	SAT-M	245	.12	.18**	−.04	.14*	N-P
(1) Amherst, males, 1963	SAT-V	246	.18**	.40***	.01	.21**	IN-P
(1)	SAT-M	246	.00	.07	*−.06	.03	----
(1) Brown, males, 1962	SAT-V	591	.25***	.34***	−.17***	.08	INT-
(1)	SAT-M	591	.06	.15***	−.16***	.02	-NT-
(1) Dartmouth, males, 1961	SAT-V	663	.12**	.36***	.01	.20***	IN-P
(1)	SAT-M	663	.05	.11**	−.03	.00	-N--
(1) Dartmouth, males, 1963	SAT-V	815	.20***	.34***	−.14***	.18***	INTP
(1)	SAT-M	815	.11**	.11**	−.11**	.00	INT-
(1) Stanford, males, 1963	SAT-V	713	.13***	.40***	.03	.22**	IN-P
(1)	SAT-M	713	.14***	.18***	−.06	.08*	IN-P
(1) Wesleyan, males, 1963	SAT-V	236	.29***	.34***	−.09	.08	IN--
(1)	SAT-M	236	.22***	.22***	−.15*	−.03	INT-
(1)	CMT	236	.29***	.28***	−.08	−.03	IN--
(1) Pembroke, females, 1962	SAT-V	240	.08	.33***	−.01	.03	-N--
(1)	SAT-M	240	.24***	−.06	−.25***	−.05	I-T-
(2) University of Florida							
(2) Florida Twelfth Grade Test		2,824	.13***	.30***	.00	.15***	IN-P
(2) SCAT-V	SCAT	3,141	.13***	.15***	−.02	.07***	IN-P
(2) SCAT-M		3,141	.10***	.08***	−.06**	.03	INT-
(2) SCAT-Total		3,141	.08***	.06	−.02	.03	----
(2)	SAT-V	1,107	.20***	.31***	−.04	.14***	IN-P
(2)	SAT-M	1,107	.14***	.18***	−.10**	.06	INT-
Engineering and science							
California Institute of Technology							
(3) Applicants, 1958	SAT-V	1,616	.11***	.46***	−.35***	.29***	INTP
(3)	SAT-M	1,616	.06	.41***	−.31***	.12***	-NTP
(3) SAT, Chemistry		1,616	.00	.45***	−.38***	.22***	-NTP
(3) SAT, English		1,616	.11***	.38***	−.30***	.16***	INTP
(3) SAT, Mathematics		1,616	.06	.47***	−.29***	.12***	-NTP
(3) SAT, Physics		1,616	.04	.41***	−.34***	.15***	-NTP
(1) Freshmen, 1962	SAT-V	201	.11	.20**	−.12	.17*	-N-P
(1)	SAT-M	201	.03	.07	−.05	−.02	----
(3) SAT, Chemistry		201	−.09	.08	−.14*	.12	--T-
(3) SAT, English		201	.09	.18*	−.12	.07	-N--
(3) SAT, Mathematics		201	.03	.13	−.03	−.05	----

(continued)

Table 8.6 Product-moment correlations of inteligence and aptitude test
with MBTI continuous scores

Source and Sample	Measure	N	EI	SN	TF	JP	Relationship
(3) SAT, Physics		201	.06	.08	−.07	−.03	----
(1) Cornell, 1964	SAT-V	498	.10*	.35***	−.01	.20***	IN-P
(1)	SAT-M	498	.01	.10***	.01	.12**	-N-P
(1) Rensselaer Polytechnic Institute, 1962	SAT-V	771	.16***	.31***	−.11**	.11**	INTP
(1)	SAT-M	771	.00	.15***	.04	.13**	-N-P
College of business							
(1) Wharton School	SAT-V	488	.10*	.30**	−.08	.08	IN--
(1)	SAT-M	488	.06	.08	−.08	-.06	----

Postbaccalaureate and Professional Samples							
<u>Law students</u>							
(4) University of California	LSAT	290	.15*	.26***	−.09	.20***	IN-P
(4) Northwestern University	LSAT	157	.17*	.04	.02	.12	I---
(4) University of Pennsylvania	LSAT	192	−.06	.26***	−.10	.18*	-N-P
(4) University of Virginia	LSAT	237	.20**	.20**	−.06	.18**	IN-P
<u>Seminary students</u>							
(5) GRE, Verbal	GRE-V	60	.24	.16	−.17	−.02	----
(5) GRE, Quantitative	GRE-Q	60	−.05	−.16	−.24	−.10	----
(5) GRE, Analytical	GRE-A	60	−.06	−.05	−.07	.05	----
<u>Physician assistant/nurse practitioners</u> Otis-Lennon Mental Ability							
(6) IQ, males	IQ	47	.15	.22	−.14	.10	----
(6) IQ, females	IQ	51	.27	.11	.07	.14	I---

*p < .05, ** p < .01, ***p < .001.
Notes: Sources and measures are given in Appendix B.
(1) Myers (1962), (2) McCaulley (1973), (3) Stricker, Schiffman, and Ross (1965),
(4) Miller (1967), (5) Harbaugh (1985), (6) Bruhn, Bunce, and Greaser (1978).

types have the greatest *natural* interest in ideas and symbols, and the ES types have the least.

The theory supplies an explanation for the fact that IN types on the whole earn higher grades than predicted from their aptitudes, and thus increase academic achievement differences between IN and ES types. ES types have an interest in learning from "real life" experiences, which leads them to place less emphasis on book learning.

Table 8.13 shows mean aptitude scores of the IN, EN, IS, and ES types for several samples. The theoretical expectation is that the means will rank in the order IN > EN > IS > ES.

In interpreting Table 8.13, it is important not to conclude that ES types are less intelligent than IN types. Scholastic aptitude tests measure the I and N aspects of intelligence particularly valuable in academic work; they are not

Table 8.7 Academic subjects significantly preferred by each type from choices on Form G answer sheet

ISTJ Mathematics Practical Skillls	**ISFJ** Practical Skillls	**INFJ** Art English Music	**INTJ** Science
ISTP Mathematics Practical Skills	**ISFP** Practical Skills	**INFP** Art English Music	**INTP** Art Science
ESTP History Mathematics Practical Skills	**ESFP** History	**ENFP** Art English Music	**ENTP** Art Science
ESTJ Mathematics Practical Skills	**ESFJ** Mathematics Music	**ENFJ** Art English Music	**ENTJ** English Science

Note: Data are from 27, 787 answer sheets in MBTI data bank for question,"Which do you like best: Math, English,science, history, practical skills, music, art?" Choices are shown if they were significantly ($p <. 05$) preferred by that type.

designed to measure the practical, applied intelligence of E and S. Note that EN and IS types often have close aptitude scores. In younger samples, extraverted groups often outscore their introverted counterparts. When the measure is of an applied rather than an academic aptitude, the differences among quadrants are often not significant.

The Sixteen Types in Liberal Arts, Engineering, and Business. The following sections describe Isabel Myers' initial research and discussion of the performance of the sixteen types in male students in liberal arts, engineering, and business. Table 8.14 shows that the three curricula have very different type distributions. Liberal arts were more attractive to NF and IN types, engineering to NJ

types, and business to ES and ST types. Of course, all types are found in all curricula but particular curricula also attract particular types. In these studies, Myers' research questions were as follows:

1. When the types are plotted for aptitude and achievement, is the pattern for the high-ranking and low-ranking types the same regardless of the field of study, or does each field of study have a characteristic pattern of high- and low-ranking types?

2. Are the types that are most interested in a field of study (highest selection ratio) also more likely to get better

Table 8.8 Frequency and mean strength of the preferences in various groups

	N	Preference for E		Preference for I		Preference for S		Preference for N	
		%	Mean E Score	%	Mean I Score	%	Mean S Score	%	Mean N Score
Males									
Junior high school									
Pre-prep, 7th-8th	100	68%	16.9	32%	17.8	72%	19.7	28%	14.9
Gifted, 7th-9th	34	50%	17.5	50%	19.9	21%	20.1	79%	29.1
Senior high school									
Vocational, 12th	701	52%	20.2	48%	18.2	85%	26.6	15%	10.7
General, 12th	148	64%	20.3	36%	18.1	81%	25.0	19%	12.8
Academic, 12th	325	62%	23.1	38%	18.3	60%	21.7	40%	19.5
National Merit									
Finalists	100	42%	20.2	58%	25.6	17%	19.6	83%	30.5
College									
Finance and									
communication	488	70%	22.8	30%	16.6	72%	26.6	28%	16. 0
Liberal arts	2177	54%	21.6	46%	21.5	38%	21.9	62%	25.3
Engineers	2389	48%	21.2	52%	22.5	33%	19.5	67%	26.0
Adult									
College graduates									
Industry-hired	350	65%	25.4	35%	19.4	50%	22.6	50%	21.0
School									
administration	124	59%		41%		58%		42%	
Creative men	115	37%	17.0	63%	23.4	3%	4.3	97%	31.8
Females									
Junior high school									
Pre-prep, 7th-8th	121	75%	21.1	25%	15.9	70%	20.5	30%	15.2
Gifted, 7th-9th	26	58%	26.5	42%	14.6	12%	17.0	88%	22.5
Senior high school									
Vocational, 12th	573	61%	22.3	39%	19.7	88%	26.9	12%	11.5
Academic, 12th	273	68%	25.3	32%	20.0	63%	21.4	37%	19.2
College									
Liberal arts	241	58%	20.6	42%	19.6	30%	16.6	70%	26.4
Adults									
School teachers	248	61%	20.6	39%	21.6	56%	24.4	44%	20.0
Creative women	28	21%	17.3	79%	24.9	4%	23.0	96%	30.3

(continued)

Table 8.8 Frequency and mean strength of the preferences in various groups

	N	Preference for T		Preference for F		Preference for J		Preference for P	
		%	Mean T Score	%	Mean F Score	%	Mean J Score	%	Mean P Score
Males									
Junior high school									
Pre-prep, 7th-8th	100	56%	15.1	44%	11.4	49%	16.1	51%	20.9
Gifted, 7th-9th	34	56%	21.0	44%	15.5	38%	23.6	62%	21.7
Senior high school									
Vocational, 12th	701	51%	13.2	49%	13.2	59%	21.3	41%	20.8
General, 12th	148	49%	11.2	51%	12.4	45%	16.8	55%	21.3
Academic, 12th	325	54%	15.3	46%	13.4	49%	21.6	51%	23.4
National Merit									
Finalists	100	42%	20.2	58%	25.6	17%	19.6	83%	30.5
College									
Finance and									
communication	488	69%	21.2	31%	18.0	53%	19.7	47%	18.9
Liberal arts	2177	54%	18.4	46%	16.9	53%	22.7	47%	24.3
Engineers	2389	68%	20.2	32%	15.0	64%	25.0	36%	22.4
Adult									
College graduates									
Industry-hired	350	82%	22.8	18%	11.4	74%	27.6	26%	19.8
School									
administration	124	55%		45%		86%		14%	
Creative men	115	59%	18.4	41%	19.3	45%	20.3	55%	25.4
Females									
Junior high school									
Pre-prep, 7th-8th	121	41%	11.7	59%	15.7	47%	19.8	53%	22.3
Gifted, 7th-9th	26	42%	13.4	58%	24.5	35%	14.1	65%	22.3
Senior high school									
Vocational, 12th	573	34%	12.3	66%	18.3	63%	23.2	37%	18.7
Academic, 12th	273	32%	14.0	68%	19.3	47%	23.0	53%	21.8
College									
Liberal arts	241	34%	16.5	66%	21.6	45%	19.2	55%	24.1
Adults									
School teachers	248	34%	16.0	66%	21.0	65%	27.8	35%	20.0
Creative women	28	43%	19.2	57%	18.4	36%	19.6	64%	25.4

grades than types less interested, or do the more academic types achieve at a higher level regardless of the curriculum?

Evidence in Chapter 7 showed that each field attracts *relatively* more of some types than others. The attracted types tend to be those types which, in theory, find the activities of the career compatible with their type preferences.

Isabel Myers noted that the influences that cause the composition of a student body or a field of study to vary are not limited to decisions of admissions committees. If the types of all applicants were known, it would be found that

Table 8.9 Product-moment correlations of academic achievement measures with MBTI continuous scores

Source Sample and Measure	*N*	EI	SN	TF	JP	Trend
Myers' Samples of High School and College Students, Grade Point Averages						
Pennsylvania high schools						
Males	3,503	.15***	.19***	−.11***	−.10***	INTJ
Females	2,511	.13***	.25***	−.03	.00	IN--
Liberal arts colleges						
Amherst, males, 1962	245	.09	.13*	−.19**	−.09	-NT-
Amherst, males, 1963	246	.03	.14*	−.05	−.14*	-N-J
Brown, males, 1962	591	.15***	.12**	−.06	−.11**	IN-J
Dartmouth, males, 1961	663	.09*	.16***	−.06	−.11**	IN-J
Dartmouth, males, 1963	815	.19***	.12***	−.02	−.12***	IN-J
Pembroke, females, 1962	240	.10	.03	−.12	−.18**	---J
Stanford, males, 1963	828	.04	.13***	.03	−.07*	-N-J
Wesleyan, males, 1963	236	.18*	.07	−.01	−.24***	I--J
Engineering colleges						
Caltech, males, 1958–61	504	.08	.02	.00	−.22***	---J
Caltech, males, 1962	201	.07	.10	−.07	−.13*	---J
Cornell, males, 1964	498	.11*	.07	−.11*	−.08	I-T-
Rensselaer Polytechnic Institute, males, 1962	771	.08*	.08*	.01	−.09*	IN-J
Finance and commerce						
Wharton School, 1957–58	488	.07	.00	−.13**	−.19***	--SJ
Samples from Other Investigators						
High school achievement						
Rank in class						
(1) Wesleyan, admitted in 1959	225	.13*	.11	−.12	−.10	----
(1) Caltech applicants, 1958	1,616	.03	.18***	−.19***	−.04	-NT-
(1) Caltech, admitted in 1958	201	.05	.06	−.10	−.10	----
(1) GPA, Caltech applicants	1,616	.09***	.40***	−.30**	.04	INT-
College and university achievement						
University of Florida students						
(2) First quarter GPA	2,499	.13***	.10**	.01	−.05**	IN-J
(2) CLEP (College Equivalency)						
(2) English	538	.11**	.24***	.06	.08	IN--
(2) Humanities	531	.15***	.29***	−.08	.08	IN--
(2) Mathematics	468	.04	.04	−.06	.01	----

(continued)

Table 8.9 Product-moment correlations of academic achievement measures with MBTI continuous scores

Source Sample and Measure	N	EI	SN	TF	JP	Trend
University of Florida students						
(2) Biological sciences	496	.13**	.19***	−.10*	.07	INT-
(2) Physical sciences	496	.17**	.20***	−.15*	.08	INT-
(2) Social sciences	542	.20***	.16***	−.15***	.06	INT-
California Institute of Technology						
(1) Four-scale GPA Contingency	201	.20**	.21**	−.11	−.34***	IN-J

Postbaccalaureate and Professional Samples						
Law students (Miller, 1966)						
(3) University of Virginia						
(3) Undergraduate GPA	233	.09	.04	.04	−.15*	---J
(3) First year law school		.24***	−.01	−.18**	−.05	I-T-
(3) University of California						
(3) Undergraduate GPA	290	−.05	−.02	.22***	−.09	--F-
(3) First year law school		.03	.17**	−.05	.10	-N--
(3) University of Pennsylvania						
(3) Undergraduate GPA	192	.02	−.17*	.07	−.31***	-S-J
(3) First year law school		−.13	.09	.02	.09	----
(3) Northwestern University						
(3) Undergraduate GPA	157	−.14	−.09	−.07	−.23**	---J
(3) First year law school		−.02	−.05	−.07	−.04	----
Seminary students (Harbaugh, 1984)						
(4) College GPA	60	.35**	.08	−.02	−.29*	I--J
(4) Seminary GPA, first quarter	60	.13	.19	.20	−.16	----
(4) Seminary GPA, first two quarters	60	.16	.19	.22	−.15	----
Physician assistants/nurse practitioners						
(5) National Board Scores, males	11	.01	.35	−.08	.21	----
(5) National Board Scores, females	13	.21	.19	−.02	.38	----
(5) GPA on graduation, males	24	.17	.23	.03	−.01	----
(5) GPA on graduation, females	27	.12	−.28	−.03	−.07	----

*p < .05, ** p < .01, ***p < .001.
Notes: Sources and measures are given in Appendix B.
Myers samples were taken from Myers (1962). (1) Stricker, Schiffman, and Ross (1965), (2) McCaulley (1973), (3) Miller (1967), (4) Harbaugh (1984), and (5) Bruhn, Bunce, and Greaser (1978).

self-selection is as important as selection by admitting officials. Similarly, in considering the scholastic success of the various types in the various fields, it is obvious that more is involved than the student's ability to do the work. The contribution made by type may be either to intellectual competence, persistence, or interest and enthusiasm for the subject.

The three college populations described by Myers are from highly selected academic institutions.[16] The effect of this selection was to truncate the distributions of aptitude for each type as compared to high school and to shorten the range of achievement. For example, the peak types in high school, INFJ and INTJ, are no longer so conspicuous.

Aptitude and Achievement in Liberal Arts Students. Selection operates to reduce the range of grades in liberal arts students compared to high school students. In the high school sample, the difference in grades between the highest- and lowest-ranking types was a full standard deviation (INTJ +.68, ESTP −.43). In the liberal arts sample, the range was only one-half as great (INTJ +.39, ESFP −.30).

As Figure 8.3 shows, one effect of the more restricted ranges in the liberal arts students is that INFJ and INTJ are not as conspicuously high as in the high school sample. Nevertheless, these two types still have the highest grades. The six types with just two of the "helpful" preferences (I, N, or J) are spread out even more widely, but rank highest of the sixteen types in grades.

TF appears to play a curious role. In high school samples, T types typically score higher than the corresponding F types. For liberal arts students with higher SAT-V

Table 8.10 Product-moment correlations of grade point averages with S and N preference scores in college samples

	Frequency		Correlation	
School and class	S Types	N Types	S Types	N Types
Liberal arts				
Amherst, 1962	96	146	.01	.10
Amherst, 1963	66	176	-.05	.11
Brown, 1962	241	334	-.04	.11
Dartmouth, 1961	341	312	.03	.18**
Dartmouth, 1963	339	457	-.06	.14**
Stanford, 1963	275	423	.02	.16**
Wesleyan, 1963	76	156	.07	.15
Engineering				
Caltech,				
1958-61,	100	398	.02	-.04
1962	18	180	.17	.05
Cornell, 1964	211	272	-.02	.13*
Rensselaer Poly-				
technic, 1962	321	435	-.05	.07
Finance and Commerce				
Wharton School	351	127	.06	.03

* *p*<.05, ** *p*<.01.

scores, T types achieve higher grades than F types. In the lower half of the sample, every F type has higher grades than the corresponding T type. Thus, not only are feeling types admitted to these liberal arts colleges in greater proportions than the corresponding thinking types but several of them (ESFP and ESFJ) seem to do better than the thinking types once they are in, even with the handicap of lower verbal ability. Since this pattern was not present in high school, it suggests that liberal arts have a special appeal for feeling types.

The liberal arts students show three relationships also found in the high school sample: Intuitives have higher aptitude scores than sensing types, judging types have higher grades, and the IN types score higher on both aptitude and grades than the ES types.

Aptitude and Achievement for Engineering Students. The range of SAT-Mathematics scores for the engineering students is narrow. Figure 8.4 shows that the −N−J and I−−J types showed the highest performance without reference to TF differences. These are the types that were most

Figure 8.3 Comparison of aptitude and achievement of the sixteen types in liberal arts

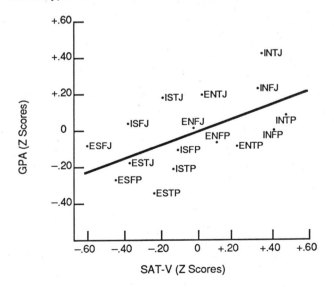

Table 8.11 Mean scores of achievement for MBTI preferences

Measure of Achievement	N	Mean	S.D.	N	Mean	S.D.	t
	Extraverts			**Introverts**			
High school students							
(1) Grades in school: Overall average	284	3.40	.70	229	3.11	.71	.02
English	269	3.10	.95	216	3.18	.95	.87
Mathematics	252	2.85	.98	206	2.94	1.0	.99
Science	213	2.93	1.2	175	2.89	1.1	.33
Social studies	226	2.91	1.1	176	2.85	1.2	.56
College and university samples							
(3) Nicholls State freshmen GPA	619	2.619	.806	389	2.674	.830	1.05
(2) University of Florida freshmen and transfers							
Cumulative GPA	1696	2.714	.583	1563	2.821	.591	5.18***
GPA from high school	1313	2.997	.498	1163	3.101	.506	5.14***
	Sensing			**Intuition**			
Junior high school students							
(4) Eighth grade math students, Stanford Achievement Test							
Math computation	143	56.4	10.5	64	64.0	15.8	3.48***
Math concepts	143	67.9	16.9	64	83.8	21.5	5.21***
Math applications	142	65.2	16.5	64	82.8	20.3	6.05***
Social studies	243	2.76	1.2	159	3.08	1.1	2.71**
College and university students							
(3) Nicholls State freshmen GPA	708	2.600	.827	300	2.736	.775	2.43**
(2) University of Florida freshmen and transfers							
Cumulative GPA	1494	2.712	.585	1765	2.810	.593	4.75***
GPA from high school	1102	3.016	.509	1374	3.069	.500	2.59**
	Thinking			**Feeling**			
High school students							
(1) Grades in school							
Overall average	149	3.15	.67	364	3.10	.72	.75
English	140	3.12	.93	345	3.14	.95	.18
Mathematics	136	2.96	.92	322	2.86	1.0	.98

(continued)

Table 8.11 Mean scores of achievement for MBTI preferences

Measure of Achievement	N	Mean	S.D.	N	Mean	S.D.	t
	Thinking			Feeling			
High school students							
(1) Grades in school							
Science	114	3.05	.97	274	2.85	1.2	1.56
Social studies	114	2.95	1.1	288	2.86	1.2	.70
College and university students							
(5) Nicholls State freshmen GPA	402	2.576	.868	606	2.683	.777	2.04*
(2) University of Florida freshmen and transfers							
Cumulative GPA	1193	2.759	.600	2066	2.768	.587	.45
GPA from high school	882	3.053	.519	1594	3.042	.498	.54
	Judgment			Perception			
High school students							
(1) Grades in school: Overall average	187	3.12	.76	326	3.11	.67	.06
English	178	3.08	.98	307	3.17	.93	.98
Mathematics	170	2.93	1.0	288	2.86	.92	.71
Science	148	2.99	1.2	240	2.87	1.1	1.00
Social studies	150	2.95	1.2	252	2.85	1.2	.85
College and university students							
(3) Nicholls State freshmen GPA	500	2.682	.868	508	2.599	.759	1.61
(2) University of Florida freshmen and transfers							
Cumulative GPA	1618	2.802	.595	1641	2.729	.585	3.53***
GPA from high school	1192	3.096	.513	1284	2.999	.492	4.83***

* $p < .05$, ** $p < .01$, *** $p < .001$.
Notes: Sources and description of samples are listed in Appendix B.
(1) McCaulley and Natter (1974), (2) McCaulley and Kainz (1974), (3) Bourg (1979),
(4) May (1971).

Figure 8.4 Aptitude and achievement of the sixteen types in engineering

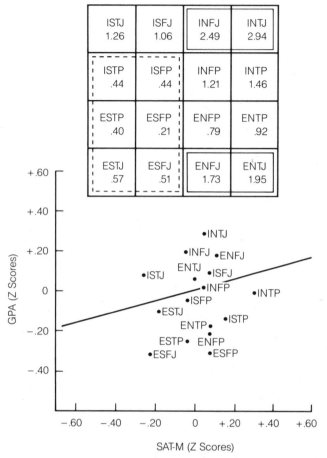

Aptitude and Achievement of Business Students. The data on students from the Wharton School of Finance and Commerce of the University of Pennsylvania (Figure 8.5) presented an informative contrast to the liberal arts and engineering patterns. The lone INFJ in the class had the highest grades despite the lowest interest in business. The following four highest-achieving types were the four "executive" TJ combinations. The highest grades were made by the NTJs, but the NTJs were less frequent in the class than the STJs. The two types who found themselves for the first time in the upper half of the class were ESTJ and ISTP; both types had positive selection ratios for business. Two F types, INFP and ENFP appeared for the first time in the lower half.

Isabel Myers hypothesized that students in fields attractive to their types would find their studies intrinsically interesting and would therefore be more successful. In Table 8.14 types are ranked in terms of theoretical predictions for success in academic studies, based on Isabel Myers' hypo-

Figure 8.5 Aptitude and achievement of the sixteen types in business

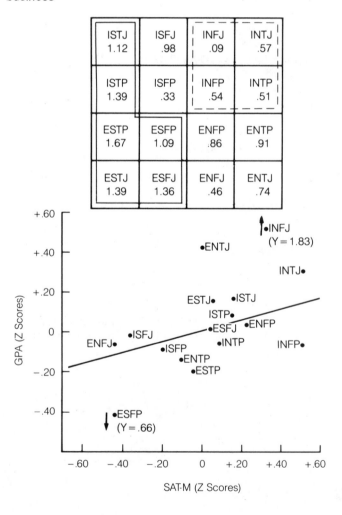

attracted to engineering in this sample. Although the IN–P types were also attracted to engineering, their grades were just average. All the other types were negatively selected (i.e., either less interested or less able to achieve admission) and also achieved below average. The ES–P types had the lowest selection ratios and also had low grades in engineering.

On aptitude measures that focus on verbal skills (such as the SAT-Verbal scores reported for liberal arts students), the difference between rankings of sensing types and intuitive types tends to be greater than on aptitude or intelligence measures when mathematics is included. It was therefore expected that the difference in aptitude among liberal arts S types and N types, estimated from SAT-Verbal, would be greater than the differences in aptitude of S types and N types of engineering or business students, estimated from SAT-Mathematics scores. All other types were less likely to be selected (or to select themselves) into engineering, and their achievement was below average. There seemed to be reasonable agreement between the "type-selection" policies of engineering schools and the achievement of the various types in engineering.

Table 8.12 Difference in achievement and intelligence of IN and ES types

Type	N	GPA Mean	IN-ES Difference	Intelligence Mean	IN-ES Difference	GPA Diff. Attributable to IQ	Residual Difference in Grades
INTJ	131	.685		.554			
			.794		.852	.399	.395
ESTJ	520	−.109		−.298			
INTP	176	.383		.529			
			.630		.742	.347	.283
ESTP	253	−.247		−.213			
INFJ	61	.523		.260			
			.801		.621	.291	.510
ESFJ	227	−.278		−.361			
INFP	131	.132		.340			
			.558		.598	.280	.278
ESFP	191	−.426		−.258			

Note: Based on male students in IN and ES types from the sample of 3,503 college preparatory students in twenty-seven Pennsylvania high schools. Data are expressed in z-score units.

thesis that preferences for N, I, and J contribute to academic achievement. For the three college groups, selection ratios and grade point averages are shown side by side, to enable comparison of interest in the field (ratio) and achievement in the field (GPA). Most comparisons show that positive interest is associated with positive achievement. An exception is found in the business sample, ESTP and ESFP had high interest but performed poorly academically, while the more academically oriented IN types had less interest but performed well.

The interpretation of Table 8.15 for INFJ would be: INFJs were a rare, high-achieving type in high school; they were 2.1% of the male college-bond high school students and they were the second-highest type in grades (.52 standard deviations above the mean of the total sample). They accounted for 5% of liberal arts students and had a high interest in liberal arts (selection ratio of 2.38 shows there were more than twice as many INFJs in liberal arts as would be expected from their numbers in high school). INFJs received higher grades than the average of their liberal arts classmates (+.21 standard scores). INFJs accounted for 5.3% of the engineering students, almost two and one-half times as many (selection ratio 2.49) as expected from their numbers in high school; their interest was matched by their performance, which was .19 standard scores over the average

of engineering students. In contrast, INFJs were rare in the business sample (actually only one person), accounting for less than 1% of the class; the selection ratio shows only about one-tenth of the INFJs one would expect from their base rate, yet despite this lack of interest, the achievement for INFJ was at the top of the class. This fact is an example of the principle that certain types may be less interested in a field and still do well academically, though one would want more data across several samples before predicting to other INFJs in business schools.

The Relationship of Type to Various Measures in Medical School. Figures 8.6 and 8.7 demonstrate the way the types in the same sample can shift depending on the measures used. Figure 8.6 compares the college grades of 370 medical students at Ohio State University with their National Medical Board averages at the end of phase II of medical school. INFJ and ISTJ stand out as having had both high grades and high Board scores. The extraverted feeling types (ESFJ and ENFJ) who have a special concern with service to others were slightly below average in both measures. An unusual pattern was shown by ESTP, a type that typically scores low in traditional liberal arts subjects. These medical school ESTPs achieved above-average grades in college and maintained this standing in their National

Table 8.13 Mean scores of aptitude and achievement for MBTI preference groups IN, EN, IS, and ES

Source of Data Measures	Introverted Intuitive			Extraverted Intuitive			Introverted Sensing			Extraverted Sensing			F
	N	Mean	SD	N	Mean	SD	N	Mean	SD	N	Mean	SD	
Aptitude Measures													
(1) Florida Eighth Grade Test													
Vocabulary	29	76.7	25.9	36	71.6	25.2	34	57.7	25.4	54	64.7	25.3	3.44**
Comprehension	30	76.4	25.7	36	68.4	23.8	35	59.7	24.3	54	64.6	25.8	2.62
Computation	30	67.7	26.3	36	61.8	25.4	35	56.2	26.8	54	63.4	24.9	1.15
Problem solving	30	75.6	25.0	36	70.1	24.9	35	63.3	25.1	54	64.5	27.6	1.64
Everyday living math	30	21.4	5.1	36	20.6	4.2	34	20.0	4.4	54	20.0	4.3	.79
Everyday living reading	31	40.5	5.6	37	40.0	4.3	34	38.4	6.6	54	39.3	5.2	.95
Study skills	31	70.2	29.6	37	66.8	28.4	34	55.7	27.4	54	60.9	25.0	1.87
(1) Florida Ninth Grade Test													
Verbal	32	81.8	15.2	39	70.1	23.8	50	54.8	26.7	42	55.3	21.0	12.33***
Quantitative	32	81.2	21.9	39	68.8	27.8	50	59.5	29.0	42	54.9	24.7	7.05***
Social studies	32	80.2	19.7	39	64.8	26.9	50	50.8	25.7	42	50.2	22.2	12.81***
English	32	75.2	19.4	39	65.6	26.3	50	55.7	25.4	42	49.5	22.5	8.33***
Mathematics #1	32	80.8	22.1	39	69.7	26.7	50	57.1	28.4	42	55.8	25.4	7.53***
Mathematics #2	32	85.0	19.7	39	72.4	26.9	50	60.1	30.0	42	63.5	24.9	6.75***
Science	32	79.9	21.5	39	61.8	26.1	50	47.9	28.0	42	47.6	21.2	13.84***
(1) Florida Twelfth Grade Placement Test													
Aptitude	17	84.2	20.9	21	68.0	27.3	29	65.2	27.3	19	51.0	23.2	5.21**
English	17	80.0	17.9	21	65.2	29.1	29	58.1	29.8	19	45.8	23.2	5.37**
Social studies	17	75.2	27.7	21	60.7	27.7	29	54.7	23.3	19	42.7	20.6	5.31**
Reading index	17	80.5	20.6	21	64.0	27.9	29	57.8	26.4	19	43.9	21.8	6.78***
Natural science	17	75.9	28.5	21	54.4	28.0	29	44.2	24.2	19	33.5	20.9	9.30***
Mathematics	17	82.7	23.6	21	66.1	28.4	29	66.7	26.0	19	54.5	20.4	3.82*
(1) PSAT													
Verbal	17	56.2	12.2	21	47.4	9.8	21	40.1	8.6	17	38.4	8.1	12.22***
Mathematics	17	63.2	7.5	22	50.6	16.4	21	52.2	12.8	17	44.2	8.2	7.12***
(1) Gates Reading Test													
Vocabulary	62	73.9	26.3	62	61.5	27.4	72	49.4	29.4	102	52.3	26.4	11.13***
Comprehension	62	73.3	30.1	62	61.8	31.4	72	52.7	29.3	102	54.3	26.9	7.13***
(1) Armed Services Vocational Aptitude Battery													
Electrical	13	52.0	28.1	18	45.8	24.4	24	41.3	23.6	20	32.3	21.1	1.99
Motor mechanical	13	44.5	22.3	18	36.2	14.9	23	36.9	18.8	17	33.2	18.2	.98
General mechanical	13	46.4	16.5	18	40.1	15.5	23	37.3	20.0	17	32.8	21.5	1.36
Clerical/administrative	13	72.2	18.3	18	70.9	14.5	23	56.1	19.7	17	63.4	9.2	4.00*
General technical	13	76.0	20.6	18	65.7	20.6	23	58.7	18.8	17	55.5	12.4	3.53*
(1) California Test of Mental Maturity													
Overall IQ	84	114.0	15.8	103	111.0	13.8	121	103.0	16.2	150	104	14.7	13.06***
(2) University of Florida freshmen and transfers													
Florida Twelfth Grade Placement Test	679	428.7	55.6	808	407.0	62.25	658	395.8	71.99	649	378.6	70.95	69.17***
SAT													
Math	343	580.5	91.09	417	553.4	84.33	278	554.1	85.51	283	534.2	87.15	15.17***
Verbal	337	560.2	82.61	410	524.1	83.37	276	514.8	85.67	282	476.4	77.98	53.51***

Table 8.13 Mean scores of aptitude and achievement for MBTI preference groups IN, EN, IS, and ES

Source of Data	Introverted Intuitive			Extraverted Intuitive			Introverted Sensing			Extraverted Sensing			
Measures	N	Mean	SD	N	Mean	SD	N	Mean	SD	N	Mean	SD	F
Aptitude Measures													
Medical School Aptitude Test													
(3) Myers' longitudinal study, 1950s													
Verbal	1217	568	92.59	1113	535	90.82	904	498	86.24	1090	477	80.47	237.00***
Quantitative	1217	549	91.43	1113	527	91.39	904	519	91.80	1090	496	91.17	65.41***
General information	1217	553	94.52	1113	526	93.03	904	493	88.36	1090	476	87.85	92.47***
Science	1217	564	89.46	1113	536	88.53	904	520	87.21	1090	493	83.18	131.89***
(4) University of Florida applicants, class of 1976													
Verbal	90	563		119	535		51	509		67	448		9.47***
Quantitative	90	629		119	602		51	560		67	538		13.53***
General information	90	568		119	534		51	524		67	488		13.30***
Science	90	563		119	551		51	519		67	496		8.09***
(4) University of Florida applicants, class of 1977													
Verbal	83	565		75	537		36	540		46	474		9.13***
Quantitative	83	633		75	604		36	559		46	572		5.56***
General information	83	567		75	550		36	547		46	497		6.58***
Science	83	600		75	576		36	554		46	528		7.00***
(4) University of Illinois freshmen, tested 1973													
Verbal	95	562		90	540		40	545		49	518		
Quantitative	95	619		90	617		40	610		49	580		
General information	95	609		90	614		40	599		49	573		
Science	95	573		90	553		40	559		49	538		
(4) University of New Mexico													
Verbal	139	578		137	554		73	550		57	547		2.95*
Quantitative	139	595		137	591		73	597		57	594		0.12
General information	139	570		137	558		73	559		57	534		2.99*
Science	139	579		137	560		73	565		57	556		2.09
(4) Ohio State University													
Verbal	266	570		260	551		181	551		157	522		(na)
Quantitative	266	625		260	614		181	626		157	592		
General information	266	584		260	569		181	560		157	541		
Science	266	592		260	575		181	580		157	559		
Achievement Measures													
(1) Grades													
Overall Average	93	3.30	.68	117	3.16	.7	136	2.98	.71	167	3.08	.70	4.13**
English	90	3.37	.91	106	3.21	1.0	126	3.04	.96	163	3.03	.89	3.13*
Mathematics	88	3.15	.89	101	2.86	1.0	118	2.78	1.10	151	2.83	.95	2.69*
Science	72	3.04	1.10	82	2.96	1.1	103	2.79	1.00	131	2.91	1.20	.78
Social studies	73	3.18	1.10	86	2.99	1.1	103	2.61	1.20	140	2.86	1.20	3.77*
(5) Nicholls State Fr.	108	2.72	.85	192	2.75	.74	281	2.66	.82	427	2.56	.83	2.78*
(2) University of Florida freshmen and transfers													
Cumulative GPA	817	2.89	.58	948	2.74	.60	746	2.75	.61	748	2.68	.56	18.44***
GPA from high school	623	3.14	.50	751	3.01	.49	540	3.06	.51	562	2.98	.51	11.94

* p<.05; ** p<.01; *** p<.001.
Notes: Prediction for ranking of means is IN>EN>IS>ES.
Sources and description of samples are listed in Appendix B.
(1) McCaulley and Natter, 1974, (2) McCaulley and Kainz, 1974, (3) McCaulley (1977),
(4) McCaulley (1976), (5) Bourg (1979).

Figure 8.6 Pre-medical point-hour ratio compared to the National Board average at the end of phase II of medical school

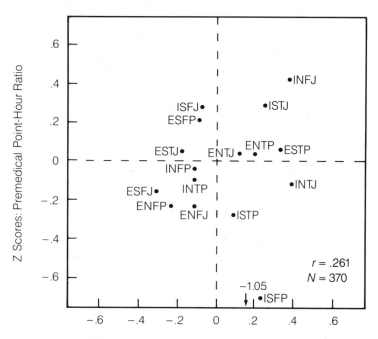

Z Scores: End of Phase II National Board Average

Board scores. Unfortunately, many counselors discourage the ESP types from trying for medical school, so they are underrepresented in premedical students. Other data on the same sample showed the ESTPs ranking high on anxiety, a possible reflection of the need for them to use much more N and J than is characteristic of their type.

Figure 8.7 shows the positions of types of the same students later in their training when they were being rated on clinical abilities. The figure compares ratings of the students on medical expertise and on enthusiastic involvement. The correlation of .89 between these two variables shows that the faculty were not making major distinctions between these two. However, the positions of the types have changed between Figure 8.6 and 8.7. In Figure 8.7, ENFJ is the star, rating highest on both medical expertise and enthusiastic involvement. Six of the eight extraverted types are rated higher for enthusiastic involvement; three of the NP independent spirits (INFP, INTP, and ENTP) received low ratings. In another analysis, they were rated lowest of the types on professional appearance. These medical school data were made available by J. Camiscioni of the Ohio State Medical School for inclusion in McCaulley (1978, pp. 154–64).

Using Type to Predict Aptitude and Grade Rankings. Stricker, Schiffman, and Ross (1965) predicted college grades, first using MBTI continuous scores and then using the sixteen types separately. Although the MBTI did not predict as well as aptitude test scores, the predictions using the sixteen types were more accurate than predictions using the four preferences. Conary (1965) established a ranking of the types based on type theory, then predicted rankings of Auburn University students for males and females separately for aptitude (the subtests and composite aptitude scores of the American College Test) and achievement (based on grade point averages). Rank-order correlations for composite ACT scores were .49 ($p<.05$) for males and .64 ($p<.01$) for females. For grades the rank-order correlations were .81 ($p<.01$) for males and .73 ($p<.01$) for females.

McCaulley (1973) reported rank-order correlations for aptitude on the Florida Twelfth Grade Placement Test (FTGPT), SCAT, SAT, and achievement (first quarter grade point average). In addition, McCaulley predicted rankings for College Level Equivalency Tests (CLEP). In these analyses, the prediction was that the ranks would correspond to those reported for intelligence scores of college preparatory high school male students in Myers (1962, p. B-10). Rank-order correlations were .94 ($p<.01$) for the FTGPT, .92 ($p<.01$) for SCAT-V, .76 ($p<.01$) for SCAT-M, .88 ($p<.01$) for SAT-V, .81 ($p<.01$) for SAT-M, and .58 ($p<.05$) for first quarter grade point averages. For the CLEP subtests, rank-order correlations were .70 ($p<.01$) for English, .82 ($p<.01$) for humanities, .59 ($p<.05$) for mathemat-

Figure 8.7 Clinical ratings for medical expertise compared to clinical ratings for enthusiastic involvement in medical students

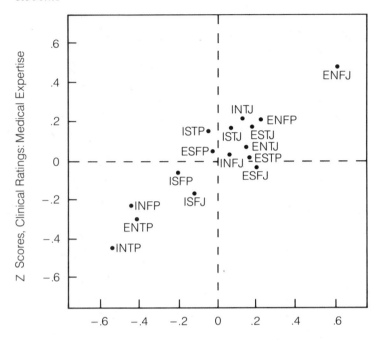

ics, .71 (*p*<.01) for social science, .75 (*p*<.01) for biology, and .67 (*p*<.01) for physical science.

Table 8.16 shows rankings of types and rank-order correlations for aptitude measures. In these analyses, the types are ordered so that N precedes S, I precedes E, T precedes F, and P precedes J. This ordering follows Isabel Myers' hypothesis that N, I, and P, and in some cases T, are important in scholastic aptitude.

Table 8.17 shows rankings of types and achievement scores. In this table, the predicted rankings are modified so that J has priority over P, since Myers considered J important in the application needed for scholastic achievement.

The rankings over samples from young students to graduate students shows that the empirical data match the theory. The rankings highlight unusual situations that alert educators and counselors to special situations. For example, INTP in the Auburn data ranks uncharacteristically low. In practice, teachers and counselors will find some outstanding students in the low-ranking types, and some marginal students in the high-ranking types. The main purpose of these data is to give baseline information from which advisers can evaluate the achievement of specific students. Advisement of typically high-achieving INTJ or INFJ students with low grades will be quite different from advisement of typically lower-ranking ESTP or ESFP with the same problem.

The complex relationship between type preferences and academic achievement can be summarized in three ways:

1. MBTI preferences are associated with academic *aptitude*. To the extent that academic work requires the ability to deal with concepts and ideas (I), and with symbols and abstractions (N), academic aptitude should be, and is, associated with a preference for introversion and intuition.

The relationships between thinking and feeling preferences and both aptitude and achievement are variable. Feeling types tend to score a little higher on aptitude measures that stress verbal abilities, and thinking types on measures that stress analysis. The patterns are less clear at the college level than in high school, and the differences tend to be slight.

The perceptive attitude (P) leads to more curiosity and wider interests. P types tend to score somewhat higher than J types in measures where breadth of information gives high aptitude scores.

Academic aptitude is therefore expected to be relatively more associated with preferences for I, N, and P.

2. *Application* to studies should lead to higher achievement. Judging types tend to be more willing to do what is required and to plan and organize their work. Through

Table 8.14 Attractiveness of five fields of study to the sixteen types

ISTJ		ISFJ		INFJ		INTJ	
High School	8.16%	High School	3.97%	High School	2.11%	High School	4.68%
Ratio		*Ratio*		*Ratio*		*Ratio*	
Engineering	1.26	Medicine	1.23	Science	2.96	Science	3.88
Business	1.12	Liberal Arts	1.06	Liberal Arts	2.38	Engineering	2.94
Liberal Arts	.91	Engineering	1.06	Engineering	2.49	Liberal Arts	1.55
Science	.68	Business	.98	Medicine	1.55	Medicine	1.15
Medicine	.62	Science	.43	Business	.09	Business	.57

ISTP		ISFP		INFP		INTP	
High School	5.14%	High School	4.37%	High School	4.17%	High School	5.97%
Ratio		*Ratio*		*Ratio*		*Ratio*	
Business	1.39	Medicine	1.17	Medicine	1.98	Science	2.92
Medicine	.97	Liberal Arts	.64	Science	1.97	Medicine	1.54
Liberal Arts	.63	Science	.49	Liberal Arts	1.92	Engineering	1.46
Science	.50	Engineering	.44	Engineering	1.21	Liberal Arts	1.31
Engineering	.44	Business	.33	Business	.54	Business	.51

ESTP		ESFP		ENFP		ENTP	
High School	7.74%	High School	6.42%	High School	7.14%	High School	7.88%
Ratio		*Ratio*		*Ratio*		*Ratio*	
Business	1.67	Business	1.09	Liberal Arts	1.43	Science	1.42
Medicine	.71	Medicine	1.09	Medicine	1.22	Liberal Arts	1.03
Liberal Arts	.48	Liberal Arts	.67	Science	1.09	Engineering	.92
Engineering	.40	Engineering	.21	Business	.86	Business	.91
Science	.22	Science	.02	Engineering	.79	Medicine	.82

ESTJ		ESFJ		ENFJ		ENTJ	
High School	15.67%	High School	6.48%	High School	3.54%	High School	6.65%
Ratio		*Ratio*		*Ratio*		*Ratio*	
Business	1.39	Business	1.36	Engineering	1.73	Engineering	1.95
Liberal Arts	.60	Medicine	1.24	Liberal Arts	1.64	Science	1.56
Engineering	.57	Liberal Arts	.92	Medicine	1.42	Liberal Arts	1.13
Medicine	.48	Engineering	.51	Science	1.08	Medicine	.87
Science	.12	Science	.17	Business	.46	Business	.74

Note: Data reported in selection ratios for populations reported in Myers (1962).

Table 8.15 Interest and achievement of the sixteen types in liberal arts, engineering, and business

Type	High School N = 3,503		Liberal Arts N = 3,676			Engineering N = 2,188			Business N = 488		
	%N	GPA	%N	Ratio	GPA	%N	Ratio	GPA	%N	Ratio	GPA
INTJ	4.7	+.68	7.3	1.55	+.39	13.8	2.94	+.28	2.7	.57	+.33
INFJ	2.1	+.52	5.0	2.38	+.21	5.3	2.49	+.19	0.2	.09	+1.83
INTP	6.0	+.38	7.8	1.31	+.12	8.7	1.46	−.01	3.1	.51	−.06
INFP	4.2	+.13	8.0	1.92	+.05	5.0	1.21	+.01	2.3	.54	−.08
ENTJ	6.6	+.26	7.5	1.13	+.17	13.0	1.95	+.06	4.9	.74	+.45
ENFJ	3.5	+.14	5.8	1.64	+.01	6.1	1.73	+.17	1.6	.46	−.07
ENTP	7.9	−.01	8.1	1.03	−.09	7.3	.92	−.18	7.2	.91	−.14
ENFP	7.1	−.00	9.6	1.34	+.07	5.7	.79	−.21	6.1	.86	+.05
ISTJ	8.1	+.16	7.3	.91	+.17	10.1	1.26	+.07	9.0	1.12	+.17
ISFJ	4.0	+.14	4.2	1.06	+.03	4.2	1.06	−.15	7.2	1.39	+.08
ISTP	5.1	−.10	3.3	.63	−.23	2.2	.44	−.05	1.4	.33	−.09
ISFP	4.4	−.26	2.8	.64	−.12	1.9	.44	−.05	1.4	.33	−.09
ESTJ	15.7	−.11	9.3	.60	−.16	9.0	.57	−.10	21.7	1.39	+.16
ESFJ	6.5	−.28	5.9	.92	−.09	3.3	.51	−.32	8.8	1.36	+.01
ESTP	7.7	−.25	3.8	.48	−.35	3.1	.40	−.26	12.9	1.67	−.20
ESFP	6.4	−.43	4.3	.67	−.30	1.3	.21	−.30	7.0	1.09	−.66

Note: Ratio is the selection ratio computed by dividing the number of types in the major by the expected frequency based on the percentage of the types in college preparatory high school students. Grade point averages are expressed in z-score units.

their application, J types often achieve higher grades than would be expected from their aptitude scores.

3. *Interest,* which comes from working with tasks that fit one's preferred style of perception and judgment should in theory, and often does in fact, supplement aptitude and application and lead to higher achievement.

Achievement as Shown by Student Programs. Achievement levels can be inferred by the types of students in remedial programs, and the students receiving scholarships or academic honors.

Students in Remedial Programs. Sensing types are more frequent in the population in general, and in poor readers. One would expect, therefore, that sensing types would be frequent in students volunteering for or assigned to remedial programs. Table 8.18 describes preferences of students in such programs.

The high school students in difficulty have a clear preference for S, F, and P. Also, the spontaneous extraverted EP types who can be expected to find traditional school constraining are frequently found among the students in difficulty. In college, the students with academic difficulty are

also likely to be S and F, but more of them are J than P. Perhaps their J persistence has enabled them to persist enough to achieve college entrance. Nisbet, Ruble, and Schurr (1982) discuss their observations of the kinds of suggestions they use with students of different types in a remedial program. Their counseling increased retention significantly. The strategies that were successful are consistent with type theory. For example:

- Sensing types needed to be taught how to generalize beyond immediate facts.

- Intuitive types needed to become more accepting of traditional instruction and testing. They had to learn not to make multiple-choice questions more complex than the instructor intended.

- SP types were the most challenging students who had to be helped to accept practice and routine. Rewards for study with risk-taking situations, such as contact sports, made learning tolerable.

- Ns were coached to pay more attention to details and not rely solely on their understanding of general concepts.

Table 8.16 Comparison of ranks predicted from theory with actual rankings of the MBTI types for aptitude

Type	Pred.	Myers[1]	Mebane[2]	Fla HS[3]	SAT-V[4]	SAT-M[5]	SAT-M[6]	Conary[7]	Conary[8]	UF Male[9]	UF Fem[10]	MCAT-V[11]	Dunning[12]
INTP	1	2.0	6	4	1	1	7	9	16	2	2	2	5
INFP	2	3.0	3.5	3	2	9	1	16	3	5	3	1	1
INTJ	3	1.0	3.5	2	3	8	2	1	1	1	1	3	8
INFJ	4	5.0	11	6	4	12	3	2	6	4	4	4	7
ENTP	5	4.0	1	1	5	4	12	3	4	3	6	5	10
ENFP	6	7.0	2	16	6	6	4	14	5	6	7	6	4
ENTJ	7	8.0	5	5	7	10	10	5	2	10	12	9	12
ENFJ	8	6.0	7	9	8	3	15	12	7	8	10	7	11
ISTP	9	9.0	12	8	10	2	5	8	15	12	11	8	8
ISFP	10	14.0	9	13	9	12	13	13	10	9	8	12	2
ISTJ	11	10.0	16	7	11	16	6	6	9	7	5	14	3
ISFJ	12	11.0	14	15	14	6	14	4	8	11	9	10	13
ESTP	13	12.0	13	11	12	12	11	10	11	13	16	13	5
ESFP	14	13.0	15	14	15	6	16	15	12	14	15	11	15
ESTJ	15	15.0	10	10	13	14	9	11	14	15	13	16	16
ESFJ	16	16.0	8	12	16	15	8	7	13	16	14	15	14
Rho		.950	.643	.682	.982	.479	.541	.174	.506	.921	.841	.947	.538
p		.01	.01	.01	.01	.05	.05		.05	.01	.01	.01	.05

Note: Details of samples will be found in Appendix B.

[1] Myers high school boys (IQ), ($N = 3,503$)
[2] Mebane eighth graders, Otis-Lennon Deviation IQ, ($N = 133$) (McCaulley and Kainz, 1976)
[3] Florida ninth through twelfth graders IQ, ($N = 458$) (McCaulley and Natter, 1974)
[4] Myers liberal arts students, SAT-V ($N = 3,676$)
[5] Myers, engineering students, SAT-M ($N = 2,188$)
[6] Myers, Wharton School, SAT-M ($N = 488$)
[7] Conary, Composite ACT, males ($N = 1,191$)
[8] Conary, Composite ACT, females ($N = 518$)
[9] UF Freshmen, follow-up, males, SAT-V ($N = 741$)
[10] UF Freshmen, follow-up females, SAT-V ($N = 564$)
[11] Myers, freshmen medical, MCAT-V ($N = 4,324$)
[12] Dunning, Scripps College students, SAT-V ($N = 611$)

- NF types benefited from personal counseling and ways to redirect extreme idealism.

Type Differences in Independent Study Programs. The previous section discussed students with problems adjusting to the academic environment which resulted in poor academic achievement. An achieving group that also resists traditional teaching is made up of students seeking independent study. Table 8.19 shows the distribution of preferences for students electing programs of independent study. The expectation from theory is that independent study will attract more Ns, more Ps and more Is, and the data confirm the prediction. Other data come from answers of high school students (McCaulley & Natter, 1974). Significantly more intuitive types answered "True" to the statements:

Self instructional courses help me. (p<.01)
I like courses that throw me on my own initiative. (p<.001)

In a cluster analysis of University of New Mexico medical students, Otis (1972) identified twelve subject types.

Table 8.17 Comparison of ranks predicted from theory with actual rankings of the MBTI types for grade point average

Type	Pred.	Myers[1]	Myers[2]	Myers[3]	Myers[4]	Conary[5]	Conary[6]	UF Male[7]	UF Fem[8]	Dunning[9]	Myers[10]	Fla HS[11]
INTJ	1	1	1	1	3	1	5	1	2	14	2	10
INFJ	2	2	2	2	1	2	1	3	1	15	3	1
INTP	3	3	5	8	10	13	12	2	11	15	7	3
INFP	4	8	6	7	12	4	4	4	8	6	4	4
ENTJ	5	4	3.5	6	2	3	2	6	4	7	5	5
ENFJ	6	6	8	3	11	5	7	8	9	1	1	9
ENTP	7	10	10.5	12	14	9	14	10	14	16	8	6
ENFP	8	9	9	13	7	8	3	11	7	9	12	7
ISTJ	9	5	3.5	4.5	4	6	9	7	3	12	14	16
ISFJ	10	6	7	4.5	9	7	15	5	5.5	3	11	13
ISTP	11	11	14	11	6	14.5	16	12	16	8	13	8
ISFP	12	14	12	9	13	11	13	15	13	4	16	15
ESTJ	13	12	13	10	5	11	6	14	10	4	10	2
ESFJ	14	15	10.5	16	8	11	8	9	5.5	11	9	11
ESTP	15	13	16	14	15	14.5	10.5	13	12	12	6	12
ESFP	16	16	15	15	16	16	10.5	16	15	10	15	14
Rho		.904	.868	.752	.479	.774	.458	.862	.536	−.021	.674	.541
p		.01	.01	.01	.05	.01	.05	.01	.05		.01	.05

Note: Details of samples will be found in Appendix B.

[1] Myers, high school Males ($N = 3,503$)
[2] Myers, liberal arts Males ($N = 3,676$)
[3] Myers, engineers ($N = 2,188$)
[4] Myers, business ($N = 488$)
[5] Conary, males ($N = 1,191$)
[6] Conary, females ($N = 518$)
[7] UF Freshmen, cumulative GPA, males ($N = 741$)
[8] UF Freshmen, cumulative GPA, females ($N = 564$)
[9] Dunning, cumulative GPA ($N = 611$)
[10] Myers, medical ($N = 4,324$)
[11] Florida, ninth through twelfth grade ($N = 513$)

Independent study was significantly preferred by the "loners" made up of ten IN–P types; by the eleven "ideal students," ten of whom were INT types; and by the thirteen "managers," nine of whom were ENTJ. Independent study was significantly disliked by the eleven "introverted pragmatists," ten of whom were IS types; and by the seven "anxious avoiders," six of whom were NP types. Independent study was neither significantly liked nor disliked by a group labeled "disillusioned idealists," which consisted entirely of NP types.

These data suggest that a preference for independent study is more likely to be found in students who prefer I, N, and P, and who are reasonably confident and satisfied with their academic progress. When entire type tables are examined, the sensing type most likely to be attracted to independent study is ISTJ.

Type Differences in Progress through School. Every college has many students who are undecided about their major field of study, or who change majors an unusual

Table 8.18 MBTI preferences of students in remedial educational programs

Source	Sample and Data

Golanty-Koel
(1978)
Middle-class students in alternative schools in California
because of problems in traditional schools:

Males	$N = 65$	55% E	71% S	52% T	71% P	41% EP
Females	$N = 82$	56% E	50% S	76% F	76% P	44% EP

Szymanski (1977) Students in an alternative school in Florida (ability to learn but
under grade level and problems with truancy or behavior):

Males	$N = 84$	51% I	69% S	73% F	64% P	32% EP
Females	$N = 34$	56% E	53% S	76% F	65% P	38% EP

Metts (1979) Adolescents living in the Northeast, 85 males and 28 females, ages
12–18, classified as learning disabled, of normal intelligence,
underachieving, and not diagnosed emotionally disturbed:

$N = 113$	50% I	67% S	59% F	62% P	30% EP

McCaulley and
Natter (1974) Mildly disruptive students in a university school:

Males	$N = 94$	53% E	62% S	64% F	67% P	34% EP
Females	$N = 62$	64% E	58% S	86% F	66% P	48% EP

Chaille (1982) Compared 100 suspended and not suspended students from the
same high school:

Suspended significantly more EP, SP; not NJ, SJ.

McCaulley (1974) Two-year sample of male and female university students in special
services and remedial program:

M & F	$N = 289$	56%E	81% S	55% F	74% J	13% EP

Bourg (1979) Entering students in small Southern university assigned to remedial
placement:

M & F	$N = 516$	61% E	80% S	54% F	54% J	28% EP

Nisbet, Ruble,
and Schurr
(1982)
Midwest university students in an academic opportunity program
for high-risk students:

Males	$N = 1071$	64% E	64% S	61% T	50% J	31% EP
Females	$N = 1064$	66% E	72% S	60% F	62% J	26% EP

Table 8.19 MBTI preferences associated with independent study

Description of Sample	Percentage of Each Preference					
	N	EI	SN	TF	JP	NP
High school students						
Barberousse (1975)						
Interdisciplinary humanities	100	50% E	79% N	75% F	77% P	66%
Independent study	42	55% I	93% N	70% F	90% P	86%
Medical students						
Ohio State						
Traditional program	765	54% I	54% N	52% F	66% J	25%
Independent study	438	58% I	75% N	50% T	52% P	43%
University of Illinois						
Traditional	222	51% E	66% N	53% T	57% J	36%
Independent scholars	72	57% I	86% N	60% F	60% P	57%

Notes: The high school students volunteered for an experimental interdisciplinary course in humanities, and a subgroup of students wished to work even more independently.

The Ohio State data were made available by J. Camiscioni. The data cover five classes 1970–74. Early (1983) reported on the two medical student programs and confirmed that the independent study students continued to have more Ns and Ps than the traditional program.

The Illinois data were made available by A. Rezler and C. Johns.

number of times. Bourg (1979) reported that P types significantly (ratio 1.26, $p<.05$) were undecided, especially the EP types (ratio 1.41, $p<.001$). McCaulley (1974) also found that P types were more likely to take longer deciding on a field of study than J types (ratio 1.10, $p<.05$). Engineering student data from a composite of eight schools (McCaulley, Kainz, Macdaid, and Harrisberger, 1982) reported that undecided students were significantly less likely to be T (ratio .91, $p<.01$) or J (ratio .87, $p<.01$).

Macdaid, Kainz, and McCaulley (1984), in a ten-year follow-up of the University of Florida Longitudinal Study, analyzed data on attrition and on the time taken to graduate. The "super-dependable" introverted sensing types had the highest rate of graduation (ISTJ ratio 1.12, $p<.01$; ISFJ ratio 1.24, $p<.001$). Four types significantly more often did not graduate (ESFP ratio 0.88, $p<.01$; ENTP ratio 0.89, $p<.05$; ENTJ ratio 0.88, $p<.05$; and ISTP ratio 0.80, $p<.01$).[17]

Only 406 or 22% of the graduates did *not* change their major, though most changes were in subspecialties of the same area of study. J types were more likely to keep their initial major (J ratio 1.11, $p<.05$). Thirty-six percent of the

original freshman class did not graduate: males who dropped out were significantly more likely to be the action-oriented innovators (EN ratio 1.19, $p<.01$) and *not* the practical matter-of-fact STs (ratio 0.81, $p<.05$) or SJs (ratio 0.85, $p<.05$). Females who did not graduate were the more academically vulnerable SP types (ratio 1.23, $p<.05$) and the sympathetic and friendly SF types (ratio 1.15, $p<.05$). The EN types who were more frequent in male dropouts were significantly less frequent in female dropouts (EN ratio 0.86, $p<.05$).

The Florida ten-year follow-up found that the FJs were most likely to graduate early (ratio 1.22, $p<.05$) and the TPs late (ratio 1.38, $p<.05$). As would be predicted from theory, the NT types were more likely to have continued to graduate school (ratio 1.30, $p<.05$). The types significantly *not* continuing to graduate school were the ES types (ratio 0.68, $p<.01$) and the SP types (ratio 0.58, $p<.01$).

Uhl, et al., (1981) make an important point in considering type differences in attrition. Different fields of study attract different types, and attrition rates for any type can best be explained by including information about the match or mismatch with modal types in the student's major. A major contribution to understanding type differences in attrition can be made by those colleges and universities who test the entire freshman classes, if they conduct follow-up studies of their students. Students successful in one school or field of study will be more likely to drop out in a different setting or major. For example, the second author (MHM) knows of a college with a religious affiliation whose students are mainly feeling types. The school loses almost all of its thinking types between the freshman and sophomore year. In another school, with many social and recreational activities, there is a high retention rate for ESFPs, a type likely to drop out of more rigorous academic environments.

Type Differences in How Students Learn

This section reports representative studies on type differences in student learning and how teachers are intervening to improve learning as a function of type. This is a relatively new and rapidly growing area of MBTI research. Early studies related learning styles to individual preferences. Later work has attempted to deal with the complexity of type differences.

Eggins (1979) carried out an aptitude by treatment by interaction study of the effects of three methods of teaching 350 sixth graders how to classify animals into vertebrate and invertebrate groups. The students were taught by slides and audiotape structured by three different learning models. The three methods were based on three concept attainment models: (*a*) an inductive approach based on Bruner's model, (*b*) a didactic approach using Ausubel's advance organizer model, that helps students see links between already familiar concepts and new material, and (*c*) a highly structured presentation using concrete examples and moving from concrete examples to more abstract concepts, following Gagne's model.

Bruner's model imposes the least structure on learners by providing an opportunity for them to see common characteristics and relationships for themselves. The Bruner approach should be helpful to intuitive types. Gagne's model presents a linear structure that should be useful for sensing types. Ausubel's model presents facts in a structured way, like Gagne, but the advanced organizer is designed to help students relate facts to concepts. The Ausubel model should be a bridge for both sensing and intuition.

Students were randomly assigned to one of the three methods of teaching animal classification. In addition to the MBTI, "crystallized intelligence" (as measured by reading comprehension), "fluid intelligence" (as measured by the Figures Analysis Test), and field dependence (as measured by the Group Embedded Figures Test) were measured. Attainment was measured by an immediate posttest and by a delayed posttest ten days later.

Key findings related to the MBTI in the complex analyses are shown in Table 8.20 and summarized below.

- Intuitive types benefited most from Bruner's less-structured, inductive approach, whether they were field dependent or field independent.

- Sensing types learned better with the Gagne method if they were field dependent and the Ausubel method if they were field independent.

- The students with higher crystallized intelligence scores all received scores on the posttest above the mean, regardless of teaching method.

- For judging types, Gagne's approach was more effective with those with low crystallized intelligence. Ausubel or Bruner was more effective for the J types with high crystallized intelligence.

- For perceptive types, Gagne was the most effective for students in the high crystallized intelligence group. Ausubel was more effective with the low intelligence group.

- Students were retested ten days after the original presentation. Eggins reports results only for those in the lower crystallized intelligence group. The NP students in the low group recalled more if they had been taught by Bruner's method.

- The SJ and NJ types succeeded with all three models. The SP and NP types were significantly affected by the instructional design. The NP types were benefitted by the inductive Bruner design; they remembered significantly less if taught by the Gagne method. The SP types, who show the greatest challenge to traditional schools, were most successful with the highly structured Gagne design, which gave them many concrete examples and took advantage of their observational skills, where success was likely to be greatest.

Eggins mentioned other significant MBTI findings, but did not give the direction or discuss them since they were not relevant to her original hypotheses. She concluded that scales of the MBTI do interact in the immediate outcome and later outcomes of learning.

The Eggins study is used to introduce this discussion of type differences in how children learn, as a reminder that many variables enter into learning. Eggins' findings with children as young as sixth grade are important because (*a*) type differences in learning can be seen in young students, (*b*) the data show the complexity of type differences in learning, and (c) they provide suggestions to teachers of ways to teach the sensing and perceptive types who are most likely to have difficulty in schools.

The MBTI is being used widely in learning and study skills centers to help students gain better control of their learning, and by teachers to understand why they reach some students more easily than others. Lawrence (1984) reviews developments in this rapidly changing use of type theory.

Extraverts in high school (McCaulley and Natter, 1974) and in adult learning groups (Haber, 1980; Kilmann and Taylor, 1974) enjoyed learning in groups. Introverts not only did not see experiential training as helpful, but were seen by peers as not participating.

Television and audiovisual aids are appreciated by sensing types (McCaulley and Natter, 1974) who may benefit from having them repeated (Golanty-Koel, 1978). Mathematics laboratory exercises are helpful to sensing types (Golliday, 1975) as are other laboratories and demonstrations (Roberts, 1982), except experiential laboratories or interpersonal laboratories, which find more favor with intuitive types (Kilmann and Taylor, 1974). Memorizing is relatively easy for sensing types (Hoffman, Waters, and Berry, 1981), but they tend to be slower to generalize from examples to concepts (Yokomoto and Ware, 1981) or from reading material to real life (Golanty-Koel, 1978). Sensing types set modest academic goals for themselves (Grant, 1965a; McCaulley and Natter, 1974; and Sachs, 1978), and they try to meet these goals by planning their time and working in a systematic way (McCaulley and Natter, 1974).

Intuitive types prefer self-paced learning and courses that let them study on their own initiative (Carlson and Levy, 1973; McCaulley and Natter, 1974; and Smith, Irey, and McCaulley, 1973). Intuitive types report feeling academically superior to other students and expect to achieve higher grades (Grant, 1965a; Sachs 1978). They like examinations that include essay questions (Grant, 1965a), and the faculty see them as making more insightful comments in class than do the sensing types (Carskadon, 1978).

The preference for objectivity and logical order of thinking types shows in their preference for structured courses with clear goals (Smith, Irey, and McCaulley, 1973) and for teacher lectures and demonstrations (McCaulley and Natter, 1974; Carlson and Levy, 1973; Smith, Irey, and McCaulley, 1973). Feeling types report preferences for working on group projects (McCaulley and Natter, 1974) and in human relations laboratories (McCaulley, 1978; Haber, 1980; and Steele, 1968). Feeling types are also more likely to report interference with their studies because of their social life (McCaulley and Natter, 1974).

Judging types, who were shown in earlier sections to have higher grades than would be predicted from their aptitude, significantly more often say that they work efficiently according to their schedules, get their assignments

Table 8.20 Effectiveness of three ways of teaching

Immediate Posttest		
	Field Dependent	Field Independent
Sensing	Gagne	Ausubel
Intuitive	Bruner	Bruner
	Lower Intelligence	Higher Intelligence
Judging	Gagne	Ausubel or Bruner
Perceptive	Ausubel	Gagne

Less Intelligent Students: Ten Day Lapse Posttest		
	Judging	Perceptive
Sensing	Ausubel, Bruner, or Gagne	Gagne
Intuitive	Ausubel, Bruner, or Gagne	Bruner

in on time (McCaulley and Natter, 1974), and benefit from study skills courses (Fretz and Schmidt, 1966). Judging types prefer to learn from material presented in an orderly way, and through workbooks, lectures, or demonstrations (McCaulley and Natter,1974; Carlson and Levy, 1973; Smith, Irey, and McCaulley, 1973).

Perceptive types are more likely to report starting too late on assignments, letting their work pile up, and having to cram at the end (McCaulley and Natter, 1974). In experiential learning situations perceptive types are seen as more open and more effective in identifying issues (Kilmann and Taylor, 1974).

This section covers only representative examples of research findings at different levels of education. Keirsey and Bates (1978) report on their observations made over the years.

As Myers predicted, the largest number of differences are between S and N. Sensing types appear to like and do better in laboratory activities that teach specific content (for example, mathematics) in an organized way. Intuitive types like human relations laboratories, where flexibility and understanding of nuances of behavior are required. In the early research on the MBTI, human relations training was clearly disliked by I, S, T, and J, and participants saw people with these preferences as less helpful to the group.

Experts in adult learning and organizational development use the MBTI extensively in organizations, and have found exercises capitalizing on type differences that are liked and appreciated by these types. Examples of such exercises can be found in Hirsh (1985) and Mitroff and Kilmann (1975).

Type Differences in Reading and Writing

Reading and writing, which are essential to academic success, involve the use of symbols to communicate ideas.

Reading. In type theory, the function concerned with symbols is intuition. The function concerned with affiliation and the wish to communicate is feeling. The attitude concerned with ideas is introversion. The prediction from theory is that reading should be associated primarily with N and secondarily with I and F. Research data and classroom observations support this theoretical prediction.

Guttinger (1974) found significantly more Ns in the top third of scores on Reading Test-A for 198 students in a university laboratory school ($p<.001$) and in a rural high school ($p<.05$). McCaulley and Natter (1974) found significant differences in the Gates Reading Test Vocabulary ($p<.01$) and Comprehension ($p<.001$) scales in favor of intuitive types in a sample of 164 university laboratory school students. Tillman (1976) reported that significantly more poor readers among 50 students in an Upward Bound program were S and T. The Fs gained more from the program that involved reading training and personal counseling. Myers (1962, B-8) reported significant correlations in the predicted direction on the Davis Reading Test for 236 Wesleyan students. Correlations for reading level were: EI .21 ($p<.01$); SN .34 ($p<.01$); TF – .02; and JP .10. For reading speed they were: EI .17 ($p<.01$); SN .31 ($p<.01$); TF – .04; and JP .14 ($p<.05$). Millott (1975) reported small but statistically significant differences on the McGraw-Hill Reading Test for 2,258 freshmen at the University of Florida in favor of I, N, and P.

Students entering the Ohio State University Medical School were asked about their interest in various kinds of remedial courses. Extraverts ($p<.01$) and sensing types ($p<.001$) significantly requested training in reading (McCaulley 1978, p. 168). Intuitive types reported reading significantly more books in samples of students in an alternative school (Golanty-Koel, 1976) and in a sample of educators (Hicks, 1984).

The size of predicted differences between sensing and intuitive types in reading varies with the homogeneity of the sample, but the data are consistent and pose important issues for educators. Since the majority of the general population are sensing types and most learning activities require reading, the failure to learn good reading skills in the early school years has significant implications to: (*a*) school achievement, (*b*) disruptive behavior (that has been shown to be more frequent with poor readers), and (*c*) school dropouts. Myers with Myers (1980) and Lawrence (1982) discuss these issues and give suggestions for solutions.

Writing. The research on styles of writing of the MBTI types is recent and much of it is concerned with writing of college students. Kramer (1977) studied expository writing of students in creative writing in Michigan and England. Kramer reported that introverts and extraverts did not differ in achievement in expository writing, but that introverts were more interested and had higher achievement in creative writing. Intuitive types achieved higher grades than sensing types. The combination of N with T and J was associated with higher achievement in expository writing, and N with T and P was associated with higher achievement in creative writing.

Held and Yokomoto (1983) reported MBTI differences in engineering technology students in a technical report writing course. The best papers were written significantly more often by NJ and EJ types. Papers of NF types were more likely to be graded average, and ISTs' papers were more likely to be graded poor. S students tended to itemize facts without an overview; N students gave a vague overview without specific facts or focus.

Jensen and DiTiberio (1984) reported on a series of studies in an ongoing effort to understand type differences in writing. Representative examples from these early findings are as follows:

Extraverts and Introverts. Extraverts write with little planning and benefit from discussing their drafts. Students with writing blocks found that giving a talk on the topic helped them focus for writing.

Introverts tend to have less difficulty writing, write more often alone, are reluctant to ask advice, and do a good deal of writing in their heads, on paper, and rewriting.

Sensing and Intuition. Sensing types like to start with factual, verifiable data and what they have learned. They need help in sorting the irrelevant facts from the relevant. Intuitive types often start with the meaning of complex events, and may overlook details essential to the reader's understanding. Intuitives write more easily than sensing types, but may be blocked in a search for originality, even in simple memoranda.

Thinking and Feeling. Thinking types are more likely to organize their writing into clear categories, and focus on clarity to the point that they forget to interest the audience.

Feeling types are less likely to follow an outline as closely as a thinking type. Feeling types may be blocked in their attempts to find the right word to capture the reader's interest and are more likely than thinking types to overstate their points for emphasis.

Judgment and Perception. Judging types tend to set goals and deadlines for their material. In writing, judging types may focus too soon or cut too much in a revision; if they have collected inadequate data before writing, their writing becomes slow and painful. Perceptive types tend to gather information indefinitely and have trouble limiting themselves to meeting deadlines. Perceptive types' first drafts are likely to be long and thorough, and to need focus and cutting for the final product.

Type and Teaching

Previous sections describe type differences in the learning process. Teachers are accustomed to taking into account differences in age, sex, development, and ability. In addition to these and other differences in students, type theory indicates that teachers have up to sixteen types to teach, each with individual patterns of aptitude, interests, and application. The teaching is complicated because a teacher falls into one of the sixteen types, and can be expected to begin with a teaching style natural to his or her own type. When type differences are taken seriously, teachers feel challenged to teach in ways not natural to themselves, in order to reach students of opposite types. Good teachers who learn about type report that in one sense they are learning what they already know: that some children do better with a step-by-step, hands-on approach (S), whereas others learn best from books that challenge their imaginations (N). Good teachers recognize that there are children for whom appreciation is essential to learning (F), and others for whom appreciation means little, but for whom clarity of presentation is everything (T). Teachers know there are children actively attuned to changes around them (E), and other quieter children who occasionally astonish them with their depth of understanding (I). And teachers know there are children who thrive on structure and clear guidelines (J) and other children who are free spirits, imprisoned by the same structure that gives security to their classmates (P). Teachers report that a knowledge of type differences makes teaching at once more complex, and more simple. The observations about differences are organized by type theory into patterns that give teachers a renewed sense of power in their teaching. Teachers report less guilt when they cannot reach certain students. Communication among teachers increases, as teachers of

opposite types use their own differences to understand puzzling students.

Lawrence (1982) introduces teachers to type theory and presents practical ways of taking type into account in teaching.

Types of Teachers at Different Levels of Education

Earlier sections of the Manual have shown the distribution of MBTI types in the population, and estimates of the types of students at different levels of education. In general, extraverts and sensing types outnumber introverts and intuitives, but the proportion of introverts and intuitives increases at higher levels of education. Table 8.21 shows data from the Form F and Form G CAPT MBTI data banks for persons describing themselves as teachers. For some types, the patterns are predictable. For example, ESFJ, extraverted feeling type with sensing as auxiliary, is in theory a nurturant type that enjoys being helpful to people day-to-day. ESFJs are most frequent among teachers in the early grades (12.2% of elementary school teachers) and become less frequent in higher grades (4.9% of college faculty). On the other hand, the scholarly and often science-minded INTJs account for only 2.1% of elementary school teachers, but are 9.6% of college faculty. For other types, such as ISTJ or ENFP, the percentage of the type is relatively constant at all educational levels. Students of some types, ISTP or ESTP, will seldom have teachers of the same type as themselves. Other types, such as ISFJ, will have teachers who speak their language throughout elementary and high school, but in college they may find the transition difficult as more professors are likely to prefer intuition.

Much needs to be learned about the ways individual types prefer to teach, and the extent to which each type can adopt teaching strategies that do not come naturally, so as to communicate with students of different preferences. It is reasonable to assume that at some stages of learning students do better with a teacher who is a kindred spirit, and at other stages students do better if stretched to understand a mind very different from their own. The models for understanding these relationships remain to be developed and tested.

Selecting and Training Teachers

Von Fange (1961) conducted an early study of educators at all levels in Canada. One of his observations was that ENFPs were highly rated as student teachers, but there were fewer ENFPs among practicing teachers than would be expected from the numbers who were trained. MBTI users in colleges of education have made similar comments, but no

Table 8.21 Percentage of teachers in each type at different levels of education

	ISTJ		ISFJ		INFJ		INTJ	
	Number	*Percent*	*Number*	*Percent*	*Number*	*Percent*	*Number*	*Percent*
Pre-school	3	3.00	20	20.00	7	7.00	4	4.00
Elementary	86	10.70	144	17.91	41	5.10	17	2.11
Middle & Jr.	126	11.70	138	12.23	56	4.96	51	4.52
High School	77	11.86	68	10.63	50	7.70	35	5.39
Adult	23	10.09	26	11.40	7	3.07	6	2.63
Jr. College	68	12.12	46	8.20	28	4.99	39	6.95
University	293	12.84	139	6.09	172	7.54	248	10.87

	ISTP		ISFP		INFP		INTP	
	Number	*Percent*	*Number*	*Percent*	*Number*	*Percent*	*Number*	*Percent*
Pre-school	0	0.00	4	4.00	8	8.00	2	2.00
Elementary	14	1.74	38	4.73	37	4.60	12	1.49
Middle & Jr.	26	2.30	36	3.19	67	5.94	27	2.39
High School	10	1.54	16	2.47	41	6.32	19	2.93
Adult	10	4.39	11	4.82	14	6.14	4	1.75
Jr. College	4	0.71	12	2.14	45	8.02	26	4.63
University	38	1.67	39	1.71	185	8.11	123	5.39

	ESTP		ESFP		ENFP		ENTP	
	Number	*Percent*	*Number*	*Percent*	*Number*	*Percent*	*Number*	*Percent*
Pre-school	0	0.00	8	8.00	12	12.00	1	1.00
Elementary	7	0.87	46	5.72	82	10.20	12	1.49
Middle & Jr.	20	1.77	43	3.81	124	10.99	44	3.90
High School	7	1.08	15	2.31	74	11.40	23	3.54
Adult	9	3.95	12	5.26	19	8.33	8	3.51
Jr. College	8	1.43	16	2.85	76	13.55	28	4.99
University	27	1.18	38	1.67	207	9.07	121	5.30

	ESTJ		ESFJ		ENFJ		ENTJ	
	Number	*Percent*	*Number*	*Percent*	*Number*	*Percent*	*Number*	*Percent*
Pre-school	6	6.00	12	12.00	8	8.00	5	5.00
Elementary	68	8.46	100	12.44	58	7.21	42	5.22
Middle & Jr.	103	9.13	130	11.52	88	7.80	49	4.34
High School	73	11.25	55	8.47	57	8.78	28	4.31
Adult	26	11.40	31	13.60	10	4.39	12	5.26
Jr. College	38	6.77	46	8.20	44	7.84	37	6.60
University	148	6.49	101	4.43	183	8.02	220	9.64

Note: Data are taken from Form F and Form G data banks of cases scored between March 1978 and December 1982. Levels are based on coding for occupations given by respondents.

systematic follow-up of type differences in attrition has yet been carried out.

Carlyn (1976) analyzed answers of 200 preservice teachers on a Teacher Personality Questionnaire and reported the following significant correlational relationships:

- F was associated with interest in teaching lower grades (F .30, $p<.01$).

- E, T, and J were associated with interest in administration (E .42, $p<.01$; T .23, $p<.01$; J .16, $p<.05$).

- N and P were associated with liking to use independence and creativity in teaching (N .32, $p<.01$; P .25, $p<.01$).

- E and N were associated with interest in planning school projects (E .39, $p<.01$; N .34, $p<.01$).

- N was associated with enjoyment of working with students in small groups (N .26, $p<.01$).

- E and F were associated with an expression of high commitment to classroom teaching (E .25, $p<.01$; F. 21, $p<.01$).

Type Differences in Teaching Styles

DeNovellis and Lawrence (1983) reported observation of seventy-six volunteer elementary and middle school teachers in the classroom. Observations used rating scales for the Florida Climate and Control System and the Coping Analysis Schedule for Educational Settings. Correlations between MBTI continuous scores and observations of teachers and students showed small but significant differences in directions consistent with theory: IS teachers were more likely to be rated as controlling the choice of activities; Ns were rated as moving more freely about the classroom; Fs were seen to attend to pupils closely, to be attending to several pupils at the same time, and to have pupils central in the activities. F teachers were also rated as giving more positive verbal and nonverbal feedback to students. NFPs were rated as showing more nonverbal disapproval. The authors commented that Ns allowed more individual activity in the classroom and attempted to control the resulting disorder with nonverbal negative behavior. Observations of students showed that productive behavior occurred in classrooms of all types of teachers; when nonproductive behavior occurred, it was likely to show in hostile or aggressive acts under the N teachers, and in withdrawal and passivity under the SJ teachers.

Thompson (1984) conducted in-depth school system interviews, following a naturalistic paradigm design. The interviews contain a wealth of detail on the ways teachers experience their roles, plan their work, teach their classes, and evaluate their students. Representative descriptions for the ST, SF, NF, and NT types are as follows:

The role of the teacher is to:

ST: Set an example for students, be a role model, and share knowledge and experience.

SF: Instruct, discipline, encourage, support, role model, and serve others.

NF: Encourage, inspire, provide variety and creativity, and motivate students to develop.

NT: Encourage, inspire, help students develop as citizens and persons.

Ideas for teaching come from:

ST: State and local curriculum guides, textbooks, and experience.

SF: Curriculum guides, manuals, textbooks, workshops, other teachers, and experience.

NF: Concepts from content of subject taught; courses, reading, knowledge of student development, and "ideas from everywhere."

NT: Concepts from subject area, knowledge of students' needs and development, synthesis of ideas from many sources.

Teaching is planned by:

ST: Making complete, detailed plans in advance for year and term with specific objectives.

SF: Establishing complete objectives and detailed teaching plans using yearly school calendar; taking students' abilities into consideration.

NF: Structuring plans around general goals, themes, and students' needs; then adapting plans to students' needs week to week.

NT: Making a plan according to an overall yearly structure; organizing by concepts or themes; determining details by student levels.

Typical method of teaching is described as:

ST: Following daily routine, directing activities.

SF: Following ordered daily pattern adjusted for person-centered interactions.

NF: Using a flexible pattern depending on topic and student need.

NT: Having a flexible daily routine that depends on topics and student need, with interaction based on expectations for order and learning.

Students' work is evaluated by:

ST: Using points and percentages in a systematic way.

SF: Using points and percentages, plus extra credit options.

NF: Using a number of factors, only one of which is grades.

NT: Using a number of factors.

The teacher feels successful if:

ST: Student grades and behavior improve.

SF: Student behavior and grades improve, and there is the feeling of having contributed to students' education.

NF: Student learning and participation increased and there is the feeling of having made a personal contribution to students' education.

NT: Students have increased involvement with learning.

The Administration of the Educational Process

The discussion thus far has been focused on students and teachers. The facts presented have important implications for those responsible for the administration of educational systems. Type provides a framework for looking at motivations of students, attrition, and blocks to academic achievement. Type provides a way to make assignments that capitalize on the strengths and minimize the blind spots of each type, to create teams that can bring more to teaching than any one teacher could do alone, and to create learning environments that increase the creativity of teachers in finding ways to motivate and instruct all sixteen types of students.

Type distributions of students show that schools have their own characteristic profile of types. Table 8.22 shows type preferences for schools that test their entire freshman class.

Colleges and universities provide in-class and out-of-class learning environments. More needs to be known about which campus learning activities are chosen by different types. Table 8.23 shows data collected at Auburn by Grant (1965). These early data show clearly that students of different types do not seek out the same activities. Administrators who know the type distribution of students in their school can make better estimates of academic and extracurricular activities most useful for the following year.

Administrators who know type can predict probable effects of changes in selection policy, and monitor to see whether these expected results occur. For example, raising the minimum aptitude score will have little effect on fields of study attractive to introverts and intuitive types, but could prevent admission of sensing types to programs attractive to them, such as business, allied health, or civil engineering, where sensing students have been succeeding, despite their lower aptitude test scores.

Type data are valuable for understanding retention in educational programs. Knowledge of the reasons different types choose to leave a school can be a tool for planning intervention strategies. One such strategy is to interview students of the vulnerable types, to learn more about the stresses in that school for that type, and how the students still in school overcame these stresses. New students of the "vulnerable" types can be alerted to these "retention strategies." Some schools have retained students of types with high dropout rates for their school by introducing students to others of their type. Simply having friends who are "kindred spirits" has made school a more positive place for many students.

There has been some interesting work using type to assign roommates or even whole dormitory floors which has met with varying success (Schroeder 1976, 1979; Schroeder, Warner, and Malone, 1980; Wentworth, 1978). Others have used type to select and train residence hall assistants (Wachowiak and Bauer, 1977). Reading and study skills programs are incorporating the MBTI for coaching students on problems specific to their type (Nisbet, et al., 1982). Such programs have shown increased achievement and decreased dropouts.

The preceding sections have discussed uses of the MBTI with students, teachers, counselors, and student personnel. The administrators have a vital role in creating a climate that permits maximum use of staff and student abilities. Table 8.24 shows the types found in educational administration.

At all levels, educational administrators have large numbers of the tough-minded TJ types found in samples of executives in business organizations. The great strengths of the TJ types are organizational ability, planning, and analysis. The data on students and on teachers show a majority of feeling types who are energized by appreciation and the challenge of service to others. TJ administrators can easily become so caught up in the technical aspects of administration that they overlook the importance of (*a*) creating structures that facilitate communication and teamwork and (*b*) recognizing and appreciating contributions of faculty in the daily stresses of coping with school tasks. Lueder (1984) in some preliminary studies of school principals is finding interesting type differences in the ways principals of different types solve problems. Sensing types focus on immediate facts and tend to solve problems by following policy guidelines; intuitives look at school-wide or district-

Table 8.22 Rankings of colleges by MBTI preferences

College	Percent	College	Percent
Extraversion-Introversion		*Thinking-Feeling*	
St. Louis University	62% E	Parks College	59% T
University of Wisconsin at Stevens Point	60% E	Franklin and Marshall College	54% F
University of Maine at Orono	59% E	Nicholls State University	57% F
Mercer University	59% E	University of Wisconsin at Stevens Point	61% F
Nicholls State University	58% E	University of North Carolina at Greensboro	61% F
Auburn University	57% E	St. Clair College	62% F
Adrian College	57% E	Mercer University	62% F
University of North Carolina at Greensboro	55% E	University of Florida	62% F
Rollins College	54% E	St. Louis University	63% F
St. Clair College	54% E	Rollins College	63% F
University of Florida	54% E	University of Maine at Orono	67% F
Hope College	53% E	Auburn University	69% F
Franklin and Marshall College	50% E	Hope College	74% F
Parks College	50% I	Concordia College	77% F
Berkshire Christian College	53% I	Adrian College	80% F
Concordia College	54% I	Berkshire Christian College	86% F
Sensing-Intuition		*Judgment-Perception*	
Nicholls State University	72% S	University of North Carolina at Greensboro	60% J
St. Clair College	68% S	Nicholls State University	54% J
Berkshire Christian College	67% S	Mercer University	54% J
Adrian College	64% S	Adrian College	53% J
Parks College	59% S	Parks College	53% J
Mercer University	59% S	Berkshire Christian College	52% J
University of Wisconsin at Stevens Point	58% S	Franklin and Marshall College	51% J
Auburn University	57% S	Concordia College	51% J
University of North Carolina at Greensboro	57% S	St. Louis University	51% P
University of Maine at Orono	55% S	Rollins College	51% P
Concordia College	54% S	University of Florida	52% P
Franklin and Marshall College	50% S	University of Wisconsin at Stevens Point	52% P
Rollins College	52% N	Hope College	53% P
St. Louis University	52% N	Auburn University	54% P
Hope College	53% N	St. Clair College	55% P
University of Florida	55% N	University of Maine at Orono	60% P

Note: Descriptions of samples appear in Appendix B.

Sources for colleges are:
Adrian (Demarest, 1979), Auburn (Grant and McCullers, 1977), Berkshire Christian (Story, 1984), Concordia (von Fange, 1982), Florida (McCaulley, 1973), Franklin and Marshall (Lacy, 1984), Hope (Demarest, 1975), Maine (Anchors, 1983), Mercer (Schroeder and Jenkins, 1981), Nicholls State (Bourg, 1982), North Carolina (Reichard and Uhl, 1979), Parks (Erickson, 1982), Rollins (Provost, 1984a), St. Clair (DesBiens, Wigle, and Peters, 1977), St. Louis (Schroeder, 1984), Wisconsin (Leafgren and Kolstad, 1984).

Table 8.23 Extracurricular activities of Auburn University freshmen
classified according to MBTI type

ISTJ	ISFJ	INFJ Movies	INTJ Lectures, Drama, or Music
ISTP Athletic Events	ISFP	INFP Movies	INTP Lectures, Drama, or Music
ESTP Social Events	ESFP Social Groups	ENFP Social Groups	ENTP Social Groups and Athletic Events
ESTJ	ESFJ Athletic Events	ENFJ Movies	ENTJ Athletic Events

Source: *Behavior of MBTI Types* by W. Harold Grant, Auburn University, 1965

wide implications and seek the advice of research and outside experts; thinking types seek fairness and consistency, often making decisions unilaterally, or seeking compromises; feeling types are more likely to involve others in the decision-making process and to seek consensus to reduce conflict. These strategies are all useful in appropriate situations, but they suggest that principals, like teachers, will have the strengths and the blind spots of their types.

Table 8.24 MBTI types of administrators in education

	ISTJ		ISFJ		INFJ		INTJ	
	Number	*Percent*	*Number*	*Percent*	*Number*	*Percent*	*Number*	*Percent*
Elementary & Secondary	128	12.50	76	7.42	40	3.91	54	5.27
College & Technical	35	10.26	18	5.28	24	7.04	29	8.50
Unspecified	63	17.03	20	5.41	13	3.51	37	10.00
Educationally Related	20	16.39	7	5.74	5	4.10	8	6.56
	ISTP		**ISFP**		**INFP**		**INTP**	
	Number	*Percent*	*Number*	*Percent*	*Number*	*Percent*	*Number*	*Percent*
Elementary & Secondary	15	1.46	27	2.64	55	5.37	26	2.54
College & Technical	6	1.76	2	0.59	22	6.45	18	5.28
Unspecified	7	1.89	4	1.08	22	5.95	12	3.24
Educationally Related	4	3.28	4	3.28	10	8.20	5	4.10
	ESTP		**ESFP**		**ENFP**		**ENTP**	
	Number	*Percent*	*Number*	*Percent*	*Number*	*Percent*	*Number*	*Percent*
Elementary & Secondary	25	2.44	28	2.73	95	9.28	38	3.71
College & Technical	8	2.35	8	2.35	32	9.38	14	4.11
Unspecified	5	1.35	12	3.24	29	7.84	15	4.05
Educationally Related	2	1.64	1	0.82	10	8.20	4	3.28
	ESTJ		**ESFJ**		**ENFJ**		**ENTJ**	
	Number	*Percent*	*Number*	*Percent*	*Number*	*Percent*	*Number*	*Percent*
Elementary & Secondary	135	13.18	108	10.55	86	8.40	88	8.59
College & Technical	34	9.97	18	5.28	24	7.04	49	14.37
Unspecified	54	14.59	18	4.86	18	4.86	41	11.08
Educationally Related	13	10.66	8	6.56	10	8.20	11	9.02

Note: Data are from the MBTI data bank and include educators who described themselves as administrators at the elementary and secondary school level ($N = 1,024$), the college and technical school level ($N = 341$), at level not specified ($N = 370$), and in educationally related fields ($N = 122$).

Chapter 9

Construction and Properties of the MBTI

The construction of the MBTI was governed by unusual requirements imposed by a working hypothesis. The hypothesis is that certain valuable differences in normal people result from their preferred ways of using perception and judgment. Each of these preferences, being a choice between opposites, is by nature "either-or," that is, a dichotomy. The MBTI contains four separate indices designed to determine the respondent's status on four dichotomies, EI, SN, TF, and JP. Each dichotomy, according to the hypothesis, produces two categories of people. An individual will belong to one or the other category based on his or her makeup and inclination. The object of the MBTI is to ascertain, as correctly as possible, the four categories to which the respondent naturally belongs, for instance ENTP or ESFJ.

Jung's theory of psychological types provided the assumptions and set the tasks for constructing the MBTI. One assumption was that "true preferences" actually exist. In persons with good type development, these preferences can be more confidently identified than in persons with inadequate type development. However, any instrument must maximize the probability that persons unsure of their preferences will be correctly assigned.

A second assumption was that persons can give an indication of the preferences that combine to form type, directly or indirectly, on a self-report inventory.

A third assumption was that the preferences are dichotomized and that the two poles of a preference are equally valuable, each in its own sphere.

These assumptions are not typical of most psychological measures. The Indicator is not trying to *measure* people, but to *sort* them into groups to which, in theory, they already belong.

Construction of the Indicator, at each stage, required success in the following tasks:

1. Determine items to reflect preferences described by Jung for extraversion or introversion (EI), sensing or intuitive perception (SN), and thinking or feeling judgment (TF).

2. Identify the dominant and auxiliary functions. (To accomplish this, Isabel Myers created the JP scale to measure the effects of the judging and perceptive attitudes, in their extraverted appearance, so that this information could be used to determine a dominant function.)

3. Write, test, weight, and select items that would achieve the widest separation and least overlap between the two kinds of people represented by each scale.

4. Achieve precision in the center of the scale, so that persons with indeterminate preferences would be more likely to be classified according to their "true" preference.

5. Find an objective check on the division points for each scale. Correct division points validate simultaneously the MBTI and the underlying hypothesis.

The Indicator was developed in a series of stages, beginning in 1942 and continuing to the publication of Form G in 1977. The issues, methods, and results in constructing the MBTI are described in the following sections.

Development of MBTI Items

Rationale for Questions

Before beginning to develop the MBTI, Isabel Myers and Katharine Briggs had thoroughly studied Jung's *Psychological Types* for descriptions and subtle clues about type preferences and their interactions. They had been "type watchers" for more than two decades, and drew on Jungian theory and their observations to generate questions that could be evaluated.

One of the first requirements imposed by the type hypothesis was that justice must be done to quite opposite viewpoints. Each dichotomy is a choice between equally legitimate alternatives. Thus, type questions have no intrinsic good or bad about them, and no right or wrong except as a certain answer is right for one respondent and wrong for another of a different type. The questions therefore needed to deal with self-reportable surface contrasts in habits, reactions, and points of view that did not imply inferiorities. The respondent should never be placed on the defensive, and should not think his or her own preference superior.

No question could be very extreme, since accuracy was more important near the middle of the distribution than at the ends. An answer that was given by people at the ends was little help, and an answer wrongly given by a lot of people near the middle was a hindrance.

Questions were sought not so much for meaning as for indicating the basic preference that influences the respondent to give it. They were directed to seemingly simple surface behaviors in the hope that they would provide reliable clues to the complex and profound patterns of behavior that could not otherwise be reached in a self-report instrument. The assumption was that preferences themselves are often not consciously formulated, in which case direct questions about them would not be answered correctly. The strategy was to use observable "straws in the wind" to make inferences about the direction of the wind itself.

Consequently, since the content of the question was only a stimulus to evoke a type of reaction, some questions seemed to be trivial. The advantage was that they could be asked without impertinence and answered in either direction without strain. As an encouragement to candor, this harmlessness was a great advantage. Sometimes this nature of the questions backfires when a testee indignantly decides that nothing significant can come out of such "worthless scraps of information."

The content areas of the questions were not meant to cover all domains of the preference. The intent was to identify any clues about preference that would empirically discriminate the two groups. The interest in questions was not in the superficial behavior reported, but in the evidence the questions could provide about the underlying preferences. Despite this intent, a range of behaviors thought to indicate each preference was included. For example, the EI questions touch on extraverted and introverted differences in sociability, friendship, and intimacy, detachment or involvement, and outspokeness or reserve.

Forced-Choice Questions

Questions were presented in forced-choice format primarily because type theory postulates dichotomies. All questions offer choices between the poles of the same preference, E or I, S or N, T or F, J or P. (No questions cut across preferences.) The forced-choice format was required because both poles of a preference are valuable. The aim was to determine which of two valuable or useful behaviors or attitudes is preferred. If each choice were presented separately, both poles could be chosen and one could not know which pole was preferred. The forced-choice format also has the advantage of avoiding the bias of acquiescent and social desirability response sets.

Phrase Questions and Word Pairs. Originally all questions were phrases followed by a choice. For example, the first question of Form G is:

When you go somewhere for the day, would you rather

(A) plan what you will do and when, or
(B) just go?

Word-pair questions were added for Forms E and F. Examples from Form G are:

Which of these words appeals to you more? (Think what the words mean, not how they look or how they sound.)

27. (A) scheduled   unplanned   (B)
28. (A) gentle   firm   (B)

The instructions in parentheses for Word Pairs were added in 1977 with Form G, because interviews with persons taking Form F revealed that some persons had answered some of the word pairs on the basis of the sound or the appearance of the words, not the meaning.

Questions Worded for Comparable Attractiveness

Early in the development and testing of questions, the authors discovered that a particular question elicited very different meanings for different types. In writing items, every effort was made to make the responses appeal to the appropriate types, for example, to make the perceptive response to a JP item as attractive to P people as the judging response is to J people. The result is that responses may be psychologically rather than logically opposed, a fact that annoys many thinking types. Item content is less important than that the words and form of the sentence should serve as a "stimulus to evoke a type response." Where the attempt to make choices equally appealing did not succeed, item weighting was adopted (discussed later in detail).

History of the Development of MBTI Forms

This section summarizes the stages of development of the MBTI, the samples used at each stage, and the changes in the forms themselves.

The Initial Stage

The initial questions were tested first on a small criterion group of about twenty relatives and friends whose type preferences seemed to the authors to be clearly evident from long acquaintance, and from a twenty-year period of "type watching." Careful observation convinced the authors that the constellation of behaviors and attitudes described for

each type by Jung actually could be reliably observed. After an initial period of identifying behaviors described by Jung, the authors noted other behaviors and characteristics. When a behavior seemed to relate to a specific preference, TF for example, the authors studied its appearance, its antecedents and effects, and its occurrence in persons thought to prefer thinking or feeling. After repeated observations and confirmations or disconfirmations of their hypotheses, they became more sure (a) that certain persons did indeed prefer thinking and (b) that specific characteristics were found associated with thinking and could be considered derivatives of thinking. By the time of the initial stages of development of the MBTI, Jung's constructs had been tested and refined by years of observation. The initial "criterion group" was made up only of those persons whose preferences were clear enough to be manifest consistently in observable behavior.

From 1942 to 1944 a large number of potential MBTI items were written and validated on the first criterion group. The authors' discussions with respondents revealed ways to change the items so as to capture the essence of the difference between the types. It became clear that the same phrase conveyed quite different meanings to different types.

Forms A and B

Items that survived the initial validation were made into a set of scales called Form A, and a rearrangement of the same items became Form B. The items were tested on progressively larger samples. These samples were mainly adults because adults were expected to have reached higher levels of type development and would, therefore, be clearer about their preferences and better able to report them.

To remain in the scales, any particular item had to be answered by at least 60% of individuals in the appropriate type ("type" was determined by the preference indicated from the total scale).

Form C

One criterion for the inclusion of items in Form C was that a question having a high validity for one index was excluded if it also had a high validity for another index. For example, an item would be excluded if it correlated well with both the EI and SN indices. It was necessary to keep the scales as uncorrelated as possible because otherwise a strong preference for a scale would distort the evidence for another scale. The Form C items were intercorrelated first on 248 adult men and later on 214 adult men. The first intercorrelation had a range of $-.17$ (EI x TF) to .18 (EI x SN) with a mean of .11. The second intercorrelation had a range of $-.14$ (EI x TF) to .19 (EI x SN) with a mean of .09.

Internal consistency analyses of Forms A and B made it clear that responses differed in popularity. To allow for unequal popularity and for omissions, responses were weighted. A prediction ratio (see below) was substituted for previous item-test consistency analyses. The ratio showed the probability that the response, if answered at all, would be given in accordance with type. The lower limit to retain an item was a prediction ratio of .60. Form C consisted of items from Forms A and B that survived this analysis, plus one new item, and six reworded items.

In 1947 Form C3 incorporated item weighting which allowed better differentiation of individuals scoring near zero. Items were weighted as a function of the prediction ratio (PR) for the item. Weights were 0 for PR less than .60, 1 for PR .60 to .69, and 2 for PR greater than or equal to .70. (See the section on the prediction ratio below for the formula.)

Form D

A second period of development occurred from 1956 to 1958, in preparation for the 1962 publication of the MBTI as a research instrument by Educational Testing Service. Over 200 new items, including word-pair questions, were submitted to a small group of people of known type who were familiar with the Indicator. Items that survived this analysis were submitted to 120 men and women who had taken Form C. The more promising items remaining after item analysis (about 130) were appended to Form C to create an experimental Form D.

When items were evaluated by the small group of people of known type, it was found that some people were more able than others to recognize their own central tendencies. If you ask introverts, "Under such and such conditions, do you tend to do (A) or (B)?" they are likely to single out the key word in (A) and the key word in (B), weigh them against each other, and decide which reaction is most like them, in accord with how the questions were designed to be answered. Extraverts respond to this question by harking back to the last time they were in a similar situation and remembering how they behaved. The extraverts' answer reflects a single occasion with many extraneous factors.

While writing items for Form D, the authors realized that the way to make respondents concentrate on key words was to give them the key words and nothing else, which formed the word pairs. For example:

Which word in each pair appeals to you more?

| (A) | build | invent | (B) |
| (A) | benefits | blessings | (B) |

| (A) | impulse | decision | (B) |

The response to the word pairs indicated that they had low face-validity, but when submitted to item analysis, they worked extremely well. Word pairs have a number of advantages. They are less distracting. They are less subject to varied interpretation, personal reticence, and conscious or unconscious censorship. They are more quickly read and answered, which made it possible to have more items without increasing the administration time. The addition of word pairs almost doubled the number of valid items in Form D.

Previous to the 1956–58 development, all analyses were based on administration of the questions to adults. A series of younger-age samplings was then conducted. Younger individuals were presumably less advanced in type development and less clear about their preferences. Each sampling was evaluated to determine the extent to which items became less efficient as samples became younger.

An internal consistency analysis was done with 385 graduate students. The lower limit of the prediction ratio required for retention of an item was raised from .60 to .63. New items meeting this criterion were added and weaker items were dropped.

An analysis with undergraduate students showed only slightly lower prediction ratios. The wording of a number of the older items was simplified and used in Forms D0 and D1 with three high school samples. When the simpler wording produced prediction ratios above .63, the revised wordings were adopted in the final experimental form, D2. Reworded items not meeting this criterion were dropped; or, in a few cases, the item was returned to the earlier wording.

In 1957, a massive internal consistency analysis of Form D was made using a sample of 2,573 Pennsylvania eleventh and twelfth grade males in college preparatory courses, and a similar sample of girls.

In order to prevent a bias in favor of any particular type, a sample of 200 males and 200 females from each type was drawn from the population. Because types differ in their liking for items predictive of their preferences, Isabel Myers did not want the weights assigned for less frequent types to be influenced by weightings derived from more frequent types. For types with sufficient numbers, a sample was drawn equally from the upper and the lower half of the students' class. Priority was given to overachievers and underachievers to diminish the difference in intelligence quotient between more and less competent students.

Items were evaluated separately by sex and by type. To correct for differences in type frequency, responses for each type were calculated and averaged by the proportion of that type responding in a particular manner. This procedure was followed in order to give the rarer introvert types equal weight with the more numerous extraverts. In addition to the prediction ratios, tetrachoric item-test correlations were computed and used as a check on item selection.

Forms E and F

The surviving items became Forms E and F which were identical except that Form F contained unscored experimental items. Item weights that had been started in Form C3 were used in these forms and made more stringent. For the first time a tie-breaking formula was adopted, and the preference scores were used instead of percentages to denote the strength of preferences. Form F was used in the large samples collected in preparation for publication by Educational Testing Service in 1962. In the early 1970s Form E was phased out, and Form F became the standard form.

Form G

Between 1975 and 1977, almost twenty years after the large-scale data collection preparing for publication of Form F, a new standardization of items was carried out. The new analyses seemed appropriate to ensure that cultural changes had not decreased the utility of items, and to make some minor modifications which two decades of experience had suggested were desirable. One goal of the restandardization was to investigate the age at which the MBTI could be validly administered to school children.

The new standardization was based on 1,114 males and 1,111 females, grades four through twelve in three public schools in Bethesda, Maryland, and in four private schools in the suburbs of Philadelphia, Pennsylvania. The analyses included a rescoring of a sample of 3,362 University of Florida freshmen tested in 1972 and 1973. The Maryland eleventh and twelfth grade sample of 1,101 students was comparable to the sample used for the original Form F item analyses, consisting largely of college preparatory students of above-average socioeconomic status.

Table 9.1 shows that item-test correlations and prediction ratios held up well, even for younger ages. The item correlations by type ranged from .92 to .22 for the three highest age groups. A few items functioned less well at the two lower-grade levels, which produced the minimum correlations in those groups. The utility of items had not diminished and most items functioned better at the elementary school level than had been anticipated.

As a result of the analyses of the restandardization, the scoring weights for the TF scale were modified for Form F, and a new revision of the MBTI, Form G, was published in 1977. Form G eliminated 38 research items not previously scored for type in Form F, added one new item, and dropped two items that no longer met the criterion for inclusion. Some items were modified to eliminate ambiguity or awkward alternatives. Items were rearranged so that all the scored items preceded unscored items. The rearrangement put the most predictive items at the beginning so that a usable approximation of type could be obtained if the first fifty questions were completed.[18]

When scored for type, the 1977 Form F and Form G are essentially interchangeable. Table 9.2 shows correlations of 1962 and 1977 item weights. Correlations of new standard Form G scoring with 1962 Form F scoring may be somewhat lower on TF because of the revision to scoring weights.

The Abbreviated Self-Scoring Version (Form AV)

The Abbreviated Version (Form AV) of the MBTI contains the first fifty items from Form G (which best predict to the total scale scores) in a format that permits self-scoring and provides some interpretive information for the client. Form AV should be used only for group situations where time pressures preclude administration and scoring of Form G and when maximum type accuracy is less important.

Form AV is a "unisex" version of the MBTI because the scoring does not provide different weights for men and women on the TF scale.[19]

Table 9.3 shows comparisons of Form G and Form AV based on a sample of 11,615 cases from the CAPT MBTI data bank as of June 1981. The data bank is composed of 51% females and 49% males with a median age of 20. Seventy percent of the sample were between 15 and 35 years of age. Eighty-six percent had graduated from high school. About 17% of the cases were engineering students in the longitudinal sample of the engineering school consortium. For the analyses, each Form G case was rescored as if the first fifty items were the entire record. More details of this study are reported in Macdaid (1984a).

Table 9.4 shows a comparison of Form AV and Form G collected by Most (1984). Three hundred and sixty-seven Foothill College students in guidance classes took the MBTI twice with a period of one week between administrations. There were four conditions: Form AV first and second (AV → AV), Form AV first and Form G second (AV → G), Form G first and Form AV second (G → AV), and Form G first and second (G → G). The number of preferences in common between administrations was the measure of the reliability of the form. The AV → AV condition was significantly less reliable than either the combined AV → G and G → AV groups or the G → G groups.

Table 9.5 shows the percentage of agreement between Form G and Form AV within each type, for males and females. Table 9.6 compares Form G and Form AV for groups based on consistency of preference score.

Table 9.1 Item-test correlations for Form F and Form G

Composition and Item-Test Correlations for Each Index of Form F

	Composition	N	Tetrachoric r 2,573 Males		Biserial r 385 Males	400 Females
			Range	Median	Median	Median
EI	Phrase questions	16	.40–.87	.60	.51	.55
	Word pairs	6	.44–.64	.56		
SN	Phrase questions	12	.41–.72	.57	.50	.48
	Word pairs	14	.41–.75	.61		
TF	Phrase questions	7	.36–.66	.58	.43	.46
	Word pairs	16	.28–.71	.58		
JP	Phrase questions	16	.48–.75	.55	.51	.55
	Word pairs	8	.45–.78	.62		

Median Item-Test Correlations for Form F and Form G

Form	Sample	N	Median r_{it}
D2	Eleventh and twelfth grade students	6014	.58
F	University of Florida freshman, 1972	3362	.63
F	Massachusetts twelfth graders	795	.50
G	Maryland eleventh and twelfth graders	1101	.61
G	Tenth and eleventh graders—two schools	192	.61
G	Eighth and ninth graders—four schools	360	.58
G	Sixth and seventh graders—five schools	309	.55
G	Fourth and fifth graders—four schools	264	.48

In general, the results confirm those reported earlier by Kaiser (1981) that Form AV is a reasonable short form for Form G. Roughly three-fourths of the response sheets yielded the same MBTI type on both Form G and Form AV when scoring weights were taken into account. Agreement is closest for persons whose preferences are clear. There are differences from type to type and the SP types show least agreement. Agreement increases with higher educational levels.

The following are aspects of Form AV that should be considered when using this form.

1. Form AV is a quick screening measure of type. Because it is less reliable than the longer MBTI forms, it should be used only in situations where time is an important

concern or where other methods of scoring are not practical.

2. Form AV predicts best when the individual has clear preferences (higher preference scores).

3. Form AV does not weight TF as a function of sex and thus is not as accurate a predictor of TF as are Forms G or F.

4. Form AV can be used as a measure to classify individuals according to type. It should not be used to measure type scores.

5. Because of the decreased reliability in Form AV, coun-

Table 9.2 Product-moment correlations of 1962 and 1977 item weights

Sample	N	EI	SN	TF	JP
University of Florida					
Combined	1,882	.993	.997	.983	1.00
Males	1,089	.992	.998	.984	1.00
Females	793	.994	.997	.990	1.00
High school (eleventh and twelfth grade)					
Combined	1,101	—	.994	—	1.00
Males	541	—	—	.983	—
Females	560	—	—	.991	—
Junior high school					
Combined	246	—	.993	—	1.00
Males	124	—	—	.976	—
Females	122	—	—	.988	—

selors should be more aware of individuals who feel they have the characteristics of contrasting preferences. There will be more "type discrepancy" than with Forms G or F.

Item Analyses and Selection of Items

Extensive item analyses were conducted for each form from Form A through Form G. The purpose of the analyses was to ensure that items (*a*) discriminated between the poles of a preference and (*b*) made a useful contribution to only one of the four indices.

Criterion Groups for Item Analyses

In order to determine whether an extraverted answer was given mainly by extraverts, it was necessary to have "criterion groups" of extraverts and introverts. In the initial stages, the small group of well-known people was sufficient, but later, samples were divided into Es and Is, Ss and Ns, and so on.

As items were grouped into scales, percentages or numbers were assigned to each respondent to indicate the preference of one pole over the other. The scales were of little interest in themselves, but were necessary steps to reach the dichotomous preferences specified in Jung's theory. Since

all persons were assigned to one pole or the other on each index, discrimination in the center of the scale, where preferences were almost evenly divided, was essential. For this reason, very broad "criterion groups" were used, including everyone in the sample studied except those with tie scores or preferences only one point away from a tie. This method of comparing almost the entire distribution of individuals is more rigorous than standard personality scale construction, which usually only compares extreme groups on the scale.

Item Analyses

An internal consistency analysis was used for Forms A through G to select items that made a contribution to only one scale. Items were analyzed on all scales, not only the scale intended. Items with high correlations on more than one scale were eliminated, and the cosine-pi formula was used to obtain the approximation of tetrachoric correlations.

In preparation for publication of Form F, Stricker and Ross (1962) computed median biserial correlations for a reanalysis of Form F items based on responses of males and females from Massachusetts high schools. More than half of the Massachusetts sample were vocational students, while the previous Pennsylvania sample was primarily college preparatory. The Massachusetts sample had more sensing types than did the balanced sample used in the 1957 analysis of the Massachusetts sample when types were given equal weight. These facts may account for the somewhat lower biserial correlations than the tetrachoric correlations of the populations used in construction of the MBTI. The item-test correlations for a series of populations collected over time, including the younger subjects tested in development of Form G, are provided in Table 9.1.

Prediction Ratio

Beginning with the development of Form C, the prediction ratio formula was used to indicate the social desirability of each item response. Prediction ratios were based only on persons in the sample who responded to the item. The scoring key item weights were derived from the prediction ratio cutoff points. The prediction ratio shows the probability that any response is given in accord with total scale score (i.e., the probability that a response designed for Js is given by Js and not given by Ps). Since precision was sought in the middle of the scale (near zero), the prediction ratio includes all cases in a class (e.g., J vs. P) in which the raw score difference between the preferences is two points or greater. Cases with a difference of one or zero are excluded from the prediction ratio. Analyses are always computed separately for males and females. Note that for each

Table 9.3 Comparison of Form G and the Abbreviated Form

Comparison	Comparisons of Point Totals							
	E	I	S	N	T	F	J	P
Maximum weighted points								
Form G	51	57	67	51	F 65	43	55	61
					M 65	39		
Form AV	33	31	43	31	F 49	31	33	35
					M 47	33		
G x AV continuous Score correlation	.95		.96		.98		.96	

Preference Changes from Form AV to Form G

	No change	One change	Two changes	Three changes	Four changes
N	8,453	2,758	382	21	1
Percent	72.8	23.7	3.3	0.2	0.0

Percentage Not Changing Preference by Sex and Education Level Completed

Male	Female	First through Eighth	Ninth and Tenth	Eleventh and Twelfth	College	Graduate School
73%	72%	68%	71%	72%	73%	76%

Sample of prediction ratio (PR) formula for items in J and P:

$$\text{PR for item } J_i = \frac{\text{Percent of J subjects giving } J_i \text{ response}}{\begin{array}{l}(\% \text{ of J subjects giving } J_i \text{ response}) \\ + (\% \text{ of P subjects giving } J_i \text{ response})\end{array}}$$

$$\text{PR for item } P_i = \frac{\text{Percent of P subjects giving } P_i \text{ response}}{\begin{array}{l}(\% \text{ of P subjects giving } P_i \text{ response}) \\ + (\% \text{ of J subjects giving } P_i \text{ response})\end{array}}$$

question, the (A) answer and the (B) answer have separate prediction ratios.

The prediction ratio gives the "goodness" of the response, that is, the relationship of the item to all the items for that preference. In order for a response to a question to appear on the scoring keys, the prediction ratio must be above .62 for a weight of 1, or .72 for a weight of 2, *and* the item popularity for the opposite preference must be below .50 (i.e., the percentage of individuals with the opposite preference giving that response). In this manner the formula takes social desirability into account. The denominator of the formula gives a measure of the popularity of the response. If the second term in the denominator of the formula goes above .50, the response has been given by more than half of those for whom that choice was *not* intended; thus, it is overpopular (socially desirable) and is likely to do more harm than it is worth by displacing people at the center of the index. A response rejected by the above criteria would be given a zero weight. A zero weight

Table 9.4 Form AV to Form G reliability comparison

Preference changes	MBTI Form and Order of Administration				
	AV → AV	AV → G	G → AV	G → G	Total
No change	17 (21%)	55 (38%)	18 (38%)	42 (45%)	132
One change	33 (41%)	63 (43%)	23 (49%)	36 (39%)	155
Two changes	25 (31%)	20 (14%)	5 (11%)	12 (13%)	62
Three changes	6 (7%)	7 (5%)	1 (2%)	2 (2%)	16
Four changes	0 (0%)	1 (0%)	0 (0%)	1 (1%)	2
N	81	146	47	93	367

Chi-square for whole table = 25.55, $p < .05$.
Chi-square AV → AV by G → G = 17.55, $p < .01$.
Chi-square AV → AV by combined AV → G and G → AV = 16.75, $p < .01$.
Chi-square combined AV → G and G → AV by G → G = 2.37, ns.
Chi-square AV → G by G → AV = 1.46, ns.

response can remain in the indicator as a counter to a weighted response, for other purposes such as its utility on special scale, or for future use in case the social desirablity of the item changes.

Weighting to Take Popularity of Responses into Account

For about one-third of MBTI questions, prediction ratios were similar for both responses and both responses were given the same weight. In another third of the questions, the responses differed somewhat in popularity; in these items, one response was weighted 1 and the other 2, based on the prediction ratio. In a final third of items, one response was much more popular than the other; these questions were given zero weight for the popular response and 1 or 2 depending on the prediction ratio for the other response.

Items had different response distributions for each of the sixteen types; thus, separate analyses were carried out for each type before the first weighted scoring in 1946, and again before publication of Form F. The popularity of each response was tabulated separately for each of the sixteen types, to guard against extreme variation and to give equal representation to the less frequent types.

Weighting for Sex Differences

Throughout the development of the MBTI, all item analyses were computed separately for males and females. In the first item analysis of 114 males and 110 females (all adults, mostly college graduates), it was discovered that some questions were valid only for one sex. The second item analysis also found sex differences in item validity. In developing Form C, items were only retained that were valid for both sexes.

In the early forms, separate keys for males and females were used for EI, SN, TF, and JP. Beginning with Forms E and F, the same keys were used for both sexes because item analyses showed that for both sexes item popularity and prediction ratios were comparable on EI, SN, and JP.

On the TF scale, it was evident that females, even those who in their behavior and attitudes indicated a clear preference for thinking, had a greater tendency to give certain feeling responses than did males. The difference was ascribed either to the possibility that certain feeling responses were more socially desirable for females than males, or to the effect of social training. Separate weights were assigned to TF items for each sex, based on the prediction ratios for each item, with checks that the criterion groups were assigned the correct preference.

Numerous studies (see section on Form D) in the late 1950s and early 1960s confirmed the weightings and the division point on TF, which tended to produce, among unselected groups of males, a distribution of about 60% T and 40% F. The females' distributions were about one-third T and two-thirds F. From the mid-1960s to the mid-1970s the distributions on the TF scale showed large changes, while the distributions of the other indices remained stable. A 1972 study of University of Florida freshmen produced only 44% T among males and 30% among females. Almost identical distributions were obtained with the 1975 high school samples used to restandardize the MBTI. In other

Table 9.5 Percentage of agreement between Form G and Form AV for males and females of each type

ISTJ				ISFJ				INFJ				INTJ		
Female	468	73.5%		Female	386	71.0%		Female	174	67.4%		Female	174	69.9%
Male	735	78.4		Male	181	77.4		Male	101	74.3		Male	288	73.7
Total	1,203	76.4		Total	567	72.9		Total	275	69.8		Total	462	72.2
	Rank 4				Rank 8				Rank 11				Rank 9	
ISTP				**ISFP**				**INFP**				**INTP**		
Female	105	67.7		Female	138	62.2		Female	256	73.6		Female	123	68.0
Male	222	66.5		Male	96	61.1		Male	220	84.3		Male	249	69.0
Total	327	66.9		Total	234	61.7		Total	476	78.2		Total	372	68.6
	Rank 13				Rank 14				Rank 3				Rank 12	
ESTP				**ESFP**				**ENFP**				**ENTP**		
Female	108	62.1		Female	204	61.3		Female	477	81.5		Female	210	80.8
Male	197	54.6		Male	102	60.4		Male	238	79.3		Male	280	70.7
Total	305	57.0		Total	306	61.0		Total	715	80.8		Total	490	74.7
	Rank 16				Rank 15				Rank 1				Rank 7	
ESTJ				**ESFJ**				**ENFJ**				**ENTJ**		
Female	482	75.3		Female	442	68.8		Female	311	78.9		Female	218	73.4
Male	633	75.5		Male	180	73.5		Male	123	81.5		Male	332	78.3
Total	1,115	75.4		Total	622	70.1		Total	434	79.6		Total	550	76.3
	Rank 6				Rank 10				Rank 2				Rank 5	

Notes: Data are based on a sample of 11,615 Form G cases in the MBTI data bank that were rescored for Form AV. In the total sample, 8, 453 or 72.8% came out the same type on Form G and Form AV.

Table 9.6 Agreement between Form G and Form AV for levels of consistency of preference score

Preference Score Level	N	Percentage of N	Agreement between G and AV
All four AV preferences > 17	651	6%	100%
All four AV preferences >11 but one preference <17	1,598	14%	98%
One and only one score <11	4,156	35%	79%
Two or more scores <11	5,210	45%	56%

words, the incidence of Ts had dropped for both males and females.

One might conclude that Ts are a vanishing species, a conclusion that would do violence to type theory, or that social/cultural changes have altered the popularity of responses in the thinking-feeling domain. The latter interpretation seems compatible with a number of sociological and psychological commentaries which suggested that feeling responses might be more acceptable or popular among young Americans than they were twenty years earlier.

In the restandardization samples, item-test correlations and prediction ratios were computed, following precisely the same system as in earlier item analyses. No changes were required for the EI, SN, and JP indices. However, feeling response choices had become more popular and therefore lost some of their weighting. Thinking responses, which were formerly penalized for overpopularity, were less popular and therefore gained added weight for that response.

With the restandardized weights, the high school male sample contained 61% T and the female sample contained 30% T. This was comparable to the earlier distributions. A rescoring of the University of Florida sample yielded 61% T for males and 30% T for females, also comparable to earlier data.

Other Comments about Weighting

In the course of the many item analyses conducted over the years, it was clear that responses for a preference are not equally popular for all types holding that preference. For example, not all thinking types are equally likely to respond to a given thinking question. In addition, weighting based on adult samples and student samples varied somewhat. Experience with Form C showed that weighting

should be virtually the same for male college students as for adult males in business or the professions, and that most items discriminated better for adults than for students. The 1975 restandardization also found some differences from one age level to the next, but on the whole, consistency was more common than difference.

These observations were taken into account throughout the development of the MBTI and governed decisions in weighting items that had varying prediction ratios based on the sample. Variation was also considered when placing the division points between poles.

Maintaining the Purity of the Scales

Item analyses always included both item-scale correlations and prediction ratios for each response to all scales, not simply the scale for which the item was designed. Any item that loaded similarly to more than one scale was eliminated. Biserial correlations computed between the retained items and the scores of other indices had a median absolute correlation range of .07 to .12, as compared to a range of .43 to .55 when correlated with the item's own index.

Independence of the Preference Scales

Intercorrelations of continuous scores (Table 9.7) for various populations show that EI, SN, TF, and JP tend to be independent of each other, except that SN and JP tend to be significantly and positively correlated. Sensing types are more likely to be J, and intuitives are more likely to be P. Isabel Myers believed that the positive correlations between SN and JP might reflect a fact about the types themselves. Sensing types typically prefer to rely on past experience, and dislike unexpected events that require a rapid assessment

Table 9.7 Intercorrelation of continuous scores for MBTI preferences

Sample	N	EI:SN	EI:TF	EI:JP	SN:TF	SN:JP	TF:JP
			Product-Moment Correlations				
	MBTI Data Banks						
Form F data bank							
Total	55,971	−.11	−.07	−.06	.09	.38	.23
Males	23,240	−.08	−.06	−.01	.16	.36	.28
Females	32,731	−.13	−.06	−.08	.06	.40	.22
Age groupings							
15–17	5,004	−.07	−.13	−.09	.08	.38	.19
18–20	14,561	−.10	−.10	−.05	.09	.36	.13
21–24	8,141	−.10	−.04	−.02	.08	.37	.19
25–29	6,383	−.11	−.04	−.05	.10	.40	.25
30–39	9,505	−.12	−.02	−.02	.12	.42	.26
40–49	5,771	−.14	−.05	−.04	.13	.41	.27
50–59	2,662	−.19	.00	−.06	.12	.42	.30
60+	821	−.17	−.04	−.06	.11	.46	.31
Form G data bank							
Total	32,671	−.08	−.07	−.07	.13	.38	.21
Males	15,791	−.05	−.06	−.04	.15	.35	.24
Females	16,880	−.11	−.05	−.10	.12	.40	.24
Age groupings							
15–17	3,948	−.07	−.10	−.06	.07	.34	.18
18–20	11,052	−.04	−.07	−.04	.10	.37	.17
21–24	2,917	−.08	−.07	−.05	.13	.36	.19
25–29	2,609	−.10	−.05	−.02	.13	.42	.21
30–39	4,807	−.10	−.06	−.03	.13	.41	.25
40–49	2,852	−.14	−.07	−.07	.21	.41	.30
50–59	1,603	−.12	−.07	−.03	.20	.43	.28
60+	520	−.12	−.10	−.02	.26	.44	.33
Data bank omissions							
Omissions sample	15,729	−.08	−.07	−.02	.15	.43	.24
No omissions	9,398	−.10	−.08	−.03	.16	.52	.25
1–14 omissions	5,810	−.05	−.06	−.01	.15	.43	.29
15–35 omissions	526	−.02	−.08	.00	.13	.38	.18
36+ omissions	241	−.08	−.02	−.04	.12	.40	.11
Data bank: Scale bias study							
Equal *N*s each type	6,144	−.04	−.04	.01	.05	.25	.12
E 75% I 25%	6,144	−.03	−.04	.00	.05	.24	.12
I 75% E 25%	6,144	−.04	−.04	.01	.04	.23	.10
S 75% N 25%	6,144	−.05	−.01	.04	.05	.22	.09
N 75% S 25%	6,144	−.02	−.05	.00	.04	.24	.12

(continued)

Table 9.7 Intercorrelation of continuous scores for MBTI preferences

Sample	N	EI:SN	EI:TF	EI:JP	SN:TF	SN:JP	TF:JP
				Product-Moment Correlations			
				MBTI Data Banks			
Data bank: Scale bias study							
Equal *N*s each type							
T 75% F 25%	6,144	−.04	−.04	.01	.05	.24	.11
F 75% T 25%	6,144	−.04	−.03	.00	−.06	.25	.11
J 75% P 25%	6,144	−.03	−.04	.00	.03	.24	.12
P 75% J 25%	6,144	−.04	−.04	.01	.06	.23	.10
Samples of students in middle, junior high, or high school							
(1) Rural Florida eighth grade							
Males	54	.01	−.22	.15	−.04	−.01	.02
Females	62	−.16	−.13	−.13	.17	−.03	−.15
(2) Pennsylvania high school							
Males	3,503	.04	−.07	.08	.06	.28	.18
Females	2,511	.06	−.05	.04	.05	.41	.16
(2) Massachusetts high school							
Males	397	−.10	.03	.09	.02	.26	.12
Females	614	−.09	−.02	.02	.10	.33	.20
(3) Small city Florida high school							
Male twelfth grade	196	.11	−.04	.12	−.04	.32	.06
Female twelfth grade	207	−.01	−.10	−.05	.13	.46	.16
(4) University laboratory							
School grades 7–12	458	.04	−.20	.07	−.00	.18	.13
Males							
IQ, 98–	64	.18	.16	−.08	.13	.10	.19
IQ, 99–115	93	.06	−.11	.16	.16	.33	.11
IQ, 116+	72	−.17	.09	−.21	.02	.28	−.03
Females							
IQ, 98–	73	.04	−.20	.07	−.00	.18	.13
IQ, 99–115	76	−.17	−.09	.04	.09	.34	.05
IQ, 116+	80	−.06	.04	−.06	.08	.29	.32
(5) University laboratory							
School grades 9–12							
Males	428	−.01	−.13	.00	.04	.38	.16
Females	418	−.07	−.12	−.11	.23	.42	.32

(continued)

Table 9.7 Intercorrelation of continuous scores for MBTI preferences

Sample	N	EI:SN	EI:TF	EI:JP	SN:TF	SN:JP	TF:JP
				Product-Moment Correlations			
				MBTI Data Banks			
				College and university students			
(2) Brown, males	591	−.03	−.03	.05	.02	.30	.10
(2) California Institute of Technology, males	201	−.13	−.14	−.12	.00	.24	.23
(2) Long Island University							
Males	300	.06	.03	.08	.02	.33	.18
Females	184	−.14	.04	.01	.06	.47	−.02
(2) Pembroke, females	240	−.09	−.19	−.05	.05	.39	.12
(2) Wesleyan, males	225	.00	−.08	.02	.14	.34	.24
(6) University of Florida							
Male freshmen	1,868	−.04	−.02	−.01	.14	.40	.26
Female freshmen	1,494	−.04	−.04	−.01	.08	.49	.20
(7) Princeton, males	102	.17	−.09	.08	−.20	.48	−.06
Preservice teachers							
(8) University of Oklahoma							
Elementary, females	65	.13	−.23	.10	−.08	.29	.29
Secondary, females	300	.03	.06	.03	.08	.28	.14
Male preservice	70	−.06	−.28	.07	.02	.09	.20
(9) Ohio State, males and females	403	−.07	.07	.02	.08	.39	.17
(10) Michigan State University							
Males	64	−.26	.20	.18	.04	.27	.33
Females	136	−.23	−.06	−.11	.16	.46	.17
Nursing students							
(11) University of New Mexico							
Admission, males and females	121	−.12	−.07	−.07	.16	.42	.17
Retest, males and females	121	−.09	.03	−.07	.20	.48	.26
				Postgraduate educational samples			
Medical students							
(12) Myers, forty-five schools	5,355	.10	−.13	.08	−.05	.21	.07
(12) University of Florida							
Applicants	342	−.03	−.06	.10	.19	.40	.34
Admitted	66	.04	−.09	.06	.24	.46	.26
(12) University of New Mexico							
Applicants	149	.07	.13	.12	.25	.42	.34
Admitted	122	.05	.03	.12	.23	.32	.16
(12) Ohio State							
1967–69	484	.02	−.12	.06	.22	.45	.17
1970–72	660	−.04	−.04	−.00	.15	.42	.14

(continued)

Table 9.7 Intercorrelation of continuous scores for MBTI preferences

Sample	N	Product-Moment Correlations					
		EI:SN	EI:TF	EI:JP	SN:TF	SN:JP	TF:JP
Postgraduate educational samples							
(13) Law students							
University of California	290	−.03	−.02	−.05	.10	.40	.19
Northwestern University	157	−.01	.06	.03	.13	.28	.33
University of Pennsylvania	192	−.27	−.08	−.14	.18	.47	.27
University of Virginia	237	.08	.01	.13	.06	.44	.33
Theology students							
(14) Boston University	79	−.01	−.22	−.04	.01	.18	.20

Notes: Descriptions of samples are given in Appendix B.
(1) McCaulley and Kainz (1976), (2) Myers (1962), (3) Morgan (1975), (4) McCaulley and Natter (1974), (5) Guttinger and McCaulley (1975), (6) McCaulley and Kainz (1974), (7) Madison, Wilder, and Studdiford (1963), (8) Richek (1969), (9) Schmidt and Fretz (1965), (10) Carlyn (1976), (11) Weiss (1980), (12) McCaulley (1978), (13) Miller (1966), (14) Kirk (1972).

of new possibilities. A preference for judging leads to a life that is planned and consistent, decreasing the numbers of such unexpected events. Intuitive types, on the other hand, are attracted to future possibilities and new constructions of events. The perceptive attitude keeps the door open to an incoming stream of these new possibilities.

Table 9.7 describes intercorrelations for a group of naturally occurring samples, and also for a group of samples from the MBTI data bank. These correlations give an estimate of the size of intercorrelations to expect, depending on the distribution of types in a particular research sample. Analyses conducted at the MBTI data bank yielded surprisingly consistent correlations. In naturally occurring samples, larger than expected scale intercorrelations can often be attributed to a greater representation than normal of a particular preference. As expected, the largest correlations are almost always between SN and JP and some samples also show a relationship between TF and JP. Other strong relationships in correlations in natural samples are rare.

Scoring and the Effect of Omissions. Omissions are permitted in the instructions of the MBTI in the belief that greater validity is achieved by the elimination of doubtful answers. Type can then be indicated by preferences to the item responses a person is reasonably sure about, uncontaminated by guessing. In practice, there are typically few omissions (see Table 9.8). Table 9.9 gives the percentages of omitted items for each type separately. More than

half of the respondents answered all the questions.

Research with other psychological measures has established individual differences in response styles, including acquiescence or general willingness to concur. On the MBTI, there is no option to say "No" directly, because of the forced-choice format. However, a person who is unable or unwilling to concur can omit an item. A few people (particularly introverted thinkers, who tend not to subscribe unreservedly to any statement short of a mathematical equation) may omit quite a number of responses. If the scoring consisted merely of counting the points for one pole of a preference (e.g., E only, or S only), with a cutoff somewhere to divide the opposites (e.g., E from I, or S from N), then these people would have low scores. Because of the omissions, they would be placed in the wrong category (e.g., they might have a low E score with no independent measure of I). In order to avoid distortion from omissions, points are counted in both directions, and each response is given the weight assigned from its item analyses. The preference can then be determined on the weight of the evidence for each item and each scale, ample or restricted as the case may be.

The MBTI is a normative instrument because it requires a choice between two contrasting responses but each response alternative is scored on a different scale. Because of this separate scoring and the omission problem, the shortcut of scoring only one part of a scale should be avoided.

Table 9.8 Cumulative percentage of omissions for Form F and Form G

	Form F				Form G			
	Males		Females		Males		Females	
	N	Cum. %	N	Cum. %	N	Cum. %	N	Cum. %
Omissions								
0	15,072	64.2	20,829	63.2	10,126	62.9	10,695	62.5
1	2,845	76.3	4,270	76.2	2,088	75.8	2,366	76.4
2	1,266	81.7	2,029	82.4	881	81.3	1,043	82.5
3	822	85.2	1,170	85.9	522	84.6	716	86.6
4	593	87.8	853	88.5	369	86.9	434	89.2
5	413	89.5	657	90.5	290	88.7	319	91.0
6	338	91.0	468	91.9	239	90.1	234	92.4
7	266	92.1	366	93.0	190	91.3	166	93.4
8	234	93.1	312	94.0	144	92.2	149	94.3
9	173	93.8	255	94.7	132	93.0	105	94.9
10	161	94.5	209	95.4	115	93.7	114	95.5
11	131	95.1	194	96.0	116	94.5	106	96.2
12	111	95.5	130	96.4	75	94.9	65	96.5
13	87	95.9	115	96.7	56	95.3	56	96.9
14	93	96.3	112	97.0	63	95.7	52	97.2
15	84	96.7	90	97.3	46	96.0	49	97.5
16	61	96.9	84	97.6	59	96.3	32	97.6
17	53	97.1	65	97.8	32	96.5	39	97.9
18	42	97.3	62	98.0	45	96.8	28	98.0
19	49	97.5	58	98.1	40	97.1	23	98.2
20	43	97.7	48	98.3	28	97.2	25	98.3
21	32	97.9	47	98.4	46	97.5	22	98.4
22	28	98.0	40	98.5	32	97.7	14	98.5
23	34	98.1	35	98.7	27	97.9	13	98.6
24	26	98.2	23	98.7	30	98.1	15	98.7
25	21	98.3	31	98.8	20	98.2	18	98.8
26	27	98.4	32	98.9				
27	23	98.5	24	99.0				
28	18	98.6	25	99.1				
29	20	98.7	21	99.1				
30	18	98.8	22	99.2				
31	22	98.9	18	99.3				
32	10	98.9	11	99.3				
33	15	99.0	13	99.3				
34	9	99.0	13	99.4				
35	12	99.1	15	99.4				
36-166 (F); 26-116 (G)	221	100.0	195	100.0	292	100.0	206	100.0

Rationale for Tie-Breaking Formula

In the early stages of the MBTI development, equal points for the poles of the same index were designated by an "x"; thus the type might be designated IxTJ, or ENFx. With Form F, a tie-breaking formula was adopted, on the suggestion of Frederick R. Kling of Educational Testing Service. The formula, given in Chapter 2, involves finding the difference between the points for each pole, doubling the difference, and adding a point if either I, N, F, or P is the

Table 9.9 Means and standard deviations of omissions for the sixteen types

	Sensing Types		Intuitive Types	
	With Thinking	With Feeling	With Feeling	With Thinking

ISTJ	ISFJ	INFJ	INTJ
N = 4,172	N = 2,470	N = 1,257	N = 1,879
% = 12.56	% = 7.44	% = 3.78	% = 5.66
Mean 2.24	Mean 1.95	Mean 2.99	Mean 2.98
S.D. 6.59	S.D. 6.09	S.D. 7.85	S.D. 7.14
Rank 5	Rank 11	Rank 1	Rank 2
ISTP	ISFP	INFP	INTP
N = 1,442	N = 1,210	N = 1,843	N = 1,698
% = 4.34	% = 3.64	% = 5.56	% = 5.11
Mean 2.22	Mean 1.99	Mean 2.20	Mean 2.96
S.D. 6.31	S.D. 6.75	S.D. 6.88	S.D. 7.40
Rank 6	Rank 10	Rank 8	Rank 3
ESTP	ESFP	ENFP	ENTP
N = 1,418	N = 1,466	N = 2,523	N = 1,809
% = 4.27	% = 4.42	% = 7.60	% = 5.45
Mean 1.79	Mean 1.25	Mean 1.62	Mean 2.21
S.D. 5.80	S.D. 3.72	S.D. 4.64	S.D. 6.45
Rank 13	Rank 16	Rank 15	Rank 7
ESTJ	ESFJ	ENFJ	ENTJ
N = 3,965	N = 2,523	N = 1,529	N = 2,003
% = 11.94	% = 7.60	% = 4.60	% = 6.03
Mean 1.85	Mean 1.70	Mean 2.05	Mean 2.50
S.D. 5.27	S.D. 5.23	S.D. 6.13	S.D. 6.67
Rank 12	Rank 14	Rank 9	Rank 4

	Number	%	Mean	S.D.	t or F
E	17,236	51.90	1.87	5.5	59.6
I	15,971	48.10	2.39	6.8	
S	18,666	56.21	1.92	5.8	46.5
N	14,541	43.79	2.38	6.6	
T	18,386	55.37	2.29	6.4	29.9
F	14,821	44.63	1.91	5.8	
J	19,798	59.62	2.19	6.2	5.6
P	13,409	40.38	2.02	6.0	
IJ	9,778	29.45	2.41	6.7	
IP	6,193	18.65	2.37	6.8	22.1
EP	7,216	21.73	1.73	5.2	
EJ	10,020	30.17	1.97	5.7	
ST	10,997	33.12	2.04	6.0	
SF	7,669	23.09	1.74	5.5	28.8
NF	7,152	21.54	2.10	6.2	
NT	7,389	22.25	2.66	6.9	
SJ	13,130	39.54	1.96	5.8	
SP	5,536	16.67	1.81	5.7	22.7
NP	7,873	23.71	2.18	6.2	
NJ	6,668	20.08	2.63	6.9	
TJ	12,019	36.19	2.27	6.3	
TP	6,367	19.17	2.32	6.5	12.9
FP	7,042	21.21	1.76	5.5	
FJ	7,779	23.43	2.06	6.1	
IN	6,677	20.11	2.76	7.2	
EN	7,864	23.68	2.06	5.9	38.2
IS	9,294	27.99	2.13	6.4	
ES	9,372	28.22	1.71	5.1	

Note: Data are from MBTI Form G data bank (N = 33,207). One-way analysis of variance df 1/33205 (F = 11.66, p = .001). All *t*s and *F*s for subgroups are significant (p = .001).

larger pole, or subtracting a point if either E, S, T, or J is the larger pole. The resulting number, accompanied by a letter denoting the pole with the greatest number of points (e.g., E 37, N 15), becomes the *preference score*, the basic scoring unit for the MBTI.

The logic behind adding a point to the I, N, or P preferences is that these are the less frequent types in the population. If a person is that close to the preference (zero difference), there is probably some environmental response pressure from the "majority" preference. This pressure can result in answers conforming to the majority and contrary to true preferences, thus the person's "true" type is probably I, N, or P.

The rationale for tie breaking on the TF scale was somewhat different. In this culture, males more frequently prefer T and are socialized toward T; females more frequently prefer F and are socialized toward F. On the possibility that the weighting of the scales may have overcorrected for social desirability, tie scores assign males to T and females to F. When Form F was published in 1962, the scoring system reflected this method. The new keys add one point on the male TF key in addition to the responses. As a result, the new scoring is simplified. Both male and female scoring handles a zero difference by subtracting one for T and adding one for F.

Ranges of Preference Scores

The ranges for the Form F and Form G scales were established with the publication of Form G in 1977. Preference scores on each index increase in either direction from zero at the center where the direction of preference changes. There are no actual zero scores, since the tie-breaking formula ensures that the lowest score for each preference is one. Scores increase by increments of two and all scores are odd numbers. These ranges are shown in Table 2.2.

Bimodality and the Problem of the Division Points

In developing an indicator based on Jung's theory two problems need to be solved. The first problem is whether each index represents two different kinds of people, each holding to a separate preference. If there are two kinds of people for each index, is the division point between the groups at the point where the two groups can be most clearly separated?

Jung's theory hypothesizes that preferences are dichotomies, based on an inner disposition which cannot be thwarted without damage to the individual's well-being and effectiveness. If Jung is correct, it is important for counselors and educators to respect the inner disposition, and to recognize it early. Accuracy in reflecting the inner disposition on each preference is, therefore, important in any type indicator. A self-report instrument that aims to accomplish the identification of Jungian types through questions and their resultant scales also has the unique problem of locating the division point, so that the two categories of people are separated with maximum accuracy.

Thus, there are two strong reasons why the division point should be as sharp and accurate as possible: (*a*) to identify the two different groups with maximum accuracy, and (*b*) to use these distinctions to obtain evidence as to

whether the preferences are, as postulated by theory, dichotomous.

From the beginning, the indices were designed to keep the division points in the "right place" as much as possible. In Form A, where all items had equal weight, the division point was the point on an index where half the items were answered for each pole. By definition this point was the boundary between people showing one preference and people showing the opposite preference. The only possible check was to see whether the people of known type were correctly classified. From that time on, whenever the scoring was changed by dropping or adding items or by assigning double weight or zero weight to responses, care was taken not to add more overall weight to one pole of the scale than to the other, lest the distribution of scores shift. Up until the completion of Form C, the people of known type were rescored at each step, to make sure that changes would not shift them to the wrong pole.

Throughout the construction of the MBTI, numerous steps were taken to deal with the issue of dichotomies and the division points. Steps already described are: (*a*) permit omissions to help avoid the effects of random guessing, (*b*) allow for omissions in the scoring formulas, (*c*) give lower weightings for overpopular items and higher weightings for the more discriminating responses, and (*d*) use inclusive groups rather than extreme groups in the item analyses. Once scales were developed, division points and dichotomies were tested as described in the following sections.

Bimodal Scales as Evidence for Dichotomies

The idea of demonstrating a dichotomy through bimodal scales is attractively simple, and a great deal of time was spent examining distributions. Clearly bimodal scales were found in a few samples of highly developed people, but these were rare. Clear bimodality would be expected only if the sample size is large and the population has very well-developed types. Unfortunately, even when bimodal populations are found, they do not indicate the location of the division point, unless there is a deep cleft division between each modal population. In developing the MBTI, a one-point correction on one index was the only change ever adopted on the basis of bimodal evidence, though mild reassurance had been at times derived from distributions that appeared to conform to the existing division point.

Comparisons of Scores on a Dependent Variable

A promising technique for showing evidence of dichotomies and the division point is to plot the means of a dependent variable upon both halves of the index. Evidence for the division point would be indicated if there is a change in *slope* or *level*, or if there is any other disparity between the two halves of the index. If possible, the dependent variable should be one in which the two categories of people behave quite differently, even with the barest difference in their scores. It is not easy to identify variables that are relevant to the index *and* relatively free of variance from the other three indices. For example, *gregariousness* is obviously a better variable for testing differences on EI than SN or JP.

When a disparity can be found, it supports the hypothesis that the index reflects a dichotomy—that two distinct categories of people, with opposite preferences, have been separated by MBTI scores. It is important to remember that the disparity and division point will be clouded by the error variance of the MBTI. When disparities occur across a number of dependent variables, there is good evidence for a meaningful division point.

It is even more difficult to place the "true" division point at zero on the Indicator. In order to pinpoint the true zero, the dependent variable needs to be sensitive to the barest amount of the preference, so that, at the point where the preference reverses, the plotted line will show a discontinuity in level as well as (or in place of) a disparity in slope. In addition, the sample needs to be very large to stabilize the group means and to make the discontinuity visible and statistically significant.

An example of this technique for identifying the division point is illustrated by the measures taken to correct the EI division point when it became displaced.

Relocation of the EI Division Point Using Grade Point Average.

When the scoring for Form F was almost completed, the zero point on EI was found to have shifted toward the extravert pole. The evidence was an unprecedented majority of "introverts" when the Pennsylvania High School sample was rescored with the new weights (see Appendix B for a description of this sample). To correct the error, external evidence was needed to find the transition on the index between the extraverts and the introverts.

During the development of Form C, the years-of-college variable had shown a satisfactory discontinuity on EI. This suggested that, as theory predicts, a preference for introversion is related to interest and/or performance in academics. This was supported by the high percentage of introverts in college populations. It therefore seemed reasonable that the intelligence measures for the Pennsylvania High School sample (5,025 males and 4,516 females) and the grade point average (standardized within each class) for the college preparatory courses (3,303 males and 2,511 females) might exhibit discontinuities that would indicate the location of the EI division point. Figure 9.1 demonstrates one of these analyses.

The mean standardized grade point average scores are plotted against the EI index in Figure 9.1. The three means

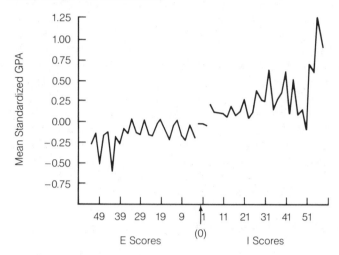

Figure 9.1 Grade-point average for levels of preference for extraversion and introversion

that appear to bracket the division point may be seen at the center, connected with each other, but separate from the E portion and I portion of the plot. The closest eighteen means of the extravert half of the distribution show no demonstrable trend; they all lie in a range of −.04 to −.29 deviations of grade point average scores. Similarly, the closest eleven means of the introvert half of the distribution show no trend and all lie in a range of +.04 to +.29 standard deviations of grade point average scores. The most reasonable location for the division point appears to be the middle one of the three linked scores, equidistant from the nearest low mean on the E side, which is −.17, and the nearest high mean on the I side, which is +.22. (The sample sizes for each EI interval plot range from 60 to 125.)

The Pennsylvania High School sample was rescored with the new EI division point, and the new location was tested by plotting IQ scores separately for males and females. For males the break, slight but evident because of the large size in the sample, came between the first and second of the groups with the three linked scores. This was the point where the division point for the EI index was finally established.

It should be noted that the change in level between E and I was in all these analyses very small, only about .25 standard deviations in grade point average and about 2 points in IQ. For such small differences to be visible, samples of 4,000–5,000 are needed.

Changes in Level or Slope as Evidence for the Division.

When plotting scores of a relevant variable on the indicator index scores, a crucial question is whether the observed disparities in level and/or slope between the two halves of the distribution are consistent with the usual assumption of a continuum or are better explained by the hypothesis of two different populations. If the plots are found to show unusual characteristics that can best be explained as reflecting a dichotomy, then both the theory and the validity of the MBTI would be supported. The conditions for these analyses are as follows:

1. *The basic trend for each half of the distribution should be clearly evident.* Stability is more essential than detail. For example, if each half of the index is divided into three parts, the three group means can show any gross curvature in the slope, and at the same time maintain maximum stability against chance variation. Samples of several thousand can, of course, be more finely divided and still yield a stable picture of the distribution slope and level.

2. *Any disparity between the halves should not be "smoothed."* No a priori assumption of a continuum should be imposed on the data by connecting the two halves. Each index half should be allowed to start at zero as though the other did not exist. The trend of each half can then be determined independently.

3. *A reversal in direction is evidence for dichotomy.* The clearest kind of disparity in slope is a reversal of direction, for example, a V-shaped or U-shaped line. According to the Jungian hypothesis, each index should divide the population into two categories. The slope of the line within each category should reflect the effect of differing degrees of preference. Because the two populations are hypothesized, there is no obligation to harmonize or connect the slopes or lines of the two categories. Between categories, therefore, there can be disparity in any combination of slope, level, and direction.

Examples of U-Shaped Distribution Plots on MBTI Indices. A series of analyses were made of a sample of 5,025 male Pennsylvania high school students and a sample of 720 male Massachusetts high school students.[20] Each analysis contained six sample groups based on the size of the preference scores (1–17, 19–35, and 37+ on each side of the midpoint).[21] In the Pennsylvania sample, mean IQ scores were computed for each preference score grouping; for the Massachusetts sample, vocabulary scores were used. Figure 9.2 shows the mean intelligence scores for the male Pennsylvania high school students, divided into six EI groups based on the strength of their EI scores, and the mean vocabulary scores for the Massachussetts high school students for the same six groupings. Figure 9.3 shows the comparable analyses for JP for Pennsylvania and Massachussetts high school students.

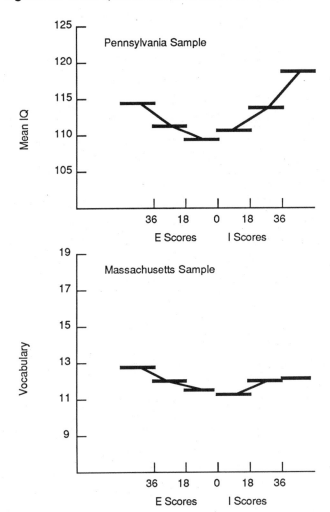

Figure 9.2 Mean aptitude scores at different levels of EI

Both EI and JP show a trend for clearer preferences (away from the midpont) to be associated with higher scores. The perceptive side of the scale is also higher than the judging side of the scale, which is typical for JP plots on aptitude/achievement data.

Figure 9.4 shows the mean IQ scores of the Pennsylvania and Massachusetts samples for the six TF groups.

Clear preferences on either thinking or feeling are associated with higher scores on both IQ and vocabulary measures. The curve shows greater discrepancy for clear and unclear (near the midpoint) preferences than the curves for EI or JP.

Figure 9.5 shows IQ scores of the Pennsylvania high school students and Massachusetts high school students for the SN groupings.

Figure 9.3 Mean aptitude scores at different levels of JP

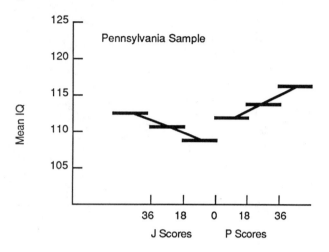

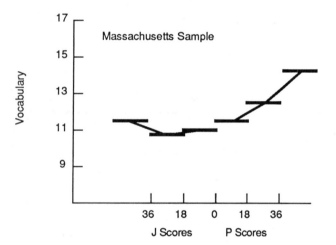

One needs, therefore, evidence for a not-too-steep slope with a significant break at the division point. The laws of probability being influenced by the size of samples, either the sample must be so large that even a modest discontinuity is significant, or the discontinuity must be so large that it is significant even for a modest sample. The comparison of liberal arts and engineering students on TF is an example of a small difference observable in a large sample. The comparison of extraverts and introverts in gregariousness is an example of a large difference in a modest sample.

Engineering Students and TF. One conspicuous contrast on the TF scale is between a sample of 2,389 engineering students and 2,177 liberal arts students tested as part of the analyses for Form F. Sixty-eight percent of engineering

Figure 9.5 shows that the SN scale does not operate the same on intelligence and vocabulary as do the other scales. Rather than clearer preferences in either pole leading to higher IQ and vocabulary scores, only clearer preferences for intuition lead to greater scores.

Examples of Discontinuities as Evidence for the Division Point. If Jung is correct about dichotomous populations, and if the MBTI correctly separates the two populations on each index, then a discontinuity at the division point is expected. In order to constitute a discontinuity, there must be a significantly greater rate of change at the point of discontinuity than on either side of that point. It is not sufficient to show that the difference in means or proportions between intervals is significant. If all differences are equally significant, they can tell nothing about the division point.

Figure 9.4 Mean aptitude scores at different levels of TF

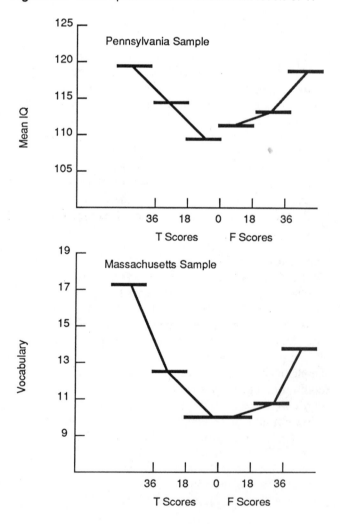

Figure 9.5 Mean aptitude scores at different levels of SN

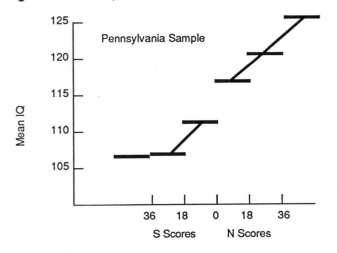

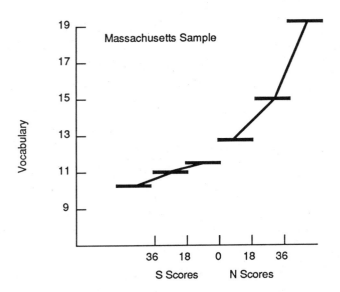

students preferred thinking, compared to only 54% of liberal arts students.

The liberal arts and engineering samples were combined, making a total sample of 4,566. The proportion of engineers was computed for each twelve-point interval along the TF index, running both directions from zero. Figure 9.6 shows this plot.

If the tendency to choose an engineering college is linked to a preference for TF, then a discontinuity in the slope should occur at the division point. If the choice of engineering is related only to the strength of the T or F preference, then the slope should be unbroken.

In the analysis of the combined sample of 2,177 liberal arts students and 2,389 engineering students, each half of the scale was divided into five rather than three divisions (1–11, 13–23, 25–35, 37–47, 49+). Of the nine successive differences between adjacent intervals, only the one that fell at the division point was statistically significant (*t* 3.25, *p*<.01). The broken line in Figure 9.6 shows the disparity between the steepness at the division point compared to the more gradual slope in the two halves of the distribution.

Faculty Ratings of Gregariousness and EI. As part of the Educational Testing Service College Student Characteristics Study, Ross (1961) obtained faculty ratings of student characteristics on a seven-point scale. Raters had no knowledge of students' MBTI results. Ross reported correlations of .50 between EI and gregariousness on a solitary-gregarious scale. The sample was a composite of students in four colleges. The subsample of 249 cases shown in Figure 9.7 had a correlation between extraversion and gregariousness of .42. When extraverts are correlated independently of introverts, the correlation was only .05. The introvert correlation independent of extraverts was –21. Figure 9.7 indicates that the faculty considered gregariousness a general characteristic of extraverts, and it was not related to the degree of extraversion. Introverts of any degree are seen as clearly less gregarious than extraverts; in addition, introverts giving the most extreme I scores on the MBTI were seen as the least gregarious.

The only significant change between contiguous groups occurred between the ranges E 1–11 and I 1–11 (*t* 2.80, *p*<.01). The change at or near zero is significantly greater than changes between any other positions on the EI index. These data support both the existence of a dichotomy on the EI index and the correctness of the location of its division point.

Preference for Reading and Differences on SN. Hicks (1984) described reports of S types and N types on the number of books read in the past year. Figure 9.8 shows the mean number of books reported for persons with different levels of preference for S or N. The largest difference appears at the midpoint; the clearer the preference for N, the more books are reported.

Figure 9.6 Proportion of engineering students at different levels of TF

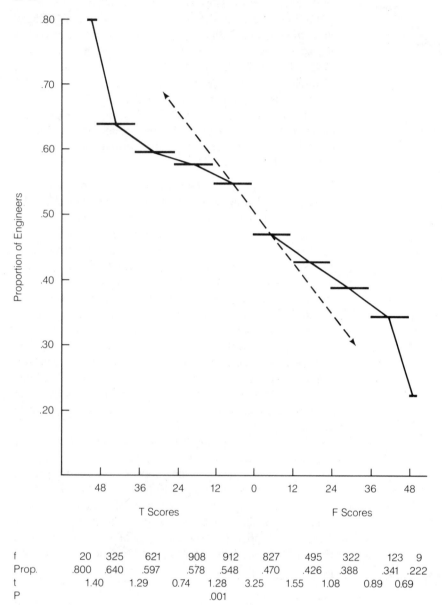

f	20	325	621	908	912	827	495	322	123	9
Prop.	.800	.640	.597	.578	.548	.470	.426	.388	.341	.222
t		1.40	1.29	0.74	1.28	3.25	1.55	1.08	0.89	0.69
P						.001				

Figure 9.7 Faculty ratings of gregariousness in students who report different levels of preference for EI

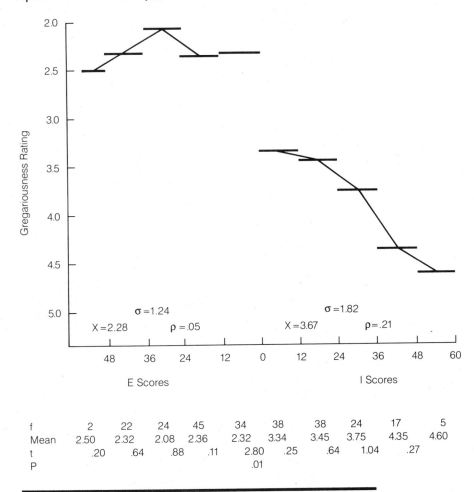

f	2	22	24	45	34	38	38	24	17	5
Mean	2.50	2.32	2.08	2.36	2.32	3.34	3.45	3.75	4.35	4.60
t		.20	.64	.88	.11	2.80	.25	.64	1.04	.27
P						.01				

Figure 9.8 Reported books read per year as a function of sensing and intuition preference scores

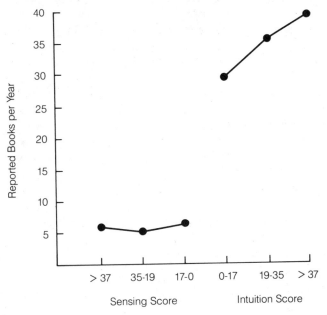

Chapter 10

Reliability

Two sets of questions are addressed in this chapter. The first set deals with the appropriateness of different estimates of internal consistency and of replicability over time. To permit reliability comparisons with other instruments, continuous score reliability estimates for the four preference scales are reported. However, MBTI scores are assumed to reflect underlying dichotomies, and the major interest of most MBTI users is in the consistency of remaining in the same type. Therefore, reliabilities that reflect these hypothesized dichotomies are also reported.

The second set of questions deals with that part of the variance in reliability estimates which is attributable to the characteristics of respondents. The reliability estimates for the MBTI are expected to vary, not only with the statistical procedures adopted, but also with the respondents' intelligence, with their understanding of themselves, and with the quality of their perception and judgment, as evidenced by their achievement.

An assumption, derived from observations made during the construction of the MBTI, is that persons with a good command of perception or judgment (i.e., with good type development) are more likely to be clear about their own preferences. They therefore will report their preferences more consistently. If these assumptions are correct, samples of older persons should have higher reliability estimates than samples of younger persons. Since the quality of perception and judgment is often evidenced by an individual's level of achievement, it is expected that in samples of persons of comparable age levels, those with higher achievement levels will also report their preferences more consistently, and thus these samples will evidence higher reliabilities than samples of their lower-achieving peers. Since the acquisition of good judgment is postulated to be the most difficult to develop, the TF index is expected to be particularly vulnerable to deficiencies in type development. Therefore, the lowest reliabilities in less effective samples are expected to occur in the TF index.

Internal Consistency Reliability Estimates

Internal Consistencies of Continuous Scores

X and Y Split-Half Scores. Split-half scores are designed primarily for use in internal consistency reliability calculations. Items were selected for the X and Y halves by a logical split-half procedure. Each index was split into halves, taking all available item statistics into consideration and pairing items that most resemble each other and correlate most highly. Consideration was given to the balancing of the halves by the expected number of responses. It was known that the responses with double weights were given less frequently, but, when given, were more predictive of

type preference. It was sometimes necessary to include three double weighted items to equate frequency of response. Each split half draws from every item content domain of each index. Table 10.1 shows the items included in the X and Y halves for Form F and Form G.

Split-Half Reliability. Table 10.2 shows split-half reliabilities of continuous scores for a number of groups. The reliabilities are consistent with those of other personality instruments, many of which have longer scales than the MBTI. The first groupings are from three samples of the CAPT data bank, showing the split-half reliabilities for subgroups from the data bank, based on the number of items omitted. Reliabilities remain stable up to thirty-five omissions for Form F, and up to twenty-five omissions for

Table 10.1 Item assignment for computation of split-half correlations

Form F				Form G			
X Half		Y Half		X Half		Y Half	
1	91	15	117	2	57	1	58
2	93	20	120	3	59	6	61
4	94	25	121	4	60	8	62
6	97	29	126	5	64	9	63
9	98	41	132	7	65	10	66
11	99	42	133	11	68	14	67
13	102	55	134	12	70	15	69
17	103	60	140	13	71	16	73
19	105	70	142	17	72	18	78
26	107	73	145	21	74	19	80
27	108	74	148	22	75	20	82
33	113	76	149	23	76	24	83
35	115	78	151	25	77	26	85
37	118	79	153	29	79	27	86
47	119	81	154	32	81	28	88
49	122	84	158	36	84	30	89
50	124	85	160	37	87	31	90
53	128	88	165	38	91	33	
58	129	92		39	92	34	
64	138	95		44	93	35	
66	147	100		45	95	40	
68		104		48		41	
72		106		49		42	
77		109		50		43	
86		111		51		46	
87		112		52		47	
89		114		53		55	
90		116		54		56	

Table 10.2 Internal consistency derived from product-moment correlations of X and Y continuous scores with Spearman-Brown prophecy formula correction

Description of Sample	Form	Sex	*N*	EI	SN	TF	JP
Samples from MBTI Data Bank							
Total Form F data bank	F	M,F	55,971	83	86	84	87
Males	F	M	23,240	82	87	84	88
Females	F	F	32,731	84	86	80	87
Traditional junior high school student	F	M,F	345	75	77	76	80
Traditional high school student	F	M,F	2,203	86	83	80	87
Adult high school dropout	F	M,F	601	79	85	81	87
Adult high school graduate, no college	F	M,F	1,943	84	85	87	88
Traditional college student	F	M,F	15,248	83	82	81	86
Nontraditional age college student	F	M,F	3,344	83	86	82	86
Adult college graduate	F	M,F	9,182	84	90	88	88
Age Groupings							
9–14	F	M,F	501	76	78	77	80
15–17	F	M,F	5,004	84	82	80	92
18–20	F	M,F	14,561	83	82	80	85
21–24	F	M,F	8,141	83	86	83	87
25–29	F	M,F	6,383	83	88	84	86
30–39	F	M,F	9,505	84	89	86	88
40–49	F	M,F	5,771	84	90	88	88
50–59	F	M,F	2,662	83	91	88	88
60+	F	M,F	821	82	90	86	88
Total Form G data bank	G	M,F	32,671	82	84	83	86
Males	G	M	15,791	82	84	82	86
Females	G	F	16,880	82	84	79	86
Traditional junior high school student	G	M,F	232	79	73	78	86
Traditional high school student	G	M,F	608	84	83	80	87
Adult high school dropout	G	M,F	378	77	86	84	84
Adult high school graduate, no college	G	M,F	1,260	82	84	84	85
Traditional college student	G	M,F	11,908	82	81	82	86
Nontraditional age college student	G	M,F	1,708	83	84	85	92
Adult college graduate	G	M,F	5,584	83	89	86	88
Age Groupings							
9–14	G	M,F	441	78	73	78	84
15–17	G	M,F	3,948	82	82	80	86
18–20	G	M,F	11,052	82	81	81	85
21–24	G	M,F	2,917	81	83	84	86
25–29	G	M,F	2,609	80	85	84	85
30–39	G	M,F	4,807	83	88	85	87
40–49	G	M,F	2,852	83	89	86	87
50–59	G	M,F	1,603	82	90	86	88
60+	G	M,F	520	83	88	85	88
Form F Sample Equal *N*s of each Type	F	M,F	9,216	84	85	83	85

(continued)

Table 10.2 Internal consistency derived from product-moment correlations of X and Y continuous scores with Spearman-Brown prophecy formula correction

Description of Sample	Form	Sex	*N*	EI	SN	TF	JP
Samples from MBTI Data Bank							
Form F Sample Equal *N*s of each Type							
	F	M	4,167	83	85	82	85
	F	F	4,559	84	85	79	85
Samples Differing in Education and Achievement Levels							
Students: Seventh to ninth grade							
(1) Underachieving seventh grade	F	M	44	60	60	57	62
	F	F	32	60	59	19	81
(1) Underachieving eighth grade	F	M	30	80	75	44	71
(2) Rural Florida eighth grade	F	M	54	65	43	49	66
	F	F	62	69	34	50	50
(1) Overachieving seventh grade	F	M	100	82	75	59	84
	F	F	100	85	73	68	85
(1) Gifted seventh to ninth grade	F	M	34	85	84	81	82
	F	F	26	81	76	84	75
(3) Educationally disadvantaged alternative school students	F	M	84	52	45	00	28
	F	F	34	80	84	41	79
High school students							
(1) Massachusetts twelfth grade							
General course	F	M	100	77	70	60	79
College preparatory course	F	M	100	79	84	76	87
		F	100	82	80	77	88
(4) Small Florida city twelfth grade	F	M	196	66	67	68	70
	F	F	207	79	74	71	76
(1) Virginia advanced placement, twelfth grade	F	F	37	87	85	84	94
(1) National Merit Finalists, 1960	F	M	100	85	86	82	89
(5) Florida future scientists	F	M	365	76	78	80	78
	F	F	307	78	78	73	75
University laboratory schools							
(6) University of Florida, grades nine through twelve	F	M	428	81	80	69	79
	F	F	418	87	81	70	83
(7) Florida State University, grades seven through twelve							
IQ 98 or lower	F	M	64	43	51	57	63
	F	F	73	70	41	47	66
IQ 99–115	F	M	93	75	75	70	66
	F	F	76	72	65	71	79
IQ 116 and higher	F	M	72	85	86	88	77
	F	F	80	82	81	75	80
College and university students							
(1) Amherst	F	M	126	82	86	80	87

(continued)

Table 10.2 Internal consistency derived from product-moment correlations of X and Y continuous scores with Spearman-Brown prophecy formula correction

Description of Sample	Form	Sex	N	EI	SN	TF	JP
Samples Differing in Education and Achievement Levels							
(1) Brown	F	M	100	81	87	86	80
(1) Long Island University	F	M	300	76	75	74	84
	F	F	184	78	80	71	81
(1) Pembroke	F	F	100	82	87	83	84
(1) Wesleyan	F	M	56	88	90	77	85
(8) University of Florida freshmen	F	M	1868	82	84	85	86
	F	F	1494	86	85	85	85
Males in aptitude groups							
First quartile	F	M	390	82	80	77	86
Second quartile	F	M	382	75	87	81	83
Third quartile	F	M	392	83	86	80	88
Fourth quartile	F	M	396	83	83	81	87
Females in aptitude groups							
First quartile	F	F	305	85	80	75	84
Second quartile	F	F	312	81	84	77	86
Third quartile	F	F	307	86	85	81	87
Fourth quartile	F	F	310	88	85	85	87
Males in achievement groups							
First quartile	F	M	394	82	84	78	85
Second quartile	F	M	368	80	86	80	85
Third quartile	F	M	393	81	82	80	87
Fourth quartile	F	M	405	84	85	81	87
Females in achievement groups							
First quartile	F	F	305	86	81	76	84
Second quartile	F	F	300	87	84	79	85
Third quartile	F	F	308	85	85	83	86
Fourth quartile	F	F	321	86	87	81	88
Student teachers							
(9) Florida State University	F	M,F	117	71	81	68	80
(10) Michigan State University	F	M	64	87	90	81	85
	F	F	136	84	85	77	87
University of New Mexico							
(11) Nursing students, New Mexico	F	M,F	121	88	87	84	85
(12) Medical students, New Mexico	F	M,F	91	86	88	80	88
(9) Teachers in Florida	F	M,F	113	63	82	67	83

Notes: Decimals omitted.
MBTI data bank analyses were conducted at different times; the later analyses have higher numbers.
Sources and description of samples appear in Appendix B.
(1) Samples reported by Isabel Briggs Myers in the first edition of this Manual or prepared for the second edition; (2) McCaulley and Kainz, 1976; (3) Szymanski, 1977; (4) Morgan and Kainz, 1975; (5) Abbot and McCaulley, 1983; (6) Guttinger and McCaulley, 1975; (7) McCaulley and Natter, 1974; (8) McCaulley and Kainz, 1974; (9) Hoffman, 1975; (10) Carlyn, 1976; (11) Weiss, 1980; (12) Otis and Quenk, 1973.

Form G. These cutoff points can be used to determine the number of omissions acceptable in research studies, that is, the point at which cases should be dropped from analyses.

The second set of groupings from the CAPT MBTI data bank shows reliability coefficients for males and females separately. The third set of groupings show reliabilities for age groups. Reliabilities tend to be somewhat lower for respondents in their teens, but stabilize from the twenties onward. One theory is that there may be lower reliabilities in midlife on the assumption that people reassess their preferences and move to higher stages of development. No such trends appear in the data bank samples.

The samples of students in high school and before high school are grouped by postulated levels of achievement. Underachieving students and rural Florida students show much lower consistency in responses than do "overachieving" or high-achieving students. The TF scale, as predicted, is the most likely to be depressed. Among the high school students, the college preparatory students in Massachusetts show higher reliabilities than their classmates in noncollege preparatory courses. Students in advanced placement in Arlington, Virginia, show even higher reliabilities. Among the Florida samples, the University of Florida laboratory school shows higher reliabilities than the seniors of the small city school, even though the laboratory school sample includes younger students.

In the Florida State University laboratory school, students are grouped by intelligence. As predicted, reliability scores are higher in the higher intelligence groups. Intelligence scores may be related to MBTI reliability in two ways. First, intelligence can be seen as a result of effective command of perception and judgment, that is, more infor-

mation is taken in accurately, and better judgments are made. Second, more intelligent students typically have a higher reading level and may have better understanding of the MBTI vocabulary. Greater understanding leads to lower likelihood of random responding and thus greater consistency.

As predicted, the college and university samples had higher reliabilities than the high school samples. When University of Florida students were grouped by aptitude, there was a slight tendency for higher aptitude students to give more consistent reponses, particularly on the TF scale.

Internal Consistency Coefficients Based on Coefficient Alpha. Table 10.3 shows internal consistency reliabilities estimated by coefficient alpha. These coefficients are roughly the same as those computed with Pearson's r.

In summary, the estimates of internal consistency reliabilities for the continuous scores of the four MBTI scales are acceptable for most adult samples. The reliabilities are adequate, if somewhat lower, for younger samples, and for other populations of persons who can be considered to be performing at lower levels of achievement or type development.

Internal Consistency of Dichotomies

Split-Half Reliabilities for Type Categories. The split-half reliabilities in Table 10.2 are derived from product-moment correlations of continuous scores for the X half and Y half of each index. They take no account of the dichotomies for which the MBTI was designed. The relia-

Table 10.3 Internal consistency of continuous scores based on coefficient alpha

Description of Sample	N	Sex	EI	SN	TF	JP
(1) Massachusetts high schools	397	M	78	77	64	78
	400	F	83	74	70	81
(1) Long Island University	399	M	76	75	74	84
	184	F	78	80	71	81
(2) MBTI data bank	9,216*	M,F	83	83	76	80
(3) IPAR data bank	100	M	82	85	82	84
	100	F	74	82	78	84

Notes: All data based on Form F. Decimals omitted.
Sources and description of samples appear in Appendix B.
(1) Stricker and Ross, 1963; (2) Kainz, 1984; (3) Gough, 1981.
*(n = 288 of each type)

bility of these dichotomous categories obviously depends on the reliability of scores in the vicinity of the division point, and may be investigated by the use of a 2 x 2 table showing how often the X half and Y half of a given index agree or differ as to type category.

Phi as an Estimate of Reliability of Type Categories. At first glance, it may seem that phi, a statistic for categorical data, is an appropriate measure for correlation of MBTI categories. However, MBTI data are not true categories; they are an end product of scoring. "Reliabilities" for type categories, computed by applying the Spearman-Brown prophecy formula to phi coefficients, are likely to understate the reliability of type categories.

Estimates of Reliabilities of Categories Using Tetrachoric Correlations. The task of determining internal consistencies for type categories is to learn whether categories derived from MBTI scores fully reflect the product-moment reliabilities for those scores. If, for any reason, the indices do not discriminate well in the center of the distribution, then the product-moment correlation, which is determined mainly by extreme scores, will not show the problem. Tetrachoric r (Guilford and Fruchter, 1973) has the advantage in that it is not affected by extreme scores, as is the product-moment correlation, but unreliability in the middle of the distribution will tend to lower the correlation. Therefore, tetrachoric correlations as estimates of reliability of categories will be sensitive precisely in the area where, in type theory, maximum sensitivity is needed for accurate type classification.

One problem in using tetrachoric correlations with MBTI data is that this statistic assumes an underlying normal distribution, and MBTI scores are typically not normally distributed. Carlyn (1976) suggests that reliabilities of type categories can be estimated by comparing phi coefficients (which tend to estimate low) and tetrachoric correlations (which tend to estimate high). Actual correlations probably fall between these two estimates. Table 10.4 shows a series of comparisons using estimates derived from applying the Spearman-Brown prophecy formula to phi coefficients and tetrachoric coefficients. Very close correspondence can probably not be expected among these correlations. The tetrachoric r (and any statistic derived from it) is considerably more variable than the product-moment r; but if the reliabilities are of the same general order of magnitude, there can have been no failure of reliability near the division point. Under these circumstances, the type categories can be assumed to be as reliable as would be expected from the reliabilities as measured by continuous scores. Since the general order of magnitude is not greatly different for the correlations in Table 10.2 and Table 10.4 one can

repose as much confidence in type categories as one would in any critical score or cutting point on other personality tests with similar reliabilities.

Test-Retest Reliability Estimates

For the MBTI, test-retest reliabilities go beyond the typical computations of correlations for the four continuous scores. The practical questions revolve around the likelihood that on retest a person will come out the same MBTI type, that is, a person will choose the same pole of all four dichotomous preferences.

Reliabilities in this section include (*a*) correlations of continuous scores, (*b*) the proportion of cases assigned the same letter (direction of preference) on retest, and (*c*) the proportion of cases reporting on retest all four preferences the same (i.e., the same type), three preferences, two preferences, one preference, or no preference the same. As in the earlier discussion, the issue of type development is expected to be a contributor to consistency of preferences.

Test-Retest Correlations of Continuous Scores

Table 10.5 shows test-retest product-moment correlations in samples from seventh grade to medical school. In eight of fourteen comparisons, the reliability coefficient for TF, as predicted by Isabel Myers, is the lowest of the four scales.

Test-Retest Reliabilities of Type Categories

Tables 10.6 and 10.7 show test-retest percentages of agreement for the EI, SN, TF, and JP categories. The tables also show the percentages of persons reporting 4, 3, 2, 1, or no preferences the same on retest. Note that the chance probability of choosing all four preferences on retest (i.e., coming out the same type) is 6.25%. The actual test-retest probabilities are significantly different from chance.

As part of a study of the effects of moods on reliabilities, Howes (1977) administered the MBTI and the 16 PF to introductory psychology student volunteers. The data (Table 10.7) showed significant elevation or lowering of their mood, but these mood changes did not significantly affect test-retest MBTI correlations. Howes reported separately reliabilities for students originally giving low, moderate, or high preference scores. This part of his study was replicated by the Center for Applications of Psychological Type on a sample of student nurses tested by J. Weiss at the College of Nursing at the University of New Mexico. Table 10.7 also contains a sample of British medical students. Table 10.7 compares the three samples showing

Table 10.4 A comparison of internal consistency of type categories using estimates from Phi Coefficients and Tetrachoric correlations, all corrected using the Spearman-Brown prophecy formula

Description of Sample	Method	*N*	Sex	EI	SN	TF	JP
Massachusetts: Twelfth grade students							
Myers (1962)							
General course	Phi	100	M	61	54	49	73
	r_{tet}			78	77	66	88
College preparatory: Male	Phi	100	M	69	65	58	75
	r_{tet}			88	81	76	91
College preparatory: Female	Phi	100	F	57	66	60	79
	r_{tet}			74	83	80	93
National merit finalists, (1960)	Phi	100	M	72	69	62	67
Myers (1962)	r_{tet}			88	87	80	84
College students							
Brown University freshmen	Phi	100	M	55	73	75	58
Myers (1962)	r_{tet}			74	88	90	76
Pembroke College freshmen	Phi	100	F	65	64	67	68
Myers (1962)	r_{tet}			81	83	84	84
Michigan State University: Student teachers							
Carlyn (1976)							
Males	Phi	64	M	79	73	67	78
	r_{tet}			92	89	83	92
Females	Phi	136	F	68	70	62	71
	r_{tet}			86	86	84	86

Notes: Decimals omitted. All data based on Form F.
Phi indicates split-half reliabilities computed by applying Spearman-Brown Prophecy Formula to Phi Coefficients. Tet indicates split-half reliabilities computed by applying Spearman-Brown Prophecy Formula to Tetrachoric Coefficients. (Phi Coefficients tend to yield low estimates of true values, and Tetrachoric Coefficients tend to yield high estimates of true values.)

the changes for subjects having low, moderate, and high initial preference scores. There is clearly a trend for the most changes to occur in cases where the original preference was low.

In conclusion, test-retest reliabilities of the MBTI show consistency over time. When subjects report a change in type, it is most likely to occur in only one preference, and in scales where the original preference was low.

Table 10.5 Test-retest product-moment correlations of continuous scores

Description of Sample	Form	Interval	N	Sex	EI	SN	TF	JP
(1) Seventh grade students	F	12 months	77	M,F	73	69	60	69
(1) Amherst: Class of 1963	F	14–16 months	126	M	75	69	60	74
(1) Wesleyan: Class of 1963	F	8 months	56	M	82	83	78	70
(2) Howard University	F	2 months	146	M	80	69	73	80
	F	2 months	287	F	83	78	82	82
(3) Wesleyan paid undergraduates	F	1 week	93	M,F	89	88	86	na
Mississippi State University Introductory psychology students								
(4) 1977 Form F study	F	7 weeks	64	M	79	79	56	76
	F	7 weeks	70	F	83	82	73	87
(5) 1979 Form G study	G	7 weeks	32	M	79	84	48	63
	G	7 weeks	24	F	86	87	87	80
(6) 1979 sex differences study	G	5 weeks	24	M	77	93	91	87
	G	5 weeks	36	F	89	85	56	89
(7) Mood manipulation study	F	5 weeks	117	M,F	82	87	78	81
Depressed mood			38	M,F	87	82	80	77
Elated mood			40	M,F	79	85	71	84
Control group			39	M,F	81	91	83	81
(8) Sub-scores study	G	5 weeks	62	F	86	85	77	89
Phrase questions					82	79	63	86
Word-pair questions					77	78	72	84
Split-half: X items					82	86	66	85
Split-half: Y items					75	78	70	86
(9) Instructions manipulation	G	4 weeks	128	M,F				
Standard-Standard			40	M,F	93	80	89	88
Vocational-Vocational			40	M,F	90	85	89	83
Standard-Vocational			48	M,F	87	78	79	88
(10) Student nurses	F	2.5 years	121	M,F	75	70	64	60
Medical students								
(1) University of New Mexico	F	9–21 months	91	M,F	78	73	67	64
(11) St. Mary's in London	F	4 years	120	M,F	51	58	45	45

Notes: Decimals omitted from correlations.

Sources and description of samples appear in Appendix B.

(1) Myers, 1973; (2) Levy, Murphy, and Carlson, 1972; (3) Steele and Kelly, 1976;
(4) Carskadon, 1977; (5) Carskadon, 1979c; (6) Carskadon, 1982; (7) Howes, 1977;
(8) McCarley and Carskadon, 1983; (9) Parham, Miller, and Carskadon, 1984;
(10) Weiss, 1980; (11) Harris, 1981.

Table 10.6 Test-retest agreement of type categories

Description of Sample	N	Sex	Test-Retest Interval	Percent of Agreement in Each MBTI Category				Percentage of Categories Unchanged on Retest				
				EI	SN	TF	JP	4	3	2	1	0
(1) Seventh grade students	77	M,F	12 months	75	74	73	79	39	na	na	na	na
(1) Amherst class of 1963	126	M	14–17 months	76	87	75	77	37	44	16	4	0
(1) Wesleyan freshmen	56	M	8 months	84	88	79	75	47	39	14	2	0
(2) Auburn University sophomores	329	M,F	2 years	74	71	73	77	31	39	22	7	0
(3) Howard University	433	M,F	2 months	Mean Agreement 85%				53	35	10	2	0
(4) Mississippi State University	177	M,F	5 weeks	81	89	83	84	48	37	13	0	0
Mood manipulation study	67	M	5 weeks	76	84	79	82	43	34	22	0	0
	50	F	5 weeks	89	92	88	84	56	42	2	0	0
(5) Mississippi State University												
Subscores study	62	F	5 weeks	86	77	79	89	47	na	na	na	na
Phrase questions				81	84	76	90	48	na	na	na	na
Word-pair questions				84	76	84	90	50	na	na	na	na
Split-half: X items				87	84	86	92	53	na	na	na	na
Spilt-half: Y items				81	77	86	89	50	na	na	na	na
(6) University of New Mexico												
nursing students	121	M,F	2.5 years	68	77	77	74	36	39	19	6	0
(7) Physician assistant students	na	M	2 years	74	78	78	78	39	39	13	9	0
	na	F	2 years	77	64	77	73	32	27	36	5	0
Medical students												
(8) University of New Mexico	91	M,F	9–21 months	80	81	76	69	42	33	20	4	1
(9) University of Utah	125	M,F	36–44 months	75	76	69	83	33	40	25	2	0
(10) St. Mary's Hospital, London	120	M,F	4.5 years	72	66	68	66	24	37	29	8	0
(11) Elementary teachers	94	M,F	6 years	83	89	90	90	61	na	na	na	na

Notes: All data based on Form F. By chance, 6.25% are expected to remain the same in all four categories; 25% to change one category; 37.5% to change two categories; 25% to change three categories; and 6.25% to change all four categories.
Sources and description of samples appear in Appendix B.
(1) Myers, 1973; (2) Stalcup, 1968; (3) Levy, Murphy, and Carlson, 1972; (4) Howes, 1977;
(5) McCarley and Carskadon, 1983; (6) Weiss, 1980; (7) Bruhn, Bunce, and Greaser, 1978;
(8) Kelley, Harris, and Coleman, 1984; (9) Harris, 1981; (10) Wright, 1967.

Table 10.7 Test-retest agreement of type categories for different levels of strength of preference

Description of Sample	Interval	Percent of Test-Retest Agreement in Each Category							
		N	EI	*N*	SN	*N*	TF	*N*	JP
Howes Mood Manipulation Study	5 weeks	117	81	117	89	117	83	117	84
Low preference score 0–15		44	68	43	74	62	71	43	70
Moderate preference score 16–29		41	83	34	94	28	96	32	88
High preference score 31 and over		32	97	40	100	27	96	42	95
Elation condition									
Low preference score 0–15		16	62	16	69	21	67	12	58
Moderate preference score 16–29		15	80	9	81	12	92	8	75
High preference score 31 and over		9	89	15	100	7	86	20	95
Depressive condition									
Low preference score 0–15		15	87	16	75	16	75	12	58
Moderate preference score 16–29		11	91	13	92	10	100	8	75
High preference score 31 and over		8	100	9	100	12	100	13	92
Control group									
Low preference score 0–15		13	54	11	82	25	72	14	79
Moderate preference score 16–29		15	80	11	100	6	100	12	100
High preference score 31 and over		11	100	16	100	27	96	9	100
University of New Mexico:									
Nursing students	5 years	121	68	121	66	121	66	121	74
Low preference score 0–15		46	63	48	62	51	69	57	60
Moderate preference score 16–29		37	78	38	84	47	79	34	82
High preference score 31 and over		38	95	35	89	23	91	30	90
Medical Students (England)	4 years	120							
Male		74							
Low preference score 1–15		32	53	27	59	38	68	22	55
Moderate preference score 16–29		27	89	26	73	25	72	17	59
Strong preference score 31 and over		15	80	21	90	11	73	35	77
Female		46							
Low preference score 1–15		18	67	20	35	26	62	18	67
Moderate preference score 16–29		20	70	17	59	16	75	12	67
Strong preference score 31 and over		8	100	9	89	4	50	16	62

Chapter 11   Validity

Because the MBTI was designed to implement Jung's theory of psychological types, its validity is determined by its ability to demonstrate relationships and outcomes predicted by theory. The theory suggests that persons are, or become, different types. The MBTI attempts to classify persons according to their "true" types. The theory postulates that the basic preferences for sensing or intuitive perception lead to different interests and that basic preferences for thinking or feeling judgment lead to differences in acting on those interests. Motivation, values, and behaviors are seen as surface indicators of the effects of the basic preferences and attitudes. If Jung's theory describes preferences that do exist, and if the MBTI adequately indicates those preferences, then surface behaviors should be in the directions predicted by the theory, allowing for measurement error, stage of development, and overriding environmental pressures that interfere with expression of type preferences.

This chapter aims to answer the following questions:

1. Do MBTI continuous scores correlate in the expected directions with other instruments that appear to be tapping the same constructs?

2. Is there evidence that the behavior of the MBTI types is consistent with behavior predicted by theory?

3. What can knowledge of type differences contribute to understanding of other issues of importance to psychology?

Content validity will not be discussed in this chapter in any detail. While the theory was taken very seriously in developing items (see Chapter 9), as was also observation of the behaviors of different types, item selection was ultimately based only on the empirical evidence that the items separate persons with opposing preferences.

Chapter 6 includes validity data related to psychological treatment and treatment modes preferred by both patient and professional as a function of type. Chapter 7 includes information related to the construct validity of interests as they relate to careers. Chapter 8 contains validity data in education, that is, aptitude, interest, application, achievement, and other aspects of teaching and learning. These topics will not be repeated here.

Evidence for Validity from Type Distributions

Type distributions are the basic method for presenting MBTI data on groups. A type table is sometimes seen as merely descriptive information before the "real" experiment. On the contrary, type tables themselves provide evidence for construct validity. For example, if the type table for a given occupation has significantly more of the types predicted by theory to have interest in, and therefore be more likely to be members of, that occupation, then the type table contributes to construct validity. Type distributions presented throughout this Manual provide evidence for the construct validity of the MBTI.

Correlation of MBTI Continuous Scores with Other Scales

Table 11.1 summarizes representative correlations from many samples and instruments. Correlations of the MBTI with measures that may be better known to the reader create a bridge for understanding the dimensions of the MBTI preferences. The left-hand columns show the actual product-moment correlations of MBTI continuous scores with scales of personality, interest, and academic tests. In addition, to make it easier to identify correlates of each preference, the right-hand columns designate the letters for preferences where correlations are at least .20 and significant at probabilities of .01 or greater. This means that there are statistically significant correlations shown in the main body of the table that are not flagged in the right-hand column. The conventional notation for MBTI correlations is followed, such that *positive correlations are associated with I, N, F, or P, and negative correlations with E, S, T, or J*. By scanning the right-hand columns, the reader can quickly identify characteristics associated with each preference and can judge whether these characteristics make sense in light of the expectations of the theory. Note that it is as important for theory that certain correlations *are not* significant as that other correlations are in the expected directions. For example, E should be positively correlated with measures of sociability; T should not.

Correlations have their limitations as evidence for construct validity. They report only the four preferences one at a time, and do not show the sixteen types as dynamic

entities. Correlations also have the problem of confounding direction and strength of preference. Finally, correlations in most cases understate the magnitude of the relationships.

Unless otherwise noted, high scores in the scales reflect the concept named by the author of the scale. For example, a scale named "spontaneity" correlates with P. High scores for spontaneity would be associated with high scores on JP and there would be a "P" in the right hand column. Not mentioned in the table, but implicit in correlations, is the fact that when high spontaneity is associated with P, low spontaneity is associated with J since both are bipolar scales. Similarly, when a scale is highly associated with J, there will be a negative correlation in the JP column and a "J" in the right-hand column.

Extraversion

In type theory, extraversion is an outward attitude in which energy flows to the environment. This outward turning is manifested in different ways which are reflected in significant correlations with other scales ranging from $-.77$ to $-.40$. The following are some examples:

- Extraversion as measured by other instruments (MMPI, 16PF, Maudsley, etc.).

- Sense of comfort in the environment, shown in measures named self-regard, self-acceptance, self-confidence, autonomy, social adjustment, well-being, personal integration, stability or ability to face reality, ego strength, and personal integration.

- Action on the environment, shown in correlations with leadership, dominance, assertiveness, enterprising, and capacity for status.

- Quick response to energy from the environment, shown in measures named venturesome, spontaneity, surgency, lability, play, and happy-go-lucky.

- Overreliance on the environment, as shown in measures of hypomania, lability, and dyscontrol.

- Freedom of expression, which appears in public speaking and talkativeness.

- Sociability in scales such as inclusion, gregariousness, outgoing, and being with people.

- Relatedness to other people, as shown in expressed affection, expressed inclusion, affiliation, liking numbers of people, and altruism.

(text continued on page 206)

Table 11.1 Correlation of MBTI continuous scores with other measures

Source Sample Description	N	Sex	EI	SN	TF	JP	Relation
			Personality Measures				

Adjective Check List (ACL) (Gough & Heilbrun, 1983)

Source Sample Description	N	Sex	EI	SN	TF	JP	Relation
(1) Self-confidence	152	M,F	−47***	36**	−26*	15	EN--
(1) Self-control	152	M,F	15	−32**	12	−46***	-S-J
(1) Lability	152	M,F	−35***	52***	10	38***	EN-P
(1) Personal adjustment	65	M	−12	−12	30**	−32**	--FJ
(1)	87	F	−12	−12	−06	−32**	---J
(1) Achievement	152	M,F	−15	17	−27**	−12	--T-
(1) Dominance	152	M,F	−52***	15	−34**	−05	E-T-
(1) Endurance	87	F	05	−27**	−28**	−47**	-STJ
(1)	65	M	05	−27**	05	−47**	-S-J
(1) Order	87	F	−06	−28**	−24**	−50***	-STJ
(1)	65	M	−06	−28**	01	−50***	-S-J
(1) Intraception	65	M	06	18	25**	−10	--F-
(1)	87	F	06	18	04	−10	----
(1) Affiliation	65	M	−33**	14	35***	−12	E-F-
(1)	87	F	−33**	14	02	−12	E---
(1) Autonomy	65	M	−34**	35***	−40***	41***	ENTP
(1)	87	F	−34**	35***	01	41***	EN-P
(1) Abasement	152	M,F	51***	−19	41***	−25**	I-FJ
(1) Deference	65	M	41***	−34**	46***	−44***	ISFJ
(1)	87	F	41***	−34**	13	−44***	IS-J

California Psychological Inventory (CPI) (Gough, 1975)

Source Sample Description	N	Sex	EI	SN	TF	JP	Relation
(2) Dominance (Do)	713	M	−53***	07	00	−06	E---
(3)	1218	M,F	−45***	12***	−07*	−08**	E---
(2) Capacity for status (Cs)	713	M	−35***	29***	02	03	EN--
(3)	1218	M,F	−44***	41***	05	15***	EN--
(2) Sociability (Sy)	713	M	−67***	05	06	−01	E---
(3)	1218	M,F	−66***	26***	07*	06*	EN--
(2) Social presence (Sp)	713	M	−47***	15***	00	22***	E--P
(3)	1218	M,F	−49***	36***	03	25***	EN-P
(2) Self-acceptance (Sa)	713	M	−53***	08*	04	09*	E---
(3)	1218	M,F	−47***	20***	00	08**	EN--
(2) Sense of well-being (Wb)	713	M	−23***	02	−06	−17***	E---
(3)	1218	M,F	−22***	−02	−14***	−15***	E---

(continued)

Table 11.1 Correlation of MBTI continuous scores with other measures

Source Sample Description	N	Sex	EI	SN	TF	JP	Relation
			Personality Measures				
(2) Responsibility (Re)	713	M	−06	03	−01	−30***	---J
(3)	1218	M,F	−07*	07	−01	−22***	---J
(2) Socialization (So)	713	M	−03	−12**	−03	−32***	---J
(3)	1218	M,F	−07*	−15***	−05	−28***	---J
(2) Self-control (Sc)	713	M	09*	−10**	−06	−34***	---J
(3)	1218	M,F	05	−14***	−13***	−28***	---J
(2) Tolerance (To)	713	M	−16***	16***	03	−08*	----
(3)	1218	M,F	−23***	19***	03	−01	E---
(2) Good impression (Gi)	713	M	−16***	02	−01	−27***	---J
(3)	1218	M,F	−23***	02	−08**	−20***	E--J
(2) Communality (Cm)	713	M	−06	−17***	−02	−24***	---J
(3)	1218	M,F	−01	−21***	−05	−21***	-S-J
(2) Achievement via conformance (Ac)							
	713	M	−16***	−01	−05	−37***	---J
(3)	1218	M,F	−20***	06*	−08**	−28***	E--J
(2) Achievement via independence (Ai)							
	713	M	10**	27***	06	00	-N--
(3)	1218	M,F	−01	31***	13***	13***	-N--
(2) Intellectual efficiency (Ie)	713	M	−21***	24***	−06	−03	EN--
(3)	1218	M,F	−25***	28***	−00	08**	EN--
(2) Psychological-mindedness (Py)							
	713	M	01	25***	−07	02	-N--
(3)	1218	M,F	−07*	30***	−09**	07**	-N--
(2) Flexibility (Fx)	713	M	04	29***	09*	45***	-N-P
(3)	1218	M,F	−07	45***	19***	44***	-N-P
(2) Femininity (Fe)	713	M	13***	−05	17***	−19***	----

Comrey Personality Scales (Comrey, 1970)

	N	Sex	EI	SN	TF	JP	Relation
(4) Trust versus defensiveness							
	102	M	−07	06	16	17	----
(4)	139	F	−16	03	35***	−08	--F-
(4) Orderliness versus lack of compulsion							
	102	M	20*	−28**	−33***	−52***	-STJ
(4)	139	F	06	−40**	−10	−54***	-S-J
(4) Social conformity versus rebellion							
	102	M	12	−39**	−16	−28**	-S-J
(4)	139	F	−23**	−41**	26**	−24**	ESFJ
(4) Activity versus lack of energy							
	102	M	−26**	04	11	−08	E---
(4)	139	F	−13	07	−07	−11	----

Table 11.1 Correlation of MBTI continuous scores with other measures

Source Sample Description	N	Sex	EI	SN	TF	JP	Relation
			Other Instruments				
(4) Emotional stability versus neuroticism							
(4)	102	M	−21*	−08	−12	−07	----
(4)	139	F	−38***	−04	03	−12	E---
(4) Extraversion versus introversion							
(4)	102	M	−69***	24*	24*	13	E---
(4)	139	F	−74***	14	12	04	E---
(4) Masculinity versus femininity							
(4)	102	M	07	−03	−23*	03	----
(4)	139	F	21*	29**	−33***	16	-NT-
(4) Empathy versus egocentrism							
(4)	102	M	−18	13	35***	10	--F-
(4)	139	F	−22**	02	33***	−03	E-F-
Edwards Personality Preference Survey (EPPS) (Edwards, 1959)							
(5) Achievement	236	M	15*	15*	−20**	−02	--T-
(5) Deference	236	M	19**	−18**	−13*	−21**	---J
(5) Order	236	M	13*	−34**	−26**	−49**	-STJ
(5) Exhibition	236	M	−24**	02	−05	22**	E--P
(5) Autonomy	236	M	06	31**	−24**	31**	-NTP
(5) Affiliation	236	M	−17**	−05	38**	02	--F-
(5) Intraception	236	M	05	13*	01	−04	----
(5) Succorance	236	M	08	−12	27**	04	--F-
(5) Dominance	236	M	−28**	02	−23**	−10	E-T-
(5) Abasement	236	M	18**	−10	23**	−01	--F-
(5) Nurturance	236	M	−04	−01	51**	06	--F-
(5) Change	236	M	−11	13*	−15*	20**	---P
(5) Endurance	236	M	06	−06	−30**	−30**	--TJ
(5) Heterosexuality	236	M	−07	05	16*	19**	----
(5) Aggression	236	M	01	06	−12	15*	----
Emotions Profile Index (Plutchik & Kellerman, 1974)							
(6) Trust	60	M,F	−38**	−05	30*	11	E-F-
(6) Dyscontrol	60	M,F	−36*	04	11	40**	E--P
(6) Timid	60	M,F	25	−27	27	−19	----
(6) Depressed	60	M,F	53***	13	−07	−39**	I--J
(6) Distrust	60	M,F	−05	08	−42**	05	--T-
(6) Controlled	60	M,F	36*	05	−09	−14	I---
(6) Aggressive	60	M,F	16	02	−23	−04	----
(6) Gregarious	60	M,F	−48***	02	23	18	E---
(6) Bias	60	M,F	−38**	−13	24	13	E---
Eysenck Personality Questionnaires (EPQ) (Eysenck & Eysenck, 1968)							
(7) Extraversion-introversion	93	M,F	74***	−13*	17*		E---
(7) Neuroticism	93	M,F	27**	−05	00		I---
(7) Psychoticism	93	M,F	05	23*	−08		----

(continued)

Table 11.1 Correlation of MBTI continuous scores with other measures

Source Sample Description	N	Sex	EI	SN	TF	JP	Relation
			Other Instruments				

Maudsley Personality Inventory (Eysenck, 1959)

Source Sample Description	N	Sex	EI	SN	TF	JP	Relation
(5) Extraversion-introversion	52	F	−63***	29*	−19	05	E---
(5) Neuroticism	52	F	36**	−31*	29*	−06	I---

FIRO-B (Schutz, 1958)

Source Sample Description	N	Sex	EI	SN	TF	JP	Relation
(8) Expressed inclusion	200	M,F	−45***	−07	08	−14*	E---
(8)	100	F	−35***	−11	02	−19	E---
(8)	100	M	−51***	−09	02	−14	E---
(3)	1,228	M,F	−46***	04	17***	−01	E---
(8) Wanted inclusion	200	M,F	−23**	−10	25***	−03	E-F-
(8)	100	F	−20*	−09	18	12	----
(8)	100	M	−22*	−16	25*	02	----
(3)	1,228	M,F	−26***	07*	15***	02	E---
(8) Expressed affection	200	M,F	−38***	−01	19**	−12	E---
(8)	100	F	−29**	−09	16	−19	E---
(8)	100	M	−56***	01	12	−09	E---
(3)	1,228	M,F	−42***	14***	28***	07*	E-F-
(8) Wanted affection	200	M,F	−17*	−11	21**	−10	--F-
(8)	100	F	−15	−25*	−24*	−21*	----
(8)	100	M	−19	−01	19	−02	----
(3)	1,228	M,F	−23***	06*	23***	05	E-F-
(8) Expressed control	200	M,F	−14*	−06	−22**	−19**	--T-
(8)	100	F	−16	−16	−19	−29**	---J
(8)	100	M	−20*	08	10	−07	E---
(3)	1,228	M,F	−16***	02	−20***	−05	--T-
(8) Wanted control	200	M,F	17*	−20**	17*	−08	-S--
(8)	100	F	31**	−18	09	−15	I---
(8)	100	M	08	−30**	16	−03	-S--
(3)	1,228	M,F	−02	−02	19***	01	----

Jungian Type Survey (Wheelwright, Wheelwright, & Buehler, 1964)

Source Sample Description	N	Sex	EI	SN	TF	JP	Relation
(5) Extraversion-introversion	47	M	79***	00	−37*	−17	I---
(5) Sensing-intuition	47	M	−24	58***	15	41**	-N-P
(5) Thinking-feeling	47	M	−20	17	60***	33*	--F-

Minnesota Multiphasic Personality Inventory (MMPI) (Dahlstrom & Welsh, 1960)

Source Sample Description	N	Sex	EI	SN	TF	JP	Relation
(2) Question (?)	225	M	−04	11	08	−30	----
(2) Lie (L)	225	M	−12	06	−17*	−11	----
(2) Validity (F)	225	M	−04	11	08	−30	----
(2) Test taking attitude (K)	225	M	−23***	06	−13*	−18**	I---
(2) Hypochondriasis (HS)	225	M	10	−05	−01	03	----
(2) Depression (D)	225	M	39***	−06	05	10	I---
(2) Hysteria (Hy)	225	M	−05	05	01	06	----
(2) Psychopathic deviate (Pd)	225	M	−08	11	12	23***	---P
(2) Masculinity and femininity (Mf)							
	225	M	22***	33***	22***	17*	INF-
(2) Paranoia (Pa)	225	M	12	04	12	03	----

Table 11.1 Correlation of MBTI continuous scores with other measures

Source Sample Description	N	Sex	EI	SN	TF	JP	Relation
			Other Instruments				
(2) Psychathenia	225	M	30***	−07	19**	13*	I---
(2) Schizophrenia (Sc)	225	M	23***	03	07	17*	I---
(2) Hypomania (Ma)	225	M	−29***	09	−06	16*	E---
(2) Social Introversion (Si)	225	M	63***	−06	02	10	I---

Omnibus Personality Inventory (OPI) (Heist, Yonge, Connelly, & Webster, 1968)

Source Sample Description	N	Sex	EI	SN	TF	JP	Relation
(9) Thinking introversion (TI)	484	M,F	−10*	53***	10*	11*	-N--
(9) (Academic interests)	648	M,F	−06	59***	04	12**	-N--
(9) Theoretical orientation (TO)	484	M,F	05	41***	−16***	07	-N--
(9) (Theoretical, logical)	648	M,F	−04	49***	−15***	10*	-N--
(9) Estheticism (Es)	484	M,F	−05	46***	29***	21***	-NFP
(9) (Artistic sensitivity)	648	M,F	−11*	48***	22***	17***	-NF-
(9) Complexity (Co)	484	M,F	03	60**	13**	57***	-N-P
(9) (Experimental, flexible)	648	M,F	-08	62***	12**	53***	-N-P
(9) Autonomy (Au)	484	M,F	11*	48***	09	37***	-N-P
(9) (Liberal, needs independence)	648	M,F	08	47***	01	33***	-N-P
(9) Religious Orientation (RO)	484	M,F	16***	20***	−15***	26***	-N-P
(9) (Skeptical, rejects orthodoxy)	648	M,F	09*	19***	−15***	25***	-N-P
(9) Social Extraversion (SE)	484	M,F	−75***	10*	06	−02	E---
(9) (Likes being with people)	648	M,F	−77***	07	01	−02	E---
(9) Impulse extraversion (IE)	484	M,F	−08	33***	07	42***	-N-P
(9) (Impulsive, imaginative)	648	M,F	−20***	29***	−06	34***	EN-P
(9) Personal integration (PI)	484	M,F	−38***	−10*	−08	−15***	E---
(9) (Not alienated or disturbed)	648	M,F	−37***	−05	−09*	−16***	E---
(9) Anxiety level (AL)	484	M,F	−20***	−07	−19***	−06	E---
(9) (Denial of anxiety or worry)	648	M,F	−23***	−02	−19***	−02	E---
(9) Altruism (AM)	484	M,F	−44***	21***	25***	−06	ENF-
(9) (Affiliative, care for others)	648	M,F	−39***	27***	29***	01	ENF-
(9) Practical outlook (PO)	484	M,F	−06	−67***	−21***	−41***	-STJ
(9) (Likes applied, concrete)	648	M,F	−03	−64***	−12**	−32***	-S-J
(9) Masculinity-femininity (MF)	484	M,F	10*	−31***	−35***	−12*	-ST-
(9) (Masculine, less social)	648	M,F	15***	−32***	−36***	−11*	-ST-
(9) Response bias (RB)	484	M,F	−26***	00	−11*	−30***	E--J
(9) (Good impression)	648	M,F	−26***	06	−09*	−32***	E--J
(9) Intellectual Disposition (IDC)	484	M,F	−03	−65***	−11*	−32***	-S-J
(9) (Learning is for practical use)	648	M,F	07	−65***	−04	−27***	-S-J

(continued)

Table 11.1 Correlation of MBTI continuous scores with other measures

Source Sample Description	N	Sex	EI	SN	TF	JP	Relation
			Other Instruments				

Personality Research Inventory (PRI) (Saunders, 1955)

Source Sample Description	N	Sex	EI	SN	TF	JP	Relation
(5) Self-insight	507	M	−03	02	05	11*	----
(5) Free-floating anxiety	507	M	22**	01	25**	12**	I-F-
(2)	722	M	09*	00	12**	00	----
(5) Self-acceptance	507	M	−16**	14**	12**	17**	----
(5) Tolerance for frustration	507	M	−11**	−02	07	−13**	----
(5) Tolerance for complexity	507	M	−02	34**	18**	47**	-N-P
(5) Compulsiveness	507	M	01	−04	−07	−10*	----
(5) Impulsiveness	507	M	−34**	24**	05	39**	EN-P
(2)	722	M	−13**	11**	−01	15**	----
(5) Altruism	507	M	−14**	01	04	−10*	----
(2)	722	M	02	−01	04	−02	----
(5) Talkativeness	507	M	−70**	15**	−11**	04	E---
(2)	722	M	−46**	05	−08*	−13**	E---
(5) Self-sufficiency	507	M	21**	15**	−17**	13**	I---
(2)	722	M	14**	−07	−14**	08*	----
(5) Gregariousness	507	M	−22**	−31**	06	−08	ES--
(2)	722	M	−18**	−18**	06	−04	----
(5) Aggressiveness	507	M	−12**	−14**	04	−28**	---J
(5) Attitude toward work	507	M	−19**	02	−22**	−36**	--TJ
(2)	722	M	−13**	10**	−07	−17**	----
(2) Foresight	507	M	−14**	01	−05	−16**	----
(5) Belief in importance of individual	507	M	−05	13**	12**	13**	----
(5) Belief in rights of groups	507	M	01	12**	−04	−07	----
(5) Social conscience	507	M	−09*	00	−03	−22**	---J
(5) Status aspiration	507	M	−13**	00	06	08	----
(5) Social know-how	507	M	−09*	−16**	02	−31**	---J
(5) Social status	507	M	−10*	−01	−01	03	----
(5) Masculine vigor	507	M	−05	−28**	−25**	−08	-ST-
(2)	722	M	13**	−07	−04	06	----
(5) Artistic versus practical	507	M	−03	42**	13**	15**	-N--

Table 11.1 Correlation of MBTI continuous scores with other measures

Source Sample Description	N	Sex	EI	SN	TF	JP	Relation
		Other Instruments					

Personality Research Inventory (PRI) (Saunders, 1955)

Source Sample Description	N	Sex	EI	SN	TF	JP	Relation
(5) Spiritual versus material	507	M	−05	00	23**	01	--F-
(2)	722	M	−13**	07	04	−06	----
(5) Progressive versus conservative							
	507	M	01	18**	−15**	11*	----
(5) Liking to use mind	507	M	−08	45**	−11*	02	-N--
(2)	722	M	−09*	26**	−08*	01	-N--

Stein Self-Description Questionnaire (Stein, 1966)

Source Sample Description	N	Sex	EI	SN	TF	JP	Relation
(10) Abasement	34	M	07	−11	21	40*	----
(10)	41	F	03	−33*	06	−32*	----
(10) Achievement	34	M	10	−29	−40*	−46**	---J
(10)	41	F	−18	13	−14	−02	----
(10) Affiliation	34	M	−37*	28	41*	33*	----
(10)	41	F	06	03	00	24	----
(10) Aggression	34	M	02	−20	−40*	−37*	----
(10)	41	F	−14	12	−19	13	----
(10) Autonomy	34	M	49**	14	−30	−01	I---
(10)	41	F	27	55***	−29	53***	-N-P
(10) Blameavoidance	34	M	03	−02	55**	49**	--FP
(10)	41	F	24	−32*	12	−25	-S--
(10) Counteraction	34	M	08	−05	−57***	−43**	--TJ
(10)	41	F	−31*	−03	−09	−03	----
(10) Defendance	34	M	51**	−07	−28	−15	I---
(10)	41	F	35*	−09	−11	−10	----
(10) Deference	34	M	−08	−20	05	09	----
(10)	41	F	06	−54***	−16	−42**	-S-J
(10) Dominance	34	M	−12	16	−45**	−37*	--T-
(10)	41	F	−59***	−03	−19	06	E---
(10) Exhibitionism	34	M	−39*	33*	30	19	----
(10)	41	F	−58***	02	04	06	E---
(10) Harmavoidance	34	M	−24	09	09	12	----
(10)	41	F	17	−24	02	−26	----
(10) Infavoidance	34	M	20	−07	17	16	----
(10)	41	F	47**	02	19	−04	I---
(10) Nurturance	34	M	−23	12	43*	32*	----
(10)	41	F	13	14	32*	−04	----

(continued)

Table 11.1 Correlation of MBTI continuous scores with other measures

Source Sample Description	N	Sex	EI	SN	TF	JP	Relation
			Other Instruments				

Stein Self-Description Questionnaire (Stein, 1966)

Source Sample Description	N	Sex	EI	SN	TF	JP	Relation
(10) Order	34	M	−13	−07	−12	−25	----
(10)	41	F	−06	−46**	−19	−59***	-S-J
(10) Play	34	M	−27	−03	34*	31	----
(10)	41	F	−09	21	25	35*	----
(10) Rejection	34	M	39*	−02	−34*	−29	----
(10)	41	F	20	11	−28	03	----
(10) Sentience	34	M	23	18	10	−06	----
(10)	41	F	−06	46**	16	50**	-N-P
(10) Sex	34	M	−39*	10	18	−12	----
(10)	41	F	−23	25	16	15	----
(10) Succorance	34	M	−08	−26	42*	42*	----
(10)	41	F	19	−00	39**	02	--F-

Bown Self-Report Inventory (SRI) (Bown & Richek, 1967)

Source Sample Description	N	Sex	EI	SN	TF	JP	Relation
(11) Self	149	F	−38**	−07	−01	−04	E---
(11) Others	149	F	−52**	−04	18*	05	E---
(11) Children	149	F	−32**	−08	14	−07	E---
(11) Authenticity	149	F	−23**	−21*	−06	−18*	E---
(11) Work	149	F	−14	−21*	−07	−37**	---J
(11) Reality (values life as a process)							
	149	F	−15	24**	13	17*	-N--
(11) Parents	149	F	−14	10	02	−04	----
(11) Hope	149	F	−32**	−20*	07	−13	E---
(11) Total	149	F	−42**	−14	08	−13	E---

Sixteen Personality Factor Questionnaire (16PF) (Cattell, Eber and Tatsuoka, 1970)

Primary factors

Source Sample Description	N	Sex	EI	SN	TF	JP	Relation
(9) A. Outgoing	66	M,F	−18	−24	01	−22	----
(9) (Affectothymia)	122	M,F	−43***	−07	−05	−13	E---
(9)	149	M,F	−22**	−01	31***	−02	E-F-
(9)	484	M,F	−40***	−08	16***	−18***	E---
(9)	645	M,F	−35***	−01	19***	−07	E---
(9) B. Intelligent	66	M,F	04	35**	22	19	-N--
(9) (Crystallized, power measure)							
	122	M,F	01	25**	−02	−05	-N--
(9)	149	M,F	−01	10	−07	01	----
(9)	484	M,F	05	14**	08	03	----
(9)	645	M,F	00	10*	−01	02	----
(9) C. Stable, faces reality	66	M,F	−30*	−22	−12	−14	----
(9) (High ego strength)	122	M,F	−23**	−17	−18*	−11	E---
(9)	149	M,F	−32**	−16*	00	−12	E---
(9)	484	M,F	−28***	−11*	−08	−08	E---
(9)	645	M,F	−31***	02	−06	09*	E---
(9) E. Assertive	66	M,F	−18	−18	−18	22	----

Table 11.1 Correlation of MBTI continuous scores with other measures

Source Sample Description	N	Sex	EI	SN	TF	JP	Relation
			Other Instruments				

Sixteen Personality Factor Questionnaire (16PF) (Cattell, Eber and Tatsuoka, (1970)

Source Sample Description	N	Sex	EI	SN	TF	JP	Relation
(9) (Dominance)	122	M,F	−08	25**	−06	32***	-N-P
(9)	149	M,F	−12	25**	−06	10	-N--
(9)	484	M,F	−21***	23***	−06	−20***	EN-P
(9)	645	M,F	−32***	29***	−18***	18***	EN-P
(9) F. Happy-go-lucky	66	M,F	−30*	09	03	10	----
(9) (Surgency)	122	M,F	−36***	33***	28***	34***	ENFP
(9)	149	M,F	−50***	03	16*	13	E---
(9)	484	M,F	−56***	12*	20***	21***	E-F?
(9)	645	M,F	−59***	13***	05	14***	E--P
(9) G. Conscientious	66	M,F	−11	−39***	−22	−54***	-S-J
(9) (Stronger superego)	122	M,F	−12	−44***	−24**	−50***	-STJ
(9)	149	M,F	−22**	−32***	−22**	−57***	ESTJ
(9)	484	M,F	−17***	−36***	−11**	−48***	-S-J
(9)	645	M,F	−11*	−38***	−06	−55***	-S-J
(9) H. Venturesome	66	M,F	−53***	03	−09	−01	E---
(9) (Parmia)	122	M,F	−67***	09	−09	01	E---
(9)	149	M,F	−63***	03	00	−14	E---
(9)	484	M,F	−64***	13**	03	04	E---
(9)	645	M,F	−76***	13***	−03	00	E---
(9) I. Tender-minded	66	M,F	05	17	29*	−01	----
(9) (Premsia)	122	M,F	−04	25**	30***	33***	-NFP
(9)	149	M,F	20*	31***	36***	33***	-NFP
(9)	484	M,F	06	31***	37***	25***	-NFP
(9)	645	M,F	−01	33***	25***	19***	-NF-
(9) L. Suspicious	66	M,F	01	12	−08	09	----
(9) (Protension)	122	M,F	19*	09	04	24**	---P
(9)	149	M,F	17*	01	−19*	00	----
(9)	484	M,F	13**	03	06	09	----
(9)	645	M,F	09*	04	−02	09*	----
(9) M. Imaginative	66	M,F	06	31*	18	21	----
(9) (Autia)	122	M,F	09	30***	19*	20**	-N-P
(9)	149	M,F	25**	34***	17*	40***	IN-P
(9)	484	M,F	26***	36***	06	21***	IN-P
(9)	645	M,F	02	36***	−03	15***	-N--
(9) Astute	66	M,F	22	−16	−06	−31*	----
(9) (Polished, socially aware)	122	M,F	01	−31***	−29**	−32***	-STJ
(9)	149	M,F	−03	−11	−25**	−28***	--TJ
(9)	484	M,F	−09	−10*	−19***	−13**	----
(9)	645	M,F	14***	−27***	−07	24***	-S-P
(9) Apprehensive	66	M,F	27*	22	11	21	----
(9) (Guilt proneness)	122	M,F	33***	−06	22*	06	I---
(9)	149	M,F	25**	−10	06	02	I---
(9)	484	M,F	20**	−11*	−12**	−10*	I-T-
(9)	645	M,F	23***	−07	16***	−03	I---

(continued)

Table 11.1 Correlation of MBTI continuous scores with other measures

Source Sample Description	N	Sex	EI	SN	TF	JP	Relation
			Other Instruments				

Sixteen Personality Factor Questionnaire (16PF) (Cattell, Eber and Tatsuoka, (1970)

(9) Q1. Experimenting	66	M,F	−02	32**	−23	22	-N--
(9) (Radicalism)	122	M,F	00	25**	−40***	12	-NT-
(9)	149	M,F	−13	28***	−10	13	-N--
(9)	484	M,F	09	31***	−15***	15***	-N--
(9)	645	M,F	02	27***	−25***	21***	-NTP
(9) Q2. Self-sufficient	66	M,F	41***	02	−03	12	I---
(9) (Self-sufficiency)	122	M,F	52***	00	00	12	I---
(9)	149	M,F	44***	22**	−03	21**	IN-P
(9)	484	M,F	41***	11*	−06	12*	I---
(9)	645	M,F	41***	14***	−11*	12**	I---
(9) Q3. Controlled	66	M,F	−05	−43***	−21	−41***	-S-J
(9) (High self-concept)	122	M,F	−11	−19*	−19*	−36***	---J
(9)	149	M,F	−01	−16*	−24**	−41***	--TJ
(9)	484	M,F	−10*	−15***	−17***	−27***	---J
(9)	645	M,F	−07	−29***	−17***	−40***	-S-J
(9) Q4. Tense	66	M,F	32**	26*	16	21	I---
(9) (High Ergic Tension)	122	M,F	22*	02	30***	06	--F-
(9)	149	M,F	28***	−03	04	02	I---
(9)	484	M,F	23***	−03	14**	−02	I---
(9)	645	M,F	26***	−02	09*	00	I---

16PF second order traits

(9) Extraversion	66	M,F	−51***	03	−05	00	E---
(9) (Exvia)	484	M,F	−70***	13**	12*	10*	E---
(9)	645	M,F	−74***	12**	03	05	E---
(9) Anxiety	66	M,F	35**	23	16	17	I---
(9) (High anxiety)	484	M,F	35***	−01	15***	04	I---
(9)	645	M,F	34***	−04	14***	06	I---
(9) Alert poise	66	M,F	−18	13	−17	23	----
(9) (Cortertia)	484	M,F	−17***	−21***	−34***	−08	-ST-
(9)	645	M,F	−30***	−06	−28***	01	E-T-
(9) Independence	66	M,F	−10	33**	−12	32**	-N-P
(9) (Independence)	484	M,F	29***	45***	−10*	36***	IN-P
(9)	645	M,F	−10*	46***	−23***	35***	-NTP

Criterion predictions

(9) Neurotic trend	66	M,F	37**	16	22	12	I---
(9) (More neurotic trend)	484	M,F	44***	−01	15***	−04	I---
(9)	645	M,F	48***	−04	18***	00	I---
(9) Leadership	66	M,F	−44***	−35**	−26*	−37**	ES-J
(9) (More leadership potential)	484	M,F	−54***	−09	−13**	−15***	E---
(9)	645	M,F	−58***	−15***	−16***	−26***	E--J

Table 11.1 Correlation of MBTI continuous scores with other measures

Source Sample Description	N	Sex	EI	SN	TF	JP	Relation
		Other Instruments					

Criterion predictions

(9) Creativity	66	M,F	12	50***	19	39***	-N-P
(9) (Creative personality)	484	M,F	43***	37***	02	25***	IN-P
(9)	645	M,F	16***	41***	−09*	25***	-N-P

STAI: State-Trait Anxiety Inventory (Spielberger, 1983)

(6) State	60	M,F	32*	−10	12	−30*	----
(6) Trait	60	M,F	38**	−06	−01	−24	I---

Study of Values (Allport, Vernon, & Lindzey, 1960)

(5) Theoretical	1,351	M	11**	26**	−37**	−05*	-NT-
(5)	236	M	14*	20**	−36**	−03	-NT-
(5)	238	M	09	22**	−35**	−02	-NT-
(9)	65	M,F	09	−16	−42***	−13	--T-
(5)	877	M	10**	28**	−38**	−07*	-NT-
(5) Economic	1,351	M	−11**	−46**	−16**	−12**	-S--
(5)	236	M	01	−52**	−24**	−14*	-ST-
(5)	238	M	−22**	−55**	−07	−06	ES--
(9)	65	M,F	08	−58***	−39**	−54***	-STJ
(5)	877	M	−11**	−41**	−16**	−13**	-S--
(5) Aesthetic	1,351	M	20**	34**	−01	16**	IN--
(5)	236	M	17**	40**	05	22**	-N-P
(5)	238	M	25**	44**	06	25**	IN-P
(9)	65	M,F	−13	50***	10	45***	-N-P
(5)	877	M	20**	30**	−05	12**	IN--
(5) Social	1,351	M	−05	−06*	34**	01	--F-
(5)	236	M	−11	00	38**	02	--F-
(5)	238	M	02	03	30**	−05	--F-
(9)	65	M,F	00	23	33**	26*	--F-
(5)	877	M	−05	−11**	34**	02	--F-
(5) Political	1,351	M	−20**	−21**	−16**	03	ES--
(5)	236	M	−12	−26**	−18**	−03	-S--
(5)	238	M	−26**	−29**	−18**	04	ES--
(9)	65	M,F	−04	−30	−19	−06	----
(5)	877	M	−20**	−17**	−14**	05	E---
(5) Religious	1,351	M	00	08**	29**	−04	--F-
(5)	236	M	−15*	04	32**	−11	--F-
(5)	238	M	08	13*	20**	−16*	--F-
(9)	65	M,F	02	15	38**	−02	--F-
(5)	877	M	01	07*	31**	01	--F-

Rokeach Dogmatism Scale (Rokeach, 1960)

(9) Close-Minded	68	M,F	28*	−32**	00	−25*	-S--

(continued)

Table 11.1 Correlation of MBTI continuous scores with other measures

Source Sample Description	N	Sex	EI	SN	TF	JP	Relation
			Interest Inventories				

OAIS: Opinion, Attitude, and Interest Scales (Fricke, 1963)

Interest scales

(9) Business	484	M,F	−34***	−36***	−05	−21***	ES-J
(9)	658	M,F	−30***	−42***	−05	−20***	ES-J
(9)	46	M,F	00	−29*	−04	−19	----
(9) Humanities	484	M,F	06	30***	14**	20***	-N-P
(9)	658	M,F	01	35***	04	19**	-N--
(9)	46	M,F	09	36*	07	41**	-N-P
(9) Social Sciences	484	M,F	−49***	26***	15**	10*	EN--
(9)	658	M,F	−53***	26***	05	13***	EN--
(9)	46	M,F	−55***	03	−01	32*	E---
(9) Physical Sciences	484	M,F	48***	−04	−25***	06	I-T-
(9)	658	M,F	49***	−04	−21***	05	I-T-
(9)	46	M,F	25	13	−25	02	----
(9) Biological Sciences	484	M,F	05	−18***	−02	−28***	---J
(9)	658	M,F	11*	−18***	08	−34***	---J
(9)	46	M,F	20	−04	02	−41**	---J

Opinion and attitude scales

(9) Achiever personality	484	M,F	17***	03	05	−25***	---J
(9)	658	M,F	14***	−02	04	−36***	---J
(9)	46	M,F	17	12	21	−28*	----
(9) Intellectual quality	484	M,F	18***	35***	05	30***	-N-P
(9)	658	M,F	20***	27***	−06	27***	IN-P
(9)	46	M,F	03	33*	−04	46***	---P
(9) Creative personality	484	M,F	−22***	43***	00	33***	EN-P
(9)	658	M,F	−27***	46***	−08	32***	EN-P
(9)	46	M,F	−27	33*	10	36*	----
(9) Social adjustment	484	M,F	−44***	−12*	14**	−13**	E---
(9)	658	M,F	−37***	−15***	23***	−13***	E-F-
(9)	46	M,F	−43**	06	24	−03	E---
(9) Emotional adjustment	484	M,F	−47***	01	−18***	−12*	E---
(9)	658	M,F	−47***	01	−15***	−12**	E---
(9)	46	M,F	−54***	−04	−20	−24	E---
(9) Masculine orientation	484	M,F	03	−09	−35***	09	--T-
(9)	658	M,F	04	−03	−33***	02	--T-
(9)	46	M,F	09	−13	−56***	−15	--T-

Kuder Occupational Interest Survey (Kuder, 1968)[a]

College major scales

(12) Agriculture	100	M	−10	−46***	−24**	−31**	-STJ
(12)	100	F(M)	−25**	24**	−09	−26**	EN-J

Table 11.1 Correlation of MBTI continuous scores with other measures

Source Sample Description	N	Sex	EI	SN	TF	JP	Relation
			Interest Inventories				

Kuder Occupational Interest Survey (Kuder, 1968)[a]

College major scales

Source Sample Description	N	Sex	EI	SN	TF	JP	Relation
(12) Animal husbandry	100	M	−08	−41***	−19*	−24**	-S-J
(12) Architecture	100	M	07	34***	01	39***	-N-P
(12)	100	F(M)	27**	−17*	−22*	40***	I--P
(12) Art and art education	100	M	18*	51***	20*	53***	-N-P
(12)	100	F	−12	19*	−04	12	----
(12) Biological science	100	M	13	28**	−07	14	-N--
(12)	100	F	−03	17*	−16*	−13	----
(12) Business, accounting, and finance	100	M	−23*	−36***	−37***	−26**	-STJ
(12) Business education and commercial	100	F	−31**	−11	14	06	E---
(12) Business, marketing	100	M	−37***	−28**	−28**	−13	EST-
(12) Business, managing	100	M	−36***	−32**	−31**	−18*	EST-
(12) Drama	100	F	−30**	16*	09	17*	E---
(12) Economics	100	M	−25**	−19*	−29**	−10	E-T-
(12)	100	F(M)	05	−09	−23*	21*	----
(12) Elementary education	100	M	−17*	12	06	12	----
(12)	100	F	−26**	−03	18*	01	E---
(12) Engineering, chemical	100	M	−07	−15	−34***	−16*	--T-
(12)	100	F(M)	−11	33***	−23*	14	-N--
(12) Engineering, civil	100	M	−05	−32**	−31**	−20*	--ST
(12)	100	F(M)	25**	−23*	−20*	24**	I--P
(12) Engineering, electrical	100	M	01	−16*	−32**	−17*	--T-
(12)	100	F(M)	16*	01	−18*	09	----
(12) Engineering, mechanical	100	M	−07	−22*	−32**	−15	--T-
(12)	100	F(M)	−06	27**	04	−01	-N--
(12) English	100	M	24**	50***	17*	43***	IN-P
(12)	100	F	−17*	08	03	04	----
(12) Foreign language	100	M	20*	49***	21*	42***	-N-P
(12)	100	F	−16*	06	04	02	----
(12) Forestry	100	M	06	−20*	−19*	−14	----
(12) General social science	100	F	−22*	07	09	03	----

(continued)

Table 11.1 Correlation of MBTI continuous scores with other measures

Source Sample Description	N	Sex	EI	SN	TF	JP	Relation
			Interest Inventories				

Kuder Occupational Interest Survey (Kuder, 1968)[a]

    College major scales

(12) Health profession	100	F	−12	11	05	−09	----
(12) History	100	M	−04	19*	03	22*	----
(12)	100	F	−12	06	−03	06	----
(12) Home economics education							
	100	F	−29**	−03	19*	−05	E---
(12) Law	100	M	−14	07	−08	16*	----
(12) Mathematics	100	M	10	04	−30**	−05	--T-
(12)	100	F	−13	07	−04	−09	----
(12) Music and music education							
	100	M	16*	50***	14	40***	-N-P
(12)	100	F	−14	05	14	00	----
(12) Nursing	100	F	−13	−02	18*	−07	----
(12) Physical education	100	M	−34***	−29**	−11	−14	ES--
(12)	100	F	−26**	03	21*	05	E---
(12) Physical sciences	100	M	25**	15	−22*	02	I---
(12)	100	F(M)	33***	−15	−25**	17*	I-T-
(12) Political science and government							
	100	M	−13	18*	−02	23*	----
(12)	100	F	−16*	15	−10	08	----
(12) Premedical, pharmacy, dentistry							
	100	M	−05	15	−11	03	----
(12) Psychology	100	M	01	38***	−04	22*	-N--
(12)	100	F	−17	28**	−08	03	-N--
(12) Sociology	100	M	−04	32**	12	31**	-N-P
(12)	100	F	−24**	11	12	07	E---
(12) Teaching sister	100	F	−00	−09	16*	−11	----
(12) U.S. Air Force cadet	100	M	−19*	−05	−15	−08	----
(12) U.S. military cadet	100	M	−26**	−17*	−24**	−04	E-T-
Occupation scales							
(12) Accountant	100	F	−10	−08	−07	−05	----
(12) Accountant, certified public							
	100	M	−25**	−27**	−31**	−21**	ESTJ
(12) Architect	100	M	10	17*	01	28**	---P
(12)	100	F(M)	32**	−22*	−21*	38***	I--P

Table 11.1 Correlation of MBTI continuous scores with other measures

Source Sample Description	N	Sex	EI	SN	TF	JP	Relation
			Interest Inventories				

Kuder Occupational Interest Survey (Kuder, 1968)[a]

Occupational scales

(12) Auto mechanic	100	M	04	−54**	−13	−25**	-S-J
(12) Auto salesman	100	M	−44***	−38***	−13	−17*	ES--
(12) Bank clerk	100	F	−14	−25**	25**	−02	-SF-
(12) Banker	100	M	−22*	−55***	−24**	−32**	-STJ
(12) Beautician	100	F	−12	−19*	21	−00	----
(12) Bookkeeper	100	F	−06	−26**	17*	−04	-S--
(12)	100	M	−01	−55***	−26**	−38***	-STJ
(12) Bookstore manager	100	F	−03	−05	−07	−00	----
(12)	100	M	14	−18*	−03	04	----
(12) Bricklayer	100	M	−07	−58***	−12	−29**	-S-J
(12) Building contractor	100	M	−04	−52***	−16*	−26**	-S-J
(12) Buyer	100	M	−27**	−48***	−23*	−27**	ES-J
(12)	100	F(M)	−18*	−08	−15	05	----
(12) Carpenter	100	M	−02	−55***	−07	−25**	-S-J
(12) Chemist	100	M	23*	12	−17*	04	----
(12)	100	F(M)	10	08	−30**	−07	--T-
(12) Clothier, retail	100	M	−34***	−42***	−14	−15	ES--
(12) Computer programmer	100	F	−08	17*	−29**	−09	--T-
(12)	100	M	23*	10	−25*	04	----
(12) Counselor, high school	100	F	−16*	−01	04	−07	----
(12)	100	M	−23*	−08	−03	−07	----
(12) County agricultural agent	100	M	−14	−44***	−12	−26**	-S-J
(12) Dean of women	100	F	−14	03	−01	−01	----
(12) Dental assistant	100	F	−12	−10	16*	−09	----
(12) Dentist	100	M	01	−21*	−10	−08	----
(12)	100	F(M)	37***	−29**	−17*	32**	IS-P
(12) Department store saleswoman	100	F	−18*	−23*	27**	00	--F-
(12) Dietitian, administrative	100	F	−17*	02	−04	−11	----
(12) Dietitian, public school	100	F	−11	−08	00	−15	----

(continued)

Table 11.1 Correlation of MBTI continuous scores with other measures

Source Sample Description	N	Sex	EI	SN	TF	JP	Relation
			Interest Inventories				

Kuder Occupational Interest Survey (Kuder, 1968)[a]

Occupational scales

(12) Electrician	100	M	−01	−53***	−16*	−26**	-S-J
(12) Engineer, civil	100	M	−01	−32**	−27**	−19*	-ST-
(12)	100	F(M)	−03	00	−29**	−02	--T-
(12) Engineer, electrical	100	M	01	−26**	−28**	−17*	-ST-
(12) Engineer, heat/air conditioning	100	M	−06	−26**	−24**	−15	-ST-
(12) Engineer, industrial	100	M	−24**	−26**	−33***	−22*	EST-
(12) Engineer, mechanical	100	M	−04	−20*	−27**	−13	--T-
(12) Engineer, mining and steel	100	M	−03	−22*	−27**	−15	--T-
(12) Florist	100	M	−25**	−46***	−10	−16*	ES--
(12)	100	F	−17*	−17*	18*	04	----
(12) Farmer	100	M	−09	−56***	−14	−32**	-S-J
(12) Forester	100	M	03	−40***	−21*	−22*	-S--
(12) Home demonstration agent	100	F	−17*	−14	13	−07	----
(12) Home economics teacher, college	100	F	−01	−04	−16*	−20*	----
(12) Insurance agent	100	M	−37***	−52***	−15	−26**	ES-J
(12)	100	F(M)	09	−31**	−09	38***	-S-P
(12) Interior decorator	100	F	−15	07	−11	11	----
(12)	100	M	−08	21*	23*	34***	---P
(12) Journalist	100	M	21*	04	−02	21*	----
(12)	100	F(M)	29**	−19*	−18*	37***	I--P
(12) Lawyer	100	M	00	−09	−07	03	----
(12)	100	F	−08	06	−18*	01	----
(12) Librarian	100	F	−01	−12	03	−04	----
(12)	100	M	24**	18*	06	21*	I---
(12) Machinist	100	M	00	−54***	−17*	−28**	-S-J
(12) Mathematician	100	M	37***	12	−14	08	I---
	100	F(M)	25**	−04	−22*	01	I---

Table 11.1 Correlation of MBTI continuous scores with other measures

Source Sample Description	N	Sex	EI	SN	TF	JP	Relation
			Interest Inventories				

Kuder Occupational Interest Survey (Kuder, 1968)[a]

Occupational scales

Source Sample Description	N	Sex	EI	SN	TF	JP	Relation
(12) Mathematics teacher, high school	100	F	−03	−12	−01	−13	----
(12)	100	M	06	−29**	−26**	−26**	-STJ
(12) Meteorologist	100	M	10	−22*	−23*	−15	----
(12) Minister	100	M	−04	23*	26**	21*	--F-
(12) Nurse	100	F	−10	−10	20*	−06	----
(12) Nurseryman	100	M	−13	−41***	−18*	20*	-S--
(12) Nutritionist	100	F	−11	05	09	−11	----
(12) Occupational therapy	100	F	−12	13	08	00	----
(12) Office clerk	100	F	−02	−28**	21*	−03	-S--
(12) Optometrist	100	M	−09	−10	−17*	−08	----
(12)	100	F(M)	30**	−29**	−18*	−30**	IS-J
(12) Osteopath	100	M	−00	−09	−05	−06	----
(12) Painter, house	100	M	02	−48***	−09	−12	-S--
(12) Pediatrician	100	M	18*	20*	06	14	----
(12)	100	F(M)	23*	−09	−13	10	----
(12) Personnel manager	100	M	−39***	−18*	−09	−06	E---
(12)	100	F(M)	13	−23*	−16*	38***	---P
(12) Pharmaceutical sales	100	M	−50***	−23*	−09	−12	E---
(12) Pharmacist	100	M	30**	−27**	−16*	35***	IS-P
(12)	100	F(M)	−09	−33***	−17*	−16*	-S--
(12) Photographer	100	M	−18*	−09	−14	06	----
(12)	100	F(M)	27**	−27**	−19*	46***	IS-P
(12) Physical therapist	100	M	−09	−05	−01	−01	----
(12)	100	F	−02	06	−01	−07	----
(12) Physician	100	M	11	−11	−06	−07	----
(12)	100	F(M)	38***	−26**	−16*	27**	IS-P
(12) Plumber	100	M	−01	−56***	−12	−24**	-S-J
(12) Plumbing contractor	100	M	−13	−54***	−20*	−28**	-S-J

(continued)

Table 11.1 Correlation of MBTI continuous scores with other measures

Source Sample Description	N	Sex	EI	SN	TF	JP	Relation
			Interest Inventories				

Kuder Occupational Interest Survey (Kuder, 1968)[a]

   Occupational scales

Source Sample Description	N	Sex	EI	SN	TF	JP	Relation
(12) Podiatrist	100	M	−30**	02	−07	−00	E---
(12) Policeman	100	M	−13	−58***	−19*	−31**	-S-J
(12) Postal clerk	100	M	−01	−58***	−17*	−34***	-S-J
(12) Primary teacher	100	F	−08	−21*	18*	−04	----
(12) Printer	100	M	09	−34***	−11	−12	-S--
(12) Psychiatrist	100	M	06	33***	08	26**	-N-P
(12)	100	F(M)	15	−05	−17*	13	----
(12) Psychiatry, professor	100	F(M)	34***	−15	−25**	22*	I-T-
(12) Psychologist	100	F	−04	18*	−22*	−05	----
(12) Psychologist, clinical	100	M	06	39***	05	30**	-N-P
(12)	100	F	−08	20*	−14	00	----
(12) Psychologist, counseling	100	M	−07	25**	−00	16*	-N--
(12) Psychologist, industrial	100	M	−20*	08	−17*	06	----
(12) Psychologist, professor	100	M	18*	28**	−10	16*	-N--
(12) Radio station manager	100	M	−28**	−24**	−15	−04	ES--
(12) Real estate agent	100	M	−27**	−44***	−17*	−18*	ES--
(12)	100	F(M)	09	−31**	−12	36***	-S-P
(12) Religious educational director							
	100	F	−14	00	12	−01	----
(12) Sales engineer, heat/air conditioning							
	100	M	−29**	−31**	−23**	−14	EST-
(12) School superintendent	100	M	−16*	−35***	−19*	−25**	-S-J
(12) School teacher, high school							
	100	M	07	−06	−18*	−15	----
(12) Science teacher, high school							
	100	F	04	10	−24**	−18*	--T-
(12) Secretary	100	F	−10	−21*	16*	−02	----
(12) Social caseworker	100	M	−16*	17*	14	19*	----
(12)	100	F	−10	07	01	−01	----
(12) Social work, psychiatrist	100	F	−12	10	−01	01	----

Table 11.1 Correlation of MBTI continuous scores with other measures

Source Sample Description	N	Sex	EI	SN	TF	JP	Relation
			Interest Inventories				

Kuder Occupational Interest Survey (Kuder, 1968)[a]

Occupational scales

(12) Social work, school	100	F	−12	02	06	00	----
(12) Social worker, group	100	F	−13	06	02	−01	----
(12)	100	M	−19*	23*	14	22*	----
(12) Social worker, medical	100	F	−11	04	02	−01	----
(12) Social worker, psychiatric	100	M	−07	25**	17*	27**	-N-P
(12) Statistician	100	M	17*	20*	−19*	09	----
(12)	100	F(M)	34***	−16*	−26**	19*	I-T-
(12) Stenographer	100	F	−06	−26**	22*	−01	-S--
(12) Supervisor foreman, industry	100	M	−14	−56***	−23*	−35***	-S-J
(12) Television repair	100	M	−06	−40***	−25**	−26**	-STJ
(12) Travel agent	100	M	−37***	−29**	−14	−05	ES--
(12)	100	F(M)	12	−30**	−15	44***	-S-P
(12) Truck driver	100	M	−06	−61***	−08	−31**	-S-J
(12) University pastor	100	M	−08	31**	20*	27**	-N-P
(12) Veterinarian	100	M	−02	−35***	−13	−16*	-S--
(12)	100	F(M)	−08	17*	−07	−09	----
(12) Welder	100	M	02	−55***	−14	−27*	-S--
(12) X-ray technician	100	F	−02	−02	07	−11	----
(12)	100	M	−04	−24**	−09	−16*	-S--
(12) YMCA secretary	100	M	−40***	−10	06	−04	E---

Strong-Campbell Interest Inventory (SVIB-SCII) (Campbell & Hansen, 1981)[22]

General Occupational Themes

(13) Realistic theme	912	M	01	03	−02	01	----
(13)	848	F	08**	13***	−05	06*	----
(14)	157	M,F	−03	−13*	−07	−07	----
(13) Investigative theme	912	M	09**	19***	−04	−10***	----
(13)	848	F	03	15***	−08*	−10**	----
(14)	157	M,F	−04	08	−18*	−04	----
(13) Artistic theme	912	M	01	38***	17***	07*	-N--
(13)	848	F	−01	43***	11***	17***	-N--
(14)	157	M,F	−01	53***	13	26***	-N-P

(continued)

Table 11.1 Correlation of MBTI continuous scores with other measures

Source Sample Description	N	Sex	EI	SN	TF	JP	Relation
			Interest Inventories				

Strong-Campbell Interest Inventory (SVIB-SCII) (Campbell & Hansen,1981)[22]

General Occupational Themes

(13) Social theme	912	M	−14***	01	24***	−07*	--F-
(13)	848	F	−17***	09**	23***	−04	--F-
(14)	157	M,F	−23**	−21*	24**	−26***	E-FJ
(13) Enterprising theme	912	M	−17***	−12***	01	−01	----
(13)	848	F	−22***	−06*	05	−03	E---
(14)	157	M,F	−40***	−22**	−04	−21**	ES-J
(13) Conventional theme	912	M	−02	−20***	−05	−17***	-S--
(13)	848	F	−02	−23***	−03	−24***	-S-J
(14)	157	M,F	−16*	−35***	−25***	−30***	-STJ

Basic Interest Scales

(13) Agriculture	912	M	−01	−03	06*	12***	----
(13)	848	F	06*	04	10**	08**	----
(15)	1,228	M,F	03	−19***	01	−01	----
(13) Nature	912	M	07*	14***	08**	00	----
(13)	848	F	10**	17***	13***	04	----
(15)	1,228	M,F	03	07*	15***	08**	----
(13) Adventure	912	M	−15***	10***	−03	21***	---P
(13)	848	F	−18***	28***	−08**	30***	-N-P
(15)	1,228	M,F	−11***	08**	−14***	14***	----
(13) Military activities	912	M	−02	−12***	−10**	−09**	----
(13)	848	F	−00	−01	−10***	−03	----
(15)	1,228	M,F	−04	−23***	−10***	−19***	-S--
(13) Mechanical activities	912	M	05	07*	−05	−03	----
(13)	848	F	09**	11***	−08*	01	----
(15)	1,228	M,F	09**	−07*	−20***	−02	--T-
(13) Science	912	M	13***	14***	−09**	−13***	----
(13)	848	F	08*	12***	−11***	−08**	----
(15)	1,228	M,F	11***	15***	−15***	−01	----
(13) Mathematics	912	M	08*	−09**	−13***	−16***	----
(13)	848	F	01	−18***	−11***	−23***	---J
(15)	1,228	M,F	09***	02	−23***	−07*	--T-
(13) Medical science	912	M	05	05	−01	−10**	----
(13)	848	F	−02	06*	−05	−05	----
(15)	1,228	M,F	−04	01***	−03	01	----
(13) Medical service	912	M	−00	01	05	−11***	----
(13)	848	F	−04	−04	02	−08**	----
(15)	1,228	M,F	−04	−01	09***	02	----

Table 11.1 Correlation of MBTI continuous scores with other measures

Source Sample Description	N	Sex	EI	SN	TF	JP	Relation
			Interest Inventories				

Strong-Campbell Interest Inventory (SVIB-SCII) (Campbell & Hansen,1981)[22]

Source Sample Description	N	Sex	EI	SN	TF	JP	Relation
(13) Music and dramatics	912	M	−04	33***	17***	02	-N--
(13)	848	F	−08**	35***	10***	14***	-N--
(15)	1,228	M,F	−16***	43***	27***	19***	-NF-
(13) Art	912	M	02	35***	17***	07*	-N--
(13)	848	F	02	38***	16***	16***	-N--
(15)	1,228	M,F	−07*	47***	21***	17***	-NF-
(13) Writing	912	M	04	32***	09**	08*	-N--
(13)	848	F	−01	38***	05	14***	-N--
(15)	1,228	M,F	−10**	44***	20***	18***	-NF-
(13) Teaching	912	M	−01	11***	17***	−06*	----
(13)	848	F	−03	10**	17***	−02	----
(15)	1,228	M,F	−06*	14***	16***	−05	----
(13) Social service	912	M	−14***	12***	26***	01	--F-
(13)	848	F	−15***	13***	26***	04	--F-
(15)	1,228	M,F	−22***	12***	28***	01	E-F-
(13) Athletics	912	M	−21***	−19***	06*	07*	E---
(13)	848	F	−14***	−09**	09**	02	----
(15)	1,228	M,F	−12***	−27***	−07**	−14***	-S--
(13) Domestic arts	912	M	−03	02	15***	−09**	----
(13)	848	F	01	−03	25***	−11***	--F-
(15)	1,228	M,F	−09**	13***	22***	08**	--F-
(13) Religious activities	912	M	−04	04	25***	−09**	--F-
(13)	848	F	−01	05	17***	−11***	----
(15)	1,228	M,F	−13***	−06*	27***	−10***	--F-
(13) Public speaking	912	M	−23***	09**	02	−02	E---
(13)	848	F	−27***	19***	−08**	04	E---
(15)	1,228	M,F	−40***	19***	08**	01	E---
(13) Law and politics	912	M	−16***	02	−05	−01	----
(13)	848	F	−18***	12***	−13***	02	----
(15)	1,228	M,F	−27***	12***	−04	−03	E---
(13) Merchandising	912	M	−12***	−12***	03	−01	----
(13)	848	F	−14***	−07*	11***	−05	----
(15)	1,228	M,F	−23***	00	03	−02	E---
(13) Sales	912	M	−13***	−15***	00	−01	----
(13)	848	F	−13***	−14***	06*	−07*	----
(15)	1,228	M,F	−26***	−11***	−09***	−06*	E---
(13) Business management	912	M	−16***	−18***	01	−07*	----
(13)	848	F	−18***	−09**	02	−09**	----
(15)	1,228	M,F	−23***	−09**	−08**	−12***	E---

(continued)

Table 11.1 Correlation of MBTI continuous scores with other measures

Source Sample Description	N	Sex	EI	SN	TF	JP	Relation
			Interest Inventories				

Strong-Campbell Interest Inventory (SVIB-SCII) (Campbell & Hansen, 1981)[22]

Source Sample Description	N	Sex	EI	SN	TF	JP	Relation
(13) Office practices	912	M	03	−15***	02	−11***	----
(13)	848	F	06*	−23***	08*	−19***	-S--
(15)	1,228	M,F	05	−20***	06*	−13***	-S--
Occupational Scales							
(13) Air Force officer	912	M	−12***	−34***	−21***	−16***	-ST-
(13)	848	F	−06*	−00	−36***	06	--T-
(13) Army officer	912	M	−15***	−29***	−11***	−13***	-S--
(13)	848	F	−12***	06*	−24***	05	--T-
(13) Navy officer	912	M	−12***	−23***	−09**	−10***	-S--
(13)	848	F	−03	04	−33***	04	--T-
(13) Police officer	912	M	−18***	−25***	03	07*	-S--
(13)	848	F	−27***	02	−10**	14***	E---
(13) Farmer	912	M	12***	−30***	−18***	−02	-S--
(13)	848	F	12***	−52***	−05	−22***	-S-J
(13) Vocational agriculture teacher							
	912	M	−03	−26***	−02	−02	-S--
(13) Forester	912	M	29***	−11***	−13***	−02	I---
(13)	848	F	13***	15***	−24***	09**	--T-
(13) Engineer	912	M	21***	−00	−19***	−13***	I---
(13)	848	F	09**	11***	−31***	−01	--T-
(13) Skilled crafts	912	M	13***	−21***	−12***	−03	-S--
(13) Licensed practical nurse	848	F	−01	−09**	07*	−18***	----
(13) X-ray technician	912	M	08**	−09**	02	−14***	----
(13)	848	F	04	−24***	−02	−15***	-S--
(13) Veterinarian	912	M	17***	−03	−02	−05	----
(13)	848	F	19***	10***	−25***	01	--T-
(13) Occupational therapist	912	M	05	30***	21***	−01	-NF-
(13)	848	F	−02	33***	05	11***	-N--
(13) Chemist	912	M	26***	15***	−12***	−17***	I---
(13)	848	F	16***	10**	−31***	−07*	--T-
(13) Physicist	912	M	29***	20***	−15***	−11***	IN--
(13)	848	F	14***	10***	−31***	−05	--T-
(13) Medical technologist	912	M	12***	04	−04	−20***	---J
(13)	848	F	13***	−07*	−16***	−17***	----

Table 11.1 Correlation of MBTI continuous scores with other measures

Source Sample Description	N	Sex	EI	SN	TF	JP	Relation
			Interest Inventories				

Strong-Campbell Interest Inventory (SVIB-SCII) (Campbell & Hansen, 1981)[22]

Source Sample Description	N	Sex	EI	SN	TF	JP	Relation
(13) Geologist	912	M	28***	15***	−13***	−03	I---
(13)	848	F	14***	15***	−32***	07*	--T-
(13) Dental hygienist	848	F	−01	−10**	04	−12***	----
(13) Dental assistant	848	F	−00	−45***	09**	−18***	-S--
(13) Dentist	912	M	09**	08*	−02	−12***	----
(13)	848	F	09**	12***	−26***	−03	--T-
(13) Optometrist	912	M	14***	05	−04	−13***	----
(13)	848	F	04	−01	−26***	−13***	--T-
(13) Physical therapist	912	M	01	−05	06*	−06*	----
(13)	848	F	−01	10***	−01	03	----
(13) Physician	912	M	13***	17***	−01	−10***	----
(13)	848	F	06*	14***	−21***	−04	--T-
(13) Registered nurse	912	M	03	−03	02	−15***	----
(13)	848	F	−28***	18***	−01	−00	E---
(13) Systems analyst	912	M	18***	−09**	−28***	−18***	--T-
(13)	848	F	11***	07*	−36***	−02	--T-
(13) Mathematics-science teacher	912	M	15***	10***	−05	−11***	----
(13)	848	F	15***	−30***	−14***	−26***	-S-J
(13) Computer programmer	912	M	36***	−07*	−13***	−10***	I---
(13)	848	F	19***	−04	−32***	−10**	--T
(13) Pharmacist	912	M	−00	−20***	−03	−17***	-S--
(13)	848	F	15***	−23***	−22***	−21***	-STJ
(13) Chiropractor	912	M	−19***	09**	06*	−06*	----
(13)	848	F	−13***	06*	−26***	−12***	--T-
(13) Geographer	912	M	26***	21***	−09**	−07*	IN--
(13)	848	F	11***	20***	−38***	06*	-NT-
(13) Biologist	912	M	26***	26***	−03	−08**	IN--
(13)	848	F	18***	14***	−29***	−02	--T-
(13) Mathematician	912	M	24***	24***	−11***	−07*	IN--
(13)	848	F	23***	08*	−31***	−09**	I-T-
(13) College professor	912	M	18***	34***	−02	−01	-N--
(13)	848	F	15***	25***	−30***	02	-NT-

(continued)

Table 11.1 Correlation of MBTI continuous scores with other measures

Source Sample Description	N	Sex	EI	SN	TF	JP	Relation
			Interest Inventories				

Strong-Campbell Interest Inventory (SVIB-SCII) (Campbell & Hansen, 1981)[22]

Source Sample Description	N	Sex	EI	SN	TF	JP	Relation
(13) Sociologist	912	M	15***	41***	02	−01	-N--
(13)	848	F	−07*	40***	−30***	13***	-NT-
(13) Architect	912	M	16***	36***	00	03	-N--
(13)	848	F	09**	20***	−31***	11***	-NT-
(13) Psychologist	912	M	09**	40***	04	−00	-N--
(13)	848	F	02	37***	−19***	10**	-N--
(13) Lawyer	912	M	−15***	19***	05	06*	----
(13)	848	F	−15***	26***	−26***	17***	-NT-
(13) Advertising executive	912	M	−17***	25***	12***	12***	-N--
(13)	848	F	−14***	16***	−17***	16***	----
(13) Public relations director	912	M	−16***	15***	09**	08**	----
(13)	848	F	−25***	25***	−17***	16***	EN--
(13) Interior decorator	912	M	−02	22***	13***	06*	-N--
(13)	848	F	−08*	23***	04	15***	-N--
(13) Musician	912	M	13***	40***	09**	10***	-N--
(13)	848	F	04	46***	−04	26***	-N-P
(13) Commercial artist	912	M	07*	37***	10***	13***	-N--
(13)	848	F	−02	39***	−12***	27***	-N-P
(13) Art teacher	912	M	02	39***	22***	10***	-NF-
(13)	848	F	−02	37***	13***	16***	-N--
(13) Fine artist	912	M	13***	31***	02	10***	-N--
(13)	848	F	−01	29***	−17***	24***	-N-P
(13) Librarian	912	M	17***	29***	08**	−04	-N--
(13)	848	F	10***	25***	−25***	03	-NT-
(13) Photographer	912	M	07*	36***	08**	15***	-N--
(13)	848	F	01	36***	−14***	26***	-N-P
(13) Foreign language teacher	912	M	09**	20***	22***	−04	-NF-
(13)	848	F	−04	18***	11***	03	----
(13) Reporter	912	M	02	29***	12***	12***	-N--
(13)	848	F	−12***	40***	−13***	26***	-N-P
(13) Speech pathologist	912	M	−09**	28***	21***	−03	-NF-
(13)	848	F	−36***	25***	03	08**	EN--
(13) English teacher	912	M	−04	31***	18***	09**	-N--
(13)	848	F	−10**	32***	09**	12***	-N--

Table 11.1 Correlation of MBTI continuous scores with other measures

Source Sample Description	N	Sex	EI	SN	TF	JP	Relation
			Interest Inventories				

Strong-Campbell Interest Inventory (SVIB-SCII) (Campbell & Hansen,1981)[22]

Source Sample Description	N	Sex	EI	SN	TF	JP	Relation
(13) Social worker	912	M	−19***	18***	21***	03	--F-
(13)	848	F	−26***	37***	04	16***	EN--
(13) Minister	912	M	−16***	24***	19***	−03	-N--
(13)	848	F	−23***	42***	03	12***	EN--
(13) Licensed practical nurse	912	M	−01	−08*	22***	−10**	--F-
(13) Elementary teacher	912	M	07*	−05	22***	−04	--F-
(13)	848	F	04	−20***	29***	−20***	-SFJ
(13) Special education teacher	912	M	−08*	07*	27***	01	--F-
(13)	848	F	−12***	10**	29***	−01	--F-
(13) Physical education teacher							
	912	M	−07*	−17***	16***	−02	----
(13)	848	F	−07*	−25***	05	−07*	-S--
(13) Recreation leader	912	M	−31***	−09**	12***	06*	E---
(13)	848	F	−42***	22***	−01	14***	EN--
(13) YMCA director	912	M	−31***	−08**	22***	00	E-F-
(13)	848	F	−34***	07*	03	−00	E---
(13) Guidance counselor	912	M	−24***	−06*	17***	−05	E---
(13)	848	F	−26***	18***	10***	−03	E---
(13) School administrator	912	M	−22***	−09**	10***	−05	E---
(13)	848	F	−33***	13***	−03	04	E---
(13) Social science teacher	912	M	−19***	−10***	14***	06*	----
(13)	848	F	−17***	14***	−01	−00	----
(13) Flight attendant	912	M	−19***	19***	21***	05	--F-
(13)	848	F	−23***	17***	13***	18***	E---
(13) Department store manager							
	912	M	−25***	−23***	04	01	ES--
(13)	848	F	−28***	−08**	−04	−00	E---
(13) Beautician	912	M	−17***	17***	19***	07*	----
(13)	848	F	−06	−39***	18***	−03	-S--
(13) Realtor	912	M	−25***	−34***	−03	01	ES--
(13)	848	F	−42***	−01	−07*	01	E---
(13) Life insurance agent	912	M	−36***	−16***	05	−02	E---
(13)	848	F	−41***	03	−04	00	E---
(13) Elected public official	912	M	−27***	−04	01	−01	E---
(13)	848	F	−34***	20***	−10**	09**	EN--

(continued)

Table 11.1 Correlation of MBTI continuous scores with other measures

Source Sample Description	N	Sex	EI	SN	TF	JP	Relation
			Interest Inventories				

Strong-Campbell Interest Inventory (SVIB-SCII) (Campbell & Hansen, 1981)[22]

Source Sample Description	N	Sex	EI	SN	TF	JP	Relation
(13) Marketing executive	912	M	−15***	−01	−11***	−01	----
(13)	848	F	−13***	03	−27***	06*	--T-
(13) Investment fund manager	912	M	−09**	−02	−17***	05	----
(13) Restaurant manager	912	M	−26***	−25***	−03	02	ES--
(13)	848	F	−27***	−09**	−07*	−04	E---
(13) Personnel director	912	M	−30***	−12***	04	−06*	E---
(13)	848	F	−34***	02	−12***	02	E---
(13) Chamber of commerce executive							
	912	M	−27***	−10**	01	−00	E---
(13)	848	F	−26***	−16***	−05	−06*	E---
(13) Buyer	912	M	−23***	−20***	03	−02	ES--
(13)	848	F	−23***	−29***	01	−19***	ES--
(13) Home economics teacher	848	F	−10***	−28***	29***	−18***	-SF-
(13) Purchasing agent	912	M	−21***	−21***	−09**	−09**	ES--
(13)	848	F	−23***	−08*	−08*	−03	E---
(13) Nursing home administrator							
	912	M	−27***	−18***	12***	−08**	E---
(13)	848	F	−34***	−21***	−08*	−14***	ES--
(13) Agribusiness manager	912	M	−05	−48***	−07*	−09**	-S--
(13) Executive housekeeper	912	M	−20***	−20***	08**	−17***	ES--
(13)	848	F	−19***	−17***	02	−15***	----
(13) Dietitian	912	M	−17*	−13***	07*	−20***	---J
(13)	848	F	−16***	−12***	−14***	−17***	----
(13) Business education teacher							
	912	M	−07*	−20**	10***	−08**	-S--
(13)	848	F	−06*	−35**	05	−19***	-S--
(13) Credit manager	912	M	−13***	−32***	−02	−08**	-S--
(13)	848	F	−12***	−36***	−10**	−21***	-S-J
(13) Banker	912	M	−19***	−35***	−08**	−09**	-S--
(13)	848	F	01	−39***	−11***	−24***	-S-J
(13) Accountant	912	M	−08*	−42***	−13***	−09**	-S--
(13)	848	F	01	−27***	−29***	−18***	-ST-
(13) Internal revenue service agent							
	912	M	−14***	−28***	−02	−07*	-S--
(13)	848	F	−14***	−08**	−11***	−10**	----

Table 11.1 Correlation of MBTI continuous scores with other measures

Source Sample Description	N	Sex	EI	SN	TF	JP	Relation
			Interest Inventories				

Strong-Campbell Interest Inventory (SVIB-SCII) (Campbell & Hansen,1981)[22]

Source Sample Description	N	Sex	EI	SN	TF	JP	Relation
(13) Secretary	848	F	−04	−27***	12***	−07*	-S--
(13) Public administration	912	M	−19***	17***	06*	−02	----
(13)	848	F	−19***	18***	−26***	10**	--T-
Special Scales							
(13) Academic comfort	848	F	08*	28***	−08*	−06*	-N--
(13)	912	M	14***	29***	00	−11***	-N--
(14)	157	M,F	02	27***	−09	00	-N--
(15)	1,228	M,F	02	40***	02	07*	-N--
(13) Introversion-Extroversion	848	F	44***	−26***	−07*	−12***	IS--
(13)	912	M	35***	−13***	−14***	−02	I---
(14)	157	M,F	44***	−15*	−12	03	I---
(15)	1,228	M,F	47***	−24***	−11***	−04	IS--

Vocational Preference Inventory (VPI) (Holland, 1978)

Source Sample Description	N	Sex	EI	SN	TF	JP	Relation
(16) Realistic	405	M,F	05	05	05	07	----
(16) Intellectual	405	M,F	04	24***	−02	06	-N--
(16) Social	405	M,F	−13**	−07	03	−06	----
(16) Conventional	405	M,F	−02	−05	−02	−05	----
(16) Enterprising	405	M,F	−11*	06	−01	06	----
(16) Artistic	405	M,F	−12**	25***	01	10*	-N--
(16) Control	405	M,F	09	−19***	06	−21***	---J
(16) Masculinity	405	M,F	06	06	−01	03	----
(16) Status	405	M,F	−09	02	01	−04	----
(16) Infrequency	405	M,F	01	−32***	05	−17***	-S--
(16) Acquiescence	405	M,F	−02	03	02	01	----

		Scales Related to Education					

Brown-Holtzman Survey of Study Habits (Brown & Holtzman, 1956)

Source Sample Description	N	Sex	EI	SN	TF	JP	Relation
(5)	236	M	−08	12	−19**	−31**	---J

Concept Mastery Test (Terman, 1956)

Source Sample Description	N	Sex	EI	SN	TF	JP	Relation
(5)	236	M	29**	28**	−08	−03	IN--

Kolb Learning Style Inventory (Kolb, 1976)

Source Sample Description	N	Sex	EI	SN	TF	JP	Relation
(17) Concrete experience (CE)	135	M,F	06	−25**	34**	−06	-SF-
(6)	60	M,F	−08	13	48***	38**	--FP
(17)	74	M,F	08	−02	08	01	----

(continued)

Table 11.1 Correlation of MBTI continuous scores with other measures

Source Sample Description	N	Sex	EI	SN	TF	JP	Relation
			Scales Related to Education				

Kolb Learning Style Inventory (Kolb, 1976)

Source Sample Description	N	Sex	EI	SN	TF	JP	Relation
(17) Reflective observation (RO)							
	135	M,F	06	−07	−02	11	----
(6)	60	M,F	41**	−21	09	08	I---
(17)	74	M,F	34**	−15	−17	−12	I---
(17) Abstract conceptualization (AC)							
	135	M,F	03	23**	−25**	−11	-NT-
(6)	60	M,F	−10	12	−31*	−37**	---J
(17)	74	M,F	03	19	00	06	----
(17) Active experimentation (AE)							
	135	M,F	−18*	−20*	05	−13	----
(6)	60	M,F	−20	−12	−15	−08	----
(17)	74	M,F	−27*	−12	−01	−05	E---
(17) AC-CE	135	M,F	−01	29**	−35**	−02	-NT-
(6)	60	M,F	−04	−05	−49***	−44***	--TJ
(17)	74	M,F	--	--	--	--	----
(17) AE-RO	135	M,F	−13	09	04	−16	----
(6)	60	M,F	−32*	08	−26*	−21	----
(17)	74	M,F	--	--	--	--	----

Science Research Temperment Scale (Kosinar, 1955)

Source Sample Description	N	Sex	EI	SN	TF	JP	Relation
(5)	236	M	−20**	46**	−05	37**	EN-P

Watson-Glaser Critical Thinking Appraisal (Watson & Glaser, 1952)

Source Sample Description	N	Sex	EI	SN	TF	JP	Relation
(9) Inference	48	M,F	06	04	−11	32*	----
(9) Recognition of assumptions	48	M,F	−09	07	14	09	----
(9) Deduction	48	M,F	−25	24	18	40*	----
(9) Interpretation	48	M,F	08	26	08	28	----
(9) Evaluation of arguments	48	M,F	−03	05	−01	13	----
(9) Total test	48	M,F	−09	22	12	35*	----

			Other Instruments				

Conflict Management [b]

Source Sample Description	N	Sex	EI	SN	TF	JP	Relation
(19) Assertiveness: MODE	86	M	−28	−09	−27*	−17	----
(19) Lawrence-Lorsch	86	M	−21	07	−41***	−13	--T-
(19) Hall	86	M	−35**	18	−11	−12	E---
(19) Cooperativeness: MODE	86	M	−13	18	25*	10	----
(19) Lawrence-Lorsch	86	M	−23*	07	07	08	----
(19) Hall	86	M	−23*	10	27*	10	----

Table 11.1 Correlation of MBTI continuous scores with other measures

Source Sample Description	N	Sex	EI	SN	TF	JP	Relation
		Other Instruments					

Conflict Management [b]

(19) Distribution:							
MODE	86	M	−16	−18	−38***	−29**	--TJ
(19) Lawrence-Lorsch	86	M	05	−02	−29**	−14	--T-
(19) Hall	86	M	−09	05	−26*	−15	----
(19) Integration:							
MODE	86	M	−29**	04	−06	−07	I---
(19) Lawrence-Lorsch	86	M	−32**	10	−20	−01	I---
(19) Hall	86	M	−43***	20	12	−02	I---
(19) Competing:							
MODE	86	M	−13	−11	−21	−17	----
(19) Lawrence-Lorsch	86	M	00	−03	−12	−10	----
(19) Hall	86	M	−07	−16	07	−15	----
(19) Collaborating:							
MODE	86	M	−16	00	−13	−08	----
(19) Lawrence-Lorsch	86	M	−20	−03	26*	−07	----
(19) Hall	86	M	−17	−05	18	−05	----
(19) Compromising:							
MODE	86	M	07	−16	08	−10	----
(19) Lawrence-Lorsch	86	M	13	−02	−11	−18	----
(19) Hall	86	M	−04	−12	17	−08	----
(19) Avoiding:							
MODE	86	M	20	−02	−02	13	----
(19) Lawrence-Lorsch	86	M	24*	−11	01	−06	----
(19) Hall	86	M	12	−19	10	−03	----
(19) Accommodating:							
MODE	86	M	07	27*	35**	23*	--F-
(19) Lawrence-Lorsch	86	M	−07	00	29**	10	--F-
(19) Hall	86	M	−01	−19	22	−06	----

Harbaugh (W)holistic Scales (Harbaugh, 1984b)

(6) Change as challenge	60	M,F	−40**	−06	07	43***	E--P
(6) Perception of choices	60	M,F	24	−09	−10	38**	---P
(6) Presence of Christ	60	M,F	23	06	−02	−05	----

Priority of Values

(6) Physical	60	M,F	−21	17	−08	14	----
(6) Mental	60	M,F	16	−06	−36**	−11	--T-
(6) Emotional	60	M,F	16	−09	21	−09	----
(6) Social	60	M,F	−27	17	16	03	----
(6) Spiritual	60	M,F	26	−25	−02	−02	----

(continued)

Table 11.1 Correlation of MBTI continuous scores with other measures

Source Sample Description	N	Sex	EI	SN	TF	JP	Relation
			Other Instruments				

Internal-External Locus of Control (Rotter, 1966)

(18) Internal-External	47	M	−00	−19	14	18	----
(18)	51	F	−06	02	−00	09	----
(18)	61	F	13	−01	12	35**	----

Intolerance of Ambiguity (Budner, 1966)

(18) Intolerance of Ambiguity	47	M	17	−41*	18	−20	----
(18)	51	F	−03	−52*	−15	−26*	----
(18)	61	F	25	−47*	−12	−47*	----

Notes: Decimals omitted from correlations.
*$p<.05.$, **$p<.01.$, ***$p<.001.$
Negative correlations are associated with E, S, T, and J; positive correlations are associated with I, N, F, and P.
Sources and description of samples appear in Appendix B.
(1) Mills, 1983, (2) Stricker and Ross, 1964, (3) Velsor and Campbell, 1984a, (4) Comrey, 1983, (5) Myers, 1962, (6) Harbaugh, 1982, (7) Steele and Kelly, 1976, (8) Mehrotra, 1968, (9) McCaulley, 1978, (10) Stein, 1976, (11) Richek and Bown, 1968, (12) Hockert, 1975, (13) Lacy, 1984, (14) Gryskiewicz and Vaught, 1975, (15) Velsor and Campbell, 1984b, (16) Morgan, 1975, (17) Kolb, 1976, (18) Bruhn, Bunce, and Greaser , 1978, (19) Kilman and Thomas, 1975, (20) Gryskiewicz, 1982.

[a] F(M) on Kuder Occupational Interest Study refers to female answers scored using male scoring keys.
[b] Thomas-Kilmann MODE (Kilmann & Thomas, 1973); Hall Conflict Management Survey (Hall, 1969); Lawrence-Lorsch Proverbs (Lawrence & Lorsch, 1967) .

- Correlations with extrapunitive measures since in the extraverted attitude the cause of events is sought in the environment.

- Correlations with interest scales such as sales of the tangible or intangible, marketing, recreation leadership, guidance counselor, travel agent, YMCA secretary, and elected public official.

Introversion

Introversion in type theory is a neutral term, referring to an inward-turning attitude, more concerned with inner than outer realities. In the personality measures of Table 11.1, the introverted attitude is often associated with scale names that have a negative connotation. To some extent introverts can be expected to report some anxiety or shyness. In theory introverts should be less at home in the environment

than extraverts. In addition, since the majority culture is extraverted, the normal characteristics of introverts would be less typical and therefore not as well understood or appreciated. Some few measures, however, will express the positive qualities of introverts such as self-sufficiency on the 16PF.

Significant correlations from .75 to .40 include the following:

- Measures of occupational introversion and social introversion.

- Measures reflecting a relative lack of comfort in the environment such as anxiety, tension, depression, abasement, infavoidance, and deference.

- Correlations with scales such as reflective observation and reality distance that show tendencies to receive from the environment rather than to act upon the environment.

- Correlations with scales such as autonomy, aloof, self-sufficient, self-control, and independence, which show a relative lack of a need for environmental stimulation.

- Correlations with quiet, silent, retiring, and solitary which show interest in privacy.

- In the introverted attitude, the cause of events is sought within the person (i.e., intrapunitive); for example, the 16PF guilt-proneness scale is correlated with MBTI introversion.

- Correlations with interest scales such as mathematician, dentist, computer programmer, physicist, statistician, psychiatrist, and chemist (occupations that require sustained attention and interest in concepts and ideas).

Sensing Perception

Sensing perception is perception by way of the senses and therefore is concerned with awareness of present realities. Characteristics expected to follow from sensing perception are realism, common sense, practicality, conservatism, preference for the concrete rather than the abstract, and pleasure in the current moment.

Scales significantly correlated with sensing in the range of −.67 to −.40 include the following:

- Practical outlook, learning for practical use, economic interests, and proper/rule-bound attitude.

- The orientation toward reality that follows from sensing perception can take different forms. For example, sensing as *managing* reality appears in correlations with leadership, achievement, order, and self-control. Sensing as *accepting* and even yielding to reality appear in correlations with deference and wanted control.

- The practical side of sensing that is related to economic gain is shown directly in correlations with scales named economic, and indirectly with scales for banker, income management, business, accounting, finance, and management.

Isabel Myers saw the SN difference as the most important preference for career satisfaction because sensing and intuition determine the aspects of life that are the most interesting. Many of the significant correlations with the SN scale in Table 11.1 are with work, not with psychological variables. Sensing is correlated with interest inventories scales (in descending order from r −.67 to r −.40 in Table 11.1) such as: truck driver, policeman, bricklayer, foreman in industry, farmer, plumber, welder, carpenter, plumbing contractor, machinist, auto mechanic, electrician, building contractor, painter, agribusiness manager, florist, retail clothier, animal husbandry, automobile salesperson, nurseryman, television repair person, and beautician. All of these occupations require expertise in dealing with tangible objects, often in a hands-on way.

White-collar occupations are attractive to sensing types as shown by correlations, in decreasing order to: postal clerk, bookkeeper, banker, insurance agent, physician assistant, purchasing agent, buyer, pharmacist, dental assistant, agricultural agent, accountant, mortician, business, accounting, and finance. All of these occupations require careful attention to detail.

Intuitive Perception

Intuition is the perception of possibilities, patterns, symbols, and abstractions. Intuition leads to interest in fields where much of the work is at a symbolic, theoretical, or abstract level, or where it is forging ground in new areas.

Some of the personality scales (in descending order from r .62 to r .40) correlated with intuition are as follows:

- Experimental/flexible, complexity, academic interests, autonomy, artistic, thinking introversion, lability, creativity, aesthetic, theoretical, artistic sensitivity, liberal, independence, creative personality, existentiality, self-actualizing, sentience, inner-directed, liking to use mind, synergy, capacity for status, and feeling reactivity.

- Occupations and fields from interest scales that are significantly correlated with intuition include: psychologist, art and art education, English, music and music education, foreign languages, science, chemistry, physician, psychiatrist, minister, sociologist, physics, and reporter.

In the original Myers study reported in McCaulley (1977), medical students were evenly divided between sensing and intuitive types. Current medical school samples have over 60% intuitives. In the interest inventories, medical scales are more highly correlated with intuition. Interest scales also correlate with intuition for the clergy, but other data (e.g., Gerhardt, 1983; Ruppart, 1985) show that denominations differ considerably in the proportion of S and N; more conservative denominations tend to have more sensing types and more liberal denominations have more intuitives.

Thinking Judgment

In theory, thinking should be associated with analytical, logical, skeptical approaches to problems, and to a coolness or distance in interpersonal relationships. Occupations attractive to thinking types should be those requiring work with material or concepts that are best understood analytically or from a cause-effect framework.

Personality characteristics are listed that correlated with thinking (r −.57 to r −40):

- Counteraction, masculine orientation, abstract conceptualization, dominance, theoretical, distrust, assertiveness, autonomy, radicalism, achievement, and aggression.

- Occupations on interest inventories correlated with thinking include geography, chemistry, business, accounting and finance, engineering, and military. (Relatively few occupations had strong correlations with preferences, so this listing includes correlations as low as r −.35.)

- Career data in Chapter 7 show substantial numbers of thinking types in the sciences, business, law, engineering, and technical fields.

Feeling Judgment

Feeling judgments are judgments made on the basis of subjective values rather than analysis or logic. Feeling is predicted to be associated with characteristics reflecting care or concern for people; interpersonal warmth, communication through the spoken word, the written word, or the arts, and a trusting rather than a skeptical approach in making decisions.

Scales significantly associated with feeling judgment (r 55 to r .40) include the following:

- Measures of concern for others, including nurturance, succorance, and social service.

- Scales concerned with interest in people including affiliation and sociability.

- Scales indicating the adaptability of feeling to others' demands including deference and abasement.

- Among dominant feeling types, difficulty in seeing aspects of situations that conflict with their values, and a tendency to avoid the unpleasant. Feeling is significantly correlated with blame avoidance.

- Interest scale occupations such as teaching, religious activities, and social service.

- In the creativity tables below, most creative fields in the arts and humanities attract a majority of feeling types.

The Judging Attitude

The JP scale is concerned with the point at which a person concludes that evidence is sufficient and a decision can be made. In the judging attitude a decision is made relatively quickly; in the perceptive attitude perception continues longer, options are kept open, and adaptability to a changing situation is preferred over following a goal-directed plan.

In theory, characteristics associated with preference for the judging attitude are decisiveness, desire for control, order, dependability, and conscientiousness. When judgment is not balanced adequately by perception, J may be correlated with prejudice or close-mindedness.

Scales for personality variables with correlations from r −.59 to r −.40 include the following:

- Order, proper/rule-bound attitude, stronger superego, endurance, self-control, achievement, and counteraction.

- Sometimes J is associated with a strong desire for order, but not necessarily the power to impose order on others; a scale that appears to be related to this aspect of J is deference.

- Few occupation scales show strong correlations with J in Table 11.1. Scales correlating at least at r .40 are female nurse practitioners and biological sciences.

- Correlations with leadership, work, and achiever personality.

- Data in Chapter 7 show that management positions and the health professions (except for counselors) tend to have a majority of J types.

The Perceptive Attitude

Type theory predicts that the perceptive attitude will be associated with spontaneity, adaptability, curiosity, and openness to new ideas. If not balanced by judgment, P may be correlated with undependability.

Scales of personality characteristics correlating with P from r .57 to r .40 are as follows:

- Complexity, flexibility, autonomy, sentience, blame avoidance, reality-distance, aesthetic, change as challenge, intellectual quality, impulse extraversion (which is related to N and P, but not E), succorance, and imaginative.

- The negative aspect of P without balancing J is shown in the correlations with blame avoidance, social undesirability, and dyscontrol.

- Occupational scales correlated with P include art, photography, travel agent, architecture, and music. Occupational interests include English, foreign languages, and the humanities.

Table 11.1 shows patterns of correlations of more than one preference. The types with S and J are found in occupations that demand system and order. The types with I and N appear in more academic fields. Types with N and T appear together in the sciences.

Comparison of the MBTI and Jungian Type Survey

The correlations between the MBTI and the Jungian Type Survey (JTS) or Gray-Wheelwright (Wheelwright, Wheelwright, and Buehler, 1964) are of special interest to the construct validity of the MBTI because the JTS was developed by two Jungian analysts independently of the MBTI, also with the purpose of identifying Jungian types. The JTS denotes its scales I–E, U–S, and T–F; there is no scale comparable to JP. Table 11.2 compares the MBTI and JTS for two small samples. The samples differed in the ways investigators computed internal consistency scores. The high correction for attenuation coefficients indicates that the MBTI and JTS have essential common true variance. In commenting on this data, Isabel Myers (1962) concluded:

> **It would therefore appear that the MBTI and the Gray-Wheelwright (as far as it goes, lacking JP), are reflecting exactly the same things, though with different reliabilities. This degree of agreement seems explicable in only two ways, one reasonable and the other not. The reasonable explanation is that both tests are reflecting the same basic realities, that is, the Jungian opposites which both were designed to reflect. If not, it must be assumed that not only did the authors of the Indicator miss their objective, but so also did the Jungian analysts Gray and Wheelwright in exactly the same ways, a coincidence which seems unlikely. (p. 22)**

Despite the relatively positive correlations for the preferences individually, Grant (1965) reported that only twenty-one percent of one hundred fifty-nine Auburn University students came out the same type on both instruments. Rich (1972) also compared the MBTI and the fifteenth edition of the JTS on a sample of ninety-eight evening division students in a course on Jung offered at the University of Minnesota. Continuous scores were not used for the analyses; instead, correlations were reported for the sums of MBTI points and the JTS scores. The correlations between the two instruments were E .68 ($p<.01$), I .66 ($p<.01$), S .54 ($p<.01$), N .47 ($p<.01$), T .33 ($p<.01$), and F .23 ($p<.05$). The two instruments appear to be tapping the same constructs, but more consistently with EI and SN than with TF.

Comparison of MBTI Types with Self-Estimates of Type

One way to validate the MBTI is to compare MBTI results with self-assessment of type preferences. By chance, one would be expected to pick the correct type once out of sixteen times, or 6.25% of the time. A critical factor in such studies is the basis on which the self-assessment was determined. Assessments have been based on brief, nonstandardized descriptions of type preferences, and on agreement with Myers' type descriptions. The expectation is that the agreement with the Myers' descriptions is the best test of the MBTI. Self-assessment based on understanding the theory and self-observation has been used as a method for validating or correcting MBTI reports (see Chapters 5 and 6 for discussion of ways of validating type).

Carskadon (1975, 1982) conducted two studies of 129 and 118 introductory psychology students. In each study, students were asked to rank five of Myers' descriptions from *Introduction to Type:* (*a*) the type reported by the MBTI, (*b*) the type with the weakest preference reversed, (*c*) the type with the same functions but EI and JP reversed, (*d*) the type with SN and TF reversed, and (*e*) the type with all four letters different from the reported type. The reported type was ranked first significantly more often than chance for both samples (35% $p<.001$, and 50% $p<.001$).

When choices for the descriptions of the reported type and the type with the closest scale reversed were combined, students rating one or the other of these first were 66% for the first study and 75% for the second study. The percentages of students giving first rank to the *opposite* of the reported type were 4% and 13% in the two studies. Students in both studies were significantly ($p<.001$) less likely to select as most accurate the description differing from the reported type on the functions SN and TF than they were to choose the type differing from the reported type on the

Table 11.2 Comparison of the MBTI and Jungian Type Survey

	N	EI:EI	SN:SU	TF:TF		
Correlation between comparable preferences						
Golden Gate students[a]	47	.79**	.58**	.60**		
Minnesota Jung class[b]	42	.55**	.66**	.66**		

		MBTI			JTS		
		EI	SN	TF	EI	SU	TF
Internal consistency[c]							
Golden Gate students[a]	47	.84	.62	.81	.64	.58	.30
Minnesota Jung class[b]	42	.65	.77	.66	.72	.59	.32

		EI	SN	TF
Correction for attenuation				
Golden Gate students	47	1.08	.97	1.22
Minnesota Jung class	42	.80	.99	1.45

Notes:
* $p<.05$, ** $p<.01$

[a] Male Golden Gate College students tested with the fourteenth edition of the JTS and reported by Stricker and Ross (1962).
[b] Male and female students and employed persons enrolled in an advanced extension course in analytical psychology at the University of Minnesota in 1977. Data reported by Davis (1978).
[c] Reliabilities for Golden Gate sample are split half (but not the logical split-half recommended by Myers), and alpha coefficients for the Minnesota sample.

attitudes (EI and JP). The authors concluded that (*a*) the idea that type descriptions other than one's reported type might be equally appealing had been refuted and (*b*) their subjects seemed to feel more confidence or certainty in their preferred functions (S, N, T, or F) and/or more flexibility in their attitudes (E, I, J, or P).

Other studies comparing self-estimates of type and the type reported by the MBTI are Carlyn (1975); Cohen, Cohen, and Cross (1981); and Anast (1966).

Studies of Behavioral Differences of the Types

Carskadon (1979b) reported on forty psychology undergraduates asked to give a five-minute talk before six judges, with only five-minutes' notice. Extraverts stood closer to judges ($p<.05$), had fewer seconds of silence ($p<.01$), and after the talk remembered more names of the judges to whom they were introduced at the onset of the experiment ($p<.001$). Thorne (1983) reported communication differences between extraverts and introverts by asking undergraduate women to chat with a stranger. Extraverts paired with extraverts served as catalysts for mutual sociability. They explored a broader range of topics, looked for a variety of ways they were similar to one another, and discussed more pleasurable topics. Introverts paired with introverts tended not to look for common ground with one another beyond their similarity as students, more often hedged in their answers, and had problem-oriented discussions. More moderate conversational patterns occurred when extraverts were paired with introverts.

The staff of the Institute for Personality Assessment and Research (IPAR) has for a number of years included behavioral ratings by the staff as part of assessments. Data reported by Gough (1981) and Helson (1975) show significant correlations between rating instruments and MBTI preferences. Ratings are based on the Adjective Check List (ACL) (Gough and Heilbrun, 1983) and the California

Q-Sort (Block, 1978). The ACL was also used by Brooks and Johnson (1979) for self-ratings of undergraduate and graduate students, and by Grant (1966) for self-ratings of specific types of college freshmen. Table 11.3 shows the staff ratings reported by Gough (1981) for 244 males and 186 females assessed at IPAR, and the self-ratings of 209 students reported by Brooks and Johnson (1979).[23] An important paper by Gough (1965) discusses how data such as these can help provide a conceptual analysis of scale meaning.

The descriptions are consistent with type theory, although some of the male thinking terms fit male STs better than male NTs. Notice that the observers described the more positive aspects of thinking in males and the more negative aspects of thinking in females. They also described the more positive aspects of feeling in females and the more negative aspects of feeling in males. These differences may come from the bias of the observers, or from the reactions of those observed because they have preferences contrary to cultural stereotypes.

Table 11.3 Self-descriptions and rater-descriptions associated with MBTI preferences

Extraversion	Introversion
Measure	*Males*
Males	ACL[a] Anxious, moody, preoccupied, aloof, apathetic, autocratic, confused, distrustful, evasive, foolish, impatient, indifferent, irritable, pessimistic, self-centered, self-pitying, slow, worrying.
ACL[a] Adaptable, alert, appreciative, good-looking, jolly, poised, warm.	
ACL[b] Outgoing (−.30), sociable (−.31), enthusiastic (−.22), optimistic (−.25), talkative (−.28), good-natured (−.26).	ACL[b] Quiet (.24), reserved (.24), aloof (.19), retiring (.20), inhibited (.19), shy (.17).
Q–Sort[b] Emphasizes being with others (−.30), is talkative (−.24), behaves in assertive fashion (−.24), has a rapid personal tempo (−.17), is facially and/or gesturally expressive (−.28).	Q–Sort[b] Keeps people at distance (.28), tends to ruminate and have preoccupying thoughts (.27), reluctant to commit self to definite course of action (.20), tends toward overcontrol of needs (.28), is introspective and concerned with self as an object (.31).
Females	*Females*
ACL[a] Active, kind, adventurous, headstrong, informal, initiative, opportunistic, sharpwitted, zany.	ACL[a] Honest, realistic, calm, complaining, fussy, lazy, methodical, modest, retiring.
ACL[b] Outgoing (−.45), sociable (−.44), enthusiastic (−.49), optimistic (−.25), talkative (−.47), good-natured (−.36).	ACL[b] Quiet (.42), reserved (.40), aloof (.36), retiring (.35), inhibited (.33), shy (.29).
Q–Sort[b] Emphasizes being with others (−.50), is talkative (−.43), behaves in assertive fashion (−.35), has a rapid personal tempo (−.41), is facially and/or gesturally expressive (−.29).	Q–Sort[b] Keeps people at distance (.48), tends to ruminate and have preoccupying thoughts (.30), reluctant to commit self to definite course of action (.41), tends toward overcontrol of needs (.48), is introspective and concerned with self as an object (.17).
Males and females	*Males and females*
ACL[a] Interests wide, enthusiastic, forgiving, frank, outgoing, quick, sociable, talkative.	ACL[a] Quiet, reserved, shy, careless, defensive,

(continued)

Table 11.3 Self-descriptions and rater-descriptions associated with MBTI preferences

inhibited, mild, silent, tense, timid, wary, withdrawn.

intellectual/cognitive matters (.25), high degree of intellectual capacity (.24), unpredictable in behavior and attitudes (.24).

Sensing

Males

ACL[a] Conservative, shy, aggressive.

ACL[b] Conventional (−.41), conservative (−.38), practical (−.37), interests narrow (−.29), simple (−.28), natural (−.27), contented (−.27), moderate (−.21), commonplace (−.20).

Q–Sort[b] Favors conservative values (−.41), judges self and others in conventional terms (−.39), uncomfortable with uncertainty and complexities (−.31), has a clear–cut, internally consistent personality (−.31), subjectively unaware of self-concern, feels satisfied with self (−.29).

Females

ACL[a] Quiet, deliberate, shy, formal.

ACL[b] Conventional (−.43), conservative (−.35), simple (−.33), interests narrow (−.31), contented (−.16), shallow (−.25), natural (−.23), practical (−.20), moderate (−.18).

Q–Sort[b] Favors conservative values (−.39), judges self and others in conventional terms (−.38), uncomfortable with uncertainty and complexities (−.26), has a clear-cut, internally consistent personality (−.22), is subjectively unaware of self concern, feels satisfied with self (−.20).

Intuition

Males

ACL[a] Adaptable, interests wide, sensitive, complicated, foresighted, idealistic, intelligent, outspoken, reflective, resourceful, sexy, talkative, trusting, unconventional.

ACL[b] Original (.40), artistic (.38), imaginative (.32), ingenious (.32), complicated (.31), unconventional (.26), reflective (.24), curious (.22), individualistic (.21), interests wide (.20).

Q–Sort[b] Associates to ideas in unusual ways (.43), rebellious and nonconforming (.36), values

Females

ACL[a] Forgiving, imaginative, absent-minded, clever, flirtatious, rebellious, resourceful.

ACL[b] Original (.22), artistic (.20), imaginative (.25), ingenious (.22), complicated (.27), unconventional (.20), reflective (.19), curious (.27), individualistic (.31), interests wide (.21).

Q–Sort[b] Associates to ideas in unusual ways (.36), high degree of intellectual capacity (.32), unpredictable in behavior and attitudes (.32), rebellious and nonconforming (.31), genuinely values intellectual matters (.31).

Thinking

Males

ACL[a] Alert, logical, assertive.

ACL[b] Conventional (−.27), conservative (−.25), moderate (−.23), interests narrow (−.21), steady (−.21).

Q–Sort[b] Prides self on being objective, rational (−.36), judges self and others in conventional terms (−.29), favors conservative values (−.25).

Females

ACL[a] Defensive, hurried.

ACL[b] Hard-hearted (−.32), fault-finding (−.30), logical (−.27), ambitious (−.26), opinionated (−.26), severe (−.26), cold (−.25), intolerant (−.25), suspicious (−.25), hostile (−.24).

Q-Sort[b] Prides self on being objective (−.32), critical, skeptical, not easily impressed (−.30), basically distrustful of people, questions their motives (−.30).

Feeling

Males

ACL[a] Curious, interests wide, kind, humorous, unselfish.

Table 11.3 Self-descriptions and rater-descriptions associated with MBTI preferences

ACL[b]   Despondent (.27), artistic (.26), original (.26), interests wide.

Q-Sort[b]   Enjoys aesthetic impressions (.27), tends to be rebellious (.20), has insight into motive and character (.19).

Females

ACL[a]   Sympathetic, soft-hearted, forgiving.

ACL[b]   Trusting (.31), affectionate (.30), pleasant (.30), sympathetic (.26), soft-hearted (.22).

Q-Sort[b]   Has warmth, capacity for close relationships (.35), tends to arouse acceptance in people (.30), is personally charming (.24).

Judgment

Males

ACL[a]   Honest, reasonable, progressive, attractive, hard-headed.

ACL[b]   Conservative (−.39), conventional (−.29), industrious (−.26), dependable (−.22), organized (−.24).

Q-Sort[b]   Favors conservative values (−.34), is fastidious (−.28), tends toward overcontrol of needs (−.23), judges self and others in conventional terms (−.32), is moralistic (−.25).

Females

ACL[a]   Cautious, sympathetic, clear-thinking, dependable, cooperative, dignified, industrious, painstaking, practical, precise.

ACL[b]   Conservative (−.39), conventional (−.37), industrious (−.33), dependable (−.32), organized (−.24).

Q-Sort[b]   Favors conservative values (−.34), is fastidious (−.37), tends toward overcontrol of needs (−.38), judges self and others in conventional terms (−.25), is moralistic (−.30).

Males and females

ACL[a]   Realistic, efficient, stable, moderate, organized, planful, thorough.

Perception

Males

ACL[a]   Forgetful.

ACL[b]   Disorderly (.28), careless (.30), adventurous (.26), pleasure-seeking (.21), lazy (.29), changeable (.23), restless (.23).

Q-Sort[b]   Tends to be rebellious (.40), enjoys sensuous experiences (.32), is unpredictable in behavior and attitudes (.22), is self-indulgent (.18), various needs tend toward relatively direct expression (.24).

Females

ACL[a]   Disorderly, fickle, pleasure-seeking, self-seeking.

ACL[b]   Disorderly (.25), careless (.29), adventurous (.26), pleasure-seeking (.31), lazy (.22), changeable (.27), restless (.23).

Q-Sort[b]   Tends to be rebellious (.32), enjoys sensuous experiences (.32), is unpredictable in behavior and attitudes (.40), is self-indulgent (.44), various needs tend toward relatively direct expression (.25).

Note: Negative correlations are associated with E, S, T, and J; positive correlations with I, N, F, and P.

[a] Brooks & Johnson (1979). Undergraduate and graduate students (106 male, 103 female) described themselves using the Adjective Check List (ACL). All adjectives discriminated significantly between preferences at least at $p<.05$. Listed are the three adjectives with the greatest differentiation plus any others unique to that preference.

[b] Gough (1981). For the 244 male sample, correlations of .13 are significant at $p<.05$, .16 at $p<.01$, and .21 at $p<.001$. For the 186 female sample, correlations of .14 are significant at $p<.05$, .19 at $p<.01$, and .24 at $p<.001$. Adjective Check Lists and Q-Sorts are based on observations by at least five staff members.

Studies of Creativity

In type theory, creation of something entirely new should be related to a preference for intuition. Intuition is the mode of perception that is oriented to possibilities and the future, and to seeing hitherto unknown patterns. Creativity, therefore, is expected to be associated primarily with a preference for intuition, and secondarily with a preference for the perceptive attitude which gives curiosity and receptiveness.

The earliest research with the MBTI and creative people was conducted at the Institute for Personality Assessment and Research (IPAR) by Donald MacKinnon and his colleagues (Gough, 1976, 1981; Helson, 1965, 1968, 1971, 1975; Helson and Crutchfield, 1970; Hall and MacKinnon, 1969; MacKinnon, 1960, 1962a, 1962b, 1965, 1971). The data below that are not included in these publications were made available by IPAR for this Manual.

The IPAR samples of creative people were selected by peer nomination from professions judged to be creative; thus, they represent highly creative people in creative fields. It is useful, therefore, to compare the type distributions of highly creative people with each other, with samples of others in creative fields, and with the distribution of types in the general public.

IPAR Studies in Creativity

Table 11.4 shows the type distributions of four of the creative male samples from the IPAR studies: forty architects, twenty mathematicians, thirty research scientists, and seventeen writers.

Table 11.5 shows the proportions of a number of creative samples, male and female, for the four MBTI preferences. The common characteristic among the four IPAR groups of creative men is their preference for intuition. The field in which they work makes little difference, although writers tend to be NF and mathematicians and scientists tend to be NT.

To be appreciated, the percentage of intuitives among creative individuals should be seen in perspective. The frequency of intuitive types in the general population is roughly estimated at 25%. In the Massachusetts vocational schools described in Chapter 8, intuitive types accounted for only 15% of males and 12% of females. In Myers' samples from academic high schools, intuitives accounted for 40% of males and 37% of females. Even among the selected group of liberal arts and engineering students from superior colleges, intuitive types were not more than two-thirds of the student body. In the creative samples, all but three of the highly creative men in the four IPAR samples preferred intuition. Comparison of this distribution with that of the selected college population yields a chi-square statistic of

more than 50.00, an occurrence that could happen by chance less than once in a million times.

If intuition is a key factor in creativity, as theory would predict, then groups rated at different levels of creativity should also differ in the proportion of intuitive types. The IPAR architect sample in Table 11.4 provides an example. In Hall and MacKinnon's (1969) data, architects in the first group were judged by other architects to be highly creative. Those in the second group were working with one of the highly creative architects. The third group was a cross-section sample of members of the American Institute of Architects, matched to the creative architects on age and geographical location. The proportion of intuitive types decreases significantly between the first, second, and third groups. The contrast between first and third groups yields a chi-square of 17.0 ($p<.001$). Not only does the proportion of intuitives increase with level of creativity, but there is also an increase in the intuition preference score. The mean score for intuition was 36.2 for the very creative group, 29.6 for their colleagues, and 27.5 for the representative sample of architects.

Table 11.5 shows consistency in the preference for intuition across all samples. Where samples differ in level of creativity, less creative samples still have a majority of intuitive types, but the proportion is lower. It may be also, as with the architects, that the most creative samples not only have more intuitives, but also express a stronger preference for intuition. Most samples have a majority of introverts, though extraverts and introverts are more nearly divided in creative samples that are associated with performance. In most of the artistic samples, feeling types are in the majority; in mathematics and science, thinking types outnumber feeling types. Isabel Myers predicted that creativity would be associated with the open, curious receptivity of the perceptive attitude. This prediction is mainly upheld. Indeed, in the samples grouped by levels of creativity, greater creativity is associated with a higher proportion of perceptive types.

An Experimental Creativity
Index Using MBTI Scores

Gough (1981) reported a series of samples ranked by an experimental MBTI Creativity Index based on twenty years of creativity research at IPAR. The experimental Creativity Index based on continuous scores is as follows:

MBTI Creativity Index = 3SN + JP – EI – .5TF.

Table 11.6 shows IPAR samples ranked by the Creativity Index. For samples in which an external or internal criteria for creativity was available, the table shows the

Table 11.4 Number in each type of MacKinnon's highly creative architects (A), mathematicians (M), research scientists (S), and writers (W).

ISTJ	ISFJ	INFJ	INTJ
		AAA	AAAAA AA
		MMM	MMMMM M
		S	SSSSS SSSSS S
WW		WWW	WW
ISTP	**ISFP**	**INFP**	**INTP**
		AAAAA AA	AAAAA AAAAA
		MMMM	MMMM M
M		SS	SSSS
		WW	
ESTP	**ESFP**	**ENFP**	**ENTP**
		AAAAA A	AA
		MM	MMMMM
		SSS	SSS
		WWWWW	WW
ESTJ	**ESFJ**	**ENFJ**	**ENTJ**
		AAAA	AA
			M
		S	SSSSS
		W	

correlation between this criterion and the Creativity Index.

Gough estimated that in IPAR samples that contain many highly creative people, males with Index scores of 350 or higher can be expected to show creative potential; men with scores of 250 or lower will be less likely to show creative talent. The Index does not work as effectively for females and it is being revised by the IPAR staff. Table 11.7 shows the experimental Creativity Index scores calculated from the MBTI data bank. These scores are substantially lower than the IPAR samples, as would be expected.

Other Studies of Creativity and Originality

A number of other researchers have studied the relationship between the MBTI and creativity. Representative studies can be found in Cropley (1965); Owen (1962); Ruane (1973); Whittemore and Heimann (1965); Burt (1968); Stephens

(1975); Erickson, Gantz, and Stephenson (1970); and Gryskiewicz (1982).

Creativity and originality in these studies continue to be associated with intuition and perception, even in early adolescence. As in the data above, the association with TF and EI is less clear, though originality may be more apparent in extraverts in younger samples.

Other Representative Studies of Type Differences

This section describes other studies relevant to Jung's theory. Studies related to careers and education are not included here.

Table 11.5 MBTI preferences of groups selected for creativity

Source	Description of Sample	EI	SN	TF	JP
Architecture					
IPAR (Hall and MacKinnon, 1969)	Entering architecture students				
	153 males	51% I	67% N	54% F	52% J
	25 females	72% I	80% N	68% T	68% P
	Practicing architects				
	40 exceptionally creative	65% I	100% N	50% T	60% P
	43 colleagues of creative	74% I	86% N	65% T	56% J
	41 Amer. Inst. of Architects	71% I	61% N	54% T	80% J
Rioux (1980)	Carleton University, Canada				
	455 first and third year students	64% I	71% N	56% F	60% P
Macdaid, Kainz, and McCaulley (1984)	University of Florida				
	44 architecture students	64% I	75% N	61% F	55% P
Fierstein and Goering (1985)	University of Maryland				
	100 architecture students	58% I	78% N	62% T	68% P
MBTI data bank	43 coded as architects	55% I	63% N	51% T	67% J
Artists					
Hulbert (1975)	Art students, Palomar College				
	20 basic design	55% I	70% N	70% F	80% P
	91 commercial art	53% I	71% N	73% F	57% P
	51 creativity	65% I	90% N	76% F	78% P
	43 graphic design	65% I	81% N	65% F	70% P
	88 watercolor	62% I	75% N	75% F	62% P
Todd and Roberts (1981)	60 art education majors	n/a	80% N	83% F	74% P
Stephens (1973)	University of Florida				
	33 seniors in fine arts	76% I	91% N	60% F	67% P
	31 seniors in art education	52% I	87% N	77% F	71% P
Fierstein and Goering (1985)	University of Maryland				
	32 students in art	69% I	88% N	63% F	56% P
Simon (1979)	Fine Artists in San Diego, Calif.				
	36 males	75% I	100% N	72% F	53% P
	78 females	55% I	87% N	69% F	54% J
	Peer ratings:				
	20 more creative	80% I	95% N	70% F	75% P
	74 middle creative	60% I	92% N	69% F	53% J
	20 less creative	50% I	85% N	75% F	70% J
Stephens (1975)	Faculty teaching art				
	19 University of Florida	79% I	79% N	---	---

Table 11.5 MBTI preferences of groups selected for creativity

Source	Description of Sample	EI	SN	TF	JP
Artists					
	25 Memphis State University	52% I	84% N	52% T	64% J
	21 Memphis Academy of Arts	71% I	81% N	71% F	52% J
MBTI data bank	16 coded as painters/sculptors	56% I	75% N	62% F	62% P
	55 coded as designers	55% E	58% N	56% F	56% J
	26 coded as commercial artists	58% I	69% N	65% F	58% J
	59 coded as photographers	58% E	73% N	63% T	51% J
Musicians					
Rossman (1979)	Morningside College Iowa				
	53 music education majors	58% E	58% N	75% F	70% J
	21 vocal music majors	57% E	67% N	81% F	57% J
	32 instrumental majors	59% E	53% N	75% F	78% J
Todd and Roberts (1981)	60 music education majors	n/a	58% N	---	58% J
Henderson (1984)	Music majors in eight North Carolina schools/colleges				
	190 BA Music	52% E	59% N	75% F	50% J
	58 music education	57% E	62% N	71% F	50% J
	61 vocalists	66% E	59% N	84% F	57% J
	49 male instrumentalists	59% I	67% N	61% F	55% P
	80 female instrumentalists	50% E	55% N	79% F	53% P
MBTI data bank	136 coded as musicians	60% E	65% N	63% F	52% J
Theater					
Belnap (1973)	Students in dance, drama, and music at the North Carolina School of Arts				
	76 males	57% I	80% N	67% F	60% P
	104 females	53% E	88% N	72% F	63% P
Ritter (1977)	Ohio State University				
	53 theater majors	51% E	79% N	64% F	62% P
	18 theater faculty	56% I	89% N	56% T	78% J
MBTI data bank	62 coded as actors	63% E	81% N	52% T	55% P
	10 coded as dancers (including teachers)	90% E	70% N	50% T	60% P
Mathematics					
IPAR (Helson and Crutchfield, 1970)	Male mathematicians				
	28 more creative	79% I	96% N	68% T	64% P
	29 less creative	83% I	97% N	55% T	55% J

(continued)

Table 11.5 MBTI preferences of groups selected for creativity

Source	Description of Sample	EI	SN	TF	JP
Mathematics					
IPAR (Helson, 1971)	Female mathematicians				
	16 more creative	81% I	100% N	50% T	62% P
	28 less creative	81% I	86% N	57% T	64% J
Science					
IPAR (Gough, 1976)	45 creative scientists	60% I	96% N	80% T	62% J
Abbott and McCaulley (1984)	High school students: Florida Future science program				
	429 males	54% I	77% N	61% T	52% P
	364 females	57% E	75% N	60% F	51% P
Literature					
IPAR (Barron)	22 creative writers	53% I	88% N	65% F	53% P
MBTI data bank	16 coded as authors	56% I	75% N	50% T	50% J

Carlson and Levy (1973) and Carlson (1980) tested type theory by predicting which types should have the maximum difference on specific variables. They selected these types for experiments testing their hypotheses.

The Carlson and Levy (1973) study tested the relationship between the MBTI and the following:

- Short-term memory using the Digit Span of the Wechsler Adult Intelligence Scale and memory for faces in the Lightfoot Facial Expression Series. They found that ITs scored higher than EFs on digit span, and EFs scored higher than ITs on recognizing faces.

- Memory task performance using geometric figures with numbers on the sides and geometric figures with fictitious names on the sides. They found that ITs were higher than EFs in the discrepancy between numbers minus names.

- Person perception using recorded judgments of twenty standardized slides, two each for ten emotions. They found NPs scored higher than SJs and females scored higher than males.

- Volunteering for social service using the amount of volunteering of ten students in a halfway house. They found seven of ten volunteers and only one of the controls were ENFP or ENTP.

Carlson (1980) tested the following relationships between the MBTI and other variables:

- Quality of affective memories was tested using blind ratings of critical incidents recalling significant personal experience by judges familiar with type theory. Carlson found that judges correctly identified eight of nine EF types and five of six IT types.

- Interpersonal closeness or distance using the same set of memories as above but rated for presence of individual or interpersonal quality. Carlson found that introverts gave more individual and extraverts more interpersonal memories of joy, excitement, and shame.

- Cognitive clarity and vividness of feeling using the same set of memories as above edited to leave only statements of personal experience, also rated blind by a new set of judges. EF memories were rated significantly more vivid in expression than IT memories in joy, excitement, and shame.

Table 11.6 Ranking of IPAR samples by the experimental MBTI Creativity Index

Sample	N	Mean	SD	r
Males				
Members, creative architectural firm	18	365.94	60.93	.33
Mathematicians	57	333.78	56.24	.22
Rated higher on creativity	28	346.46	56.13	—
Rated lower on creativity	29	321.53	54.50	—
Student playwrights	5	340.30	29.27	.54
Creative writers	19	325.66	74.36	—
Research scientists	454	320.88	72.83	.07
Architects	124	303.00	91.89	.45
Highly creative	40	357.38	52.33	.22
Control subsample	41	301.40	96.83	.32
Random subsample	43	253.94	89.29	.03
Berkeley college students	71	293.51	104.85	.34
Students of architecture	165	290.47	90.84	—
Medical school students	39	275.63	78.94	.51
Engineering students	66	275.47	87.64	.46
Commercial writers	8	261.38	88.37	—
Inventors	14	257.86	92.96	—
Marin County residents	25	225.86	101.42	.53
Business executives	37	221.07	78.40	.36
Females				
Student playwrights	5	380.70	30.56	.50
Law school students	40	355.85	73.83	.10
High aptitude college seniors	26	331.15	60.93	.05
Rated higher on creativity	13	388.58	67.58	−.24
Rated lower on creativity	13	323.73	55.20	.00
Commercial writers	8	316.22	47.73	—
Creative writers	3	313.17	53.68	—
Mathematicians	41	312.38	78.59	.11
Rated higher on creativity	15	300.57	84.86	.25
Rated lower on creativity	26	319.19	75.61	.44

(continued)

Table 11.6 Ranking of IPAR samples by the experimental MBTI Creativity Index

Sample	N	Mean	SD	r
Students of architecture	27	309.17	70.17	—
Berkeley college students	70	300.69	91.18	.41
Members, architectural firm	4	298.00	94.35	.86
Bay Area college students	158	293.88	94.26	—
Medical school students	10	279.80	79.90	—
Inventors	4	268.25	115.14	—
Marin County residents	25	259.46	82.50	.23

- Type differences in personal constructs using judges' blind ratings of concrete or inferential constructs on an abbreviated version of the Role Construct Repertory Test (Kelly, 1955). Judges identified inferential constructs on sixteen of twenty N types and three of fourteen S types. See also Howland (1971) for a similar study.

A number of researchers have looked at the relationship between the MBTI and various variables. Representative studies are Bush (1968), on the feeling of the closeness or distance of reality; Haber (1980), on the response to learning by fantasy or nonverbal communication; and Emanuel (1972), on the response to empathy as measured by an Affective Sensitivity Scale.

Type Differences in Orientation to Time

Type theory predicts that sensing types are more oriented to present events since the present is what can be perceived by the senses. Intuitive types are more attuned to the future, since intuition is the function that sees possibilities beyond the immediate present. Thinking types are expected to be more concerned with the sequence of time from past through present to future, since thinking is concerned with cause-effect sequences. Feeling types are expected to be more oriented toward the past, since values are transmitted as the heritage of the past. For each type, the two functions may complement or conflict with one another. For example, SF is concerned with the present moment, but the present moment is colored by past values. Thus one would expect SF types to be relatively more conservative. The NF group, however, can be seen as pulled toward the future by intuition and toward the past by feeling. These contrasting forces can be expected to differ in the four NF types, as a result of the interplay of the dominant and intuitive functions, and depending on whether these are extraverted or introverted. Time perspective of the Jungian functions is discussed in Mann, Siegler, and Osmond (1968).

There are fewer hypotheses about time and the attitudes, though one would expect extraverts to be more aware of time changes in the world around them, and to see time in more discrete units. Introverts should be more oriented toward ideas that have more continuity, and relatively less aware of changes in the world around them. Thus, introverts may be expected to be less accurate in evaluating the time of events.

Isabel Myers hypothesized that intuitives are less accurate than sensing types in projecting how long any given task will require. Seeing possibilities in a sudden flash, intuitives would underestimate the time it takes to work out necessary details and to bring the possibility to completion. Organized judging types can be expected to take time more seriously than spontaneous perceptive types, and to be more effective in making deadlines.

Evans (1976) and Yang (1981) supported theoretical connections between S and the present, N and the future, F and the past, and T and no time zone. Studies of type differences in ease of visualizing the future found longer extensions with N and T, and shorter with S and F (Harrison, 1984; Nightingale, 1973; Seiden, 1970; and Smith, 1976).

One would expect extraverts to experience the world in discrete units of time. This expectation was supported by

Table 11.7 IPAR experimental MBTI Creativity Index percentiles calculated from the CAPT MBTI data bank

Group	N	25%	50%	75%	100%	Mean	SD
Form F females	32,731	159	231	308	529	232.55	100.36
Form F males	23,240	167	239	313	521	239.54	99.79
Form G females	16,880	161	232	305	521	232.70	98.07
Form G males	15,791	170	237	309	522	238.75	95.69

Note: Scores range from −69 to 529.
Table prepared by G. Macdaid from the CAPT MBTI data bank.

Seiden (1970), who found that extraverts related their identity to events or ceremonies that represented change. Extraverts were also more accurate in autokinetic time perception (Veach and Touhey, 1971). Introverts who are oriented to ideas that are more continuous than external events, see time as more continuous (Seiden, 1970) or oceanic (Knapp and Lapuc, 1965). Nightingale (1973) found that introverts extend time farther back into the past; extraverts extend time farther forward into the future.

Organized judging types can be expected to take time more seriously than spontaneous perceptive types and can be expected to be more effective in making deadlines. Evidence for JP differences in time management appear in Jaffe (1980), in which S, T, and J managers were more successful with management by objectives. In student populations, Table 11.1 shows significant correlations between J and planning and control, which are essential elements of time management. Judging students took fewer incompletes (Smith, Irey, and McCaulley, 1973), and judging medical school applicants completed their applications earlier (Kainz and McCaulley, 1975).

The studies provide support for the predicted differences in the experience and use of time for different MBTI types. Sex differences also appear to be important. Marcus (1976) and Squyres (1980) also found differences in the populations they studied.

Fantasy and Imagery

Fantasy and imagery are ways of suspending time. Representative studies of fantasy and imagery and MBTI types are Edmunds (1982), Ireland and Kernan-Schloss (1983), O'Haire and Marcia (1980), and Palmiere (1972). These studies found that, as predicted, both fantasy and imagery are of more interest to intuitive types. In addition, significant differences are found concerning the content and affect of images.

Introversion and the Preference for Privacy

Marshall (1971) studied preference for privacy using a newly developed scale called the Preference for Privacy Scale (PPS), which relates to a number of psychological and life behavior measures. The two preferences most closely associated with affiliation on the PPS are extraversion and feeling. Grant (1965) found that the four EF types among Auburn students were the only types that stated significantly more often that they dated more than once a week, and had no trouble finding dates. The introverts and especially the IT types were dating less or not at all. The two preferences most closely associated with a need for privacy are introversion and thinking.

Marshall's data show a consistent tendency for introverts to prefer privacy on all the subscales of the PPS, but the most important aspects of privacy for both introverts and thinking types are personal space and lack of pressure for self-disclosure. Laypeople sometimes interpret introversion and thinking as being associated with a dislike of or a lack of need for people. The data are more consistent with the idea that introverts and thinking types enjoy the company of others, so long as they have their needed privacy, or are not under great stress.

Optimism and Pessimism

Isabel Myers believed that sensing and intuition are often related to a pessimistic or optimistic attitude. In a difficult situation, the tendency of sensing is to assume that what is will not change. Clinicians (e.g., von Franz 1971) note that types with sensing dominant often find that when intuitions do occur to them, these are negative and pessimistic. (In the dynamics of type theory, intuition in a dominant sensing type would be less conscious and differentiated, and therefore less adept at coping with reality problems.) The more optimistic tendency of intuitive types is to assume that the situation may be difficult now, but that some hitherto unseen possibility will turn up.

Extraversion and introversion can be related to optimism for a different reason. Extraverts in theory are more at home in the world, and thus they may also report themselves as more competent to cope with its demands.

Quenk (1966) looked at type differences as part of a study of fantasy and personal outlook in relation to optimism, pessimism, realism, and anxiety. Responses of the twenty-five male and thirty-two female subjects who recorded daydreams for ten days showed consistent sex differences. Significant MBTI findings were that optimists were more E in both sexes; female optimists were more N, males were more T; anxious females were more I and N, anxious males were more F. In another aspect of the study, students reporting realistic fantasies were reported to have a stronger preference for S, as would be predicted.

Vaughan and Knapp (1963) reported a study of dimensions of pessimism in which a number of instruments, including the MBTI, were administered to seventy-five male Wesleyan University undergraduates. Pessimism was significantly associated with I and T, confirming the EI difference found by Quenk but not the male TF difference.

Type Differences in Anxiety and Conformity

Some researchers have looked at the relationship between type preferences and anxiety or conformity. Representative studies are Shapiro and Alexander (1969), Krapu (1981), and Cooper and Scalise (1974).

Correlations with Factor Scores
Derived from Other Measures

Mitchell (1981) reported on data from 475 bank employees at all levels of the organization in a study concerned with the social climate of the organization. Data included FIRO-B (Schutz, 1978), Strong-Campbell Interest Inventory (SCII) (Campbell and Hansen, 1981), Edwards Personality Preference Schedule (EPPS) (Edwards, 1954), Super's Work Values Inventory (WVI) (Super, 1970), and data about job level, type of job, and performance. Factor analysis was used to derive factors from the items of FIRO-B, SCII, EPPS, and WVI. The author describes the factors as *group* phenomena that report value orientations in the group process and the experience of the organization. Factor scores were then created for each person in the sample, and MBTI differences on these factors were identified. Mitchell extended the analyses beyond correlations of the four MBTI preference scales to identification of

specific types and type groupings based on the FIRO-B, SCII, EPPS, and WVI. Factor scores were generated for each person. Analysis of variance was used to investigate type differences in factor scores. Note that the MBTI was not included in the original factor analyses. The sample was 55% E, 70% S, 57% T, and 68% J. Mitchell cautioned about generalizing from these data because of the relatively few Ns and Ps. Preferences and types significantly associated with each factor include:

Factor 1: Happy family (harmonious interpersonal relationships with pleasant material surroundings). Highest types were ESFJ, ISFP, ISFJ, and ESFP. Lowest type was ENTP.

Factor 2: Variety and challenge (latitude to work creatively on intellectually stimulating problems). Highest type was ENTP. Lowest types were ISFJ and ISFP.

Factor 3: Achievement within the system (orientation toward climbing the corporate ladder). Highest type was ESTJ. Lowest types were ESFP, ESTP, and ENFP. (The highest six types are all Js, the lowest six are all Ps.)

Factor 4: Visible autonomy (free expression of views even when at odds with the social milieu). Highest types were ESTP, INTP, and ENTP. Lowest types were ISTJ and ISFJ.

Factor 5: Outgoing affiliation (satisfaction in being part of a group). Highest type was ESFJ. Lowest type was ISTP. (Top three types were all EFs; bottom three were all ITs.)

Factor 6: Business sociability (sociability with a purpose). Highest type was ESFJ. Lowest type was INTJ. (Top four types were all EJ; bottom three were all IN.)

Factor 7: Financial analysis (scientific and intellectual curiosity about economic and financial matters). Highest types were NTJ types. Lowest types were STP types.

Factor 8: Nurturing affiliation. Highest types were ENFJ and INFP. Lowest type was ENTJ. (Top seven types were F, bottom five were T.)

In the Mitchell study, consistent with theoretical predictions, sociability and concern for others were associated with E and F; focus on achievement with J; independence, autonomy, and intellectual achievement with N and P.[24]

Prediction of Specialty Choices in Medicine

Isabel Myers' medical sample provides an example of long-term prediction of type differences. She followed up her longitudinal sample of 5,355 medical students over a decade from admission to medical school and found specialty choices significantly in the directions predicted by type theory. McCaulley (1977) followed up the sample a decade later and found that those who changed specialty significantly more often moved to specialties appropriate for their types; the effect was greater for intuitives than for sensing types.

Type and Culture

Jung's theory is concerned with perception and judgment, which are information gathering and decision making, or taking in the stimulus and making the response. Because most behavior is concerned with perception or with judgment, type differences can be expected to occur across a very broad range of life events. Jung believed he was describing mental processes common to the entire human species. To the extent that he was correct, type differences should be consistent across cultures.

The Carlson and Levy (1973) studies are of interest to the cross-cultural hypothesis because they successfully tested Jungian theory with subjects who were black college students. Myers (in McCaulley, 1977, pp. 66-70) developed

a scale to predict success in medical school internships. The scale was developed on mainly black physicians from Howard Medical School and cross-validated on mainly white physicians from the University of New Mexico.

Ohsawa (1975, 1981) reported on data with the Japanese version of the MBTI. In Japan as in this country ST types are found in production management, SF types in sales, and NT types in long-range planning. TJ types are in top executive jobs in both societies. As more translations of the MBTI are completed, cross-cultural construct validity studies will be important.

MBTI Research Resources

Many researchers have used the MBTI to look at the relationship between behavior and the Jungian concepts measured by the MBTI. This chapter has reported only some of the better research and some of the more explored research topics. Many topics were not covered for a number of reasons.

For those interested in research not covered in this Manual, CAPT is the main research center for the MBTI. An extensive bibliography of MBTI research is available from CAPT as well as material describing how to conduct MBTI research and computer programs for standard methods.

MBTI researchers are encouraged to share their research and use the resources available from the Center for Applications of Psychological Type, Gainesville, Florida.

Appendix A

Glossary

The following terms have special uses in connection with the MBTI. This listing provides uniform definitions for researchers and those not familiar with Jungian or MBTI concepts and terminology.

Terms Related to Jung's Theory of Psychological Types

Attitudes. Extraversion and introversion in Jung's theory. The term *attitudes* can also refer to judgment and perception in MBTI usage.

Auxiliary function or process. The function or process that is second in importance and that provides balance (*a*) between perception and judgment and (*b*) between extraversion and introversion.

Dominant function or process. The function or process that is assumed to be first developed, most conscious and differentiated, and which becomes the governing force dominating and unifying one's life.

Extraversion. The attitude that orients attention and energy to the outer world.

Feeling. One of the two judging functions that makes decisions by ordering choices in terms of personal values.

Functions. The four basic mental processes or powers of sensing, intuition, thinking, and feeling.

Inferior function. The opposite of the dominant function, also called the *fourth function*. The inferior function is assumed to be nearest to the unconscious, the least differentiated, and a source of both problems and potential for growth.

Introversion. The attitude that orients attention and energy to the inner world.

Intuition. One of the two perceptive functions that attends to meanings, relationships, symbols, and possibilities.

Judgment. A term that refers to the two judging functions, thinking and feeling. *Judgment* also describes how thinking and feeling appear in observable behavior.

Perception. A term that refers to the two perceptive functions, sensing and intuition. *Perception* also describes how sensing and intuition appear in observable behavior.

Preference. One of the four basic dichotomies that in type theory structure the individual's personality. The four preferences are extraversion or introversion, sensing or intuition, thinking or feeling, and judgment or perception.

Process. Same as function. *Function* (defined above) is the more technical term; process is the term used in descriptions for the general public.

Sensing. One of the two perceptive functions that attends to experiences available to the senses. (Used as a noun and as an adjective.)

Thinking. One of the two judging functions that makes decisions by ordering choices in terms of cause-effect or impersonal logical analysis.

Terms Used to Describe MBTI Scores and Data

APT. Association for Psychological Type. An MBTI users' group that also conducts training workshops.

CAPT. Center for Applications of Psychological Type, Inc. A nonprofit public organization for education, research, and services relating to the MBTI.

CPP. Consulting Psychologists Press, Inc. Publisher of the MBTI and related MBTI materials as well as a number of psychological instruments.

Continuous score. A transformation of a preference score such that the midpoint is set at 100 and preference scores for E, S, T, J are subtracted from 100 while preference scores for I, N, F, or P are added to 100. Continuous scores are used mainly in correlational analyses of the preferences.

Dropout ratio. A selection ratio when the ratio compares the proportion of a type that drops out to the proportion in the original population.

Form F, Form G, and Form AV. The forms of the MBTI in current use. Form G is the standard form for general use. Form F is comparable to Form G but has additional unscored research items. Form AV is the abbreviated, self-scoring version that should be used only when time or scoring constraints preclude using the other forms.

Index. Two letters to refer to one of the four preferences—EI, SN, TF, or JP. (Note that the indices are written EI, not E-I, etc.)

MBTI. The Myers-Briggs Type Indicator. The MBTI is sometimes referred to as the *Indicator*.

MBTI data bank. A research bank of cases generated by MBTI computer scoring at CAPT. The MBTI data bank is described in Appendix B.

Omissions. Questions in which none of the choices were answered. In research, cases are dropped if omissions exceed 25 in Form G or 35 in Form F.

Phrase questions. Questions in Parts I and III of Form F or Form G that present sentences or phrases for comparison.

Points. The eight weighted sums of the values for each item on each scale, as obtained from the handscoring keys.

Prediction ratio. The formula used for item analysis of the MBTI. The prediction ratio is designed to indicate how well any item discriminates between choices for its scored preference.

Preference score. The basic score for the MBTI that consists of a letter to denote the direction of preference and a number to indicate the strength or consistency of preference. The preference score is derived by formula from points for each pole of the index.

Selection ratio. The ratio of the number occurring in a type or group of types compared to the number expected to occur.

Selection ratio type table (SRTT). A type table on a group that has been compared to another population. The table shows the number, percent, selection ratio, and a probability level for each type and type grouping.

Split-half scores (also called X-half and Y-half scores). Scores developed from logical split halves of the full scale used for computing split-half reliabilities. Half of the questions are assigned to the X scale and half to the Y scale.

Type. One of sixteen combinations of four preferences, each with specific characteristics postulated from the dynamics of the theory. *Type* is not used to denote a single preference.

Type formula. The four letters used to denote a type, for example, ESTJ or INFJ.

Type table. A display of the sixteen types in the format developed by Isabel Myers. The type table may have only the sixteen types, or may be supplemented with a column at the side showing the type groupings.

Word pairs. The choices in Part II of Forms F and G consisting of two single words.

Appendix B

Sources and Description of Samples

Appendix B is divided into three sections. The first section describes the MBTI data bank and the studies from the data bank that appear throughout this Manual. The second section describes the samples reported by Isabel Myers in the first edition of this Manual. The third section describes samples of other investigators. Samples are listed alphabetically by the senior author or researcher.

The MBTI data bank

The MBTI data bank is a computer data bank of more than 250,000 MBTI records. The data bank is generated from the MBTI scoring program at The Center for Applications of Psychological Type, Inc. (CAPT) in Gainesville, Florida. These MBTI records are an aggregate and constantly expanding archive of answer sheets processed beginning in 1971 by the computer scoring service originally authorized by Educational Testing Service (ETS) at the Typology Laboratory in the Department of Clinical Psychology of the University of Florida. Computer scoring was continued by CAPT beginning in 1975. The data bank is divided into five main sections: (a) the initial Form F data bank from 1971 to March of 1978, (b) the Form F data bank from March 1978 when new item weights were begun up until December 1982 when the data bank was closed for the analyses going into this Manual; (c) the Form G data bank comparable to (b), and (d) and (e) the Form F and Form G cases scored since January 1983.

The data bank was established by Isabel Myers and Mary McCaulley and is maintained by CAPT to make possible large-scale psychometric and normative analyses of the MBTI. Occupations are coded if reported on the answer sheets. The coding follows the *Dictionary of Occupational Titles* (U.S. Department of Labor, 1977) with some refinements to achieve greater precision. These codings were used in the career tables in Appendix D. Other data from the answer sheets are stored and are reported in tables coded for age and education differences.

CAPT conducted a number of analyses over several years in preparation for the second edition of this Manual. The numbers in the samples vary, sometimes because samples in later analyses were larger than samples from earlier analyses, and sometimes because subgroups of the data bank were selected for specific studies (for example, Form F or Form G and cases reporting age, education level, or occupation). Except where selected subsets are noted, larger sample sizes indicate analyses performed later and include all cases reported for earlier analyses. The largest subset consists of MBTIs administered after revisions to the TF scale item weights were introduced in 1977.

Chapters 9 and 10 report data bank analyses on reliabilities and independence of the scales. In one of the studies, Richard Kainz created subsamples randomly selected to yield equal numbers in each type. From this subsample, further samples were then chosen with the intent of determining the effects of one-sided sampling by randomly selecting cases so that 75% held one preference and only 25% the opposite preference. Richard Kainz and Gerald Macdaid with the help of Glenn Granade conducted studies during the development of Form G and Form AV to compare the older and the newer forms, and for this Manual analyzed the effect on reliability of omissions, determined internal consistency Alpha coefficients for equal and biased samples, determined frequencies of age and occupation groups, analyzed discrepancy scores for phrase questions and word pairs, and analyzed mean preference scores for samples at different educational levels.

The available sample size in the MBTI data bank is the largest in existence for normative studies of the distributions of MBTI preference scores, and other basic analyses of samples differing in age and educational level. It is important, however, to keep in mind that these analyses must be interpreted in the framework of the inherent limitations imposed by the various and uncontrolled sources of the records. For example, the career data are limited by the precision with which individuals described their occupations. The coders made educated guesses in borderline cases and these guesses doubtless contain error. A substantial majority of the records were submitted to CAPT for computer scoring by professionals in counseling, student personnel, career advisement, or organizational development. The data bank necessarily will reflect sampling biases of populations who are more likely to participate in such services. A more subtle, undocumented bias occurs even within groups that are well represented; that is, all of the records are from individuals who chose to complete the MBTI. Individuals, and perhaps MBTI types, who are not inclined to cooperate with psychological testing, will be underrepresented in the data bank.

The ages reported for MBTI records in the MBTI data bank are approximately: 8% under 18, 35% 18–24, 43% 25–39, 12% 40–59, and 1% 60 or older. In the current Form F and Form G data banks the range of persons reporting at least one year of college is 50% to 63%.

The MBTI data bank appears to provide reasonable estimates of the frequencies of the types in the populations who interest most MBTI users. The data bank shows consistent trends. As predicted by theory, males more frequently express a preference for thinking, while females prefer feeling. The STJ types are most common among males; the SFJ types are most common among females. Though the more academically oriented IN types are relatively rare among high school samples, the proportion of IN types increases with education level.

Samples Reported by Isabel Myers in the First Edition

In the 1962 Manual, Isabel Myers reported data from three sources: (*a*) data she had collected over the twenty years she developed the MBTI; (*b*) data shared with Isabel Myers by other MBTI users; and (*c*) data made available by ETS from the large studies ETS conducted before it published the 1962 Manual.

The High School Samples

The Pennsylvania High School Samples. During the original construction of the MBTI, Myers collected large samples of high school students, mainly from twenty-seven schools with a large proportion of college preparatory students in the suburbs around Philadelphia. Data for the twenty-seven schools were collected in the spring of 1957 with Form D2. In some samples, three other schools were added, two tested with Form D0 and one with Form D1. All were scored using the original unweighted provisional scoring.

Measures of intelligence and grades were made available to Myers for students in the Pennsylvania high school sample and were converted within each class, to a normalized zero-to-nine scale, with nominal intervals of one-half a standard deviation to indicate where each student stood in the relation to the student's class. The mean for the whole class was set at 4.5. For males, the mean IQ was 4.6 and the mean grades were 4.2. These normalized scores were then merged across classes and schools for further analyses.

The major samples were:

Males: **For the twenty-seven schools, *N* = 5,025 (1,483 non-college preparatory, 3,542 college preparatory). For males where both** aptitude and achievement measures were available, $N = 4,933$ (1,430 non-college preparatory, 3,503 college preparatory). For some tables Isabel Myers used a sample 5,584 in thirty schools made up by adding three schools to the original twenty-seven. In this population, 1,552 were not preparing for college, and 4,032 were in college preparatory courses. For item-test correlations, a sample of 2,573 from the thirty schools was drawn, with 200 of each type unless the type had less than 200, in which case all available cases were used.

Females: The total number of females was 4,387 (1,884 not preparing for college, 2,155 in college preparatory courses, and 348 from an advanced high school).

The Massachusetts High School Samples. In preparation for publication of the first edition of this Manual, ETS administered the MBTI to a number of student populations. Some of these data were reported in the first edition, and also in Stricker and Ross (1962, 1964). ETS made available to Isabel Myers MBTI records of Forms E and F for high school seniors from eight schools, vocabulary test scores from tenth grade, and high school grades from twelfth grade. A combined sample of 397 males and 614 females in academic, vocational, and general courses answered Forms E and F in the spring of 1958. The distribution is as follows:

Course	*n* for males	*n* for females
Forms E and F		
Academic	325	273
General	148	273
Vocational	701	573
Form F only		
All three courses	397	614
Random college preparatory	100	100
Random nonpreparatory	100	—
Sample for item-test correlations	395	400

The Academically Gifted High School Samples. Swarthmore High School, Pennsylvania (Myers). Tested spring, 1957, Form D1; $N = 100$ males and 121 females in college preparatory program in seventh and eighth grade; mean IQ for eighth grade was 114.

Gifted students from Arlington County, Virginia (Richard G. Wiggin). Tested fall, 1961, Form F; $N = 34$ males and 26 females in special classes for the gifted in seventh, eighth, and ninth grades. The criteria were very high IQ scores and a rank of 95th percentile or better on all achievement tests. Advanced twelfth grade students from same school system; $N = 37$ females in advanced placement classes in English or in an art-literature-music seminar.

National Merit Finalists (John Holland). Tested spring of 1960, Form F. Total sample of 671 males, 330 females. For computation of split-half reliabilities, a random sample ($N = 100$) of students was used, with each type represented in proportion to its frequency in the total sample.

Underachieving eighth grade students (Marian Price). Students from Huntington School, San Marino, California, selected for outstanding mental ability but underachieving in eighth grade; Form D2; $N = 30$ males.

College and University Samples

The college and university samples were collected by ETS (Stricker and Ross, 1962, 1964) with further analyses by Isabel Myers.

Amherst (Stricker and Ross). Aptitude/achievement analyses include the class of 1962 tested as freshmen, Form F ($N = 245$), and the class of 1963 tested as freshmen, Form F ($N = 246$). The composite sample of liberal arts students includes class of 1963 ($N = 258$). The composite sample for the Allport-Vernon-Lindzey correlations includes the class of 1963 ($N = 238$). In 1973 Isabel Myers reanalyzed the data for the class of 1963 for reliability studies ($N = 126$).

Brown (Stricker and Ross). The class of 1962 tested as freshmen, Form E ($N = 591$). This entire sample was included in the aptitude/achievement analyses. A random sample ($N = 100$) was used in split-half reliability estimates. Concept Mastery scores were reported for a sample of 525.

California Institute of Technology (Stricker and Ross). Classes of 1958–61 were tested as freshmen; Form D ($N = 504$). Class of 1962 tested as freshmen; Form F ($N = 201$).

Cornell (Stricker and Ross). Class of 1964 engineering students tested as freshmen; Form F. Composite sample for aptitude/achievement analyses includes $N = 498$. Correlations with PRI scales include $N = 507$.

Dartmouth (Stricker and Ross). Class of 1961 tested as

freshmen; Form D (N = 663). Class of 1963 tested as freshmen; Form F (N = 815).

Golden Gate (Stricker and Ross). Male students, half day and half evening, age range 19–55 (N = 47). Used in comparing MBTI and Jungian Type Survey.

Long Island University (Stricker and Ross). Form F. Freshmen entering in 1959; males (N = 300) and females (N = 184).

Pembroke (Stricker and Ross). Form E. Class of 1962 tested as freshmen; females (N = 240). Also reported as liberal arts females with one additional student (N = 241). A random sample (N = 100) was used for comparisons of samples on split-half reliability.

University of Pennsylvania, Wharton School of Finance and Commerce (Myers). Forms D and D2. Undergraduates tested 1956–57 (N = 488).

Rensselaer Polytechnic Institute (Stricker and Ross). Form F. Class of 1962 tested as freshmen. Composite aptitude/achievement samples (N = 771). Composite sample for Allport-Vernon-Lindzey correlations (N = 877).

Stanford (Stricker and Ross). Form F. Class of 1963 tested as freshmen. Sample for Aptitude/Achievement composite (N = 713).

Wesleyan (Stricker and Ross). Form F. Class of 1963 tested as freshmen (N = 236). Composite sample for comparison with Allport-Vernon-Lindzey, Edwards Personal Preference Survey, Concept Mastery Test, Brown-Holtzman Survey of Study Habits, Davis Reading Test, and Science Research Temperament Scale were all based on N = 236. In 1973 Isabel Myers reanalyzed data from the class of 1963 for reliability studies (N = 56).

Male freshmen in liberal arts programs. Amherst (N = 258), Dartmouth (N = 821), Stanford (N = 844), and Wesleyan (N = 254).

Male freshmen in engineering programs (Stricker and Ross). Total sample N = 2,389. Some of the schools represented were California Institute of Technology, 1963 (N = 201), Cornell University, 1964 (N = 515), and Massachusetts Institute of Technology, 1962 (N = 792).

Composite of liberal arts and engineering freshmen. Consisted of the sum of the two previous groups, less four students missing on TF (N = 4,562).

Male freshmen in aptitude/achievement comparisons. Samples included freshmen for whom MBTI, SAT, and GPA were all available. Amherst, 1962 (N = 245) and 1963 (N = 246); Brown, 1962 (N = 591); Dartmouth, 1961 (N = 663) and 1963 (N = 815); Stanford, 1963 (N = 713); Wesleyan, 1963 (N = 236). Engineering students were from California Institute of Technology, 1958–61 (N = 204) and 1962 (N = 201); Cornell, 1964 (N = 498); Rensselaer Polytechnic Institute, 1962 (N = 771).

Samples of Employed Persons

School Administrators (von Fange, 1961). Form E, tested in 1960. (See following section for descriptions).

Elementary School Teachers, Covina, California (Educational Testing Service). Form E. Tested 1948 (N = 248 females).

Creative men (MacKinnon and IPAR associates). Forms D and F. Tested 1957–61. Total sample of most creative males (N = 124). Architect samples (N = 124); most creative (n = 40), less creative (n = 43), and least creative (n = 41). Mathematician sample (N = 28). Research scientists sample (N = 30), upper and middle thirds of a sample of 45. Sample of writers (N = 17).

Creative women (MacKinnon, Helson, and others at IPAR). Forms D and F. Tested 1957–61 (N = 28); mathematicians (n = 15), writers (n = 3), college seniors (n = 10).

Washington Gas Light (Laney). Form C. All males (N = 598) hired in 1945, 1946, and 1947, tested at time of hire. MBTI data were not used in selection or job assignment, nor communicated to supervisors or employees. Males were included in analyses if points for preferred preferences were three points or more higher than points for nonpreferred preferences. Turnover analyses were based on employees remaining with the company on December 15, 1948.

Westinghouse. Form F. College graduates newly hired by Westinghouse for technical and nontechnical positions from June through August 1959 (N = 300).

Later Samples of Other Investigators

Abbott & McCaulley (1983). Form F. High school students recommended by their schools to attend summer programs for scientifically gifted students to work with

University of Florida faculty. Data reported for programs in years 1974 through 1982 (males $N = 429$, females $N = 364$).

Anchors (1983). Entering students at the University of Maine at Orono answering the MBTI by mail or in summer orientation for the years 1981 and 1982 ($N = 4,035$).

Barberousse (1975). Form F. High school seniors ($N = 100$) were selected for an interdisciplinary humanities pilot program in a high school in the Washington suburbs during 1969–70; a subgroup ($n = 30$) found the humanities program too restricting and selected independent study.

Barron (see IPAR).

Belnap (1973). Form F. First year students at the North Carolina School of the Arts ($N = 180$) in music, dance, and drama. Grade levels ranged from eighth grade to college sophomores. School is open by audition to students who are considered to have exceptional talent in dance, design, production, drama, and music.

Bourg (1979). Full-time freshmen ($N = 1,041$) enrolled at Nicholls State University, Louisiana, who completed the MBTI fall semester 1978. The MBTI was administered in freshman English (seventy-one sections).

Bourg (1982). Freshmen entering Nicholls State University in 1979, 1980, 1981, and 1982 ($N = 4,150$).

Braun (1971). Staff members from twelve Veteran's Administration mental hygiene clinics who had at least five years experience (eleven clinical psychologists and fourteen social workers) and twenty-three trainees in clinical psychology who had completed at least two years of their traineeships. Of the forty-eight, twenty-seven were males, and twenty-one were females.

Brooks & Johnson (1979). Undergraduate and graduate students at North Texas State University ($N = 209$; males $n = 106$, females $n = 103$; age range 18–50) who described themselves using the Adjective Check List. Adjectives listed discriminated between MBTI preferences at least $p < .05$. Table 11.3 shows three adjectives with highest difference plus any other adjectives on the preference.

Bruhn, Bunce, & Greaser (1978). Physician assistants ($N = 98$) and nurse practitioners ($N = 61$) enrolled at the University of Texas Medical Branch at Galveston.

Burt (1968). Form F. Fine arts students ($N = 92$) at the Richmond Professional Institute, of whom sixty supplied five paintings each for rating by independent judges.

Cacioppe (1980). Postgraduate students in business administration ($N = 228$) at Management Studies Centre, MacQuarie University, in New South Wales, Australia.

Camiscioni (1974). Data made available from the Longitudinal Medical Studies of the Ohio State University College of Medicine. Students answered Form F at the time of entrance. Two samples on which many analyses were based were 484 students from the classes of 1967–68–69 and 645 students from the classes of 1970–71–72.

Carlson & Levy (1973). Form F. The four studies used Howard University undergraduates. Short Term Memory: females in undergraduate psychology ($N = 24$, 6 each IT, IF, ET, EF). Memory Task Performance: female undergraduates, ($N = 32$, 16 EF, 16 IT). Person Perception: male and female undergraduates ($N = 98$) 56 NP (male $n = 14$, and female, $n = 26$) and 42 SJ (male $n = 14$, and female $n = 26$). Volunteers: student volunteers ($n = 10$) at halfway house for disturbed adolescents in Washington, D.C.; nonvolunteer students ($n = 10$) matched for sex, age, parent occupation, siblings, and ordinal position.

Carlyn, M. (1976). Form F. Data collected in 1975. Seniors majoring in elementary or secondary education at Michigan State University ($N = 200$; males $n = 64$, females $n = 136$).

Chaille (1982). Students attending South Lakes High School, Reston, Virginia. Students suspended from school ($N = 100$) compared to a random sample of students ($N = 100$).

Child (1965). Form F. Yale students paid volunteers ($N = 138$; undergraduates $n = 137$, graduate student $n = 1$).

Coan (1979). Form F. Data collected in 1972. Psychologists listed in Directory of American Psychological Association (APA) ($N = 114$; males $n = 61$, females $n = 43$). The sample was one of a series of studies of psychologists in which subjects were chosen by taking consecutive names from the APA Directory.

Comrey (1983). Volunteer subjects recruited from faculty, staff, and students at University of California at Los Angeles, $N = 241$ (males $n = 102$ mean age 33.7, and females $n = 139$ mean age 31.9). About 65 percent were college students; the majority were upper middle class and college educated.

Conary (1965) Form F. Students admitted to Auburn University were tested in the summer or fall of 1964. Grade point averages used in analyses based on initial term at Auburn (A = 3, B = 2, C = 1, D = 0).

Cropley (1965). Entire seventh grade population (N = 354) of a large Edmonton, Alberta, Canada, junior high school tested in an extra day of school in June with a wide variety of tests related to originality. The entire battery was completed by 320 students (males n = 170, mean Verbal IQ 115, and females n = 150, mean Verbal IQ 114). Divided into three groups based on IQ and scores of some Guilford originality measures: high originals (N = 32; males n = 20, females n = 12); low originals (N = 32; males n = 16, females n = 16); low originals with average IQ (N = 39; males n = 17, females n = 22).

Davis (1978). Form F. Male and female students (N = 42) enrolled in 1977 in an advanced extension course in analytical psychology at the University of Minnesota. Coefficient alpha used to estimate reliability.

Desbiens, Peters, & Wigle (1977). Data collected as part of a comprehensive study at St. Clair College of Applied Arts and Technology, Windsor, Ontario, a community college. The total of students participating was N = 2,602; the MBTI was answered by n = 1,979.

Demarest (1975). Form F. Incoming freshmen at Hope College, Holland, Michigan (N = 1,505). For classes entering in 1973 (n = 570), 1974 (n = 546), and 1975 (n = 509).

Demarest (1979). Incoming freshmen at Adrian College, Adrian, Michigan, tested in 1978 (N = 198).

Dietl (1981). Form F. (Data collected 1981). Executives from the top three levels of management at Northwestern Bell Telephone Company in Omaha, Nebraska, randomly selected in 1981 (N = 125). Participating executives (n = 101) were 11% top level, 22% second level, and 67% third level managers.

Dunning (1971). Form F. Entering class at Scripps College, California, a school with a strong emphasis on humanities.

Eggins (1979). Form G. Sixth grade students in two middle schools in Bloomington, Indiana, were chosen from a potential sample (N = 400). None had yet been taught the biological system of classification of animals. The final sample (n = 328) was divided into three groups, one for each teaching method.

Elliott (1975). Salaried staff members in thirty-eight centers to serve runaway youth in New Jersey, Pennsylvania, Washington, D.C., Maryland, Virginia, New York, Michigan, Illinois, Minnesota, and Wisconsin (male N = 58, female N = 61).

Erickson (1982). Incoming students at Parks College of St. Louis University (a school with a special emphasis on aeronautical support occupations) entering in 1982 (N = 405; males n = 375, females n = 30).

Erickson, Gantz, & Stephenson (1970). Form F. Research scientists and engineers (N = 117) divided into high and low "creative" groups on the basis of a brief life history form (the BIRST).

Evered (1973). Form F. The first students in a professional master's program initiated in 1971 at the Graduate School of Management of the University of California at Los Angeles. The sample consisted of the 96 who survived the first year, from an initial class of 108 (female n = 14, foreign-born but fluent in English n = 16).

Fierstein & Goering (1985). Architecture students, juniors or seniors at the University of Maryland (N = 100).

Fretz & Schmidt (1967). Form F. Entering freshmen at Ohio State University enrolled in the educational skills course (N = 144). Comparison group of dormitory residents (N = 74) matched for sex, college, curriculum, and aptitude score.

Gaster, Tobacyk, & Dawson (1984). Male managers of a national mass merchandising retail firm (n = 316 out of a total N = 333). Median age 26, median educational level 13.5 years.

Golanty-Koel (1975). Form F. Students in a continuation high school for students who failed in the traditional high schools in an upper middle-class area in northern California. The sample included 147 of 160 students, ages sixteen to eighteen (males n = 65, females n = 82). Seventy-six percent were able to read at the seventh grade level.

Golliday (1974). Form F. Students (N = 129, of whom 94 participated) and three instructors of seven classes of freshmen in a required mathematics course at Santa Fe Community College, Gainesville, Florida. Classes were included in the study if their instructors taught two sections on the same days.

Grant (1965a). Form F. Auburn University freshmen (N = 1,413) who had answered MBTI Form F in summer orientation and then answered a questionnaire their third quarter at the university. Type descriptions were created to summarize significant answers for each type. Type tables were created from those answers.

Grant (1965b). Form F. Auburn University students (*N* = 159) entering in the winter quarter, 1966. The students also answered the Grey-Wheelwright (Jungian Type Survey).

Grant (1975). Entering freshmen at Auburn University tested mainly in summer before beginning classes (*N* = 10,342).

Gryskiewicz (1982). Managers (*N* = 438; males *n* = 355, females *n* = 83) who attended leadership development courses at the Center for Creative Leadership, Greensboro, North Carolina, beginning in 1976. Fifty-five percent were top or upper-middle managers.

Gryskiewicz, Vaught, & Johansson (1975). Form F. Participants (*N* = 157) in week-long Creative Leadership Development Programs at the Center for Creative Leadership, Greensboro, North Carolina.

Guttinger & McCaulley (1975). Form F. 846 students (males *n* = 428 , females *n* = 418) of the University of Florida P. K. Yonge Laboratory School. MBTI administered in 1970s, usually in ninth grade.

Haber (1980). Students (*N* = 175) in graduate courses in education at a Southeastern university. Classes included experiential training using guided fantasy (seven classes) or nonverbal communication (seven classes).

Harbaugh (1984a). Students at Trinity Lutheran Seminary, Columbus, Ohio. Data collected in 1982.

Harris (1981). Form F. University of Manchester, England, medical students tested on admission in 1971 at ages eighteen to ninteen. Of the original class (*N* = 159), those who completed their studies without interruption or dropout were retested in 1976 (*N* = 120, males *n* = 74, females *n* = 46).

Harris, Kelley, & Coleman (1984). Form F. University of Utah medical students from the graduating classes of 1980 (*N* = 99) and 1981 (*N* = 99) answered the MBTI during freshman orientation. Some retook the MBTI at the end of their senior year (*n* = 35 in the class of 1980 and *n* = 90 in the class of 1981) at intervals of thirty-six to forty-two months.

Helson (See IPAR).

Henderson (1984). Students majoring in music from eight schools representing the fifty-four North Carolina colleges and universities offering a BA in music (*N* = 190).

Hicks (1984). Form F. White-collar employees of the public school system of Humphreys County, Mississippi (*N* = 104, sensing *n* = 52; intuitive *n* = 52), average age 37.4 years. The sample included 33 males and 71 females, 20 blacks and 84 whites. From the total sample, subsamples of sensing types and intuitive types were randomly selected.

Hoffman (1975). Form F. Student teachers enrolled in the fall quarter of 1973 at Florida State University (*N* = 117) and their supervising teachers (*N* = 113). Grades ranged from kindergarten to twelfth grade.

Hoffman, Waters, & Berry (1981). Students in a military installation (*N* = 155; males *n* = 100, females *n* = 55) for seven consecutive classes in a fast-paced computer-assisted program that included learning Morse code.

Howes (1977). Form F. Undergraduates (*N* = 117) enrolled in introductory psychology at Mississippi State University. Participation in research was a course requirement.

Hoy & Hellriegel (1982). Managers (*N* = 150) randomly selected from companies that met six criteria for a survey of small manufacturing and retailing firms in Texas with five to fifty employees. Managers had to be able to influence the organizations' goals and processes directly. The type table was not in the article but was made available by F. Hoy.

Hulbert (1975). Form F. Students enrolled in art and creativity classes at Palomar College, San Marcos, California, between 1972 and 1975 (*N* = 301).

IPAR. Institute for Personality Assessment and Research at the University of California at Berkeley. Persons assessed at the Center answered a number of personality instruments including the MBTI and were observed and rated by staff members, using the Adjective Check List, California Q-Sort, and other measures. The creativity studies involved samples of persons rated high for creativity by others in their fields. MacKinnon shared his early work on creative architects, Helson and Crutchfield's work on mathematicians, Gough's on scientists, and Barron's on writers with Isabel Myers for the first edition of this Manual. Gough (personal communication, 1981) made available type distributions of later IPAR samples. Gough (1979) reported alpha reliabilities given in Chapter 10 and the California Q-sort and ACL correlations in Chapter 11.

Kainz (1976). Seniors (N = 405 from a class of 548) in a comprehensive high school that reflected the demographic mix of a central Florida county in 1973. Of the tested sample reported by Morgan (1975) a smaller sample (males n = 195, and females n = 201) completed both MBTI Form F and the Vocational Preference Inventory.

Kauppi (1982). Montgomery College students, Rockville, Maryland, who were selected from 11,000 full-time students if they were residents of Montgomery County, under age 26, and had a grade point average of 3.2 to 4.0. Of students meeting these criteria (N = 241), 134 (males n = 60, females n = 74) agreed to participate and completed all research protocols.

Kilmann & Taylor (1974). Business administration students (N = 95) in a graduate laboratory course in Behavioral Sciences for Management at the University of Pittsburgh.

Kilmann & Thomas (1975). Graduate students in two sections of a course in Behavioral Science for Management at the University of Pittsburgh (N = 86 males).

Kirk (1972). Students enrolled from 1966 to 1971 in a Th.M. program at the Boston University School of Theology (N = 85 males).

Kolb (1976). Form F. Correlations cited in the Learning Style Inventory Manual. Kent State undergraduates (N = 135) reported to Kolb by Taylor (1973). University of Wisconsin students in program for Masters of Business Administration (N = 74) reported to Kolb by Wynne (1976).

Lacy (1984). Students entering Franklin and Marshall College, Pennsylvania (males n = 912, females n = 848) in 1980, 1981, 1982, and 1983.

Leafgren & Kolstad (1984). Students entering the University of Wisconsin at Stevens Point in 1983 (N = 1,195; males n = 442, females n = 753).

Levell (1965). Form F. Counselor trainees attending in 1963 to 1964 four National Defense Education Act Counseling and Guidance Institutes for graduate instruction of secondary school counselors; institutes were from East, South, Midwest, and West. High- and low-rated counselors were identified by a composite (N =117) of peer and faculty.

Levin (1978). Mail sample in 1977 of 295 clinical psychologists and psychiatrists selected from membership listings in professional associations all with more than five years experience and with field of specialization given first or second choice. Sampling resulted in 94 subjects (15 of 70 psychoanalytic, 15 of 60 behavioral, 24 of 65 rational-emotive, 15 of 43 gestalt, and 25 of 37 experiential) 76 males and 15 females, 21 M.D. and 70 Ph.D. The mean age of the sample was 47.6 years.

Levy, Murphy, & Carlson (1972). (N = 758) Black Howard University students (311 males, 447 females) from various courses. Original administration of the MBTI was spring semester; second administration to 433 students (146 males, 287 females) approximately two months later.

Macdaid, Kainz, & McCaulley (1984). Form F. University of Florida freshmen (N = 2,514) tested prior to admission in 1971–73 and followed up in 1983–84 to determine which students graduated (N = 1,878), the majors in which they graduated, and the years to graduation.

MacKinnon (see IPAR).

Madison, Wilder, & Studdiford (1963). Random sample of 102 Princeton University male freshmen in fall of 1962.

Margerison & Lewis (1981). Managers attending business short courses in the United Kingdom sponsored by the Cranfield School of Management (N = 849).

McCarley & Carskadon (1983). Female undergraduate psychology students (N = 62) attending Mississippi State University. Participated in the experiment that included the MBTI as a course requirement.

McCaulley (1973). Form F. Entering freshmen in 1972 (N = 2,514).

McCaulley (1977). Myers' Longitudinal sample of 5,355 medical students from forty-five medical schools tested with MBTI Forms between 1951 and 1959. Isabel Myers followed up the sample to study aptitude and achievement, attrition, specialty choice, internship performance, and deaths. McCaulley followed up in 1972–73 and identified 4,977 cases. The follow-up included specialty choice, specialty change, professional activities, board certification, professorial appointments, membership in societies, state of residence, size of community, and service in medically underserved areas.

McCaulley (1978). A series of studies giving data on medicine and other health professions from the MBTI data bank and contributions of other researchers, to provide frequencies of 32,371 students and practitioners in health fields and data on aptitude, achievement, specialty choice, and career satisfaction.

McCaulley & Kainz (1974). Form F. Follow-up of University of Florida freshmen and transfer students, originally tested in 1970 and 1971. In 1974 the original records were matched with current University of Florida records of choice of major and grades.

McCaulley & Kainz (1976). Middle school students in a Florida school with both rural and suburban students whose school provided a number of academic and achievement measures. Data collected in 1976 ($N = 116$ in eighth grade; $N = 168$ in seventh grade).

McCaulley & Natter (1974). Form F. Students from seventh grade through twelfth grade in the Florida State University Laboratory School ($N = 521$) tested in 1974 with the MBTI and learning style questions. The school provided academic records on aptitude and grades.

Mehrotra (1968). All students enrolled in introductory educational psychology at Ohio State University in spring 1964. Age range was 17–25. Random samples of 100 males and 100 females.

Metts (1979). Adolescents diagnosed by their schools as learning disabled ($N = 113$; males $n = 85$, females $n = 28$) from a suburban public high school ($n = 40$), from a private residential summer tutorial program but regularly attending public or private classes for the learning disabled ($n = 66$), and students known through clinical contacts ($n = 7$). All had IQs within the normal range and a marked discrepancy between expected and actual academic achievement. Records showed no personality or behavior disorders consistent with a diagnosis of emotional disturbance. MBTI administered by reading aloud or tape recording.

Miller (1965). Form F. First year law students from Northwestern University ($N = 157$), University of California at Berkeley ($N = 309$), University of Pennsylvania ($N = 192$), and University of Virginia ($N = 238$) tested September 1963.

Miller (1966). Form F. First year law students from five law schools tested in September 1965 ($N = 1,352$). Some data reported with combined 1963 and 1965 samples ($N = 2,248$).

Mills (1983). Gifted adolescents in the seventh grade to tenth grade with scores at ninety-eighth percentile or higher on ability tests (males $n = 65$, females $n = 87$). Students were enrolled in a South-Central Pennsylvania program for gifted students in 1981 and 1982 at Franklin and Marshall College in Pennsylvania.

Morgan (1975). Form F. Senior high school students of a comprehensive high school that reflected the demographic mix of a central Florida county, tested in 1973 (48% male, 52% female; 25% black, 75% white). Of the total in the senior class ($N = 548$), the MBTI and General Aptitude Test Battery were completed by 418 students.

Mitchell, W. (1981). Employees from all levels of the organization at a large Southeast bank ($N = 800$) who attended a two and one-half day career development program for employees. Four hundred seventy-five participants answered the MBTI.

Most, (1985). Form G and Form AV. Students in guidance classes at Foothill College, California ($N = 367$).

Nisbet, Ruble, & Schurr (1981). Ball State University high-risk or remedial/developmental students enrolled in an Academic Opportunity Program in 1978 ($N = 473$), 1979 ($N = 760$), and 1980 ($N = 902$).

Ohsawa (1981). Top executives ($N = 118$) of large Japanese companies (tested with Japanese translation by Nippon Recruit Center of Tokyo).

Otis & Quenk (1973). Test-retest data of University of New Mexico medical students, used by Isabel Myers for test-retest reliability study.

Owen (1962). Elementary students in Palo Alto, California, School District judged for performance in art on a scale with a range of 0–70. The range observed was 26–64. The 62 scoring above 50 were considered potentially gifted. Potentially gifted students from this sample participated in a study at Terman Junior High School to develop creativity (experimental $N = 30$, control $N = 30$).

Parham, Miller, & Carskadon (1984). Male and female college students ($N = 128$) enrolled in introductory psychology at Mississippi State University. Participation in the research was a course requirement. Students were randomly assigned to three groups that received standard instructions or "vocational instructions" ("The test is designed to measure vocational preferences; answer as you prefer to act on the job"). All groups answered the MBTI twice under these instructions: group one received standard-standard instructions ($N = 40$), group two vocational-vocational instructions (N = 40), and group three standard-vocational instructions (N = 48).

Perelman (1978). Graduate students in counseling (N = 8) reporting personal experience of counseling practice.

Perry (1974). Form F. Psychologists selected from American Psychological Association 1973 Directory. Perry selected 55 psychologists at random for each of three groupings of APA divisions: experimental (from divisions of Experimental, Comparative, and Experimental Analysis of Behavior); clinical (from divisions of Clinical Psychology, Counseling Psychology, Psychotherapy, and Humanistic Psychology); and a "buffer group" (from divisions of Developmental, Educational, Personality, and Social). Final sample (N = 72) was divided: Experimental n = 30 of 45 surveyed, clinical n = 25 of 45 surveyed, and buffer n = 17 of 45 surveyed.

Provost (1984). Incoming freshmen at Rollins College, Florida (N = 395; males n = 173, females n = 222).

Quenk & Albert (1975). Form F. An initial sample of physicians from fourteen specialties (N = 1,900) from five states representing different areas of the country in communities from under 5,000 to more than 100,000. Participants responded to a mail request (N = 477; males n = 445, females n = 32).

Reichard & Uhl (1979). Form F. Incoming freshmen at University of North Carolina, Greensboro (N = 2,492) entering in 1976 (n = 366), 1977 (n = 662), 1978 (n = 716), and 1979 (n = 748).

Rezler & Johns (1975). Form F. Medical students at the University of Illinois in the traditional program (N = 222) and a special program for independent scholars (N = 72).

Richek (1969). Form F. Junior and senior students (males n = 70, females n = 365) at the University of Oklahoma in education programs preparing for elementary and secondary school teaching.

Richek & Bown (1968). One hundred forty-nine female students in an experimental education program of the Personality and Teaching Behavior Project in the Department of Educational Psychology at the University of Texas. All students were prospective teachers (N = 149; elementary n = 71, and secondary n = 78).

Ritter (1977). Form F. Department of Theater at the Ohio State University: students majoring in theater (N = 53) and theater faculty (N = 18).

Rioux (1981). Form F. Students attending Carelton University, Canada School of Architecture, tested in first or third years between 1975 and 1979 (N = 455).

Roberts (1982). First term community college freshmen (N = 335) from an unspecified number of schools who ranked thirteen instructional media in order of preference for learning.

Rossman (1979). Students at Morningside College, Iowa, majoring in music education (N = 53; vocal n = 32, instrumental n = 32).

Ruane (1973). Form F. High school students in Roanoke, Virginia, in 1971. Teachers permitted students in their classes to be tested (N = 146 students; art classes n = 53, classes other than art n = 93).

Ruppart (1985). Male clergy from protestant denominations (N = 1,458) drawn from a total sample of persons active in religious professional careers (N = 5,472).

Sachs (1978). Data from the Entering Resources Questionnaire answered by incoming medical students at the Ohio State University (N = 1,345) as part of a longitudinal medical study. The data were analyzed by McCaulley and Kainz and reported in McCaulley (1978).

Schmidt & Fretz (1965). Form F. All students enrolled in an educational skills course at Ohio State University during the fall and winter of 1964–65. Modal student was eighteen years old, male, freshman, from Arts and Science, and had an ACT percentile 41.

Schroeder (1984). Incoming freshmen at St. Louis University (N = 535; males n = 245, females n = 290).

Schroeder & Jenkins (1981). Incoming freshmen at Mercer University, Macon, Georgia (N = 1,506) for classes entering in 1978 (n = 323), 1979 (n = 310), 1980 (n = 445) (data collected by Schroeder), and 1981 (n = 428) (data collected by Jenkins).

Simon (1979). Professional fine artists who met the high standards for PFA by members of the Fine Arts Guild of the Fine Arts Society of San Diego. Volunteers were requested in Art Guild magazine. One hundred fourteen responded (55% of the membership; N = 114; males n = 36, females n = 78). Creativity was rated by fellow PFA members on a 1–5 scale.

Smith, Irey, & McCaulley (1973). Form F. Engineering students (N = 58) at the University of Florida enrolled in a thermodynamics course offering eighteen self-paced instructional modules with different ways to cover the material.

Steele (1968). Form F. Sample includes: manager participants in two-week human relations summer laboratory sponsored by National Training Laboratories ($N = 72$ of total of 84) and middle managers who went through a two-week "Grid" laboratory (Blake and Mouton) as part of a year at a graduate school of business administration ($N = 39$ of a possible 58). Managers came from a wide variety of organizations and occupations.

Steele & Kelly (1976). Form F. Paid volunteer undergraduates ($N = 93$; males $n = 39$, females $n = 54$; ages 18–22).

Stein (1976). Form F. University of Florida students in introductory psychology ($N = 75$; males $n = 34$, females $n = 41$) who answered the Self-Directed Search and MBTI in 1971.

Stephens (1973). Form F. Seniors in advanced studio courses at the University of Florida ($N = 93$) majoring in fine arts ($n = 33$), art education ($n = 31$), and occupational therapy ($n = 29$).

Stephens (1975). Form F. Full-time art faculty from Memphis State University ($N = 25$ of a total faculty of 27), the Memphis Academy of Arts ($N = 21$ of 24), and an earlier population of art faculty from the University of Florida ($N = 19$).

Story (1983). Incoming students at Berkshire Christian College, Lenox, Massachusetts, who entered as freshmen or transfers from 1974 through 1982 ($N = 403$).

Stricker & Ross (1964). Entering class of students at Wesleyan University ($N = 254$), and entering class of male students at Stanford University ($N = 889$ of whom 713 answered the CPI, and of whom 727 answered both the MBTI and SVIB).

Stricker, Schiffman, & Ross (1965). Male freshmen entering Wesleyan University in 1959 ($N = 225$), applicants to the California Institute of Technology in 1958 ($N = 1,616$), and those applicants admitted to California Institute of Technology ($N = 201$).

Szymanski (1977). Form F. Students ($N = 118$; male $n = 84$, female $n = 34$) and teachers ($N = 42$) at Escambia County Florida's Exemplary Program for Educationally Disadvantaged Youth in Pensacola Florida. The student sample included students from the total population of 630 who read at or above sixth grade level; sixty percent were white and forty percent were black; the modal age was fifteen; all were at least two years below grade level in reading and mathematics but considered capable of earning a high school diploma.

Terrill (1969). Full-time counselors from ten typical junior and ten senior high schools in heavily populated suburbs in the Denver area ($N = 58$).

Todd & Roberts (1981). Students in art education ($N = 60$) and in music education ($N = 60$).

Velsor & Campbell (1984a). Participants (mainly managers in business organizations) in Leadership Development Programs 1979–83 at the Center for Creative Leadership, Greensboro, North Carolina, and who completed both the MBTI and the California Personality Inventory ($N = 1,218$).

Velsor & Campbell (1984b). Participants (mainly managers in business organizations) in Leadership Development Programs 1979–83 at the Center for Creative Leadership, Greensboro, North Carolina, and who completed the MBTI, the Strong-Campbell Interest Inventory, and the FIRO-B ($N = 1,228$).

von Fange (1961). Form E. Canadian male school administrators ($N = 124$). Superintendents ($n = 66$) tested at the Short Course for Superintendents at Banff in 1960; median age 48, experience in education 26 years and in their present position four years; all had responsibilities at a system or provincial level. Principals ($n = 58$) tested at the Fifth Annual Leadership Course for Principals in Edmonton, July 1960; median age 41.5, experience in education sixteen years, in present position three years. Schools consisted of thirteen elementary, twenty-four elementary-junior high, sixteen elementary-high, three junior-senior high, one senior high school. The number of classrooms in the schools ranged from two to forty, median fourteen.

von Fange (1982). Form F. Incoming students at Concordia Lutheran College in Ann Arbor, Michigan, entering between 1975 and 1981 ($N = 1,699$; males $n = 836$, females $n = 863$). Sixty-eight percent of these students were planning church-related vocations.

Walsh (1984). Male and female students at Universities of Guelph and Waterloo in Canada for whom both MBTI and SCII were administered ($N = 314$); tested April 1982 through May 1984.

Warrick (1983). Nationwide sample ($N = 1105$; males $n = 446$, females $n = 659$) tested in 1983 as part of SRI-VALS study designed mainly for media research. The sample is described in Chapter 4.

Weiss, (1980). Form F. Nursing students (N = 121) at the University of New Mexico, tested on admission and several years later near end of their training.

Whittemore & Heimann (1965). Form F. From a sample of male freshmen at the University of Arizona whose aptitude scores were in the top ten percent of their class (N = 80). The ten highest and ten lowest were identified on the basis of composite scores on measures of originality (Minnesota Test of Creative Thinking, Consequences Test, Anagrams Test).

Williams (1982). One hundred sixty residents of rural and small town areas in southern Alabama. Stressed group (N = 80) was presented to hospitals or physicians with stress-related complaints and were given preliminary diagnosis of psychosomatic or stress-related disorder. Normal comparison group (N = 80) was randomly selected from employees of largest local hospital with no medical history of psychosomatic or stress-related disease in preceding year.

Witzig (1978). Professional staff of public mental health clinics in Oregon (N = 102) whose type was estimated from a narrative using MBTI questions.

Yokomoto & Ware (1981). Students in a sophomore-level engineering course in linear circuit analysis at Indiana University-Purdue University in Indianapolis. Data reported in five case studies (N = 64, N = 43, N = 24, N = 19, and N = 30).

Wright (1967). Form F. From a total population of kindergarten to sixth grade teachers (N = 310) in the Covina, California, Unified School District, the MBTI was answered in 1964–65 (N =257; males n = 32, females n = 225). Scores were compared with data supplied by Educational Testing Service which had administered the MBTI in the same school district in 1958.

Appendix C

Mean Preference Scores for MBTI Preferences by Age Groups

Appendix D gives the means and standard deviations for preference scores separately for the Form F and Form G MBTI data banks by age groupings for males and females.

Type theory assumes that in midlife people normally gain more respect for hitherto neglected third and fourth functions and therefore develop them further. One effect might be to divide answers on the MBTI more evenly and to move scores toward the midpoint.

The MBTI Manual data are cross-sectional and therefore do not provide the longitudinal samples that would be needed to test the hypothesis of movement toward the center of the scale in midlife. However, the data shown below in the tables from the MBTI data bank support the opposite hypothesis—that with maturity people report their preferences with greater consistency.

Nevertheless, it is quite possible, and Myers believed it was probable, that persons do indeed develop less preferred functions at a point in their lives when they are secure in their dominant and auxiliary functions. This security appears in more consistent scores. In behavior, however, more tolerance for and enjoyment of the less-preferred functions and attitudes become evident. In other words, when preferences are clear, one feels confident of being on solid ground, and therefore feels safer in exploring new territory.

MBTI Form F Data Bank

	Extraversion			Introversion		
Age	N	Mean	S.D.	N	Mean	S.D.
15–17	2,829	22.9	13.96	2,175	21.5	14.40
18–20	8,445	23.1	13.98	6,116	20.1	13.84
21–24	4,524	22.2	13.50	3,617	20.9	13.76
25–29	3,123	21.0	13.16	3,260	22.4	14.26
30–39	4,826	21.2	13.17	4,679	22.6	14.49
40–49	2,960	20.9	12.79	2,811	22.9	14.33
50–59	1,401	20.7	12.95	1,261	22.1	14.43
60 plus	401	19.5	12.85	420	21.9	13.94

	Sensing			Intuition		
15–17	2,791	20.7	13.68	2,213	20.6	13.74
18–20	8,965	22.0	14.30	5,596	18.9	13.16
21–24	4,390	22.7	15.00	3,751	21.1	13.59
25–29	3,204	23.7	15.51	3,179	23.0	13.84
30–39	4,942	26.3	16.46	4,563	23.9	14.17
40–49	3,166	27.5	16.69	2,605	24.6	14.45
50–59	1,535	28.7	17.12	1,127	24.1	14.41
60 plus	525	30.9	16.73	296	22.7	14.00

	Thinking			Feeling		
15–17	1,973	18.1	14.12	3,031	17.3	10.75
18–20	5,534	17.0	13.47	9,027	18.1	10.93
21–24	3,758	19.5	14.19	4,383	17.2	10.72
25–29	3,321	20.0	14.22	3,062	16.9	10.86
30–39	5,007	22.7	15.24	4,498	17.7	11.96
40–49	3,209	24.4	15.80	2,562	18.2	11.22
50–59	1,349	22.2	15.35	1,313	18.4	11.05
60 plus	385	20.2	14.62	436	18.6	11.33

	Judgment			Perception		
15–17	2,207	19.8	13.71	2,797	24.5	15.89
18–20	7,837	21.3	13.74	6,724	21.9	14.99
21–24	4,902	23.9	14.55	3,239	21.3	15.07
25–29	3,937	24.5	14.74	2,446	20.9	14.98
30–39	6,226	26.6	15.11	3,279	21.9	15.59
40–49	3,979	27.7	14.87	1,792	21.5	15.25
50–59	1,829	28.8	15.05	833	21.1	14.91
60 plus	626	31.1	14.77	195	19.8	14.73

MBTI Form G Data Bank

Age	Extraversion			Introversion		
	N	Mean	S.D.	*N*	Mean	S.D.
15–17	2,289	22.0	13.5	1,659	19.9	13.9
18–20	6,107	21.4	13.1	4,945	20.5	13.7
21–24	1,466	19.2	12.6	1,451	20.8	13.4
25–29	1,244	19.0	12.3	1,365	21.4	14.0
30–39	2,208	19.4	12.7	2,599	22.3	14.3
40–49	1,388	19.6	12.4	1,464	22.5	14.2
50–59	758	18.9	12.1	845	22.1	14.2
60 plus	233	18.3	12.0	287	20.9	14.6

Age	Sensing			Intuition		
15–17	2,301	21.5	13.9	1,647	19.8	13.7
18–20	6,569	22.2	14.1	4,483	19.5	13.5
21–24	1,682	22.6	14.7	1,235	19.5	13.2
25–29	1,359	23.4	15.3	1,250	21.6	13.9
30–39	2,496	25.1	16.3	2,311	23.4	13.9
40–49	1,487	27.4	16.4	1,365	24.7	14.5
50–59	927	28.1	16.5	676	24.2	14.6
60 plus	311	30.7	16.3	209	22.1	14.0

Age	Thinking			Feeling		
15–17	2,100	19.8	14.8	1,848	15.1	10.1
18–20	6,133	20.6	14.6	4,919	15.1	10.1
21–24	1,743	22.5	15.2	1,174	15.6	10.4
25–29	1,478	22.2	15.6	1,131	16.1	10.7
30–39	2,711	22.2	15.2	2,096	17.1	11.1
40–49	1,513	22.5	15.4	1,339	18.0	11.2
50–59	865	21.6	15.3	738	18.1	11.4
60 plus	257	21.7	15.2	263	17.8	11.5

Age	Judgment			Perception		
15–17	2,001	20.6	13.5	1,947	23.4	15.7
18–20	6,130	21.2	13.4	4,922	22.3	15.6
21–24	1,757	24.0	14.2	1,160	20.4	15.1
25–29	1,625	23.9	14.6	984	21.1	14.4
30–39	3,178	26.3	14.7	1,629	21.2	14.9
40–49	1,919	27.2	14.8	933	20.3	15.2
50–59	1,153	28.9	14.9	450	20.6	14.8
60 plus	382	30.0	15.2	138	21.1	14.5

Appendix D

Types of Populations

Appendix D shows tables of occupations empirically attractive to EI, SN, TF, JP, and to the sixteen types. The data for these tables come from the CAPT MBTI data bank (described in Appendix B). MBTI response sheets contain a line for individuals to write their occupation. When these response sheets are sent to CAPT for scoring, the occupations are coded by a system modified from the *Dictionary of Occupational Titles* (U.S. Department of Labor, 1977). Data are included in the Appendix D tables when an occupation is represented by at least fifty people. In addition to the percentages for the occupation, the percentages of males and females in the MBTI data bank whose answer sheets show twelfth grade (high school graduate) or sixteenth grade (college graduate) as the highest grade completed are included to provide reference points.

To create these occupational tables for each of the sixteen types, a type table was created for each occupation showing the percentage in each type making up the total number in the occupation. These type percentages were then ranked from high to low. Data were collected from response sheets scored in the 1970's until 1984.

No attempt has been made to group occupations by families because it is often instructive to see which occupations attract people of the same preference. Note that these are samples of convenience, not randomly selected samples. In addition, respondents differ in the precision with which they name their occupation. Despite these limitations, the listings are consistent with the theory and common sense understanding of the occupation and the MBTI. Readers with a special interest in medicine and other health occupations will find similar summary information in McCaulley and Morgan (1982) and McCaulley (1977, 1978).

Individual occupations appear in lowercase. Composites of related occupations appear in capital letters. The totals for the composites may be greater than the sum of the individual occupations on the table, because composites can include occupations with fewer than fifty people. Normative data from the CAPT data bank are indicated by **.

Guidelines for Using the Career Listings in Appendix D

1. Look at the occupations at the top and the bottom of the table. Notice how they are different.

2. Consider whether any of the occupations at the high preference end of the table are attractive to the person seeking career information. Consider also the attractiveness of occupations at the bottom of the table.

3. Discuss how the high and low attraction occupations are or are not related to type preferences. This discussion and the search for patterns can be the most enlightening use of the data for career planning.

4. Notice the number of cases in the data bank for occupations of particular interest. Percentages for occupations with several hundred cases are more likely to be stable. Percentages can change when new cases are added to small samples. All of the occupations listed contain at least fifty cases.

Ranking of occupations by preference for EI

Percent Extravert	Percent Introvert	N	Sample Description
74.70	25.30	83	Marketing personnel
69.31	30.69	101	Insurance agents, brokers, and underwriters
68.38	31.62	136	Credit investigators and mortgage brokers
67.59	32.41	108	Sales clerks, retail trade
67.04	32.96	179	Sales representatives, unspecified
66.67	33.33	312	Managers: Restaurant, cafeteria, bar, and food service
66.29	33.71	89	Public relations workers and publicity writers
64.71	35.29	51	Restaurant workers: Table setting and cleaning
64.41	35.59	177	Resident housing assistants
63.86	36.14	83	Managers: Sales, not specified
63.79	36.21	58	Home management advisors and home economists
62.90	37.10	62	Actors
62.00	38.00	100	Receptionists
61.98	38.02	192	Consultants: Type unknown
61.83	38.17	1,750	SALES WORKERS
61.67	38.33	60	Dental hygienists
61.24	38.76	756	Bank officers and financial managers
60.78	39.22	102	Office managers
60.29	39.71	136	Musicians and composers
59.72	40.28	1,147	Nuns and miscellaneous religious workers

Ranking of occupations by preference for EI

Percent Extravert	Percent Introvert	N	Sample Description
59.71	40.29	139	Construction laborers, except carpenters' helpers
59.44	40.56	673	Counselors: Vocational and educational
59.12	40.88	274	Cashiers
58.89	41.11	1,024	Administrators: Elementary and secondary school
58.49	41.51	106	Speech pathologists
58.43	41.57	166	Real estate agents and brokers
58.21	41.79	67	Sales agents, retail trade
58.20	41.80	378	ARTISTS AND ENTERTAINERS
58.18	41.82	55	Child care workers, except private household
57.73	42.27	783	PERSONAL SERVICE WORKERS
57.69	42.31	52	Journalists
57.68	42.32	534	Clergy, all denominations
57.63	42.37	59	Photographers
57.56	42.44	2,010	RELIGIOUS WORKERS, ALL DENOMINATIONS
57.35	42.65	211	Lifeguards, attendants, recreation and amusement
57.29	42.71	96	Hairdressers and cosmetologists, manicurists
57.24	42.76	1,803	COUNSELORS
57.14	42.86	70	Optometrists
56.98	43.02	172	Coordinators: Not specified
56.80	43.20	250	Business: General, self-employed
56.67	43.33	7,463	MANAGERS AND ADMINISTRATORS
56.48	43.52	540	Waiters, waitresses
56.30	43.70	238	Public service aides and community health workers
56.01	43.99	932	Counselors: General
55.93	44.07	177	Counselors: Rehabilitation
55.74	44.26	3,678	Administrators: Managers and supervisors miscellaneous
55.74	44.26	61	Food counter and fountain workers
55.70	44.30	228	Teachers: Adult education
55.21	44.79	96	Teachers: Reading
55.18	44.82	1,082	FOOD SERVICE WORKERS
54.91	45.09	173	Teachers: Special education
54.88	45.12	82	Professional, technical, and kindred workers, misc.
54.84	45.16	341	Administrators: Colleges and technical institutes
54.62	45.38	119	Teachers: Trade, industrial, and technical
54.55	45.45	55	Designers
54.44	45.56	90	Personnel and labor relations workers
54.43	45.57	79	Religion: Educator, all denominations
54.43	45.57	79	Medical assistants
54.41	45.59	68	Secretaries: Medical

Ranking of occupations by preference for EI

Percent Extravert	Percent Introvert	N	Sample Description
54.29	45.71	606	**High school graduates, males
54.27	45.73	164	Teachers: Coaching
53.85	46.15	52	Factory and site supervisors, miscellaneous
53.81	46.19	223	Teachers: Health
53.75	46.25	80	Employment development specialists
53.73	46.27	67	Stock clerks and storekeepers
53.58	46.42	782	LABORERS
53.42	46.58	146	Nursing: Consultants
53.41	46.59	264	MILITARY PERSONNEL
53.28	46.72	1,128	Teachers: Middle and junior high school
53.27	46.73	107	Typists
53.16	46.84	190	Engineers: Mining
53.12	46.87	128	Judges
53.06	46.94	245	Therapists: Occupational
53.02	46.98	530	WRITERS AND JOURNALISTS
52.97	47.03	472	Miscellaneous laborers
52.62	47.38	840	CLERICAL AND KINDRED WORKERS
52.58	47.42	213	Teachers: Art, drama, and music
52.52	47.48	139	Physicians: Family practice, general practice
52.42	47.58	765	HEALTH CARE THERAPISTS
52.31	47.69	65	Operations and systems researchers and analysts
52.25	47.75	333	Secretaries: Executive and administrative assistants
52.23	47.77	561	Teachers: Junior college
52.00	48.00	100	Teachers: Preschool
51.98	48.02	202	Administrators: Health
51.89	48.11	370	Administrators: School level unspecified
51.85	48.15	297	Computer and peripheral equipment operators
51.79	48.21	112	Food service workers, miscellaneous; except private
51.79	48.21	56	Clerical supervisors, miscellaneous
51.69	48.31	89	Consultants: Management analysts
51.62	48.38	804	Teachers: Elementary school
51.59	48.41	157	Teachers: Speech pathology and therapy
51.59	48.41	126	Radiologic technologists and technicians
51.54	48.46	2,499	Clerical workers, miscellaneous
51.48	48.52	169	Service workers, except private household, miscellaneous
51.47	48.53	68	Corrections officers, probation officers
51.39	48.61	72	FARMERS
51.39	48.61	72	Dental assistants
51.16	48.84	649	Teachers: High school
51.11	48.89	900	HEALTH SERVICE WORKERS
51.09	48.91	4,905	OFFICE MACHINE OPERATORS

Ranking of occupations by preference for EI

Percent Extravert	Percent Introvert	N	Sample Description
51.05	48.95	143	Auditors
51.00	49.00	402	PSYCHOLOGISTS
50.94	49.06	479	Social workers
50.64	49.36	314	Nurses: Aides, orderlies, and attendants
50.62	49.38	81	Research workers, not specified
50.51	49.49	16,678	TEACHERS
50.39	49.61	3,064	PRIVATE HOUSEHOLD WORKERS
50.33	49.67	608	PROTECTIVE SERVICE WORKERS
50.27	49.73	4,446	**College graduates, males
50.07	49.93	669	MECHANICS
50.00	50.00	84	Library attendants and assistants
50.00	50.00	54	Engineers: Aeronautical
50.00	50.00	52	Engineers: Chemical
49.68	50.32	155	Police and detectives
49.59	50.41	490	SOCIAL SCIENTISTS
49.58	50.42	4,736	**College graduates, females
49.52	50.48	208	Writers, artists, entertainers, and agents, miscellaneous
49.44	50.56	180	Cooks, except private household
49.31	50.69	432	Teachers' aides, except school monitors
49.23	50.77	323	Dietitians, nutritionists
49.16	50.84	179	Teachers: English
48.93	51.07	1,126	Secretaries: Not specified
48.85	51.15	305	Nursing: Educators
48.72	51.28	195	Therapists: Respiratory
48.67	51.33	150	Bookkeepers
48.62	51.38	109	Carpenters
48.36	51.64	122	Administrators: Educationally related
48.08	51.92	52	Computer specialists
48.00	52.00	175	ENGINEERING AND SCIENCE TECHNICIANS
47.92	52.08	144	TRANSPORTATION OPERATIVES
47.87	52.13	94	Nursing: Administrators
47.76	52.24	268	Technicians: Miscellaneous
47.67	52.33	986	ENGINEERS
47.62	52.38	105	Police supervisors
47.57	52.43	3,103	NURSES
47.57	52.43	1,337	**High school graduates, females
47.42	52.58	97	MISCELLANEOUS OPERATIVES AND FACTORY WORKERS
47.37	52.63	57	Scientists: Biological
47.30	52.70	148	Therapists: Physical
47.23	52.77	559	CRAFT WORKERS
47.06	52.94	85	Dentists
46.92	53.08	260	Nurses: Licensed practical
46.75	53.25	77	Engineers: Mechanical
46.60	53.40	191	Pharmacists
46.58	53.42	73	Air force personnel
46.51	53.49	172	Teaching assistants
46.51	53.49	86	Guards and watch keepers

Ranking of occupations by preference for EI

Percent Extravert	Percent Introvert	N	Sample Description
46.38	53.62	1,880	Nursing: Registered nurses, no specialty stated
46.02	53.98	113	Editors and reporters
46.01	53.99	1,291	HEALTH TECHNOLOGISTS AND TECHNICIANS
45.79	54.21	2,282	Teachers: University
45.78	54.22	83	Nursing: Public health
45.66	54.34	219	Priests, monks
45.63	54.37	206	SPECIALIZED: OPERATIVES
45.20	54.80	427	Accountants
45.09	54.91	519	LAWYERS AND JUDGES
44.78	55.22	67	CLEANING SERVICES
44.69	55.31	226	SCIENTISTS: LIFE AND PHYSICAL
44.44	55.56	54	Consultants: Education
44.29	55.71	70	Electricians
44.26	55.74	61	Physicians: Pathology
44.19	55.81	86	Computer systems analysts, support representatives
44.12	55.88	68	Physicians: Psychiatry
43.39	56.61	2,072	DOCTORS OF MEDICINE
43.28	56.72	67	Research assistants
43.26	56.74	638	Medical technologists
42.86	57.14	105	Steelworkers, miscellaneous
42.86	57.14	84	Attorneys: Administrators, nonpracticing
42.59	57.41	54	Chain, rod, and ax workers; surveying
42.31	57.69	338	COMPUTER SPECIALISTS
42.25	57.75	71	Teachers: Mathematics
42.11	57.89	57	Technicians: Electrical and electronic engineering
41.70	58.30	223	Clinical laboratory technologists and technicians
41.33	58.67	271	Lawyers
40.57	59.43	106	Media specialists
40.00	60.00	200	Computer programmers
39.37	60.63	127	Mechanics and repairers, not specified
39.33	60.67	267	Librarians
39.26	60.74	270	LIBRARIANS, ARCHIVISTS, AND CURATORS
37.70	62.30	61	Scientists: Chemistry
37.66	62.34	77	Secretaries: Legal
37.04	62.96	54	Engineers: Electrical and electronic

Ranking of occupations by preference for SN

Percent Sensing	Percent Intuition	N	Sample Description
85.71	14.29	105	Steelworkers, miscellaneous

Ranking of occupations by preference for SN

Percent Sensing	Percent Intuition	N	Sample Description
85.16	14.84	155	Police and detectives
84.62	15.38	52	Factory and site supervisors, miscellaneous
83.00	17.00	606	**High school graduates, males
81.51	18.49	238	Public service aides and community health workers
76.39	23.61	72	FARMERS
76.12	23.88	67	CLEANING SERVICES
75.00	25.00	608	PROTECTIVE SERVICE WORKERS
74.05	25.95	1,337	**High school graduates, females
73.85	26.15	260	Nurses: Licensed practical
73.61	26.39	144	TRANSPORTATION OPERATIVES
73.21	26.79	112	Food service workers, miscellaneous; except private
72.38	27.62	105	Police supervisors
72.22	27.78	432	Teachers' aides, except school monitors
72.19	27.81	169	Service workers, except private household, misc.
71.96	28.04	107	Typists
71.47	28.53	312	Managers: Restaurant, cafeteria, bar and food service
70.93	29.07	86	Guards and watch keepers
70.83	29.17	96	Hairdressers and cosmetologists, manicurists
70.73	29.27	164	Teachers: Coaching
69.59	30.41	559	CRAFT WORKERS
69.29	30.71	127	Mechanics and repairers, not specified
69.07	30.93	97	MISCELLANEOUS OPERATIVES AND FACTORY WORKERS
68.00	32.00	150	Bookkeepers
67.86	32.14	56	Clerical supervisors, miscellaneous
66.91	33.09	139	Construction laborers, except carpenters' helpers
66.67	33.33	72	Dental assistants
66.18	33.82	68	Correctional officers, probation officers
65.87	34.13	126	Radiologic technologists and technicians
65.48	34.52	840	CLERICAL AND KINDRED WORKERS
65.48	34.52	84	Library attendants and assistants
65.45	34.55	55	Child care workers, except private household
65.32	34.68	669	MECHANICS
65.08	34.92	756	Bank officers and financial managers
64.97	35.03	314	Nurses: Aides, orderlies, and attendants
64.94	35.06	77	Secretaries: Legal
64.91	35.09	228	Teachers: Adult education
64.89	35.11	900	HEALTH SERVICE WORKERS

Ranking of occupations by preference for SN

Percent Sensing	Percent Intuition	N	Sample Description
64.89	35.11	94	Nursing: Administrators
64.71	35.29	119	Teachers: Trade, industrial and technical
64.71	35.29	68	Secretaries: Medical
64.39	35.61	264	MILITARY PERSONNEL
64.18	35.82	67	Stock clerks and storekeepers
63.87	36.13	274	Cashiers
63.59	36.41	206	SPECIALIZED: OPERATIVES
63.38	36.62	71	Teachers: Mathematics
63.17	36.83	782	LABORERS
63.03	36.97	211	Lifeguards, attendants, recreation and amusement
63.01	36.99	73	Air force personnel
62.56	37.44	804	Teachers: Elementary school
62.30	37.70	427	Accountants
62.08	37.92	472	Miscellaneous laborers
62.07	37.93	783	PERSONAL SERVICE WORKERS
62.01	37.99	179	Sales representatives, unspecified
61.60	38.40	638	Medical technologists
61.47	38.53	109	Carpenters
61.43	38.57	70	Electricians
61.33	38.67	3,064	PRIVATE HOUSEHOLD WORKERS
61.28	38.72	1,126	Secretaries: Not specified
60.94	39.06	128	Judges
60.84	39.16	166	Real estate agents and brokers
60.59	39.41	1,147	Nuns and miscellaneous religious workers
60.51	39.49	157	Teachers: Speech pathology and therapy
60.00	40.00	4,905	OFFICE MACHINE OPERATORS
60.00	40.00	100	Receptionists
60.00	40.00	85	Dentists
59.76	40.24	82	Professional, technical, and kindred workers, misc.
59.70	40.30	67	Sales agents, retail trade
59.57	40.43	1,291	HEALTH TECHNOLOGISTS AND TECHNICIANS
59.26	40.74	108	Sales clerks, retail trade
59.04	40.96	83	Managers: Sales, not specified
58.82	41.18	2,499	Clerical workers, miscellaneous
58.57	41.43	70	Optometrists
58.44	41.56	77	Engineers: Mechanical
57.97	42.03	3,678	Administrators: Managers and supervisors, miscellanous
57.95	42.05	195	Therapists: Respiratory
57.89	42.11	323	Dietitians, nutritionists
57.83	42.17	83	Nursing: Public health
57.58	42.42	297	Computer and peripheral equipment operators
57.43	42.57	101	Insurance agents, brokers, and underwriters
57.38	42.62	61	Food counter and fountain workers
56.91	43.09	1,880	Nursing: Registered nurses, no specialty stated

Ranking of occupations by preference for SN

Percent Sensing	Percent Intuition	N	Sample Description
56.90	43.10	58	Home management advisors and home economists
56.72	43.28	268	Technicians: Miscellaneous
56.64	43.36	143	Auditors
56.32	43.68	7,463	MANAGERS AND ADMINISTRATORS
56.29	43.71	1,750	SALES WORKERS
56.25	43.75	96	Teachers: Reading
56.14	43.86	57	Technicians: Electrical and electronic engineering
56.11	43.89	180	Cooks, except private household
56.04	43.96	3,103	NURSES
55.77	44.23	52	Computer specialists
55.70	44.30	79	Medical assistants
55.61	44.39	223	Clinical laboratory technologists and technicians
55.56	44.44	333	Secretaries: Executive and administrative assistants
55.56	44.44	90	Personnel and labor relations workers
55.43	44.57	175	ENGINEERING AND SCIENCE TECHNICIANS
55.41	44.59	148	Therapists: Physical
55.14	44.86	1,128	Teachers: Middle and junior high school
54.90	45.10	102	Office managers
54.71	45.29	1,082	FOOD SERVICE WORKERS
54.21	45.79	190	Engineers: Mining
54.10	45.90	61	Physicians: Pathology
54.00	46.00	250	Business: General, self-employed
53.85	46.15	52	Engineers: Chemical
53.70	46.30	270	LIBRARIANS, ARCHIVISTS, AND CURATORS
53.56	46.44	267	Librarians
53.42	46.58	146	Nursing: Consultants
53.40	46.60	191	Pharmacists
53.24	46.76	139	Physicians: Family practice, general practice
53.00	47.00	100	Teachers: Preschool
52.93	47.07	1,024	Administrators: Elementary and secondary school
52.64	47.36	986	ENGINEERS
51.85	48.15	54	Engineers: Electrical and electronic
50.98	49.02	51	Restaurant workers: Table setting and cleaning
50.85	49.15	16,678	TEACHERS
50.56	49.44	540	Waiters, waitresses
50.50	49.50	202	Administrators: Health
50.00	50.00	106	Media specialists
50.00	50.00	60	Dental hygienists
49.87	50.13	4,446	**College graduates, males
49.61	50.39	649	Teachers: High school
49.46	50.54	370	Administrators: School level unspecified
49.42	50.58	172	Coordinators: Not specified

Ranking of occupations by preference for SN

Percent Sensing	Percent Intuition	N	Sample Description
49.30	50.70	2,010	RELIGIOUS WORKERS, ALL DENOMINATIONS
49.15	50.85	765	HEALTH CARE THERAPISTS
48.65	51.35	2,072	DOCTORS OF MEDICINE
48.36	51.64	122	Administrators: Educationally related
48.26	51.74	172	Teaching assistants
48.15	51.85	54	Chain, rod, and ax workers; surveying
48.04	51.96	4,736	**College graduates, females
47.06	52.94	136	Credit investigators and mortgage brokers
46.84	53.16	79	Religion: Educator, all denominations
46.75	53.25	338	COMPUTER SPECIALISTS
46.56	53.44	305	Nursing: Educators
46.51	53.49	86	Computer systems analysts, support representatives
46.15	53.85	65	Operations and systems researchers and analysts
45.66	54.34	173	Teachers: Special education
45.31	54.69	245	Therapists: Occupational
44.50	55.50	200	Computer programmers
43.40	56.60	106	Speech pathologists
42.92	57.08	226	SCIENTISTS: LIFE AND PHYSICAL
42.62	57.38	61	Scientists: Chemistry
42.59	57.41	54	Engineers: Aeronautical
42.42	57.58	561	Teachers: Junior college
41.82	58.18	55	Designers
41.81	58.19	177	Counselors: Rehabilitation
40.45	59.55	89	Public relations workers and publicity writers
40.00	60.00	80	Employment development specialists
39.76	60.24	83	Marketing personnel
39.46	60.54	223	Teachers: Health
39.33	60.67	89	Consultants: Management analysts
39.31	60.69	519	LAWYERS AND JUDGES
38.83	61.17	479	Social workers
38.63	61.37	673	Counselors: Vocational and educational
38.36	61.64	219	Priests, monks
37.85	62.15	177	Resident housing assistants
37.83	62.17	341	Administrators: Colleges and technical institutes
37.38	62.62	1,803	COUNSELORS
36.84	63.16	57	Scientists: Biological
36.06	63.94	2,282	Teachers: University
35.84	64.16	932	Counselors: General
35.75	64.25	179	Teachers: English
34.90	65.10	192	Consultants: Type unknown
34.56	65.44	136	Musicians and composers
32.10	67.90	81	Research workers, not specified
31.86	68.14	113	Editors and reporters
31.48	68.52	54	Consultants: Education

Ranking of occupations by preference for SN

Percent Sensing	Percent Intuition	N	Sample Description
30.95	69.05	378	ARTISTS AND ENTERTAINERS
30.71	69.29	534	Clergy, all denominations
30.63	69.37	271	Lawyers
29.11	70.89	213	Teachers: Art, drama, and music
28.85	71.15	52	Journalists
27.38	72.62	84	Attorneys: Administrators, nonpracticing
27.12	72.88	59	Photographers
26.42	73.58	530	WRITERS AND JOURNALISTS
25.00	75.00	68	Physicians: Psychiatry
19.40	80.60	67	Research assistants
19.35	80.65	62	Actors
17.76	82.24	490	SOCIAL SCIENTISTS
14.93	85.07	402	PSYCHOLOGISTS
13.94	86.06	208	Writers, artists, entertainers, and agents, miscellaneous

Ranking of occupations by preference for TF

Percent Thinking	Percent Feeling	N	Sample Description
79.52	20.48	83	Managers: Sales, not specified
78.46	21.54	65	Operations and systems researchers and analysts
77.23	22.77	606	**High school graduates, males
76.74	23.26	86	Computer systems analysts, support representatives
75.52	24.48	143	Auditors
75.00	25.00	756	Bank officers and financial managers
74.29	25.71	105	Steelworkers, miscellaneous
73.53	26.47	136	Credit investigators and mortgage brokers
72.78	27.22	169	Service workers, except private household, misc.
72.13	27.87	61	Scientists: Chemistry
71.15	28.85	52	Engineers: Chemical
70.83	29.17	72	FARMERS
70.59	29.41	119	Teachers: Trade, industrial and technical
70.56	29.44	4,446	**College graduates, males
70.13	29.87	77	Engineers: Mechanical
69.05	30.95	84	Attorneys: Administrators, nonpracticing
68.85	31.15	61	Physicians: Pathology
68.42	31.58	57	Technicians: Electrical and electronic engineering
68.39	31.61	155	Police and detectives
67.46	32.54	338	COMPUTER SPECIALISTS
66.67	33.33	54	Engineers: Electrical and electronic

Ranking of occupations by preference for TF

Percent Thinking	Percent Feeling	N	Sample Description
65.93	34.07	226	SCIENTISTS: LIFE AND PHYSICAL
65.56	34.44	90	Personnel and labor relations workers
64.94	35.06	271	Lawyers
64.50	35.50	200	Computer programmers
64.16	35.84	519	LAWYERS AND JUDGES
64.06	35.94	128	Judges
63.89	36.11	3,678	Administrators: Managers and supervisors, miscellaneous
63.81	36.19	105	Police supervisors
63.78	36.22	312	Managers: Restaurant, cafeteria, bar and food service
63.59	36.41	986	ENGINEERS
63.46	36.54	52	Computer specialists
63.24	36.76	370	Administrators: School level unspecified
62.71	37.29	59	Photographers
61.56	38.44	7,463	MANAGERS AND ADMINISTRATORS
61.51	38.49	608	PROTECTIVE SERVICE WORKERS
61.45	38.55	83	Marketing personnel
61.18	38.82	85	Dentists
59.65	40.35	57	Scientists: Biological
59.25	40.75	427	Accountants
59.15	40.85	71	Teachers: Mathematics
58.40	41.60	250	Business: General, self-employed
58.21	41.79	67	Sales agents, retail trade
57.53	42.47	73	Air force personnel
57.42	42.58	559	CRAFT WORKERS
57.35	42.65	68	Corrections officers, probation officers
57.23	42.77	166	Real estate agents and brokers
57.20	42.80	264	MILITARY PERSONNEL
57.14	42.86	175	ENGINEERING AND SCIENCE TECHNICIANS
57.14	42.86	70	Electricians
56.98	43.02	179	Sales representatives, unspecified
56.60	43.40	341	Administrators: Colleges and technical institutes
55.77	44.23	52	Factory and site supervisors, miscellaneous
55.06	44.94	89	Consultants: Management analysts
55.04	44.96	238	Public service aides and community health workers
54.92	45.08	122	Administrators: Educationally related
54.88	45.12	82	Professional, technical, and kindred workers, misc.
54.26	45.74	94	Nursing: Administrators
53.75	46.25	80	Employment development specialists
53.73	46.27	67	CLEANING SERVICES

Ranking of occupations by preference for TF

Percent Thinking	Percent Feeling	N	Sample Description
53.65	46.35	192	Consultants: Type unknown
53.47	46.53	101	Insurance agents, brokers, and underwriters
53.37	46.63	2,282	Teachers: University
53.33	46.67	195	Therapists: Respiratory
52.99	47.01	268	Technicians: Miscellaneous
52.62	47.38	669	MECHANICS
52.24	47.76	67	Stock clerks and storekeepers
51.83	48.17	164	Teachers: Coaching
51.69	48.31	472	Miscellaneous laborers
51.61	48.39	62	Actors
51.49	48.51	202	Administrators: Health
51.31	48.69	191	Pharmacists
50.52	49.48	97	MISCELLANEOUS OPERATIVES AND FACTORY WORKERS
50.39	49.61	127	Mechanics and repairers, not specified
50.38	49.62	782	LABORERS
50.36	49.64	139	Construction laborers, except carpenters' helpers
50.00	50.00	206	SPECIALIZED: OPERATIVES
50.00	50.00	144	TRANSPORTATION OPERATIVES
49.71	50.29	1,024	Administrators: Elementary and secondary school
49.44	50.56	180	Cooks, except private household
49.42	50.58	2,072	DOCTORS OF MEDICINE
49.42	50.58	172	Coordinators: Not specified
48.31	51.69	89	Public relations workers and publicity writers
48.15	51.85	81	Research workers, not specified
48.05	51.95	77	Secretaries: Legal
46.51	53.49	86	Guards and watch keepers
46.30	53.70	54	Chain, rod, and ax workers; surveying
46.23	53.77	1,750	SALES WORKERS
45.71	54.29	490	SOCIAL SCIENTISTS
45.71	54.29	70	Optometrists
45.59	54.41	68	Physicians: Psychiatry
45.54	54.46	112	Food service workers, miscellaneous; except private
45.37	54.63	108	Sales clerks, retail trade
45.29	54.71	223	Clinical laboratory technologists and technicians
44.95	55.05	109	Carpenters
44.58	55.42	323	Dietitians, nutritionists
44.55	55.45	211	Lifeguards, attendants, recreation and amusement
44.53	55.47	402	PSYCHOLOGISTS
44.21	55.79	561	Teachers: Junior college
44.18	55.82	378	ARTISTS AND ENTERTAINERS
43.84	56.16	333	Secretaries: Executive and administrative assistants
43.84	56.16	146	Nursing: Consultants
43.64	56.36	55	Designers
43.40	56.60	106	Media specialists

Ranking of occupations by preference for TF

Percent Thinking	Percent Feeling	N	Sample Description
43.33	56.67	1,147	Nuns and miscellaneous religious workers
43.28	56.72	67	Research assistants
43.02	56.98	530	WRITERS AND JOURNALISTS
42.98	57.02	228	Teachers: Adult education
42.48	57.52	113	Editors and reporters
42.45	57.55	1,291	HEALTH TECHNOLOGISTS AND TECHNICIANS
42.45	57.55	245	Therapists: Occupational
42.16	57.84	638	Medical technologists
42.15	57.85	783	PERSONAL SERVICE WORKERS
42.00	58.00	16,678	TEACHERS
41.91	58.09	649	Teachers: High school
41.64	58.36	305	Nursing: Educators
41.44	58.56	765	HEALTH CARE THERAPISTS
41.35	58.65	208	Writers, artists, entertainers, and agents, misc.
41.26	58.74	223	Teachers: Health
41.11	58.89	4,736	**College graduates, females
40.74	59.26	54	Engineers: Aeronautical
40.70	59.30	172	Teaching assistants
40.62	59.37	96	Hairdressers and cosmetologists, manicurists
40.46	59.54	173	Teachers: Special education
39.68	60.32	126	Radiologic technologists and technicians
39.54	60.46	1,128	Teachers: Middle and junior high school
39.22	60.78	102	Office managers
39.09	60.91	1,082	FOOD SERVICE WORKERS
38.89	61.11	54	Consultants: Education
38.46	61.54	52	Journalists
37.70	62.30	61	Food counter and fountain workers
37.25	62.75	51	Restaurant workers: Table setting and cleaning
37.04	62.96	297	Computer and peripheral equipment operators
36.76	63.24	136	Musicians and composers
36.69	63.31	139	Physicians: Family practice, general practice
36.22	63.78	3,103	NURSES
36.16	63.84	177	Resident housing assistants
35.96	64.04	673	Counselors: Vocational and educational
35.91	64.09	479	Social workers
35.75	64.25	179	Teachers: English
35.44	64.56	79	Medical assistants
34.89	65.11	1,880	Nursing: Registered nurses, no specialty stated
34.72	65.28	72	Dental assistants
34.53	65.47	2,010	RELIGIOUS WORKERS, ALL DENOMINATIONS
34.52	65.48	84	Library attendants and assistants
34.48	65.52	58	Home management advisors and home economists

Ranking of occupations by preference for TF

Percent Thinking	Percent Feeling	N	Sample Description
34.17	65.83	1,803	COUNSELORS
34.05	65.95	840	CLERICAL AND KINDRED WORKERS
34.03	65.97	432	Teachers' aides, except school monitors
33.96	66.04	106	Speech pathologists
33.82	66.18	68	Secretaries: Medical
33.70	66.30	270	LIBRARIANS, ARCHIVISTS, AND CURATORS
33.33	66.67	540	Waiters, waitresses
33.33	66.67	177	Counselors: Rehabilitation
33.33	66.67	96	Teachers: Reading
33.26	66.74	932	Counselors: General
33.07	66.93	4,905	OFFICE MACHINE OPERATORS
32.96	67.04	267	Librarians
32.83	67.17	1,337	**High school graduates, females
32.73	67.27	55	Child care workers, except private household
32.71	67.29	107	Typists
32.67	67.33	900	HEALTH SERVICE WORKERS
32.09	67.91	804	Teachers: Elementary school
31.92	68.08	260	Nurses: Licensed practical
31.45	68.55	2,499	Clerical workers, miscellaneous
30.41	69.59	148	Therapists: Physical
30.29	69.71	274	Cashiers
30.12	69.88	83	Nursing: Public health
30.00	70.00	150	Bookkeepers
29.84	70.16	1,126	Secretaries: Not specified
29.30	70.70	157	Teachers: Speech pathology and therapy
28.64	71.36	213	Teachers: Art, drama, and music
28.57	71.43	56	Clerical supervisors, miscellaneous
28.33	71.67	60	Dental hygienists
27.71	72.29	314	Nurses: Aides, orderlies, and attendants
25.79	74.21	190	Engineers: Mining
25.72	74.28	3,064	PRIVATE HOUSEHOLD WORKERS
25.11	74.89	219	Priests, monks
22.78	77.22	79	Religion: Educator, all denominations
22.00	78.00	100	Receptionists
21.35	78.65	534	Clergy, all denominations
21.00	79.00	100	Teachers: Preschool

Ranking of occupations by preference for JP

Percent Judging	Percent Perception	N	Sample Description
78.85	21.15	52	Engineers: Chemical

Ranking of occupations by preference for JP

Percent Judging	Percent Perception	N	Sample Description
78.72	21.28	94	Nursing: Administrators
77.59	22.41	58	Home management advisors and home economists
76.24	23.76	606	**High school graduates, males
75.90	24.10	83	Managers: Sales, not specified
75.32	24.68	312	Managers: Restaurant, cafeteria, bar, and food service
74.79	25.21	119	Teachers: Trade, industrial, and technical
74.75	25.25	202	Administrators: Health
74.37	25.63	238	Public service aides and community health workers
74.22	25.78	128	Judges
74.12	25.88	85	Dentists
73.33	26.67	105	Steelworkers, miscellaneous
71.43	28.57	756	Bank officers and financial managers
71.35	28.65	370	Administrators: School level unspecified
70.55	29.45	146	Nursing: Consultants
70.50	29.50	139	Physicians: Family practice, general practice
70.49	29.51	61	Physicians: Pathology
70.42	29.58	71	Teachers: Mathematics
69.82	30.18	1,024	Administrators: Elementary and secondary school
69.77	30.23	86	Guards and watch keepers
69.52	30.48	105	Police supervisors
69.35	30.65	323	Dietitians, nutritionists
69.32	30.68	7,463	MANAGERS AND ADMINISTRATORS
69.32	30.68	427	Accountants
69.23	30.77	65	Operations and systems researchers and analysts
69.15	30.85	804	Teachers: Elementary school
69.12	30.88	136	Credit investigators and mortgage brokers
69.05	30.95	84	Attorneys: Administrators, nonpracticing
68.94	31.06	4,446	**College graduates, males
68.85	31.15	61	Scientists: Chemistry
68.79	31.21	157	Teachers: Speech pathology and therapy
68.57	31.43	70	Optometrists
68.43	31.57	3,678	Administrators: Managers and supervisors, miscellaneous
68.42	31.58	608	PROTECTIVE SERVICE WORKERS
68.41	31.59	649	Teachers: High school
68.03	31.97	638	Medical technologists
67.83	32.17	143	Auditors
67.74	32.26	341	Administrators: Colleges and technical institutes
67.71	32.29	96	Hairdressers and cosmetologists, manicurists
67.65	32.35	68	Secretaries: Medical
67.31	32.69	260	Nurses: Licensed practical

Ranking of occupations by preference for JP

Percent Judging	Percent Perception	N	Sample Description
67.31	32.69	52	Factory and site supervisors, miscellaneous
67.31	32.69	52	Computer specialists
67.21	32.79	122	Administrators: Educationally related
67.16	32.84	67	CLEANING SERVICES
67.12	32.88	4,736	**College graduates, females
67.07	32.93	82	Professional, technical, and kindred workers, misc.
67.04	32.96	179	Teachers: English
66.67	33.33	432	Teachers' aides, except school monitors
66.67	33.33	96	Teachers: Reading
66.67	33.33	90	Personnel and labor relations workers
66.45	33.55	155	Police and detectives
66.43	33.57	1,147	Nuns and miscellaneous religious workers
66.37	33.63	226	SCIENTISTS: LIFE AND PHYSICAL
66.27	33.73	83	Nursing: Public health
66.21	33.79	219	Priests, monks
65.91	34.09	2,282	Teachers: University
65.90	34.10	305	Nursing: Educators
65.69	34.31	1,128	Teachers: Middle and junior high school
65.64	34.36	16,678	TEACHERS
65.12	34.88	2,010	RELIGIOUS WORKERS, ALL DENOMINATIONS
65.12	34.88	86	Computer systems analysts, support representatives
65.00	35.00	100	Teachers: Preschool
64.91	35.09	57	Scientists: Biological
64.74	35.26	173	Teachers: Special education
64.71	35.29	102	Office managers
64.62	35.38	2,072	DOCTORS OF MEDICINE
64.46	35.54	166	Real estate agents and brokers
64.44	35.56	270	LIBRARIANS, ARCHIVISTS, AND CURATORS
64.29	35.71	84	Library attendants and assistants
64.17	35.83	1,337	**High school graduates, females
64.04	35.96	267	Librarians
64.04	35.96	89	Consultants: Management analysts
63.95	36.05	172	Coordinators: Not specified
63.87	36.13	191	Pharmacists
63.69	36.31	179	Sales representatives, unspecified
63.59	36.41	1,291	HEALTH TECHNOLOGISTS AND TECHNICIANS
63.58	36.42	3,103	NURSES
63.41	36.59	164	Teachers: Coaching
63.16	36.84	57	Technicians: Electrical and electronic engineering
63.06	36.94	268	Technicians: Miscellaneous
62.96	37.04	54	Engineers: Electrical and electronic

Ranking of occupations by preference for JP

Percent Judging	Percent Perception	N	Sample Description
62.96	37.04	54	Consultants: Education
62.92	37.08	534	Clergy, all denominations
62.82	37.18	1,880	Nursing: Registered nurses, no specialty stated
62.78	37.22	223	Teachers: Health
62.47	37.53	3,064	PRIVATE HOUSEHOLD WORKERS
62.45	37.55	245	Therapists: Occupational
62.43	37.57	519	LAWYERS AND JUDGES
62.34	37.66	77	Secretaries: Legal
62.34	37.66	77	Engineers: Mechanical
62.21	37.79	172	Teaching assistants
62.03	37.97	79	Religion: Educator, all denominations
61.98	38.02	192	Consultants: Type unknown
61.86	38.14	333	Secretaries: Executive and administrative assistants
61.84	38.16	228	Teachers: Adult education
61.76	38.24	68	Correctional officers, probation officers
61.74	38.26	264	MILITARY PERSONNEL
61.68	38.32	561	Teachers: Junior college
61.32	38.68	106	Media specialists
61.25	38.75	80	Employment development specialists
61.11	38.89	900	HEALTH SERVICE WORKERS
60.71	39.29	112	Food service workers, miscellaneous; except private
60.49	39.51	81	Research workers, not specified
60.45	39.55	986	ENGINEERS
60.00	40.00	250	Business: General, self-employed
59.95	40.05	1,126	Secretaries: Not specified
59.81	40.19	107	Typists
59.79	40.21	97	MISCELLANEOUS OPERATIVES AND FACTORY WORKERS
59.29	40.71	840	CLERICAL AND KINDRED WORKERS
59.26	40.74	783	PERSONAL SERVICE WORKERS
59.03	40.97	144	TRANSPORTATION OPERATIVES
59.02	40.98	61	Food counter and fountain workers
58.92	41.08	314	Nurses: Aides, orderlies, and attendants
58.90	41.10	73	Air force personnel
58.88	41.12	338	COMPUTER SPECIALISTS
58.33	41.67	108	Sales clerks, retail trade
58.33	41.67	72	FARMERS
58.33	41.67	60	Dental hygienists
58.00	42.00	150	Bookkeepers
57.85	42.15	223	Clinical laboratory technologists and technicians
57.66	42.34	274	Cashiers
57.40	42.60	169	Service workers, except private household, miscellaneous

Ranking of occupations by preference for JP

Percent Judging	Percent Perception	N	Sample Description
57.14	42.86	56	Clerical supervisors, miscellaneous
57.07	42.93	559	CRAFT WORKERS
57.00	43.00	4,905	OFFICE MACHINE OPERATORS
56.76	43.24	148	Therapists: Physical
56.73	43.27	765	HEALTH CARE THERAPISTS
56.72	43.28	67	Sales agents, retail trade
56.44	43.56	101	Insurance agents, brokers, and underwriters
56.36	43.64	55	Designers
56.35	43.65	126	Radiologic technologists and technicians
56.18	43.82	89	Public relations workers and publicity writers
56.00	44.00	175	ENGINEERING AND SCIENCE TECHNICIANS
56.00	44.00	100	Receptionists
55.71	44.29	70	Electricians
55.56	44.44	72	Dental assistants
55.42	44.58	83	Marketing personnel
55.34	44.66	206	SPECIALIZED: OPERATIVES
55.02	44.98	2,499	Clerical workers, miscellaneous
54.98	45.02	673	Counselors: Vocational and educational
54.86	45.14	1,750	SALES WORKERS
54.80	45.20	177	Resident housing assistants
54.72	45.28	106	Speech pathologists
54.55	45.45	55	Child care workers, except private household
54.43	45.57	79	Medical assistants
54.36	45.64	195	Therapists: Respiratory
54.26	45.74	669	MECHANICS
54.07	45.93	479	Social workers
54.00	46.00	200	Computer programmers
53.87	46.13	271	Lawyers
53.70	46.30	54	Engineers: Aeronautical
52.86	47.14	297	Computer and peripheral equipment operators
52.21	47.79	136	Musicians and composers
52.08	47.92	1,803	COUNSELORS
51.97	48.03	127	Mechanics and repairers, not specified
51.66	48.34	211	Lifeguards, attendants, recreation, and amusement
51.18	48.82	932	Counselors: General
51.17	48.83	213	Teachers: Art, drama, and music
51.11	48.89	180	Cooks, except private household
51.08	48.92	139	Construction laborers, except carpenters' helpers
50.85	49.15	59	Photographers
50.79	49.21	378	ARTISTS AND ENTERTAINERS
50.00	50.00	68	Physicians: Psychiatry
49.39	50.61	490	SOCIAL SCIENTISTS
48.01	51.99	402	PSYCHOLOGISTS
47.76	52.24	67	Stock clerks and storekeepers
47.41	52.59	1,082	FOOD SERVICE WORKERS
47.06	52.94	782	LABORERS

Ranking of occupations by preference for JP

Percent Judging	Percent Perception	N	Sample Description
47.03	52.97	472	Miscellaneous laborers
46.27	53.73	67	Research assistants
45.16	54.84	62	Actors
44.26	55.74	540	Waiters, waitresses
44.21	55.79	190	Engineers: Mining
44.07	55.93	177	Counselors: Rehabilitation
43.40	56.60	530	WRITERS AND JOURNALISTS
43.36	56.64	113	Editors and reporters
43.12	56.88	109	Carpenters
41.18	58.82	51	Restaurant workers: Table setting and cleaning
38.94	61.06	208	Writers, artists, entertainers, and agents, miscellaneous
38.89	61.11	54	Chain, rod, and ax workers; surveying
38.46	61.54	52	Journalists

Occupational choices of ST

Percent Sensing-Thinking	N	Sample Description
66.67	105	Steelworkers, miscellaneous
65.02	606	**High school graduates, males
57.42	155	Police and detectives
55.03	169	Service workers, except private household, miscellaneous
52.10	119	Teachers: Trade, industrial and technical
51.43	105	Police supervisors
51.39	72	FARMERS
50.53	756	Bank officers and financial managers
49.25	67	CLEANING SERVICES
48.52	608	PROTECTIVE SERVICE WORKERS
48.08	52	Factory and site supervisors, miscellaneous
48.05	77	Engineers: Mechanical
47.06	238	Public service aides and community health workers
46.15	143	Auditors
45.51	312	Managers: Restaurant, cafeteria, bar and food service
44.58	83	Managers: Sales, not specified
43.47	559	CRAFT WORKERS
42.62	61	Physicians: Pathology
42.47	73	Air force personnel
42.42	264	MILITARY PERSONNEL
42.19	128	Judges
39.40	3,678	Administrators: Managers and supervisors, miscellaneous
39.36	94	Nursing: Administrators
39.34	427	Accountants
38.89	144	TRANSPORTATION OPERATIVES

Occupational choices of ST

Percent Sensing-Thinking	N	Sample Description
38.55	179	Sales representatives, unspecified
38.37	86	Guards and watch keepers
38.35	4,446	**College graduates, males
37.80	127	Mechanics and repairers, not specified
37.65	85	Dentists
37.52	669	MECHANICS
37.38	7,463	MANAGERS AND ADMINISTRATORS
37.20	164	Teachers: Coaching
36.84	57	Technicians: Electrical and electronic engineering
36.67	90	Personnel and labor relations workers
36.63	101	Insurance agents, brokers, and underwriters
36.54	52	Engineers: Chemical
36.21	986	ENGINEERS
36.08	97	MISCELLANEOUS OPERATIVES AND FACTORY WORKERS
35.82	67	Stock clerks and storekeepers
35.71	112	Food service workers, miscellaneous; except private household
35.68	782	LABORERS
35.38	472	Miscellaneous laborers
35.29	136	Credit investigators and mortgage brokers
35.29	68	Corrections officers, probation officers
35.21	71	Teachers: Mathematics
35.19	54	Engineers: Electrical and electronic
34.88	86	Computer systems analysts, support representatives
34.86	370	Administrators: School level unspecified
34.53	139	Construction laborers, except carpenters' helpers
34.44	180	Cooks, except private household
34.40	250	Business: General, self-employed
34.34	166	Real estate agents and brokers
34.29	70	Electricians
33.96	268	Technicians: Miscellaneous
33.85	65	Operations and systems researchers and analysts
33.03	109	Carpenters
32.86	70	Optometrists
32.69	52	Computer specialists
32.52	206	SPECIALIZED: OPERATIVES
32.00	175	ENGINEERING AND SCIENCE TECHNICIANS
31.97	122	Administrators: Educationally related
30.81	211	Lifeguards, attendants, recreation and amusement
30.47	338	COMPUTER SPECIALISTS
30.21	96	Hairdressers and cosmetologists, manicurists
29.87	77	Secretaries: Legal
29.84	191	Pharmacists
29.82	228	Teachers: Adult education
29.74	195	Therapists: Respiratory
29.59	1,024	Administrators: Elementary and secondary school

Occupational choices of ST

Percent Sensing-Thinking	N	Sample Description
29.51	61	Scientists: Chemistry
29.27	82	Professional, technical, and kindred workers, miscellaneous
28.92	83	Marketing personnel
28.79	323	Dietitians, nutritionists
28.70	108	Sales clerks, retail trade
28.53	333	Secretaries: Executive and administrative assistants
28.48	783	PERSONAL SERVICE WORKERS
28.36	67	Sales agents, retail trade
28.25	223	Clinical laboratory technologists and technicians
28.09	89	Consultants: Management analysts
28.01	432	Teachers' aides, except school monitors
28.00	200	Computer programmers
27.94	519	LAWYERS AND JUDGES
27.88	226	SCIENTISTS: LIFE AND PHYSICAL
27.60	1,750	SALES WORKERS
27.33	172	Coordinators: Not specified
27.23	202	Administrators: Health
26.74	2,072	DOCTORS OF MEDICINE
26.72	1,291	HEALTH TECHNOLOGISTS AND TECHNICIANS
26.65	638	Medical technologists
26.50	1,147	Nuns and miscellaneous religious workers
26.19	126	Radiologic technologists and technicians
26.03	146	Nursing: Consultants
25.86	58	Home management advisors and home economists
25.73	649	Teachers: High school
25.23	107	Typists
25.12	840	CLERICAL AND KINDRED WORKERS
25.00	84	Library attendants and assistants
24.76	1,337	**High school graduates, females
24.62	260	Nurses: Licensed practical
24.53	106	Media specialists
24.51	102	Office managers
24.38	1,128	Teachers: Middle and junior high school
24.34	341	Administrators: Colleges and technical institutes
23.99	271	Lawyers
23.80	16,678	TEACHERS
23.75	80	Employment development specialists
23.66	1,082	FOOD SERVICE WORKERS
23.36	274	Cashiers
23.23	297	Computer and peripheral equipment operators
22.92	192	Consultants: Type unknown
22.81	57	Scientists: Biological
22.67	172	Teaching assistants
22.67	150	Bookkeepers
22.47	89	Public relations workers and publicity writers
22.22	72	Dental assistants
22.22	54	Chain, rod, and ax workers; surveying
22.17	2,282	Teachers: University

Occupational choices of ST

Percent Sensing-Thinking	N	Sample Description
22.11	900	HEALTH SERVICE WORKERS
21.77	804	Teachers: Elementary school
21.59	4,905	OFFICE MACHINE OPERATORS
21.52	79	Medical assistants
21.27	3,103	NURSES
21.18	765	HEALTH CARE THERAPISTS
21.03	561	Teachers: Junior college
20.92	4,736	**College graduates, females
20.85	1,880	Nursing: Registered nurses, no specialty stated
20.59	68	Secretaries: Medical
20.33	305	Nursing: Educators
20.25	1,126	Secretaries: Not specified
20.14	139	Physicians: Family practice, general practice
20.01	2,499	Clerical workers, miscellaneous
20.00	270	LIBRARIANS, ARCHIVISTS, AND CURATORS
20.00	245	Therapists: Occupational
20.00	55	Designers
19.59	148	Therapists: Physical
19.48	267	Librarians
19.43	314	Nurses: Aides, orderlies, and attendants
19.28	223	Teachers: Health
19.15	2,010	RELIGIOUS WORKERS, ALL DENOMINATIONS
19.12	68	Physicians: Psychiatry
18.57	673	Counselors: Vocational and educational
18.50	173	Teachers: Special education
18.42	190	Engineers: Mining
18.15	540	Waiters, waitresses
18.08	177	Counselors: Rehabilitation
18.03	61	Food counter and fountain workers
17.86	84	Attorneys: Administrators, nonpracticing
17.86	56	Clerical supervisors, miscellaneous
17.65	51	Restaurant workers: Table setting and cleaning
17.36	1,803	COUNSELORS
17.33	479	Social workers
17.20	157	Teachers: Speech pathology and therapy
16.97	3,064	PRIVATE HOUSEHOLD WORKERS
16.95	59	Photographers
16.87	83	Nursing: Public health
16.67	96	Teachers: Reading
16.67	60	Dental hygienists
16.67	54	Engineers: Aeronautical
16.52	932	Counselors: General
16.36	55	Child care workers, except private household
16.20	179	Teachers: English
16.04	106	Speech pathologists
15.25	177	Resident housing assistants
15.04	113	Editors and reporters
15.00	100	Receptionists
14.81	378	ARTISTS AND ENTERTAINERS
14.81	81	Research workers, not specified

Occupational choices of ST

Percent Sensing-Thinking	N	Sample Description
14.81	54	Consultants: Education
13.70	219	Priests, monks
13.46	52	Journalists
13.24	136	Musicians and composers
13.21	530	WRITERS AND JOURNALISTS
12.90	62	Actors
12.66	79	Religion: Educator, all denominations
11.74	213	Teachers: Art, drama, and music
9.00	100	Teachers: Preschool
8.98	490	SOCIAL SCIENTISTS
8.96	67	Research assistants
7.71	402	PSYCHOLOGISTS
7.21	208	Writers, artists, entertainers, and agents, miscellaneous
7.12	534	Clergy, all denominations

Occupational choices of SF

Percent Sensing-Feeling	N	Sample Description
50.00	56	Clerical supervisors, miscellaneous
49.29	1,337	**High school graduates, females
49.23	260	Nurses: Licensed practical
49.09	55	Child care workers, except private household
46.73	107	Typists
45.54	314	Nurses: Aides, orderlies, and attendants
45.33	150	Bookkeepers
45.00	100	Receptionists
44.44	72	Dental assistants
44.35	3,064	PRIVATE HOUSEHOLD WORKERS
44.21	432	Teachers' aides, except school monitors
44.12	68	Secretaries: Medical
44.00	100	Teachers: Preschool
43.31	157	Teachers: Speech pathology and therapy
42.78	900	HEALTH SERVICE WORKERS
41.03	1,126	Secretaries: Not specified
40.96	83	Nursing: Public health
40.80	804	Teachers: Elementary school
40.62	96	Hairdressers and cosmetologists, manicurists
40.51	274	Cashiers
40.48	84	Library attendants and assistants
40.36	840	CLERICAL AND KINDRED WORKERS
39.68	126	Radiologic technologists and technicians
39.58	96	Teachers: Reading
39.34	61	Food counter and fountain workers
38.82	2,499	Clerical workers, miscellaneous
38.41	4,905	OFFICE MACHINE OPERATORS

Occupational choices of SF

Percent Sensing-Feeling	N	Sample Description
37.50	112	Food service workers, miscellaneous; except private household
36.54	52	Factory and site supervisors, miscellaneous
36.06	1,880	Nursing: Registered nurses, no specialty stated
35.81	148	Therapists: Physical
35.79	190	Engineers: Mining
35.09	228	Teachers: Adult education
35.06	77	Secretaries: Legal
34.95	638	Medical technologists
34.77	3,103	NURSES
34.72	144	TRANSPORTATION OPERATIVES
34.45	238	Public service aides and community health workers
34.34	297	Computer and peripheral equipment operators
34.18	79	Religion: Educator, all denominations
34.18	79	Medical assistants
34.09	1,147	Nuns and miscellaneous religious workers
34.08	267	Librarians
33.70	270	LIBRARIANS, ARCHIVISTS, AND CURATORS
33.59	783	PERSONAL SERVICE WORKERS
33.54	164	Teachers: Coaching
33.33	60	Dental hygienists
33.33	51	Restaurant workers: Table setting and cleaning
33.09	139	Physicians: Family practice, general practice
32.99	97	MISCELLANEOUS OPERATIVES AND FACTORY WORKERS
32.84	1,291	HEALTH TECHNOLOGISTS AND TECHNICIANS
32.56	86	Guards and watch keepers
32.41	540	Waiters, waitresses
32.37	139	Construction laborers, except carpenters' helpers
32.23	211	Lifeguards, attendants, recreation and amusement
31.50	127	Mechanics and repairers, not specified
31.34	67	Sales agents, retail trade
31.07	206	SPECIALIZED: OPERATIVES
31.05	1,082	FOOD SERVICE WORKERS
31.03	58	Home management advisors and home economists
30.88	68	Corrections officers, probation officers
30.76	1,128	Teachers: Middle and junior high school
30.56	108	Sales clerks, retail trade
30.49	82	Professional, technical, and kindred workers, miscellaneous
30.39	102	Office managers
30.15	2,010	RELIGIOUS WORKERS, ALL DENOMINATIONS
29.10	323	Dietitians, nutritionists
28.69	1,750	SALES WORKERS

Occupational choices of SF

Percent Sensing-Feeling	N	Sample Description
28.44	109	Carpenters
28.36	67	Stock clerks and storekeepers
28.21	195	Therapists: Respiratory
28.17	71	Teachers: Mathematics
27.97	765	HEALTH CARE THERAPISTS
27.80	669	MECHANICS
27.74	155	Police and detectives
27.49	782	LABORERS
27.40	146	Nursing: Consultants
27.36	106	Speech pathologists
27.35	223	Clinical laboratory technologists and technicians
27.17	173	Teachers: Special education
27.14	70	Electricians
27.11	4,736	**College graduates, females
27.04	16,678	TEACHERS
27.03	333	Secretaries: Executive and administrative assistants
26.87	67	CLEANING SERVICES
26.69	472	Miscellaneous laborers
26.51	166	Real estate agents and brokers
26.48	608	PROTECTIVE SERVICE WORKERS
26.23	305	Nursing: Educators
26.12	559	CRAFT WORKERS
25.96	312	Managers: Restaurant, cafeteria, bar and food service
25.93	54	Engineers: Aeronautical
25.93	54	Chain, rod, and ax workers; surveying
25.71	70	Optometrists
25.58	172	Teaching assistants
25.53	94	Nursing: Administrators
25.47	106	Media specialists
25.31	245	Therapists: Occupational
25.00	72	FARMERS
24.66	219	Priests, monks
23.88	649	Teachers: High school
23.73	177	Counselors: Rehabilitation
23.60	534	Clergy, all denominations
23.56	191	Pharmacists
23.46	179	Sales representatives, unspecified
23.43	175	ENGINEERING AND SCIENCE TECHNICIANS
23.34	1,024	Administrators: Elementary and secondary school
23.27	202	Administrators: Health
23.08	52	Computer specialists
22.95	427	Accountants
22.76	268	Technicians: Miscellaneous
22.60	177	Resident housing assistants
22.35	85	Dentists
22.09	172	Coordinators: Not specified
21.97	264	MILITARY PERSONNEL
21.91	2,072	DOCTORS OF MEDICINE
21.82	55	Designers
21.67	180	Cooks, except private household
21.50	479	Social workers

Occupational choices of SF

Percent Sensing-Feeling	N	Sample Description
21.39	561	Teachers: Junior college
21.32	136	Musicians and composers
20.95	105	Police supervisors
20.79	101	Insurance agents, brokers, and underwriters
20.55	73	Air force personnel
20.18	223	Teachers: Health
20.06	673	Counselors: Vocational and educational
20.02	1,803	COUNSELORS
19.60	250	Business: General, self-employed
19.55	179	Teachers: English
19.31	932	Counselors: General
19.30	57	Technicians: Electrical and electronic engineering
19.05	105	Steelworkers, miscellaneous
18.93	7,463	MANAGERS AND ADMINISTRATORS
18.89	90	Personnel and labor relations workers
18.75	128	Judges
18.57	3,678	Administrators: Managers and supervisors, miscellaneous
17.99	606	**High school graduates, males
17.98	89	Public relations workers and publicity writers
17.37	213	Teachers: Art, drama, and music
17.31	52	Engineers: Chemical
17.28	81	Research workers, not specified
17.16	169	Service workers, except private household, miscellaneous
16.81	113	Editors and reporters
16.67	54	Engineers: Electrical and electronic
16.67	54	Consultants: Education
16.50	200	Computer programmers
16.43	986	ENGINEERS
16.39	122	Administrators: Educationally related
16.27	338	COMPUTER SPECIALISTS
16.25	80	Employment development specialists
16.14	378	ARTISTS AND ENTERTAINERS
15.38	52	Journalists
15.04	226	SCIENTISTS: LIFE AND PHYSICAL
14.59	370	Administrators: School level unspecified
14.55	756	Bank officers and financial managers
14.46	83	Managers: Sales, not specified
14.04	57	Scientists: Biological
13.89	2,282	Teachers: University
13.49	341	Administrators: Colleges and technical institutes
13.21	530	WRITERS AND JOURNALISTS
13.11	61	Scientists: Chemistry
12.61	119	Teachers: Trade, industrial and technical
12.31	65	Operations and systems researchers and analysts
11.98	192	Consultants: Type unknown
11.76	136	Credit investigators and mortgage brokers
11.63	86	Computer systems analysts, support representatives
11.52	4,446	**College graduates, males

Occupational choices of SF

Percent Sensing-Feeling	N	Sample Description
11.48	61	Physicians: Pathology
11.37	519	LAWYERS AND JUDGES
11.24	89	Consultants: Management analysts
10.84	83	Marketing personnel
10.49	143	Auditors
10.45	67	Research assistants
10.39	77	Engineers: Mechanical
10.17	59	Photographers
9.52	84	Attorneys: Administrators, nonpracticing
8.78	490	SOCIAL SCIENTISTS
7.21	402	PSYCHOLOGISTS
6.73	208	Writers, artists, entertainers, and agents, miscellaneous
6.64	271	Lawyers
6.45	62	Actors
5.88	68	Physicians: Psychiatry

Occupational choices of NF

Percent Intuition-Feeling	N	Sample Description
55.06	534	Clergy, all denominations
53.99	213	Teachers: Art, drama, and music
51.92	208	Writers, artists, entertainers, and agents, miscellaneous
50.23	219	Priests, monks
48.53	68	Physicians: Psychiatry
48.26	402	PSYCHOLOGISTS
47.42	932	Counselors: General
46.27	67	Research assistants
46.15	52	Journalists
45.81	1,803	COUNSELORS
45.51	490	SOCIAL SCIENTISTS
44.69	179	Teachers: English
44.44	54	Consultants: Education
43.98	673	Counselors: Vocational and educational
43.77	530	WRITERS AND JOURNALISTS
43.04	79	Religion: Educator, all denominations
42.94	177	Counselors: Rehabilitation
42.59	479	Social workers
41.94	62	Actors
41.91	136	Musicians and composers
41.24	177	Resident housing assistants
40.71	113	Editors and reporters
39.68	378	ARTISTS AND ENTERTAINERS
38.68	106	Speech pathologists
38.57	223	Teachers: Health
38.42	190	Engineers: Mining
38.33	60	Dental hygienists

Occupational choices of NF

Percent Intuition-Feeling	N	Sample Description
35.32	2,010	RELIGIOUS WORKERS, ALL DENOMINATIONS
35.00	100	Teachers: Preschool
34.57	81	Research workers, not specified
34.55	55	Designers
34.48	58	Home management advisors and home economists
34.40	561	Teachers: Junior college
34.38	192	Consultants: Type unknown
34.26	540	Waiters, waitresses
34.21	649	Teachers: High school
33.78	148	Therapists: Physical
33.72	172	Teaching assistants
33.71	89	Public relations workers and publicity writers
33.71	89	Consultants: Management analysts
33.33	54	Engineers: Aeronautical
33.00	100	Receptionists
32.96	267	Librarians
32.73	2,282	Teachers: University
32.59	270	LIBRARIANS, ARCHIVISTS, AND CURATORS
32.37	173	Teachers: Special education
32.24	245	Therapists: Occupational
32.13	305	Nursing: Educators
31.78	4,736	**College graduates, females
31.13	106	Media specialists
30.96	16,678	TEACHERS
30.59	765	HEALTH CARE THERAPISTS
30.39	102	Office managers
30.38	79	Medical assistants
30.22	139	Physicians: Family practice, general practice
30.00	80	Employment development specialists
29.93	3,064	PRIVATE HOUSEHOLD WORKERS
29.91	341	Administrators: Colleges and technical institutes
29.85	1,082	FOOD SERVICE WORKERS
29.73	2,499	Clerical workers, miscellaneous
29.70	1,128	Teachers: Middle and junior high school
29.41	51	Restaurant workers: Table setting and cleaning
29.20	274	Cashiers
29.13	1,126	Secretaries: Not specified
29.13	333	Secretaries: Executive and administrative assistants
29.04	1,880	Nursing: Registered nurses, no specialty stated
29.00	3,103	NURSES
28.92	83	Nursing: Public health
28.89	180	Cooks, except private household
28.77	146	Nursing: Consultants
28.69	122	Administrators: Educationally related
28.67	2,072	DOCTORS OF MEDICINE
28.62	297	Computer and peripheral equipment operators

Occupational choices of NF

Percent Intuition-Feeling	N	Sample Description
28.57	70	Optometrists
28.52	4,905	OFFICE MACHINE OPERATORS
28.49	172	Coordinators: Not specified
28.41	271	Lawyers
27.78	54	Chain, rod, and ax workers; surveying
27.71	83	Marketing personnel
27.39	157	Teachers: Speech pathology and therapy
27.35	223	Clinical laboratory technologists and technicians
27.12	59	Photographers
27.11	804	Teachers: Elementary school
27.08	96	Teachers: Reading
26.95	1,024	Administrators: Elementary and secondary school
26.75	314	Nurses: Aides, orderlies, and attendants
26.61	109	Carpenters
26.32	323	Dietitians, nutritionists
26.32	57	Scientists: Biological
25.74	101	Insurance agents, brokers, and underwriters
25.60	840	CLERICAL AND KINDRED WORKERS
25.25	202	Administrators: Health
25.13	191	Pharmacists
25.09	1,750	SALES WORKERS
25.00	84	Library attendants and assistants
24.71	1,291	HEALTH TECHNOLOGISTS AND TECHNICIANS
24.67	150	Bookkeepers
24.56	900	HEALTH SERVICE WORKERS
24.47	519	LAWYERS AND JUDGES
24.27	783	PERSONAL SERVICE WORKERS
24.25	268	Technicians: Miscellaneous
24.07	108	Sales clerks, retail trade
23.22	211	Lifeguards, attendants, recreation and amusement
22.95	61	Food counter and fountain workers
22.88	638	Medical technologists
22.58	1,147	Nuns and miscellaneous religious workers
22.16	370	Administrators: School level unspecified
22.12	782	LABORERS
22.06	68	Secretaries: Medical
22.00	250	Business: General, self-employed
21.93	228	Teachers: Adult education
21.92	73	Air force personnel
21.76	432	Teachers' aides, except school monitors
21.61	472	Miscellaneous laborers
21.43	84	Attorneys: Administrators, nonpracticing
21.43	56	Clerical supervisors, miscellaneous
20.93	86	Guards and watch keepers
20.83	264	MILITARY PERSONNEL
20.83	72	Dental assistants
20.63	126	Radiologic technologists and technicians
20.56	107	Typists
20.21	94	Nursing: Administrators
19.98	986	ENGINEERS
19.67	61	Physicians: Pathology

Occupational choices of NF

Percent Intuition-Feeling	N	Sample Description
19.58	669	MECHANICS
19.55	179	Sales representatives, unspecified
19.51	7,463	MANAGERS AND ADMINISTRATORS
19.48	77	Engineers: Mechanical
19.43	175	ENGINEERING AND SCIENCE TECHNICIANS
19.40	67	Stock clerks and storekeepers
19.40	67	CLEANING SERVICES
19.03	226	SCIENTISTS: LIFE AND PHYSICAL
19.00	200	Computer programmers
18.93	206	SPECIALIZED: OPERATIVES
18.85	260	Nurses: Licensed practical
18.75	96	Hairdressers and cosmetologists, manicurists
18.46	195	Therapists: Respiratory
18.18	55	Child care workers, except private household
18.11	127	Mechanics and repairers, not specified
17.93	4,446	**College graduates, males
17.88	1337	**High school graduates, females
17.80	427	Accountants
17.54	3,678	Administrators: Managers and supervisors, miscellaneous
17.27	139	Construction laborers, except carpenters' helpers
17.19	128	Judges
16.96	112	Food service workers, miscellaneous; except private household
16.88	77	Secretaries: Legal
16.81	119	Teachers: Trade, industrial, and technical
16.67	54	Engineers: Electrical and electronic
16.49	97	MISCELLANEOUS OPERATIVES AND FACTORY WORKERS
16.47	85	Dentists
16.46	559	CRAFT WORKERS
16.27	338	COMPUTER SPECIALISTS
16.27	166	Real estate agents and brokers
15.71	70	Electricians
15.56	90	Personnel and labor relations workers
15.28	144	TRANSPORTATION OPERATIVES
15.24	105	Police supervisors
14.75	61	Scientists: Chemistry
14.71	136	Credit investigators and mortgage brokers
14.63	164	Teachers: Coaching
14.63	82	Professional, technical, and kindred workers, miscellaneous
13.99	143	Auditors
13.46	52	Computer specialists
12.68	71	Teachers: Mathematics
12.28	57	Technicians: Electrical and electronic engineering
12.01	608	PROTECTIVE SERVICE WORKERS
11.76	68	Corrections officers, probation officers
11.63	86	Computer systems analysts, support representatives
11.54	52	Engineers: Chemical

Occupational choices of NF

Percent Intuition-Feeling	N	Sample Description
10.50	238	Public service aides and community health workers
10.45	756	Bank officers and financial managers
10.45	67	Sales agents, retail trade
10.26	312	Managers: Restaurant, cafeteria, bar, and food service
10.06	169	Service workers, except private household, miscellaneous
9.23	65	Operations and systems researchers and analysts
7.69	52	Factory and site supervisors, miscellaneous
6.67	105	Steelworkers, miscellaneous
6.02	83	Managers: Sales, not specified
4.79	606	**High school graduates, males
4.17	72	FARMERS
3.87	155	Police and detectives

Occupational choices of NT

Percent Intuition-Thinking	N	Sample Description
51.19	84	Attorneys: Administrators, nonpracticing
45.76	59	Photographers
44.62	65	Operations and systems researchers and analysts
42.62	61	Scientists: Chemistry
41.86	86	Computer systems analysts, support representatives
40.96	271	Lawyers
38.71	62	Actors
38.24	136	Credit investigators and mortgage brokers
38.05	226	SCIENTISTS: LIFE AND PHYSICAL
36.98	338	COMPUTER SPECIALISTS
36.84	57	Scientists: Biological
36.82	402	PSYCHOLOGISTS
36.73	490	SOCIAL SCIENTISTS
36.50	200	Computer programmers
36.22	519	LAWYERS AND JUDGES
34.94	83	Managers: Sales, not specified
34.62	52	Engineers: Chemical
34.33	67	Research assistants
34.13	208	Writers, artists, entertainers, and agents, miscellaneous
33.33	81	Research workers, not specified
32.53	83	Marketing personnel
32.26	341	Administrators: Colleges and technical institutes
32.21	4,446	**College graduates, males

Occupational choices of NT

Percent Intuition-Thinking	N	Sample Description
31.58	57	Technicians: Electrical and electronic engineering
31.48	54	Engineers: Electrical and electronic
31.20	2,282	Teachers: University
30.77	52	Computer specialists
30.73	192	Consultants: Type unknown
30.00	80	Employment development specialists
29.85	67	Sales agents, retail trade
29.81	530	WRITERS AND JOURNALISTS
29.37	378	ARTISTS AND ENTERTAINERS
29.37	143	Auditors
28.89	90	Personnel and labor relations workers
28.38	370	Administrators: School level unspecified
27.43	113	Editors and reporters
27.38	986	ENGINEERS
26.97	89	Consultants: Management analysts
26.47	68	Physicians: Psychiatry
26.23	61	Physicians: Pathology
25.84	89	Public relations workers and publicity writers
25.61	82	Professional, technical, and kindred workers, miscellaneous
25.14	175	ENGINEERING AND SCIENCE TECHNICIANS
25.00	52	Journalists
24.50	3,678	Administrators: Managers and supervisors, miscellaneous
24.47	756	Bank officers and financial managers
24.26	202	Administrators: Health
24.17	7,463	MANAGERS AND ADMINISTRATORS
24.07	54	Engineers: Aeronautical
24.07	54	Consultants: Education
24.07	54	Chain, rod, and ax workers; surveying
24.00	250	Business: General, self-employed
23.94	71	Teachers: Mathematics
23.64	55	Designers
23.59	195	Therapists: Respiratory
23.53	136	Musicians and composers
23.53	85	Dentists
23.17	561	Teachers: Junior college
22.95	122	Administrators: Educationally related
22.89	166	Real estate agents and brokers
22.86	70	Electricians
22.68	2,072	DOCTORS OF MEDICINE
22.45	245	Therapists: Occupational
22.09	172	Coordinators: Not specified
22.08	77	Engineers: Mechanical
22.06	68	Corrections officers, probation officers
21.97	223	Teachers: Health
21.97	173	Teachers: Special education
21.88	128	Judges
21.47	191	Pharmacists
21.31	305	Nursing: Educators
20.90	177	Resident housing assistants
20.26	765	HEALTH CARE THERAPISTS
20.19	4,736	**College graduates, females

Occupational choices of NT

Percent Intuition-Thinking	N	Sample Description
20.12	1,024	Administrators: Elementary and secondary school
19.91	427	Accountants
19.67	61	Food counter and fountain workers
19.61	51	Restaurant workers: Table setting and cleaning
19.55	179	Teachers: English
19.44	72	FARMERS
19.03	268	Technicians: Miscellaneous
18.87	106	Media specialists
18.63	1,750	SALES WORKERS
18.58	479	Social workers
18.49	119	Teachers: Trade, industrial, and technical
18.44	179	Sales representatives, unspecified
18.27	312	Managers: Restaurant, cafeteria, bar and food service
18.19	16,678	TEACHERS
18.18	77	Secretaries: Legal
18.02	172	Teaching assistants
17.92	106	Speech pathologists
17.81	146	Nursing: Consultants
17.75	169	Service workers, except private household, miscellaneous
17.48	206	SPECIALIZED: OPERATIVES
17.38	673	Counselors: Vocational and educational
17.04	223	Clinical laboratory technologists and technicians
16.90	213	Teachers: Art, drama, and music
16.83	1,147	Nuns and miscellaneous religious workers
16.83	101	Insurance agents, brokers, and underwriters
16.81	1,803	COUNSELORS
16.74	932	Counselors: General
16.67	108	Sales clerks, retail trade
16.67	96	Teachers: Reading
16.55	139	Physicians: Family practice, general practice
16.42	67	Stock clerks and storekeepers
16.36	55	Child care workers, except private household
16.31	472	Miscellaneous laborers
16.18	649	Teachers: High school
15.83	139	Construction laborers, except carpenters' helpers
15.79	323	Dietitians, nutritionists
15.72	1,291	HEALTH TECHNOLOGISTS AND TECHNICIANS
15.52	638	Medical technologists
15.43	1,082	FOOD SERVICE WORKERS
15.37	2,010	RELIGIOUS WORKERS, ALL DENOMINATIONS
15.32	333	Secretaries: Executive and administrative assistants
15.25	177	Counselors: Rehabilitation
15.19	540	Waiters, waitresses
15.16	1,128	Teachers: Middle and junior high school

Occupational choices of NT

Percent Intuition-Thinking	N	Sample Description
15.10	669	MECHANICS
15.07	73	Air force personnel
15.00	180	Cooks, except private household
14.95	3,103	NURSES
14.89	94	Nursing: Administrators
14.77	264	MILITARY PERSONNEL
14.71	782	LABORERS
14.71	102	Office managers
14.63	164	Teachers: Coaching
14.43	97	MISCELLANEOUS OPERATIVES AND FACTORY WORKERS
14.23	534	Clergy, all denominations
14.04	1,880	Nursing: Registered nurses, no specialty stated
13.95	559	CRAFT WORKERS
13.92	79	Medical assistants
13.80	297	Computer and peripheral equipment operators
13.74	211	Lifeguards, attendants, recreation and amusement
13.70	270	LIBRARIANS, ARCHIVISTS, AND CURATORS
13.67	783	PERSONAL SERVICE WORKERS
13.49	126	Radiologic technologists and technicians
13.48	267	Librarians
13.25	83	Nursing: Public health
13.24	68	Secretaries: Medical
13.16	228	Teachers: Adult education
12.99	608	PROTECTIVE SERVICE WORKERS
12.86	70	Optometrists
12.60	127	Mechanics and repairers, not specified
12.50	72	Dental assistants
12.38	105	Police supervisors
12.21	606	**High school graduates, males
12.10	157	Teachers: Speech pathology and therapy
12.00	100	Teachers: Preschool
11.93	109	Carpenters
11.67	60	Dental hygienists
11.48	4,905	OFFICE MACHINE OPERATORS
11.44	2,499	Clerical workers, miscellaneous
11.42	219	Priests, monks
11.11	144	TRANSPORTATION OPERATIVES
10.97	155	Police and detectives
10.81	148	Therapists: Physical
10.71	56	Clerical supervisors, miscellaneous
10.56	900	HEALTH SERVICE WORKERS
10.42	96	Hairdressers and cosmetologists, manicurists
10.32	804	Teachers: Elementary school
10.13	79	Religion: Educator, all denominations
9.82	112	Food service workers, miscellaneous; except private household
9.59	1,126	Secretaries: Not specified
9.52	84	Library attendants and assistants
8.93	840	CLERICAL AND KINDRED WORKERS
8.75	3,064	PRIVATE HOUSEHOLD WORKERS

Occupational choices of NT

Percent Intuition- Thinking	N	Sample Description
8.62	58	Home management advisors and home economists
8.28	314	Nurses: Aides, orderlies, and attendants
8.14	86	Guards and watch keepers
8.08	1,337	**High school graduates, females
7.98	238	Public service aides and community health workers
7.69	52	Factory and site supervisors, miscellaneous
7.62	105	Steelworkers, miscellaneous
7.48	107	Typists
7.37	190	Engineers: Mining
7.33	150	Bookkeepers
7.31	260	Nurses: Licensed practical
7.00	100	Receptionists
6.93	274	Cashiers
6.02	432	Teachers' aides, except school monitors
4.48	67	CLEANING SERVICES

Occupations attractive to ISTJ

Percent ISTJ	N	Sample Description
31.43	105	Steelworkers, miscellaneous
22.61	606	**High school graduates, males
22.35	85	Dentists
21.90	105	Police supervisors
21.29	155	Police and detectives
20.28	143	Auditors
20.14	427	Accountants
20.00	70	Electricians
19.48	77	Engineers: Mechanical
19.40	67	CLEANING SERVICES
19.30	57	Technicians: Electrical and electronic engineering
18.49	119	Teachers: Trade, industrial, and technical
18.31	71	Teachers: Mathematics
17.81	73	Air force personnel
17.76	608	PROTECTIVE SERVICE WORKERS
17.32	127	Mechanics and repairers, not specified
17.31	52	Factory and site supervisors, miscellaneous
17.12	4,446	**College graduates, males
17.03	370	Administrators: School level unspecified
17.02	94	Nursing: Administrators
16.93	756	Bank officers and financial managers
16.92	65	Operations and systems researchers and analysts
16.82	559	CRAFT WORKERS
16.67	54	Engineers: Electrical and electronic

Occupations attractive to ISTJ

Percent ISTJ	N	Sample Description
16.49	97	MISCELLANEOUS OPERATIVES AND FACTORY WORKERS
16.42	268	Technicians: Miscellaneous
16.39	238	Public service aides and community health workers
16.39	122	Administrators: Educationally related
16.39	61	Scientists: Chemistry
15.98	169	Service workers, except private household, miscellaneous
15.88	3,678	Administrators: Managers and supervisors, miscellaneous
15.56	90	Personnel and labor relations workers
15.52	986	ENGINEERS
15.38	52	Engineers: Chemical
15.28	72	FARMERS
15.24	164	Teachers: Coaching
15.18	112	Food service workers, miscellaneous; except private household
14.94	7,463	MANAGERS AND ADMINISTRATORS
14.86	175	ENGINEERING AND SCIENCE TECHNICIANS
14.84	128	Judges
14.75	61	Physicians: Pathology
14.56	206	SPECIALIZED: OPERATIVES
14.46	83	Managers: Sales, not specified
14.16	226	SCIENTISTS: LIFE AND PHYSICAL
14.02	264	MILITARY PERSONNEL
13.95	86	Computer systems analysts, support representatives
13.89	144	TRANSPORTATION OPERATIVES
13.85	195	Therapists: Respiratory
13.60	250	Business: General, self-employed
13.48	89	Consultants: Management analysts
13.46	312	Managers: Restaurant, cafeteria, bar and food service
13.46	52	Computer specialists
13.17	638	Medical technologists
13.03	2,072	DOCTORS OF MEDICINE
12.99	77	Secretaries: Legal
12.96	54	Consultants: Education
12.91	333	Secretaries: Executive and administrative assistants
12.87	202	Administrators: Health
12.86	70	Optometrists
12.84	2,282	Teachers: University
12.79	86	Guards and watch keepers
12.73	55	Designers
12.56	223	Clinical laboratory technologists and technicians
12.50	1,024	Administrators: Elementary and secondary school
12.50	96	Hairdressers and cosmetologists, manicurists
12.41	669	MECHANICS
12.33	519	LAWYERS AND JUDGES
12.28	57	Scientists: Biological

Occupations attractive to ISTJ		
Percent ISTJ	N	Sample Description
12.21	172	Teaching assistants
12.20	82	Professional, technical, and kindred workers, miscellaneous
12.13	338	COMPUTER SPECIALISTS
12.12	561	Teachers: Junior college
12.05	166	Real estate agents and brokers
11.94	67	Stock clerks and storekeepers
11.90	84	Library attendants and assistants
11.90	84	Attorneys: Administrators, nonpracticing
11.86	649	Teachers: High school
11.76	68	Corrections officers, probation officers
11.63	172	Coordinators: Not specified
11.62	1,291	HEALTH TECHNOLOGISTS AND TECHNICIANS
11.52	191	Pharmacists
11.48	61	Food counter and fountain workers
11.44	271	Lawyers
11.32	106	Media specialists
11.25	16,678	TEACHERS
11.17	1,128	Teachers: Middle and junior high school
11.11	270	LIBRARIANS, ARCHIVISTS, AND CURATORS
11.11	126	Radiologic technologists and technicians
11.00	200	Computer programmers
10.90	211	Lifeguards, attendants, recreation and amusement
10.88	432	Teachers' aides, except school monitors
10.86	267	Librarians
10.84	83	Nursing: Public health
10.81	472	Miscellaneous laborers
10.70	804	Teachers: Elementary school
10.53	323	Dietitians, nutritionists
10.34	58	Home management advisors and home economists
10.29	68	Secretaries: Medical
10.27	146	Nursing: Consultants
10.26	341	Administrators: Colleges and technical institutes
10.24	4,736	**College graduates, females
10.24	840	CLERICAL AND KINDRED WORKERS
10.19	108	Sales clerks, retail trade
10.14	148	Therapists: Physical
10.09	228	Teachers: Adult education
10.00	180	Cooks, except private household
10.00	150	Bookkeepers
9.85	274	Cashiers
9.65	1,337	**High school graduates, females
9.64	3,103	NURSES
9.59	782	LABORERS
9.57	1,880	Nursing: Registered nurses, no specialty stated
9.56	136	Credit investigators and mortgage brokers
9.51	305	Nursing: Educators
9.45	783	PERSONAL SERVICE WORKERS
9.38	192	Consultants: Type unknown
9.33	1,147	Nuns and miscellaneous religious workers
9.26	54	Engineers: Aeronautical

Occupations attractive to ISTJ		
Percent ISTJ	N	Sample Description
9.23	260	Nurses: Licensed practical
9.17	109	Carpenters
9.15	765	HEALTH CARE THERAPISTS
9.13	219	Priests, monks
8.75	297	Computer and peripheral equipment operators
8.75	80	Employment development specialists
8.67	173	Teachers: Special education
8.63	139	Construction laborers, except carpenters' helpers
8.57	245	Therapists: Occupational
8.56	479	Social workers
8.54	4,905	OFFICE MACHINE OPERATORS
8.52	223	Teachers: Health
8.38	179	Teachers: English
8.17	1,126	Secretaries: Not specified
8.13	1,082	FOOD SERVICE WORKERS
8.11	900	HEALTH SERVICE WORKERS
7.84	102	Office managers
7.60	2,499	Clerical workers, miscellaneous
7.59	79	Medical assistants
7.48	107	Typists
7.46	67	Research assistants
7.43	673	Counselors: Vocational and educational
7.41	54	Chain, rod, and ax workers; surveying
7.37	1,750	SALES WORKERS
7.35	68	Physicians: Psychiatry
7.32	314	Nurses: Aides, orderlies, and attendants
7.29	96	Teachers: Reading
7.27	55	Child care workers, except private household
7.26	179	Sales representatives, unspecified
7.21	2,010	RELIGIOUS WORKERS, ALL DENOMINATIONS
7.08	113	Editors and reporters
6.94	72	Dental assistants
6.93	101	Insurance agents, brokers, and underwriters
6.71	1,803	COUNSELORS
6.67	540	Waiters, waitresses
6.44	932	Counselors: General
6.43	3,064	PRIVATE HOUSEHOLD WORKERS
6.37	157	Teachers: Speech pathology and therapy
6.02	83	Marketing personnel
6.00	100	Receptionists
5.82	378	ARTISTS AND ENTERTAINERS
5.63	213	Teachers: Art, drama, and music
5.26	190	Engineers: Mining
5.08	177	Counselors: Rehabilitation
5.08	59	Photographers
5.04	139	Physicians: Family practice, general practice
4.94	81	Research workers, not specified
4.84	62	Actors
4.72	106	Speech pathologists
4.48	67	Sales agents, retail trade
4.34	530	WRITERS AND JOURNALISTS

Occupations attractive to ISTJ

Percent ISTJ	N	Sample Description
4.08	490	SOCIAL SCIENTISTS
3.92	51	Restaurant workers: Table setting and cleaning
3.85	52	Journalists
3.80	79	Religion: Educator, all denominations
3.57	56	Clerical supervisors, miscellaneous
3.37	89	Public relations workers and publicity writers
3.00	100	Teachers: Preschool
2.99	402	PSYCHOLOGISTS
2.94	136	Musicians and composers
2.82	177	Resident housing assistants
2.81	534	Clergy, all denominations
2.40	208	Writers, artists, entertainers, and agents, miscellaneous
0	60	Dental hygienists

Occupations attractive to ISTP

Percent ISTP	N	Sample Description
9.72	72	FARMERS
9.59	73	Air force personnel
9.45	127	Mechanics and repairers, not specified
9.26	54	Engineers: Electrical and electronic
8.77	57	Technicians: Electrical and electronic engineering
8.57	105	Steelworkers, miscellaneous
8.33	144	TRANSPORTATION OPERATIVES
8.33	60	Dental hygienists
8.28	169	Service workers, except private household, miscellaneous
7.93	782	LABORERS
7.92	669	MECHANICS
7.79	77	Secretaries: Legal
7.58	264	MILITARY PERSONNEL
7.46	67	CLEANING SERVICES
7.41	54	Chain, rod, and ax workers; surveying
7.35	68	Corrections officers, probation officers
7.34	109	Carpenters
7.20	472	Miscellaneous laborers
7.19	139	Construction laborers, except carpenters' helpers
6.67	180	Cooks, except private household
6.56	61	Physicians: Pathology
6.49	77	Engineers: Mechanical
6.44	559	CRAFT WORKERS
6.27	606	**High school graduates, males
6.00	200	Computer programmers
5.92	608	PROTECTIVE SERVICE WORKERS
5.90	271	Lawyers

Occupations attractive to ISTP

Percent ISTP	N	Sample Description
5.81	155	Police and detectives
5.71	175	ENGINEERING AND SCIENCE TECHNICIANS
5.71	70	Optometrists
5.66	106	Media specialists
5.56	72	Dental assistants
5.34	206	SPECIALIZED: OPERATIVES
4.97	986	ENGINEERS
4.82	519	LAWYERS AND JUDGES
4.76	105	Police supervisors
4.73	338	COMPUTER SPECIALISTS
4.68	427	Accountants
4.67	107	Typists
4.65	86	Guards and watch keepers
4.62	195	Therapists: Respiratory
4.62	65	Operations and systems researchers and analysts
4.48	67	Stock clerks and storekeepers
4.48	67	Sales agents, retail trade
4.39	228	Teachers: Adult education
4.27	164	Teachers: Coaching
4.21	190	Engineers: Mining
4.19	191	Pharmacists
4.17	96	Hairdressers and cosmetologists, manicurists
4.12	97	MISCELLANEOUS OPERATIVES AND FACTORY WORKERS
4.04	297	Computer and peripheral equipment operators
3.96	101	Insurance agents, brokers, and underwriters
3.91	179	Sales representatives, unspecified
3.91	128	Judges
3.85	52	Engineers: Chemical
3.84	756	Bank officers and financial managers
3.75	80	Employment development specialists
3.61	83	Managers: Sales, not specified
3.57	112	Food service workers, miscellaneous; except private household
3.57	84	Attorneys: Administrators, nonpracticing
3.54	226	SCIENTISTS: LIFE AND PHYSICAL
3.50	314	Nurses: Aides, orderlies, and attendants
3.50	143	Auditors
3.49	86	Computer systems analysts, support representatives
3.46	260	Nurses: Licensed practical
3.45	58	Home management advisors and home economists
3.39	177	Counselors: Rehabilitation
3.39	59	Photographers
3.38	148	Therapists: Physical
3.37	89	Consultants: Management analysts
3.36	268	Technicians: Miscellaneous
3.33	150	Bookkeepers
3.33	90	Personnel and labor relations workers
3.28	122	Administrators: Educationally related
3.28	61	Scientists: Chemistry

Percent ISTP	N	Sample Description
3.26	1,750	SALES WORKERS
3.24	4,446	**College graduates, males
3.23	1,082	FOOD SERVICE WORKERS
3.20	250	Business: General, self-employed
3.11	1,126	Secretaries: Not specified
3.11	900	HEALTH SERVICE WORKERS
3.10	323	Dietitians, nutritionists
3.07	1,337	**High school graduates, females
3.05	3,678	Administrators: Managers and supervisors, miscellaneous
2.94	136	Credit investigators and mortgage brokers
2.94	102	Office managers
2.91	172	Teaching assistants
2.86	840	CLERICAL AND KINDRED WORKERS
2.84	211	Lifeguards, attendants, recreation and amusement
2.82	71	Teachers: Mathematics
2.77	4,905	OFFICE MACHINE OPERATORS
2.74	146	Nursing: Consultants
2.69	7,463	MANAGERS AND ADMINISTRATORS
2.69	223	Teachers: Health
2.65	2,072	DOCTORS OF MEDICINE
2.61	765	HEALTH CARE THERAPISTS
2.55	432	Teachers' aides, except school monitors
2.52	119	Teachers: Trade, industrial and technical
2.45	1,880	Nursing: Registered nurses, no specialty stated
2.42	3,103	NURSES
2.41	540	Waiters, waitresses
2.41	166	Real estate agents and brokers
2.41	83	Marketing personnel
2.38	84	Library attendants and assistants
2.36	2,499	Clerical workers, miscellaneous
2.30	1,128	Teachers: Middle and junior high school
2.30	783	PERSONAL SERVICE WORKERS
2.30	305	Nursing: Educators
2.25	267	Librarians
2.23	179	Teachers: English
2.22	270	LIBRARIANS, ARCHIVISTS, AND CURATORS
2.21	136	Musicians and composers
2.19	274	Cashiers
2.13	94	Nursing: Administrators
2.09	1,291	HEALTH TECHNOLOGISTS AND TECHNICIANS
2.04	932	Counselors: General
2.04	638	Medical technologists
2.01	16,678	TEACHERS
1.98	202	Administrators: Health
1.96	51	Restaurant workers: Table setting and cleaning
1.94	1,803	COUNSELORS
1.92	1,147	Nuns and miscellaneous religious workers
1.92	208	Writers, artists, entertainers, and agents, miscellaneous
1.92	52	Factory and site supervisors, miscellaneous

Percent ISTP	N	Sample Description
1.92	52	Computer specialists
1.91	157	Teachers: Speech pathology and therapy
1.89	370	Administrators: School level unspecified
1.89	106	Speech pathologists
1.88	213	Teachers: Art, drama, and music
1.85	378	ARTISTS AND ENTERTAINERS
1.85	108	Sales clerks, retail trade
1.82	55	Designers
1.82	55	Child care workers, except private household
1.80	3,064	PRIVATE HOUSEHOLD WORKERS
1.80	333	Secretaries: Executive and administrative assistants
1.79	223	Clinical laboratory technologists and technicians
1.77	113	Editors and reporters
1.76	341	Administrators: Colleges and technical institutes
1.74	804	Teachers: Elementary school
1.74	172	Coordinators: Not specified
1.69	177	Resident housing assistants
1.67	2,282	Teachers: University
1.64	61	Food counter and fountain workers
1.60	312	Managers: Restaurant, cafeteria, bar, and food service
1.59	126	Radiologic technologists and technicians
1.56	192	Consultants: Type unknown
1.54	649	Teachers: High school
1.49	673	Counselors: Vocational and educational
1.49	402	PSYCHOLOGISTS
1.47	68	Secretaries: Medical
1.47	68	Physicians: Psychiatry
1.46	1,024	Administrators: Elementary and secondary school
1.43	490	SOCIAL SCIENTISTS
1.43	70	Electricians
1.39	4,736	**College graduates, females
1.39	2,010	RELIGIOUS WORKERS, ALL DENOMINATIONS
1.32	530	WRITERS AND JOURNALISTS
1.27	79	Religion: Educator, all denominations
1.27	79	Medical assistants
1.26	238	Public service aides and community health workers
1.23	81	Research workers, not specified
1.22	82	Professional, technical, and kindred workers, miscellaneous
1.12	89	Public relations workers and publicity writers
1.04	479	Social workers
1.04	96	Teachers: Reading
.75	534	Clergy, all denominations
.72	139	Physicians: Family practice, general practice
.71	561	Teachers: Junior college
.58	173	Teachers: Special education
.46	219	Priests, monks

Occupations attractive to ISTP

Occupations attractive to ISTP

Percent ISTP	N	Sample Description
.41	245	Therapists: Occupational
0	100	Teachers: Preschool
0	100	Receptionists
0	85	Dentists
0	83	Nursing: Public health
0	67	Research assistants
0	62	Actors
0	57	Scientists: Biological
0	56	Clerical supervisors, miscellaneous
0	54	Engineers: Aeronautical
0	54	Consultants: Education
0	52	Journalists

Occupations attractive to ESTP

Percent ESTP	N	Sample Description
9.64	83	Marketing personnel
8.39	155	Police and detectives
8.28	169	Service workers, except private household, miscellaneous
8.26	109	Carpenters
7.41	108	Sales clerks, retail trade
6.99	143	Auditors
6.98	559	CRAFT WORKERS
6.94	72	FARMERS
6.78	782	LABORERS
6.57	472	Miscellaneous laborers
6.47	139	Construction laborers, except carpenters' helpers
6.30	238	Public service aides and community health workers
6.25	144	TRANSPORTATION OPERATIVES
6.19	97	MISCELLANEOUS OPERATIVES AND FACTORY WORKERS
5.97	67	Stock clerks and storekeepers
5.88	51	Restaurant workers: Table setting and cleaning
5.81	86	Guards and watch keepers
5.77	52	Computer specialists
5.71	105	Steelworkers, miscellaneous
5.71	105	Police supervisors
5.59	608	PROTECTIVE SERVICE WORKERS
5.45	606	**High school graduates, males
5.36	112	Food service workers, miscellaneous; except private household
5.31	113	Editors and reporters
5.03	179	Sales representatives, unspecified
4.80	250	Business: General, self-employed
4.74	211	Lifeguards, attendants, recreation and amusement

Occupations attractive to ESTP

Percent ESTP	N	Sample Description
4.48	67	Sales agents, retail trade
4.47	783	PERSONAL SERVICE WORKERS
4.44	90	Personnel and labor relations workers
4.41	136	Credit investigators and mortgage brokers
4.41	68	Corrections officers, probation officers
4.29	1,750	SALES WORKERS
4.29	70	Optometrists
4.29	70	Electricians
4.23	756	Bank officers and financial managers
4.19	191	Pharmacists
4.10	195	Therapists: Respiratory
4.04	669	MECHANICS
4.00	200	Computer programmers
3.97	126	Radiologic technologists and technicians
3.96	101	Insurance agents, brokers, and underwriters
3.95	228	Teachers: Adult education
3.90	77	Engineers: Mechanical
3.85	52	Journalists
3.85	52	Factory and site supervisors, miscellaneous
3.75	986	ENGINEERS
3.70	1,082	FOOD SERVICE WORKERS
3.68	190	Engineers: Mining
3.65	192	Consultants: Type unknown
3.64	55	Child care workers, except private household
3.61	166	Real estate agents and brokers
3.60	139	Physicians: Family practice, general practice
3.57	84	Library attendants and assistants
3.55	338	COMPUTER SPECIALISTS
3.53	85	Dentists
3.37	89	Public relations workers and publicity writers
3.36	119	Teachers: Trade, industrial, and technical
3.33	180	Cooks, except private household
3.28	61	Physicians: Pathology
3.27	245	Therapists: Occupational
3.23	62	Actors
3.03	264	MILITARY PERSONNEL
2.94	3,678	Administrators: Managers and supervisors, miscellaneous
2.88	765	HEALTH CARE THERAPISTS
2.88	312	Managers: Restaurant, cafeteria, bar, and food service
2.86	840	CLERICAL AND KINDRED WORKERS
2.86	175	ENGINEERING AND SCIENCE TECHNICIANS
2.82	177	Resident housing assistants
2.79	1,147	Nuns and miscellaneous religious workers
2.79	323	Dietitians, nutritionists
2.78	72	Dental assistants
2.74	73	Air force personnel
2.71	7,463	MANAGERS AND ADMINISTRATORS
2.70	148	Therapists: Physical

Occupations attractive to ESTP		

Percent ESTP	N	Sample Description
2.69	223	Clinical laboratory technologists and technicians
2.68	2,499	Clerical workers, miscellaneous
2.64	530	WRITERS AND JOURNALISTS
2.63	4,446	**College graduates, males
2.62	1,337	**High school graduates, females
2.60	77	Secretaries: Legal
2.55	274	Cashiers
2.51	4,905	OFFICE MACHINE OPERATORS
2.48	1,291	HEALTH TECHNOLOGISTS AND TECHNICIANS
2.44	1,024	Administrators: Elementary and secondary school
2.44	164	Teachers: Coaching
2.44	82	Professional, technical, and kindred workers, miscellaneous
2.41	540	Waiters, waitresses
2.41	83	Managers: Sales, not specified
2.40	1,126	Secretaries: Not specified
2.40	333	Secretaries: Executive and administrative assistants
2.35	341	Administrators: Colleges and technical institutes
2.34	128	Judges
2.31	432	Teachers' aides, except school monitors
2.21	136	Musicians and composers
2.17	2,072	DOCTORS OF MEDICINE
2.11	427	Accountants
2.08	96	Hairdressers and cosmetologists, manicurists
2.04	638	Medical technologists (4 year)
1.97	1,880	Nursing: Registered nurses, no specialty stated
1.94	206	SPECIALIZED: OPERATIVES
1.93	932	Counselors: General
1.92	260	Nurses: Licensed practical
1.89	106	Speech pathologists
1.87	268	Technicians: Miscellaneous
1.85	54	Engineers: Aeronautical
1.82	55	Designers
1.80	3,103	NURSES
1.79	2,010	RELIGIOUS WORKERS, ALL DENOMINATIONS
1.79	56	Clerical supervisors, miscellaneous
1.77	1,128	Teachers: Middle and junior high school
1.75	57	Scientists: Biological
1.74	172	Coordinators: Not specified
1.72	58	Home management advisors and home economists
1.70	3,064	PRIVATE HOUSEHOLD WORKERS
1.69	177	Counselors: Rehabilitation
1.67	900	HEALTH SERVICE WORKERS
1.64	122	Administrators: Educationally related
1.59	378	ARTISTS AND ENTERTAINERS
1.55	1,803	COUNSELORS
1.54	65	Operations and systems researchers and analysts

Occupations attractive to ESTP		

Percent ESTP	N	Sample Description
1.53	16,678	TEACHERS
1.49	202	Administrators: Health
1.47	68	Secretaries: Medical
1.47	68	Physicians: Psychiatry
1.46	479	Social workers
1.43	561	Teachers: Junior college
1.41	71	Teachers: Mathematics
1.35	370	Administrators: School level unspecified
1.33	226	SCIENTISTS: LIFE AND PHYSICAL
1.33	150	Bookkeepers
1.31	305	Nursing: Educators
1.27	314	Nurses: Aides, orderlies, and attendants
1.27	79	Religion: Educator, all denominations
1.23	81	Research workers: Not specified
1.19	84	Attorneys: Administrators, nonpracticing
1.18	2,282	Teachers: University
1.16	173	Teachers: Special education
1.16	86	Computer systems analysts, support representatives
1.08	649	Teachers: High school
1.06	94	Nursing: Administrators
1.04	673	Counselors: Vocational and educational
1.04	96	Teachers: Reading
1.01	297	Computer and peripheral equipment operators
1.00	100	Receptionists
.96	519	LAWYERS AND JUDGES
.94	213	Teachers: Art, drama, and music
.93	107	Typists
.90	223	Teachers: Health
.87	804	Teachers: Elementary school
.84	4,736	**College graduates, females
.79	127	Mechanics and repairers, not specified
.75	267	Librarians
.74	270	LIBRARIANS, ARCHIVISTS, AND CURATORS
.68	146	Nursing: Consultants
.64	157	Teachers: Speech pathology and therapy
.61	490	SOCIAL SCIENTISTS
.58	172	Teaching assistants
.50	402	PSYCHOLOGISTS
.46	219	Priests, monks
.37	271	Lawyers
.19	534	Clergy, all denominations
0	208	Writers, artists, entertainers, and agents, miscellaneous
0	179	Teachers: English
0	106	Media specialists
0	102	Office managers
0	100	Teachers: Preschool
0	89	Consultants: Management analysts
0	83	Nursing: Public health
0	80	Employment development specialists
0	79	Medical assistants
0	67	Research assistants
0	67	CLEANING SERVICES
0	61	Scientists: Chemistry

Occupations attractive to ESTP

Percent ESTP	N	Sample Description
0	61	Food counter and fountain workers
0	60	Dental hygienists
0	59	Photographers
0	57	Technicians: Electrical and electronic engineering
0	54	Engineers: Electrical and electronic
0	54	Consultants: Education
0	54	Chain, rod, and ax workers; surveying
0	52	Engineers: Chemical

Occupations attractive to ESTJ

Percent ESTJ	N	Sample Description
30.69	606	**High school graduates, males
27.73	119	Teachers: Trade, industrial, and technical
27.56	312	Managers: Restaurant, cafeteria, bar, and food service
25.53	756	Bank officers and financial managers
25.00	52	Factory and site supervisors, miscellaneous
24.10	83	Managers: Sales, not specified
23.11	238	Public service aides and community health workers
22.49	169	Service workers, except private household, miscellaneous
22.39	67	CLEANING SERVICES
22.35	179	Sales representatives, unspecified
21.94	155	Police and detectives
21.78	101	Insurance agents, brokers, and underwriters
21.09	128	Judges
20.95	105	Steelworkers, miscellaneous
19.44	72	FARMERS
19.24	608	PROTECTIVE SERVICE WORKERS
19.15	94	Nursing: Administrators
19.05	105	Police supervisors
18.38	136	Credit investigators and mortgage brokers
18.18	77	Engineers: Mechanical
18.03	61	Physicians: Pathology
17.80	264	MILITARY PERSONNEL
17.54	3,678	Administrators: Managers and supervisors, miscellaneous
17.31	52	Engineers: Chemical
17.04	7,463	MANAGERS AND ADMINISTRATORS
16.28	86	Computer systems analysts, support representatives
16.27	166	Real estate agents and brokers
15.38	143	Auditors
15.36	4,446	**College graduates, males
15.24	164	Teachers: Coaching
15.12	86	Guards and watch keepers

Occupations attractive to ESTJ

Percent ESTJ	N	Sample Description
14.93	67	Sales agents, retail trade
14.61	89	Public relations workers and publicity writers
14.59	370	Administrators: School level unspecified
14.44	180	Cooks, except private household
13.73	102	Office managers
13.43	67	Stock clerks and storekeepers
13.41	82	Professional, technical, and kindred workers, miscellaneous
13.33	90	Personnel and labor relations workers
13.24	559	CRAFT WORKERS
13.18	1,024	Administrators: Elementary and secondary school
13.15	669	MECHANICS
12.80	250	Business: General, self-employed
12.69	1,750	SALES WORKERS
12.68	71	Teachers: Mathematics
12.66	79	Medical assistants
12.50	56	Clerical supervisors, miscellaneous
12.47	1,147	Nuns and miscellaneous religious workers
12.41	427	Accountants
12.38	323	Dietitians, nutritionists
12.33	146	Nursing: Consultants
12.33	73	Air force personnel
12.32	211	Lifeguards, attendants, recreation and amusement
12.31	268	Technicians: Miscellaneous
12.27	432	Teachers' aides, except school monitors
12.26	783	PERSONAL SERVICE WORKERS
12.23	139	Construction laborers, except carpenters' helpers
12.21	172	Coordinators: Not specified
12.15	107	Typists
11.97	986	ENGINEERS
11.76	85	Dentists
11.76	68	Corrections officers, probation officers
11.61	112	Food service workers, miscellaneous; except private household
11.54	52	Computer specialists
11.46	96	Hairdressers and cosmetologists, manicurists
11.41	333	Secretaries: Executive and administrative assistants
11.40	228	Teachers: Adult education
11.38	782	LABORERS
11.25	649	Teachers: High school
11.25	80	Employment development specialists
11.24	89	Consultants: Management analysts
11.21	223	Clinical laboratory technologists and technicians
10.89	202	Administrators: Health
10.84	83	Marketing personnel
10.81	472	Miscellaneous laborers
10.79	139	Physicians: Family practice, general practice
10.77	65	Operations and systems researchers and analysts

Occupations attractive to ESTJ		
Percent ESTJ	**N**	**Sample Description**
10.68	206	SPECIALIZED: OPERATIVES
10.66	122	Administrators: Educationally related
10.53	1,291	HEALTH TECHNOLOGISTS AND TECHNICIANS
10.42	144	TRANSPORTATION OPERATIVES
10.34	58	Home management advisors and home economists
10.24	127	Mechanics and repairers, not specified
10.06	338	COMPUTER SPECIALISTS
10.00	260	Nurses: Licensed practical
10.00	70	Optometrists
9.97	341	Administrators: Colleges and technical institutes
9.95	191	Pharmacists
9.84	61	Scientists: Chemistry
9.83	519	LAWYERS AND JUDGES
9.52	126	Radiologic technologists and technicians
9.43	297	Computer and peripheral equipment operators
9.42	1,337	**High school graduates, females
9.40	638	Medical technologists
9.28	97	MISCELLANEOUS OPERATIVES AND FACTORY WORKERS
9.26	108	Sales clerks, retail trade
9.26	54	Engineers: Electrical and electronic
9.22	900	HEALTH SERVICE WORKERS
9.17	840	CLERICAL AND KINDRED WORKERS
9.13	1,128	Teachers: Middle and junior high school
9.01	16,678	TEACHERS
8.88	2,072	DOCTORS OF MEDICINE
8.85	226	SCIENTISTS: LIFE AND PHYSICAL
8.82	68	Physicians: Psychiatry
8.77	57	Technicians: Electrical and electronic engineering
8.77	57	Scientists: Biological
8.76	2,010	RELIGIOUS WORKERS, ALL DENOMINATIONS
8.76	274	Cashiers
8.62	673	Counselors: Vocational and educational
8.60	1,082	FOOD SERVICE WORKERS
8.57	175	ENGINEERING AND SCIENCE TECHNICIANS
8.57	70	Electricians
8.47	59	Photographers
8.46	804	Teachers: Elementary school
8.45	4,736	**College graduates, females
8.33	192	Consultants: Type unknown
8.33	60	Dental hygienists
8.28	157	Teachers: Speech pathology and therapy
8.26	109	Carpenters
8.09	173	Teachers: Special education
8.00	150	Bookkeepers
8.00	100	Receptionists
7.91	177	Resident housing assistants
7.91	177	Counselors: Rehabilitation
7.77	4,905	OFFICE MACHINE OPERATORS
7.76	245	Therapists: Occupational

Occupations attractive to ESTJ

Percent ESTJ	**N**	**Sample Description**
7.55	106	Speech pathologists
7.55	106	Media specialists
7.41	3,103	NURSES
7.41	81	Research workers, not specified
7.41	54	Chain, rod, and ax workers; surveying
7.36	2,499	Clerical workers, miscellaneous
7.35	68	Secretaries: Medical
7.32	314	Nurses: Aides, orderlies, and attendants
7.29	96	Teachers: Reading
7.21	305	Nursing: Educators
7.18	195	Therapists: Respiratory
7.17	223	Teachers: Health
7.15	1,803	COUNSELORS
7.14	84	Library attendants and assistants
7.05	3,064	PRIVATE HOUSEHOLD WORKERS
7.00	200	Computer programmers
6.98	172	Teaching assistants
6.94	72	Dental assistants
6.86	1,880	Nursing: Registered nurses, no specialty stated
6.77	561	Teachers: Junior college
6.67	540	Waiters, waitresses
6.57	1,126	Secretaries: Not specified
6.54	765	HEALTH CARE THERAPISTS
6.49	2,282	Teachers: University
6.49	77	Secretaries: Legal
6.33	79	Religion: Educator, all denominations
6.27	271	Lawyers
6.26	479	Social workers
6.12	932	Counselors: General
6.02	83	Nursing: Public health
6.00	100	Teachers: Preschool
5.93	270	LIBRARIANS, ARCHIVISTS, AND CURATORS
5.88	136	Musicians and composers
5.88	51	Restaurant workers: Table setting and cleaning
5.77	52	Journalists
5.62	267	Librarians
5.59	179	Teachers: English
5.56	378	ARTISTS AND ENTERTAINERS
5.56	54	Engineers: Aeronautical
5.26	190	Engineers: Mining
4.92	61	Food counter and fountain workers
4.91	530	WRITERS AND JOURNALISTS
4.84	62	Actors
3.65	219	Priests, monks
3.64	55	Designers
3.64	55	Child care workers, except private household
3.38	148	Therapists: Physical
3.37	534	Clergy, all denominations
3.29	213	Teachers: Art, drama, and music
2.88	208	Writers, artists, entertainers, and agents, miscellaneous
2.86	490	SOCIAL SCIENTISTS
2.74	402	PSYCHOLOGISTS

Occupations attractive to ESTJ

Percent ESTJ	N	Sample Description
1.85	54	Consultants: Education
1.49	67	Research assistants
1.19	84	Attorneys: Administrators, nonpracticing
.88	113	Editors and reporters

Occupations attractive to ISFJ

Percent ISFJ	N	Sample Description
22.31	260	Nurses: Licensed practical
21.43	56	Clerical supervisors, miscellaneous
20.00	100	Teachers: Preschool
19.75	157	Teachers: Speech pathology and therapy
19.44	432	Teachers' aides, except school monitors
19.43	314	Nurses: Aides, orderlies, and attendants
19.15	1,337	**High school graduates, females
19.10	267	Librarians
18.89	270	LIBRARIANS, ARCHIVISTS, AND CURATORS
18.24	3,064	PRIVATE HOUSEHOLD WORKERS
18.07	83	Nursing: Public health
17.91	804	Teachers: Elementary school
17.44	86	Guards and watch keepers
17.27	139	Physicians: Family practice, general practice
17.11	900	HEALTH SERVICE WORKERS
16.82	107	Typists
16.67	96	Teachers: Reading
16.39	61	Food counter and fountain workers
16.00	150	Bookkeepers
15.99	638	Medical technologists
15.74	1,880	Nursing: Registered nurses, no specialty stated
15.63	1,126	Secretaries: Not specified
15.48	84	Library attendants and assistants
15.00	60	Dental hygienists
14.89	94	Nursing: Administrators
14.73	3,103	NURSES
14.71	68	Corrections officers, probation officers
14.55	55	Child care workers, except private household
14.40	840	CLERICAL AND KINDRED WORKERS
14.29	77	Secretaries: Legal
14.19	148	Therapists: Physical
14.02	1,291	HEALTH TECHNOLOGISTS AND TECHNICIANS
13.93	323	Dietitians, nutritionists
13.89	72	Dental assistants
13.54	96	Hairdressers and cosmetologists, manicurists
13.50	274	Cashiers

Occupations attractive to ISFJ

Percent ISFJ	N	Sample Description
13.45	238	Public service aides and community health workers
13.43	67	Sales agents, retail trade
13.27	4,905	OFFICE MACHINE OPERATORS
13.19	144	TRANSPORTATION OPERATIVES
13.13	2,499	Clerical workers, miscellaneous
12.96	54	Engineers: Aeronautical
12.86	70	Electricians
12.70	126	Radiologic technologists and technicians
12.68	71	Teachers: Mathematics
12.50	112	Food service workers, miscellaneous; except private household
12.46	305	Nursing: Educators
12.46	297	Computer and peripheral equipment operators
12.33	146	Nursing: Consultants
12.23	1,128	Teachers: Middle and junior high school
12.14	4,736	**College graduates, females
12.00	100	Receptionists
11.88	202	Administrators: Health
11.76	68	Secretaries: Medical
11.68	608	PROTECTIVE SERVICE WORKERS
11.54	52	Factory and site supervisors, miscellaneous
11.54	52	Computer specialists
11.49	783	PERSONAL SERVICE WORKERS
11.40	228	Teachers: Adult education
11.39	79	Religion: Educator, all denominations
11.21	223	Clinical laboratory technologists and technicians
11.10	16,678	TEACHERS
10.63	649	Teachers: High school
10.59	85	Dentists
10.48	105	Police supervisors
10.37	164	Teachers: Coaching
10.32	155	Police and detectives
10.31	97	MISCELLANEOUS OPERATIVES AND FACTORY WORKERS
10.14	2,072	DOCTORS OF MEDICINE
10.13	79	Medical assistants
10.11	1,147	Nuns and miscellaneous religious workers
10.06	179	Teachers: English
10.00	190	Engineers: Mining
10.00	70	Optometrists
9.95	191	Pharmacists
9.88	172	Teaching assistants
9.84	559	CRAFT WORKERS
9.84	427	Accountants
9.83	173	Teachers: Special education
9.76	82	Professional, technical, and kindred workers, miscellaneous
9.62	52	Engineers: Chemical
9.59	219	Priests, monks
9.50	2,010	RELIGIOUS WORKERS, ALL DENOMINATIONS
9.47	264	MILITARY PERSONNEL
9.43	106	Media specialists

Occupations attractive to ISFJ

Percent ISFJ	N	Sample Description
9.42	669	MECHANICS
9.41	765	HEALTH CARE THERAPISTS
9.26	54	Engineers: Electrical and electronic
8.98	245	Therapists: Occupational
8.97	312	Managers: Restaurant, cafeteria, bar, and food service
8.96	67	CLEANING SERVICES
8.88	169	Service workers, except private household, miscellaneous
8.82	102	Office managers
8.62	58	Home management advisors and home economists
8.59	128	Judges
8.57	105	Steelworkers, miscellaneous
8.52	223	Teachers: Health
8.33	72	FARMERS
8.25	206	SPECIALIZED: OPERATIVES
8.22	73	Air force personnel
8.21	195	Therapists: Respiratory
8.20	561	Teachers: Junior college
8.05	534	Clergy, all denominations
8.00	200	Computer programmers
8.00	175	ENGINEERING AND SCIENCE TECHNICIANS
7.99	338	COMPUTER SPECIALISTS
7.93	479	Social workers
7.82	179	Sales representatives, unspecified
7.81	333	Secretaries: Executive and administrative assistants
7.60	250	Business: General, self-employed
7.59	606	**High school graduates, males
7.50	80	Employment development specialists
7.43	1,750	SALES WORKERS
7.42	1,024	Administrators: Elementary and secondary school
7.34	177	Counselors: Rehabilitation
7.34	109	Carpenters
7.23	166	Real estate agents and brokers
7.19	139	Construction laborers, except carpenters' helpers
7.09	268	Technicians: Miscellaneous
7.02	57	Technicians: Electrical and electronic engineering
6.98	172	Coordinators: Not specified
6.93	1,082	FOOD SERVICE WORKERS
6.78	782	LABORERS
6.78	177	Resident housing assistants
6.60	106	Speech pathologists
6.39	673	Counselors: Vocational and educational
6.30	127	Mechanics and repairers, not specified
6.28	7,463	MANAGERS AND ADMINISTRATORS
6.19	113	Editors and reporters
6.16	1,803	COUNSELORS
6.16	211	Lifeguards, attendants, recreation, and amusement
6.14	472	Miscellaneous laborers
6.12	3,678	Administrators: Managers and supervisors, miscellaneous

Occupations attractive to ISFJ

Percent ISFJ	N	Sample Description
6.10	213	Teachers: Art, drama, and music
6.09	2,282	Teachers: University
6.09	986	ENGINEERS
5.97	67	Research assistants
5.88	68	Physicians: Psychiatry
5.81	86	Computer systems analysts, support representatives
5.75	226	SCIENTISTS: LIFE AND PHYSICAL
5.74	122	Administrators: Educationally related
5.69	932	Counselors: General
5.62	89	Public relations workers and publicity writers
5.56	540	Waiters, waitresses
5.56	54	Chain, rod, and ax workers; surveying
5.41	370	Administrators: School level unspecified
5.28	341	Administrators: Colleges and technical institutes
5.26	57	Scientists: Biological
5.15	136	Musicians and composers
5.04	119	Teachers: Trade, industrial and technical
5.00	180	Cooks, except private household
4.94	81	Research workers, not specified
4.90	143	Auditors
4.63	108	Sales clerks, retail trade
4.62	519	LAWYERS AND JUDGES
4.62	65	Operations and systems researchers and analysts
4.50	4,446	**College graduates, males
4.49	89	Consultants: Management analysts
4.44	90	Personnel and labor relations workers
4.41	136	Credit investigators and mortgage brokers
4.17	192	Consultants: Type unknown
3.96	530	WRITERS AND JOURNALISTS
3.92	51	Restaurant workers: Table setting and cleaning
3.85	52	Journalists
3.84	756	Bank officers and financial managers
3.70	54	Consultants: Education
3.64	55	Designers
3.57	84	Attorneys: Administrators, nonpracticing
3.44	378	ARTISTS AND ENTERTAINERS
3.28	61	Scientists: Chemistry
3.28	61	Physicians: Pathology
2.99	67	Stock clerks and storekeepers
2.97	101	Insurance agents, brokers, and underwriters
2.60	77	Engineers: Mechanical
2.58	271	Lawyers
2.49	402	PSYCHOLOGISTS
2.45	490	SOCIAL SCIENTISTS
2.41	83	Managers: Sales, not specified
1.92	208	Writers, artists, entertainers, & agents, miscellaneous
1.69	59	Photographers
1.61	62	Actors
0	83	Marketing personnel

Occupations attractive to ISFP

Percent ISFP	N	Sample Description
13.43	67	Stock clerks and storekeepers
12.96	54	Chain, rod, and ax workers; surveying
10.71	56	Clerical supervisors, miscellaneous
10.24	127	Mechanics and repairers: Not specified
9.72	72	Dental assistants
9.33	150	Bookkeepers
9.22	206	SPECIALIZED: OPERATIVES
8.96	67	CLEANING SERVICES
8.26	109	Carpenters
8.08	260	Nurses: Licensed practical
8.04	112	Food service workers, miscellaneous; except private household
7.94	126	Radiologic technologists and technicians
7.93	1,337	**High school graduates, females
7.79	77	Secretaries: Legal
7.78	180	Cooks, except private household
7.59	540	Waiters, waitresses
7.59	79	Medical assistants
7.48	107	Typists
7.43	148	Therapists: Physical
7.22	97	MISCELLANEOUS OPERATIVES AND FACTORY WORKERS
7.02	1,082	FOOD SERVICE WORKERS
6.93	1,126	Secretaries: Not specified
6.89	900	HEALTH SERVICE WORKERS
6.79	840	CLERICAL AND KINDRED WORKERS
6.76	3,064	PRIVATE HOUSEHOLD WORKERS
6.69	314	Nurses: Aides, orderlies, and attendants
6.64	211	Lifeguards, attendants, recreation and amusement
6.47	139	Construction laborers, except carpenters' helpers
6.45	155	Police and detectives
6.40	297	Computer and peripheral equipment operators
6.32	4,905	OFFICE MACHINE OPERATORS
6.12	2,499	Clerical workers, miscellaneous
6.02	432	Teachers' aides, except school monitors
6.02	83	Nursing: Public health
5.97	67	Sales agents, retail trade
5.95	84	Library attendants and assistants
5.93	472	Miscellaneous laborers
5.75	782	LABORERS
5.71	175	ENGINEERING AND SCIENCE TECHNICIANS
5.71	70	Electricians
5.66	106	Media specialists
5.64	1,880	Nursing: Registered nurses, no specialty stated
5.58	3,103	NURSES
5.56	108	Sales clerks, retail trade
5.53	669	MECHANICS
5.45	55	Child care workers, except private household
5.38	223	Clinical laboratory technologists and technicians
5.34	1,291	HEALTH TECHNOLOGISTS AND TECHNICIANS

Occupations attractive to ISFP

Percent ISFP	N	Sample Description
5.33	638	Medical technologists
5.26	190	Engineers: Mining
5.11	333	Secretaries: Executive and administrative assistants
5.04	139	Physicians: Family practice, general practice
5.02	219	Priests, monks
4.98	783	PERSONAL SERVICE WORKERS
4.90	102	Office managers
4.88	82	Professional, technical, and kindred workers, miscellaneous
4.85	268	Technicians: Miscellaneous
4.82	228	Teachers: Adult education
4.80	1,750	SALES WORKERS
4.73	804	Teachers: Elementary school
4.72	106	Speech pathologists
4.62	238	Public service aides and community health workers
4.58	765	HEALTH CARE THERAPISTS
4.52	177	Resident housing assistants
4.52	177	Counselors: Rehabilitation
4.49	245	Therapists: Occupational
4.47	559	CRAFT WORKERS
4.41	68	Secretaries: Medical
4.41	68	Corrections officers, probation officers
4.38	274	Cashiers
4.23	71	Teachers: Mathematics
4.22	166	Real estate agents and brokers
4.17	96	Teachers: Reading
4.17	72	FARMERS
4.12	534	Clergy, all denominations
4.12	267	Librarians
4.07	270	LIBRARIANS, ARCHIVISTS, AND CURATORS
4.00	100	Teachers: Preschool
4.00	100	Receptionists
3.98	427	Accountants
3.93	2,010	RELIGIOUS WORKERS, ALL DENOMINATIONS
3.92	1,147	Nuns and miscellaneous religious workers
3.92	51	Restaurant workers: Table setting and cleaning
3.90	77	Engineers: Mechanical
3.85	52	Journalists
3.85	52	Factory and site supervisors, miscellaneous
3.85	52	Computer specialists
3.82	157	Teachers: Speech pathology and therapy
3.70	81	Research workers: Not specified
3.70	54	Consultants: Education
3.66	191	Pharmacists
3.66	164	Teachers: Coaching
3.64	55	Designers
3.61	83	Marketing personnel
3.61	83	Managers: Sales, not specified
3.59	195	Therapists: Respiratory
3.55	338	COMPUTER SPECIALISTS

Occupations attractive to ISFP

Percent ISFP	N	Sample Description
3.51	57	Technicians: Electrical and electronic engineering
3.50	200	Computer programmers
3.49	172	Coordinators: Not specified
3.49	86	Computer systems analysts, support representatives
3.47	144	TRANSPORTATION OPERATIVES
3.45	58	Home management advisors and home economists
3.42	146	Nursing: Consultants
3.33	90	Personnel and labor relations workers
3.29	16,678	TEACHERS
3.29	608	PROTECTIVE SERVICE WORKERS
3.29	213	Teachers: Art, drama, and music
3.28	122	Administrators: Educationally related
3.28	61	Scientists: Chemistry
3.21	312	Managers: Restaurant, cafeteria, bar, and food service
3.19	1,128	Teachers: Middle and junior high school
3.11	932	Counselors: General
3.10	323	Dietitians, nutritionists
3.04	4,736	**College graduates, females
2.94	2,072	DOCTORS OF MEDICINE
2.89	173	Teachers: Special education
2.88	1,803	COUNSELORS
2.86	105	Steelworkers, miscellaneous
2.80	3,678	Administrators: Managers and supervisors, miscellaneous
2.69	223	Teachers: Health
2.65	113	Editors and reporters
2.64	1,024	Administrators: Elementary and secondary school
2.54	986	ENGINEERS
2.53	7,463	MANAGERS AND ADMINISTRATORS
2.51	479	Social workers
2.50	80	Employment development specialists
2.47	649	Teachers: High school
2.38	84	Attorneys: Administrators, nonpracticing
2.30	305	Nursing: Educators
2.26	530	WRITERS AND JOURNALISTS
2.25	89	Public relations workers and publicity writers
2.25	89	Consultants: Management analysts
2.23	673	Counselors: Vocational and educational
2.15	606	**High school graduates, males
2.14	561	Teachers: Junior college
2.13	94	Nursing: Administrators
2.12	756	Bank officers and financial managers
2.08	96	Hairdressers and cosmetologists, manicurists
1.98	101	Insurance agents, brokers, and underwriters
1.91	4,446	**College graduates, males
1.90	105	Police supervisors
1.85	54	Engineers: Electrical and electronic
1.84	490	SOCIAL SCIENTISTS
1.78	169	Service workers, except private household, miscellaneous

Occupations attractive to ISFP

Percent ISFP	N	Sample Description
1.74	172	Teaching assistants
1.71	2,282	Teachers: University
1.69	59	Photographers
1.68	119	Teachers: Trade, industrial, and technical
1.64	61	Food counter and fountain workers
1.60	250	Business: General, self-employed
1.59	378	ARTISTS AND ENTERTAINERS
1.56	192	Consultants: Type unknown
1.54	65	Operations and systems researchers and analysts
1.52	264	MILITARY PERSONNEL
1.48	271	Lawyers
1.47	136	Musicians and composers
1.44	208	Writers, artists, entertainers, and agents, miscellaneous
1.43	70	Optometrists
1.40	143	Auditors
1.37	73	Air force personnel
1.24	402	PSYCHOLOGISTS
1.18	85	Dentists
1.16	519	LAWYERS AND JUDGES
1.16	86	Guards and watch keepers
1.12	179	Teachers: English
1.12	179	Sales representatives, unspecified
1.08	370	Administrators: School level unspecified
.88	226	SCIENTISTS: LIFE AND PHYSICAL
.59	341	Administrators: Colleges and technical institutes
0	202	Administrators: Health
0	136	Credit investigators and mortgage brokers
0	128	Judges
0	79	Religion: Educator, all denominations
0	68	Physicians: Psychiatry
0	67	Research assistants
0	62	Actors
0	61	Physicians: Pathology
0	60	Dental hygienists
0	57	Scientists: Biological
0	54	Engineers: Aeronautical
0	52	Engineers: Chemical

Occupations attractive to ESFP

Percent ESFP	N	Sample Description
14.55	55	Child care workers, except private household
11.00	100	Receptionists
10.42	144	TRANSPORTATION OPERATIVES
10.37	540	Waiters, waitresses
10.00	190	Engineers: Mining
9.62	52	Factory and site supervisors, miscellaneous

Occupations attractive to ESFP

Percent ESFP	N	Sample Description
9.52	84	Library attendants and assistants
9.49	274	Cashiers
9.09	55	Designers
8.93	56	Clerical supervisors, miscellaneous
8.41	107	Typists
8.08	1,337	**High school graduates, females
8.06	211	Lifeguards, attendants, recreation and amusement
8.00	100	Teachers: Preschool
7.93	164	Teachers: Coaching
7.86	1,082	FOOD SERVICE WORKERS
7.84	51	Restaurant workers: Table setting and cleaning
7.69	195	Therapists: Respiratory
7.59	79	Religion: Educator, all denominations
7.46	67	Stock clerks and storekeepers
7.41	54	Engineers: Aeronautical
7.35	68	Secretaries: Medical
7.33	150	Bookkeepers
7.26	840	CLERICAL AND KINDRED WORKERS
7.23	83	Nursing: Public health
7.14	112	Food service workers, miscellaneous; except private household
7.14	70	Electricians
6.99	472	Miscellaneous laborers
6.93	101	Insurance agents, brokers, and underwriters
6.88	2,499	Clerical workers, miscellaneous
6.73	297	Computer and peripheral equipment operators
6.69	314	Nurses: Aides, orderlies, and attendants
6.67	60	Dental hygienists
6.56	61	Food counter and fountain workers
6.48	4,905	OFFICE MACHINE OPERATORS
6.47	139	Construction laborers, except carpenters' helpers
6.42	109	Carpenters
6.40	1,750	SALES WORKERS
6.39	782	LABORERS
6.33	79	Medical assistants
6.30	3,064	PRIVATE HOUSEHOLD WORKERS
6.25	96	Hairdressers and cosmetologists, manicurists
6.21	177	Counselors: Rehabilitation
6.19	97	MISCELLANEOUS OPERATIVES AND FACTORY WORKERS
6.15	179	Sales representatives, unspecified
6.10	1,147	Nuns and miscellaneous religious workers
5.72	804	Teachers: Elementary school
5.56	126	Radiologic technologists and technicians
5.56	108	Sales clerks, retail trade
5.56	72	FARMERS
5.51	127	Mechanics and repairers: Not specified
5.42	166	Real estate agents and brokers
5.38	669	MECHANICS
5.37	559	CRAFT WORKERS
5.36	783	PERSONAL SERVICE WORKERS
5.31	113	Editors and reporters

Occupations attractive to ESFP

Percent ESFP	N	Sample Description
5.26	228	Teachers: Adult education
5.22	900	HEALTH SERVICE WORKERS
5.15	1,126	Secretaries: Not specified
5.11	333	Secretaries: Executive and administrative assistants
5.03	378	ARTISTS AND ENTERTAINERS
4.93	223	Clinical laboratory technologists and technicians
4.88	82	Professional, technical, and kindred workers, miscellaneous
4.86	432	Teachers' aides, except school monitors
4.85	206	SPECIALIZED: OPERATIVES
4.84	62	Actors
4.80	250	Business: General, self-employed
4.71	85	Dentists
4.59	479	Social workers
4.58	2,010	RELIGIOUS WORKERS, ALL DENOMINATIONS
4.55	264	MILITARY PERSONNEL
4.48	67	Sales agents, retail trade
4.41	136	Musicians and composers
4.17	312	Managers: Restaurant, cafeteria, bar, and food service
4.17	96	Teachers: Reading
4.17	72	Dental assistants
4.11	73	Air force personnel
4.10	268	Technicians: Miscellaneous
4.05	148	Therapists: Physical
4.03	1,291	HEALTH TECHNOLOGISTS AND TECHNICIANS
3.94	1,803	COUNSELORS
3.92	765	HEALTH CARE THERAPISTS
3.90	77	Secretaries: Legal
3.86	673	Counselors: Vocational and educational
3.85	260	Nurses: Licensed practical
3.85	52	Computer specialists
3.82	157	Teachers: Speech pathology and therapy
3.81	1,128	Teachers: Middle and junior high school
3.81	105	Police supervisors
3.78	1,880	Nursing: Registered nurses, no specialty stated
3.77	3,103	NURSES
3.70	54	Chain, rod, and ax workers; surveying
3.61	638	Medical technologists
3.61	83	Managers: Sales, not specified
3.58	530	WRITERS AND JOURNALISTS
3.54	932	Counselors: General
3.51	57	Scientists: Biological
3.49	172	Teaching assistants
3.49	172	Coordinators: Not specified
3.47	173	Teachers: Special education
3.41	323	Dietitians, nutritionists
3.40	16,678	TEACHERS
3.37	267	Librarians
3.37	89	Public relations workers and publicity writers
3.36	238	Public service aides and community health workers

Occupations attractive to ESFP

Percent ESFP	N	Sample Description
3.33	270	LIBRARIANS, ARCHIVISTS, AND CURATORS
3.33	90	Personnel and labor relations workers
3.28	305	Nursing: Educators
3.28	61	Scientists: Chemistry
3.28	61	Physicians: Pathology
3.24	370	Administrators: School level unspecified
3.23	155	Police and detectives
3.19	94	Nursing: Administrators
3.14	986	ENGINEERS
3.14	223	Teachers: Health
3.12	608	PROTECTIVE SERVICE WORKERS
3.07	3,678	Administrators: Managers and supervisors, miscellaneous
3.00	4,736	**College graduates, females
2.99	67	Research assistants
2.96	169	Service workers, except private household, miscellaneous
2.94	68	Corrections officers, probation officers
2.86	175	ENGINEERING AND SCIENCE TECHNICIANS
2.86	70	Optometrists
2.85	561	Teachers: Junior college
2.83	106	Speech pathologists
2.82	213	Teachers: Art, drama, and music
2.82	71	Teachers: Mathematics
2.80	7,463	MANAGERS AND ADMINISTRATORS
2.78	180	Cooks, except private household
2.73	1,024	Administrators: Elementary and secondary school
2.48	202	Administrators: Health
2.43	534	Clergy, all denominations
2.41	83	Marketing personnel
2.35	341	Administrators: Colleges and technical institutes
2.33	86	Guards and watch keepers
2.31	649	Teachers: High school
2.26	177	Resident housing assistants
2.22	2,072	DOCTORS OF MEDICINE
2.09	191	Pharmacists
2.07	338	COMPUTER SPECIALISTS
2.00	200	Computer programmers
1.98	756	Bank officers and financial managers
1.98	606	**High school graduates, males
1.96	102	Office managers
1.92	208	Writers, artists, entertainers, and agents, miscellaneous
1.92	52	Journalists
1.90	105	Steelworkers, miscellaneous
1.89	106	Media specialists
1.85	54	Engineers: Electrical and electronic
1.85	54	Consultants: Education
1.77	226	SCIENTISTS: LIFE AND PHYSICAL
1.75	57	Technicians: Electrical and electronic engineering
1.72	58	Home management advisors and home economists

Occupations attractive to ESFP

Percent ESFP	N	Sample Description
1.69	59	Photographers
1.68	119	Teachers: Trade, industrial, and technical
1.67	2,282	Teachers: University
1.63	490	SOCIAL SCIENTISTS
1.63	245	Therapists: Occupational
1.56	192	Consultants: Type unknown
1.56	128	Judges
1.55	4,446	**College graduates, males
1.54	519	LAWYERS AND JUDGES
1.54	65	Operations and systems researchers and analysts
1.49	67	CLEANING SERVICES
1.48	271	Lawyers
1.44	139	Physicians: Family practice, general practice
1.41	427	Accountants
1.40	143	Auditors
1.37	146	Nursing: Consultants
1.25	80	Employment development specialists
1.24	402	PSYCHOLOGISTS
1.16	86	Computer systems analysts, support representatives
1.12	179	Teachers: English
.91	219	Priests, monks
.82	122	Administrators: Educationally related
.74	136	Credit investigators and mortgage brokers
0	89	Consultants: Management analysts
0	84	Attorneys: Administrators, nonpracticing
0	81	Research workers, not specified
0	77	Engineers: Mechanical
0	68	Physicians: Psychiatry
0	52	Engineers: Chemical

Occupations attractive to ESFJ

Percent ESFJ	N	Sample Description
20.59	68	Secretaries: Medical
18.75	96	Hairdressers and cosmetologists, manicurists
18.00	100	Receptionists
17.65	51	Restaurant workers: Table setting and cleaning
17.24	58	Home management advisors and home economists
16.67	72	Dental assistants
15.92	157	Teachers: Speech pathology and therapy
15.19	79	Religion: Educator, all denominations
15.00	260	Nurses: Licensed practical
14.81	108	Sales clerks, retail trade
14.75	61	Food counter and fountain workers

Occupations attractive to ESFJ		

Occupations attractive to ESFJ		

Percent ESFJ	N	Sample Description
14.71	102	Office managers
14.58	96	Teachers: Reading
14.55	55	Child care workers, except private household
14.14	1,337	**High school graduates, females
14.02	107	Typists
13.95	1,147	Nuns and miscellaneous religious workers
13.89	432	Teachers' aides, except school monitors
13.60	228	Teachers: Adult education
13.56	900	HEALTH SERVICE WORKERS
13.49	126	Radiologic technologists and technicians
13.32	1,126	Secretaries: Not specified
13.21	106	Speech pathologists
13.14	274	Cashiers
13.05	3,064	PRIVATE HOUSEHOLD WORKERS
13.03	238	Public service aides and community health workers
12.74	314	Nurses: Aides, orderlies, and attendants
12.69	2,499	Clerical workers, miscellaneous
12.67	150	Bookkeepers
12.44	804	Teachers: Elementary school
12.33	4,905	OFFICE MACHINE OPERATORS
12.23	139	Construction laborers, except carpenters' helpers
12.14	2,010	RELIGIOUS WORKERS, ALL DENOMINATIONS
12.00	100	Teachers: Preschool
11.90	840	CLERICAL AND KINDRED WORKERS
11.75	783	PERSONAL SERVICE WORKERS
11.67	60	Dental hygienists
11.63	86	Guards and watch keepers
11.59	164	Teachers: Coaching
11.54	52	Factory and site supervisors, miscellaneous
11.52	1,128	Teachers: Middle and junior high school
11.43	70	Optometrists
11.37	211	Lifeguards, attendants, recreation and amusement
10.98	173	Teachers: Special education
10.98	82	Professional, technical, and kindred workers, miscellaneous
10.90	1,880	Nursing: Registered nurses, no specialty stated
10.70	3,103	NURSES
10.55	1,024	Administrators: Elementary and secondary school
10.53	190	Engineers: Mining
10.47	172	Teaching assistants
10.29	136	Musicians and composers
10.27	146	Nursing: Consultants
10.20	245	Therapists: Occupational
10.14	148	Therapists: Physical
10.13	79	Medical assistants
10.07	765	HEALTH CARE THERAPISTS
10.06	1,750	SALES WORKERS
10.03	638	Medical technologists
9.82	112	Food service workers, miscellaneous; except private household
9.64	166	Real estate agents and brokers
9.64	83	Nursing: Public health
9.62	312	Managers: Restaurant, cafeteria, bar, and food service
9.52	84	Library attendants and assistants
9.45	1,291	HEALTH TECHNOLOGISTS AND TECHNICIANS
9.45	127	Mechanics and repairers: Not specified
9.35	139	Physicians: Family practice, general practice
9.28	97	MISCELLANEOUS OPERATIVES AND FACTORY WORKERS
9.25	16,678	TEACHERS
9.24	1,082	FOOD SERVICE WORKERS
9.13	219	Priests, monks
9.09	77	Secretaries: Legal
9.04	177	Resident housing assistants
9.01	333	Secretaries: Executive and administrative assistants
8.99	534	Clergy, all denominations
8.93	4,736	**College graduates, females
8.93	56	Clerical supervisors, miscellaneous
8.91	202	Administrators: Health
8.91	101	Insurance agents, brokers, and underwriters
8.89	540	Waiters, waitresses
8.82	68	Corrections officers, probation officers
8.75	297	Computer and peripheral equipment operators
8.74	206	SPECIALIZED: OPERATIVES
8.72	195	Therapists: Respiratory
8.67	323	Dietitians, nutritionists
8.64	81	Research workers, not specified
8.59	128	Judges
8.57	782	LABORERS
8.49	106	Media specialists
8.47	649	Teachers: High school
8.45	71	Teachers: Mathematics
8.39	608	PROTECTIVE SERVICE WORKERS
8.38	179	Sales representatives, unspecified
8.20	561	Teachers: Junior college
8.20	305	Nursing: Educators
8.14	172	Coordinators: Not specified
7.85	191	Pharmacists
7.78	90	Personnel and labor relations workers
7.74	155	Police and detectives
7.73	427	Accountants
7.69	52	Engineers: Chemical
7.64	144	TRANSPORTATION OPERATIVES
7.63	472	Miscellaneous laborers
7.58	673	Counselors: Vocational and educational
7.49	267	Librarians
7.47	669	MECHANICS
7.46	67	Sales agents, retail trade
7.46	67	CLEANING SERVICES

Occupations attractive to ESFJ

Percent ESFJ	N	Sample Description
7.41	270	LIBRARIANS, ARCHIVISTS, AND CURATORS
7.41	54	Consultants: Education
7.32	7,463	MANAGERS AND ADMINISTRATORS
7.26	179	Teachers: English
7.04	1,803	COUNSELORS
7.02	57	Technicians: Electrical and electronic engineering
6.97	932	Counselors: General
6.94	72	FARMERS
6.86	175	ENGINEERING AND SCIENCE TECHNICIANS
6.85	73	Air force personnel
6.74	89	Public relations workers and publicity writers
6.72	268	Technicians: Miscellaneous
6.64	226	SCIENTISTS: LIFE AND PHYSICAL
6.62	136	Credit investigators and mortgage brokers
6.61	2,072	DOCTORS OF MEDICINE
6.61	756	Bank officers and financial managers
6.58	3,678	Administrators: Managers and supervisors, miscellaneous
6.56	122	Administrators: Educationally related
6.47	479	Social workers
6.44	559	CRAFT WORKERS
6.44	264	MILITARY PERSONNEL
6.42	109	Carpenters
6.27	606	**High school graduates, males
6.11	180	Cooks, except private household
6.08	378	ARTISTS AND ENTERTAINERS
5.88	85	Dentists
5.83	223	Teachers: Health
5.83	223	Clinical laboratory technologists and technicians
5.77	52	Journalists
5.71	105	Steelworkers, miscellaneous
5.65	177	Counselors: Rehabilitation
5.60	250	Business: General, self-employed
5.56	54	Engineers: Aeronautical
5.45	55	Designers
5.32	94	Nursing: Administrators
5.28	341	Administrators: Colleges and technical institutes
5.26	57	Scientists: Biological
5.16	213	Teachers: Art, drama, and music
5.08	59	Photographers
5.00	80	Employment development specialists
4.92	61	Physicians: Pathology
4.86	370	Administrators: School level unspecified
4.82	83	Marketing personnel
4.82	83	Managers: Sales, not specified
4.76	105	Police supervisors
4.69	192	Consultants: Type unknown
4.67	986	ENGINEERS
4.62	65	Operations and systems researchers and analysts
4.49	89	Consultants: Management analysts

Occupations attractive to ESFJ

Percent ESFJ	N	Sample Description
4.48	67	Stock clerks and storekeepers
4.43	2,282	Teachers: University
4.20	119	Teachers: Trade, industrial, and technical
4.05	519	LAWYERS AND JUDGES
3.90	77	Engineers: Mechanical
3.85	52	Computer specialists
3.70	54	Engineers: Electrical and electronic
3.70	54	Chain, rod, and ax workers; surveying
3.57	84	Attorneys: Administrators, nonpracticing
3.55	4,446	**College graduates, male
3.55	169	Service workers, except private household, miscellaneous
3.40	530	WRITERS AND JOURNALISTS
3.28	61	Scientists: Chemistry
3.00	200	Computer programmers
2.86	490	SOCIAL SCIENTISTS
2.80	143	Auditors
2.66	338	COMPUTER SPECIALISTS
2.65	113	Editors and reporters
2.24	402	PSYCHOLOGISTS
1.49	67	Research assistants
1.44	208	Writers, artists, entertainers, and agents, miscellaneous
1.43	70	Electricians
1.16	86	Computer systems analysts, support representatives
1.11	271	Lawyers
0	68	Physicians: Psychiatry
0	62	Actors

Occupations attractive to INFJ

Percent INFJ	N	Sample Description
15.53	219	Priests, monks
14.81	54	Consultants: Education
11.61	534	Clergy, all denominations
11.48	61	Physicians: Pathology
10.06	179	Teachers: English
9.43	106	Media specialists
9.39	213	Teachers: Art, drama, and music
8.86	79	Religion: Educator, all denominations
8.82	68	Physicians: Psychiatry
8.14	479	Social workers
7.70	649	Teachers: High school
7.56	2,010	RELIGIOUS WORKERS, ALL DENOMINATIONS
7.54	2,282	Teachers: University
7.46	67	Research assistants
7.23	83	Marketing personnel
7.14	490	SOCIAL SCIENTISTS

Occupations attractive to INFJ

Percent INFJ	N	Sample Description
7.12	267	Librarians
7.04	341	Administrators: Colleges and technical institutes
7.04	270	LIBRARIANS, ARCHIVISTS, AND CURATORS
7.02	57	Scientists: Biological
7.00	100	Teachers: Preschool
6.97	402	PSYCHOLOGISTS
6.94	173	Teachers: Special education
6.93	202	Administrators: Health
6.90	58	Home management advisors and home economists
6.87	932	Counselors: General
6.86	4,736	**College graduates, females
6.74	89	Public relations workers and publicity writers
6.74	89	Consultants: Management analysts
6.67	60	Dental hygienists
6.60	106	Speech pathologists
6.52	2,072	DOCTORS OF MEDICINE
6.47	139	Physicians: Family practice, general practice
6.33	79	Medical assistants
6.17	81	Research workers, not specified
6.13	16,678	TEACHERS
6.12	245	Therapists: Occupational
6.05	1,803	COUNSELORS
5.97	67	Stock clerks and storekeepers
5.96	1,880	Nursing: Registered nurses, no specialty stated
5.90	305	Nursing: Educators
5.88	68	Secretaries: Medical
5.83	223	Teachers: Health
5.76	191	Pharmacists
5.56	90	Personnel and labor relations workers
5.56	54	Engineers: Aeronautical
5.54	271	Lawyers
5.49	638	Medical technologists
5.48	3,064	PRIVATE HOUSEHOLD WORKERS
5.45	55	Designers
5.39	519	LAWYERS AND JUDGES
5.37	540	Waiters, waitresses
5.26	323	Dietitians, nutritionists
5.26	190	Engineers: Mining
5.23	172	Coordinators: Not specified
5.22	3,103	NURSES
5.21	192	Consultants: Type unknown
5.19	77	Secretaries: Legal
5.10	804	Teachers: Elementary school
5.10	157	Teachers: Speech pathology and therapy
5.08	177	Counselors: Rehabilitation
5.05	673	Counselors: Vocational and educational
5.00	100	Receptionists
4.99	561	Teachers: Junior college
4.96	1,128	Teachers: Middle and junior high school
4.92	61	Scientists: Chemistry

Occupations attractive to INFJ

Percent INFJ	N	Sample Description
4.88	82	Professional, technical, and kindred workers, miscellaneous
4.84	765	HEALTH CARE THERAPISTS
4.82	83	Nursing: Public health
4.80	1,126	Secretaries: Not specified
4.69	128	Judges
4.67	150	Bookkeepers
4.65	172	Teaching assistants
4.65	86	Guards and watch keepers
4.57	1,291	HEALTH TECHNOLOGISTS AND TECHNICIANS
4.52	177	Resident housing assistants
4.50	378	ARTISTS AND ENTERTAINERS
4.44	2,499	Clerical workers, miscellaneous
4.42	226	SCIENTISTS: LIFE AND PHYSICAL
4.42	113	Editors and reporters
4.41	136	Musicians and composers
4.34	530	WRITERS AND JOURNALISTS
4.33	208	Writers, artists, entertainers, and agents, miscellaneous
4.32	4,905	OFFICE MACHINE OPERATORS
4.32	139	Construction laborers, except carpenters' helpers
4.26	94	Nursing: Administrators
4.20	119	Teachers: Trade, industrial, and technical
4.18	1,147	Nuns and miscellaneous religious workers
4.17	144	TRANSPORTATION OPERATIVES
4.17	72	Dental assistants
4.11	146	Nursing: Consultants
4.10	122	Administrators: Educationally related
4.00	900	HEALTH SERVICE WORKERS
4.00	200	Computer programmers
3.96	101	Insurance agents, brokers, and underwriters
3.94	432	Teachers' aides, except school monitors
3.91	1,024	Administrators: Elementary and secondary school
3.90	77	Engineers: Mechanical
3.85	52	Journalists
3.85	52	Engineers: Chemical
3.85	52	Computer specialists
3.74	107	Typists
3.69	840	CLERICAL AND KINDRED WORKERS
3.65	274	Cashiers
3.60	1,082	FOOD SERVICE WORKERS
3.60	333	Secretaries: Executive and administrative assistants
3.59	1,337	**High school graduates, female
3.59	223	Clinical laboratory technologists and technicians
3.57	112	Food service workers, miscellaneous; except private household
3.57	84	Library attendants and assistants
3.57	84	Attorneys: Administrators, nonpracticing
3.55	338	COMPUTER SPECIALISTS
3.53	85	Dentists
3.51	427	Accountants

Occupations attractive to INFJ

Percent INFJ	N	Sample Description
3.51	370	Administrators: School level unspecified
3.46	260	Nurses: Licensed practical
3.41	264	MILITARY PERSONNEL
3.39	59	Photographers
3.38	148	Therapists: Physical
3.26	4,446	**College graduates, male
3.20	250	Business: General, self-employed
3.14	986	ENGINEERS
3.12	96	Teachers: Reading
3.11	7,463	MANAGERS AND ADMINISTRATORS
3.08	195	Therapists: Respiratory
3.08	65	Operations and systems researchers and analysts
3.07	228	Teachers: Adult education
3.03	297	Computer and peripheral equipment operators
2.99	67	CLEANING SERVICES
2.94	782	LABORERS
2.94	102	Office managers
2.86	70	Optometrists
2.81	783	PERSONAL SERVICE WORKERS
2.80	143	Auditors
2.75	109	Carpenters
2.74	73	Air force personnel
2.69	3,678	Administrators: Managers and supervisors, miscellaneous
2.55	314	Nurses: Aides, orderlies, and attendants
2.51	1,750	SALES WORKERS
2.38	126	Radiologic technologists and technicians
2.37	211	Lifeguards, attendants, recreation and amusement
2.33	559	CRAFT WORKERS
2.33	472	Miscellaneous laborers
2.33	86	Computer systems analysts, support representatives
2.24	268	Technicians: Miscellaneous
2.23	179	Sales representatives, unspecified
2.10	238	Public service aides and community health workers
2.08	96	Hairdressers and cosmetologists, manicurists
2.06	97	MISCELLANEOUS OPERATIVES AND FACTORY WORKERS
1.96	51	Restaurant workers: Table setting and cleaning
1.94	669	MECHANICS
1.90	105	Police supervisors
1.85	108	Sales clerks, retail trade
1.85	54	Engineers: Electrical and electronic
1.83	164	Teachers: Coaching
1.81	608	PROTECTIVE SERVICE WORKERS
1.79	56	Clerical supervisors, miscellaneous
1.71	175	ENGINEERING AND SCIENCE TECHNICIANS
1.64	61	Food counter and fountain workers
1.61	62	Actors
1.60	312	Managers: Restaurant, cafeteria, bar, and food service

Occupations attractive to INFJ

Percent INFJ	N	Sample Description
1.43	70	Electricians
1.41	71	Teachers: Mathematics
1.25	80	Employment development specialists
1.20	166	Real estate agents and brokers
1.16	606	**High school graduates, males
1.11	180	Cooks, except private household
1.06	756	Bank officers and financial managers
.97	206	SPECIALIZED: OPERATIVES
.95	105	Steelworkers, miscellaneous
.79	127	Mechanics and repairers: Not specified
.74	136	Credit investigators and mortgage brokers
.65	155	Police and detectives
.59	169	Service workers, except private household, miscellaneous
0	83	Managers: Sales, not specified
0	72	FARMERS
0	68	Corrections officers, probation officers
0	67	Sales agents, retail trade
0	57	Technicians: Electrical and electronic engineering
0	55	Child care workers, except private household
0	54	Chain, rod, and ax workers; surveying
0	52	Factory and site supervisors, miscellaneous

Occupations attractive to INFP

Percent INFP	N	Sample Description
20.59	68	Physicians: Psychiatry
16.81	113	Editors and reporters
16.42	67	Research assistants
16.35	208	Writers, artists, entertainers, and agents, miscellaneous
15.38	52	Journalists
14.68	402	PSYCHOLOGISTS
13.92	79	Religion: Educator, all denominations
13.88	490	SOCIAL SCIENTISTS
13.58	530	WRITERS AND JOURNALISTS
12.96	54	Consultants: Education
12.56	223	Clinical laboratory technologists and technicians
12.45	932	Counselors: General
12.21	213	Teachers: Art, drama, and music
11.93	109	Carpenters
11.92	1,803	COUNSELORS
11.76	51	Restaurant workers: Table setting and cleaning
11.48	479	Social workers
11.32	106	Media specialists
11.30	177	Counselors: Rehabilitation

Occupations attractive to INFP

Percent INFP	N	Sample Description
11.29	673	Counselors: Vocational and educational
11.29	62	Actors
11.11	81	Research workers: Not specified
11.05	190	Engineers: Mining
10.61	179	Teachers: English
10.56	180	Cooks, except private household
10.53	57	Scientists: Biological
10.49	267	Librarians
10.47	172	Teaching assistants
10.38	106	Speech pathologists
10.37	270	LIBRARIANS, ARCHIVISTS, AND CURATORS
10.05	378	ARTISTS AND ENTERTAINERS
10.00	80	Employment development specialists
9.64	83	Nursing: Public health
9.56	136	Musicians and composers
9.38	96	Teachers: Reading
9.31	333	Secretaries: Executive and administrative assistants
9.26	54	Engineers: Aeronautical
9.26	54	Chain, rod, and ax workers; surveying
9.09	55	Designers
9.04	177	Resident housing assistants
8.92	2,499	Clerical workers, miscellaneous
8.89	540	Waiters, waitresses
8.78	148	Therapists: Physical
8.66	127	Mechanics and repairers: Not specified
8.43	534	Clergy, all denominations
8.33	84	Attorneys: Administrators, nonpracticing
8.22	219	Priests, monks
8.21	1,291	HEALTH TECHNOLOGISTS AND TECHNICIANS
8.20	2,072	DOCTORS OF MEDICINE
8.20	122	Administrators: Educationally related
8.15	4,905	OFFICE MACHINE OPERATORS
8.14	86	Guards and watch keepers
8.13	1,082	FOOD SERVICE WORKERS
8.11	2,282	Teachers: University
8.05	323	Dietitians, nutritionists
8.02	561	Teachers: Junior college
8.00	100	Teachers: Preschool
8.00	100	Receptionists
7.94	126	Radiologic technologists and technicians
7.90	1,126	Secretaries: Not specified
7.87	89	Consultants: Management analysts
7.84	472	Miscellaneous laborers
7.77	206	SPECIALIZED: OPERATIVES
7.71	765	HEALTH CARE THERAPISTS
7.59	79	Medical assistants
7.58	211	Lifeguards, attendants, recreation and amusement
7.55	1,880	Nursing: Registered nurses, no specialty stated
7.54	3,103	NURSES
7.54	782	LABORERS
7.50	200	Computer programmers
7.46	67	CLEANING SERVICES
7.41	4,736	**College graduates, females

Occupations attractive to INFP

Percent INFP	N	Sample Description
7.35	68	Secretaries: Medical
7.32	314	Nurses: Aides, orderlies, and attendants
7.14	70	Electricians
7.13	16,678	TEACHERS
7.09	268	Technicians: Miscellaneous
7.01	157	Teachers: Speech pathology and therapy
6.98	3,064	PRIVATE HOUSEHOLD WORKERS
6.94	245	Therapists: Occupational
6.93	202	Administrators: Health
6.89	305	Nursing: Educators
6.86	102	Office managers
6.85	73	Air force personnel
6.78	59	Photographers
6.73	669	MECHANICS
6.71	432	Teachers' aides, except school monitors
6.67	105	Police supervisors
6.67	60	Dental hygienists
6.64	271	Lawyers
6.62	2,010	RELIGIOUS WORKERS, ALL DENOMINATIONS
6.51	338	COMPUTER SPECIALISTS
6.49	77	Engineers: Mechanical
6.47	139	Physicians: Family practice, general practice
6.45	341	Administrators: Colleges and technical institutes
6.36	173	Teachers: Special education
6.32	649	Teachers: High school
6.27	638	Medical technologists
6.25	192	Consultants: Type unknown
6.19	986	ENGINEERS
6.17	519	LAWYERS AND JUDGES
6.16	146	Nursing: Consultants
6.15	195	Therapists: Respiratory
6.15	179	Sales representatives, unspecified
6.14	228	Teachers: Adult education
6.13	783	PERSONAL SERVICE WORKERS
6.11	1,750	SALES WORKERS
6.10	82	Professional, technical, and kindred workers, miscellaneous
6.08	559	CRAFT WORKERS
6.06	297	Computer and peripheral equipment operators
6.06	264	MILITARY PERSONNEL
5.95	840	CLERICAL AND KINDRED WORKERS
5.95	370	Administrators: School level unspecified
5.95	84	Library attendants and assistants
5.94	1,128	Teachers: Middle and junior high school
5.89	900	HEALTH SERVICE WORKERS
5.88	68	Corrections officers, probation officers
5.83	223	Teachers: Health
5.77	52	Computer specialists
5.76	191	Pharmacists
5.71	70	Optometrists
5.61	107	Typists
5.56	90	Personnel and labor relations workers
5.56	54	Engineers: Electrical and electronic
5.47	274	Cashiers

Occupations attractive to INFP

Percent INFP	N	Sample Description
5.45	55	Child care workers, except private household
5.42	166	Real estate agents and brokers
5.37	1,024	Administrators: Elementary and secondary school
5.36	56	Clerical supervisors, miscellaneous
5.33	169	Service workers, except private household, miscellaneous
5.33	150	Bookkeepers
5.31	1,337	**High school graduates, females
5.31	226	SCIENTISTS: LIFE AND PHYSICAL
5.14	175	ENGINEERING AND SCIENCE TECHNICIANS
4.92	61	Physicians: Pathology
4.86	144	TRANSPORTATION OPERATIVES
4.71	1,147	Nuns and miscellaneous religious workers
4.65	86	Computer systems analysts, support representatives
4.60	804	Teachers: Elementary school
4.57	4,446	**College graduates, males
4.56	7,463	MANAGERS AND ADMINISTRATORS
4.44	608	PROTECTIVE SERVICE WORKERS
4.40	250	Business: General, self-employed
4.30	3,678	Administrators: Managers and supervisors, miscellaneous
4.20	119	Teachers: Trade, industrial, and technical
4.17	96	Hairdressers and cosmetologists, manicurists
4.17	72	FARMERS
4.17	72	Dental assistants
4.12	97	MISCELLANEOUS OPERATIVES AND FACTORY WORKERS
4.07	172	Coordinators: Not specified
3.98	427	Accountants
3.96	101	Insurance agents, brokers, and underwriters
3.90	77	Secretaries: Legal
3.85	52	Factory and site supervisors, miscellaneous
3.85	52	Engineers: Chemical
3.70	108	Sales clerks, retail trade
3.60	139	Construction laborers, except carpenters' helpers
3.51	57	Technicians: Electrical and electronic engineering
3.46	260	Nurses: Licensed practical
3.37	89	Public relations workers and publicity writers
3.28	61	Scientists: Chemistry
3.19	94	Nursing: Administrators
3.12	128	Judges
3.05	164	Teachers: Coaching
2.94	238	Public service aides and community health workers
2.82	71	Teachers: Mathematics
2.78	756	Bank officers and financial managers
2.41	83	Marketing personnel

Occupations attractive to INFP

Percent INFP	N	Sample Description
2.35	85	Dentists
2.21	136	Credit investigators and mortgage brokers
2.10	143	Auditors
1.79	112	Food service workers, miscellaneous; except private household
1.72	58	Home management advisors and home economists
1.64	61	Food counter and fountain workers
1.49	67	Stock clerks and storekeepers
1.49	67	Sales agents, retail trade
1.28	312	Managers: Restaurant, cafeteria, bar, and food service
1.20	83	Managers: Sales, not specified
.95	105	Steelworkers, miscellaneous
.83	606	**High school graduates, males
.65	155	Police and detectives
0	65	Operations and systems researchers and analysts

Occupations attractive to ENFP

Percent ENFP	N	Sample Description
21.15	52	Journalists
20.34	177	Counselors: Rehabilitation
19.72	213	Teachers: Art, drama, and music
19.40	67	Research assistants
19.23	208	Writers, artists, entertainers, and agents, miscellaneous
18.41	402	PSYCHOLOGISTS
17.92	932	Counselors: General
17.69	1,803	COUNSELORS
17.51	177	Resident housing assistants
17.23	534	Clergy, all denominations
17.17	530	WRITERS AND JOURNALISTS
16.91	136	Musicians and composers
16.79	673	Counselors: Vocational and educational
16.73	490	SOCIAL SCIENTISTS
16.32	190	Engineers: Mining
16.16	297	Computer and peripheral equipment operators
16.13	62	Actors
15.73	89	Public relations workers and publicity writers
15.69	51	Restaurant workers: Table setting and cleaning
15.24	479	Social workers
15.08	378	ARTISTS AND ENTERTAINERS
15.00	540	Waiters, waitresses
15.00	100	Receptionists
15.00	60	Dental hygienists
14.81	54	Engineers: Aeronautical

Occupations attractive to ENFP

Percent ENFP	N	Sample Description
14.81	54	Consultants: Education
14.81	54	Chain, rod, and ax workers; surveying
14.15	106	Speech pathologists
13.86	101	Insurance agents, brokers, and underwriters
13.73	102	Office managers
13.55	561	Teachers: Junior college
13.45	223	Teachers: Health
13.29	173	Teachers: Special education
13.14	274	Cashiers
13.03	1,082	FOOD SERVICE WORKERS
12.79	219	Priests, monks
12.74	314	Nurses: Aides, orderlies, and attendants
12.66	79	Religion: Educator, all denominations
12.66	79	Medical assistants
12.39	113	Editors and reporters
12.36	89	Consultants: Management analysts
12.29	179	Teachers: English
12.24	245	Therapists: Occupational
12.00	100	Teachers: Preschool
11.96	2,499	Clerical workers, miscellaneous
11.81	271	Lawyers
11.63	172	Teaching assistants
11.63	172	Coordinators: Not specified
11.50	765	HEALTH CARE THERAPISTS
11.49	148	Therapists: Physical
11.48	61	Food counter and fountain workers
11.46	192	Consultants: Type unknown
11.40	649	Teachers: High school
11.34	4,905	OFFICE MACHINE OPERATORS
11.25	80	Employment development specialists
11.19	1,126	Secretaries: Not specified
11.14	2,010	RELIGIOUS WORKERS, ALL DENOMINATIONS
11.11	180	Cooks, except private household
11.03	1,750	SALES WORKERS
11.00	900	HEALTH SERVICE WORKERS
10.99	1,128	Teachers: Middle and junior high school
10.96	73	Air force personnel
10.91	55	Designers
10.82	305	Nursing: Educators
10.43	211	Lifeguards, attendants, recreation and amusement
10.40	250	Business: General, self-employed
10.34	58	Home management advisors and home economists
10.29	68	Physicians: Psychiatry
10.22	783	PERSONAL SERVICE WORKERS
10.20	804	Teachers: Elementary school
10.19	108	Sales clerks, retail trade
10.17	59	Photographers
10.15	3,064	PRIVATE HOUSEHOLD WORKERS
10.01	16,678	TEACHERS
10.00	150	Bookkeepers
9.88	840	CLERICAL AND KINDRED WORKERS
9.88	81	Research workers: Not specified
9.72	72	Dental assistants

Occupations attractive to ENFP

Percent ENFP	N	Sample Description
9.64	83	Marketing personnel
9.59	146	Nursing: Consultants
9.57	4,736	**College graduates, females
9.41	1,880	Nursing: Registered nurses, no specialty stated
9.38	341	Administrators: Colleges and technical institutes
9.28	3,103	NURSES
9.28	1,024	Administrators: Elementary and secondary school
9.21	782	LABORERS
9.17	109	Carpenters
9.14	175	ENGINEERING AND SCIENCE TECHNICIANS
9.07	2,282	Teachers: University
9.01	333	Secretaries: Executive and administrative assistants
8.96	67	Stock clerks and storekeepers
8.71	264	MILITARY PERSONNEL
8.57	70	Optometrists
8.47	472	Miscellaneous laborers
8.33	228	Teachers: Adult education
8.33	96	Teachers: Reading
8.28	157	Teachers: Speech pathology and therapy
8.22	669	MECHANICS
8.20	122	Administrators: Educationally related
8.09	519	LAWYERS AND JUDGES
8.08	260	Nurses: Licensed practical
7.94	126	Radiologic technologists and technicians
7.91	139	Physicians: Family practice, general practice
7.91	139	Construction laborers, except carpenters' helpers
7.87	2,072	DOCTORS OF MEDICINE
7.84	370	Administrators: School level unspecified
7.76	1,147	Nuns and miscellaneous religious workers
7.55	106	Media specialists
7.49	267	Librarians
7.48	107	Typists
7.41	432	Teachers' aides, except school monitors
7.41	270	LIBRARIANS, ARCHIVISTS, AND CURATORS
7.41	54	Engineers: Electrical and electronic
7.35	68	Secretaries: Medical
7.29	96	Hairdressers and cosmetologists, manicurists
7.28	206	SPECIALIZED: OPERATIVES
7.26	179	Sales representatives, unspecified
7.23	83	Nursing: Public health
7.14	56	Clerical supervisors, miscellaneous
7.09	268	Technicians: Miscellaneous
7.06	85	Dentists
7.02	57	Technicians: Electrical and electronic engineering
6.97	1,291	HEALTH TECHNOLOGISTS AND TECHNICIANS
6.93	7,463	MANAGERS AND ADMINISTRATORS

Occupations attractive to ENFP

Percent ENFP	N	Sample Description
6.80	986	ENGINEERS
6.71	164	Teachers: Coaching
6.62	136	Credit investigators and mortgage brokers
6.50	323	Dietitians, nutritionists
6.44	3,678	Administrators: Managers and supervisors, miscellaneous
6.30	127	Mechanics and repairers: Not specified
6.29	143	Auditors
6.28	223	Clinical laboratory technologists and technicians
6.25	112	Food service workers, miscellaneous; except private household
6.15	195	Therapists: Respiratory
6.15	65	Operations and systems researchers and analysts
6.09	427	Accountants
6.06	1,337	**High school graduates, females
5.95	84	Library attendants and assistants
5.94	4,446	**College graduates, males
5.94	202	Administrators: Health
5.80	638	Medical technologists
5.75	226	SCIENTISTS: LIFE AND PHYSICAL
5.72	559	CRAFT WORKERS
5.50	200	Computer programmers
5.32	94	Nursing: Administrators
5.24	191	Pharmacists
5.15	97	MISCELLANEOUS OPERATIVES AND FACTORY WORKERS
4.81	312	Managers: Restaurant, cafeteria, bar, and food service
4.41	68	Corrections officers, probation officers
4.29	70	Electricians
4.22	166	Real estate agents and brokers
4.20	119	Teachers: Trade, industrial, and technical
4.14	338	COMPUTER SPECIALISTS
3.91	128	Judges
3.90	77	Engineers: Mechanical
3.85	52	Factory and site supervisors, miscellaneous
3.85	52	Computer specialists
3.81	105	Steelworkers, miscellaneous
3.81	105	Police supervisors
3.78	238	Public service aides and community health workers
3.70	756	Bank officers and financial managers
3.64	55	Child care workers, except private household
3.57	84	Attorneys: Administrators, nonpracticing
3.51	57	Scientists: Biological
3.33	90	Personnel and labor relations workers
2.99	67	CLEANING SERVICES
2.82	71	Teachers: Mathematics
2.80	608	PROTECTIVE SERVICE WORKERS
2.60	77	Secretaries: Legal
2.44	82	Professional, technical, and kindred workers, miscellaneous
2.37	169	Service workers, except private household, miscellaneous

Occupations attractive to ENFP

Percent ENFP	N	Sample Description
2.33	86	Guards and watch keepers
2.08	144	TRANSPORTATION OPERATIVES
1.92	52	Engineers: Chemical
1.64	61	Physicians: Pathology
1.49	606	**High school graduates, males
1.49	67	Sales agents, retail trade
1.29	155	Police and detectives
1.20	83	Managers: Sales, not specified
1.16	86	Computer systems analysts, support representatives
0	72	FARMERS
0	61	Scientists: Chemistry

Occupations attractive to ENFJ

Percent ENFJ	N	Sample Description
17.79	534	Clergy, all denominations
15.52	58	Home management advisors and home economists
13.70	219	Priests, monks
13.45	223	Teachers: Health
12.90	62	Actors
12.68	213	Teachers: Art, drama, and music
12.02	208	Writers, artists, entertainers, and agents, miscellaneous
11.73	179	Teachers: English
11.46	192	Consultants: Type unknown
11.43	70	Optometrists
11.03	136	Musicians and composers
10.85	673	Counselors: Vocational and educational
10.19	932	Counselors: General
10.17	177	Resident housing assistants
10.15	1,803	COUNSELORS
10.14	148	Therapists: Physical
10.05	378	ARTISTS AND ENTERTAINERS
10.00	2,010	RELIGIOUS WORKERS, ALL DENOMINATIONS
10.00	60	Dental hygienists
9.52	84	Library attendants and assistants
9.35	139	Physicians: Family practice, general practice
9.09	55	Designers
9.09	55	Child care workers, except private household
8.90	146	Nursing: Consultants
8.82	68	Physicians: Psychiatry
8.78	649	Teachers: High school
8.68	530	WRITERS AND JOURNALISTS
8.52	305	Nursing: Educators
8.43	83	Marketing personnel

Occupations attractive to ENFJ

Percent ENFJ	N	Sample Description
8.40	1,024	Administrators: Elementary and secondary school
8.38	191	Pharmacists
8.33	108	Sales clerks, retail trade
8.21	402	PSYCHOLOGISTS
8.20	122	Administrators: Educationally related
8.20	61	Food counter and fountain workers
8.02	2,282	Teachers: University
8.00	100	Teachers: Preschool
7.94	4,736	**College graduates, females
7.87	267	Librarians
7.87	89	Public relations workers and publicity writers
7.84	561	Teachers: Junior college
7.84	268	Technicians: Miscellaneous
7.80	1,128	Teachers: Middle and junior high school
7.78	270	LIBRARIANS, ARCHIVISTS, AND CURATORS
7.76	490	SOCIAL SCIENTISTS
7.72	479	Social workers
7.69	16,678	TEACHERS
7.59	79	Religion: Educator, all denominations
7.56	172	Coordinators: Not specified
7.55	106	Speech pathologists
7.50	80	Employment development specialists
7.46	67	Sales agents, retail trade
7.45	94	Nursing: Administrators
7.41	81	Research workers: Not specified
7.31	3,064	PRIVATE HOUSEHOLD WORKERS
7.23	83	Nursing: Public health
7.21	804	Teachers: Elementary school
7.21	333	Secretaries: Executive and administrative assistants
7.14	56	Clerical supervisors, miscellaneous
7.08	113	Editors and reporters
7.04	341	Administrators: Colleges and technical institutes
7.01	157	Teachers: Speech pathology and therapy
6.98	172	Teaching assistants
6.96	3,103	NURSES
6.94	245	Therapists: Occupational
6.93	274	Cashiers
6.86	102	Office managers
6.78	59	Photographers
6.74	89	Consultants: Management analysts
6.56	61	Scientists: Chemistry
6.54	765	HEALTH CARE THERAPISTS
6.50	323	Dietitians, nutritionists
6.25	96	Teachers: Reading
6.21	177	Counselors: Rehabilitation
6.12	1,880	Nursing: Registered nurses, no specialty stated
6.11	180	Cooks, except private household
6.08	2,072	DOCTORS OF MEDICINE
6.07	840	CLERICAL AND KINDRED WORKERS
5.97	67	CLEANING SERVICES
5.95	84	Attorneys: Administrators, nonpracticing

Occupations attractive to ENFJ

Percent ENFJ	N	Sample Description
5.93	1,147	Nuns and miscellaneous religious workers
5.81	86	Guards and watch keepers
5.79	190	Engineers: Mining
5.78	173	Teachers: Special education
5.77	52	Journalists
5.63	71	Teachers: Mathematics
5.47	128	Judges
5.45	202	Administrators: Health
5.43	1,750	SALES WORKERS
5.42	166	Real estate agents and brokers
5.36	112	Food service workers, miscellaneous; except private household
5.33	638	Medical technologists
5.26	57	Scientists: Biological
5.24	1,126	Secretaries: Not specified
5.21	96	Hairdressers and cosmetologists, manicurists
5.19	77	Secretaries: Legal
5.19	77	Engineers: Mechanical
5.15	136	Credit investigators and mortgage brokers
5.15	97	MISCELLANEOUS OPERATIVES AND FACTORY WORKERS
5.11	783	PERSONAL SERVICE WORKERS
5.08	1,082	FOOD SERVICE WORKERS
5.00	540	Waiters, waitresses
5.00	100	Receptionists
4.96	1291	HEALTH TECHNOLOGISTS AND TECHNICIANS
4.93	223	Clinical laboratory technologists and technicians
4.92	7,463	MANAGERS AND ADMINISTRATORS
4.86	370	Administrators: School level unspecified
4.82	519	LAWYERS AND JUDGES
4.71	4,905	OFFICE MACHINE OPERATORS
4.67	150	Bookkeepers
4.43	271	Lawyers
4.40	2,499	Clerical workers, miscellaneous
4.39	228	Teachers: Adult education
4.22	427	Accountants
4.20	119	Teachers: Trade, industrial, and technical
4.17	144	TRANSPORTATION OPERATIVES
4.16	4,446	**College graduates, males
4.14	314	Nurses: Aides, orderlies, and attendants
4.11	3,678	Administrators: Managers and supervisors, miscellaneous
4.00	250	Business: General, self-employed
3.96	101	Insurance agents, brokers, and underwriters
3.91	179	Sales representatives, unspecified
3.85	986	ENGINEERS
3.85	260	Nurses: Licensed practical
3.80	79	Medical assistants
3.74	107	Typists
3.70	432	Teachers' aides, except school monitors
3.70	54	Engineers: Aeronautical
3.70	54	Chain, rod, and ax workers; surveying
3.67	900	HEALTH SERVICE WORKERS

Occupations attractive to ENFJ

Percent ENFJ	N	Sample Description
3.61	83	Managers: Sales, not specified
3.54	226	SCIENTISTS: LIFE AND PHYSICAL
3.53	85	Dentists
3.49	86	Computer systems analysts, support representatives
3.43	175	ENGINEERING AND SCIENCE TECHNICIANS
3.37	297	Computer and peripheral equipment operators
3.08	195	Therapists: Respiratory
3.05	164	Teachers: Coaching
2.99	67	Stock clerks and storekeepers
2.99	67	Research assistants
2.97	472	Miscellaneous laborers
2.96	608	PROTECTIVE SERVICE WORKERS
2.92	1,337	**High school graduates, females
2.91	756	Bank officers and financial managers
2.91	206	SPECIALIZED: OPERATIVES
2.86	105	Police supervisors
2.86	70	Electricians
2.84	211	Lifeguards, attendants, recreation and amusement
2.83	106	Media specialists
2.80	143	Auditors
2.78	72	Dental assistants
2.75	109	Carpenters
2.69	669	MECHANICS
2.65	264	MILITARY PERSONNEL
2.56	312	Managers: Restaurant, cafeteria, bar, and food service
2.43	782	LABORERS
2.38	126	Radiologic technologists and technicians
2.36	127	Mechanics and repairers: Not specified
2.33	559	CRAFT WORKERS
2.07	338	COMPUTER SPECIALISTS
2.00	200	Computer programmers
1.92	52	Engineers: Chemical
1.85	54	Engineers: Electrical and electronic
1.85	54	Consultants: Education
1.78	169	Service workers, except private household, miscellaneous
1.75	57	Technicians: Electrical and electronic engineering
1.68	238	Public service aides and community health workers
1.64	61	Physicians: Pathology
1.47	68	Secretaries: Medical
1.47	68	Corrections officers, probation officers
1.44	139	Construction laborers, except carpenters' helpers
1.37	73	Air force personnel
1.32	606	**High school graduates, males
1.29	155	Police and detectives
1.22	82	Professional, technical, and kindred workers, miscellaneous
1.11	90	Personnel and labor relations workers
.95	105	Steelworkers, miscellaneous

Occupations attractive to ENFJ

Percent ENFJ	N	Sample Description
0	72	FARMERS
0	65	Operations and systems researchers and analysts
0	52	Factory and site supervisors, miscellaneous
0	52	Computer specialists
0	51	Restaurant workers: Table setting and cleaning

Occupations attractive to INTJ

Percent INTJ	N	Sample Description
17.86	84	Attorneys: Administrators, nonpracticing
15.13	271	Lawyers
14.75	61	Scientists: Chemistry
13.58	81	Research workers: Not specified
12.96	54	Engineers: Electrical and electronic
12.83	226	SCIENTISTS: LIFE AND PHYSICAL
12.79	86	Computer systems analysts, support representatives
12.33	519	LAWYERS AND JUDGES
11.86	59	Photographers
11.54	52	Engineers: Chemical
10.87	2,282	Teachers: University
10.70	402	PSYCHOLOGISTS
10.61	490	SOCIAL SCIENTISTS
10.53	57	Technicians: Electrical and electronic engineering
10.36	338	COMPUTER SPECIALISTS
10.00	370	Administrators: School level unspecified
10.00	200	Computer programmers
9.68	62	Actors
9.64	83	Managers: Sales, not specified
9.62	208	Writers, artists, entertainers, and agents, miscellaneous
9.56	4,446	**College graduates, males
9.26	378	ARTISTS AND ENTERTAINERS
9.23	65	Operations and systems researchers and analysts
9.09	143	Auditors
8.82	136	Musicians and composers
8.77	57	Scientists: Biological
8.50	341	Administrators: Colleges and technical institutes
8.49	530	WRITERS AND JOURNALISTS
8.20	61	Physicians: Pathology
8.14	172	Teaching assistants
8.09	136	Credit investigators and mortgage brokers
7.96	113	Editors and reporters
7.87	89	Consultants: Management analysts

Occupations attractive to INTJ

Percent INTJ	N	Sample Description
7.71	986	ENGINEERS
7.69	52	Journalists
7.69	52	Computer specialists
7.62	223	Teachers: Health
7.50	80	Employment development specialists
7.46	67	Research assistants
7.41	54	Engineers: Aeronautical
7.41	54	Consultants: Education
7.27	55	Designers
7.24	2,072	DOCTORS OF MEDICINE
7.21	305	Nursing: Educators
7.06	85	Dentists
7.04	71	Teachers: Mathematics
6.95	561	Teachers: Junior college
6.85	73	Air force personnel
6.67	180	Cooks, except private household
6.56	122	Administrators: Educationally related
6.49	77	Engineers: Mechanical
6.38	94	Nursing: Administrators
6.36	173	Teachers: Special education
6.33	79	Religion: Educator, all denominations
6.25	192	Consultants: Type unknown
6.12	245	Therapists: Occupational
5.97	268	Technicians: Miscellaneous
5.88	68	Physicians: Psychiatry
5.83	223	Clinical laboratory technologists and technicians
5.81	172	Coordinators: Not specified
5.79	4,736	**College graduates, females
5.64	7,463	MANAGERS AND ADMINISTRATORS
5.62	89	Public relations workers and publicity writers
5.59	179	Teachers: English
5.56	54	Chain, rod, and ax workers; surveying
5.39	649	Teachers: High school
5.38	3,678	Administrators: Managers and supervisors, miscellaneous
5.27	1,024	Administrators: Elementary and secondary school
5.26	323	Dietitians, nutritionists
5.24	191	Pharmacists
5.22	16,678	TEACHERS
4.89	756	Bank officers and financial managers
4.82	166	Real estate agents and brokers
4.80	333	Secretaries: Executive and administrative assistants
4.72	106	Media specialists
4.71	297	Computer and peripheral equipment operators
4.69	128	Judges
4.62	195	Therapists: Respiratory
4.57	175	ENGINEERING AND SCIENCE TECHNICIANS
4.55	638	Medical technologists
4.52	1,128	Teachers: Middle and junior high school
4.49	1,291	HEALTH TECHNOLOGISTS AND TECHNICIANS

Occupations attractive to INTJ

Percent INTJ	N	Sample Description
4.46	202	Administrators: Health
4.44	765	HEALTH CARE THERAPISTS
4.44	90	Personnel and labor relations workers
4.38	479	Social workers
4.31	534	Clergy, all denominations
4.23	213	Teachers: Art, drama, and music
4.22	427	Accountants
4.20	119	Teachers: Trade, industrial, and technical
4.19	3,103	NURSES
4.11	146	Nursing: Consultants
4.08	932	Counselors: General
4.07	270	LIBRARIANS, ARCHIVISTS, AND CURATORS
4.00	100	Teachers: Preschool
3.96	101	Insurance agents, brokers, and underwriters
3.93	2,010	RELIGIOUS WORKERS, ALL DENOMINATIONS
3.92	51	Restaurant workers: Table setting and cleaning
3.90	77	Secretaries: Legal
3.78	1,880	Nursing: Registered nurses, no specialty stated
3.77	106	Speech pathologists
3.75	1,147	Nuns and miscellaneous religious workers
3.75	267	Librarians
3.66	1,803	COUNSELORS
3.66	164	Teachers: Coaching
3.64	55	Child care workers, except private household
3.61	83	Nursing: Public health
3.60	1,082	FOOD SERVICE WORKERS
3.60	139	Physicians: Family practice, general practice
3.57	84	Library attendants and assistants
3.52	540	Waiters, waitresses
3.39	177	Counselors: Rehabilitation
3.35	179	Sales representatives, unspecified
3.29	669	MECHANICS
3.26	1,750	SALES WORKERS
3.20	219	Priests, monks
3.15	127	Mechanics and repairers: Not specified
3.12	673	Counselors: Vocational and educational
3.12	96	Hairdressers and cosmetologists, manicurists
3.09	97	MISCELLANEOUS OPERATIVES AND FACTORY WORKERS
3.03	264	MILITARY PERSONNEL
3.00	4,905	OFFICE MACHINE OPERATORS
2.99	67	Sales agents, retail trade
2.96	2,499	Clerical workers, miscellaneous
2.94	102	Office managers
2.94	68	Secretaries: Medical
2.94	68	Corrections officers, probation officers
2.93	1,126	Secretaries: Not specified
2.91	206	SPECIALIZED: OPERATIVES
2.86	105	Police supervisors

Occupations attractive to INTJ

Percent INTJ	N	Sample Description
2.86	70	Optometrists
2.82	177	Resident housing assistants
2.80	250	Business: General, self-employed
2.78	144	TRANSPORTATION OPERATIVES
2.78	72	FARMERS
2.78	72	Dental assistants
2.70	148	Therapists: Physical
2.63	228	Teachers: Adult education
2.54	472	Miscellaneous laborers
2.50	559	CRAFT WORKERS
2.41	83	Marketing personnel
2.39	1,337	**High school graduates, females
2.37	211	Lifeguards, attendants, recreation and amusement
2.37	169	Service workers, except private household, miscellaneous
2.33	86	Guards and watch keepers
2.31	606	**High school graduates, males
2.30	608	PROTECTIVE SERVICE WORKERS
2.25	3,064	PRIVATE HOUSEHOLD WORKERS
2.17	783	PERSONAL SERVICE WORKERS
2.17	782	LABORERS
2.11	804	Teachers: Elementary school
2.08	96	Teachers: Reading
1.94	155	Police and detectives
1.92	312	Managers: Restaurant, cafeteria, bar, and food service
1.92	52	Factory and site supervisors, miscellaneous
1.90	105	Steelworkers, miscellaneous
1.83	109	Carpenters
1.79	56	Clerical supervisors, miscellaneous
1.72	58	Home management advisors and home economists
1.68	238	Public service aides and community health workers
1.67	840	CLERICAL AND KINDRED WORKERS
1.67	60	Dental hygienists
1.59	126	Radiologic technologists and technicians
1.58	190	Engineers: Mining
1.54	260	Nurses: Licensed practical
1.44	900	HEALTH SERVICE WORKERS
1.44	139	Construction laborers, except carpenters' helpers
1.43	70	Electricians
1.33	150	Bookkeepers
1.27	157	Teachers: Speech pathology and therapy
1.27	79	Medical assistants
1.22	82	Professional, technical, and kindred workers, miscellaneous
.93	108	Sales clerks, retail trade
.93	107	Typists
.89	112	Food service workers, miscellaneous; except private household
.64	314	Nurses: Aides, orderlies, and attendants
.46	432	Teachers' aides, except school monitors
.36	274	Cashiers

Occupations attractive to INTJ

Percent INTJ	N	Sample Description
0	100	Receptionists
0	67	Stock clerks and storekeepers
0	67	CLEANING SERVICES
0	61	Food counter and fountain workers

Occupations attractive to INTP

Percent INTP	N	Sample Description
13.11	61	Scientists: Chemistry
12.50	208	Writers, artists, entertainers, and agents, miscellaneous
11.94	67	Research assistants
10.00	200	Computer programmers
9.96	271	Lawyers
9.84	61	Food counter and fountain workers
9.30	86	Computer systems analysts, support representatives
9.26	54	Chain, rod, and ax workers; surveying
8.98	490	SOCIAL SCIENTISTS
8.96	67	Sales agents, retail trade
8.88	338	COMPUTER SPECIALISTS
8.77	57	Scientists: Biological
8.68	530	WRITERS AND JOURNALISTS
8.47	59	Photographers
8.46	402	PSYCHOLOGISTS
8.45	71	Teachers: Mathematics
8.41	226	SCIENTISTS: LIFE AND PHYSICAL
8.09	519	LAWYERS AND JUDGES
8.06	62	Actors
7.69	65	Operations and systems researchers and analysts
7.33	191	Pharmacists
7.18	195	Therapists: Respiratory
7.08	113	Editors and reporters
7.03	128	Judges
6.80	250	Business: General, self-employed
6.56	61	Physicians: Pathology
6.49	77	Secretaries: Legal
6.29	175	ENGINEERING AND SCIENCE TECHNICIANS
6.19	986	ENGINEERS
5.97	67	Stock clerks and storekeepers
5.95	84	Attorneys: Administrators, nonpracticing
5.89	2,072	DOCTORS OF MEDICINE
5.88	85	Dentists
5.88	68	Physicians: Psychiatry
5.77	52	Factory and site supervisors, miscellaneous
5.71	70	Electricians
5.62	89	Public relations workers and publicity writers

Occupations attractive to INTP

Percent INTP	N	Sample Description
5.58	4,446	**College graduates, males
5.56	54	Engineers: Electrical and electronic
5.56	54	Engineers: Aeronautical
5.39	2,282	Teachers: University
5.38	223	Clinical laboratory technologists and technicians
5.34	206	SPECIALIZED: OPERATIVES
5.33	169	Service workers, except private household, miscellaneous
5.31	245	Therapists: Occupational
5.29	378	ARTISTS AND ENTERTAINERS
5.28	341	Administrators: Colleges and technical institutes
5.26	57	Technicians: Electrical and electronic engineering
5.22	268	Technicians: Miscellaneous
5.15	136	Musicians and composers
5.15	97	MISCELLANEOUS OPERATIVES AND FACTORY WORKERS
5.04	119	Teachers: Trade, industrial, and technical
5.01	479	Social workers
5.00	80	Employment development specialists
4.90	143	Auditors
4.88	82	Professional, technical, and kindred workers, miscellaneous
4.84	765	HEALTH CARE THERAPISTS
4.72	127	Mechanics and repairers, not specified
4.69	213	Teachers: Art, drama, and music
4.63	561	Teachers: Junior college
4.59	305	Nursing: Educators
4.48	223	Teachers: Health
4.45	427	Accountants
4.29	559	CRAFT WORKERS
4.24	472	Miscellaneous laborers
4.22	166	Real estate agents and brokers
4.21	190	Engineers: Mining
4.17	72	FARMERS
4.16	1,082	FOOD SERVICE WORKERS
4.10	122	Administrators: Educationally related
4.07	172	Coordinators: Not specified
4.05	3,678	Administrators: Managers and supervisors, miscellaneous
3.95	177	Counselors: Rehabilitation
3.92	638	Medical technologists
3.92	51	Restaurant workers: Table setting and cleaning
3.90	77	Engineers: Mechanical
3.85	52	Journalists
3.85	52	Computer specialists
3.80	79	Medical assistants
3.79	211	Lifeguards, attendants, recreation and amusement
3.71	782	LABORERS
3.70	108	Sales clerks, retail trade
3.70	81	Research workers, not specified
3.68	136	Credit investigators and mortgage brokers
3.66	164	Teachers: Coaching

Occupations attractive to INTP

Percent INTP	N	Sample Description
3.65	192	Consultants: Type unknown
3.64	1,291	HEALTH TECHNOLOGISTS AND TECHNICIANS
3.64	55	Child care workers, except private household
3.58	7,463	MANAGERS AND ADMINISTRATORS
3.57	673	Counselors: Vocational and educational
3.57	56	Clerical supervisors, miscellaneous
3.55	4,736	**College graduates, females
3.52	540	Waiters, waitresses
3.49	172	Teaching assistants
3.47	173	Teachers: Special education
3.44	1,803	COUNSELORS
3.43	1,750	SALES WORKERS
3.42	146	Nursing: Consultants
3.39	177	Resident housing assistants
3.35	16,678	TEACHERS
3.33	932	Counselors: General
3.33	90	Personnel and labor relations workers
3.31	756	Bank officers and financial managers
3.24	370	Administrators: School level unspecified
3.23	155	Police and detectives
3.20	219	Priests, monks
3.18	157	Teachers: Speech pathology and therapy
3.17	126	Radiologic technologists and technicians
3.13	3,103	NURSES
3.00	267	Librarians
3.00	100	Receptionists
2.97	202	Administrators: Health
2.97	101	Insurance agents, brokers, and underwriters
2.96	270	LIBRARIANS, ARCHIVISTS, AND CURATORS
2.94	783	PERSONAL SERVICE WORKERS
2.93	1,880	Nursing: Registered nurses, no specialty stated
2.93	649	Teachers: High school
2.92	2,499	Clerical workers, miscellaneous
2.88	139	Physicians: Family practice, general practice
2.83	106	Speech pathologists
2.81	606	**High school graduates, males
2.79	179	Teachers: English
2.78	180	Cooks, except private household
2.75	109	Carpenters
2.70	148	Therapists: Physical
2.69	669	MECHANICS
2.69	297	Computer and peripheral equipment operators
2.68	112	Food service workers, miscellaneous; except private household
2.54	1,024	Administrators: Elementary and secondary school
2.53	4,905	OFFICE MACHINE OPERATORS
2.47	608	PROTECTIVE SERVICE WORKERS
2.40	333	Secretaries: Executive and administrative assistants

Occupations attractive to INTP		
Percent INTP	N	Sample Description
2.39	1,128	Teachers: Middle and junior high school
2.35	1,147	Nuns and miscellaneous religious workers
2.33	900	HEALTH SERVICE WORKERS
2.33	86	Guards and watch keepers
2.29	2,010	RELIGIOUS WORKERS, ALL DENOMINATIONS
2.25	534	Clergy, all denominations
2.25	89	Consultants: Management analysts
2.13	94	Nursing: Administrators
2.00	100	Teachers: Preschool
1.96	102	Office managers
1.92	52	Engineers: Chemical
1.91	314	Nurses: Aides, orderlies, and attendants
1.90	105	Steelworkers, miscellaneous
1.90	105	Police supervisors
1.89	106	Media specialists
1.82	55	Designers
1.79	840	CLERICAL AND KINDRED WORKERS
1.75	228	Teachers: Adult education
1.66	3,064	PRIVATE HOUSEHOLD WORKERS
1.60	1,126	Secretaries: Not specified
1.55	323	Dietitians, nutritionists
1.54	260	Nurses: Licensed practical
1.52	264	MILITARY PERSONNEL
1.49	804	Teachers: Elementary school
1.47	68	Secretaries: Medical
1.47	68	Corrections officers, probation officers
1.46	274	Cashiers
1.44	139	Construction laborers, except carpenters' helpers
1.43	70	Optometrists
1.39	144	TRANSPORTATION OPERATIVES
1.39	72	Dental assistants
1.35	1,337	**High school graduates, females
1.33	150	Bookkeepers
1.28	312	Managers: Restaurant, cafeteria, bar, and food service
1.26	238	Public service aides and community health workers
1.20	83	Nursing: Public health
1.20	83	Marketing personnel
1.20	83	Managers: Sales, not specified
1.19	84	Library attendants and assistants
1.12	179	Sales representatives, unspecified
1.04	96	Teachers: Reading
1.04	96	Hairdressers and cosmetologists, manicurists
.69	432	Teachers' aides, except school monitors
0	107	Typists
0	79	Religion: Educator, all denominations
0	73	Air force personnel
0	67	CLEANING SERVICES
0	60	Dental hygienists
0	58	Home management advisors and home economists
0	54	Consultants: Education

Occupations attractive to ENTP		
Percent ENTP	N	Sample Description
16.95	59	Photographers
13.25	83	Marketing personnel
11.94	67	Sales agents, retail trade
11.54	52	Journalists
11.29	62	Actors
10.47	86	Computer systems analysts, support representatives
10.29	136	Credit investigators and mortgage brokers
10.29	68	Physicians: Psychiatry
9.62	52	Engineers: Chemical
9.35	139	Construction laborers, except carpenters' helpers
9.09	77	Engineers: Mechanical
8.99	89	Public relations workers and publicity writers
8.73	378	ARTISTS AND ENTERTAINERS
8.64	81	Research workers, not specified
8.57	70	Electricians
8.49	271	Lawyers
8.33	192	Consultants: Type unknown
8.28	169	Service workers, except private household, miscellaneous
8.20	61	Food counter and fountain workers
7.87	89	Consultants: Management analysts
7.84	51	Restaurant workers: Table setting and cleaning
7.69	338	COMPUTER SPECIALISTS
7.69	208	Writers, artists, entertainers, and agents, miscellaneous
7.69	65	Operations and systems researchers and analysts
7.50	200	Computer programmers
7.41	54	Engineers: Aeronautical
7.36	530	WRITERS AND JOURNALISTS
7.35	68	Corrections officers, probation officers
7.27	55	Child care workers, except private household
7.23	83	Managers: Sales, not specified
7.02	57	Technicians: Electrical and electronic engineering
7.02	57	Scientists: Biological
6.94	72	FARMERS
6.94	72	Dental assistants
6.74	519	LAWYERS AND JUDGES
6.67	90	Personnel and labor relations workers
6.64	226	SCIENTISTS: LIFE AND PHYSICAL
6.61	756	Bank officers and financial managers
6.60	106	Speech pathologists
6.33	79	Medical assistants
6.29	175	ENGINEERING AND SCIENCE TECHNICIANS
6.15	195	Therapists: Respiratory
6.10	82	Professional, technical, and kindred workers, miscellaneous
6.02	166	Real estate agents and brokers
5.98	986	ENGINEERS
5.97	402	PSYCHOLOGISTS

Occupations attractive to ENTP

Percent ENTP	N	Sample Description
5.95	84	Attorneys: Administrators, nonpracticing
5.94	101	Insurance agents, brokers, and underwriters
5.88	136	Musicians and composers
5.83	1750	SALES WORKERS
5.81	172	Coordinators: Not specified
5.72	472	Miscellaneous laborers
5.65	4,446	**College graduates, males
5.63	782	LABORERS
5.61	107	Typists
5.59	179	Sales representatives, unspecified
5.59	143	Auditors
5.56	540	Waiters, waitresses
5.56	126	Radiologic technologists and technicians
5.56	54	Engineers: Electrical and electronic
5.51	490	SOCIAL SCIENTISTS
5.48	73	Air force personnel
5.45	1,082	FOOD SERVICE WORKERS
5.45	312	Managers: Restaurant, cafeteria, bar, and food service
5.45	55	Designers
5.36	56	Clerical supervisors, miscellaneous
5.31	113	Editors and reporters
5.30	2,282	Teachers: University
5.30	264	MILITARY PERSONNEL
5.23	765	HEALTH CARE THERAPISTS
5.23	669	MECHANICS
5.21	96	Hairdressers and cosmetologists, manicurists
5.00	80	Employment development specialists
5.00	60	Dental hygienists
4.99	561	Teachers: Junior college
4.92	3,678	Administrators: Managers and supervisors, miscellaneous
4.92	61	Scientists: Chemistry
4.89	7,463	MANAGERS AND ADMINISTRATORS
4.88	164	Teachers: Coaching
4.75	673	Counselors: Vocational and educational
4.72	106	Media specialists
4.59	479	Social workers
4.55	1,803	COUNSELORS
4.52	177	Counselors: Rehabilitation
4.52	155	Police and detectives
4.51	932	Counselors: General
4.49	267	Librarians
4.48	67	Stock clerks and storekeepers
4.48	67	CLEANING SERVICES
4.46	112	Food service workers, miscellaneous; except private household
4.44	270	LIBRARIANS, ARCHIVISTS, AND CURATORS
4.34	783	PERSONAL SERVICE WORKERS
4.27	211	Lifeguards, attendants, recreation and amusement
4.23	71	Teachers: Mathematics
4.17	144	TRANSPORTATION OPERATIVES
4.17	96	Teachers: Reading

Occupations attractive to ENTP

Percent ENTP	N	Sample Description
4.11	341	Administrators: Colleges and technical institutes
4.08	4,736	**College graduates, females
4.05	370	Administrators: School level unspecified
4.05	173	Teachers: Special education
4.04	297	Computer and peripheral equipment operators
4.04	223	Teachers: Health
4.01	1,147	Nuns and miscellaneous religious workers
4.00	250	Business: General, self-employed
4.00	150	Bookkeepers
3.98	427	Accountants
3.95	608	PROTECTIVE SERVICE WORKERS
3.95	177	Resident housing assistants
3.91	128	Judges
3.90	1,128	Teachers: Middle and junior high school
3.89	180	Cooks, except private household
3.85	52	Computer specialists
3.71	1,024	Administrators: Elementary and secondary school
3.70	108	Sales clerks, retail trade
3.70	54	Consultants: Education
3.70	54	Chain, rod, and ax workers; surveying
3.66	191	Pharmacists
3.65	274	Cashiers
3.64	16,678	TEACHERS
3.64	1291	HEALTH TECHNOLOGISTS AND TECHNICIANS
3.58	559	CRAFT WORKERS
3.54	649	Teachers: High school
3.51	228	Teachers: Adult education
3.49	172	Teaching assistants
3.49	86	Guards and watch keepers
3.47	202	Administrators: Health
3.46	1,880	Nursing: Registered nurses, no specialty stated
3.43	2,072	DOCTORS OF MEDICINE
3.36	268	Technicians: Miscellaneous
3.33	840	CLERICAL AND KINDRED WORKERS
3.29	213	Teachers: Art, drama, and music
3.28	122	Administrators: Educationally related
3.28	61	Physicians: Pathology
3.27	245	Therapists: Occupational
3.14	223	Clinical laboratory technologists and technicians
3.13	2,010	RELIGIOUS WORKERS, ALL DENOMINATIONS
3.12	2,499	Clerical workers, miscellaneous
3.00	333	Secretaries: Executive and administrative assistants
2.99	67	Research assistants
2.98	638	Medical technologists
2.94	102	Office managers
2.91	206	SPECIALIZED: OPERATIVES
2.90	4,905	OFFICE MACHINE OPERATORS
2.90	3,103	NURSES
2.81	606	**High school graduates, males

Occupations attractive to ENTP

Percent ENTP	N	Sample Description
2.79	179	Teachers: English
2.78	900	HEALTH SERVICE WORKERS
2.78	432	Teachers' aides, except school monitors
2.75	109	Carpenters
2.74	219	Priests, monks
2.70	148	Therapists: Physical
2.62	305	Nursing: Educators
2.60	77	Secretaries: Legal
2.55	157	Teachers: Speech pathology and therapy
2.52	119	Teachers: Trade, industrial, and technical
2.41	83	Nursing: Public health
2.36	127	Mechanics and repairers, not specified
2.31	260	Nurses: Licensed practical
2.19	3,064	PRIVATE HOUSEHOLD WORKERS
2.17	323	Dietitians, nutritionists
2.13	94	Nursing: Administrators
2.10	238	Public service aides and community health workers
2.06	97	MISCELLANEOUS OPERATIVES AND FACTORY WORKERS
2.05	146	Nursing: Consultants
2.00	100	Receptionists
1.90	105	Police supervisors
1.78	1,126	Secretaries: Not specified
1.69	534	Clergy, all denominations
1.49	804	Teachers: Elementary school
1.47	68	Secretaries: Medical
1.44	139	Physicians: Family practice, general practice
1.43	70	Optometrists
1.42	1,337	**High school graduates, females
1.27	79	Religion: Educator, all denominations
1.19	84	Library attendants and assistants
1.18	85	Dentists
1.05	190	Engineers: Mining
1.00	100	Teachers: Preschool
.96	314	Nurses: Aides, orderlies, and attendants
.95	105	Steelworkers, miscellaneous
0	58	Home management advisors and home economists
0	52	Factory and site supervisors, miscellaneous

Occupations attractive to ENTJ

Percent ENTJ	N	Sample Description
21.43	84	Attorneys: Administrators, nonpracticing
20.00	65	Operations and systems researchers and analysts
16.87	83	Managers: Sales, not specified
16.18	136	Credit investigators and mortgage brokers

Occupations attractive to ENTJ

Percent ENTJ	N	Sample Description
15.66	83	Marketing personnel
15.38	52	Computer specialists
14.44	90	Personnel and labor relations workers
14.37	341	Administrators: Colleges and technical institutes
13.41	82	Professional, technical, and kindred workers, miscellaneous
13.37	202	Administrators: Health
12.96	54	Consultants: Education
12.50	192	Consultants: Type unknown
12.50	80	Employment development specialists
12.28	57	Scientists: Biological
11.94	67	Research assistants
11.69	402	PSYCHOLOGISTS
11.63	490	SOCIAL SCIENTISTS
11.54	52	Engineers: Chemical
11.43	4,446	**College graduates, males
11.08	370	Administrators: School level unspecified
10.73	177	Resident housing assistants
10.40	250	Business: General, self-employed
10.29	68	Corrections officers, probation officers
10.18	226	SCIENTISTS: LIFE AND PHYSICAL
10.14	3,678	Administrators: Managers and supervisors, miscellaneous
10.06	7,463	MANAGERS AND ADMINISTRATORS
10.06	338	COMPUTER SPECIALISTS
9.84	61	Scientists: Chemistry
9.79	143	Auditors
9.68	62	Actors
9.66	756	Bank officers and financial managers
9.64	2,282	Teachers: University
9.62	312	Managers: Restaurant, cafeteria, bar, and food service
9.41	85	Dentists
9.38	96	Teachers: Reading
9.30	86	Computer systems analysts, support representatives
9.09	55	Designers
9.06	519	LAWYERS AND JUDGES
9.02	122	Administrators: Educationally related
9.00	200	Computer programmers
8.99	89	Consultants: Management analysts
8.77	57	Technicians: Electrical and electronic engineering
8.63	139	Physicians: Family practice, general practice
8.59	1,024	Administrators: Elementary and secondary school
8.47	59	Photographers
8.38	179	Teachers: English
8.38	179	Sales representatives, unspecified
8.33	108	Sales clerks, retail trade
8.22	146	Nursing: Consultants
8.20	61	Physicians: Pathology
8.09	173	Teachers: Special education
8.00	175	ENGINEERING AND SCIENCE TECHNICIANS
7.83	166	Real estate agents and brokers

Occupations attractive to ENTJ

Percent ENTJ	N	Sample Description
7.76	245	Therapists: Occupational
7.55	106	Media specialists
7.51	986	ENGINEERS
7.41	81	Research workers, not specified
7.41	54	Engineers: Electrical and electronic
7.38	271	Lawyers
7.35	68	Secretaries: Medical
7.26	427	Accountants
7.14	70	Optometrists
7.14	70	Electricians
7.08	113	Editors and reporters
6.90	58	Home management advisors and home economists
6.89	305	Nursing: Educators
6.86	102	Office managers
6.81	323	Dietitians, nutritionists
6.78	4,736	**College graduates, females
6.72	119	Teachers: Trade, industrial, and technical
6.71	1,147	Nuns and miscellaneous religious workers
6.60	561	Teachers: Junior college
6.40	172	Coordinators: Not specified
6.31	206	SPECIALIZED: OPERATIVES
6.25	128	Judges
6.13	2,072	DOCTORS OF MEDICINE
6.11	1,750	SALES WORKERS
6.08	378	ARTISTS AND ENTERTAINERS
6.02	2,010	RELIGIOUS WORKERS, ALL DENOMINATIONS
6.02	83	Nursing: Public health
5.99	534	Clergy, all denominations
5.98	16,678	TEACHERS
5.97	67	Stock clerks and storekeepers
5.97	67	Sales agents, retail trade
5.94	673	Counselors: Vocational and educational
5.83	223	Teachers: Health
5.75	765	HEALTH CARE THERAPISTS
5.71	105	Police supervisors
5.64	195	Therapists: Respiratory
5.62	89	Public relations workers and publicity writers
5.56	72	FARMERS
5.56	54	Chain, rod, and ax workers; surveying
5.28	530	WRITERS AND JOURNALISTS
5.26	228	Teachers: Adult education
5.24	191	Pharmacists
5.22	804	Teachers: Elementary school
5.19	77	Secretaries: Legal
5.16	1,803	COUNSELORS
5.11	333	Secretaries: Executive and administrative assistants
5.10	157	Teachers: Speech pathology and therapy
5.00	100	Teachers: Preschool
5.00	60	Dental hygienists
4.92	264	MILITARY PERSONNEL
4.83	932	Counselors: General
4.78	314	Nurses: Aides, orderlies, and attendants
4.74	3,103	NURSES
4.72	106	Speech pathologists

Occupations attractive to ENTJ

Percent ENTJ	N	Sample Description
4.69	213	Teachers: Art, drama, and music
4.59	479	Social workers
4.59	109	Carpenters
4.48	268	Technicians: Miscellaneous
4.41	68	Physicians: Psychiatry
4.34	1,128	Teachers: Middle and junior high school
4.33	208	Writers, artists, entertainers, and agents, miscellaneous
4.31	649	Teachers: High school
4.29	606	**High school graduates, males
4.28	608	PROTECTIVE SERVICE WORKERS
4.26	94	Nursing: Administrators
4.23	71	Teachers: Mathematics
4.21	783	PERSONAL SERVICE WORKERS
4.12	97	MISCELLANEOUS OPERATIVES AND FACTORY WORKERS
4.08	638	Medical technologists
4.00	900	HEALTH SERVICE WORKERS
3.96	101	Insurance agents, brokers, and underwriters
3.95	1,291	HEALTH TECHNOLOGISTS AND TECHNICIANS
3.92	51	Restaurant workers: Table setting and cleaning
3.89	669	MECHANICS
3.88	1,880	Nursing: Registered nurses, no specialty stated
3.81	472	Miscellaneous laborers
3.70	54	Engineers: Aeronautical
3.68	136	Musicians and composers
3.60	139	Construction laborers, except carpenters' helpers
3.58	559	CRAFT WORKERS
3.57	84	Library attendants and assistants
3.39	177	Counselors: Rehabilitation
3.32	211	Lifeguards, attendants, recreation and amusement
3.29	1,126	Secretaries: Not specified
3.20	782	LABORERS
3.17	126	Radiologic technologists and technicians
3.06	4,905	OFFICE MACHINE OPERATORS
2.94	238	Public service aides and community health workers
2.92	1,337	**High school graduates, females
2.91	172	Teaching assistants
2.86	105	Steelworkers, miscellaneous
2.78	144	TRANSPORTATION OPERATIVES
2.74	73	Air force personnel
2.70	148	Therapists: Physical
2.69	223	Clinical laboratory technologists and technicians
2.64	3,064	PRIVATE HOUSEHOLD WORKERS
2.60	77	Engineers: Mechanical
2.59	540	Waiters, waitresses
2.53	79	Religion: Educator, all denominations
2.53	79	Medical assistants
2.44	2,499	Clerical workers, miscellaneous
2.44	164	Teachers: Coaching

Occupations attractive to ENTJ		
Percent ENTJ	N	Sample Description
2.36	297	Computer and peripheral equipment operators
2.36	127	Mechanics and repairers, not specified
2.28	219	Priests, monks
2.25	267	Librarians
2.22	1,082	FOOD SERVICE WORKERS
2.22	270	LIBRARIANS, ARCHIVISTS, AND CURATORS
2.14	840	CLERICAL AND KINDRED WORKERS
2.08	432	Teachers' aides, except school monitors
2.00	100	Receptionists
1.92	260	Nurses: Licensed practical
1.92	52	Journalists
1.82	55	Child care workers, except private household
1.79	112	Food service workers, miscellaneous; except private household
1.78	169	Service workers, except private household, miscellaneous

Occupations attractive to ENTJ		
Percent ENTJ	N	Sample Description
1.67	180	Cooks, except private household
1.64	61	Food counter and fountain workers
1.46	274	Cashiers
1.39	72	Dental assistants
1.29	155	Police and detectives
1.04	96	Hairdressers and cosmetologists, manicurists
.93	107	Typists
.67	150	Bookkeepers
.53	190	Engineers: Mining
0	86	Guards and watch keepers
0	67	CLEANING SERVICES
0	56	Clerical supervisors, miscellaneous
0	52	Factory and site supervisors, miscellaneous

Notes

1. The notation EI means E *or* I, rather than "from E to I." The notation is EI rather than E–I, since the latter might be read "E minus I."
2. The formula for calculating preference scores from points is: For E, S, T, and J multiply 2 times (larger points minus smaller points) *minus* 1; for I, N, F, and P multiply 2 times (larger points minus smaller points) *plus* 1; for ties, the preference score will be I 01, N 01, F 01, or P 01.
3. Counselors have reported that it is useful to let counselees who are uncomfortable with their reported type retake the MBTI. They can take the MBTI with any of several frames of reference. For example, they can answer for their "true self," "ideal self," "work self," "home self," "present self," or "the child my parents thought they had." It is sometimes useful for clients to indicate responses about which they felt sure and then to have the MBTI scored for just those items. Clients should be warned that when retaking the MBTI after having their type explained they are no longer naive about the questions, and the validity of their type measurement will be affected.
4. Type theory is but one part of Jung's personality theory; it does not directly consider other parts of Jung's theory, for example, the animus, anima, archetypes, or the collective unconscious.
5. The term *function* is used in technical language; the term *process* is used when describing the theory in lay terms. In this Manual, the two terms are used interchangeably.
6. Type theory assumes that all types have unique and valuable gifts. By definition, however, *creativity* means the creation of something new which has not existed before. Perception of the new is in the domain of intuition. All intuition is not creative; intuition can also include the merest hunches or unfounded suspicions. True creativity requires a highly differentiated awareness of many observations by the senses, from which intuition develops new patterns.
7. The JP index is sometimes referred to as an orientation to the outer world, and sometimes JP is classified as an "attitude." In Jungian terminology the term *attitude* is restricted to EI. In MBTI terminology *attitude* can include EI and also JP.

8. An example of the admission of the least developed process to conscious use in the service of the dominant process is an ENFP trying to accomplish a goal that has captured intuition and is important to feeling. The ENFP might temporarily lay aside the glitter of the NF vision in order to consciously look at the realities of the immediate situation (S) and the logical outcomes of various courses of action being considered (T). The fourth function (S) and the third function (T) would be allowed into consciousness to help the NF vision come true. In this process of using S and T consciously and purposefully to help N and F, the S and T would also become better developed.

9. Note that all MBTI choices are between pairs of the *same* preference. There are no comparisons of I with S, or T with N, for example. The reason is that the MBTI aims to assess preferences between poles of the same index as described in Jung's theory.

10. Myers followed Jung's comment, "The counterbalancing functions of feeling, intuition and sensation are comparatively unconscious and inferior, and therefore have a primitive extraverted character that accounts for all the troublesome influences from the outside to which the introverted thinker is prone." (p. 387, 1971). She therefore considered the second, third, and fourth functions to be in the attitude opposite to the dominant. Some MBTI interpreters (e.g., Grant, Thompson, and Clark, 1983) consider the third function to be in the same attitude as the dominant function.

11. The *inferior function* is sometimes referred to as the *shadow* function in Jungian terminology. This terminology is discouraged in MBTI theory. In Jung's total theory, the term *shadow* refers to an archetype that contains repressed, rejected, undesirable views of oneself. The inferior function has no content by itself, but may give form to the contents of the shadow. The term *inferior function* is more precise.

12. To be precise, one can use E–TJ types to stand for extraverted thinking types; usually, the dashes are omitted and the extraverted thinking types are referred to as ETJ types. In this section where the model is being described, precise terminology is used. Elsewhere, standard notation (without dashes) is used.

13. Osmond and his associates (Osmond, Siegler, and Smoke, 1977) describe their observations of characteristics of ST, SF, NF, and NT. Keirsey and Bates (1978) describe their observations of NF, NT, SJ, and SP in terms of their theory of temperaments.

14. As translations now under way are completed and used, it will be possible to compare distributions of types across cultures. It is expected that all sixteen types will appear in all cultures, but that the distributions of types will differ from culture to culture.

15. Computer software known as the Selection Ratio Type Table Program (SRTT) compares two type distributions with each other and generates ratios and significance tests to compare each of the sixteen types and the type groupings. This software is available from the Center for Applications of Psychological Type, 2720 N.W. 6th Street, Suite A, Gainesville, FL 32609.

16. The samples were: 3,676 male liberal arts students enrolled at Amherst, Brown, Dartmouth, Stanford, and Wesleyan; 2,188 freshman engineering students at Cornell, Massachusetts Institute of Technology, and California Polytechnic Institute; and 488 undergraduate business students at the Wharton School of the University of Pennsylvania.

17. The word *ratio* referred to in this paragraph is the selection ratio described in Chapter 6. Ratios greater than 1.00 indicate more of the type than expected compared to the frequency of the type in the base population. Numbers less than 1.00 indicate fewer than expected from the base population. In the data in the paragraph, therefore, ISTJ had a higher than expected retention rate, and ESFP a lower than expected retention rate, or a higher than expected attrition rate.

18. In the development of Form G, item 25 on Form F was dropped from the EI index. A new item 71 on Form G was substituted for Form F item 55 on the SN index. Nine Form F items were revised or modified slightly to simplify wording or to clarify awkward or ambiguous alternatives. These modifications can be examined by comparing the following items: F6 and G7, F13 and G74, F26 and G21, F42 and G8, F66 and G72, F126 and G19, F129 and G77, F140 and G85, and F149 and G18. Item weights were revised for the TF index for both Form F and Form G.

19. If self-scoring the MBTI is not crucial, the regular Form G booklets, response sheets, and keys may be used, responding to only the first fifty items in the booklet. These items are identical with those in Form AV. If this method is employed, the scorer may use the separate keys for men and women for TF preference. In Form AV, a "unisex" scoring is used for TF; specifically, in the feeling scoring, items 6 and 43 on Form G were given the male weights while items 30 and 32 were given the female weights. The thinking scoring is balanced by scoring Form G item 6 with the female weight and item 32 with the male weight.

20. The Pennsylvania sample consisted of students from 27 high schools; 3,542 were in college preparatory courses, and 1,483 were in noncollege preparatory curricula. Comparable analyses were conducted for females but are not reported in this Manual. The Massachusetts students included students from both academic and vocational schools (see Stricker and Ross, 1962, p. 180).

21. The unequal size of the 37+ interval on different preferences, because of different maximum values of the indices, is recognized on the figures by the placement of the midpoint.

22. Other researchers correlating the MBTI and the SCII are: J. A. Aanstadt (raw data available through CAPT, 1974); Charles Broussard at Foothill College in Los Altos Hills, CA; Tamara Nelson at the University of Minnesota; and

Shel Weissman at California State University, Sacramento, who has occupational scales loading on each of the sixteen types.

23. An expanded analysis of the MBTI with data such as that in Table 11.2 and other evaluations of the MBTI scales is contained in a forthcoming monograph by H.G. Gough and A. Thorne to be published by Consulting Psychologists Press.

24. Another study in which MBTI differences were shown on factors developed independently of type is Quenk and Albert (1975).

References

Abbott, E. F., & McCaulley, M. H. (1983). [High school students in Florida Future Scientist Program 1974–1982.] Unpublished raw data.

Allen, J., Myers, I. B., & Kainz, R. I. (1976). *The Selection Ratio Type Table Program*. Gainesville, FL: Center for Applications of Psychological Type Inc.

Allport, G. W., Vernon, P. E., & Lindzey, G. (1960). *Study of values: A scale for measuring the dominant interests in personality* (3rd ed.). Boston: Houghton Mifflin.

Anast, P. (1966) Similarity between self and fictional character choice. *The Psychological Record, 16,* 535-539.

Anchors, S. (1983). [Type distributions of freshmen students in 1981 and 1982 at the University of Maine at Orono.] Unpublished raw data.

Andrea, M. C. (1983). Imagery and psychological type. *Research in Psychological Type, 6,* 68–75.

Arain, A. A. (1968). Relationships among counseling clients' personalities, expectations, and problems (Doctoral dissertation, Rutgers University, 1967). *Dissertation Abstracts International, 29,* 4903A–4904A. (University Microfilms No. 68–8640)

Barberousse, E. M. (1975). Humanities Pilot Program at Walt Whitman High School in School Session 1969–70. Data prepared for First National Conference on the Uses of the Myers-Briggs Type Indicator, Gainesville, FL.

Beck, F. S. (1973). Affective sensitivity of counselor supervisors as a dimension of growth in their trainee groups (Doctoral dissertation, University of Southern California, 1972). *Dissertation Abstracts International, 33,* 3277A. (University Microfilms No. 73-720)

Belnap, D. D. (1973). *A study of the personality types of artistically talented students*. Unpublished master's thesis, Wake Forest University, Winston-Salem, NC.

Bissiri, G. R. (1971). Adolescent negativism, field-independence and the development of integrated structures (Doctoral dissertation, Claremont University, 1971). *Dissertation Abstracts International, 32,* 2981B. (University Microfilms No. 71-29, 635)

Block, J. (1978). *The Q-Sort Method.* Palo Alto, CA: Consulting Psychologists Press.

Bourg, B. J. (1979). *A study of the academic success of college freshmen in terms of Jungian psychological type.* Louisiana State University and Agricultural and Mechanical College, Shreveport.

Bourg, B. J. (1982). [Type distributions of Nicholls State University freshmen 1979–1982.] Unpublished raw data.

Bown, O. H., & Richek, H. G. (1967). The Bown Self-Report Inventory: A quick screening instrument for mental health professionals. *Comprehensive Psychiatry, 8,* 45–52.

Bradway, K. (1964). Jung's psychological types: Classification by test versus classification by self. *Journal of Analytical Psychology, 9,* 129-135.

Braun, J. A. (1971). The empathic ability of psychotherapists as related to therapist perceptual flexibility and professional experience, patient insight, and therapist-patient similarity (Doctoral dissertation, Fordham University). *Dissertation Abstracts International, 32,* 2391B. (University Microfilms No. 71-26, 956)

Brooks, F. R., & Johnson, R. W. (1979). Self-descriptive adjectives associated with a Jungian personality inventory. *Psychological Reports, 44* (3, pt. 1), 747–750.

Brown, W. F., & Holtzman, W. H. (1956). *Brown-Holtzman Survey of Study Habits and Attitudes.* New York: The Psychological Corporation.

Bruhn, J. G., Bunce, H., & Greaser, R. C. (1978). Predictors of academic performance among physician assistants. *The P. A. Journal, 8* (3), 181–187.

Budner, S. (1962). Intolerance of ambiguity as a personality variable. *Journal of Personality, 30,* 29–50.

Burt, M. A. (1981). *Counselor response time utilization within the counseling session as a correlate of counselor effectiveness and personality.* Unpublished doctoral dissertation, University of Florida, Gainesville, FL.

Burt, R. B. (1968). An exploratory study of personality manifestations in paintings. (Doctoral dissertation, Duke University, 1968). *Dissertation Abstracts International, 29,* 1493B. (University Microfilms No. 68-14, 298)

Bush, M. (1968). A study of reality-closeness, reality-distance: A directional study of attention deployment (Doctoral dissertation, University of Michigan, 1968). *Dissertation Abstracts International, 29,* 1168B. (University Microfilms No. 68-13, 290)

Cacioppe, R. L. (1980). [Type distributions of Australian samples.] Unpublished raw data.

Camiscioni, J. S. (1974, November). The prediction of academic and clinical competence. In M. H. McCaulley (Chair), *The Myers-Briggs Type Indicator in Medical Education and Practice.* Symposium conducted at the annual meeting of the Association of American Medical Colleges, Chicago.

Campbell, D. P. (1977). *Manual for the SVIB-SCII Strong-Campbell Interest Inventory* (2nd ed.). Stanford, CA: Stanford University Press.

Campbell, D. P., & Hansen, J.C. (1981). *Manual for the SVIB-SCII Strong-Campbell Interest Inventory* (3rd ed.). Stanford, CA: Stanford University Press.

Carlson, R. (1980). Studies of Jungian typology: II. Representations of the personal world. *Journal of Personality and Social Psychology, 38* (5), 801–810.

Carlson, R., & Levy, N. (1973). Studies in Jungian Typology: I. Memory, social perception and social action. *Journal of Personality, 41* (4), 559–576.

Carlyn, M. (1975, October). *A comparison of two methods of assessing a subject's dominant process.* Paper presented at the First National Conference on the Myers-Briggs Type Indicator, Gainesville, FL.

Carlyn, M. (1976). The relationship between Myers-Briggs personality characteristics and teaching preferences of prospective teachers (Doctoral dissertation, Michigan State University, 1976). *Dissertation Abstracts International, 37,* 3493A. (University Microfilms No. 76-27, 081)

Carlyn, M. (1977). An assessment of the Myers-Briggs Type Indicator. *Journal of Personality Assessment, 41* (5), 461–473.

Carskadon, T. G. (1975). Myers-Briggs Type Indicator characterizations: A Jungian horoscope? *Research in Psychological Type, 1,* 88–89. (Reprinted in Volume 5, 87–88).

Carskadon, T. G. (1977). Test-retest reliabilities of continuous scores on the Myers-Briggs Type Indicator. *Psychological Reports, 41,* 1011–1012.

Carskadon, T. G. (1978). Uses of the Myers-Briggs Type Indicator in psychology courses and discussion groups. *Teaching of Psychology, 5* (3), 140–142.

Carskadon, T. G. (1979a). Clinical and counseling aspects of the Myers-Briggs Type Indicator: A research review. *Research in Psychological Type, 2,* 2–31.

Carskadon, T. G. (1979b). Behavioral differences between extraverts and introverts as measured by the Myers-Briggs Type Indicator: An experimental demonstration. *Research in Psychological Type, 2,* 78–82.

Carskadon, T. G. (1979c). Test-retest reliabilities of continuous scores on Form G of the Myers-Briggs Type Indicator. *Research in Psychological Type, 2,* 83–84.

Carskadon, T. G. (1982). Sex differences in test-retest reliabilities on Form G of the Myers-Briggs Type Indicator. *Research in Psychological Type, 5,* 78–79.

Carskadon, T. G., and Cook, D. D. (1982). Validity of MBTI type descriptions as perceived by recipients unfamiliar with type. *Research in Psychological Type, 5,* 89–94.

Casas, E., & Hamlet, J. (1984). *Les Types Psychologiques des Clients, des Etudiants-Conseillers et des Superviseurs dans un Centre d'Entrainement Clinique: Etude sur la Compatibility Client-Conseiller et l'Apprentissage de la Therapie* [Psychological Types of Clients, Student-Counselors and Supervisors in a Clinical Training Center: Study of Client-Counselor Compatibility and Therapy Internship]. Interim Report, CRSHC, Subvention No. 410 834 0428, University of Ottawa, Canada.

Cattell, R. B., Eber, H. W., & Tatsuoka, M. M. (1970). *Handbook for the Sixteen Personality Factor Questionnaire (16 PF).* Champaign, IL: Institute for Personality and Ability Testing.

Center for Applications of Psychological Type, Inc. (1985). *Atlas of Type Tables.* Gainesville, FL: Center for Applications of Psychological Type, Inc.

Center for Applications of Psychological Type, Inc. (1985). *Bibliography: The Myers-Briggs Type Indicator.* Gainesville, FL: Center for Applications of Psychological Type, Inc.

Chaille, C. M. (1982). The relationship of personality type to unacceptable student behavior (Doctoral dissertation, George Peabody College for Teachers). *Dissertation Abstracts International, 43/06,* 1917A.

Child, I. L. (1965). Personality correlates of aesthetic judgment in college students. *Journal of Personality, 33,* 476–511.

Coan, R. W. (1979). *Psychologists: Personal and Theoretical Pathways.* New York: Irvington Publishers, Inc.

Cohen, D., Cohen, M., & Cross, H. (1981). A construct validity study of the Myers-Briggs Type Indicator. *Educational and Psychological Measurement, 41* (3), 883–891.

Comrey, A. L. (1970). *Manual for the Comrey Personality Scales.* San Diego, CA: Educational and Industrial Testing Service.

Comrey, A. L. (1983). An evaluation of the Myers-Briggs Type Indicator. *Academic Psychology Bulletin, 5,* 115–129.

Conary, F. M. (1965). An investigation of the variability of behavioral response of Jungian psychological types to select educational variables (Doctoral dissertation, Auburn University, 1965). *Dissertation Abstracts International, 26,* 5222. (University Microfilms No. 82-06, 181)

Cooper, J., & Scalise, C. J. (1974). Dissonance produced by deviations from life styles: The interaction of Jungian typology and conformity. *Journal of Personality and Social Psychology, 19* (4), 566-571.

Cropley, A. J. (1965). *Originality, personality and intelligence.* Unpublished doctoral dissertation, University of Alberta.

Dahlstrom, W. G., & Welsh, G. S. (1972). *An MMPI Handbook.* Minneapolis, MN: University of Minnesota Press.

Davis, F. B., & Davis, C. C. (1962). *Davis Reading Test: Manual.* New York: The Psychological Corporation.

Davis, M. F. (1978). *An investigation of the reliability and validity of the Gray-Wheelwright Jungian Type Survey.* Unpublished paper, Master of Arts Program, University of Minnesota.

Demarest (1975). [Type distributions of Hope College freshmen for classes entering 1973–1975]. Unpublished raw data.

Demarest (1979). [Type distributions of Adrian College freshmen for classes entering 1979]. Unpublished raw data.

DeNovellis, R., & Lawrence, G. (1983). Correlates of teacher personality variables (Myers-Briggs) and classroom observation data. *Research in Psychological Type, 6,* 37–46.

Desbiens, B., Peters, L., & Wigle, M. (1977). [Supplementary data from the final report on the Demographic Study of St. Clair College of Applied Arts and Technology, Windsor, Ontario.] Unpublished raw data.

Dietl, J. A. (1980). A study reflecting the dominant personality style most successful in exemplifying effective situational leadership within a corporate organization (Doctoral dissertation, United States International University). *Dissertation Abstracts International, 42,* (10), 4509A.

DiTiberio, J. K. (1977). The strength of sensing-intuition preference on the Myers-Briggs Type Indicator as related to empathic discrimination of overt or covert feeling messages of others (Doctoral dissertation, Michigan State University, 1976). *Dissertation Abstracts International, 37,* 5599A. (University Microfilms No. 77-5789)

Doering, R. D. (1972). New dimensions for staff talents: Enlarging scientific task team creativity. *Personnel, 49* (02), 43–52.

Duch, R. G. (1980). *The inservice preparation for Catholic secondary school principals for a leadership role in local staff development.* Unpublished doctoral dissertation, University of Pittsburgh.

Duch, R. G. (1982). Introducing type theory into a school system. In G. D. Lawrence (Ed.), *People types and tiger stripes* (pp. 87–93).

Dunning, J. E. (1971). Values and humanities study: An operational analysis of the humanities using the Myers-Briggs Type Indicator (Doctoral dissertation, Claremont Graduate School and University Center, 1970). *Dissertation Abstracts International, 32,* 785A. (University Microfilms No. 71-21, 639)

Early, L. A. (1983). A study of student characteristics, academic achievement, and residency selection of students in an independent study program compared to students in a lecture discussion program in medical school (Doctoral dissertation, Ohio State University). *Dissertation Abstracts International, 44* (1) 102B.

Edmunds, M. (1982). Jungian personality type and imagery ability within a holistic health context (Doctoral dissertation, Pennsylvania State University). *Dissertation Abstracts International, 43* (3), 868B.

Edwards, A. L. (1954). *Manual for the EPPS.* New York: The Psychological Corporation.

Eggins, J. A. (1979). *The interaction between structure in learning materials and the personality type of learners.* Unpublished doctoral dissertation, Indiana University.

Elliott, G. V. (1975). A descriptive study of characteristics and personality types of counselors of runaway youth (Doctoral dissertation, University of Maryland, 1975). *Dissertation Abstracts International, 36,* 3119B–3120B. (University Microfilms No. 75-28, 741)

Ellsworth, R. B. (1981). *Profile of Adaptation to Life—Holistic Scale Manual.* Palo Alto, CA: Consulting Psychologists Press.

Emanual, G. V. (1972). Affective sensitivity (empathy) as a function of therapist experience level, personality type, and client cue source (Doctoral dissertation, Southern Illinois University, Carbondale, IL). *Dissertation Abstracts International, 33,* 2342B. (University Microfilms No. 72-28, 535)

Erickson, C., Gantz, B. S., & Stephenson, R. W. (1970). Logical and construct validation of a short-form biographical inventory predictor of scientific creativity. *Proceedings of the 78th Annual Convention of the American Psychological Association, 5* (1), 151–152.

Erickson, L. (1982). [Parks College data.] Unpublished raw data.

Evans, L. N. (1976). A psycho-temporal theory of personality: A study of the relationship between temporal orientation, affect, and personality type (Doctoral dissertation, United States International University, 1976). *Dissertation Abstracts International, 37,* 1875B. (University Microfilms No. 76-22, 381)

Evered, R. D. (1973). Conceptualizing the future: Implications for strategic management in a turbulent environment (Doctoral dissertation, University of California, 1973). *Dissertation Abstracts International, 34,* 3625A–3626A. (University Microfilms No. 73-32, 663)

Evered, R. D. (1977). Organizational activism and its relation to "reality" and mental imagery. *Human Relations, 30* (4), 311–334.

Eysenck, H. J., & Eysenck, S. B. G. (1968). *Eysenck Personality Inventory.* San Diego, CA: Educational and Industrial Testing Service.

Fierstein, R. F., & Goering, J. (1985). *A descriptive study of psychological type preferences among upper-division students at the University of Maryland.* (Unpublished manuscript).

Frederick, A. H. (1975). Self-actualization and personality type: A comparative study of doctoral majors in educational administration and the helping relations (Doctoral dissertation, University of Alabama, 1974). *Dissertation Abstracts International, 35,* 7055A–7056A. (University Microfilms No. 75-9896)

Fretz, B. R., & Schmidt, L. D. (1966). Effects of teacher-student similarity in an educational skills program (Abstract). *Proceedings of the 74th Annual Convention of the American Psychological Association, 1,* 271–272.

Fretz, B. R., & Schmidt, L. D. (1967). Comparison of improvers and nonimprovers in an educational skills course. *Journal of Counseling Psychology, 14,* 175–176.

Fricke, B. G. (1963). *OAIS handbook* (preliminary edition). Ann Arbor, MI: OAIS Testing Program.

Galvin, M. D. (1976). Facilitative conditions and psychological type in intake interviews by professionals and paraprofessionals (Doctoral dissertation, University of Florida, 1975). *Dissertation Abstracts International, 36,* 6378B. (University Microfilms No. 76-12, 078)

Gaster, W. D. (1982). A study of personality type as a predictor of success in retail store management (Doctoral dissertation, Louisiana Technical University). *Dissertation Abstracts International, 43,* (12), 4020A.

Gerhardt, R. (1983). Liberal religion and personality type. *Research in Psychological Type, 6,* 47–53.

Golanty-Koel, R. (1978). The relationship of psychological types and mass media preferences to the values of non-academic high school students. (Doctoral dissertation, University of California, Berkeley). *Dissertation Abstracts International, 38,* 4683A. (University Microfilms No. 73-29, 395)

Golliday, J. M. (1975). An investigation of the relative effectiveness of three methods of utilizing laboratory activities in selected topics of junior college mathematics (Doctoral dissertation, University of Florida, 1974). *Dissertation Abstracts International, 36* (02), 611A. (University Microfilms No. 75-16, 383)

Gough, H. G. (1965). Conceptual analysis of psychological test scores and other diagnostic variables. *Journal of Abnormal Psychology, 70,* 294–302.

Gough, H. G. (1975). *Manual for the California Psychological Inventory*. Palo Alto, CA: Consulting Psychologists Press.

Gough, H. G. (1976). Studying creativity by means of word association tests. *Journal of Applied Psychology, 61,* 348–353.

Gough, H. G. (1981, July). *Studies of the Myers-Briggs Type Indicator in a personality assessment research institute*. Paper presented at the Fourth National Conference on the Myers-Briggs Type Indicator, Stanford University, CA.

Gough, H. G., & Heilbrun, A. B. (1983). *The Adjective Check List Manual*. Palo Alto, CA: Consulting Psychologists Press.

Grant, W. H. (1965a). *Behavior of MBTI Types (Research report)*. Auburn, AL: Auburn University, Student Counseling Service. [Available from the Center for Applications of Psychological Type, Gainesville FL]

Grant, W. H. (1965b). *Comparability of the Gray-Wheelwright Psychological Type Questionnaire and the Myers-Briggs Type Indicator*. Auburn, AL: Research Report, Student Counseling Service, Auburn University.

Grant, W. H. (1966a). *Personal problems of the Myers-Briggs types*. Auburn, AL: Research Report, Student Counseling Service, Auburn University.

Grant, W. H. (1966b). *Self-description by MBTI types on the Adjective Check List*. Auburn Unversity: Office of Student Development.

Grant, W. H., Thompson, M., & Clark, T. (1983). *From image to likeness: A Jungian path in the Gospel journey*. Ramsey, NJ: Paulist Press.

Gryskiewicz, S. S., & Vaught, R. S. (1975, October). *Describing the creative leader*. Paper presented at the First National Conference on the Uses of the Myers-Briggs Type Indicator, Gainesville, FL.

Gryskiewicz, S. S. (1982, January). *Creative leadership development and the Kirton Adaption-Innovation Inventory*. Paper delivered at the 1982 Occupational Psychology Conference of the British Psychological Society: "Breaking Set: New Directions in Occupational Psychology."

Guilford, J. & Fructer (1973). *Manual for the Guildford-Zimmerman Temperament Survey*. Beverly Hills, CA: Sheridan Psychological Services.

Guttinger, H. I. (1974). *Patterns of perceiving: Factors which affect individualized reading instruction at the high school level*. Paper presented at the meeting of the American Education Research Association, Chicago.

Guttinger, H. I., & McCaulley, M. H. (1975). [MBTI preferences of University of Florida Laboratory School students: Supplementary analyses.] Unpublished raw data.

Haber, R. A. (1980). Different strokes for different folks: Jung's typology and structured experiences. *Group and Organizational Studies, 5,* 113–119.

Hall, W. B., & MacKinnon, D. W. (1969). Personality inventory correlates of creativity among architects. *Journal of Applied Psychology, 53* (4), 322–326.

Harbaugh, G. L. (1984a). [The admission and training of seminary students.] Unpublished raw data.

Harbaugh, G. L. (1984b). *(W)holistic scales.* (Available from Gary L. Harbaugh, Ph.D., Trinity Lutheran Seminary. 2199 East Main Street, Columbus, OH 43209)

Harris, C. M. (1981). [Test-retest reliabilities of medical students at St. Mary's Hospital Medical School.] Unpublished raw data.

Harris, D. L., Kelley, K., & Coleman, M. (1984). The stability of personality types and their usefulness in medical student career guidance. *Family Medicine, XIV* (6) 203–205.

Harrison, D. F. (1984). *The temporal dimensions of Jung's psychological typology: Testing an instructional theory of future studies with middle school students.* Unpublished doctoral dissertation, University of Florida, Gainesville, FL.

Hay, J. E. (1964). The relationship of certain personality variables to managerial level and job performance among engineering managers (Doctoral dissertation, Temple University, 1964). *Dissertation Abstracts International, 25,* 3973. (University Microfilms No. 64-13, 684)

Heist, P.A., McConnell, T. R., Webster, H., & Yonge, G. D. (1963). *Omnibus Personality Inventory.* New York: The Psychological Corporation.

Held, J. S., & Yokomoto, C. F. (1983). Technical report writing: Effects of personality differences in learning. *Proceedings of Annual Conference of American Society of Engineering Education.*

Helson, R. (1965). Childhood interest clusters related to creativity in women. *Journal of Consulting Psychology, 29* (4), 352–361.

Helson, R. (1968). Effect of sibling characteristics and parental values on creative interest and achievement. *Journal of Personality, 36* (4), 589–607.

Helson, R. (1971). Women mathematicians and the creative personality. *Journal of Consulting and Clinical Psychology, 36* (2), 210–220.

Helson, R. (1975, October). *Studying typological patterns in "real" contexts: Research styles in women mathematicians.* Paper presented at First National Conference on the Uses of the Myers-Briggs Type Indicator, Gainesville, FL.

Helson, R., & Crutchfield, R. S. (1970). Creative types in mathematics. *Journal of Personality, 38* (2), 177–197.

Henderson, B. B. N. (1984). *Music major matriculants in North Carolina colleges and universities: Their personality types as measured by the Myers-Briggs Type Indicator.* Unpublished doctoral dissertation, University of North Carolina at Greensboro.

Hicks, E. (1984) Conceptual and empirical analysis of some assumptions of an explicitly typological theory. *Journal of Personality and Social Psychology, 46* (5), 1118–1131.

Hirsh, S. K. (1985). *Using the Myers-Briggs Type Indicator in organizations: A resource book.* Palo Alto, CA: Consulting Psychologists Press.

Hoffman, J. L., & Betkouski, M. (1981). A summary of Myers-Briggs Type Indicator research applications in education. *Research in Psychological Type, 3,* 3–41.

Hoffman, J. L., Waters, K., & Berry, M. (1981). Personality types and computer assisted instruction in a self-paced technical training environment. *Research in Psychological Type, 3,* 81–85.

Holland, J. L. (1978). *Vocational Preference Inventory: Manual.* Palo Alto, CA: Consulting Psychologists Press.

Howes, R. J. (1977). *Reliability of the Myers-Briggs Type Indicator as a function of mood manipulation.* Unpublished master's thesis, Mississippi State University.

Howland, A. (1971). *Personal constructs and psychological types.* Unpublished master's thesis, University of Florida, Gainesville.

Hoy, F., & Hellriegel, D. (1982). The Kilmann and Herden model of organizational effectiveness criteria for small business managers. *Academy of Management Journal, 25* (2), 308–322.

Hulbert, J. C. (1975, October). A comparison of the frequency of types in six different community college art classes based on 301 samplings. Data prepared for the First National Conference on the Uses of the Myers-Briggs Type Indicator, Gainesville, FL.

Ieland, M. S., & Kernan-Schloss, L. (1983). Pattern analysis of recorded daydreams, memories, and personality type. *Perceptual and Motor Skills, 56* (1), 119–125.

Jaffe, J. M. (1980). The relationship of Jungian psychological predispositions to the implementation of management by objectives: A sociotechnical perspective (Doctoral dissertation, University of Southern California). *Dissertation Abstracts International, 41* (11), 4833A.

Jensen, G. H., & DiTiberio, J. K. (1984). Personality and individual writing processes. *College Composition and Communication, 35* (3), 285–300.

Jones, J. H., & Sherman, R. G. (1979). Clinical uses of the Myers-Briggs Type Indicator. *Research in Psychological Type, 2,* 32–45.

Jung, C. G. (1971). *Psychological types* (H. G. Baynes, Trans. revised by R. F. C. Hull). Volume 6 of *The collected works of C. G. Jung.* Princeton, NJ: Princeton University Press. (Original work published in 1921.)

Kainz, R. I. (1976). *A comparison of the Myers-Briggs Type Indicator and the Vocational Preference Inventory in 405 high school seniors.* Unpublished paper.

Kainz, R. I. (1978). *An investigation of response style in the Myers-Briggs Type Indicator, a Jungian typology inventory.* Unpublished manuscript.

Kainz, R. I., & McCaulley, M. H. (1975). [Type differences in selection to medical school]. Unpublished raw data.

Kainz, R. I., & Morgan, M. K. (1975). [Supplementary data from the high school project of academic and career data.] Unpublished raw data.

Kaiser, K. M. (1981). Use of the first 50 items as a surrogate measure of the Myers-Briggs Type Indicator Form G. *Research in Psychological Type, 4,* 55–61.

Kauppi, R. J. (1982). Jungian type and field-dependence-independence as related to the career orientations of high-achieving college students (Doctoral dissertation, University of Maryland). *Dissertation Abstracts International, 42* (8), 3427-B. (University Microfilms No. 8202847)

Keirsey, D., & Bates, M. (1978). *Please understand me: Character and temperament types* (3rd ed.). Del Mar, CA: Prometheus Nemesis Books.

Kelley., K., & Harris, D. L. (1981, November). *Medical student personality changes from freshmen to seniors.* Paper presented at Annual Conference of Association of American Medical Colleges, Washington, D. C.

Kelly, G. A. (1955). *The psychology of personal constructs.* New York: Norton.

Kilmann, R. H., & Taylor, V. (1974). A contingency approach to laboratory learning: Psychological types versus experimental norms. *Human Relations, 27* (9), 891–909.

Kirk, J. S. (1972). The relationship of personality type to choice of academic major in seminary education (Doctoral dissertation, Boston University, 1972). *Dissertation Abstracts International,* 1065A. (University Microfilms No. 72-75, 294)

Kirton, M. J. (1976). Adaptors and innovators: A description and measure. *Journal of Applied Psychology, 61,* 622–629.

Klein, K. C. D. (1975). Housing style preferences and personality (Doctoral dissertation, Illinois Institute of Technology, 1975). *Dissertation Abstracts International, 36,* 6539B. (University Microfilms No. 76-13, 162)

Knapp, R. H. (1962). *Manual: Maudsley Personality Inventory.* San Diego, CA: Educational and Industrial Testing Service.

Knapp, R. H. (1964). An experimental study of a triadic hypothesis concerning the sources of aesthetic imagery. *Journal of Projective Techniques and Personality Assessment, 28,* 49–54.

Knapp, R. H., & Lapuc, P. S. (1965). Time imagery, introversion and fantasied preoccupations in simulated isolation. *Perceptual and Motor Skills, 20,* 327–330.

Knapp, R. H., & Wulff, A. (1963). Preferences for abstract and representational art. *Journal of Social Psychology, 60,* 255–262.

Kolb, D. A. (1976). *Learning Style Inventory: Technical manual.* Boston: McBer and Company.

Kosinar, W. C. (1955). *Science Research Temperament Scale.* Munster, IN: Psychometric Affiliates.

Kramer, H. W. (1977). The relationship between personality type and achievement in expository and creative writing (Doctoral dissertation, The University of Michigan, 1977). *Dissertation Abstracts International, 38,* 3384A. (University Microfilms No. 77-26, 283)

Krapu, T. M. (1981). Extraversion, introversion and anxiety in relation to affiliation in college students (Doctoral dissertation, University of North Dakota, Grand Forks). *Dissertation Abstracts International, 42,* (04), 1551A.

Kuder, G. F. (1968). *Kuder Occupational Interest Survey: Manual.* Chicago: Science Research Associates, Inc.

Lacy, O. W. (1984). [Myers-Briggs Type Indicator and Strong-Campbell Interest Inventory]. Unpublished raw data.

Laney, A. R. (1949). *Occupational implications of the Jungian personality function-types as identified by the Myers-Briggs Type Indicator.* Unpublished master's thesis, George Washington University.

Lawler, N. K. (1984). *The imposter phenomenon in high achieving persons and Jungian personality variables.* Unpublished doctoral dissertation, Georgia State University, Atlanta.

Lawrence, G. D. (1982). *People types and tiger stripes* (2nd ed.). Gainesville, FL: Center for Applications of Psychological Type.

Lawrence, G. D. (1984). A synthesis of learning style research involving the MBTI. *Journal of Psychological Type, 8,* 2–15.

Lawrence, P. R., & Lorsch, J. W. (1967). *Organization and management.* Boston: Graduate School of Business Administration, Harvard University.

Leafgren, F., & Kolstad, D. (1984). [Type distribution of entering students at the University of Wisconsin at Stevens Point.] Unpublished raw data.

Lepes, N. L. (1983). Time estimation and individual differences in junior high school students (Doctoral dissertation, Fordham University). *Dissertation Abstracts International, 43,* (12), 3849A.

Levell, J. P. (1965). Secondary school counselors: A study of differentiating characteristics (Doctoral dissertation, University of Oregon, 1965). *Dissertation Abstracts International, 26,* 4452. (University Microfilms No. 65-12, 227)

Levin, L. S. (1978). Jungian personality variables of psychotherapists of five different theoretical orientations (Doctoral dissertation, Georgia State University, 1978). *Dissertation Abstracts International, 39* 4042B–4043B. (University Microfilms No. 79-01, 823)

Levy, N., Murphy, C., Jr., & Carlson, R. (1972), Personality types among negro college students. *Educational and Psychological Measurement, 32,* 641–653.

Lindner, B. J. (1972). Patterning of psychological type, interpersonal understanding, and marital happiness (Doctoral dissertation, University of Florida, 1972). *Dissertation Abstracts International, 34,* 417B. (University Microfilms No. 73-15, 517)

Lueder, D. C. (1984). *Principals' personalities and problem-solving strategies.* Unpublished manuscript, Peabody College, Vanderbilt University, Nashville, TN.

Macdaid, G. P. (1984a). Recommended uses of the abbreviated version (Form AV) of the Myers-Briggs Type Indicator and comparisons with Form G. *Journal of Psychological Type, 7,* 49–55.

Macdaid, G. P. (1984b). *Types of volunteer phone counselors in a crisis center.* (Unpublished paper.)

Macdaid, G. P., Kainz, R. I., & McCaulley, M. H. (1984). *The University of Florida Longitudinal Study: Ten-year followup.* (Unpublished paper.)

MacKinnon, D. W. (1960). The highly effective individual. *Teachers College Record, 61,* 367–378.

MacKinnon, D. W. (1962a). The nature and nurture of creative talent. *American Psychologist, 17,* 484–495.

MacKinnon, D. W. (1962b). The personality correlates of creativity: A study of American architects. In G. S. Nielsen (Ed.), *Personality Research, Proceedings of the XIV International Congress of Applied Psychology, 2,* 11–39. Copenhagen, 1961, Copenhagen: Munksgaard Ltd.

MacKinnon, D. W. (1965). Personality and the realization of creative potential. *American Psychologist, 20,* 273–281.

MacKinnon, D. W. (1971). Creativity and the transliminal experience. *The Journal of Creative Behavior, 5* (4), 227–241.

Madison, P., Wilder, D. H., & Studdiford, W. B. (1963). The Myers-Briggs Type Indicator in academic counseling (Statistical Unit Research Report No. 13). Princeton, NJ: Princeton University, Counseling Service.

Mann, H., Siegler, M., & Osmond, H. (1968). The many worlds of time. *Journal of Analytical Psychology, 13* (1), 33–56.

Marcus, S. K. (1976). Jungian typology and time orientation (Doctoral dissertation, United States International University, 1976). *Dissertation Abstracts International, 37(03),* 1409B. (University Microfilms No. 76-19, 756)

Margerison, C., & Lewis, R. (1981). Mapping managerial styles. *International Journal of Manpower, 2,* 1–24.

Marshall, N.J. (1971). Orientations toward privacy: Environmental and personality components (Doctoral dissertation, University of California, 1970). *Dissertation Abstracts International, 31,* 4315B. (University Microfilms No. 71-815)

May, D. C. (1971). *An investigation of the relationship between selected personality characteristics of eighth-grade students and their achievement in mathematics.* Doctoral dissertation, University of Florida. (University Microfilms No. 72-21, 080)

McCarley, N. G., & Carskadon, T. G. (1983). Test-retest

reliabilities of scales and subscales of the Myers-Briggs Type Indicator and of criteria for clinical interpretive hypotheses involving them. *Research in Psychological Type, 6,* 24–36.

McCary, P. W. (1970). The effects of small self-understanding groups on the self-concept and anxiety level when group composition has been varied (Doctoral dissertation, University of Michigan, 1970). *Dissertation Abstracts International, 31,* 2112A. (University Microfilms No. 70-20, 491)

McCaulley, M. H. (1973). *Myers-Briggs Type Indicator applications.* Report of Committee 13, Counseling Study. Gainesville, FL: University of Florida, Department of Clinical Psychology.

McCaulley, M. H. (1974). [MBTI types of students in remedial programs at the University of Florida]. Unpublished raw data.

McCaulley, M. H. (1977). *The Myers Longitudinal Medical Study* (Monograph II). Gainesville, FL: Center for Applications of Psychological Type Inc.

McCaulley, M. H. (1978). *Application of the Myers-Briggs Type Indicator to medicine and other health professions* (Monograph I). Gainesville, FL: Center for Applications of Psychological Type.

McCaulley, M. H. (1981). Jung's theory of psychological types and the Myers-Briggs Type Indicator. In P. McReynolds, (Ed.), *Advances in Psychological Assessment (Volume V)* (pp. 294–352). San Francisco: Jossey Bass, Inc.

McCaulley, M. H. (1983, October). *Sample set of type tables* (2nd ed.). Gainesville, FL: Center for Applications of Psychological Type.

McCaulley, M. H., & Kainz, R. I. (1974). *The University of Florida Longitudinal Study: First follow-up.* Unpublished study.

McCaulley, M. H., & Kainz, R. I. (1976). [MBTI and achievement in a Florida middle school.] Unpublished raw data.

McCaulley, M. H., Kainz, R. I., Granade, J. G., & Harrisberger, L. (1983). *ASEE-MBTI Engineering Consortium: Report of the first three years.* Gainesville, FL: Center for Applications of Psychological Type.

McCaulley, M. H., Kainz, R. I., Macdaid, G. P., & Harrisberger, L. (1982). *ASEE-MBTI Engineering Consortium: Report of the first two years.* Gainesville, FL: Center for Applications of Psychological Type.

McCaulley, M. H., Macdaid, G. P., & Kainz, R. I. (1986). *Myers-Briggs Type Indicator atlas.* Gainesville, FL: Center for Applications of Psychological Type, Inc.

McCaulley, M. H., & Morgan, M. K. (1982). Health professionals: Characteristics and student self-assessment. In M. V. Boyles, M. K. Morgan, & M. H. McCaulley, (Eds.), *The Health Professions* (pp. 57–78). Philadelphia: W. B. Saunders.

McCaulley, M. H., & Natter, F. L. (1974). Psychological (Myers-Briggs) type differences in education. In F.L. Natter, & S.A. Rollin, (Eds.), *The Governor's Task Force on Disruptive Youth: Phase II Report.* Tallahassee, FL: Office of the Governor. [Report out of print. This chapter available from Center for Applications of Psychological Type, Gainesville, FL.]

Mendelsohn, G. A. (1966). Effects of client personality and client-counselor similarity on the duration of counseling: A replication and extension. *Journal of Counseling Psychology, 13* (2), 228–232.

Mendelsohn, G. A., & Geller, M. H. (1963). Effects of counselor-client similarity on the outcome of counseling. *Journal of Counseling Psychology, 10* (1), 71–77.

Mendelsohn, G. A., & Geller, M. H. (1965). Structure of client attitudes toward counseling and their relation to client-counselor similarity. *Journal of Consulting Psychology, 29* (1), 63–72.

Mendelsohn, G. A., & Geller, M. H. (1967). Similarity, missed sessions, and early termination. *Journal of Counseling Psychology, 14,* (3), 210–215.

Mendelsohn, G. A., & Kirk, B. A. (1962). Personality differences between students who do and do not use a counseling facility. *Journal of Counseling Psychology, 9,* (4), 341–346.

Miller, P. V. (1966). The contribution of non-cognitive variables to the prediction of student performance in law school (Doctoral dissertation, University of Pennsylvania, 1965). *Dissertation Abstracts, 27,* 1679A. (University Microfilms No. 66-4630)

Miller, P. V. (1967). *A follow-up study of personality factors as predictors of law student performance.* Unpublished report to the LSAT Council, 1966–1967. Princeton, NJ: Educational Testing Service.

Millott, R. (1974). *Reading performance as a correlate of the personality type of college freshmen.* Unpublished doctoral dissertation, University of Florida.

Mills, C. J. (1983, April). *Personality characteristics of gifted adolescents and their parents: Comparisons and implications for achievement and counseling.* Paper presented at the Annual Meeting of the American Educational Research Association, Montreal.

Mitchell, A. (1983). *The nine American lifestyles.* New York: Macmillan Publishing Company.

Mitchell, W. D. (1981). *A study of type and social climate in a large organization.* Unpublished manuscript.

Mitroff, I. I., & Kilmann, R. H. (1975). Stories managers tell: A new tool for organizational problem solving. *Management Review, 64* (7), 18–28.

Morgan, M. K. (1975). *The MBTI, Holland's VPI, the GATB, and other measures of academic aptitude.* Unpublished manuscript, University of Florida, College of Education.

Most, R. B. (1984). [A test-retest comparison of Form AV and Form G of the Myers-Briggs Type Indicator.] Unpublished raw data.

Myers, I. B. (1958). *Some findings with regard to type and manual for Myers-Briggs Type Indicator Form E* (preliminary edition). Unpublished manuscript.

Myers, I. B. (1962). *Manual: The Myers-Briggs Type Indicator.* Princeton, NJ: Educational Testing Service. [Distributed by Consulting Psychologists Press, Palo Alto, CA.]

Myers, I. B. (1973). *Retest reliability of the Type Indicator.* Unpublished manuscript.

Myers, I. B. (1993). *Introduction to Type* (5th ed.). Palo Alto, CA: Consulting Psychologists Press.

Myers, I. B. with Myers, P. B. (1980). *Gifts Differing.* Palo Alto, CA: Consulting Psychologists Press

Nechworth, J. A., & Carskadon, T. G. (1979). Experimental validation of an assumption underlying the clinical interpretation of discrepancies between Myers-Briggs Type Indicator scores computed separately from word-pair and phrased question items. *Research in Psychological Type, 2,* 56–59.

Nelson, M. J., & Denny, E. C. (1960). *The Nelson-Denny Reading Test.* Boston: Houghton Mifflin Co.

Newman, L. E. (1975). Counselor characteristics and training as related to the process of empathy and its manifestation (Doctoral dissertation, University of Florida, 1975). *Dissertation Abstracts International, 37,* 4138A–4139A. (University Microfilms No. 77-114)

Newman, L. E. (1979). Personality types of therapist and client and their use in counseling. *Research in Psychological Type, 2,* 46–55.

Nightingale, J. A. (1973). The relationship of Jungian type to death concern and time perspective (Doctoral dissertation, University of South Carolina, 1972). *Dissertation Abstracts International, 33,* 3956B. (University Microfilms No. 73-3609)

Nisbet, J. A., Ruble, V. E., & Schurr, K. T. (1981, March). *Myers-Briggs Type Indicator: A key to diagnosing learning styles and developing desirable learning behaviors in high risk college students.* Paper presented at 5th Annual National Conference on Remedial Developmental Studies in Post-Secondary Institutions, Dayton, OH.

Nisbet, J. A., Ruble, V. E., & Schurr, K. T. (1982). Predictors of academic success with high risk college students. *Journal of College Student Personnel, 23* (3), 227–235.

O'Haire, T. D., & Marcia, J. E. (1980). Some personality characteristics associated with Ananda Marga meditations: A pilot study. *Perceptual and Motor Skills, 51,* 447–452.

Ohnmacht, F. W. (1970). Personality and cognitive referents of creativity: A second look. *Psychological Reports, 26* (1), 336–338.

Ohsawa, T. (1975, October). *MBTI experiences in Japan: Career choice, selection, placement, and counseling for individual development.* Paper presented at the 1st National Conference on the Myers-Briggs Type Indicator, Gainesville, FL.

Ohsawa, T. (1981). *A profile of top executives of Japanese companies.* Paper presented at the 4th National Conference on the Myers-Briggs Type Indicator, Palo Alto, CA: Stanford University.

Osmond, H., Siegler, M., & Smoke, R. (1977). Typology revisited: A new perspective. *Psychological Perspectives, 8* (2), 206–219.

Otis, G. D. (1972). *Types of medical students.* (Contract 71-4066), USPHS, National Institutes of Health.

Owen, C. (1962). An investigation of creative potential at the junior high level. *Studies in Art Education, 3,* 16–22.

Page, E. C. (1983). *Looking at type.* Gainesville, FL: Center for Applications of Psychological Type.

Palmiere, L. (1972). Intro-extra-version as an organizing principle in fantasy production. *Journal of Analytical Psychology, 17* (2), 116–131.

Parham, M., Miller, D. I., & Carskadon, T. G. (1984). Do "job types" differ from "life types"?: The effects of standard vs. vocationally specific instructions on the reliability of MBTI scores. *Journal of Psychological Type, 7,* 46–48.

Perelman, S. G. (1978). A phenomenological investigation of the counselor's personal experience of his counseling practice and its relationship to specific constructs in Jungian analytical psychology (Doctoral dissertation, University of Pittsburgh, 1977). *Dissertation Abstracts International, 38,* 5258A. (University Microfilms No. 7801874)

Perry, H. W. (1975). Interrelationships among selected personality variables of psychologists and their professional orientation (Doctoral dissertation, Notre Dame University, 1974). *Dissertation Abstracts International, 35,* 6080B. (University Microfilms No. 75-13,100)

Peters, C. E. (1981). An investigation of the relationship between Jungian psychological type and preferred styles of inquiry (Doctoral dissertation, Ohio State University). *Dissertation Abstracts International, 44* (06), 1974B

Plutchik, R., & Kellerman, H. (1984). *The Emotions Profile Index: Manual.* Los Angeles, CA: Western Psychological Services.

Provost, J. (1984a). [Type distributions of freshmen students at Rollins College.] Unpublished raw data.

Provost, J. (1984b). *Applications of the Myers-Briggs Type Indicator in Counseling.* Gainesville, FL: Center for Applications of Psychological Type.

Quenk, N. L. (1966). Fantasy and personal outlook: A study of daydreaming as a function of optimism, pessimism, realism and anxiety (Doctoral dissertation, University of California, Berkeley). *Dissertation Abstracts International, 27,* 970B. (University Microfilms No. 66-8364)

Quenk, N. L. (1975). *Sources of physician satisfaction* (Report to Bureau of Health Manpower, Health Resources Administration, Contract No. 1-MI-24197). Albuquerque, NM: University of New Mexico, Longitudinal Study.

Quenk, N. L., & Albert, M. (1975). *A Taxonomy of physician work settings* (Health Resources Administration, Contract No. 1-MI-24197: Study Report #2). Albuquerque, NM: University of New Mexico, Longitudinal Study.

Reichard, D. J., & Uhl, N. P. (1979, October). *The use of the Myers-Briggs Type Indicator in institutional research.* Paper presented at the Annual Conference of the Southern Association for Institutional Research, Orlando, FL. [Supplementary data provided by the authors.]

Rezler, A. G., & Johns, C. (1975). *Data on University of Illinois College of Medicine Program for Independent Scholars.* Presented at Conference of the Myers-Briggs Type Indicator in Medical Education. University of Florida.

Rich, B. (1972). *A correlational study of the Myers-Briggs Type Indicator and the Jungian Type Survey.* Unpublished paper prepared for course in Jung at University of Minnesota.

Richek, H. G. (1969). Note on intercorrelation of scales of the Myers-Briggs Type Indicator. *Alberta Journal of Educational Research (Canada), 15* (3), 159–173.

Richek, H. G., & Bown, O. H. (1968). Phenomenological correlates of Jung's typology. *Journal of Analytical Psychology, 13* (1), 57–65.

Rioux, C. (1980). *Design preferences and architectural studio performance.* Unpublished manuscript.

Ritter, C. C. (1977, November). Types of university theater faculty and students. Data prepared for the Second National Conference on the Myers-Briggs Type Indicator, Michigan State University, East Lansing, MI.

Roberts, D. Y. (1982). Personality and media preferences of community college students. *Research in Psychological Type, 5,* 84–86.

Rokeach, M. (1960). *The Open and Closed Mind.* New York: Basic Books.

Ross, J. (1961). *Progress report on the College Student Characteristics Study: June 1961.* Research Memorandum 61-11. Princeton, NJ: Educational Testing Service.

Rossman, R. L. (1979, October). *MBTI types of music education students: Morningside College, Sioux City, IA.* Paper presented at the Third National Conference on the Myers-Briggs Type Indicator, Philadelphia, PA.

Rotter, J. B. (1966). Generalized expectancies for internal versus external control of reinforcement. *Psychological Monographs, 80,* (1) (Whole No. 609).

Ruane, F. V. (1973). An investigation of the relationship of response modes in the perception of paintings to selected variables (Doctoral dissertation, Pennsylvania State University, 1973). *Dissertation Abstracts International, 34,* 5031A. (University Microfilms No. 74-4285)

Ruppart, R. (1985). *Psychological types and occupational choices among religious professionals: A psychosocial, historical perspective.* Doctoral dissertation, New York University, New York City.

Sachs, L. (1978). [Entering Resources Questionnaire data for Ohio State University medical students.] Unpublished raw data.

Saunders, D. R. (1955). *Some preliminary interpretive material for the PRI.* Research Memorandum RR-15. Princeton, NJ: Educational Testing Service.

Schilling, K. L. (1972). *Myers-Briggs Type Indicator and the helping person.* Unpublished master's thesis, University of Florida, Gainesville, FL.

Schmidt, L., & Fretz, B. R. (1965, September). *The effects of teacher-student similarity in an educational skill course* (USOE Cooperative Research Project No. S-217). Columbus, OH: Ohio State University.

Schroeder, C. C. (1976). New strategies for structuring residential environments. *The Journal of College Student Personnel, 17* (5), 386–390.

Schroeder, C. C. (1979). Designing ideal staff environments through milieu management. *The Journal of College Student Personnel, 19,* 129–135.

Schroeder, C. C. (1984). [Type distributions of St. Louis University freshmen.] Unpublished raw data.

Schroeder, C. C., & Jenkins, J. B. (1981). [Type distributions of Mercer University freshmen.] Unpublished raw data.

Schroeder, C. C., Warner, R., & Malone, D. R. (1980). Effects of assignment to living units by personality types on environmental perceptions and student development. *The Journal of College Student Personnel, 21* (5), 443–449.

Schutz, W. (1978). *FIRO Awareness Scales manual.* Palo Alto, CA: Consulting Psychologists Press.

Seiden, H. M. (1970). Time perspective and styles of consciousness (Doctoral dissertation, New School for Social Research, 1969). *Dissertation Abstracts International, 31,* 386B (University Microfilms No. 70-11, 275)

Shapiro, K. J., & Alexander, I. E. (1969). Extraversion-introversion, affiliation and anxiety. *Journal of Personality, 37* (3), 387–406.

Sherman, R. (1982). Psychological typology and satisfactions in intimate relationships (Doctoral dissertation, Humanistic Psychology Institute, 1981). *Dissertation Abstracts International, 42,* (05), 2084B.

Sherman, R. G. (1981). Typology and problems in intimate relationships. *Research in Psychological Type, 4,* 4–23.

Simon, R. S. (1979). *Jungian types and creativity of professional fine artists.* Unpublished doctoral dissertation, United States International University, 1979.

Smith, A., Irey, R., & McCaulley, M. H. (1973). Self-paced instruction and college student's personality. *Engineering Education, 63* (6), 435–440.

Smith, N. P. (1976). The influence of structural information characteristics of Jungian personality type on time horizons in decision–making (Doctoral dissertation, University of California, 1976). *Dissertation Abstracts International, 37,* 2297A–2298A. (University Microfilms No. 76-22, 715)

Spielberger, C. D. (1983). *Manual for the State-Trait Anxiety Inventory (Form Y).* Palo Alto, CA: Consulting Psychologists Press.

Squyres, E. M. (1980). *Time orientation and Jung's concept of psychological wholeness.* Unpublished master's thesis, Georgia State University.

Stalcup, D. L. (1968). An investigation of the personality of students who do participate and those who do not participate in campus activities (Doctoral dissertation, Auburn University). *Dissertation Abstracts International, 28,* 4452A. (University Microfilms No. 72-33, 131)

Stein, M. I. (1966). *Volunteers for peace.* New York: Wiley.

Stein, M. I. (1972, November). *Notes on two studies involving the Myers-Briggs Type Indicator and the Stein Self-Description Questionnaire.* Paper presented at invitational workshop on the Uses of Type Concepts in Medical Education at the meeting of the Association of American Medical Colleges, Miami Beach, FL.

Stephens, W. B. (1973). Relationship between selected personality characteristics of senior art students and their area of art study (Doctoral dissertation, University of Florida, 1972). *Dissertation Abstracts International, 34,* 149A. (University Microfilms No. 75-15, 599)

Stephens, W. B. (1975, April). *University art department and academies of art: The relation of artists' psychological types to their specialties and interests.* Paper presented at the National Art Education Association Conference, Miami, FL.

Steele, F. I. (1968). Personality and the "laboratory style". *Journal of Applied Behavioral Science, 4,* 25–45.

Story, G. (1984). [Type distributions of freshmen students at Berkshire Christian College.] Unpublished raw data.

Stricker, L. J., & Ross, J. (1962). *A description and evaluation of the Myers-Briggs Type Indicator.* Research Bulletin RB-62-6. Princeton, NJ: Educational Testing Service.

Stricker, L. J., Schiffman, H., & Ross, J. (1965). Prediction of college performance with the Myers-Briggs Type Indicator. *Educational and Psychological Measurement, 25,* (4), 1081–1095.

Super, D. E. (1970). *The Work Values Inventory*. Boston: Houghton Mifflin.

Szymanski, M. D. (1977). The successful teacher in an alternative school: A study of student preference and student and teacher personality type. Unpublished doctoral dissertation, Georgia State University.

Taylor, F. C. (1973). *Relationship between student personality and performance in an experiential theoretical group dynamics course*. Faculty Working Paper #132, Kent State University.

Terman, L. M. (1956). *Concept Mastery Test: Manual*. New York: The Psychological Corporation.

Terrill, J. L. (1970). Correlates of counselor role perception (Doctoral dissertation, University of Colorado, 1969). *Dissertation Abstracts International, 31*, 166A. (University Microfilms No. 70-5898)

Thompson, L. L. (1984). *An investigation of the relationship of the personality theory of C. G. Jung and teachers' self-reported perceptions and decisions*. Unpublished doctoral dissertation, Ohio State University.

Thorne, A. (1983). Disposition in interpersonal constraint: A study of conversations between introverts and extraverts (Doctoral dissertation, University of California, Berkeley). *Dissertation Abstracts International, 44* (08), 2601B.

Tillman, C. (1976). Personality types and reading gain for upward bound students. *Journal of Reading, 12*, 302–306.

Todd, M., & Roberts, D. (1981). A comparative study of Jungian psychological traits of art education and music education majors. *Research in Psychological Type, 3*, 73–77.

Uhl, N. P., et al. (1981). *Personality type and congruence with environment: Their relationship to college attrition and changing of major*. Paper presented at the Annual Forum of the Association for Institutional Research, Minneapolis, MN.

U.S. Department of Labor (1977). *Dictionary of Occupational Titles*. Washington, D.C.: U.S. Government Printing Office.

Van der Hoop, J. H. (1939). *Conscious Orientation: A study of personality types in relation to neurosis and psychosis*. London: Kegan Paul, Trench, Trubner & Co. Ltd.

Vaughan, J. A., & Knapp, R. H. (1963). A study in pessimism. *Journal of Social Psychology, 59*, 77–92.

Vaught, R. S., Gryskiewicz, S. S., & Kuleck, W. J. (undated). *Phenomenological validation by cross-test prediction: The SCII, MBTI and creativity*. Unpublished manuscript, Center for Creative Leadership, Greensboro, NC 27402.

Veach, T. L., & Touhey, J. C. (1971). Personality correlates of accurate time perception. *Perceptual and Motor Skills, 33* (3), 765–766.

Velsor, E. V., & Campbell, D. (1984a). [Pearson correlations: Myers-Briggs continuous scores and California Personality Inventory.] Unpublished raw data.

Velsor, E. V., & Campbell, D. (1984b). [Pearson correlations: Myers-Briggs continuous scores and Strong Campbell.] Unpublished raw data.

von Fange, E. A. (1961). *Implications for school administration of the personality structure of educational personnel*. Unpublished doctoral dissertation, University of Alberta.

von Fange, E. A. (1982). [Type distributions of incoming students at Concordia Lutheran College, Ann Arbor, MI, from 1975 through 1981.] Unpublished raw data.

von Franz, M-L. (1971). The inferior function. In M-L. von Franz & J. Hillman (Eds.), *Lectures on Jung's Typology* (5th corrected printing) (pp. 1–72). Dallas, TX: Spring Publications, Inc.

Wachowiak, D., & Bauer, G. (1977). The use of the Myers-Briggs Type Indicator for the selection and evaluation of residence hall advisors. *Journal of College and University Housing, 2* (2), 34–37.

Walsh, R. (1984). [MBTI types at Universities of Waterloo and Guelph]. Unpublished raw data.

Warrick, B. H. (1983). [MBTI data from the Values and Lifestyles Program, SRI International, Menlo Park, CA.] Unpublished raw data.

Watson, G., & Glaser, E. M. (1952). *Watson-Glaser Critical Thinking Appraisal*. New York: Harcourt, Brace & World.

Weir, D. M. (1976). The relationship of four Jungian personality types to stated preference for high unconditional positive regard as a counseling approach (Doctoral dissertation, Southern Illinois University, 1975). *Dissertation Abstracts International, 36*, 7881A. (University Microfilms No. 76-13, 298)

Weiss, J. (1980). [Longitudinal data of University of New Mexico Nursing Program.] Unpublished raw data.

Wentworth, M. G. (1978). *The relationship between roommate satisfaction and personality type as measured by the*

Myers-Briggs Type Indicator. (revised by D. P. Campbell). Stanford, CA: Stanford University Press.

Wentworth, M. T. (1981). The relationship of marital adjustment and Jungian psychological types of college students (Doctoral dissertation, University of Florida, 1980). *Dissertation Abstracts International, 41* (9), 3893-A. (University Microfilms No. 81-05, 629)

Wheelwright, J. B., Wheelwright, J. H., & Buehler, H. A. (1964). *Jungian Type Survey. The Gray-Wheelwright test* (16th revision). San Francisco: Society of Jungian Analysts of Northern California.

Whittemore, R. G., & Heimann, R. A. (1965). Originality responses in academically talented male university freshmen. *Psychological Reports, 16,* 439–442.

Williams, B. T., & Carskadon, T. G. (1983). Validity of three MBTI clinical interpretive hypotheses in normal and psychosomatically stressed adults. *Research in Psychological Type, 6,* 81–86.

Wilson, J. T. (1972). The relationship between personality type and student perception of head resident effectiveness (Doctoral dissertation, University of North Colorado, 1971). *Dissertation Abstracts International, 32,* 3735A. (University Microfilms No. 72-3320)

Witzig, J. S. (1978). Jung's typology and classification of psychotherapies. *Journal of Analytical Psychology, 23* (4) 315–331.

Wynne, B. E. (1976). *Abstraction, reflection, and insight—situation coping style measurement dimensions.* Working Paper, School of Business Administration, Winter 1975–76, University of Wisconsin, Milwaukee.

Yang, A. I. (1981). Psychological temporality: A study of temporal orientation, attitude, mood states, and personality type (Doctoral dissertation, University of Hawaii). *Dissertation Abstracts International, 42* (04), 1677B.

Yankelovich, D. (1981). *New rules: Searching for self-fulfillment in a world turned upside down.* New York, Random House.

Yeakley, F. R. (1982). Communication style preferences and adjustments as an approach to studying effects of similarity in psychological type. *Research in Psychological Type, 5,* 30–48.

Yeakley, F. R. (1983). Implications of communication style research for psychological type theory. *Research in Psychological Type, 6,* 5–23.

Yokomoto, C.F., & Ware, J. R. (1982). Improving problem solving performance using the MBTI. *Proceedings of the 1982 American Society of Engineering Education Annual Conference,* 163–167.